Ultimate Study Guide: Foundations
Microsoft Project 2010

Dale A. Howard
Gary L. Chefetz

Ultimate Study Guide: Foundations
Microsoft Project 2010

Copyright © 2010 Chefetz LLC dba MSProjectExperts

Publisher:	Chefetz LLC dba MSProjectExperts
Authors:	Dale A. Howard and Gary L. Chefetz
Cover Design:	Emily Baker
Copy Editor:	Rodney L. Walker
Cover Photo:	Peter Hurley

ISBN: 978-1-934240-13-7

Library of Congress Control Number: 2010932705

Published and distributed by Chefetz LLC dba MSProjectExperts, 90 John Street, Suite 404, New York, NY 10038. (646) 736-1688 http://www.msprojectexperts.com

MSProjectExperts publishes a complete series of role-based training/reference manuals for Microsoft's Enterprise Project Management software including Microsoft Project and Microsoft Project Server. Use our books for self-study or for classroom learning delivered by professional trainers and corporate training programs. To learn more about our books and courseware series for Administrators, Implementers, Project Managers, Resource Managers, Executives, Team Members, and Developers, or to obtain instructor companion products and materials, contact MSProjectExperts by phone (646) 736-1688 or by email info@msprojectexperts.com.

Contents

Contents

Contents

Contents

Introduction

Welcome to the *Ultimate Study Guide: Foundations Microsoft Project 2010*. You picked up the right manual if you seek a complete learning experience and reference to managing projects using the Microsoft Project 2010 desktop application. Our goal in writing this book is to teach you how to use the software effectively.

We take a systematic approach to the topical ordering in this book, in which every module teaches you foundational skills by following the project life cycle. In these modules, you learn how to define a new project; plan your project with tasks, resources, and assignments, analyze the Critical Path, baseline your project, enter actual progress, analyze variance, revise your project, report about project progress, and then close the project.

Throughout each module, we provide a generous amount of information notes, warnings, and best practices. Information notes call your attention to important additional information about a subject. Warnings help you to avoid the most common problems experienced by others, while best practices provide tips for using the tool based on our field experience.

Microsoft Project 2010 introduces exciting new features representing profound changes to the software functionality, including the ability to manually schedule tasks, a feature added to ease the transition for people who use Excel to manage their projects. From the new ribbon-based user interface and backstage, to the incredibly handy new *Timeline* and *Team Planner* views, Microsoft Project 2010 is packed with new features and changes that you can use to enrich your scheduling experience.

Be sure to download the practice files and work your way through the hands-on lessons. You will be up to speed in no time. Enjoy!

Dale A. Howard, Microsoft Project MVP

Gary L. Chefetz, Microsoft Project MVP

MSProjectExperts

Download the Sample Files

Before working on any of the Hands On Exercises in this book, you must download and unzip the sample files required for each exercise. You can download these sample files from the following URL:

http://www.msprojectexperts.com/foundations2010

Module 01

Project Management Overview

Learning Objectives

After completing this module, you will be able to:

- Understand the PMI definition of a project
- Comprehend the project management process as defined by PMI

Inside Module 01

What is a Project?

According to *A Guide to the Project Management Body of Knowledge* (PMBOK Guide, 2000) from the Project Management Institute (PMI), a project is "a temporary endeavor undertaken to create a unique product or service." According to this definition, a project is:

- **Temporary** – Every project has a definite beginning and end.

- **Unique** – Every project is something your organization has not done before, or has not done in this manner.

Understanding the Project Management Process

Because Microsoft Project 2010 is a project management tool, you use the software most effectively in the context of the normal project management process. Therefore, it is important to become acquainted with each of the phases of the project management process and with the activities that take place during each phase. According to the Project Management Institute, the project management process consists of five phases including: definition, planning, execution, control, and closure.

Definition

The definition phase of a project authorizes the creation of the project and is a part of the project's scope management process. The definition phase of a project usually includes the creation of definition documents that include one or more of the following:

- The **Project Charter** is a high-level document that recognizes the existence of the project. This document usually includes the product or service description, the analysis of the business need, and the authority to assign resources to the project. Developed by senior management and stakeholders, the Project Charter feeds the development of the Statement of Work document.

- The **Statement of Work** (SOW) document defines the project and the product or service produced by the project. Other names for this document are proposal, business plan, Scope of Work, or scoping document. The Statement of Work can include one or more of the following sections:

  - Executive Summary

  - Phases, Deliverables, and Activities (Tasks)

  - Sponsor Responsibilities (Rules of Engagement)

  - Assumptions and History

  - Acceptance Criteria

  - Change Control Policies and Procedures

- A **Work Breakdown Structure** (WBS) document breaks the project work into meaningful components, including phases and deliverables. You can see the WBS in the *Task Sheet* view for any project in Microsoft Project 2010.

MSProjectExperts recommends that you carefully define your project and do not stop the definition process until you fully understand your project requirements. In a famous Dilbert™ cartoon, the pointy-haired boss asks Dilbert to start a project to create a new product for a customer. When Dilbert complains that he does not know the customer's product requirements, the pointy-haired boss replies, "start working on the project and we'll come up with the requirements later."

Planning

The planning phase is typically when the project manager becomes directly involved with the project. This phase is of major importance to the potential success of any project. According to the PMBOK Guide, the planning phase can include any of the following processes:

- Scope Planning and Definition

- Activity Definition

- Activity Sequencing

- Activity Duration and Work Estimating

- Resource Planning

- Schedule Development

- Cost Planning and Budgeting

- Risk Management Planning

- Project Plan Development

MSProjectExperts strongly recommends that you perform risk management planning in every project. In the real world, things go wrong and you must plan for them.

Execution

The execution phase of a project is the process of moving forward with the project by performing the activities (tasks) associated with the project. Execution also involves coordinating the resources to carry out the project plan. Execution includes each of the following processes:

- **Saving a Project Baseline** – Prior to beginning work on the project, you must save a baseline for your project. Use the baseline to compare project progress with your original project estimates and then to analyze project variance. You should save the project baseline at the beginning of the project, and you should never change the original project baseline without good reason and without stakeholder agreement.

- **Tracking Project Progress** – Collecting actual project data is critical to controlling the project. Ideally, you should gather and update actual progress from your project team on a weekly basis, or at any other frequency tuned to your project lifecycle.

- **Analyzing Project Variance** – Throughout the life of the project, you must analyze project variance between the current project schedule and the original baseline schedule, and identify trouble spots in the project.

- **Revising the Project Plan** – Based on the results of variance analysis, you may need to make revisions to the project to stay within its predefined scope, schedule, and budget.

- **Reporting Project Progress** –Throughout the life of the project, you should seek to identify the reporting needs of all project participants, and then create custom views and reports in Microsoft Project 2010 to meet these needs.

Control

During the execution phase of the project, various interested parties may request changes, including your customer, your project stakeholders, your project executives, your fellow project managers, and even your project team members. In the face of relentless change requests, you must maintain control over the project to ensure that your project meets its objectives. Some of the common aspects of project control are the following:

- **Change Control** –Change control is the process of managing changes to the predefined scope of the project.

- **Continued Communication** –A critical component of controlling any project is communication. You must keep communication lines open at all times with all project participants.

 MSProjectExperts recommends that your organization define a formal change control process to manage project changes. Every project change can potentially increase the project cost and delay the project finish date. Without a change control process in place, you may not be able to reject changes that are not beneficial to the project's goals and objectives, needlessly driving up your project costs and delaying the completion of your project!

Closure

The closure phase of the project formalizes the acceptance of the project and then closes the project. At the conclusion of project closure, release your resources from the project team to work on other projects. The project closure phase can include any of the following:

- **Project Closure Methodologies** are the processes through which you formally close your project. They must clearly define the "exit criteria" which are critical to measuring the success of your project.

- A **Lessons Learned** meeting (aka "post mortem" meeting) is a wise practice to evaluate the successes and failures during the project life cycle. From this meeting, you should document the lessons learned and then use this information when you plan future projects. The goal of every lessons learned meeting is to determine "how we can do better the next time."

- Use a **Template Creation** process to create project templates from successful projects for similar project types. It is part of your job as a project manager to define project types, build templates to meet other project needs, and modify templates to meet the unique needs of each project.

Once you understand the project management process, you are ready to begin learning how to use Microsoft Project 2010. In the remainder of this book, I show you how to harness the power of the software by using best practices during each stage of the project management life cycle. During the definition stage, I show you how to define a new project using a six-step process. During the planning stage, I show you how to conduct task, resource, and assignment planning. During the execution stage, I show you how to view the Critical Path, baseline your project, enter task progress, perform variance analysis, revise your project, report on your project, and handle change control issues. Finally, during the closure stage, I show you how to save a completed project as a template and how to use the *Compare Projects* utility.

Module 02

Microsoft Project 2010 Overview

Learning Objectives

After completing this module, you will be able to:

- Understand the purpose of the Global.mpt file in Microsoft Project 2010

- Understand the features of the Microsoft Project 2010 user interface

- Understand the features of the ribbon

- Use the *File* tab to access the *Backstage*

- Customize the ribbon

- Customize the *Quick Access Toolbar*

- Use navigation tricks to better navigate the Microsoft Project 2010 environment

- Understand the symbols used in the *Gantt Chart* view

- Read and understand a Gantt chart

- Create and use a three-tiered timescale

Inside Module 02

Introducing the Global.mpt File

Microsoft Project 2010 uses the Global.mpt file as the template to create all new project files. When you launch Microsoft Project 2010, the software opens the Global.mpt file from your hard drive and loads it into memory. This file contains the default objects that ship with Microsoft Project 2010, including default views, tables, filters, groups, reports, calendars, toolbars, etc. You can also use the Global.mpt file to store any custom personal objects you create, such as custom views, tables, filters, groups, reports, etc. Storing your custom personal objects in the Global.mpt file makes them available to all current and future projects.

Although you cannot view the Global.mpt file directly, you can view it indirectly by clicking the *File* tab and then clicking the *Organizer* button in the *Info* tab of the *Backstage*. The system displays the *Organizer* dialog shown in Figure 2 - 1. The list on the left side of the dialog shows the default and custom objects in the Global.mpt file.

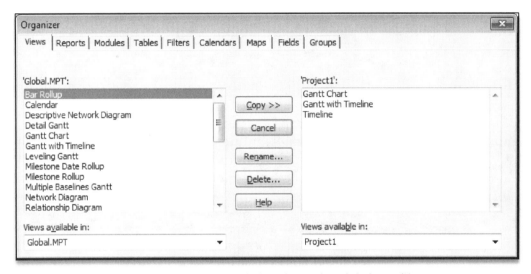

Figure 2 - 1: Organizer dialog shows the Global.mpt file

When you use Microsoft Project 2010 with Microsoft Project Server 2010, the system uses two global files. The system opens the **Global.mpt** file from your PC's hard drive and the **Enterprise Global** file from Project Server, and then merges these two global files into a single cached global file for the current session. Organizations use the *Enterprise Global* to distribute enterprise custom objects, such as enterprise views, tables, filters, groups, reports, and macros to all users quickly and easily.

Understanding the User Interface

To the experienced user, the most striking new feature of Microsoft Project 2010 is the user interface, which conforms to the standard of other applications in the Microsoft Office 2010 suite, such as Word, Excel, or PowerPoint. Previous users of Microsoft Office 2007 should find this user interface familiar. Figure 2 - 2 displays the Microsoft Project 2010 user interface after starting the application.

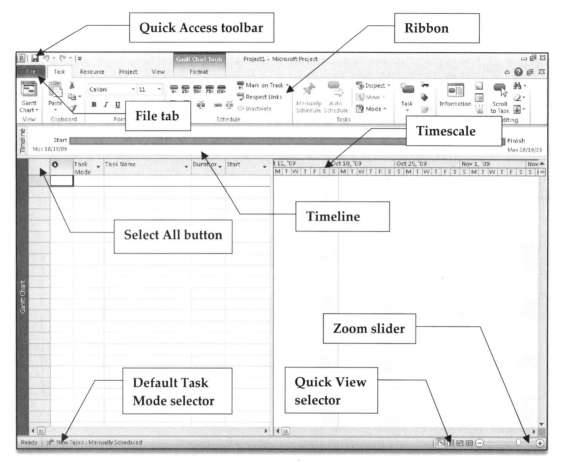

Figure 2 - 2: Features of the Microsoft Project 2010 User Interface

You use these user interface features as follows:

- Use the *ribbon* to access commands found on menus in previous versions of Microsoft Project.

- Use the *File* tab to access all file-related commands, such as open, save, print, etc.

- Use the *Quick Access Toolbar* to display frequently used commands such as open, undo, save, etc.

- Use the *Timeline* to view the current progress of the project in any task view, such as the *Gantt Chart* view or the *Tracking Gantt* view.

- Use the *Select All* button to select all items in the current view. You can also right-click on the *Select All* button to select a different table in a shortcut menu of the most commonly-used tables.

- Use the *Timescale* to determine the current level of zoom applied to the active project.

- Use the *Zoom slider* to quickly zoom to pre-set levels of zoom in the *Gantt Chart* view.

- Use the *Quick View* selector to apply four of the most commonly used views.

- Use the *Default Task Mode* selector to determine the default *Task Mode* for new tasks in the project.

I discuss each of these features in this module and succeeding modules.

Understanding the Ribbon

The most noticeable new feature is the *ribbon*, which replaces the familiar system of menus found in all previous versions of Microsoft Project. These familiar menus included *File, Edit, View, Insert, Format*, etc. Replacing these menus are a series of *ribbon* tabs that display the *Task* ribbon, the *Resource* ribbon, the *Project* ribbon, the *View* ribbon, and the *Format* ribbon for the current view.

Using the Task Ribbon

Microsoft Project 2010 displays the *Task* ribbon by default on application startup. The *Task* ribbon contains all of the buttons and commands you need for task planning. Figure 2 - 3 shows the *Task* ribbon.

Figure 2 - 3: Task ribbon

The system organizes the buttons and commands on the *Task* ribbon into eight sections, which include the *View, Clipboard, Font, Schedule, Tasks, Insert, Properties*, and *Editing* sections. The *Font* section also includes the *Font Dialog Launcher* icon, shown in Figure 2 - 4.

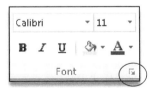

Figure 2 - 4: Font Dialog Launcher icon

When you click the *Font Dialog Launcher* icon, Microsoft Project 2010 displays the *Font* dialog shown in Figure 2 - 5. This dialog is the same *Font* dialog used in Microsoft Office Project 2007.

Figure 2 - 5: Font dialog

Table 2 - 1 documents the corresponding Microsoft Office Project 2007 locations for the buttons and commands you see on the *Task* ribbon.

Microsoft Project 2010 Feature	Microsoft Office Project 2007 Location
View section	*View* menu View ➢ More Views
Clipboard section	*Cut, Copy, Paste,* and *Format Painter* buttons on the *Standard* toolbar
Font section	*Font* and *Font Size* pick list buttons, *Bold, Italic,* and *Underline* buttons on the *Formatting* toolbar Format ➢ Font
Schedule section	View ➢ Toolbars ➢ Tracking (for the progress buttons shown on the top row of the *Schedule* section) *Outdent* and *Indent* buttons on the *Formatting* toolbar *Split Task, Link Tasks,* and *Unlink Tasks* buttons on the *Standard* toolbar
Tasks section	No corresponding feature in 2007
Insert section	Insert ➢ Task
View section	*View* menu

Microsoft Project 2010 Feature	Microsoft Office Project 2007 Location
Properties section	Project ➤ Task Information *Task Information* button on the *Standard* toolbar Project ➤ Task Notes *Task Notes* button on the *Standard* toolbar
Editing section	*Scroll to Task* button on the *Standard* toolbar Edit ➤ Find and Edit ➤ Replace Edit ➤ Clear Edit ➤ Fill

Table 2 - 1: Corresponding Features for the Task ribbon

If you do not see a corresponding location in Microsoft Office Project 2007 for a button or command on a Microsoft Project 2010 ribbon section in the preceding table, then that means the button or command is a new feature in Microsoft Project 2010.

Using the Resource Ribbon

Click the *Resource* tab to display the *Resource* ribbon shown in Figure 2 - 6. Use the *Resource* ribbon with any resource view (such as the *Resource Sheet* view) to manage the resources in your project. The exception to this statement is the *Assign Resources* button, which you can use with any task view (such as the *Gantt Chart* view) to assign resources to tasks.

Figure 2 - 6: Resource ribbon

Table 2 - 2 documents the corresponding Microsoft Office Project 2007 locations for the buttons and commands found on the *Resource* ribbon.

Project 2010 Feature	Microsoft Office Project 2007 Location
View section	*View* menu
	View ➤ More Views
Assignments section	*Assign Resources* button on the *Standard* toolbar
	Tools ➤ Resource Sharing
	Tools ➤ Substitute Resources (available only when used with Project Server 2007 and 2010)
Insert section	Insert ➤ New Resource
	Insert ➤ New Resource From…
Properties section	Project ➤ Resource Information
	Resource Information button on the *Standard* toolbar
	Project ➤ Resource Notes
	Resource *Notes* button on the *Standard* toolbar
Level section	Tools ➤ Level Resources

Table 2 - 2: Corresponding Features for the Resource ribbon

Using the Project Ribbon

Click the *Project* tab to display the *Project* ribbon shown in Figure 2 - 7. Use the *Project* ribbon to specify high-level information about your project or to generate reports for your project.

Figure 2 - 7: Project ribbon

Table 2 - 3 documents the corresponding Microsoft Office Project 2007 locations for the buttons and commands found on the *Project* ribbon.

Project 2010 Feature	Microsoft Office Project 2007 Location
Insert section	Insert ➤ Project
Properties section	Project ➤ Project Information
	Tools ➤ Customize ➤ Fields
	Tools ➤ Links Between Projects
	Project ➤ WBS
	Tools ➤ Change Working Time
Schedule section	Tools ➤ Options ➤ Calculation and then click the *Calculate Now* button
	Tools ➤ Tracking ➤ Set Baseline
	View ➤ Toolbars ➤ Analysis and then click the *Adjust Dates* button
Status section	Project ➤ Project Information and enter a date in the *Status Date* field
	Tools ➤ Tracking ➤ Update Project
Reports section	Report ➤ Visual Reports
	Report ➤ Reports
	View ➤ Toolbars ➤ Compare Project Versions
Proofing section	*Spelling* button on the *Standard* toolbar

Table 2 - 3: Corresponding Features for the Project ribbon

Using the View Ribbon

Click the *View* tab to display the *View* ribbon shown in Figure 2 - 8. Use the *View* ribbon to apply different views in your project, and to apply features of views, including tables, filters, and groups.

Figure 2 - 8: View ribbon

Table 2 - 4 documents the corresponding Microsoft Office Project 2007 locations for the buttons and commands found on the *View* ribbon.

Project 2010 Feature	Microsoft Office Project 2007 Location
Task Views section	View ➤ More Views
Resource Views section	View ➤ More Views
Data section	Project ➤ Sort
	Project ➤ Outline (or click the *Show* button on the *Formatting* toolbar)
	View ➤ Table 1 - ➤ More Tables
	Project ➤ Filtered For ➤ More Filters and click the *Highlight* button
	Filter pick list on the *Formatting* toolbar
	Project ➤ Group By ➤ More Groups (or click the *Group By* pick list on the *Standard* toolbar)
Zoom section	View ➤ Zoom
	Zoom In and *Zoom Out* buttons on the *Standard* toolbar
Split View section	Window ➤ Split
	View ➤ More Views ➤ Task Entry
Window section	Window ➤ New Window
	Window ➤ Select any open project
	Window ➤ Arrange All
	Window ➤ Hide
Macros section	Tools ➤ Macro

Table 2 - 4: Corresponding Features for the View ribbon

Using the Format Ribbon

You can only use the *Format* ribbon with the current view applied in the active project. Before you click the *Format* tab, select a view to format (such as the *Gantt Chart* view), and then click the *Format* tab. Microsoft Project 2010 displays the *Format* ribbon for the current view, and allows you to customize that view. Figure 2 - 9 shows the *Format* ribbon for the *Gantt Chart* view. Notice in Figure 2 - 9 that the software indicates I am editing the *Gantt Chart* view by the *Gantt Chart Tools* header above the *Format* tab.

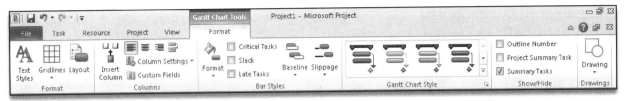

Figure 2 - 9: Format ribbon for the Gantt Chart view

Table 2 - 5 documents the corresponding Microsoft Office Project 2007 locations for the buttons and commands found on the *Format* ribbon.

Microsoft Project 2010 Feature	Microsoft Office Project 2007 Location
Format section	Format ➤ Text Styles Format ➤ Gridlines Format ➤ Layout
Columns section	Insert ➤ Column Tools ➤ Customize ➤ Fields
Bar Styles section	Format ➤ Bar Format ➤ Bar Styles *Gantt Chart Wizard* button on the *Formatting* toolbar
Gantt Chart Style section	Format ➤ Bar Styles
Show/Hide section	Tools ➤ Options ➤ View
Drawings section	View ➤ Toolbars ➤ Drawing

**Table 2 - 5: Corresponding Features for the
Format Ribbon, Gantt Chart Tools**

Remember that the *Format* ribbon shows the appropriate formatting options for your current view. This means that the buttons and commands on the *Format* ribbon vary widely depending on the formatting options available for the current view. For instance, Figure 2 - 10 shows the *Format* ribbon for the *Task Usage* view.

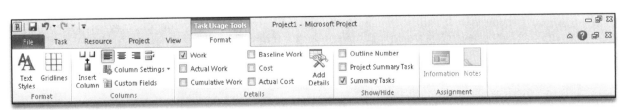

Figure 2 - 10: Format ribbon for the Task Usage view

Figure 2 - 11 shows the *Format* ribbon for the *Resource Sheet* view. Notice that the *Format* ribbon shows very few options for formatting the *Resource Sheet* view.

Figure 2 - 11: Format ribbon for the Resource Sheet view

Figure 2 - 12 shows the *Format* ribbon for the *Team Planner* view. The *Team Planner* view is a powerful new view included in Microsoft Project 2010. Notice that the *Format* ribbon for this view includes a number of buttons and commands not available when formatting other views.

Figure 2 - 12: Format ribbon for the Team Planner view

Figure 2 - 13 shows the *Format* ribbon for the *Calendar* view. Notice that the *Format* ribbon shows very few options for formatting the *Calendar* view

Figure 2 - 13: Format ribbon for the Calendar view

I do not document the buttons and commands available on the *Format* ribbon for every view. Keep in mind that every view offers a unique set of options for formatting. All task views, such as the *Gantt Chart* view and the *Task Sheet* view, include a common set of task formatting options. Likewise, all resource views, such as the *Resource Sheet* view and the *Resource Graph* view, offer a common set of resource formatting options.

Collapsing the Ribbon

Microsoft Project 2010 allows you to expand and collapse the *ribbon* by double-clicking any *ribbon* tab. For example, Figure 2 - 14 shows Microsoft Project 2010 with an open project after I collapsed the *ribbon*. Because of this, the application allows me to see more tasks in the active project.

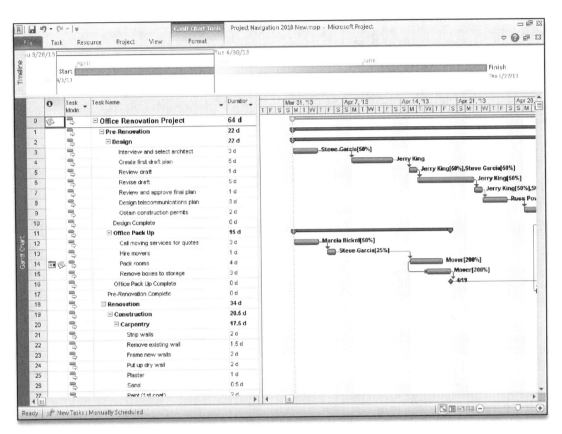

Figure 2 - 14: Microsoft Project 2010 with the ribbon collapsed

 You can also collapse the ribbon by right-clicking on any ribbon tab and selecting the *Minimize the Ribbon* item on the shortcut menu.

Using the Backstage (File Tab)

As I noted earlier in this module, you click the *File* tab to access the most commonly used file commands, such as *Open, Save,* and *Print.* When you click the *File* tab, Microsoft Project 2010 displays the *Backstage* shown in Figure 2 - 15.

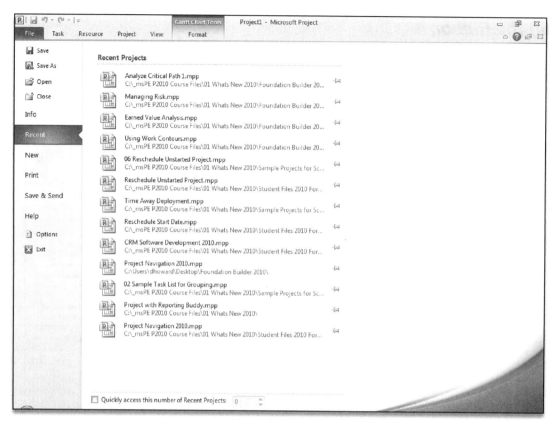

Figure 2 - 15: Microsoft Project 2010 Backstage

Notice in Figure 2 - 15 that the *Backstage* defaults to the *Recent* tab, and shows the list of files you opened recently. The menu on the left side of the *Backstage* contains five tabs, as well as several commands above and below the five tabs. In the *Backstage*, you can perform any of the following actions:

- Save a project file.

- Save a project file using a different file type.

- Open a project file.

- Close a project file.

- Specify information about a project file, such as the properties for the project.

- Open a recently used project file and specify the number of recently used files.

- Create a new project file.

- Print a project file.

- Share a project file with others.

- Access Microsoft Project 2010 Help topics.

- Specify options settings for the active project and for the application.

- Exit Microsoft Project 2010.

You may also see an *Add-ins* command item below the *Options* item in the *Backstage* menu if your system has an Add-In that Microsoft Project 2010 recognizes, such as a Bluetooth device.

To save the active project file, click the *Save* command from the *Backstage* menu. Microsoft Project 2010 saves the active project and then exits the *Backstage*.

To save the active project as an alternate file type, click the *Save As* item in the *Backstage* menu. The system exits the *Backstage* and displays the *Save As* dialog shown in Figure 2 - 16. This dialog allows you to save your project using an alternate file type, such as a Microsoft Excel workbook or a PDF file. Select your alternate file type and location, and then click the *Save* button. The system exits the *Save As* dialog and returns to your active project.

Warning: Although the *Save As* dialog indicates that you can save your project to an ODBC compliant database by the presence of the *ODBC* button, this feature was deprecated in Microsoft Project 2007 and remains unavailable in Microsoft Project 2010. The presence of the *ODBC* button is a bug in Microsoft Project 2010.

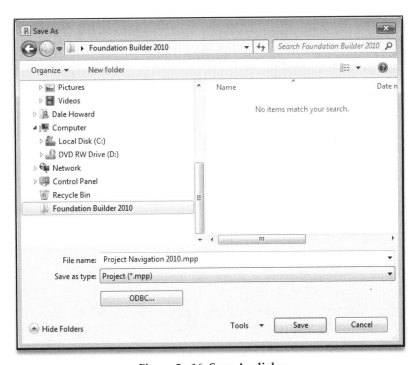

Figure 2 - 16: Save As dialog

To open any existing project, click the *File* tab and then click the *Open* item in the *Backstage* menu. Microsoft Project 2010 closes the *Backstage* and displays the *Open* dialog shown in Figure 2 - 17. The *Open* dialog offers you a number of ways to locate an existing project, including the following:

- Click one of the folders shown in the *Breadcrumb* bar at the top of the dialog.

- Click the *Previous Locations* pick list button at the right end of the *Breadcrumb* bar.

- Enter a search term in the *Search* field in the upper right corner of the dialog.

- Select a link in the *Favorite Links* list on the left side of the dialog.

- Click the *Folders* button at the bottom of the *Favorite Links* list and select the drive and folder.

- Click the *Type* pick list in the lower right corner of the dialog, and choose an alternate file type, such as an Excel workbook file.

Select the project file you want to open and then click the *Open* button. The system closes the dialog and opens the selected project in read/write mode.

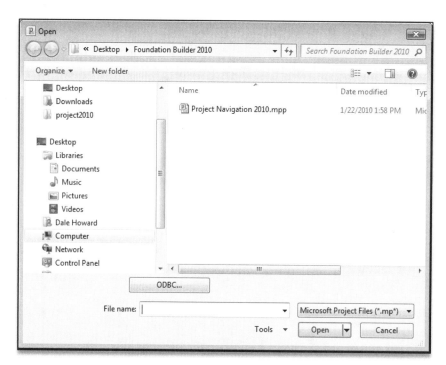

Figure 2 - 17: Open dialog

 You can also click the *Open* pick list selector on the *Open* button to open the project file read-only, to open a copy of the selected project, or to show previous versions of the project file.

To close the active project file, click the *Close* item in the *Backstage* menu. The system exits the *Backstage* and returns you to your Microsoft Project 2010 application window.

To specify information about the active project, click the *Info* tab in the *Backstage*. Microsoft Project 2010 displays the *Information* page for the selected project, as shown in Figure 2 - 18. Notice the following about the *Information* page:

- The system displays the name and file path for the active project at the top of the page.

- The system displays statistics for the active project on the right side of the page.

- The system allows you to create and manage Project Server 2010 login accounts (available **only** in the Professional version of Microsoft Project 2010).

- The system allows you to access the *Organizer* dialog.

- The system allows you to specify project information about the active project.

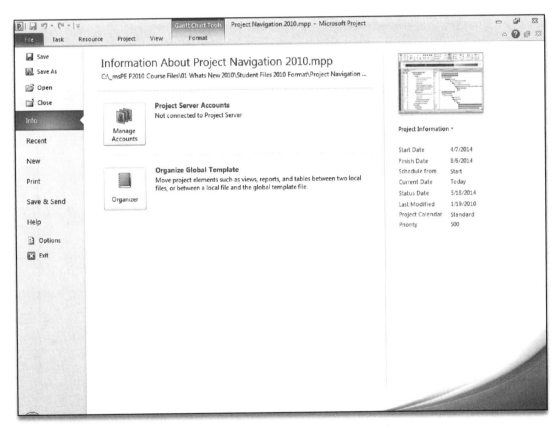

Figure 2 - 18: Information page for the selected project

When you click the *Project Server Accounts* button on the *Information* page of the *Backstage*, the system displays the *Project Server Accounts* dialog shown in Figure 2 - 19. This feature is **only** available in Microsoft Project 2010 Professional, and you use this feature to specify login information for your organization's Project Server 2010 instances.

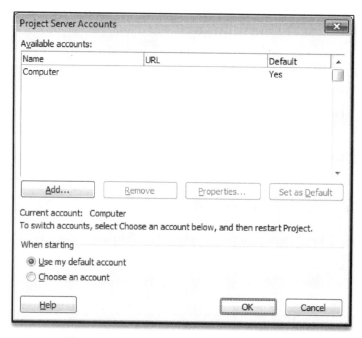

Figure 2 - 19: Project Server Accounts dialog

When you click the *Organizer* button on the *Information* page of the *Backstage*, the system displays the *Organizer* dialog shown in Figure 2 - 20. You use the *Organizer* dialog to manage default and custom objects in Microsoft Project 2010, such as views, tables, filters, groups, reports, etc.

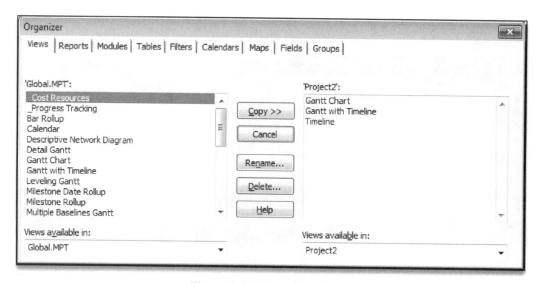

Figure 2 - 20: Organizer dialog

When you click the *Project Information* pick list in the upper right corner of the *Information* page in the *Backstage*, the system displays the pick list shown in Figure 2 - 21. Select the *Advanced Properties* item on the list to display the *Properties* dialog, where you can enter custom properties for the selected project. Select the *Project Statistics* item on the list to display the *Project Statistics* dialog.

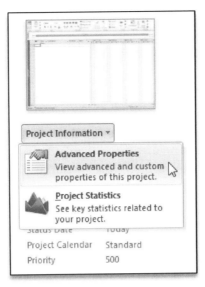

Figure 2 - 21: Project Information
pick list in the Backstage

To open a recently opened project file, click the *Recent* tab in the *Backstage*. The system displays the recently used projects in the *Recent Projects* page shown previously in Figure 2 - 15. To add a specific number of recently used project files to the list shown on the left side of the *Backstage* page, select the *Quickly Access This Number of Recent Projects* option and then specify a number for this field. The system adds these projects to the menu on the left side of the page, as shown in Figure 2 - 22. Notice in the figure that I chose to display eight projects in the menu.

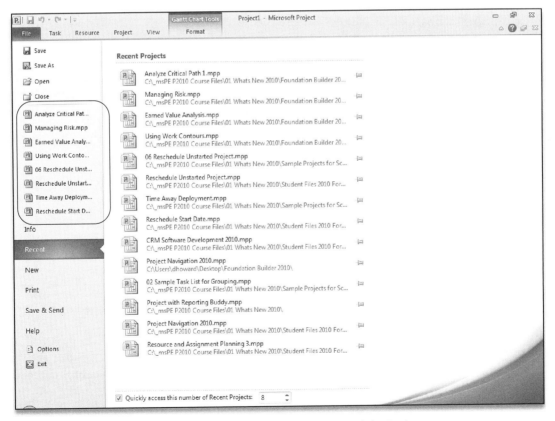

Figure 2 - 22: Recent files shown on the left side of the Backstage page

Microsoft Project 2010 limits you to no more than **17 files** in the *Quickly access this number of Recent Projects* field.

For any project file shown on the recently used file list, you can "pin" the file so that the system always displays this file at the top of the *Recent Projects* list. To "pin" a recently used project file, click the "pushpin" icon to the right of the project file name in the *Recent Project* list. The system moves the project file to the top of the *Recent Projects* list and displays an "unpin" icon, as shown in Figure 2 - 23. Notice that I "pinned" four recently used project files.

 If you right-click on any of the projects shown in the *Recent Projects* list, the system displays a shortcut menu that allows you to perform additional actions such as removing a project from the display list or clearing the list of all unpinned projects.

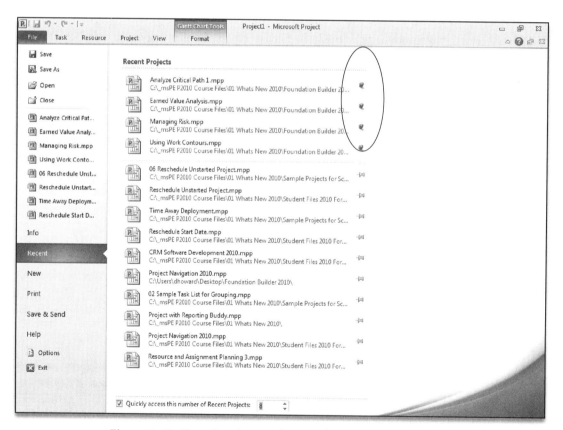

Figure 2 - 23: Pinned projects at the top of the Recent Projects list

To create a new project, click the *New* tab in the *Backstage*. The system displays the *Available Templates* page in the *Backstage* shown in Figure 2 - 24. Notice that you can create a new project in a variety of ways, including the following:

- Click the *Blank Project* button to create a new blank project.

- Click the *Recent Templates* button to create a new project from a template you used recently.

- Click the *My Templates* button to create a new project from a custom project template you created.

- Click the *New from Existing Project* button to create a new project from an existing project.

- Click the *New from Excel Workbook* button to import a new Microsoft Project 2010 file from an existing Microsoft Excel file.

- Click the *New from SharePoint Task List* button to create a new project from a task list in an existing SharePoint 2010 site (available only in Microsoft Project 2010 Professional).

- Click one of the icons in the *Office.com Templates* section to display available templates on Office.com.

- Type one or more key words in the *Search Office.com For Templates* field and click the *Start Searching* button to search Office.com for customized project templates.

Figure 2 - 24: Available Templates page in the Backstage

To print the active project, click the *Print* tab in the *Backstage*. The system displays the *Print* page shown in Figure 2 - 25. On the *Print* page, you can control any of the following printing options:

- Specify the number of copies to print in the *Copies* field.

- Select an available printer in the *Printer* pick list.

- Set printer options by clicking the *Printer Properties* link.

- Specify the date range for printing project information by clicking the *Settings* pick list and choosing a pre-defined date range.

- Manually enter a date range in the *Dates* and *To* fields.

- Specify the number of pages to print by selecting a value in the *Pages* and *To* fields.

- Specify the orientation of the printout on the *Print Orientation* pick list.

- Specify the paper size on the *Paper Size* pick list.

- Display the *Page Setup* dialog by clicking the *Page Setup* link.

- View the print preview of the project in the right side of the page.

- Navigate in the print preview using the buttons in the lower right corner of the page.

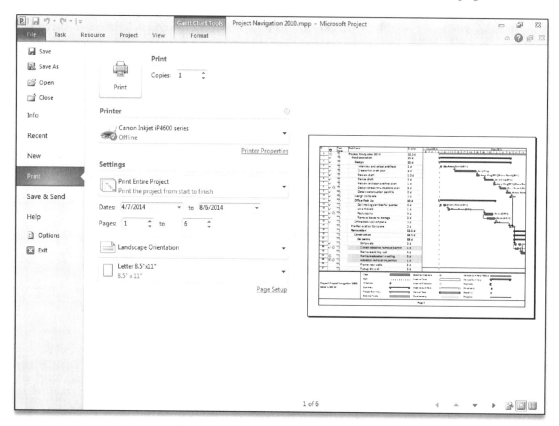

Figure 2 - 25: Print page in the Backstage

To share a project with others, click the *Save & Send* tab in the *Backstage*. The system displays the *Save & Send* page in the *Backstage*, shown in Figure 2 - 26. Notice on the *Save & Send* page that Microsoft Project 2010 allows you to share your project file in a number of ways, including each of the following:

- Send the project file as an e-mail attachment.

- Synchronize the tasks in the project file with a tasks list in a SharePoint 2010 site (available **only** in Microsoft Project 2010 Professional).

- Save the project file in a SharePoint 2010 site (available only in Microsoft Project 2010 Professional).

- Share the project with others using the Microsoft Project Online service.

- Save the project file to an alternate file type.

- Save the project file as a PDF document or an XPS document.

XPS documents are electronic paper documents saved according to X̲ML P̲aper S̲pecification standard. Hardware, software, and people can all read XPS documents.

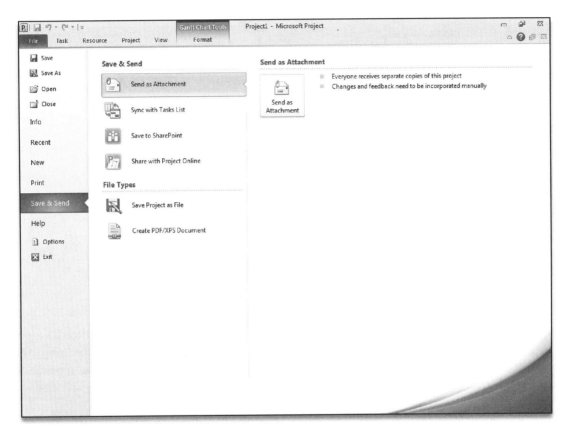

Figure 2 - 26: Save & Send page in the Backstage

Click the *Help* tab to display the *Help* page in the *Backstage*, shown in Figure 2 - 27. Notice that the *Help* page contains four sections of options, including the following:

- The *Support* section contains icons that offer you help articles and allow you to contact Microsoft.

- The *Tools for Working with Office* section contains icons that allow you to display the *Project Options* dialog and to help you to get the latest updates for the software.

- The *Product Activation* section shows you the activation status of your software.

- The *About Microsoft Project* section shows you the version of Microsoft Project 2010 you are using.

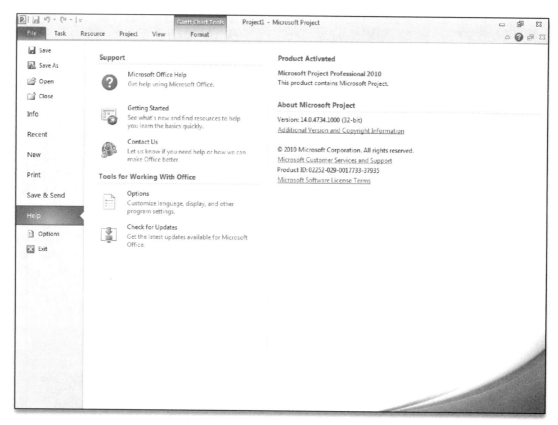

Figure 2 - 27: Help page in the Backstage

To specify options settings for the active project and for the Microsoft Project 2010 application, click the *Options* item in the *Backstage* menu. The system displays the *Project Options* dialog shown in Figure 2 - 28. In the *Project Options* dialog, you can specify settings for the active project as well as for the Microsoft Project 2010 desktop application. Notice that the *Project Options* dialog offers eleven sections in which to specify options settings. These sections include:

- The *General* section allows you to specify general settings for the Microsoft Project 2010 application.

- The *Display* section allows you to specify how Microsoft Project 2010 displays application content.

- The *Schedule* section allows you to specify options related to scheduling, calendars, and calculations for the active project.

- The *Proofing* section allows you to specify how the Microsoft Project 2010 application proofs and formats text in your project files.

- The *Save* section allows you to specify how and where the Microsoft Project 2010 application saves your project files.

- The *Language* section allows you to specify the language used in your Microsoft Project 2010 application.

- The *Advanced* section allows you to specify advanced options for the active project and for the Microsoft Project 2010 application.

- The *Customize Ribbon* section allows you to customize the *ribbon* by adding or removing tabs and buttons on the *ribbon*.

- The *Quick Access Toolbar* section allows you to customize the *Quick Access Toolbar* by adding or removing buttons.

- The *Add-Ins* section allows you to add and remove COM Add-Ins for Microsoft Project.

- The *Trust Center* section allows you to specify your level of security for macros written in the VBA programming language.

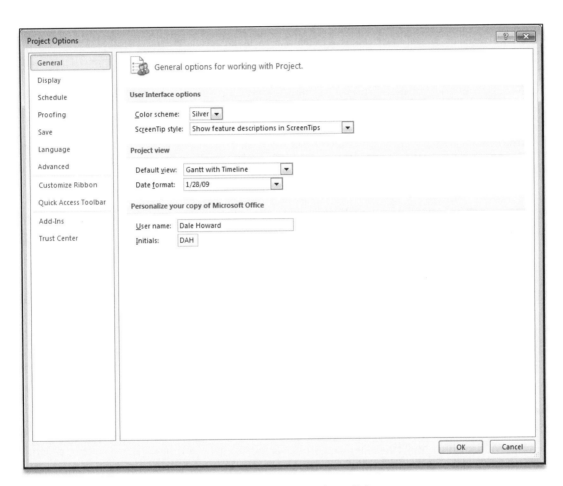

Figure 2 - 28: Project Options dialog

I present an in-depth discussion of many of these *Backstage* features in succeeding modules in this book. To close the *Backstage* without taking any other actions, click the *File* tab again or click any other tab on the *ribbon*.

Hands On Exercise

Exercise 2-1

Explore the *ribbon* and the *Backstage* in Microsoft Project 2010.

1. Launch Microsoft Project 2010, if necessary.

2. Click the *File* tab and then click the *Open* item in the *Backstage* menu.

3. Navigate to your student folder and then open the **Project Navigation 2010.mpp** sample file.

4. Click the *Task, Resource, Project, View,* and *Format* tabs individually and study the buttons available on each *ribbon*.

5. Click the *File* tab again to display the *Backstage*.

6. In the *Information* page of the *Backstage*, click the *Project Information* pick list (upper right corner of the page) and choose the *Advanced Properties* item on the list.

7. Enter your name in the *Author* field and then click the *OK* button.

8. Click *Recent, New, Print, Save & Send,* and *Help* tabs in the *Backstage* and study the options available on each page.

9. Click the *Save* button to save the **Project Navigation 2010.mpp** sample file and exit the *Backstage*.

Using Navigation Features

Microsoft Project 2010 offers four new types of navigation options to help you navigate in the active project. These options include improved shortcut menus and keyboard shortcuts, zooming the *Timescale*, and using the *View Slider*. I discuss each of the navigation features individually.

Using Shortcut Menus

If you are a previous user of Microsoft Office Project 2007, you are probably already familiar with the shortcut menu that the software displays when you right-click any object such as a task or a Gantt bar. Microsoft expanded the short-cut menu in Microsoft Project 2010 to include a longer menu of options and an additional shortcut menu section called the *Mini Toolbar*. When you right-click on any object, the system displays the *Mini Toolbar* and the shortcut menu simultaneously. For example, Figure 2 - 29 shows the *Mini Toolbar* and the shortcut menu when I right-click a task.

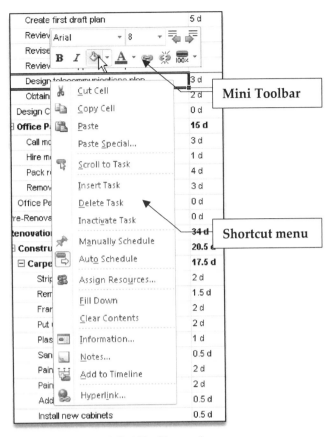

**Figure 2 - 29: Mini Toolbar and
shortcut menu for tasks**

Notice in Figure 2 - 29 that the *Mini Toolbar* has buttons for the following actions: *Font, Font Size, Indent, Outdent, Bold* text, *Italic* text, *Cell Background Color, Font Color, Link Tasks, Unlink Tasks*, and *Percent Complete*. If you right-click on any graphical object in the *Gantt Chart* view, such as a Gantt bar, the system displays the shortcut menu and *Mini Toolbar* shown in Figure 2 - 30.

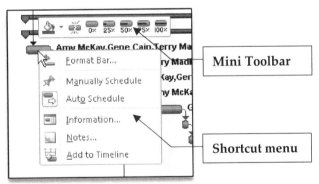

**Figure 2 - 30: Mini Toolbar and
shortcut menu for a Gantt bar**

Notice in Figure 2 - 30 that the *Mini Toolbar* has buttons for the following actions: *Bar Color, Split Task, 0% Complete, 25% Complete, 50% Complete, 75% Complete,* and *100% Complete*. Likewise, if you right-click on a resource, such as in the *Resource Sheet* view, the *Mini Toolbar* and shortcut menu offer a set of features exclusively for working with resource information.

Using Built-In Keyboard Shortcuts

For users who prefer using the keyboard to the mouse, Microsoft Project 2010 offers two types of keyboard shortcuts. The first type includes the same set of keyboard shortcuts found in previous Microsoft Project versions. You can continue to use keyboard shortcuts such as **Ctrl + S** to save a file and **Ctrl + C** to copy information to the Windows Clipboard. The second type includes keyboard shortcuts called **KeyTips** for use with the tabs on the *ribbon* and for the buttons on each *ribbon* and on the *Quick Access Toolbar*. To activate these keyboard shortcuts, press the **Alt** key on your computer keyboard. The system displays the *KeyTips* for each tab on the *ribbon* and for each button on the *Quick Access Toolbar*, as shown in Figure 2 - 31.

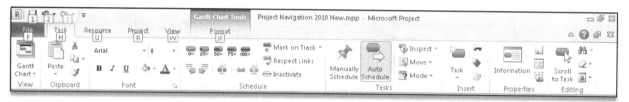

Figure 2 - 31: Ribbon with KeyTips for tabs

Notice in Figure 2 - 31 that **F** is the *KeyTip* for the *File* tab, **U** is the *KeyTip* for the *Resource* tab on the *ribbon*, and **2** is the *KeyTip* for the *Undo* button on the *Quick Access Toolbar*. With *KeyTips* activated, press the keyboard shortcut key for the *KeyTip* you want to use. When you press the shortcut key for a *ribbon* tab, the system displays the *KeyTips* for each button on the selected *ribbon*. For example, Figure 2 - 32 shows the *KeyTips* for the *Task* ribbon. Therefore, to activate the *Paste* button I must click the **V** key on my computer keyboard.

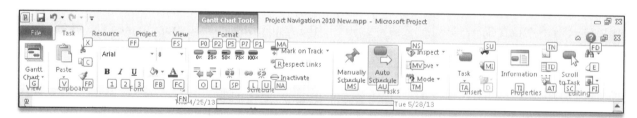

Figure 2 - 32: Ribbon with KeyTips for buttons

Zooming the Timescale

Microsoft Office Project 2007provided you with two quick ways to zoom the *Timescale* using the *Zoom In* button and the *Zoom Out* button on the *Standard* toolbar, or clicking View ➤ Zoom to display the *Zoom* dialog. Microsoft Project 2010 now offers a single *Zoom* pick list button in the *Zoom* section of the *View* ribbon, which allows you to zoom in and zoom out, and offers two new zooming options: the *Zoom Entire Project* button and the *Zoom Selected Tasks* button. To zoom the *Timescale*, first apply any task view, such as the *Gantt Chart* view. When you click the *Zoom Entire Project* button, the system zooms the *Timescale* to display the entire time span of the project in the *Gantt Chart* view, as shown in Figure 2 - 33.

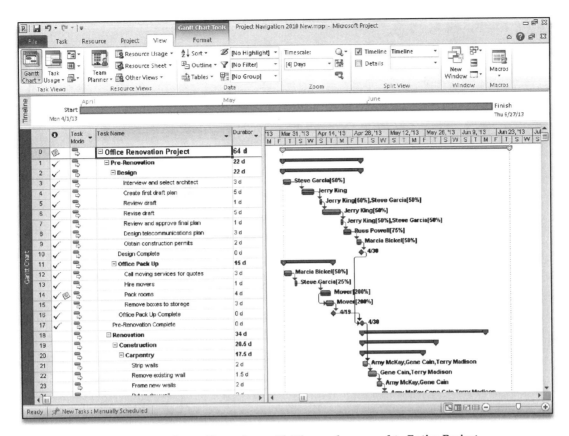

Figure 2 - 33: Gantt Chart view with Timescale zoomed to Entire Project

In the project shown in the figure above, the current level of zoom for the project is "2-Week Time Periods Over 4-Day Time Periods." To determine the current level of Zoom in a project, double-click anywhere in the *Timescale*. In the *Timescale* dialog, examine the zoom information on the *Middle Tier* tab and the *Bottom Tier* tab to determine the current level of Zoom applied to the project.

If you select a block of tasks and then click the *Zoom Selected Tasks* button, the system zooms the *Timescale* for the time span of the selected tasks. In Figure 2 - 34, I zoomed the *Timescale* to the time span for the tasks I selected in the Design deliverable section of the project.

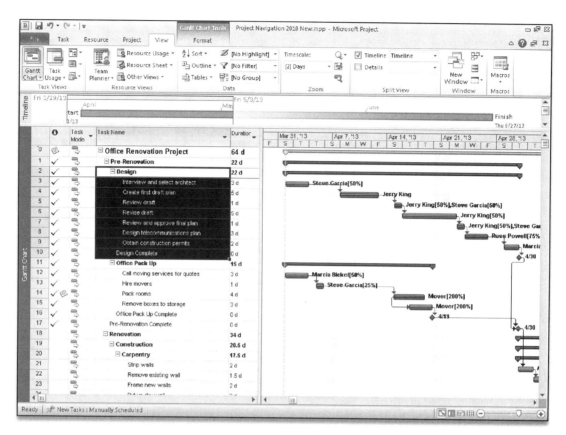

Figure 2 - 34: Gantt Chart view with Timescale zoomed to the selected tasks

 In the project shown in Figure 2 - 34, the current level of zoom for the project is "Weeks Over 2-Day Time Periods."

Microsoft Project 2010 also provides a handy *Zoom Slider* for zooming the *Timescale* in your projects. Shown in Figure 2 - 35, you find the *Zoom Slider* in the lower right corner of the Microsoft Project 2010 application window. The *Zoom Slider* allows you to change the current level of zoom quickly by sliding the zoom control manually to the left (to zoom out) or right (to zoom in). You can also click the *Zoom In* button and *Zoom Out* button in the *Zoom Slider*.

Figure 2 - 35: Zoom Slider

 You can use the *Zoom Slider* in any view containing a Gantt chart, such as the *Gantt Chart* and *Tracking Gantt* view, and in the *Task Usage, Resource Usage*, and *Calendar* views.

Tips for Using the Scroll Bars

Drag the vertical scroll box up and down to scroll to exact task ID numbers and task names. Drag the horizontal scroll box left and right to scroll to precise dates in any task view.

Using the Scroll to Task button

Select any task and then click the *Scroll to Task* button in the *Editing* section of the *Task* ribbon to bring the left end of the selected task's Gantt bar into view.

Using Screen Tips and Tool Tips

You can display many helpful screen tips and tool tips in Microsoft Project 2010 by floating your mouse pointer over many of the objects in the user interface. For example, float the mouse pointer over the *Select All* button, column headers, Gantt bars, and link lines between dependent tasks. Figure 2 - 36 shows the tool tip displayed when you float the mouse pointer over the *Select All* button, while Figure 2 - 37 shows the screen tip displayed while hovering over the *Task Mode* column header.

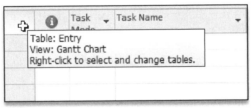

**Figure 2 - 36: Tool tip for the
Select All button**

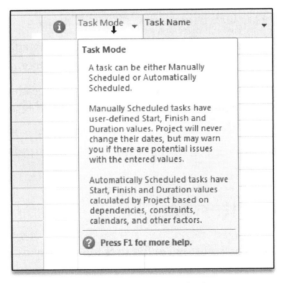

**Figure 2 - 37: Screen tip for
the Task Mode column**

To access a Help article about any column in Microsoft Project 2010, float your mouse pointer over the column header and then press the **F1** function key on your computer keyboard.

Hands On Exercise

Exercise 2-2

Explore the new navigation features in Microsoft Project 2010.

1. Return to your **Project Navigation 2010.mpp** sample file.

2. Right-click on task ID #3, *Interview and select architect*, to display the shortcut menu and the *Mini Toolbar*.

3. In the *Mini Toolbar*, click the *Background Color* pick list button and choose the *Blue, Lighter 80%* color in the *Theme Colors* section of the palette.

4. Select task ID #23, *Remove existing wall*, and then click the *Scroll to Task* button on the *Tasks* ribbon.

5. In the Gantt chart, right-click on the Gantt bar for the *Remove existing wall* task and then click the *100% Complete* button in the *Mini Toolbar*.

6. Press the **Alt ≻ W ≻ Q ≻ O** on your computer keyboard to use the built-in *KeyTips* to select the *View* ribbon and then zoom out one level in the *Timescale*.

7. In the *Zoom* section of the *View* ribbon, click the *Zoom Entire Project* button.

8. Select all of the tasks in the *Carpentry* section of the project (task ID #20 - #38) and then click the *Zoom Selected Tasks* button in the *Zoom* section of the *View* ribbon.

9. In the lower right corner of your Microsoft Project 2010 application window, click and hold the slider control in the *Zoom Slider* section, and then zoom the *Timescale* in and out to see more and less detail in the Gantt chart.

10. Click the *File* tab, then save and close your **Project Navigation 2010.mpp** sample file.

Customizing the User Interface

Microsoft Project 2010 offers you two ways to customize the user interface by modifying the *ribbon* and the *Quick Access Toolbar*. I discuss each of these topics separately.

Customizing the Ribbon

You can customize the *ribbon* by adding *ribbon* tabs, *ribbon* groups, and *ribbon* buttons. To begin the process of customizing the *ribbon*, complete the following steps:

1. Click the *File* tab.

2. In the *Backstage*, click the *Options* item.

3. In the *Project Options* dialog, click the *Customize Ribbon* section in the left side of the dialog.

The fastest way to access the *Customize Ribbon* section of the *Project Options* dialog is to right-click on any ribbon tab and then click the *Customize the Ribbon* item on the shortcut menu.

The system displays the *Project Options* dialog with the *Customize Ribbon* section displayed, as shown in Figure 2 - 38. Notice in the figure that the *Customize Ribbon* section of the *Project Options* dialog contains two sections:

- Use the *Choose Commands From* section to locate the commands you want to add to the *ribbon*.

- Use the *Customize the Ribbon* section to display the *ribbon(s)* you want to customize.

Click the *Choose Commands From* pick list to choose the type of commands you want to add to the *ribbon*. The pick list offers you the following choices: *Popular Commands* (the default setting), *Commands Not in the Ribbon*, *All Commands*, *Macros, File Tab, All Tabs, Main Tabs, Tool Tabs*, and *Custom Tabs and Groups*. Select your option on the *Choose Commands From* pick list.

Click the *Customize the Ribbon* pick list and choose which *ribbon* tabs to display in the dialog. You have three choices: *Main Tabs* (the default setting), *Tool Tabs* (used for formatting views), and *All Tabs* (offers both the *Main Tabs* and the *Tool Tabs*). Select your option on the *Customize the Ribbon* pick list.

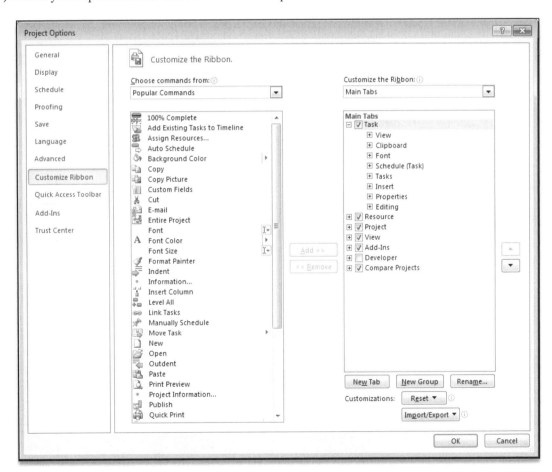

Figure 2 - 38: Project Options dialog, Customize Ribbon section

After you select your options on the *Choose Commands From* pick list and the *Customize the Ribbon* pick list, you are ready to customize the *ribbon*. The software offers you multiple choices for customizing the *ribbon*:

- Show or hide a *ribbon* tab.

- Create a new *ribbon* tab.

- Create a *ribbon* group in a new or existing *ribbon* tab.

- Add or remove buttons on a default or custom *ribbon* tab.

- Rename a *ribbon* tab, a *ribbon* group, or a button.

- Move buttons, *ribbon* groups, and *ribbon* tabs on the *ribbon*.

- Reset the *ribbon* to its default settings.

- Import or export the customized *ribbon* and *Quick Access Toolbar* settings to a file.

Showing/Hiding a Ribbon Tab

To show or hide a *ribbon* tab, select or deselect the option checkbox to the left of the *ribbon* tab. For example, if you are a software developer, you might want to show the *Developer* tab so that you can create macros in the Office VBA programming language for Microsoft Project 2010. In this case, select the option checkbox for the *Developer* tab.

Creating a New Ribbon Tab

To create a new *ribbon* tab, select an existing *ribbon* tab in the location where you want to insert the new *ribbon* tab, and then click the *New Tab* button. The system inserts the new *ribbon* tab **below** the selected *ribbon* tab, as shown in Figure 2 - 39. Notice in the figure that the new *ribbon* tab also includes a custom *ribbon* group as well. Every default and custom *ribbon* tab **must** contain at least one *ribbon* group, but you can also create additional *ribbon* groups.

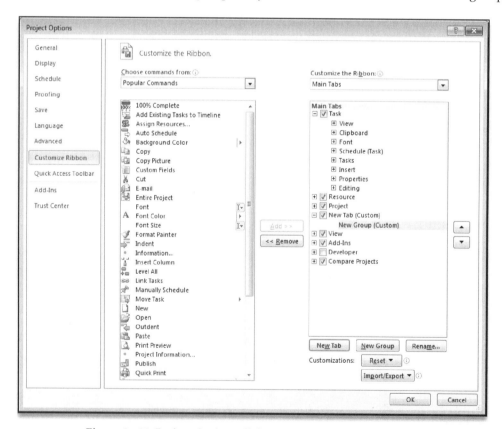

**Figure 2 - 39: Project Options dialog, Customize Ribbon section
after inserting a custom ribbon tab below the Project tab**

Renaming a Ribbon Tab, Group, or Button

After creating a new *ribbon* tab or *ribbon* group, you should immediately rename it. To rename a *ribbon* tab, click the name of the *ribbon* tab and then click the *Rename* button. Microsoft Project 2010 displays the *Rename* dialog shown in Figure 2 - 40. Enter the name of the new *ribbon* tab in the *Display Name* field and then click the *OK* button.

**Figure 2 - 40: Rename dialog for a
new custom ribbon tab**

To rename a *ribbon* group, click the name of the *ribbon* group and then click the *Rename* button. Microsoft Project 2010 displays the *Rename* dialog shown in Figure 2 - 41. Enter the name of the new *ribbon* group in the *Display Name* field and then click the *OK* button.

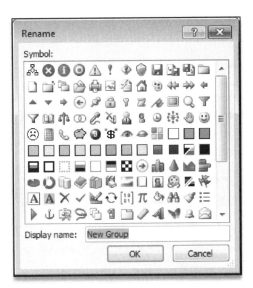

**Figure 2 - 41: Rename dialog for a
new custom ribbon group**

To rename a button, click the name of the button and then click the *Rename* button. Microsoft Project 2010 displays the *Rename* dialog shown previously in Figure 2 - 41. Enter the new name of the button in the *Display Name* field, select a symbol for the button in the *Symbol* list, and then click the *OK* button.

When you rename a *Ribbon* group in the *Rename* dialog, selecting a symbol in the *Symbol* list has no effect on the *Ribbon* group. Selecting a symbol in the *Symbol* list only applies to renaming buttons.

Creating a New Ribbon Group

To create a new custom *ribbon* group, select an existing *ribbon* tab or *ribbon* group, and then click the *New Group* button. The system adds the new custom *ribbon* group **below** the selected *ribbon* tab or *ribbon* group. After creating the new *ribbon* group, you should rename the *ribbon* group immediately by clicking the *Rename* button and entering a name for the *ribbon* group. You should create a custom *ribbon* group for every section of buttons and options you want to display on your custom *ribbon* tab.

Adding/Removing Buttons on a Ribbon Tab

After creating a new custom *ribbon* tab and adding custom *ribbon* groups, you are ready to add buttons to your new custom *ribbon* tab. To add a button to a *ribbon* tab, select the button in the list of buttons on the left, select the *ribbon* group in the list of *ribbon* tabs and groups on the right, and then click the *Add* button. Microsoft Project 2010 adds the button to the selected *ribbon* group.

 Warning: You cannot add a button to any default *ribbon* tab **unless** you create a custom *ribbon* group on that *ribbon* tab. This means that you cannot add buttons to a default *ribbon* group on any default *ribbon* tab.

To remove a button on a *ribbon* tab, select the button in the list on the right and then click the *Remove* button. You can also remove a custom *ribbon* tab or *ribbon* group using the same process.

Moving Items in the Ribbon

Microsoft Project 2010 allows you to move default and custom *ribbon* tabs, *ribbon* groups, and buttons to a different location. To move any of these, select the object you want to move and then click the *Move Up* or *Move Down* button. Figure 2 - 42 shows a new custom *ribbon* tab with multiple *ribbon* groups. I created this *ribbon* tab to help me perform the six steps needed to define a new project.

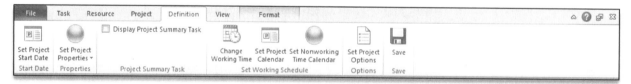

Figure 2 - 42: New custom ribbon tab

Resetting the Ribbon

Microsoft Project 2010 allows you to reset the entire *ribbon* back to its default settings, or to reset any default *ribbon* tab to its default settings. To reset only a single *ribbon* tab, select the *ribbon* tab in the list on the right, click the *Reset* pick list button and choose the *Reset Only Selected Ribbon Tab* item on the list. The system resets the selected *ribbon* tab immediately. To reset the entire *ribbon*, click the *Reset* pick list button and choose the *Reset All Customizations* item on the list. The system displays the warning dialog shown in Figure 2 - 43. Click the *Yes* button to confirm the reset action.

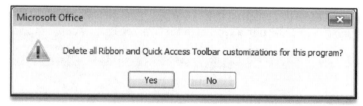

**Figure 2 - 43: Warning dialog to reset all
customizations to the ribbon**

Warning: Notice in the dialog shown in the figure above that the system is about to reset all of the customizations to **both** the *ribbon* **and** the *Quick Access Toolbar*. If you do not want to reset customizations to the *Quick Access Toolbar*, then **do not** select the *Reset All Customizations* option.

Hands On Exercise

Exercise 2-3

Customize the *ribbon* by adding a new *ribbon* tab and *ribbon* buttons.

1. Click the *File* tab, click the *New* tab, and then double-click the *Blank Project* icon to open a new blank project.

2. Right-click anywhere in the *ribbon* and choose the *Customize the Ribbon* item on the shortcut menu.

3. In the *Customize Ribbons* section of the *Project Options* dialog, click the *Choose Commands From* pick list and select the *All Commands* item on the list.

4. In the list of *ribbon* tabs on the right side of the dialog, select the *Compare Projects* item and then click the *New Tab* button.

5. Select the *New Tab (Custom)* item, click the *Rename* button, enter *Definition* in the *Display Name* field, and then click the *OK* button.

6. Select the *New Group (Custom)* item, click the *Rename* button, enter *Define a New Project* in the *Display Name* field, and then click the *OK* button.

7. Add the following buttons to the new *Define a New Project* group:

   - Project Information

   - Document Properties

   - Project Summary Task

   - Nonworking Time

   - Options

   - Save

8. Click the *OK* button to close the *Project Options* dialog.

9. Click the *Definition* tab to view your new *ribbon* tab, your new *ribbon* group, and the buttons you added to the *ribbon* group.

Customizing the Quick Access Toolbar

Like the *ribbon*, Microsoft Project 2010 allows you to customize the *Quick Access Toolbar*. By default, the *Quick Access Toolbar* appears **above** the *ribbon*, in the upper left corner of the application window, as shown in Figure 2 - 44. Notice in the figure that the *Quick Access Toolbar* contains only a few buttons, including the *Save*, *Undo*, and *Redo* buttons.

Figure 2 - 44: Quick Access Toolbar above the ribbon

You use the *Quick Access Toolbar* to provide quick access to the buttons you use most often. For example, many users like to add the *Open* and *Print* buttons to the *Quick Access Toolbar*. Microsoft Project 2010 allows you to customize the *Quick Access Toolbar* in two ways:

- Move the *Quick Access Toolbar* below the *ribbon*.

- Add or remove buttons on the *Quick Access Toolbar*.

To customize the *Quick Access Toolbar*, click the *Customize Quick Access Toolbar* button at the right end of the toolbar, just to the right of the *Redo* button. The system displays the pick list shown in Figure 2 - 45.

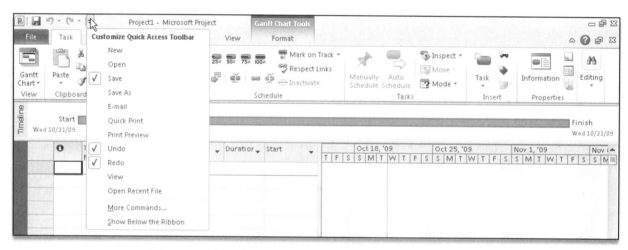

**Figure 2 - 45: Click the Customize Quick Access toolbar button
to customize the Quick Access Toolbar**

To display the *Quick Access Toolbar* below the *ribbon*, click the *Show Below the Ribbon* item on the pick list menu. The system moves the *Quick Access Toolbar* below the *ribbon* as shown in Figure 2 - 46.

Figure 2 - 46: Quick Access Toolbar displayed below the ribbon

To add or remove buttons on the *Quick Access Toolbar*, click the *Customize Quick Access Toolbar* button again. Notice that the pick list menu contains a number of frequently used buttons such as the *New, Open,* and *Print Preview* buttons. Select any one of these buttons to add it to the *Quick Access Toolbar*. To add other buttons, click the *More Commands* item on the pick list menu. The system displays the *Project Options* dialog with the *Quick Access Toolbar* section selected, as shown in Figure 2 - 47.

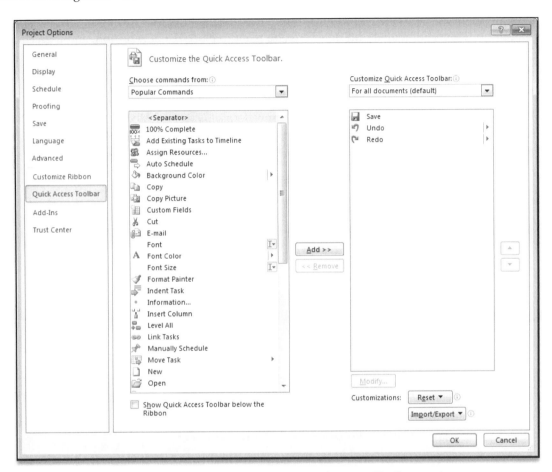

Figure 2 - 47: Project Options dialog, Quick Access Toolbar section

The process of customizing the *Quick Access Toolbar* is very similar to the process of customizing the *ribbon*. Click the *Choose Commands From* pick list to choose the type of commands you want to add to the *Quick Access Toolbar*. The pick list offers you a number of choices, including *Popular Commands* (the default setting), *Commands Not in the Ribbon, All Commands,* and *Macros,* plus the commands found on each of the available *ribbon* tabs. Select your option on the *Choose Commands From* pick list.

Click the *Customize the Quick Access Toolbar* pick list and choose how to customize the *Quick Access Toolbar*. The choices on the pick list allow you to customize the *Quick Access Toolbar* for all projects or only for the active project. The second option means that you can have a customized *Quick Access Toolbar* for each project, based on your project management needs for each project. Select your option on the *Customize the Quick Access Toolbar* pick list.

After you select your options on the *Choose Commands From* pick list and the *Customize the Quick Access Toolbar* pick list, you are ready to customize the *Quick Access Toolbar*. The software offers you the following customization choices:

- Add/remove buttons and separators on the *Quick Access Toolbar*.

- Change the order of buttons on the *Quick Access Toolbar*.

- Reset the *Quick Access Toolbar* to its default settings.

- Import or export the customized *ribbon* and *Quick Access Toolbar* settings to a file.

Adding/Removing Buttons on the Quick Access Toolbar

To add a button to the *Quick Access Toolbar*, select the button in the list of buttons on the left. In the list of buttons on the right, select a button representing the location where you want to place the new button, and then click the *Add* button. The system adds the new button **below** the selected button. To add a separator to organize the buttons into groups, select the <*Separator*> item at the top of the list on the left and click the *Add* button. You place separators in the list to add gridlines between buttons and separate the buttons into groups.

If you add a button for a macro to the *Quick Access Toolbar*, the system activates the *Modify* button on the *Quick Access Toolbar* section of the *Project Options* dialog. Click the *Modify* button to change the icon displayed for the button on the *Quick Access Toolbar*. The system displays the *Modify Button* dialog shown Figure 2 - 48.

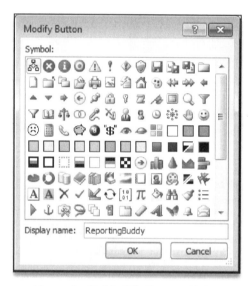

Figure 2 - 48: Modify Button dialog

To remove a button or separator on the *Quick Access Toolbar*, select the item in the list of buttons on the right, and then click the *Remove* button.

Tip: To add a button to the *Quick Access Toolbar* quickly, you do not need to use the *Project Options* dialog. Instead, right-click on any button on the *ribbon* and then select the *Add to Quick Access Toolbar* item on the shortcut menu.

Moving Items in the Quick Access Toolbar

Microsoft Project 2010 allows you to move the buttons and separators on the *Quick Access Toolbar* into the order you want to see them. To move any of these, select the item you want to move and then click the *Move Up* or *Move Down* button. Figure 2 - 49 and Figure 2 - 50 together, show the custom setup of my *Quick Access Toolbar*. I included the buttons I most commonly use, and then I organized the buttons into groups of similar functionality.

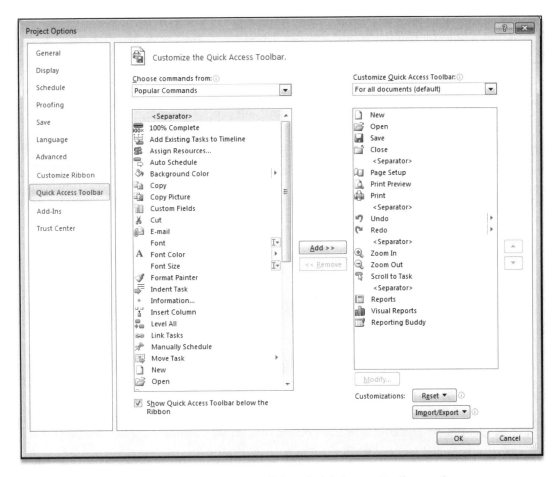

**Figure 2 - 49: Project Options dialog, Quick Access Toolbar section
after adding, moving, and renaming buttons to the Quick Access Toolbar**

Figure 2 - 50: Customized Quick Access Toolbar

Resetting the Quick Access Toolbar

Microsoft Project 2010 allows you to reset the *Quick Access Toolbar* to its default settings, or to reset **both** the *Quick Access Toolbar* and the *ribbon* to their default settings. To reset only the *Quick Access Toolbar*, click the *Reset* pick list button and choose the *Reset Only Quick Access Toolbar* item on the list. The system displays the *Reset Customizations* dialog shown in Figure 2 - 51. Click the *Yes* button to reset the *Quick Access Toolbar* to its default settings.

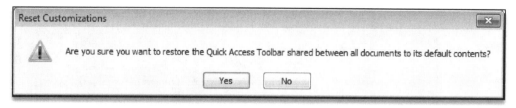

Figure 2 - 51: Confirmation dialog to restore the Quick Access Toolbar

To reset both the *Quick Access Toolbar* and the *ribbon,* click the *Reset* pick list button and choose the *Reset All Customizations* item on the list. The system displays the confirmation dialog shown in Figure 2 - 52. Click the *Yes* button to confirm the reset action.

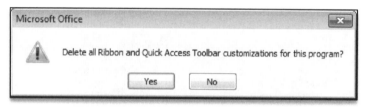

**Figure 2 - 52: Confirmation dialog to reset
the ribbon and Quick Access Toolbar**

 Warning: Notice in the dialog shown in the figure above that the system is about to reset all of the customizations to **both** the ribbon **and** the *Quick Access Toolbar*. If you do not want to reset customizations to the *ribbon* and the *Quick Access Toolbar*, then **do not** select the *Reset All Customizations* option.

 # Hands On Exercise

Exercise 2-4

Customize the *Quick Access Toolbar.*

1. At the right end of the *Quick Access Toolbar,* click the *Customize Quick Access Toolbar* pick list button and select the *Show Below the Ribbon* item on the list.

2. Click the *Customize Quick Access Toolbar* pick list button again and select the *More Commands* item on the list.

3. In the *Quick Access Toolbar* section of the *Project Options* dialog, click the *Choose Commands From* pick list and select the *All Commands* item on the list.

4. Add the following buttons to your *Quick Access Toolbar* and then move them into the order shown below:

- New

- Open

- Save (already on the Quick Access Toolbar)

- Close

- <Separator>

- Page Setup

- Print Preview

- Print

- <Separator>

- Undo (already on the Quick Access Toolbar)

- Redo (already on the Quick Access Toolbar)

- <Separator>

- Assign Resources

- Zoom In

- Zoom Out

- Scroll to Task

5. Click the *OK* button to close the *Project Options* dialog, and then examine the new buttons on your *Quick Access Toolbar*.

Importing/Exporting a Custom Ribbon

Microsoft Project 2010 allows you to export the *ribbon* and *Quick Access Toolbar* customization settings to a file. You can then give the file to other users who can import the customization settings into their own Microsoft Project 2010 application. To export these settings to a file, click the *Import/Export* pick list button and select the *Export All Customizations* item on the pick list. The system displays the *File Save* dialog shown in Figure 2 - 53. In the *File Save* dialog, enter a name for the customization file, select a destination for the file, and then click the *Save* button.

Notice in the following figure that ***.exportedUI** is file extension for the exported customization file.

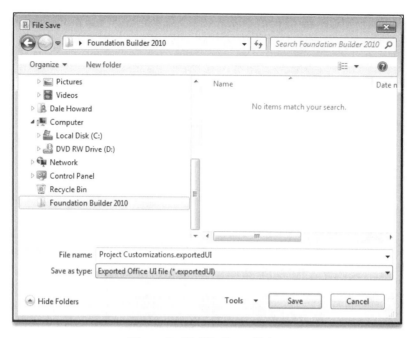

Figure 2 - 53: File Save dialog

To import a customized *ribbon*, click the *Import/Export* pick list button and select the *Import Customization File* item on the pick list. The system displays the *File Open* dialog shown in Figure 2 - 54. In the *File Open* dialog, navigate to the location of the customization file and select it, and then click the *Open* button.

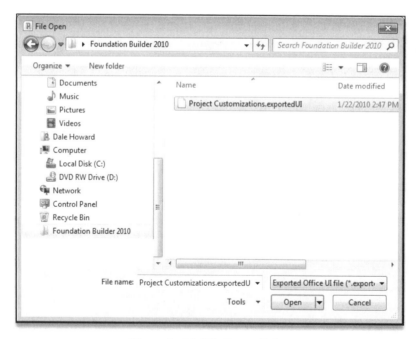

Figure 2 - 54: File Open dialog

The system displays the confirmation dialog shown in Figure 2 - 55. In the confirmation dialog, click the *Yes* button to import the customized *ribbon* and *Quick Access Toolbar* settings, and replace your current *ribbon* and *Quick Access Toolbar*. Click the *OK* button to close the *Project Options* dialog and view your new customized *ribbon* and *Quick Access Toolbar*.

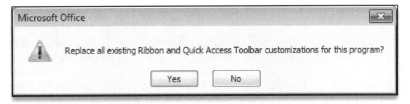

Figure 2 - 55: Warning dialog when importing a customized ribbon

 Hands On Exercise

Exercise 2-5

Export the *ribbon* and *Quick Access Toolbar* customization settings to a file.

1. Right-click anywhere on the *ribbon* and select the *Customize the Ribbon* item on the shortcut menu.

2. Click the *Import/Export* pick list button and select the *Export All Customizations* item on the list.

3. In the *File Save* dialog, leave the default name **Project Customizations.exportedUI** in the *File Name* field, and then click the *Save* button.

4. Click the *Reset* pick list button and select the *Reset All Customizations* item on the list.

5. When prompted in the confirmation dialog, click the *Yes* button to delete all customizations to the *ribbon* and the *Quick Access Toolbar*.

Notice how the system removed all of your customization settings to the *ribbon* and the *Quick Access Toolbar*.

6. Click the *Import/Export* pick list button again and select the *Import Customization File* item on the list.

7. In the *File Open* dialog, select the **Project Customizations.exportedUI** file, and then click the *Open* button.

8. When prompted in the confirmation dialog, click the *Yes* button to replace all current customization to the *ribbon* and the *Quick Access Toolbar*.

9. Click the *OK* button to close the *Project Options* dialog.

Notice how the system imports all of your previous customization settings.

As a bonus, the sample files for this book include a customization file containing the custom *Quick Access Toolbar* settings and the expanded *ribbon* customization recommended by MsProjectExperts. To apply these customizations to your own copy of Microsoft Project 2010, use the steps documented in the previous section with the **Custom Ribbon and Quick Access Menu.exportedUI** file during the import process. When prompted in a confirmation dialog, click the *Yes* button to import the customizations for the *ribbon* and the *Quick Access Toolbar*.

Understanding the Planning Wizard

The *Planning Wizard* is an interactive help feature in Microsoft Project 2010 that presents you with advice as you work on your project. The *Planning Wizard* offers guidance in three areas:

- Using Microsoft Project

- Scheduling

- Errors

The software displays the *Planning Wizard* any time you take an action that causes it to activate in any of the preceding three categories. For example, setting a *Finish No Later Than* constraint on a successor task displays the *Planning Wizard* message about scheduling shown in Figure 2 - 56.

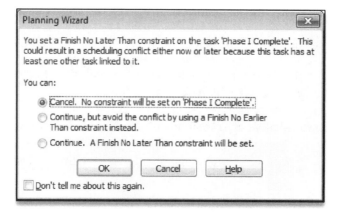

**Figure 2 - 56: Planning Wizard
message about scheduling**

You control the function of the *Planning Wizard* through options settings in the *Project Options* dialog. Click the *File* tab and then click the *Options* item in the *Backstage* menu to display the *Project Options* dialog. Click the *Advanced* tab in the *Project Options* dialog and examine the options in the *Planning Wizard* section shown in Figure 2 - 57.

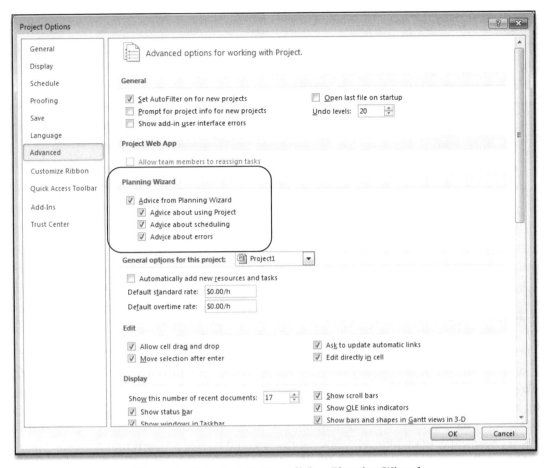

**Figure 2 - 57: Project Options dialog, Planning Wizard
options on the Advanced page**

Understanding Gantt Chart Symbols

To a new user of Microsoft Project 2010, understanding the symbols used in the *Gantt Chart* view can be a daunting task. The easiest way to learn about the symbols used in the *Gantt Chart* view is to open any project, print the *Gantt Chart* view of the project, and then study the *Legend* area at the bottom of any page. The *Legend* displays a simple key for understanding the symbols used in the *Gantt Chart* view, as shown in Figure 2 - 58.

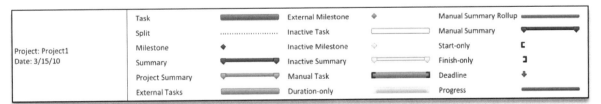

Figure 2 - 58: Legend for the Gantt Chart view

The only symbol the *Legend* does not explain is the arrow line drawn from one task to another, called the link line symbol. This symbol represents the dependency relationship between the two tasks, and models the order in which team members perform the two dependent tasks.

Reading a Gantt Chart

Once you understand Gantt chart symbols, you can begin to read and understand the Gantt chart. Consider the *Gantt Chart* view for the very simple project shown in Figure 2 - 59.

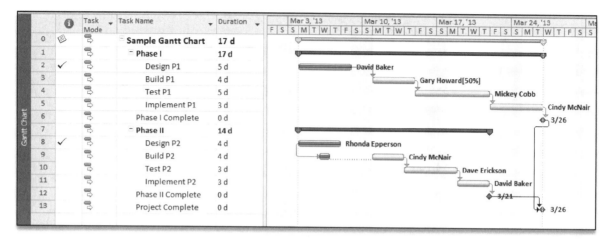

Figure 2 - 59: Gantt Chart view for a simple project

For this simple project, the Gantt chart visually reveals that the project structure includes two phases named Phase I and Phase II. You can quickly see that these two phases run parallel, meaning that the phases run concurrently. The summary Gantt bar for Phase I, represented by the black "jagged" Gantt bar, indicates that this phase runs from Monday, March 4, through Tuesday, March 26. The milestone symbol for the Phase I Complete task confirms that the finish date for this phase is Tuesday, March 26. The summary Gantt bar for Phase II indicates that this phase runs from Monday, March 4 through Thursday, March 21. The milestone symbol for the Phase II Complete task confirms that the finish date of this phase is Thursday, March 21. The summary Gantt bar for the Project Summary Task (Row 0), represented by the gray "jaggy" Gantt bar, indicates that the project runs from Monday, March 4, through Tuesday, March 26. The milestone symbol for the Project Complete task confirms that the scheduled finish date for the project is Tuesday, March 26.

The Gantt bar for each task reveals the current task schedule. For example, Microsoft Project 2010 schedules the Design P1 task from Monday, March 4, through Friday, March 8. The software schedules the Build P1 task from Monday, March 11, through Thursday, March 14. Remember that you can float your mouse pointer over any Gantt bar to learn its current scheduled start and finish dates. Microsoft Project 2010 determines the length of each Gantt bar based on the value shown for the task in the *Duration* column on the left side of the *Gantt Chart* view.

The progress bar (black stripe) running completely through the Gantt bars for the Design P1 and Design P2 tasks indicates that these two tasks are 100% complete. The progress bar for the Build P2 task runs only partially through its Gantt bar, indicating that this task is only partially complete. The split symbol (...) in the middle of Gantt bar for the Build P2 task indicates that the resource worked one day on the task, skipped the next two days (perhaps due to illness), and the remainder of the work is scheduled for the first three days of the next week.

 Do not be alarmed by the task split task symbol (...) in the Gantt bar for the Build P2 task. This symbol means that work started, stopped, and resumes at the current schedule date.

The link lines between the tasks in the *Gantt Chart* view indicate that all tasks must occur sequentially in the project, with the exception of the Design P2 and Build P2 tasks in Phase II. These two tasks must occur in parallel, with the Build P2 task starting two days after the Design P2 task starts. To model this relationship, I set a Start-to-Start (SS) dependency with two days of *Lag* time between these two tasks. Notice also that I linked both the Phase I Complete and Phase II Complete milestone tasks to the Project Complete milestone task. This guarantees that the Project Complete milestone shows the correct finish date of the entire project.

The Gantt chart reveals that all resources work full-time on tasks in this project, except for Gary Howard's assignment on the Build P1 task. To the right of his name on the task's Gantt bar, notice the *[50%]* notation. This indicates that Gary works half-time on this task, working approximately 4 hours per day for each of the 4 days. If you do not see a percentage notation to the right of the resource's name on any task's Gantt bar, this means the resource works full-time on the task.

Understanding Gantt-Optimized Scheduling Benefits

One of the unfortunate habits of many Microsoft Project 2010 users (and of many users of previous versions, as well) is that they simply use the tool to draw a *Gantt Chart* view of the project, and nothing more. It is a shame that people undervalue the best practice of using Gantt-optimized scheduling.

Referring back to Figure 2 - 59, notice the "waterfall structure" of tasks in the Phase I and Phase II sections of the project. Whether you want to schedule a project that uses an "agile" methodology like SCRUM, or you want to schedule a project that uses a formal phase-gate structure, your goal is to build a waterfall structure when you use Gantt-optimized scheduling. The benefit is that this forces you to build a schedule structure that also optimizes readability and analysis. Most notably, a clean waterfall structure allows you to avoid going overboard on dependency relationships revealing the true work paths in your project or process model. Simplicity is easier to manage; less is more.

One of the reasons why Microsoft Office Project 2010 users have a difficult time applying Gantt-optimized scheduling is because **organizational pressure** often seeks to represent the project process by organizational unit. You should design your project WBS to represent actual work paths and work flows. Designing a project schedule structure around organizational unit contributions is less productive compared to an integrated work path approach. MSProjectExperts recommends that you provide your users with an organizational-oriented project view to meet egocentric reporting demands.

Creating a Three-Tiered Timescale

The three-tiered *Timescale* allows you to display a different time unit on each tier. For example, an organization might need to show the fiscal year on one tier and the calendar year on the other two tiers. The default setting of the *Timescale* in Microsoft Project 2010 shows only two tiers, formatted with weeks on the top tier and days on the bottom tier. Each tier of the *Timescale* shows the time units displayed in the *Gantt Chart* view at the current level of zoom. To add a third tier to the *Timescale*, complete the following steps:

1. Double-click anywhere on the *Timescale*. The software displays the *Timescale* dialog shown in Figure 2 - 60.

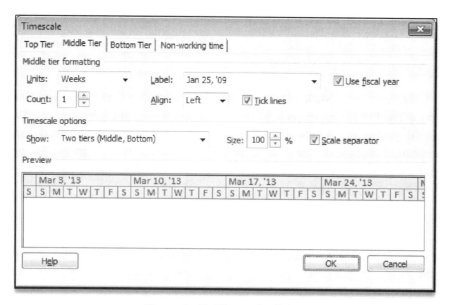

Figure 2 - 60: Timescale dialog

2. Click the *Top Tier* tab.

3. Click the *Show* pick list in the *Timescale options* section and select the *Three tiers (Top, Middle, Bottom)* item from the list.

4. Select your time *Units* and *Label* in the *Top Tier Formatting* section.

5. Click the *OK* button when finished.

Displaying Fiscal Year in a Three-Tiered Timescale

If your company uses a fiscal year different from the calendar year, you can use the three-tiered *Timescale* to display the fiscal year against the calendar year. Complete these steps to add a third tier to display the fiscal year:

1. Click the *File* tab and then click the *Options* item in the *Backstage* menu to display the *Project Options* dialog.

2. In the *Project Options* dialog, click the *Schedule* tab.

3. In the *Calendar options for this project* section of the *Schedule* page, click the *Fiscal year starts in* pick list and choose the beginning month for your organization's fiscal year.

4. Select the *Use starting year for FY number* checkbox, if necessary to display your organization's fiscal year correctly.

5. Click the *OK* button to close the *Project Options* dialog.

6. Double-click anywhere in the *Timescale* to display the *Timescale* dialog.

7. Click the *Show* pick list in the *Timescale options* section of the dialog and select the *Three tiers (Top, Middle, Bottom)* item from the list.

8. On the *Top Tier* page, set the *Units* value to *Years*, and leave the *Use fiscal year* option selected.

9. On the *Middle Tier* and *Bottom Tier* pages, select your desired *Units* options, then deselect the *Use fiscal year* option and click the *OK* button.

Figure 2 - 61 shows the three-tiered *Timescale* set to display the fiscal year on the top tier and the calendar year on the middle and bottom tiers. Notice in the top tier that the fiscal year 2014 begins in October 2013.

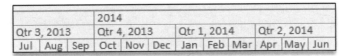

Figure 2 - 61: Three-Tiered Timescale

 The settings on the *Timescale* apply to only the current view in the active project. To apply the three-tiered *Timescale* to every future project, you must modify the *Timescale* settings for each project template that you use.

 Hands On Exercise

Exercise 2-6

Display the fiscal year on the top tier of a three-tiered timescale.

1. Navigate to the folder containing your student sample files and then open the **Format the Timescale.mpp** sample file.

2. Click the *File* tab and then click the *Options* item in the *Backstage* menu to display the *Project Options* dialog.

3. In the *Project Options* dialog, click the *Schedule* tab.

4. In the *Calendar options for this project* section of the *Schedule* page, click the *Fiscal year starts in* pick list and choose *April* as the beginning month for the organization's fiscal year.

5. Click the *OK* button to close the *Project Options* dialog.

6. Double-click anywhere in the *Timescale* to display the *Timescale* dialog.

7. In the *Timescale* dialog, click the *Show* pick list in the *Timescale options* section, and then select the *Three tiers (Top, Middle, Bottom)* item from the list.

8. Click the *Top Tier* tab to apply the *Top Tier* page.

9. On the *Top Tier* page, set the *Units* value to *Years*, and leave the *Use fiscal year* option selected.

10. Click the *Middle Tier* tab to apply the *Middle Tier* page.

11. On the *Middle Tier* page, specify the following values:

Field Name	Value to Set
Units	Months
Label	January 2009
Use fiscal year	**Deselected**

12. On the *Bottom Tier* page select the following values:

Field Name	Value to Set
Units	Weeks
Label	Jan 25, Feb 1, ...
Use fiscal year	**Deselected**

13. Click the *OK* button to close the *Timescale* dialog.

Examine the *Timescale* at the beginning of the project. Notice how the top tier of the *Timescale* displays the Fiscal Year (2015), while the middle tier displays the current month and calendar year (April 2014).

14. Save and close the **Format the Timescale.mpp** sample file.

Module 03

Inside Microsoft Project 2010

Learning Objectives

After completing this module, you will be able to:

- Understand the organization of data in the Microsoft Project data model
- Describe how the Microsoft Project data model affects views, tables, filters, and groups
- Describe the new views, filters, and groups in Microsoft Project 2010
- Use appropriate views, tables, filters, and groups
- Apply standard filters and highlight filters

Inside Module 03

Understanding the Microsoft Project Data Model

Figure 3 - 1 displays the simplified Microsoft Project data model as it affects views, tables, filters, and groups. Notice that Microsoft Project 2010 recognizes two separate and distinct types of data: *Task* data and *Resource* data. Each type of data has its own unique set of views, tables, filters, and groups.

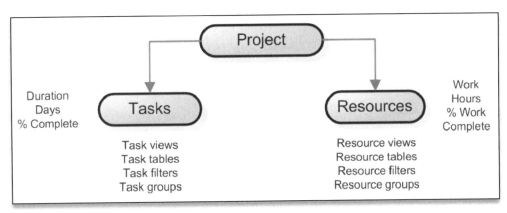

**Figure 3 - 1: Simplified Microsoft Office
Project 2010 Data Model**

Task data carries *Duration* values measured in days by default. Microsoft Project 2010 measures the percentage of the duration completed to date in the *% Complete* field. *Resource* data carries *Work* (or Effort) values, measured in hours by default. Microsoft Project 2010 measures the percentage of work completed to date in the *% Work Complete* field.

 It might be less confusing to some if Microsoft renamed the *% Complete* field as *the % Duration Complete* field because this field actually measures the percentage of the duration consumed to date.

Understanding Views

Microsoft Project 2010 includes 27 default views, of which 21 are task views and 6 are resource views. Software users often define views as "different ways of looking at my project data." Microsoft Project 2010 formally defines a view as:

View = Table + Filter + Group + Screen

In the preceding definition of a view, the *Table* displays the columns you wish to see, the *Filter* acts on the data to display only the rows you wish to see, the *Group* organizes the data rows into groups, and the *Screen* determines what appears on the right side of the view. Specifically, the *Screen* determines whether you see a Gantt chart, a timephased grid, or no screen at all on the right side of the view.

Removed from Microsoft Project 2010 are four PERT analysis views included in all previous versions of the software. These four views include the *PA_PERT Entry Sheet*, *PA_Optimistic Gantt*, *PA_Expected Gantt*, and *PA_Pessimistic Gantt* views.

Microsoft Project 2010 includes three new views, along with a new way to apply views. These three new views include the following:

- Gantt with Timeline
- Timeline
- Team Planner

The *Gantt with Timeline* view is the new default view Microsoft Project 2010 displays when you launch the software application. The *Gantt with Timeline* view is a combination view that consists of two separate views, each displayed in its own pane. The *Gantt with Timeline* view includes the *Timeline* view in the top pane and the *Gantt Chart* view in the bottom pane. Figure 3 - 2 shows the *Gantt with Timeline* view.

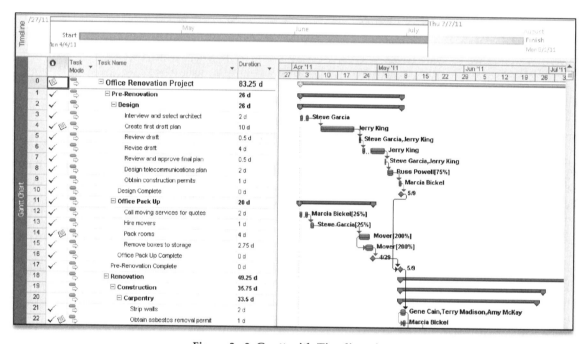

Figure 3 - 2: Gantt with Timeline view

 Warning: If you apply any other view after applying the *Gantt with Timeline* view, Microsoft Project 2010 continues to display the *Timeline* view in the top pane. To close the *Timeline* pane, double-click the bottom edge of the *Timeline* pane, or click the *View* tab and deselect the *Timeline* checkbox.

To apply any view, use any of the following methods:

- Click the *Task* tab to apply the *Task* ribbon. Click the *Gantt Chart* pick list button in the *View* section of the *Task* ribbon. Select any view on the list or select the *More Views* item on the list.

- Click the *Resource* tab to apply the *Resource* ribbon. Click the *Team Planner* pick list button in the *View* section of the *Resource* ribbon. Select any view on the list or select the *More Views* item on the list.

- Click the *View* tab to apply the *View* ribbon. Click any button in the *Task Views* or *Resource Views* sections of the *View* ribbon. You can also click the pick list selector on any button in these two sections and select a view on the list or select the *More Views* item on the list.

- Right-click on the *View Bar* and select the view directly from the list if available, or select the *More Views* item on the pick list. In the *More Views* dialog, select a view and click the *Apply* button. The *View Bar* is the gray bar that displays the name of the view on the left side of the screen. For example, you see that the *View Bar* displays the name *Gantt Chart* in Figure 3 - 2 shown previously.

Figure 3 - 3 shows the views available on the *Gantt Chart* pick list in the *Task Views* section of the *View* ribbon.

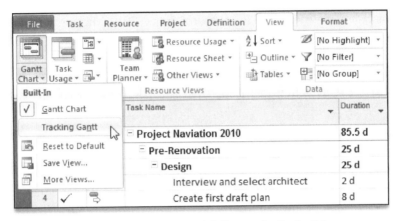

Figure 3 - 3: Gantt Chart pick list on the Task ribbon

When you click the *More Views* item on any pick list, the system displays the *More Views* dialog shown in Figure 3 - 4. In the *More Views* dialog, select any default or custom view and click the *Apply* button.

Figure 3 - 4: More Views dialog

By default, the *Gantt with Timeline* view does not appear on any view pick list, and appears only in the *More Views* dialog. To change this setting, display the *More Views* dialog, select the *Gantt with Timeline* view in the dialog, and then click the *Edit* button. In the *View Definition* dialog, select the *Show on Menu* checkbox and then click the *OK* button. After making this selection, you can select the *Gantt with Timeline* view from any view pick list, such as on the *Gantt Chart* pick list button on the *Task* ribbon.

In the *More Views* dialog, Microsoft Project 2010 allows you to edit any view by selecting it and then clicking the *Edit* button. Although the software allows you to do this, msProjectExperts recommends that you do not modify any of the default views included with the software. Instead, if no default view meets your reporting needs, copy a view that comes close and then modify that new view to meet your reporting needs.

The *Timeline* view is the second new view included in Microsoft Project 2010. Microsoft designed this view for use in combination with a task view, such as the *Gantt Chart* view, or with a resource view that also displays task or assignment information, such as the *Resource Usage* view. Applied alone, the *Timeline* view makes little sense unless you have already defined the items that appear on it. You need a data grid element to determine which items in the schedule appear on the view. I discuss in detail how to use and customize the *Timeline* view in Module 11, Project Reporting.

The third new view in Microsoft Project 2010 is the *Team Planner* view, shown in Figure 3 - 5. To display the *Team Planner* view, click the *Resource* tab and then click the *Team Planner* button. The *Team Planner* view is a new way for you to analyze resource assignment information in your projects. This new view is a very special type of resource view that shows the resources in your project team, along with the assigned and unassigned tasks in the project. Notice these details about the *Team Planner* view example shown in Figure 3 - 5:

- I previously assigned the Design task to Calvin Baker.

- I have not assigned the Build task to any team member.

- The Test and Implement tasks are *Unscheduled Tasks.*

- I have not assigned any tasks to David Dyer, Karly Brack, or Mickey Cobb.

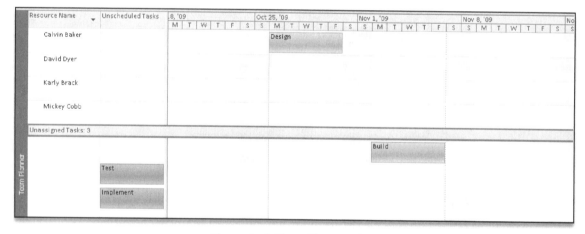

Figure 3 - 5: Team Planner view

I discuss in detail how to use and customize the *Team Planner* view in Module 07, Project Assignment Planning.

Using Single Views and Combination Views

In Microsoft Project 2010, a *Single* view is any view that displays in a single window. You commonly use *Single* views such as the *Gantt Chart* and *Resource Sheet* views.

In Microsoft Project 2010, a *Combination* view is any view that contains two views, displayed in a split-screen format with each view in its own pane. The view in the secondary pane (usually the bottom pane) displays detailed information about the selected task, resource, or assignment in the view contained in the primary pane (usually the top pane). The most commonly used *Combination* views are the *Task Entry* view and the new *Gantt with Timeline* view.

In the *Gantt with Timeline* view, the *Timeline* view is in the top pane, but this pane is the secondary pane. The *Gantt Chart* view is in the bottom pane, but this pane is the primary pane. This differs from all other *Combination* views, such as the *Task Entry* view.

Figure 3 - 6 shows a *Single* view, the *Tracking Gantt* view. Figure 3 - 7 shows a *Combination* view, the *Resource Allocation* view. The *Resource Allocation* view includes the *Resource Usage* view in the primary pane (top pane) and the *Leveling Gantt* view in the secondary pane (bottom pane). You can use the *Resource Allocation* view for leveling resource overallocations.

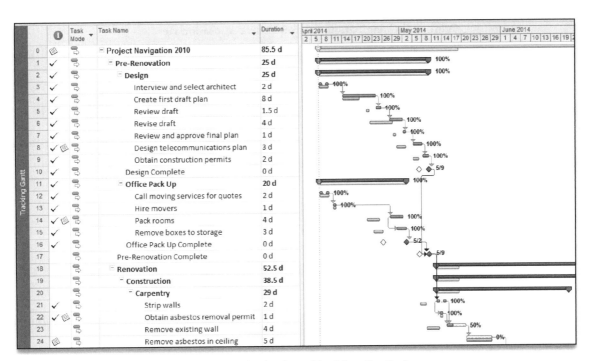

Figure 3 - 6: Single view - Tracking Gantt view

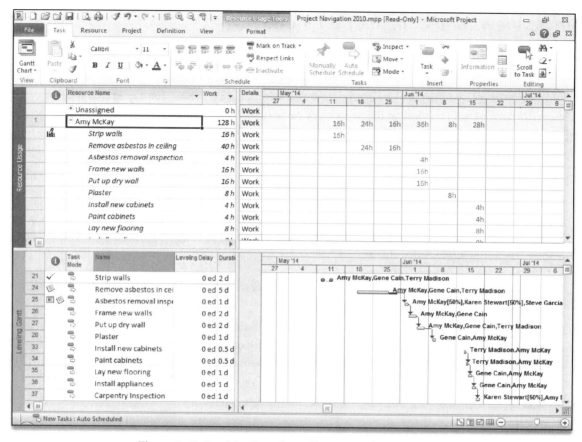

Figure 3 - 7: Combination view - Resource Allocation view

Hands On Exercise

Exercise 3-1

Apply task and resource views in Microsoft Project 2010.

1. Open the **Software Project in Development 2010.mpp** sample file.

Notice that this sample project **does not** show the *Gantt with Timeline* view.

2. Click the *Task* tab, click the *Gantt Chart* pick list button, and then select the *More Views* item on the pick list.

3. In the *More Views* dialog, select the *Gantt with Timeline* view, and then click the *Apply* button.

4. Using the *Gantt Chart* pick list button on the *Task* ribbon, apply the *Calendar* view.

5. Click the *View* tab to display the *View* ribbon.

6. In the *Task Views* section of the *View* ribbon, click the *Task Usage* button to apply the *Task Usage* view.

7. In the *Split View* section of the *View* ribbon **deselect** the *Timeline* checkbox to close the *Timeline* view pane.

8. Click the *Resource* tab to display the *Resource* ribbon.

9. Using the *Team Planner* pick list button on the *Resource* ribbon, apply and examine each of the following resource views:

   - Resource Sheet

   - Resource Usage

   - Team Planner

10. Study the task assignments for each resource in the *Team Planner* view, including unscheduled tasks, and study the tasks shown in the *Unassigned Tasks* section as well.

11. Click the *View* tab to display the *View* ribbon again.

12. In the *Resource Views* section of the *View* ribbon, click the *Other Views* pick list button and then select the *More Views* item in the list.

13. In the *More Views* dialog, select the *Task Entry* view and then click the *Apply* button.

14. In the upper pane (*Gantt Chart* view), select task ID #2, *Conduct needs analysis*.

15. In the lower pane (*Task Form* view), examine the assignment information for the resource assigned to this task.

16. In the *Split View* section of the *View* ribbon, **deselect** the *Details* checkbox to close the lower viewing pane.

17. In the *Task Views* section of the *View* ribbon, click the *Gantt Chart* pick list button and select the *More Views* item in the list.

18. In the *More Views* dialog, select the *Task Sheet* view and then click the *Apply* button.

Notice that the *Task Sheet* view includes a table (set of columns) on the left side but **does not** include any screen on the right side of the view.

19. Save but do not close the **Software Project in Development 2010.mpp** sample file.

Understanding Tables

Microsoft Project 2010 includes 27 default tables, of which 17 are task tables and 10 are resource tables. By definition, a table is a collection of columns (fields) and the name of each table describes the type of columns in the collection. For example, the task *Cost* table contains columns showing the cost data associated with each task in the project. Because Microsoft Project 2010 displays tables within views, you **must** use task tables with task views and resource tables with resource views.

Microsoft Project 2010 does not include any new tables, but several of the default task tables now include the *Task Mode* column, and you apply tables using a new method. The *Task Mode* column allows you to specify whether tasks are *Auto Scheduled* or *Manually Scheduled*. For *Auto Scheduled* tasks, the software calculates the start and finish dates automatically. For *Manually Scheduled* tasks, the software does not specify a default duration value, and does not calculate the start and finish dates. This leaves *Manually Scheduled* tasks as unscheduled.

The default task tables that include the *Task Mode* column are the *Entry*, *Rollup*, *Schedule*, and *Summary* tables. Figure 3 - 8 shows the *Entry* table applied in the *Gantt Chart* view. Notice that I set the *Task Mode* value to *Auto Scheduled* for the first two tasks and to *Manually Scheduled* for the last two tasks. Notice how Microsoft Project 2010 displays the Gantt bars for these tasks in the Gantt chart, as solid bars for *Auto Scheduled* tasks, and as hollow bars for *Manually Scheduled* tasks.

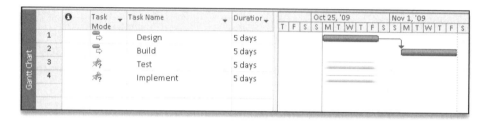

Figure 3 - 8: Entry table shows the Task Mode column

In addition to the tables that now contain the *Task Mode* column, Microsoft also changed one of the default columns displayed in the task *Baseline* table. In all previous versions of the software, the *Baseline* table includes the *Baseline Duration* column to the right of the *Task Name* column. In Microsoft Project 2010, the *Baseline* table now includes the *Baseline Estimated Duration* column in place of the *Baseline Duration* column. Do not be confused by the column header of the *Baseline Estimated Duration* column becuase Microsoft added a *Title* to the column so that *Baseline Duration* appears in the column header instead of *Baseline Estimated Duration*.

In addition to the changes in several default tables, Microsoft Project 2010 uses a new method to apply a table. To apply any table in the current view, use one of the following methods:

- Right-click on the *Select All* button (upper left corner of the *Task Sheet* or *Resource Sheet*) and then choose one of the commonly used tables shown on the shortcut menu.

- Right-click on the *Select All* button and then choose the *More Tables* item the shortcut menu. In the *More Tables* dialog, select a table and then click the *Apply* button.

- Click the *View* tab and then click the *Table* pick list in the *Data* section of the *View* ribbon. On the *Table* pick list, choose one of the commonly used tables on the list, or select the *More Tables* item on the list.

Figure 3 - 9 shows the list of available tables on the *Tables* pick list in the *Data* section of the *View* ribbon.

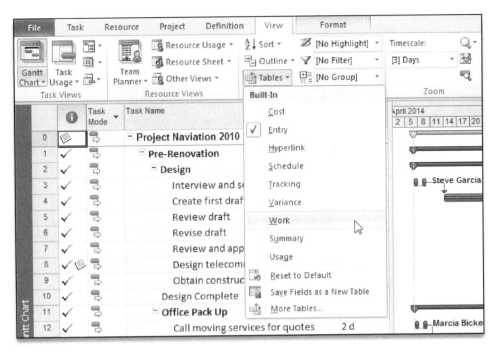

Figure 3 - 9: Tables pick list on the View ribbon

When you select the *More Tables* item on any menu, the system displays the *More Tables* dialog shown in Figure 3 - 10. In the *More Tables* dialog, select any table and click the *Apply* button.

Figure 3 - 10: More Tables dialog

Warning: While in a task view, such as the *Gantt Chart* view, the *More Tables* dialog only allows you to apply task tables, such as the *Schedule* table. While in a resource view, such as the *Resource Sheet* view, the *More Tables* dialog only allows you to apply resource tables, such as the *Usage* table. Keep in mind that the Microsoft Project data model governs this behavior.

In the *More Tables* dialog, Microsoft Project 2010 allows you to edit any table by selecting it and then clicking the *Edit* button. Although the software allows you to do this, MSProjectExperts recommends that you do not modify any of the default tables included with the software. Instead, if no default table meets your reporting needs, copy a table that comes close and then modify that new table to meet your reporting needs.

Figure 3 - 11 shows the task *Schedule* table applied in the *Task Sheet* view. Figure 3 - 12 shows the resource *Work* table applied in the *Resource Sheet* view.

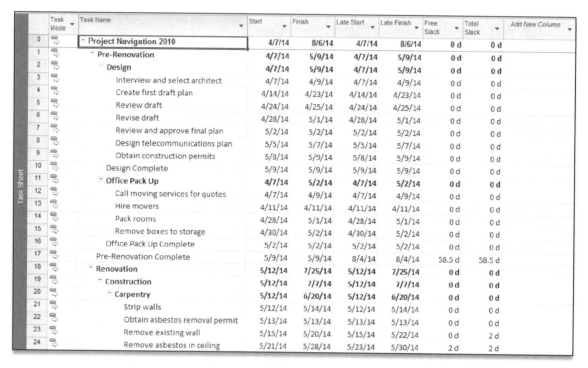

	Task Mode	Task Name	Start	Finish	Late Start	Late Finish	Free Slack	Total Slack	Add New Column
0		− Project Navigation 2010	4/7/14	8/6/14	4/7/14	8/6/14	0 d	0 d	
1		− Pre-Renovation	4/7/14	5/9/14	4/7/14	5/9/14	0 d	0 d	
2		− Design	4/7/14	5/9/14	4/7/14	5/9/14	0 d	0 d	
3		Interview and select architect	4/7/14	4/9/14	4/7/14	4/9/14	0 d	0 d	
4		Create first draft plan	4/14/14	4/23/14	4/14/14	4/23/14	0 d	0 d	
5		Review draft	4/24/14	4/25/14	4/24/14	4/25/14	0 d	0 d	
6		Revise draft	4/28/14	5/1/14	4/28/14	5/1/14	0 d	0 d	
7		Review and approve final plan	5/2/14	5/2/14	5/2/14	5/2/14	0 d	0 d	
8		Design telecommunications plan	5/5/14	5/7/14	5/5/14	5/7/14	0 d	0 d	
9		Obtain construction permits	5/8/14	5/9/14	5/8/14	5/9/14	0 d	0 d	
10		Design Complete	5/9/14	5/9/14	5/9/14	5/9/14	0 d	0 d	
11		− Office Pack Up	4/7/14	5/2/14	4/7/14	5/2/14	0 d	0 d	
12		Call moving services for quotes	4/7/14	4/9/14	4/7/14	4/9/14	0 d	0 d	
13		Hire movers	4/11/14	4/11/14	4/11/14	4/11/14	0 d	0 d	
14		Pack rooms	4/28/14	5/1/14	4/28/14	5/1/14	0 d	0 d	
15		Remove boxes to storage	4/30/14	5/2/14	4/30/14	5/2/14	0 d	0 d	
16		Office Pack Up Complete	5/2/14	5/2/14	5/2/14	5/2/14	0 d	0 d	
17		Pre-Renovation Complete	5/9/14	5/9/14	8/4/14	8/4/14	58.5 d	58.5 d	
18		− Renovation	5/12/14	7/25/14	5/12/14	7/25/14	0 d	0 d	
19		− Construction	5/12/14	7/7/14	5/12/14	7/7/14	0 d	0 d	
20		− Carpentry	5/12/14	6/20/14	5/12/14	6/20/14	0 d	0 d	
21		Strip walls	5/12/14	5/14/14	5/12/14	5/14/14	0 d	0 d	
22		Obtain asbestos removal permit	5/13/14	5/13/14	5/13/14	5/13/14	0 d	0 d	
23		Remove existing wall	5/15/14	5/20/14	5/15/14	5/22/14	0 d	2 d	
24		Remove asbestos in ceiling	5/21/14	5/28/14	5/23/14	5/30/14	2 d	2 d	

Figure 3 - 11: Schedule table displayed in the Task Sheet view

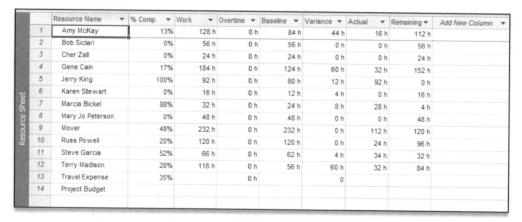

	Resource Name	% Comp.	Work	Overtime	Baseline	Variance	Actual	Remaining	Add New Column
1	Amy McKay	13%	128 h	0 h	84 h	44 h	16 h	112 h	
2	Bob Siclari	0%	56 h	0 h	56 h	0 h	0 h	56 h	
3	Cher Zall	0%	24 h	0 h	24 h	0 h	0 h	24 h	
4	Gene Cain	17%	184 h	0 h	124 h	60 h	32 h	152 h	
5	Jerry King	100%	92 h	0 h	80 h	12 h	92 h	0 h	
6	Karen Stewart	0%	16 h	0 h	12 h	4 h	0 h	16 h	
7	Marcia Bickel	88%	32 h	0 h	24 h	8 h	28 h	4 h	
8	Mary Jo Peterson	0%	48 h	0 h	48 h	0 h	0 h	48 h	
9	Mover	48%	232 h	0 h	232 h	0 h	112 h	120 h	
10	Russ Powell	20%	120 h	0 h	120 h	0 h	24 h	96 h	
11	Steve Garcia	52%	66 h	0 h	62 h	4 h	34 h	32 h	
12	Terry Madison	28%	116 h	0 h	56 h	60 h	32 h	84 h	
13	Travel Expense	35%		0 h		0			
14	Project Budget								

Figure 3 - 12: Work table displayed in the Resource Sheet view

Notice in the tables shown in Figure 3 - 11 and Figure 3 - 12 that each table includes an extra column labeled *Add New Column* at the right end of the table. This extra column is a new virtual column that appears by default in every table you apply in Microsoft Project 2010. The *Add New Column* virtual column allows you to add a default column to the current table, or to create a custom column. I discuss how to use the *Add New Column* virtual column feature in Module 09, Variance Analysis.

Hands On Exercise

Exercise 3-2

Apply task and resource tables in Microsoft Project 2010.

1. Return to the **Software Project in Development 2010.mpp** sample file.

Notice the *Task Mode* column to the left of the *Task Name* column. Microsoft Project 2010 includes this column by default in the task *Entry* table, shown currently in the *Task Sheet* view.

2. Right-click on the *Select All* button and successively select each of the following task tables:

   - Cost

   - Work

   - Schedule

3. Click the *View* tab to display the *View* ribbon, if necessary.

4. In the *Data* section of the *View* ribbon, click the *Tables* pick list and select the *More Tables* item on the list.

5. In the *More Tables* dialog, select the *Baseline* table and then click the *Apply* button.

6. Float your mouse pointer over the *Baseline Dur.* column header to determine the real name of this column

Notice in the tool tip that the real name of this column is actually *Baseline Duration*, while its *Title* (or abbreviated name) is *Baseline Dur*.

7. Right-click on the *Select All* button again and select the *Entry* table.

8. In the *Resource Views* section of the *View* ribbon, click the *Resource Sheet* button to apply the *Resource Sheet* view.

9. Right-click on the *Select All* button and successively select each of the following task tables:

   - Cost

   - Work

   - Summary

10. In the *Task Views* section of the *View* ribbon, click the *Gantt Chart* button to reapply the *Gantt Chart* view.

11. Save and close the **Software Project in Development 2010.mpp** sample file.

Understanding Filters

Microsoft Project 2010 ships with 60 default filters, of which 35 are task filters and 25 are resource filters. Filters allow you to extract specific information from tables according to the criteria in the filter. Because Microsoft Project 2010 applies filters within views, you must use task filters with task views and resource filters with resource views. Microsoft Project 2010 includes four new task filters, along with a new way to apply both standard filters and highlight filters. The four new filters include the following:

- Active Tasks

- Late Tasks

- Manually Scheduled Tasks

- Tasks Without Dates

You use the *Active Tasks* filter in conjunction with the new *Inactivate Task* feature that allows you to cancel tasks no longer needed in the project. The *Active Tasks* filter, therefore, displays all tasks with a *Yes* value in the *Active* field, which allows you to filter out cancelled (*Inactive*) tasks.

 The *Inactivate Task* feature is **only** available in Microsoft Project 2010 Professional.

You use the *Late Tasks* filter to identify any task where progress is behind schedule. The *Late Tasks* filter displays only those tasks with a *Late* value in the *Status* field. By default, the software calculates a *Late* value in the *Status* field when the timephased cumulative Percent Complete (represented by the black progress line in a Gantt bar) does not reach the *Status Date* you specify for the project.

You use the *Manually Scheduled Tasks* filter to locate tasks with this setting in your project. The *Manually Scheduled* filter displays only those tasks with a *Manually Scheduled* value in the *Task Mode* field.

You use the *Tasks Without Dates* filter to locate tasks that do not have a date in the *Start* or *Finish* fields. By default, *Manually Scheduled* tasks do not have a system-calculated start date or a finish date, but may contain these date and duration values that you enter manually. At some point during the life of your project, however, you must convert *Manually Scheduled* tasks to *Auto Scheduled* in order for the system to calculate these dates based on dependency links or resource availability. You use the *Tasks Without Dates* filter to locate *Manually Scheduled* tasks that do not yet have a system-calculated start date or finish date.

Applying a Standard Filter

In addition to the four new filters, Microsoft Project 2010 introduces a new method for applying filters. To apply any filter as a standard filter, click the *View* tab. In the *Data* section of the *View* ribbon, click the *Filter* pick list and select a standard filter, as shown in Figure 3 - 13.

Figure 3 - 13: Apply a Standard Filter

Notice in Figure 3 - 13 that the *Filter* pick list allows you to choose from a list of most commonly used filters, and allows you other filtering options such as *Clear Filter* to remove filtering criteria, *New Filter* to create a new filter from scratch, *More Filters* to display the *More Filters* dialog, and *Display AutoFilter* to turn on the *AutoFilter* feature in the data grid. On the *Filter* pick list, click the name of the filter you want to apply as a standard filter. When you apply a standard filter, the software displays only those tasks that meet your filtering criteria.

Any filter name that ends with an ellipsis (**...**) is an **interactive filter** that prompts you for additional information before you can apply the filter. Interactive filters on the *Filter* pick list include the *Date Range*, *Task Range*, and *Using Resource* filters.

If you click the *More Filter* item on the *Filter* pick list, the system displays the *More Filters* dialog shown in Figure 3 - 14. This dialog displays all available default and custom filters. Select any filter and click the *Apply* button to apply the filter as a standard filter, or click the *Highlight* button to apply the filter as a highlight filter. When you apply a filter as a highlight filter, Microsoft Project 2010 displays all tasks (or resources) in the project, and highlights only the data that meet your filtering criteria using yellow cell background formatting. I discuss highlight filters in more detail in the following section of this module.

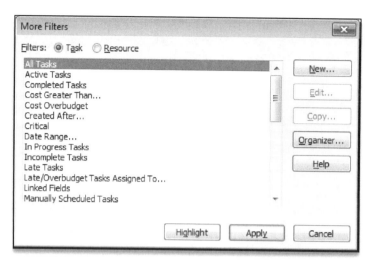

Figure 3 - 14: More Filters dialog

 In the *More Filters* dialog, Microsoft Project 2010 allows you to edit any filter by selecting it and then clicking the *Edit* button. Although the software allows you to do this, MSProjectExperts recommends that you do not modify any of the default filters included with the software. Instead, if no default filter meets your reporting needs, copy a filter that comes close and then modify that new filter to meet your reporting needs.

To remove a filter and reapply the *[No Filter]* filter, click the *Filter* pick list again and choose either the *[No Filter]* item or the *Clear Filter* item on the pick list.

 Keyboard Shortcut: Press the **F3** function key on your keyboard to apply the *All Tasks* standard filter in any task view or the *All Resources* standard filter in any resource view.

Figure 3 - 15 shows the *Resource Group...* filter applied as a standard filter to a project, filtering for members of the *Architect* group. Notice that the filter extracts five tasks in *Pre-Renovation* phase and *Design* deliverable sections of the project.

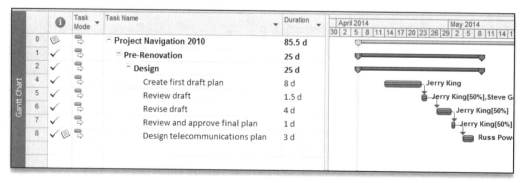

Figure 3 - 15: Resource Group... filter applied as a standard filter

Applying a Highlight Filter

In addition to standard filters, Microsoft Project 2010 uses a new method for applying highlight filters. When you apply a highlight filter in a task view, the system displays all tasks in the project, but highlights all tasks that meet the filter criteria using yellow cell background formatting. When you apply a highlight filter in a resource view, the system displays all resources in the project, but highlights all resources that meet the filter criteria using yellow cell background formatting. To apply any filter as a highlight filter, click the *View* tab. In the *Data* section of the *View* ribbon, click the *Highlight* pick list and select a highlight filter, as shown in Figure 3 - 16.

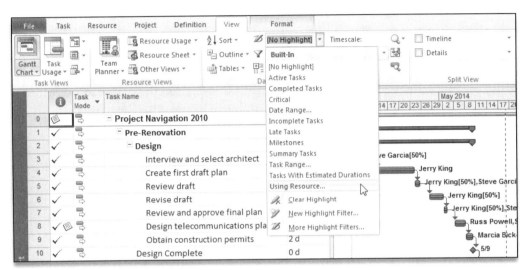

Figure 3 - 16: Apply a Highlight Filter

Notice in Figure 3 - 16 that the *Highlight* pick list allows you to choose from a list of the most commonly used filters, and provides other filtering options such as *Clear Highlight* to remove the highlight filter, *New Highlight Filter* to create a new highlight filter, and *More Highlight Filters* that opens the *More Highlight Filters* dialog. On the *Highlight* pick list, click the name of the filter you want to apply as a highlight filter.

The list of filters shown on the *Highlight* pick list and the *Filter* pick list are identical. When you create a new filter and select the option to show it on the menu, Microsoft Project 2010 displays the new filter on **both** the *Highlight* pick list **and** the *Filter* pick list automatically.

To remove a highlight filter and reapply the *[No Filter]* filter, click the *Highlight* pick list again and choose either the *[No Highlight]* item or the *Clear Highlight* item on the pick list.

You can also press the **F3** keyboard shortcut to to remove the current highlight filter and reapply the *All Tasks* or *All Resources* highlight filter.

Figure 3 - 17 shows the *Resource Group...* filter applied as a highlight filter to a project, again filtering for members of the *Architect* group. Notice that the highlight filter displays all tasks in the project, but highlights five tasks in the Pre-Renovation phase and Design deliverable sections of the project.

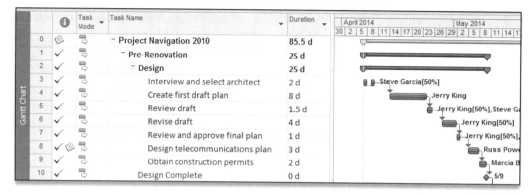

Figure 3 - 17: Resource Group... filter applied as a Highlight filter

Hands On Exercise

Exercise 3-3

Explore the new filters in Microsoft Project 2010.

1. Open the **CRM Software Development 2010.mpp** sample file.

2. Click the *View* tab to apply the *View* ribbon, if necessary.

3. In the *Data* section of the *View* ribbon, click the *Filter* pick list and select the *Active Tasks* filter.

Notice that the *Active Tasks* filter **excludes** task ID #21, Re-Test Modified Code, because this task is an *Inactive* (cancelled) task.

4. Click the *Filter* pick list and select the *Late Tasks* filter.

Notice that the *Late Tasks* filter displays only task IDs #13 and #14, the Develop Code and Developer Testing tasks. The software considers both tasks late because their progress line falls short of the *Status Date* line, indicated by the red-dashed vertical line in the *Gantt Chart* view.

5. Click the *Highlight* pick list and click the *More Highlight Filters* item on the list.

6. In the *More Filters* dialog, select the *Manually Scheduled Tasks* filter and then click the *Highlight* button.

Notice that when you apply the *Manually Scheduled Tasks* filter as a highlight filter, the software highlights all of the tasks in the *Testing* phase with the yellow cell background color.

7. Click the *Highlight* pick list and click the *More Highlight Filters* item on the list.

8. In the *More Filters* dialog, select the *Tasks Without Dates* filter and then click the *Highlight* button.

Notice that the software highlights only task ID #20, Modify Code.

9. Pull your split bar to the right of the *Finish* column to see that the Modify Code task has no *Start* date or *Finish* date.

10. Press the **F3** function key to reapply the *[No Filter]* filter.

11. Save and close the **CRM Software Development 2010.mpp** sample file.

Exercise 3-4

Apply a standard filter and a highlight filter in Microsoft Project 2010.

1. Open the **Project Navigation 2010.mpp** sample file.

2. Click the *View* tab to apply the *View* ribbon, if necessary.

3. In the *Data* section of the *View* ribbon, click the *Filter* pick list and select the *Using Resource…* filter.

4. In the *Using Resource* dialog, select the resource named Russ Powell and then click the *OK* button.

Notice how applying this filter as a standard filter displays only those tasks assigned to Russ Powell in the three phases of the project.

5. Press the **F3** function key to reapply the *[No Filter]* filter.

6. In the *Data* section of the *View* ribbon, click the *Highlight* pick list and select the *Using Resource…* filter.

7. In the *Using Resource* dialog, select *Russ Powell* again and click the *OK* button.

Notice how applying this filter as a highlight filter displays all tasks, but highlights all of Russ Powell's tasks using the yellow cell background color.

8. Press the **F3** function key to reapply the *[No Filter]* filter.

9. Save and close the **Project Navigation 2010.mpp** sample file.

Understanding Groups

Microsoft Project 2010 ships with 20 default groups, of which 13 are task groups and 7 are resource groups. You use groups to organize and sort task or resource information. Because Microsoft Project 2010 applies groups within views, you must use task groups with task views and resource groups with resource views. The system includes four new groups for task data, along with a new method for applying a group. These four new groups include:

- Active v. Inactive

- Auto Scheduled v. Manually Scheduled

- Resource

- Status

The *Active v. Inactive* group organizes tasks into two groups according to each task's value in the *Active* field. Remember that you can set an unneeded task as inactive in your project by selecting a *No* value in the *Active* field.

The *Auto Scheduled v. Manually Scheduled* group organizes tasks into two groups according to each task's value in the *Task Mode* field. Remember that the value you specify in the *Task Mode* field for a task determines whether the software calculates the *Start* date and *Finish* date for the task automatically, or whether you have to enter a *Start* date and *Finish* date manually.

The *Resource* group organizes tasks into groups according to the names of the resource(s) assigned to each task, as listed in the *Resource Names* field. Figure 3 - 18 shows the *Resource* group applied to the *Task Sheet* view in a project.

	❶	Task Mode	Task Name	Duration	Start	Finish	Predecessors	Resource Names	Add New Column
			⊞ **Resource Names: No Value**	**0d**	Fri 4/29/11	Mon 8/1/11			
			⊟ **Resource Names: Amy McKay,Gene Cain,Terry Madison**	**5d**	Wed 5/18/1:	Tue 5/24/11		**Amy McKay,Gene**	
24	📝		Remove asbestos in ceilings	5 d	Wed 5/18/11	Tue 5/24/11	23,22	Amy McKay,Gene Ca	
			⊟ **Resource Names: Bob Siclari**	**5d**	Tue 6/7/11	Wed 6/15/1:		**Bob Siclari**	
48			Install pipes	5 d	Tue 6/7/11	Mon 6/13/11	40SS+2 d	Bob Siclari	
49			Install sink and faucets	1 d	Tue 6/14/11	Tue 6/14/11	48	Bob Siclari	
50			Connect appliances	0.25 d	Wed 6/15/11	Wed 6/15/11	49	Bob Siclari	
			⊟ **Resource Names: Cher Zall**	**1d**	Fri 7/1/11	Wed 7/13/1:		**Cher Zall**	
64			Order new furniture	1 d	Fri 7/1/11	Tue 7/5/11	63	Cher Zall[50%]	
65			Order Blinds	1 d	Tue 7/5/11	Tue 7/5/11	64SS	Cher Zall[50%]	
66			Install blinds	1 d	Wed 7/13/11	Wed 7/13/11	65FS+5 d	Cher Zall	
			⊟ **Resource Names: Gene Cain**	**2d**	Tue 6/14/11	Mon 6/20/1:		**Gene Cain**	
29			Sand	0.5 d	Tue 6/14/11	Tue 6/14/11	28	Gene Cain	
30			Paint (1st coat)	2 d	Wed 6/15/11	Thu 6/16/11	29	Gene Cain	
31			Paint (2nd coat)	2 d	Fri 6/17/11	Mon 6/20/11	30	Gene Cain	
			⊟ **Resource Names: Gene Cain,Amy McKay**	**2d**	Wed 6/1/11	Fri 6/24/11		**Gene Cain,Amy Mc**	
26			Frame new walls	2 d	Wed 6/1/11	Thu 6/2/11	25	Gene Cain,Amy McK	
28			Plaster	1 d	Mon 6/13/11	Tue 6/14/11	27	Gene Cain,Amy McK	
35			Lay new flooring	1 d	Wed 6/22/11	Thu 6/23/11	34	Gene Cain,Amy McK	
36			Install appliances	1 d	Thu 6/23/11	Fri 6/24/11	35	Gene Cain,Amy McK	
			⊟ **Resource Names: Gene Cain,Terry Madison,Amy McKay**	**2.5d**	Tue 5/10/11	Mon 6/13/1:		**Gene Cain,Terry M**	
21	✓		Strip walls	2 d	Tue 5/10/11	Wed 5/11/11	17	Gene Cain,Terry Mac	
27			Put up dry wall	2.5 d	Fri 6/3/11	Mon 6/13/11	26	Gene Cain,Terry Mac	
			⊟ **Resource Names: Jerry King**	**10d**	Mon 4/11/1:	Tue 5/3/11		**Jerry King**	
4	✓📝		Create first draft plan	10 d	Mon 4/11/11	Fri 4/22/11	3	Jerry King	
6	✓		Revise draft	4 d	Tue 4/26/11	Tue 5/3/11	5	Jerry King	

Figure 3 - 18: Resource group applied to the Task Sheet view

The *Status* group organizes tasks into four groups, according to the value in the *Status* field for each task. Microsoft Project 2010 automatically calculates the values in the *Status* field and selects one of four values for each task. The four possible values in the *Status* field include *Future Task, On Schedule, Late,* and *Complete*.

> When you apply the *Status* group to a project, this group includes the summary tasks automatically, and maintains the task hierarchy. In addition, Microsoft Project 2010 displays the outline number value for each summary task and formats each summary task with a light blue cell background formatting.

Applying a Group

In addition to providing four new groups, Microsoft Project 2010 provides a new method for applying groups. To apply a group to your project data, click the *View* tab. In the *Data* section of the *View* ribbon, click the *Group By* pick list and select a group or select the *More Groups* item, as shown in Figure 3 - 19.

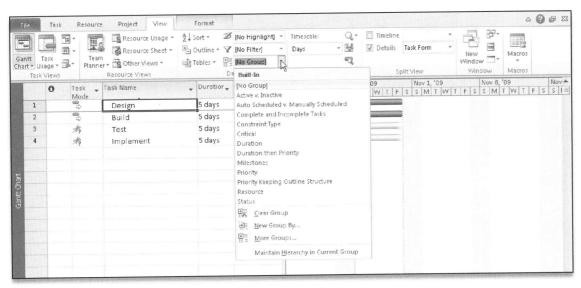

Figure 3 - 19: Apply a group

If you select the *More Groups* item on the *Group By* pick list, the system displays the *More Groups* dialog shown in Figure 3 - 20. In the *More Groups* dialog, select any default or custom group and then click the *Apply* button.

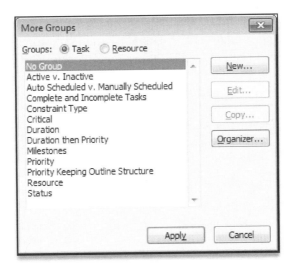

Figure 3 - 20: More Groups dialog

In the *More Groups* dialog, Microsoft Project 2010 allows you to edit any group by selecting it and then clicking the *Edit* button. Although the software allows you to do this, msProjectExperts recommends that you do not modify any of the default groups included with the software. Instead, if no default group meets your reporting needs, copy a group that comes close and then modify that new group to meet your reporting needs.

Another new feature on the *Group By* pick list is the *Maintain Hierarchy in Current Group* item at the bottom of the list. When you apply a group in any task view, most of the default groups do not display the work breakdown structure

(WBS) of summary tasks for the grouped tasks. This can create a confusing situation when you use same-named tasks in different summary task sections of your project. For example, Figure 3 - 21 shows a list of tasks in a project that includes summary tasks representing the phase and deliverable sections of the project. Notice that the Deliverable 1 and Deliverable 2 summary sections each contain four same-named tasks (Design, Build, Test, and Implement).

	❶	Task	Task Name	Duration	Start	Finish	Predecessors
1			⊟ **Phase I**	**29 d**	**11/6/09**	**12/16/09**	
2			⊟ **Deliverable 1**	**15 d**	**11/6/09**	**11/26/09**	
3			Design	3 d	11/6/09	11/10/09	
4			Build	5 d	11/11/09	11/17/09	3
5			Test	4 d	11/18/09	11/23/09	4
6			Implement	3 d	11/24/09	11/26/09	5
7			Deliverable 1 Complete	0 d	11/26/09	11/26/09	6
8			⊟ **Deliverable 2**	**14 d**	**11/27/09**	**12/16/09**	
9			Design	4 d	11/27/09	12/2/09	7
10			Build	4 d	12/3/09	12/8/09	9
11			Test	3 d	12/9/09	12/11/09	10
12			Implement	3 d	12/14/09	12/16/09	11
13			Deliverable 2 Complete	0 d	12/16/09	12/16/09	12
14			Phase I Complete	0 d	12/16/09	12/16/09	13

Figure 3 - 21: Task list includes same-named tasks

In Figure 3 - 22, I applied the *Auto Scheduled v. Manually Scheduled* group to the task list shown previously in Figure 3 - 21. Notice how each grouping includes only regular tasks and milestone tasks, and does not include summary tasks. This means that I can see two tasks named Design in the *Auto Scheduled* group, but I cannot determine the WBS for either of these Design tasks.

	❶	Task	Task Name	Duration	Start	Finish	Predecessors
			⊟ **Task Mode: Auto Scheduled**	**5d**	**11/6/09**	**12/16/09**	
3			Design	3 d	11/6/09	11/10/09	
4			Build	5 d	11/11/09	11/17/09	3
7			Deliverable 1 Complete	0 d	11/26/09	11/26/09	6
9			Design	4 d	11/27/09	12/2/09	7
10			Build	4 d	12/3/09	12/8/09	9
13			Deliverable 2 Complete	0 d	12/16/09	12/16/09	12
14			Phase I Complete	0 d	12/16/09	12/16/09	13
			⊟ **Task Mode: Manually Scheduled**	**4d**	**11/18/09**	**12/16/09**	
5			Test	4 d	11/18/09	11/23/09	4
6			Implement	3 d	11/24/09	11/26/09	5
11			Test	3 d	12/9/09	12/11/09	10
12			Implement	3 d	12/14/09	12/16/09	11

**Figure 3 - 22: Auto Scheduled v. Manually Scheduled
group does not include summary tasks**

To eliminate the confusion about the WBS for each Design task, I click the *Group By* pick list again and select the *Maintain Hierarchy in Current Group* item. Figure 3 - 23 shows the result. Notice in the figure that the groupings now include the Phase and Deliverable summary sections for each regular task and milestone task. Because of this, I can now determine the WBS for each Design task in the *Auto Scheduled* group.

	❶	Task	Task Name	Duration	Start	Finish	Predecessors
			⊟ **Task Mode: Auto Scheduled**	**5d**	**11/6/09**	**12/16/09**	
			⊟ **1 Phase I**	**5d**	**11/6/09**	**12/16/09**	
14		🖥⇨	Phase I Complete	0 d	12/16/09	12/16/09	13
			⊟ **1.1 Deliverable 1**	**5d**	**11/6/09**	**11/26/09**	
3		🖥⇨	Design	3 d	11/6/09	11/10/09	
4		🖥⇨	Build	5 d	11/11/09	11/17/09	3
7		🖥⇨	Deliverable 1 Complete	0 d	11/26/09	11/26/09	6
			⊟ **1.2 Deliverable 2**	**4d**	**11/27/09**	**12/16/09**	
9		🖥⇨	Design	4 d	11/27/09	12/2/09	7
10		🖥⇨	Build	4 d	12/3/09	12/8/09	9
13		🖥⇨	Deliverable 2 Complete	0 d	12/16/09	12/16/09	12
			⊟ **Task Mode: Manually Scheduled**	**4d**	**11/18/09**	**12/16/09**	
			⊟ **1 Phase I**	**4d**	**11/18/09**	**12/16/09**	
			⊟ **1.1 Deliverable 1**	**4d**	**11/18/09**	**11/26/09**	
5		📌	Test	4 d	11/18/09	11/23/09	4
6		📌	Implement	3 d	11/24/09	11/26/09	5
			⊟ **1.2 Deliverable 2**	**3d**	**12/9/09**	**12/16/09**	
11		📌	Test	3 d	12/9/09	12/11/09	10
12		📌	Implement	3 d	12/14/09	12/16/09	11

**Figure 3 - 23: Auto Scheduled v. Manually Scheduled
group with "Maintain Hierarchy" applied**

After you select the *Maintain Hierarchy in Current Group* item for any task group, the software continues to show the task hierarchy automatically each time you reapply that group in the current project. If you do not want to see the task hierachy, you must click the *Group By* pick list again and then click the *Maintain Hierarchy in Current Group* item to deselect this option.

If you want to create your own custom groups, Microsoft Project 2010 offers you the option to include the hierarchy as a part of the group definition. To create a new custom group, click the *Group By* pick list and select the *New Group By* item on the list. The software displays the *Group Definition* dialog shown in Figure 3 - 24.

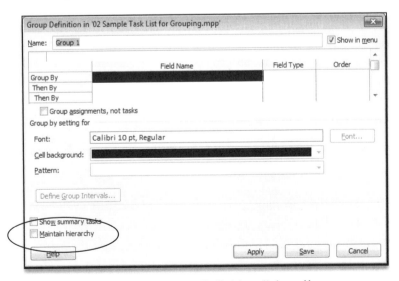

**Figure 3 - 24: Group Definition dialog offers
the Maintain hierarchy option**

In Figure 3 - 24, notice the *Maintain hierarchy* option in the lower left of the *Group Definition* dialog. If you want to display the WBS for the tasks in a new task group, select the *Maintain hierarchy* option when you create your custom group.

The *Maintain hierarchy* option is available only for task groups. You cannot display the hierarchy information for resource groups because resources do not have work breakdown structure information. This means that the software disables the the *Maintain Hierarchy in Current Group* item on the *Group By* pick list in any resource view, and disables the *Maintain hierarchy* option in the *Group Definition* dialog when creating a resource group.

When you have a group applied in any task or resource view, you can remove the group by clicking the *Group By* pick list and selecting either the *[No Group]* item or the *Clear Group* item on the pick list.

Keyboard Shortcut: Press **Shift + F3** on your keyboard to remove the current group and reapply the group called *No Group*.

Hands On Exercise

Exercise 3- 5

Experiment with the new groups in Microsoft Project 2010.

1. Open the **CRM Software Development 2010.mpp** sample file.

2. Click the *Tasks* tab to apply the *Task* ribbon.

3. In the *Task* ribbon, click the *Gantt Chart* pick list button and select the *Task Sheet* view.

4. Click the *View* tab to apply the *View* ribbon.

5. In the *Data* section of the *View* ribbon, click the *Group By* pick list and select the *Active v. Inactive* group.

Notice how the software groups the tasks in the project into two groups, the *Inactive* (Active: No) and *Active* (Active: Yes) groups.

6. Click the *Group By* pick list and select the *Auto Scheduled v. Manually Scheduled* group.

Notice how the software groups the tasks in the project into the *Auto Scheduled* and *Manually Scheduled* groups, but does not display the task hierarchy of summary tasks to reveal the WBS of each task.

7. Click the *Group By* pick list and select the *Maintain Hierarchy in Current Group* item at the bottom of the list.

Notice how the software shows the work breakdown structure (WBS) for every task in each group, as indicated by groups using the light blue cell background color.

8. Click the *Group By* pick list and select the *Resource* group.

Notice how the software now groups the tasks in the project into groups corresponding with the resource(s) assigned to each task, but does not display the task hierarchy of summary tasks to reveal the WBS of each task.

9. Click the *Group By* pick list again and select the *Maintain Hierarchy in Current Group* item at the bottom of the list.

10. Click the *Group By* pick list and select the *Status* group.

Notice how the software groups the tasks by their status and displays the task hierarchy of summary tasks automatically to reveal the WBS of each task.

11. Click the *Group By* pick list and select the *[No Group]* item on the list.

12. In the *Task Views* section of the *View* ribbon, click the *Gantt Chart* button to reapply the *Gantt Chart* view.

13. Save and close the **CRM Software Development 2010.mpp** sample file.

Exercise 3-6

Apply a resource group in Microsoft Project 2010.

1. Reopen the **Project Navigation 2010.mpp** sample file.

2. Click the *View* tab to display the *View* ribbon.

3. In the *Resource Views* section of the *View* ribbon, click the *Resource Usage* button to apply the *Resource Usage* view.

4. Click the *Group By* pick list button and select the *Resource Group* item on the list.

5. Scroll down to the *Construction* grouping.

Notice that this group, when applied in the *Resource Usage* view, shows you the total amount of *Work* assigned to the resources in the *Construction* group (532 hours).

6. In the *Task Views* section of the *View* ribbon, click the *Gantt Chart* button to apply the *Gantt Chart* view.

7. Save and close the **Project Navigation 2010.mpp** sample file.

84

Module 04

Project Definition

Learning Objectives

After completing this module, you will be able to:

- Create a new project from a SharePoint task list or an Office.com template
- Define a new project using the six-step method recommended by MSProjectExperts
- Set nonworking time and the working schedule on the Standard calendar
- Create new base calendars
- Specify the Task Mode setting for new tasks
- Specify options settings for a project
- Save your project using an alternate file type
- Save your project to a SharePoint workspace
- Share your project with others via e-mail

Inside Module 04

Creating a New Project from a Template

To create a new project in Microsoft Project 2010, click the *File* tab to display the *Backstage. Click* the *New* tab to display the *Available Templates* page shown in Figure 4 - 1.

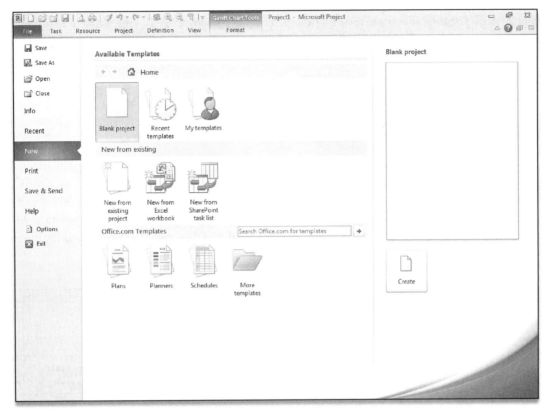

Figure 4 - 1: Available Templates page in the Backstage

Notice in the *Available Templates* page shown in Figure 4 - 1 that the software offers you a number of ways to create a new project, including each of the following:

- Click the *Blank project* button to create a new blank project.

- Click the *Recent templates* button to create a new project from a recently used template.

- Click the *My templates* button to create a new project from a custom project template that you created or that you downloaded from Office.com.

- Click the *New from existing project* button to create a new project from an existing project.

- Click the *New from Excel workbook* button to create a new project from an existing Microsoft Excel workbook file using the *Import/Export Wizard.*

- Click the *New from SharePoint task list* button to create a new project from a task list in an existing SharePoint site (available **only** in the Professional version of Microsoft Project 2010).

- Click one of the icons in the *Office.com Templates* section to search Office.com for customized project templates.

In this module, I discuss each of the preceding methods for creating a new project, except for creating a new project from an Excel workbook using the *Import/Export Wizard*. Because the *Import/Export Wizard* is a very complex tool with many options, I devote an entire module to the import/export process in this book's companion volume, *Microsoft Project 2010 Ultimate Learning Guide: Advanced*.

Creating a New Project Using a Template

Microsoft Project 2010 offers several ways to create a new project from a template. To create a new blank project using the blank project template included with the software, click the *Blank Project* button on the *Available Templates* page and then click the *Create* button in the preview sidepane on the right side of the page. The system creates a new blank project and applies the default *Gantt with Timeline* view.

To create a project from a pre-defined template, you must download a template from Office.com. Unlike previous versions of the software, Microsoft Project 2010 **does not** ship with any pre-defined project templates. Instead, Microsoft offers a continuously-updated list of project templates through its Office.com website.

On the *Available Templates* page, the system displays the current list of template types and categories in the *Office.com Templates* section at the bottom of the page. Microsoft updates this section continuously so that you always have the "latest and greatest" project templates available to you. To create a new project from a pre-defined project template, click the name of a project type and sub-category, as needed, until you see a list of available templates. Alternately, you can also enter key words in the *Search Office.com for templates* field and then click the *Start Searching* button. Figure 4 - 2 shows the list of templates available in the *Plans* section and *Business* sub-category.

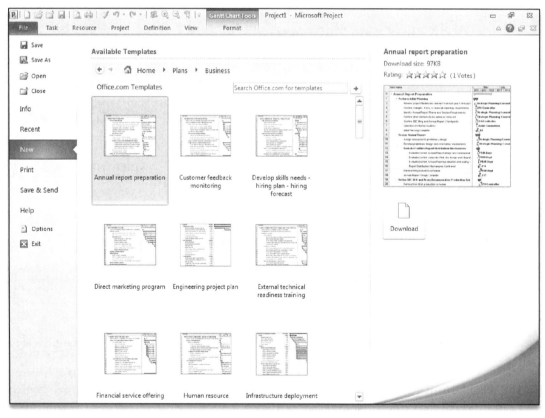

Figure 4 - 2: Available Templates page shows Business templates available for download in Office.com

To create a new project from a pre-defined template in Office.com, select the name of the template. In the preview sidepane on the right side of the *Available Templates* page, the system shows you the full name of the template, the size of the file, the rating of the template based on feedback from users, and a preview picture of the template, if available. Notice in Figure 4 - 2 that I selected the *Annual report preparation* template. The file size of this template is 97 Kb, it has a rating of five stars out of six based on the feedback of one user, and you can see a preview of the template. To download the template and create a new project from the template, click the *Create* button.

If an organization other than Microsoft created the template in Office.com, the sidepane on the right side of the page also shows the name of the organization that created the template.

Microsoft Project 2010 downloads the template from the Office.com website and creates a new project from the template. In addition, the software saves the template in your *Templates* folder and makes it available for future use by clicking the *My Templates* button on the *Available Templates* page of the *Backstage*.

Understanding the Changing Face of Help Content in Project 2010

As part of a larger initiative that blankets the entire Microsoft product stack, users of Office, Visio, and Project 2010 will see a steady evolution toward community-authored content when they access Help or other application content, such as templates. Microsoft's new model of enriching connected-Help sources with continuously evolving content from both Microsoft and non-Microsoft sources is a compelling reason to always favor using connected Help over the static Help files that ship with the products.

To create a project from a custom template you created, or from a pre-defined project template you downloaded from Office.com, click the *My templates* button in the *Available Templates* page. Microsoft Project 2010 displays the *New* dialog. Notice that the *New* dialog in Figure 4 - 3 shows a list of seven templates, one of which I created, and six of which I downloaded from Office.com. Select any template in the *New* dialog and then click the *OK* button to create a new project from the template.

In Windows Vista and Windows 7, the location of the templates shown in the *New* dialog is:
C:\Users\YourUserID\AppData\Roaming\Microsoft\Templates

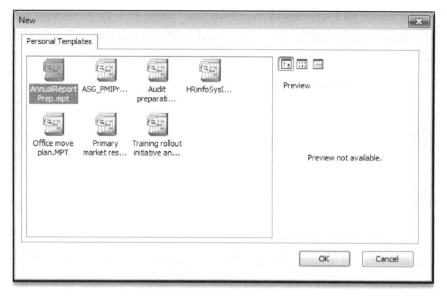

Figure 4 - 3: New dialog

To create a project from a template you used recently, click the *Recent templates* button in the *Available Templates* page. The system displays the *Available Templates* page with a list of recently used templates, as shown in Figure 4 - 4. Notice that my *Available Templates* page shows three templates I used recently. Select one of the recently used templates and then click the *Create* button in the preview sidepane on the right side of the page.

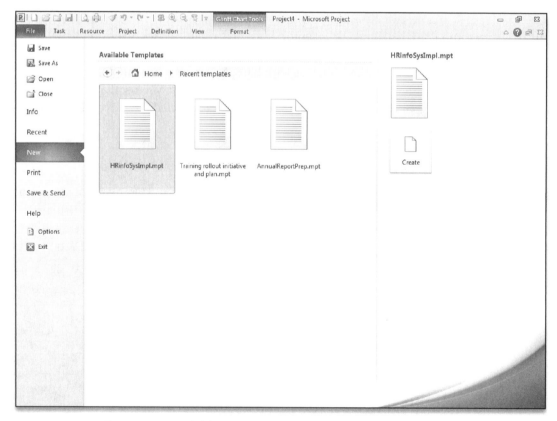

Figure 4 - 4: Available Templates page with recently used templates

Before a template can qualify as a "recently used" template, you must create a new project from the template using the *New* dialog or create a new project from an existing project. When you create a new project by downloading a template from Office.com, this action does not qualify the template as a "recently used" template.

Creating a New Project from an Existing Project

To create a new project from an existing project, click the *New from existing project* button in the *Available Templates* page. Microsoft Project 2010 displays the *New from Existing Project* dialog shown in Figure 4 - 5. In the dialog, navigate to the folder containing existing projects, select a project, and then click the *Open* button.

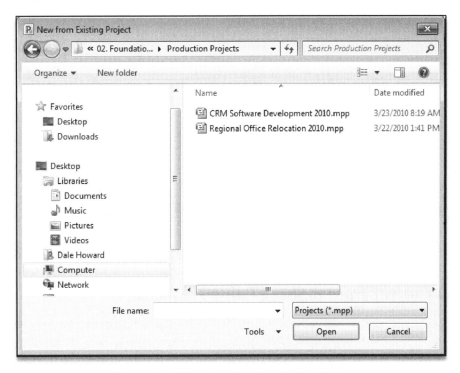

Figure 4 - 5: New from Existing Project dialog

When you use this method to create a new project, the system makes an **exact copy** of the existing project using the file name of the existing project. This means that the new project contains all of the data in the existing project, including task progress, constraints, deadline dates, resource names, resource assignments, baseline data, etc. At this point, you must clean up the project by performing actions such as removing task progress and removing/editing constraints and deadline dates.

When you are ready to save the new project created from an existing project, Microsoft Project 2010 displays the *Save As* dialog using the name of the existing project, as shown in Figure 4 - 6. In the *Save As* dialog, be sure to change the name of the project file before you save it; otherwise, you overwrite the original existing project with your new project.

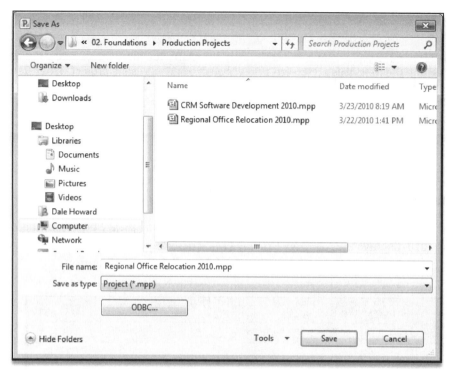

**Figure 4 - 6: Save As dialog after creating
a new project from an existing project**

When you create a new project from an existing project, Microsoft Project 2010 adds the name of the project to the list of recently used templates in the *Available Templates* page.

Creating a New Project from a SharePoint Task List

If your organization uses Microsoft SharePoint Foundation 2010 or Microsoft SharePoint Server (MSS) 2010, but does not use the enterprise tool Microsoft Project Server 2010, you can leverage the power of SharePoint by creating a new project in Microsoft Project 2010 from a task list in a SharePoint site. This feature can be useful to your organization if you need to create a new project from a standard list of tasks defined by your organization. Before you can create a new project from a task list in SharePoint, your organization must meet the following requirements:

- You or your SharePoint administrator must create a SharePoint site for you and add you to the list of users in the SharePoint site.

- Your SharePoint administrator must supply you with the URL of the site.

- In the SharePoint site, a knowledgeable person must create a new *Task List* containing the names of tasks for a standard project. Ideally, the *Task List* should include task dependencies, if possible.

- You must navigate to the SharePoint site and copy the URL to your Windows clipboard.

Warning: Your organization **must** use either Microsoft SharePoint Foundation 2010 or Microsoft SharePoint Server 2010 before you can create a new project from a task list in SharePoint. You **cannot** use any previous version of Windows SharePoint Services for this functionality. Furthermore, your organization must create a new *Task List* item rather than a *List* item for this purpose only.

Figure 4 - 7 shows a Microsoft SharePoint Server 2010 site with a custom *Task List* named *Project Tasks*. Notice that the *Project Tasks* list includes four standard tasks including Design, Build, Test, and Implement, plus one milestone task named Project Complete.

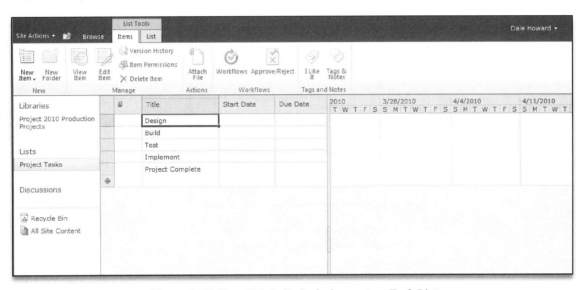

Figure 4 - 7: SharePoint site includes custom Task List

To create a new project from a list of tasks in a SharePoint site, complete the following steps:

1. Click the *File* tab and then click the *New* tab in the *Backstage*.

2. On the *Available Templates* page in the *Backstage*, click the *New from SharePoint Task List* button. Microsoft Project 2010 displays the *Import SharePoint Tasks List* dialog shown in Figure 4 - 8.

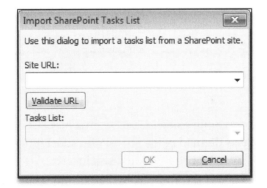

**Figure 4 - 8: Import SharePoint
Tasks List dialog**

3. In the *Import SharePoint Tasks List* dialog, enter the URL of the SharePoint site in the *Site URL* field.

After you create at least one new project from a task list in SharePoint, Microsoft Project 2010 populates the *Site URL* field automatically by adding the URL of the SharePoint site to the pick list. When you create new projects from multiple SharePoint sites, the *Site URL* field displays a pick list containing the entire URL history.

4.   Click the *Validate URL* button in the *Import SharePoint Tasks List* dialog. If your URL is valid, the system activates the *Tasks List* pick list with a list of *Task List* items, as shown in Figure 4 - 9.

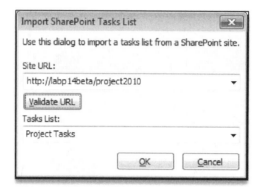

**Figure 4 - 9: Tasks List populated
with available Task List items**

5.   Click the *Tasks List* pick list and choose an available *Task List* item, if needed, and then click the *OK* button. As Microsoft Project 2010 collects the *Task List* information, the system displays the *SharePoint Synchronization* dialog shown in Figure 4 - 10.

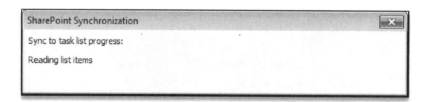

Figure 4 - 10: SharePoint Synchronization dialog

After the system completes the process of creating a new project from a *Task List* in SharePoint, Microsoft Project 2010 creates the new project using the list of tasks defined in the SharePoint site. Figure 4 - 11 shows a new project created from the *Project Tasks* list shown previously in Figure 4 - 7. Microsoft Project 2010 creates each task as a *Manually Scheduled* task and sets dependencies on the tasks if the *Task List* in SharePoint contains dependency information in the *Predecessors* field. The system also sets the date in the *Start* field to the current date, unless the *Task List* in SharePoint includes a date in the *Start Date* field.

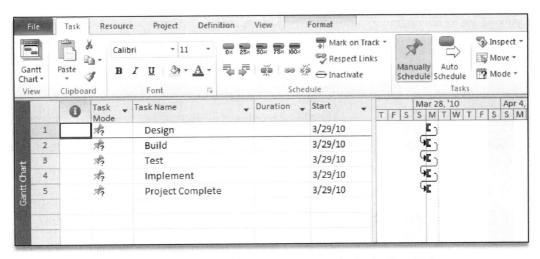

Figure 4 - 11: New project created from a Task List in SharePoint

Warning: When you create a new project from a task list in SharePoint, the process creates a new project with *Manually Scheduled* tasks. After you create your project, you may want to convert the tasks to *Auto Scheduled* tasks.

Hands On Exercise

Exercise 4-1

Create a new project from an Office.com template.

1. Click the *File* tab and then click the *New* tab in the *Backstage*.

2. In the *Office.com Templates* section of the *Available Templates* page in the *Backstage*, search for and then select the *Annual Report Preparation* template (if not available, select any available project template).

3. Click the *Download* button.

4. In the new project, drag the split bar to the right edge of the *Duration* column.

5. Scroll down through the project and examine the task list.

Notice any tasks that display a "burning man" indicator in the *Indicators* column. This indicator tells you that these tasks have overallocated resources assigned to them. I discuss resource overallocations and leveling in Module 07, Project Assignment Planning.

6. If you see a "burning man" indicator in the *Indicators* column for any tasks, float your mouse pointer over one of the indicators to view the tooltip about overallocated resources.

7. Click the *File* tab and then click the *Close* item in the *Backstage* menu.

8. When prompted in a warning dialog to save changes, click the *No* button.

9. Click the *File* tab and then click the *New* tab in the *Backstage*.

10. Click the *Blank Project* button and then click the *Create* button in the preview pane to create a new blank project.

Defining a New Project

After you determine your project requirements, you are ready to define the project in Microsoft Project 2010 using the six-step method recommended by MSProjectExperts. You should use this six-step method when you open a new blank project or create a new project from a project template. The six-step method includes the following mandatory and optional steps:

1. Set the project start date.

2. Enter the project properties.

3. Display the Project Summary Task (Row 0).

4. Set the project working schedule.

5. Set project options unique to this project (optional).

6. Save the project according to your company's naming standards.

After completing the six-step definition process, you are ready to begin the planning process. In this module, I discuss each of these steps as a major topical section.

Step #1 - Set the Project Start Date

When you define a new project in Microsoft Project 2010, you must set the start date of the project. When you set a project's start date, you allow the software to calculate an estimated finish date based on the information you enter during the task, resource, and assignment planning process.

 Although it may seem more logical to set a project finish date and to let Microsoft Project 2010 calculate the start date, this can result in an estimated start date in the past. Remember the lesson from the past: on many Y2K projects scheduled backwards from a finish date, project managers discovered that their projects should have started months or even years earlier than they were scheduled to start!

To enter the start date for a new project, complete the following steps:

1. Click the *Project* tab to display the *Project* ribbon.

2. Click the *Project Information* button in the *Properties* section of the *Project* ribbon. The system displays the *Project Information* dialog shown in Figure 4 - 12.

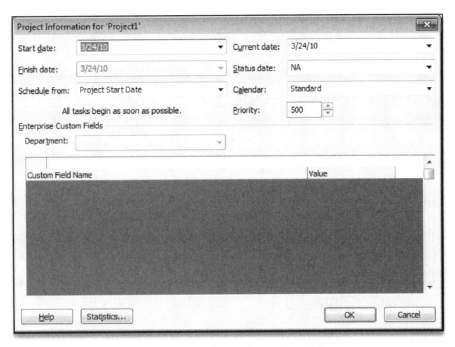

Figure 4 - 12: Project Information dialog

3. Enter your desired project start date in the *Start date* field and then click the *OK* button.

> In the *Project Information* dialog, you do not see an *Enterprise Custom Fields* section in the bottom half of the dialog if you are using the **Standard** version of Microsoft Project 2010. You only see an *Enterprise Custom Fields* section in the dialog if you are using the **Professional** version of the software.

Hands On Exercise

Exercise 4-2

You are the project manager of the Training Advisor Rollout project. The purpose of this project is to implement a new enterprise Learning Management System (LMS) that allows employees to create and manage their own professional development program by taking in-house and external training classes. You estimate the project start date at January 6, 2014. The target finish date for the project is June 27, 2014.

1. Open the **Training Advisor 04.mpp** sample file.

2. Click the *Project* tab to display the *Project* ribbon.

3. Click the *Project Information* button in the *Properties* section of the *Project* ribbon.

4. Enter *January 6, 2014* in the *Start date* field.

5. Click the *OK* button.

Notice how Microsoft Project 2010 scrolls the Gantt chart to the start date of the project.

6. Save but **do not** close the **Training Advisor 04.mpp** project file.

Step #2 - Enter the Project Properties

Although you may not enter file properties information when you create a new Word document or Excel spreadsheet, you should enter the properties information for each new project you create in Microsoft Project 2010. When you enter properties information for a project, this causes the software to display the properties information **automatically** in various places throughout the project, such as in the headers and footers of printed views and reports. To enter the properties for a new project, complete the following steps:

1. Click the *File* tab to display the *Backstage*.

2. Click the *Info* tab to display the *Info* page in the *Backstage*, as shown in Figure 4 - 13.

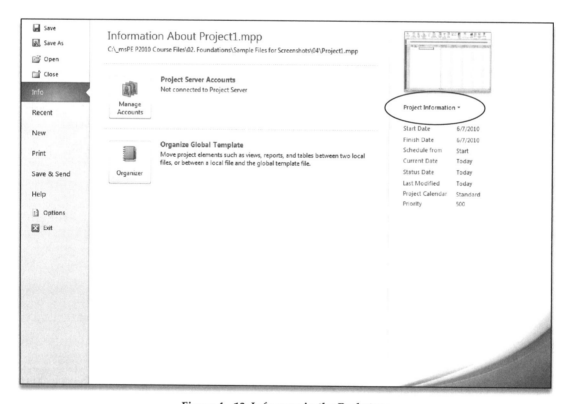

Figure 4 - 13: Info page in the Backstage

3. In the sidepane on the right side of the *Info* page, click the *Project Information* pick list and select the *Advanced Properties* item on the list, as shown in Figure 4 - 14.

**Figure 4 - 14: Project
Information pick list**

The system displays the *Properties* dialog for the new project shown in Figure 4 - 15.

Figure 4 - 15: Properties dialog

4. Click the *Summary* tab, if necessary, and enter values in each of the fields.

5. Click the *OK* button when finished.

Table 4 - 1 provides descriptions and recommendations for using the fields in the *Properties* dialog.

Field Name	Description and Recommendations
Title	Displays as the task name for the Project Summary Task (Row 0), as the task name for subprojects inserted in a master project, and in the headers or footers of printed views and reports.
Subject	Used only for file searching when you save the project as an MPP file (not used with Project Server 2010).
Author	Enter your name. Optionally displayed in the headers or footers of printed views and reports.
Manager	Enter your name, or the name of the person to whom you report (your manager). Displayed in the headers and footers of printed views and reports.
Company	Enter the name of your company. Displayed in the headers and footers of printed views and reports.
Category	Used only for file searching when you save the project as an MPP file (not used with Project Server 2010).
Keywords	Used only for file searching when you save the project as an MPP file (not used with Project Server 2010).
Comments	Displayed in the *Notes* field of the Project Summary Task (Row 0).
Hyperlink base	Used as the base path address for all relative hyperlinks inserted within the project (not used with Project Server 2010).
Template	Displays the name of the template you used to create the project plan. The system disables this field if you create the project as a new blank project.
Save preview picture	Displays a preview picture of your project file in the *Open* dialog (not used with Project Server 2010).

Table 4 - 1: Project Properties fields

Hands On Exercise

Exercise 4-3

Enter the properties information for a project.

1. Return to your **Training Advisor 04.mpp** sample file.

2. Click the *File* tab to display the *Backstage*, and then click the *Info* tab.

3. In the sidepane on the right side of the *Info* page, click the *Project Information* pick list and select the *Advanced Properties* item on the list.

4. In the *Properties* dialog, enter the information shown in Table 4 - 2.

Field Name	Description and Recommendations
Title	Training Advisor Rollout
Subject	enterprise software implementation
Author	Your name
Manager	Your name
Company	Name of your organization or company
Category	enterprise software implementation
Keywords	enterprise software implementation
Comments	Implement the Training Advisor software to allow employees to plan and direct their own continuing education program.
Hyperlink base	Leave blank
Template	Unused
Save preview picture	Leave deselected

Table 4 - 2: Properties information for the Training Advisor project

5. Click the *OK* button.

6. Click the *Save* item in the *Backstage* menu, but **do not** close the **Training Advisor 04.mpp** sample file.

Step #3 - Display the Project Summary Task

The Project Summary Task, also known as Row 0 or Task 0, is the highest-level summary task in your project. The Project Summary Task summarizes or "rolls up" all task values in the entire project. For example, the value in the *Duration* column for the Project Summary Task represents the duration of the entire project, while the values in the *Work* and the *Cost* columns represent the total work and total cost for the entire project. By default, Microsoft Project 2010 **does not** display the Project Summary Task automatically in any new blank project, so you must display it manually. To display the Project Summary Task, complete the following steps:

1. Apply the *Gantt Chart* view, if necessary.

2. Click the *Format* tab to display the *Format* ribbon with the *Gantt Chart Tools* applied.

3. In the *Show/Hide* section of the *Format* ribbon, select the *Project Summary Task* option. The system displays the Project Summary Task (Row 0) in the current project, as shown in Figure 4 - 16.

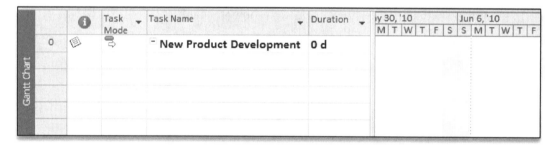

Figure 4 - 16: Project Summary Task (Row 0)

4. Widen the *Task Name* column, if necessary, to "best fit" the task name of the Project Summary Task.

5. If you widen the *Task Name* column, drag the split bar to the right side of the *Duration* column, as needed.

Notice the name of the Project Summary Task shown in Figure 4 - 16. Microsoft Project 2010 uses the text you enter in the *Title* field of the *Properties* dialog as the task name of the Project Summary Task. Notice also the note indicator in the *Indicators* column to the left of the *Task Name* column. The system uses the text you enter in the *Comments* field of the *Properties* dialog as the body of the note for the Project Summary Task.

Hands On Exercise

Exercise 4-4

Display the Project Summary Task in a project.

1. Return to your **Training Advisor 04.mpp** sample file.

2. Apply the *Gantt Chart* view, if necessary.

3. Click the *Format* tab to display the *Format* ribbon with the *Gantt Chart Tools* applied.

4. In the *Show/Hide* section of the *Format* ribbon, select the *Project Summary Task* checkbox option.

5. Widen the *Task Name* column and then drag the split bar to the right edge of the *Duration* column.

Notice that the system uses the *Title* information from the *Properties* dialog as the task name of the Project Summary Task.

6. Float your mouse pointer over the note indicator in the *Indicators* column for the Project Summary Task.

Notice that the system uses the *Comments* information from the *Properties* dialog as the body of the note for the Project Summary Task.

7. Save but **do not** close the **Training Advisor 04.mpp** sample file.

Step #4 - Set the Project Working Schedule

To achieve a realistic working schedule for your project, you likely need to do one of more of the following:

- Add nonworking time to the *Standard* calendar to reflect your company holidays.

- Modify the *Standard* calendar in your project to reflect your company's working schedule, if different from the default working schedule.

- Create new base calendars to represent unique working schedules.

- Specify the *Project Calendar* and the *Nonworking Time Calendar* for your project.

I discuss each of these as its own sub-topical section.

Adding Nonworking Time to the Standard Calendar

To add nonworking time representing company holidays to the *Standard* calendar in a project, complete the following steps:

1. Click the *Project* tab to display the *Project* ribbon.

2. In the *Properties* section of the *Project* ribbon, click the *Change Working Time* button. The software opens the *Change Working Time* dialog, as shown in Figure 4 - 17.

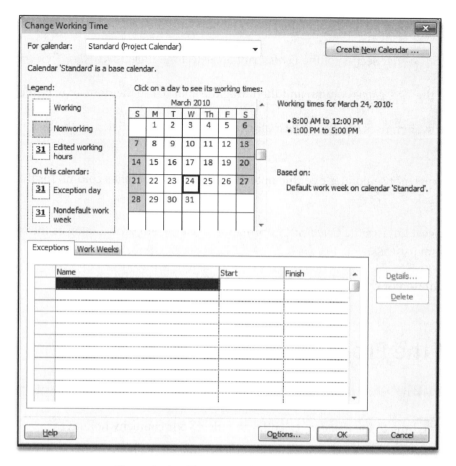

Figure 4 - 17: Change Working Time dialog

3. Click the *For calendar* pick list at the top of the dialog and make sure you have the *Standard* calendar selected.

4. In the *Calendar* grid at the top of the *Change Working Time* dialog, select the date of the next company holiday, such as Memorial Day.

To set consecutive nonworking days, drag your mouse pointer over the dates in the calendar grid to select a block of days. For example, some companies mark as nonworking time the week between Christmas Day and New Year's Day. To select noncontiguous dates, select the first date, press and hold the *Control* key on your keyboard, and then select additional dates.

5. On the *Exceptions* data grid at the bottom of the dialog, enter a name for the holiday, such as Memorial Day, and then press either the *Right-Arrow* key or the *Tab* key on your keyboard.

Microsoft Project 2010 sets the date as nonworking time, as shown in Figure 4 - 18.

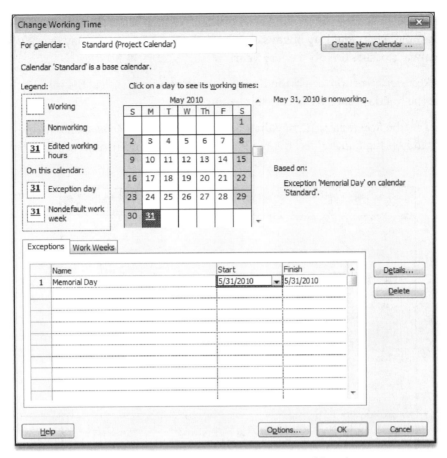

Figure 4 - 18: Memorial Day set as nonworking time

6. With the new holiday selected in the *Exceptions* data grid, click the *Details* button. The software displays the *Details* dialog for the selected holiday, as shown in Figure 4 - 19.

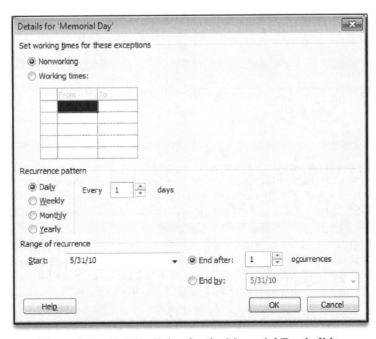

Figure 4 - 19: Details dialog for the Memorial Day holiday

7. In the *Recurrence Pattern* section, select the *Yearly* option and then select the pattern of recurrence for the holiday. For example, Memorial Day always occurs on the last Monday of May every year, while Independence Day always occurs on July 4 every year.

8. In the *Range of Recurrence* section, select the *End after* option and then select the number of years for which you want to set the holiday (such as 5 years, for example).

Figure 4 - 20 shows that I set the *Recurrence pattern* values to *Yearly* on the *Last Monday* of *May* (the official date of Memorial Day every year) and set the *Range of recurrence* values to *End after 5* occurrences.

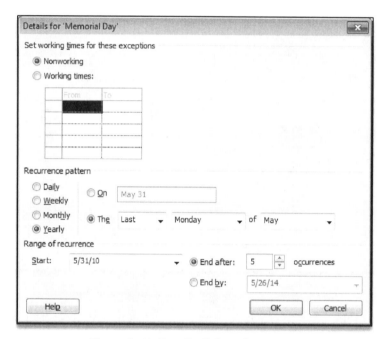

**Figure 4 - 20: Details dialog after setting
Memorial Day recurrence for 5 years**

9. Click the *OK* button.

10. Repeat the preceding set of steps for each company holiday.

Warning: When you set a hard date as nonworking time, such as the New Year's day holiday on January 1, and then set the holiday to occur multiple times, some of the nonworking dates may fall on a weekend. Microsoft Project 2010 does not automatically reset a Saturday holiday to the previous Friday, or reset a Sunday holiday to the following Monday. Instead, you must set these weekend occurrences as individual instances in the *Exceptions* grid.

After you set a recurring company holiday on a hard date, such as January 1, scroll through the calendar grid looking for weekend occurrences and then set individual exceptions according to your organization's policies. For example, notice in Figure 4 - 21 that I set an additional Independence Day holiday for Monday, July 5, 2010 because July 4, 2010 occurs on a Sunday.

Figure 4 - 21 shows the *Change Working Time* dialog after setting company holidays as nonworking days for the next 5 years through 2014.

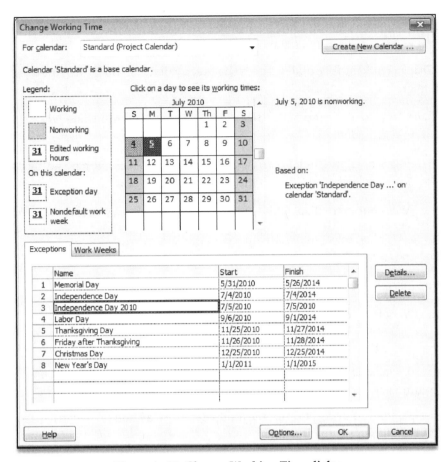

**Figure 4 - 21: Change Working Time dialog
with company holidays set as nonworking time**

11. Click the *OK* button.

After you set your holidays as nonworking time on the *Standard* calendar, Microsoft Project 2010 schedules no task work on any date specified as nonworking time.

Hands On Exercise

Exercise 4-5

Set a company holiday that occurs on a fixed date every year on the *Standard* calendar.

1. Return to the **Training Advisor 04.mpp** sample file.

2. Click the *Project* tab to display the *Project* ribbon.

3. In the *Properties* section of the *Project* ribbon, click the *Change Working Time* button.

4. Examine the list of company holidays already entered for the *Standard* calendar.

Notice that the holidays recur through 2015 with additional exceptions entered when a holidays occurs on a Saturday or Sunday (such as Christmas Day 2010).

5. In the *Change Working Time* dialog, select the first available blank line at the bottom of the *Exceptions* data grid.

6. In the *Calendar* grid at the top of the dialog, scroll to and select the date *July 4, 2010* in the calendar (it occurs on a Sunday).

7. In the *Exceptions* data grid, enter *Independence Day* in the *Name* column and then press the *Right-Arrow* key on your keyboard to select the date in the *Start* column.

8. Click the *Details* button to display the *Details* dialog for the *Independence Day* exception.

9. In the *Details* dialog, select the *Yearly* option in the *Recurrence pattern* section, and make sure the *On July 4* option remains selected as well.

10. Select the *End after* option and then select *6 occurrences*.

11. Click the *OK* button to close the *Details* dialog.

12. In the *Calendar* grid at the top of the dialog, select *July 5, 2010* (it occurs on a Monday).

13. On the next available blank line of the *Exceptions* data grid, enter *Independence Day 2010* in the *Name* column and then press the *Right-Arrow* key to select the date in the *Start* column.

Note: You just set an individual exception for the Independence Day holiday when it occurs on a weekend by setting the following Monday as the holiday.

Exercise 4-6

Set a company holiday that occurs on a designated day of the week every year on the *Standard* calendar.

1. Make sure you have the *Change Working Time* dialog open for the **Training Advisor 04.mpp** sample file.

2. In the *Calendar* grid at the top of the dialog, scroll to and select *November 25, 2010* (the fourth Thursday of November is Thanksgiving Day).

3. On the next available blank line of the *Exceptions* data grid, enter *Thanksgiving Day* in the *Name* column and then press the *Right-Arrow* key to select the date in the *Start* column.

4. Click the *Details* button to display the *Details* dialog for the *Thanksgiving Day* exception.

5. In the *Details* dialog, select the *Yearly* option in the *Recurrence pattern* section, and select the *Fourth Thursday of November* option.

6. Select the *End after* option and then select *6 occurrences*.

7. Click the *OK* button to close the *Details* dialog.

Exercise 4-7

Create a partial working day on the *Standard* calendar.

1. Make sure you have the *Change Working Time* dialog open for the **Training Advisor 04.mpp** sample file.

2. In the *Calendar* grid at the top of the dialog, scroll to and select *August 13, 2010*.

3. On the next available blank line of the *Exceptions* data grid, enter *Annual Company Picnic* in the *Name* column and then press the *Right-Arrow* key to select the date in the *Start* column.

4. Click the *Details* button to display the *Details* dialog for the *Annual Company Picnic* exception.

5. In the *Details* dialog, select the *Working Time* option at the top of the dialog.

6. In the *Working Time* data grid, select the line containing the *1:00 PM to 5:00 PM* working schedule and press the *Delete* key on your keyboard to **delete** the afternoon work.

Note: The organization holds its annual company picnic in the afternoon of the 2nd Friday of August, but the morning is working time.

7. Select the *Yearly* option in the *Recurrence pattern* section, and select the *Second Friday of August* option.

8. Select the *End after* option and then select *6 occurrences*.

9. Click the *OK* button to close the *Details* dialog.

10. Click the *OK* button to close the *Change Working Time* dialog.

11. Save but **do not** close the **Training Advisor 04.mpp** sample file.

Setting the Working Schedule

After entering your company holidays as nonworking time, you may also need to set your company's daily working schedule on the *Standard* calendar. By default, Microsoft Project 2010 assumes a daily working schedule of 8:00 AM – 5:00 PM with one hour off for lunch, Monday through Friday, with Saturday and Sunday as nonworking times. To set any other type of daily working schedule, such as from 7:00 AM – 3:30 PM with a half-hour for lunch, you must complete the following steps:

1. Click the *Project* tab to display the *Project* ribbon.

2. In the *Properties* section of the *Project* ribbon, click the *Change Working Time* button.

3. In the *Change Working Time* dialog, click the *Work Weeks* tab as shown in Figure 4 - 22.

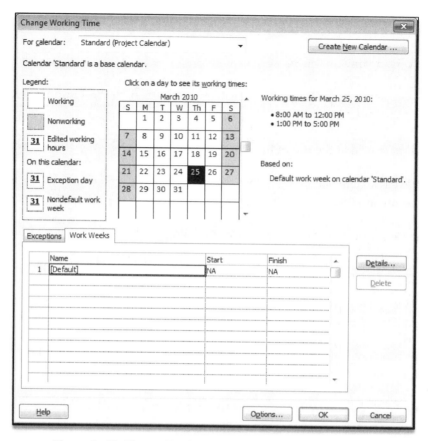

Figure 4 - 22: Change Working Time dialog, Work Weeks tab

4. In the *Work Weeks* data grid, select the *[Default]* item and then click the *Details* button. The system displays the *Details* dialog for the default working schedule, as shown in Figure 4 - 23.

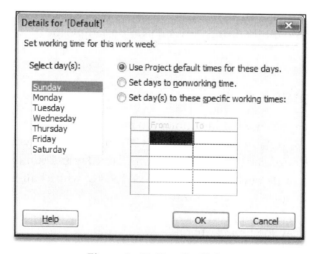

Figure 4 - 23: Details dialog

5. In the *Select day(s)* section, select and drag from *Monday* through *Friday* in the list of days.

6. Select the *Set day(s) to these specific working times* option. The software displays the default 8:00 AM – 12:00 PM and 1:00 PM – 5:00 PM working time in the working times grid shown in Figure 4 - 24.

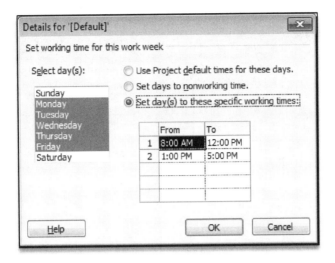

**Figure 4 - 24: Default working schedule
in the Details dialog**

7. Change the first *From* value to *7:00 AM*.

8. Leave the first *To* value set to *12:00 PM*.

9. Change the second *From* value to *12:30 PM*.

10. Change the second *To* value to *3:30 PM*.

11. Click the *OK* button to close the *Details* dialog.

To view the alternate working schedule, select any date in the *Calendar* grid and then examine the schedule shown in the upper right corner of the *Change Working Time* dialog. Notice that the dialog shown in Figure 4 - 25 reveals the alternate working schedule of 7:00 AM – 12:00 PM and 12:30 PM – 3:30 PM.

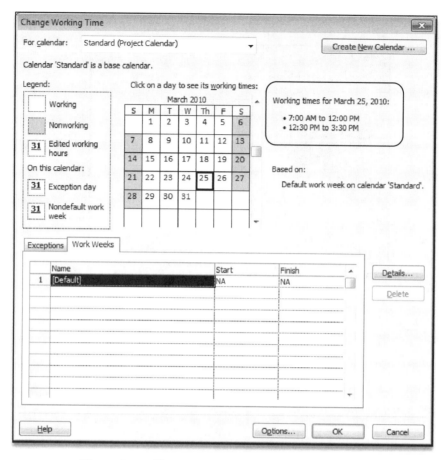

Figure 4 - 25: Change Working Time dialog shows the 7:00 AM – 3:30 PM alternate working schedule

12. Click the *OK* button in the *Change Working Time* dialog.

Hands On Exercise

Exercise 4-8

Change the default working schedule on a calendar for staff members who work on the second shift from 3:00 PM – Midnight each day.

1.   Return to the **Training Advisor 04.mpp** sample file.

2.   Click the *Project* tab to display the *Project* ribbon.

3.   In the *Properties* section of the *Project* ribbon, click the *Change Working Time* button.

4.   In the *Change Working Time* dialog, click the *For calendar* pick list at the top of the dialog and select the *Second Shift* calendar.

Notice that the *Second Shift* base calendar already contains all company holidays, including the *Annual Company Picnic* partial working day.

5. In the *Change Working Time* dialog, click the *Work Weeks* tab.

6. In the *Work Weeks* data grid, select the *[Default]* item and then click the *Details* button.

7. In the *Select day(s)* section of the *Details* dialog, select and drag from *Monday* through *Friday* in the list of days.

8. Select the *Set day(s) to these specific working times* option.

9. Set the first *From* time to *3:00 PM* and set the first *To* time to *7:00 PM*.

10. Set the second *From* time to *8:00 PM* and set the second *To* time to *12:00 AM*.

11. Click the *OK* button to close the *Details* dialog and then click the *OK* button to close the *Change Working Time* dialog.

12. Save but **do not** close the **Training Advisor 04.mpp** sample file.

Creating a New Base Calendar

A base calendar is a master calendar that represents a unique working schedule for your organization. Microsoft Project 2010 uses base calendars to schedule all work for tasks in a project and to set the working schedule for each resource as well. The software offers three predefined base calendars: the *24 Hours* calendar, the *Night Shift* calendar, and the *Standard* calendar. The software defaults to the *Standard* calendar as the *Project Calendar* for all new projects.

Because of unique scheduling needs in your project, you may need to create additional base calendars beyond the three default calendars that ship with the tool. For example, you may need to schedule work to occur only on a weekend, to occur on a 7-day work week schedule, or to occur on a 4-day work week (10 hours/day and 4 days/week). For each of these scheduling needs, you must create a new base calendar. To create a new base 4-day work week calendar, complete the following steps:

1. Click the *Project* tab to display the *Project* ribbon.

2. In the *Properties* section of the *Project* ribbon, click the *Change Working Time* button.

3. In the *Change Working Time* dialog, click the *Create New Calendar* button in the upper right corner of the dialog.

The software displays the *Create New Base Calendar* dialog as shown in Figure 4 - 26.

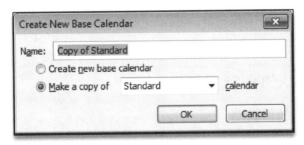

Figure 4 - 26: Create New Base Calendar dialog

4. In the *Name* field, enter a name for your new base calendar.

5. To copy the existing schedule of company holidays, select the *Make a copy of Standard calendar* option. To create an entirely new calendar without company holidays, select the *Create new base calendar* option.

6. Click the *OK* button.

7. Set the working and nonworking schedule for the new calendar using the steps detailed in the previous two topical sections.

8. Click the *OK* button in the *Change Working Time* dialog.

Figure 4 - 27 shows a custom *4x10 Work Week* base calendar I created. This calendar schedules work for 10 hours per day, Monday through Thursday, with every Friday marked as nonworking time.

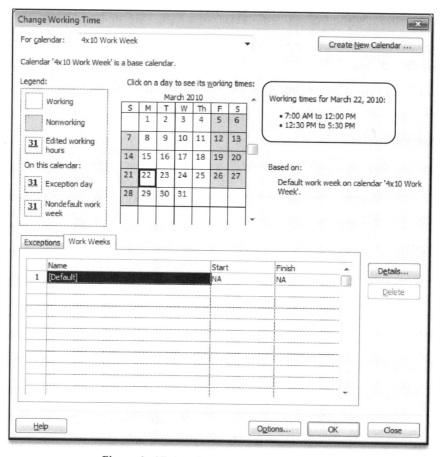

Figure 4 - 27: 4x10 Work Week base calendar

Hands On Exercise

Exercise 4-9

You need a new base calendar called *Weekend Work Only* to schedule work that occurs only on a Saturday or Sunday.

1. Return to the **Training Advisor 04.mpp** sample file.

2. Click the *Project* tab to display the *Project* ribbon.

3. In the *Properties* section of the *Project* ribbon, click the *Change Working Time* button.

4. In the *Change Working Time* dialog, click the *Create New Calendar* button.

5. In the *Create New Calendar* dialog, select the *Create new base calendar* option.

6. Enter the name *Weekend Work Only* in the *Name* field and click the *OK* button.

7. Click the *Work Weeks* tab, make sure you have the *[Default]* item selected in the data grid, and then click the *Details* button.

8. Using the *Control* key on your keyboard, select the *Sunday* and *Saturday* items in the *Select days* section of the *Details* dialog, and then release the *Control* key.

9. Select the *Set days to these specific working time* option.

10. In the *From* and *To* fields, enter the working schedule of *8:00 AM* to *12:00 PM* and *1:00 PM* to *5:00 PM*.

11. In the *Select days* section of the dialog, drag your mouse pointer to select the *Monday* through *Friday* items as a block of selected days.

12. Select the *Set days to nonworking time* option.

13. Click the *OK* button to close the *Details* dialog.

14. In the *Change Working Time* dialog, examine the working schedule for your new custom *Weekend Work Only* base calendar.

Note: Leave the *Change Working Time* dialog open for the next Hands On Exercise.

Exercise 4-10

Create a base calendar called *7-Day Work Week* that schedules work every day of the week.

1. In the *Change Working Time* dialog, click the *Create New Calendar* button.

2. In the *Create New Calendar* dialog, select the *Create new base calendar* option.

3. Enter the name *7-Day Work Week* in the *Name* field and click the *OK* button.

4. When prompted to save changes to the *Weekend Work Only* base calendar, click the *Yes* button.

5. Click the *Work Weeks* tab, make sure you have the *[Default]* item selected in the data grid, and then click the *Details* button.

6. Using the *Control* key on your keyboard, select the *Sunday* and *Saturday* items in the *Select days* section of the *Details* dialog, and then release the *Control* key.

7. Select the *Set days to these specific working time* option.

8. In the *From* and *To* fields, enter the working schedule of *8:00 AM* to *12:00 PM* and *1:00 PM* to *5:00 PM*.

9. Click the *OK* button to close the *Details* dialog.

10. In the *Change Working Time* dialog, examine the working schedule for your new custom *7-Day Work Week* base calendar.

11. Click the *OK* button to close the *Change Working Time* dialog.

12. Save but **do not** close the **Training Advisor 04.mpp** sample file.

Setting the Project Calendar

Setting the *Project* calendar is an optional step, and is only required if your project schedule does not follow the schedule specified on the *Standard* calendar. For example, suppose that you work for an international company that has its headquarters in the United States. Although you work in the United States, you are the manager of a project in which most of the team members are from Canada. Because most team members are from Canada, the Canadian working schedule with Canadian holidays should drive the project schedule. In a situation like this, the project manager must change both the *Project* calendar and the *Non-Working Time* calendar to a calendar that contains Canadian holidays by completing the following steps:

1. Click the *Project* tab to display the *Project* ribbon.

2. Click the *Project Information* button in the *Properties* section of the *Project* ribbon.

3. In the *Project Information* dialog, click the *Calendar* pick list and select the calendar with Canadian holidays, as shown in Figure 4 - 28.

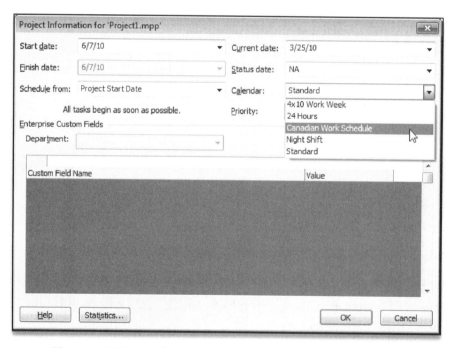

Figure 4 - 28: Project Information dialog – Set the Project Calendar

4. Click the *OK* button.

The preceding steps set the *Canadian Work Schedule* calendar as the *Project* calendar, which is the master calendar for scheduling all tasks in the project. This means that Microsoft Project 2010 automatically schedules all tasks according to the working schedule shown on this calendar. If a task occurs on a Canadian national holiday, the system automatically reschedules the task to the next working day.

After setting the *Project* calendar for the project, you must also set the *Non-Working Time* calendar as well. This calendar displays the nonworking time from the *Project* calendar in the Gantt chart, and shows this nonworking time as gray shaded bands. Setting the *Non-Working Time* calendar to the *Canadian Work Schedule* calendar allows you to see Canadian national holidays in the Gantt chart. To set the *Non-Working Time* calendar, complete the following steps:

1. Double-click anywhere in the *Timescale* bar. The system displays the *Timescale* dialog.

2. In the *Timescale* dialog, select the *Non-working time* tab.

 The fastest way to display the *Timescale* dialog with the *Non-working time* tab selected is to zoom to Weeks Over Days and then double-click anywhere in a gray shaded band in the Gantt chart.

3. On the *Non-working time* page of the dialog, click the *Calendar* pick list and select the alternate calendar with Canadian holidays as shown in Figure 4 - 29.

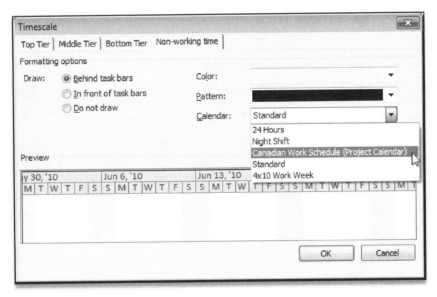

Figure 4 - 29: Timescale dialog, Non-working time tab

4. Click the *OK* button.

 Warning: You must complete **both sets of steps** to set an alternate working schedule for your project. If you set the *Project* calendar but fail to select the *Non-Working Time* calendar, Microsoft Project 2010 schedules each task correctly, but you cannot confirm this schedule because you cannot see the holidays as gray shaded bands on the Gantt chart.

Always keep in mind that the *Project* calendar sets the **initial schedule** for every task in the project. When you assign resources to tasks, Microsoft Project 2010 schedules each task according to the personal calendars of the assigned resources. Therefore, even though the *Canadian Work Schedule* calendar governs the initial task schedule, if I assign an American worker to a task, the system reschedules the task according to the American working schedule.

Hands On Exercise

Exercise 4-11

Examine the *Project* calendar and *Non-Working Time* calendar for a project.

1. Return to the **Training Advisor 04.mpp** sample file.

2. Click the *Project* tab to display the *Project* ribbon.

3. In the *Properties* section of the *Project* ribbon, click the *Project Information* button.

4. In the *Project Information* dialog, click the *Calendar* pick list and examine the available calendars for use as the *Project* calendar.

5. Leave the *Standard* calendar selected on the *Calendar* pick list and click the *OK* button.

6. Double-click anywhere in the *Timescale* bar and then click the *Non-working time* tab.

7. On the *Non-working time* page of the *Timescale* dialog, click the *Calendar* pick list and examine the available calendars for use as the *Non-Working Time* calendar.

8. Leave the *Standard (Project Calendar)* item selected in the *Calendar* pick list and click the *OK* button.

9. Save but **do not** close the **Training Advisor 04.mpp** sample file.

Step #5 - Set Options Unique to this Project

You need to specify two types of options for your new project. I discuss each of these types of options individually:

- Set the *Task Mode* option.

- Set options in the *Project Options* dialog.

Setting the Task Mode Option

One of the major changes to Microsoft Project 2010 is the *Task Mode* setting that allows you to specify tasks as either *Auto Scheduled* or *Manually Scheduled*. *Auto Scheduled* tasks were the default type of tasks in all previous versions of the software. *Manually Scheduled* tasks are a new feature in Microsoft Project 2010. You can use this new feature for tasks that you know you need to include in the project, but for which you may not have enough information to properly schedule, and you can use these for top-down planning exercises. Other potential purposes for this feature include more relaxed scheduling approaches that are preferable when modeling schedules for sprints in the SCRUM methodology.

The default *Task Mode* setting in Microsoft Project 2010 is the *Manually Scheduled* option, which specifies all new tasks as *Manually Scheduled* tasks. Every time you launch the software, you see this default *Task Mode* setting as a ScreenTip on the *Status* bar in the lower left corner of the application window, as shown in Figure 4 - 30.

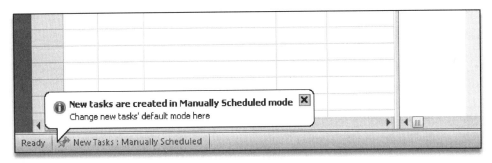

Figure 4 - 30: Task Mode option set to
Manually Scheduled for all new tasks

To change the *Task Mode* setting and specify that all tasks must be *Auto Scheduled* in your new project, use either of the following methods:

- Click the *New Tasks* button on the Status bar and select the *Auto Scheduled* option.

- In the *Tasks* section of the *Task* ribbon, click the *Task Mode* pick list button and choose the *Auto Schedule* item on the pick list, as shown in Figure 4 - 31.

After selecting this option, when you create new tasks in your new project, Microsoft Project 2010 creates them as *Auto Scheduled* tasks. If you want to specify the default *Task Mode* setting for all new blank projects, you must specify this setting in the *Project Options* dialog. I discuss this setting in the next section of this module.

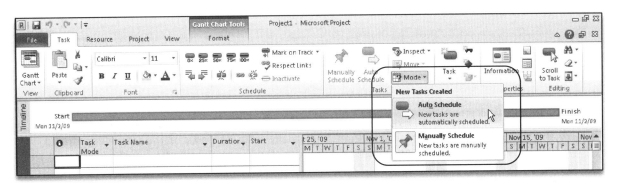

Figure 4 - 31: Task Mode pick list

Setting Options in the Project Options Dialog

After you specify the *Task Mode* setting for your new project, you are ready to specify options in the *Project Options* dialog. Microsoft Project 2010 allows you to specify three types of options settings in the *Project Options* dialog as follows:

- Application options that control how the software looks and works.

- Options specific to any project currently open.

- Options for all new projects created from a blank project.

To specify all three types of options settings, click the *File* tab and then click the *Options* item in the *Backstage* menu. The software displays the *General* page of the *Project Options* dialog shown in Figure 4 - 32.

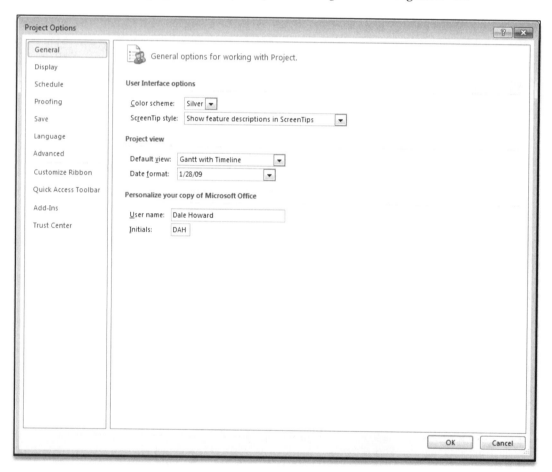

Figure 4 - 32: Project Options dialog, General page

Because Microsoft provides excellent Help articles for all of the options found in the *Project Options* dialog, I do not discuss each of these options individually. Instead, I focus on the new options found in Microsoft Project 2010, and I document other important options of which you should be aware. To access Help for any option, press the *F1* function key or click the *Help* button (**?** button) in the upper right corner of the *Project Options* dialog.

Notice in Figure 4 - 32 that the *Project Options* dialog includes tabs for the following eleven pages of options: *General, Display, Schedule, Proofing, Save, Language, Advanced, Customize Ribbon, Quick Access Toolbar, Add-Ins,* and *Trust Center.* With the exception of the *Customize Ribbon* and *Quick Access Toolbar* pages, which I discussed previously in Module 02, I discuss all of the other pages in detail below.

Setting General Options

The *General* page of the *Project Options* dialog, shown previously in Figure 4 - 32, contains application options only. Remember that these options control how the software looks, works, and displays every project you open. The *User Interface options* section of the *General* page includes two new options for Microsoft Project 2010, the *Color Scheme* and *ScreenTip Style* options.

Use the *Color Scheme* option to control the color scheme that the system applies to all display elements in the Microsoft Project 2010 application window. These elements include the *Title Bar, Quick Access Toolbar,* ribbon, column headers and row headers, *Timescale* bar, vertical and horizontal scroll bars, *View Bar* (displayed along the left side of every view), and *Status* bar. Click the *Color Scheme* pick list and choose the *Blue, Silver,* or *Black* item. The *Silver* item is the default setting for the *Color Scheme* option.

When you float your mouse pointer over an object in the Microsoft Project 2010 application window, the software displays a *ScreenTip* to give you more information about that object. For example, the system displays *ScreenTips* for objects in the Gantt chart, such as Gantt bars or link lines, column headers for the columns shown in the current table, and buttons on the active ribbon. Figure 4 - 33 shows the *ScreenTip* for the *Project Information* button in the *Properties* section of the *Project* ribbon.

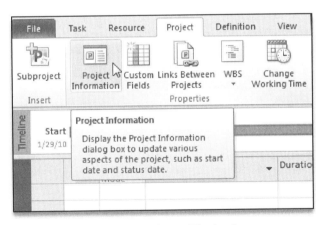

Figure 4 - 33: ScreenTip for the
Project Information button

When you click the *ScreenTip Style* pick list in the *Project Options* dialog, the software offers you three settings. Leave the default *Show Feature Descriptions in ScreenTips* setting selected to show the most information possible in every *ScreenTip,* as shown for the *Project Information* button in Figure 4 - 33. Choose the *Don't Show Feature Descriptions in ScreenTips* setting to display only a minimum amount of information in the *ScreenTip.* Choose the *Don't Show Screen-Tips* setting to disable the display of *ScreenTips.* When you choose the last setting, you **do not** see a *ScreenTip* for any object when you float your mouse pointer over it in the Microsoft Project 2010 application window.

Table 4 - 3 shows the non-default options settings recommended by MSProjectExperts on the *General* page of the *Project Options* dialog.

Option	Setting
Date format	1/28/09
User name	Your name
Initials	Your initials

Table 4 - 3: Recommended options on the General page

Setting Display Options

Click the *Display* tab in the *Project Options* dialog to view the options on the *Display* page shown in Figure 4 - 34. As indicated at the top of the *Display* page, use the options on this page to control how Microsoft Project 2010 displays project data on the screen.

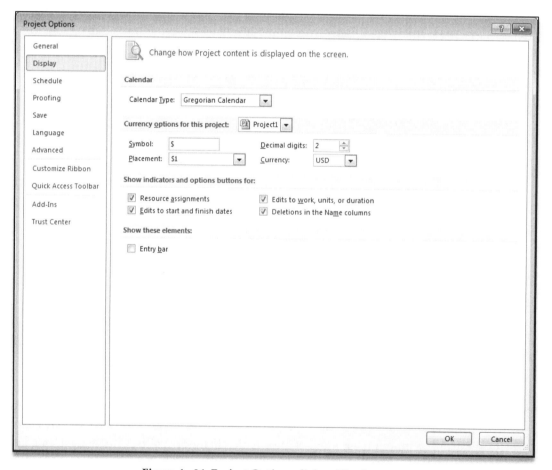

Figure 4 - 34: Project Options dialog, Display page

A new feature in Microsoft Project 2010 allows you to specify option settings for any project currently open, regardless of whether that project is the active project or not. You see this new feature on the *Display* page in the *Currency options for this project* section. Click the *Currency options for this project* pick list to view a list of projects currently open, and then select one of the open projects. By default, the pick list pre-selects the active project, but you can choose any other open project and then specify the *Currency options for this project* setting for that project. This new functionality means that you can specify a unique set of options settings for each open project without the nuisance of continually selecting a new active project and opening and closing the *Project Options* dialog for each project.

Setting Schedule Options

Click the *Schedule* tab in the *Project Options* dialog to view the options on the *Schedule* page shown in the Figure 4 - 35. As indicated at the top of the *Schedule* page, you use the options on this page to control scheduling, calendars, and calculations in Microsoft Project 2010. Notice in Figure 4 - 35 that the *Schedule* page includes sections in which you may specify the following types of options: *Calendar, Schedule, Scheduling,* and *Schedule Alerts,* along with two sections for *Calculation* options.

Notice in Figure 4 - 35 that four of the six sections include the new ability to select any open project from a pick list. The pick lists on the *Schedule* page, however, differ slightly from the pick list shown on the *Display* page. For example, if you click the *Calendar options for this project* pick list, the list includes all projects currently open, plus an *All New Projects* item as well. If you select the *All New Projects* item, the system allows you to specify an options setting for all future projects created from a new blank project.

There are new options on the *Schedule* page in Microsoft Project 2010 in the *Scheduling options for this project* section and the *Schedule Alerts Options* section. In the *Scheduling options for this project* section, new options include the *New tasks created* option, the *Update Manually Scheduled tasks when editing links* option, and the *Keep task on nearest working day when changing to Automatically Scheduled mode* option.

The *New tasks created* option affects the default *Task Mode* setting for new tasks you add to your project. When you click the *New tasks created* pick list, the system offers you two ways to set the task mode for new tasks, *Manually Scheduled* and *Auto Scheduled*. On the *Auto scheduled tasks scheduled on* pick list, you can select the *Project Start Date* or *Current Date* options. The system creates *Auto Scheduled* tasks with dates in the *Start* and *Finish* fields and with a default duration value of *1 day* in the *Duration* field; the system creates all *Manually Scheduled* tasks with no values in the *Duration, Start,* and *Finish* fields.

Although not entirely obvious, you can use the *New Tasks Created* pick list to set the default *Task Mode* option to *Auto Scheduled* for **every new blank project** you create. To do this, click the *Scheduling options for this project* pick list and select the *All New Projects* item. Then click the *New tasks created* pick list and select the *Auto Scheduled* item. Click the *Auto scheduled tasks scheduled on* pick list and select either the *Project Start Date* or the *Current Date* option. When you click the *OK* button, Microsoft Project 2010 sets the default *Task Mode* option to *Auto Scheduled* for every new blank project you create from this point forward.

Another new option in the *Scheduling Options* section is the *Update manually scheduled tasks when editing links* option, which works as you might expect. When you select this option and you link two *Manually Scheduled* tasks with a task dependency, the system reschedules the successor task automatically. If you deselect this option, and you link two *Manually Scheduled* tasks with a task dependency, the system **does not** reschedule the successor task but leaves it at its original start date instead.

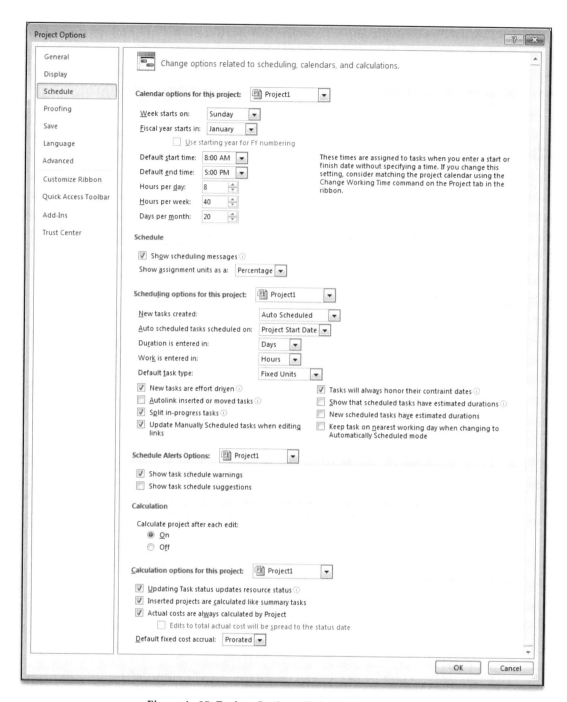

Figure 4 - 35: Project Options dialog, Schedule page

The final change in the *Scheduling Options* section is the *Keep task on the nearest working day when changing to Automatically Scheduled mode* option. You can see how this option affects a task when you convert it from *Manually Scheduled* to *Auto Scheduled* in the example I show you in Figure 4 - 36. Notice that I have two *Manually Scheduled* tasks, Task A and Task B. In this example, I manually scheduled Task A to start on Monday and Task B to start on Wednesday.

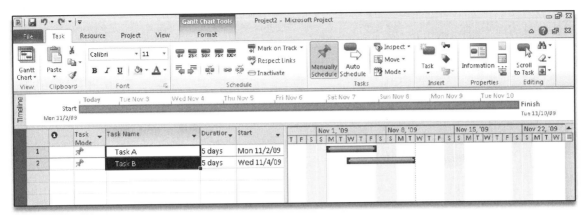

Figure 4 - 36: Two Manually Scheduled tasks

Figure 4 - 37 shows the result of the operation when I change the *Task Mode* setting to *Auto Schedule* for both Task A and Task B with the *Keep task on the nearest working day when changing to Automatically Scheduled mode* option **deselected** (the default setting). Notice that Microsoft Project 2010 schedules Task A and Task B to start on Monday, in spite of the fact that I indicated I want Task B to start on Wednesday.

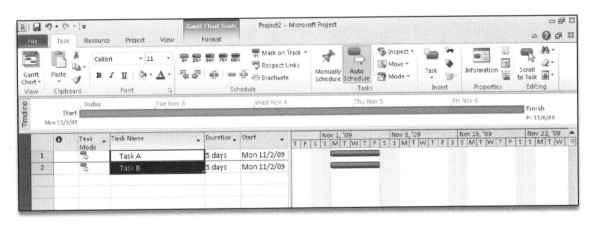

Figure 4 - 37: Convert Manually Scheduled Tasks
to Auto Scheduled tasks with the Option DESELECTED

Figure 4 - 38 shows the result of changing the *Task Mode* setting to *Auto Schedule* for these two tasks after **selecting** the *Keep task on the nearest working day when changing to Automatically Scheduled mode* option. Notice in Figure 4 - 38 that there is an indicator showing to the left of each task in the *Indicators* column. This indicator represents a Start No Earlier Than (SNET) constraint placed by Microsoft Project 2010 on each task to enforce my start dates. This means that Task A continues to start on Monday and Task B continues to start on Wednesday, as I specified when I created these two tasks as *Manually Scheduled* tasks.

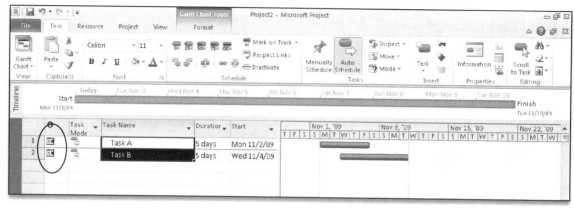

**Figure 4 - 38: Convert Manually Scheduled Tasks
to Auto Scheduled tasks with the Option SELECTED**

Two other options in the *Scheduling Options* section change their default settings from selected to deselected in Microsoft Project 2010. These options are the *New tasks are effort driven* option and the *Autolink inserted or moved tasks* option. In Microsoft Project 2007, the system selected these two options by default.

If the majority of tasks in your projects are Effort Driven tasks, MSProjectExperts recommends that you do the following early in your use of Microsoft Project 2010:

1. Create a new blank project.

2. Click the *Scheduling options for this project* pick list and choose the *All New Projects* item.

3. Select the *New tasks are effort driven* option.

4. Click the *OK* button.

Completing the preceding steps sets the default value for all tasks to *Effort Driven* in all of the new blank projects you create from this point forward. If you use project templates to create new projects, you should also complete the above steps in each of your existing project templates.

The remaining new options you find on the *Schedule* page of the *Project Options* dialog are the two options in the *Schedule Alerts Options* section of the page. Both of these options control the information shown in the *Task Information* pane when you use the *Task Inspector* tool to analyze schedule problems. The *Task Inspector* pane, which started as the *Task Drivers* feature in Project 2007, shows the factors controlling the start date of any task, along with Warnings and Suggestions for correcting task schedule problems. By default, the system selects the *Show task schedule warnings* option and **deselects** the *Show task schedule suggestions* option. To take maximum advantage of the new *Schedule Alerts* feature, I recommend you select **both of these options** for the current project and for all new projects. I discuss the *Task Inspector* tool in detail in Module 05, Project Task Planning.

Table 4 - 4 shows the non-default options settings recommended by MSProjectExperts on the *Schedule* page of the *Project Options* dialog. Furthermore, MSProjectExperts recommends you set these options for all open projects and for all new projects as well.

Option	Setting
New tasks created	Auto Scheduled
New tasks are effort driven	Selected
Show that scheduled tasks have estimated durations	Deselected
New scheduled tasks have estimated durations	Deselected
Show task schedule suggestions	Selected

Table 4 - 4: Recommended options on the Schedule page for all current and future project

Setting Proofing Options

Click the *Proofing* tab in the *Project Options* dialog to view the options on the *Proofing* page shown in Figure 4 - 39. As indicated at the top of the *Proofing* page, use the options on this page to control how Microsoft Project 2010 corrects and formats text in your projects.

The only new option on this page is the *Spanish modes* option, set to the *Tuteo verb forms only* option by default. If you use the Spanish version of Microsoft Project 2010, click the *Spanish modes* pick list and choose your preferred option for working with the Spanish language. Your options are as follows:

- Tuteo Verb Forms Only (the default option)

- Tuteo and Voseo Verb Forms

- Voseo Verb Forms Only

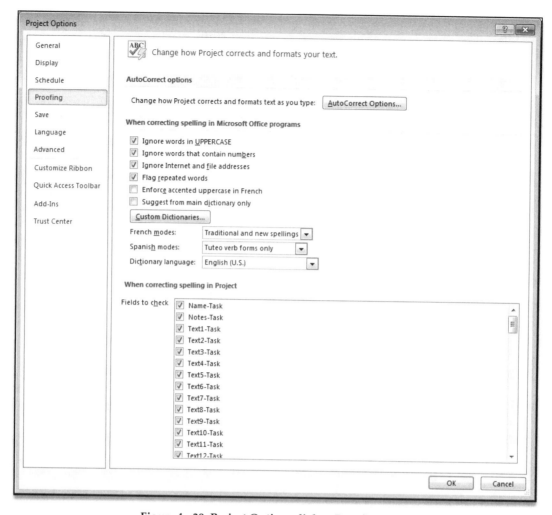

Figure 4 - 39: Project Options dialog, Proofing page

Setting Save Options

Click the *Save* tab in the *Project Options* dialog to view the options on the *Save* page shown in Figure 4 - 40. As indicated at the top of the *Save* page, use the options on this page to determine options for saving a project in Microsoft Project 2010.

The only new options on the *Save* page are those found in the *Cache* section at the bottom of the page. These options are available **only** in the Professional version of Microsoft Project 2010, and for use only with Microsoft Project Server 2010. If you have the Standard version of the software, you do not see a *Cache* section on this page.

Warning: If you like to perform a "what if" analysis in your project, and you select the *Auto save every ___ minutes* option, be sure to leave the *Prompt before saving* option **selected**. Otherwise, you risk the possibility of ovewriting your production project with the "what if" changes, with no recourse to use the *Undo* button since the save action clears the *Undo* cache.

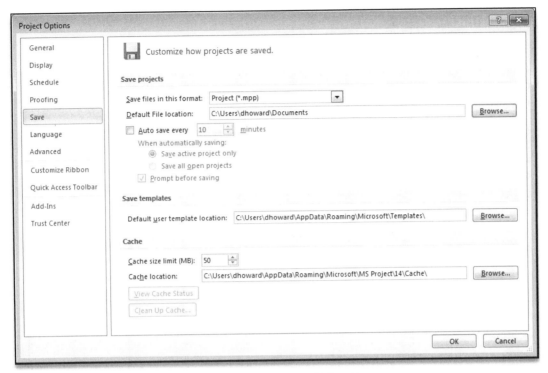

Figure 4 - 40: Project Options dialog, Save page

Backward Compatibility and Save Option Behavior

As with prior versions, Microsoft designed Project 2010 to be backward compatible through at least two generations. Microsoft Project 2010 is capable of saving projects in both 2007 and 2000-2003 formats. Although the *Save files in this format* pick list in the *Save Projects* section is not a new option, it has a profoundly different effect on the behavior of your project client when you choose to save in an older project format as your default save option.

When you select either of the older project formats as the default, the system creates all new blank projects in your selected format, and disables many of the new features in Microsoft Project 2010, including the ability to use *Manually Scheduled* tasks. When you create a new blank project the system presents the project in *Compatibility Mode*, which the system displays rather subtly as shown in Figure 4 - 41.

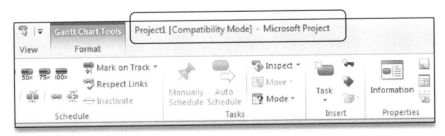

Figure 4 - 41: Compatibility Mode display

You cannot create *Manually Scheduled* tasks in new blank projects when you set your default to save in older formats. The same is true when you open projects saved in legacy formats. The system does not convert these for you automatically. Instead, it respects the limits of the legacy format and disables new scheduling features in Project 2010 for those projects. You can, however, continue to use these features when you open projects previously saved in the new Project 2010 file format and for new blank projects and existing projects saved in a legacy format after you deliberately save the project to the new 2010 format. I discuss these limitations in more depth later in this module.

Setting Language Options

Click the *Language* tab in the *Project Options* dialog to view and set options on the *Language* page shown in Figure 4 - 42. As indicated at the top of the *Language* page, use the options on this page to specify your language preference(s) for all of your Microsoft Office 2010 applications and Microsoft Project 2010. The *Language* page is common to all Microsoft Office applications, as well as to Microsoft Visio and Microsoft Project.

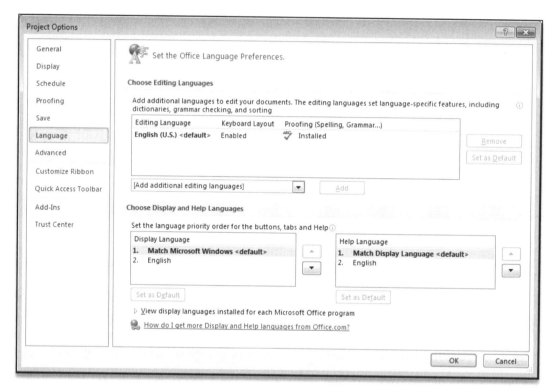

Figure 4 - 42: Project Options dialog, Language page

Before you can use the *Language* page, you must install one or more *Language Packs* for Microsoft Office 2010 applications. After installing at least one *Language Pack*, you can specify the language you want to use for editing your projects, and choose the language the software uses to display your application and to display *Help* dialogs. If you do not install at least one *Language Pack*, the software limits you to the default options shown on the *Language* page. The corresponding *Language* options in Microsoft Project 2007 are located at Start ➢ Programs ➢ Microsoft Office ➢ Microsoft Office Tools ➢ Microsoft Office 2007 Language Tools.

Setting Advanced Options

Click the *Advanced* tab in the *Project Options* dialog to view the options on the *Advanced* page shown in Figure 4 - 43. As indicated at the top of the *Advanced* page, use the options on this page to specify advanced settings for Microsoft Project 2010.

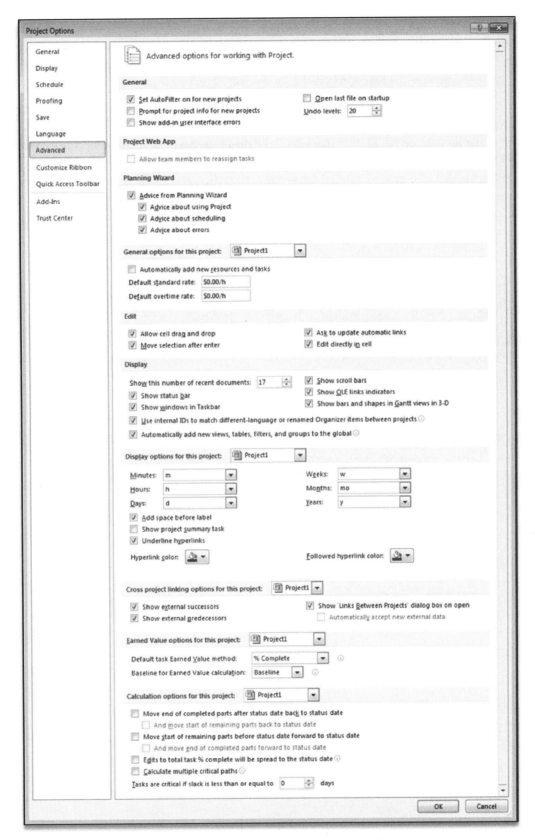

Figure 4 - 43: Project Options dialog, Advanced page

Notice in Figure 4 - 43 that the *Advanced* page includes sections where you specify the following types of options: *General, Project Web App, Planning Wizard, General options for this project, Edit, Display, Display options for this project, Cross project linking, Earned Value,* and *Calculation.* The *Project Web App* section is available **only** in the Professional version of Microsoft Project 2010. If you have the Standard version of the software, you do not see the *Project Web App* section.

Microsoft Project 2010 includes two new options on the *Advanced* page: the *Show add-in user interface errors* option in the *General* section, and the *Automatically add new views, tables, filters, and groups to the global* option in the *Display* section. The first option displays errors originating from Project Add-ins in the project client interface. When you select the *Automatically add new views, tables, filters, and groups to the global* option (the default), the software automatically adds new views, tables, filters, and groups, to your Global.mpt file when you create them, making them available to all current and future projects. If you want to create custom views, tables, filters, and groups on a per-project basis, or if you want to manually control the content available in the Global.mpt file using the *Organizer* dialog, you should **deselect** the *Automatically add new views, tables, filters, and groups to the global* option.

 Although not a new option, the *Show Project Summary Task* option offers a new setting state. To display the Project Summary Task in all new blank projects, click the *Display options for this project* pick list and choose the *All New Projects* item, and then select the *Show Project Summary Task* option. In prior versions of Microsoft Project, the system required you to select this option for each project individually.

Table 4 - 5 shows the non-default options settings recommended by MSProjectExperts on the *Advanced* page of the *Project Options* dialog. Furthermore, MSProjectExperts recommends you set these options for all open projects and for all new projects as well.

Option	Setting
Automatically add new resources and tasks	Deselected
Minutes	m
Hours	h
Days	d
Weeks	w
Months	mo
Years	y
Show project summary task	Selected

Table 4 - 5: Recommended options on the
Advanced page for all current and future project

Setting Add-Ins Options

Click the *Add-Ins* item in the *Project Options* dialog to view the options on the *Add-Ins* page shown in Figure 4 - 44. As indicated at the top of the *Add-Ins* page, use the options on this page to view and manage COM Add-Ins for Microsoft Office 2010.

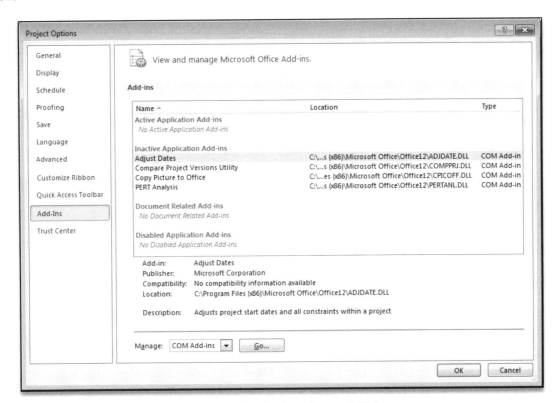

Figure 4 - 44: Project Options dialog, Add-Ins page

 Microsoft Project 2010 **does not** include any of the pre-built macros found in previous versions. Note in the *Inactive Application Add-ins* section of the *Add-Ins* page, that the familiar macros from Project 2007 display in this section because I also have Project 2007 installed on my system.

Setting Trust Center Options

Click the *Trust Center* tab in the *Project Options* dialog to view the options on the *Trust Center* page shown in Figure 4 - 45. As indicated at the top of the *Trust Center* page, use the options on this page to provide security for your project and for your computer. The *Trust Center* page in the *Project Options* dialog provides three sections of security-related information:

- Protecting your privacy
- Security & more
- Microsoft Office Project Trust Center

The *Protecting your privacy* section includes three links, the *Show the Microsoft Office Project privacy statement*, the *Office.com privacy statement*, and the *Customer Experience Improvement Program* links. I do not discuss these options, as they are self-explanatory. The *Security & more* section includes the *Microsoft Trustworthy Computing* link that displays the Microsoft Trustworthy Computing website. Again, I do not discuss this option, as it self-explanatory.

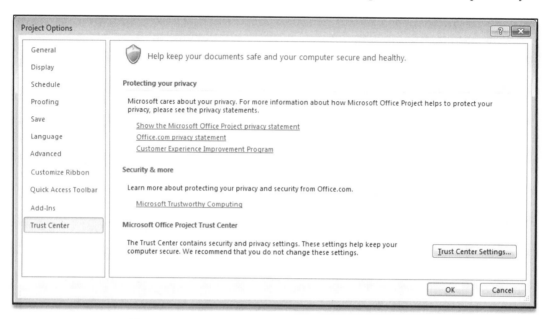

Figure 4 - 45: Project Options dialog, Trust Center page

In the *Microsoft Office Project Trust Center* section, click the *Trust Center Settings* button to specify a range of security settings. The system displays the *Macro Settings* page of the *Trust Center* dialog shown in Figure 4 - 46. Use the *Macro Settings* page to set your level of macro security. By default, Microsoft Project 2010 selects the *Disable all macros with notification* option, which prevents you from running macros in the application. The software notifies you in a warning dialog about this limitation when you attempt to run a macro. To avoid the security warnings, select the *Disable all macros without notification* option. To specify a lower level of macro security, select the *Disable all macros except digitally signed macros* option or the *Enable all macros* option. Notice in the dialog shown in Figure 4 - 46 that Microsoft does not recommend selecting the *Enable all macros* option.

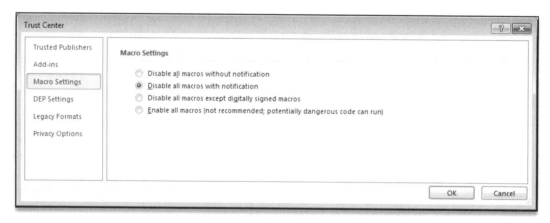

Figure 4 - 46: Trust Center dialog, Macro Settings page

Select the *Trusted Publishers* tab to display the *Trusted Publishers* page in the *Trust Center* dialog shown in Figure 4 - 47. The *Trusted Publishers* page shows macro authors whose VBA code you trust. Notice in the dialog shown in Figure 4 - 47 that I do not currently have a formal macro trust relationship with any macro authors.

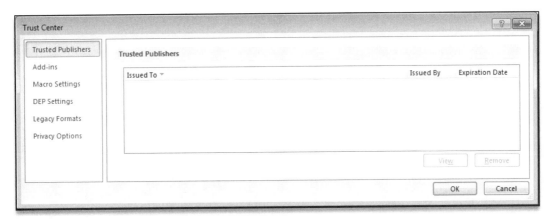

Figure 4 - 47: Trust Center dialog, Trusted Publishers page

Click the *Add-Ins* tab to display the *Add-Ins* page in the *Trust Center* dialog shown in Figure 4 - 48. The *Add-Ins* page offers three options for working with COM Add-Ins, and none of these options are enabled by default. I do not discuss these options because they are self-explanatory.

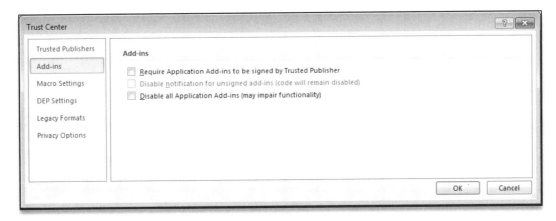

Figure 4 - 48: Trust Center dialog, Add-Ins page

Click the *DEP Settings* tab to display the *Data Execution Prevention* page in the *Trust Center* dialog shown in Figure 4 - 49. Data Execution Prevention (DEP) is a set of hardware and software technologies that protect your computer memory from malicious software code exploits. By default, the single option on the page enables Data Execution Prevention.

If you use Microsoft Project 2010 while connected to Project Server 2010, the *Trust Center* dialog does not contain a *DEP Settings* tab.

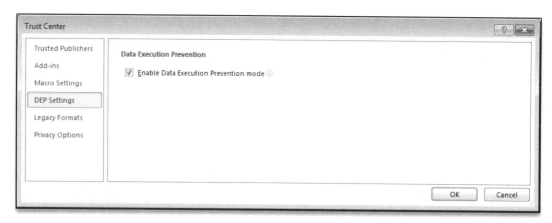

Figure 4 - 49: Trust Center dialog, Data Execution Prevention page

Click the *Legacy Formats* tab to display the *Legacy Formats* page in the *Trust Center* dialog shown in Figure 4 - 50. The options on the *Legacy Formats* page control how Microsoft Project 2010 works with non-default and legacy file formats. Legacy formats controlled by this setting include:

- Microsoft Project Database files

- Microsoft Excel .XLS workbook files

- Microsoft Access databases

- Project Exchange Format .MPX files

- Text files .TXT

- Comma Delimited .CSV files

The default *Do not open/save file with legacy or non-default file formats in Project* option prevents you from opening or closing files that are non-default or legacy format. If you need to work with non-default or legacy files, select either the *Prompt when loading files with legacy or non-default file format* option or the *Allow loading files with legacy or non-default file format* option in the dialog.

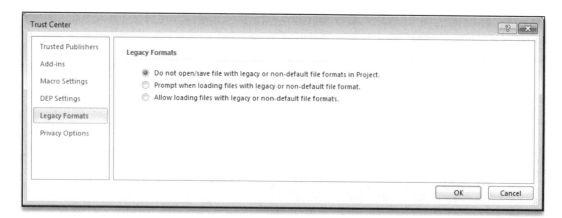

Figure 4 - 50: Trust Center dialog, Legacy Formats page

Warning: If you do not change the default option setting in the *Legacy Formats* page of the *Trust Center* dialog, the system prevents you from either importing or exporting with a legacy or non-default file format such as the Microsoft Office Excel workbook format. If you want to export your Microsoft Project 2010 data to an Excel workbook, be sure to select either the second or third option on the *Legacy Formats* page.

Click the *Privacy Options* tab to display the *Privacy Options* page in the *Trust Center* dialog shown in Figure 4 - 51. As the name of the page implies, use the settings on the *Privacy Options* page to control how much information Microsoft Project 2010 shares with Microsoft and other outside organizations. The *Privacy Options* page contains six application options and one project-specific option. The names of the six application options reveal their function, so I do not discuss them individually. If you select the *Remove personal information from file properties on save* option, the single project-specific option, the system clears the *Author, Manager, Company* and *Last Saved By* fields in the *Properties* dialog each time you save the project.

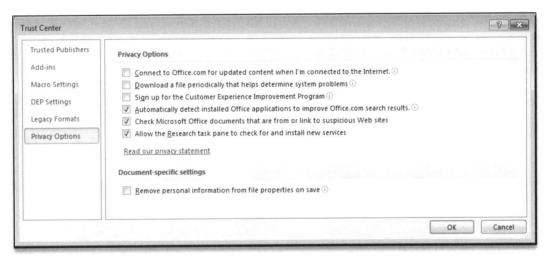

Figure 4 - 51: Trust Center dialog, Privacy Options page

After selecting your options in the *Trust Center* dialog, click the *OK* button to close the dialog. Click the *OK* button to close the *Project Options* dialog as well.

Table 4 - 6 shows the non-default options settings recommended by MSProjectExperts on the *Trust Center* page of the *Project Options* dialog.

Option	Setting
Macro Settings	Disable all macros without notification
Legacy Formats	Disable all macros without notification

Table 4 - 6: Recommended options for the Trust Center page

Hands On Exercise

Exercise 4-12

In your new project, specify the settings recommended by MSProjectExperts in the *Project Options* dialog.

1. Return to the **Training Advisor 04.mpp** sample file.

2. Click the *File* tab and then click the *Options* item in the *Backstage* menu.

3. On the *General* page of the *Project Options* dialog, click the *Date Format* pick list and select the *1/28/09* setting.

4. On the *Schedule* page, set the following options for the active project in the *Scheduling options for this project* section:

New tasks created	Auto Scheduled
New tasks are effort driven	Selected
Show that scheduled tasks have estimated durations	Deselected
New scheduled tasks have estimated durations	Deselected

5. On the *Schedule* page, click the *Scheduling options for this project* pick list, select the *All New Projects* item, and then set the following options for all new projects:

New tasks are effort driven	Selected
Show that scheduled tasks have estimated durations	Deselected
New scheduled tasks have estimated durations	Deselected

6. On the *Schedule* page, select the *Show task schedule suggestions* option for the active project in the *Schedule Alert Options* section.

7. On the *Schedule* page, click the *Schedule Alert Options* pick list, select the *All New Projects* item, and then select the *Show task schedule suggestions* option again for all new projects.

8. On the *Advanced* page, deselect the *Automatically Add New Resources and Tasks* option for the active project in the *General Options for this Project* section.

9. On the *Advanced* page, click the *General options for this project* pick list, select the *All New Projects* item, and then deselect the *Automatically add new resources and tasks* option for all new projects.

10. On the *Advanced* page, set the following options for the active project in the *Display options for this project* section:

Minutes	m
Hours	h
Days	d
Weeks	w
Months	mo
Years	y
Show Project Summary Task	Selected

11. On the *Advanced* page, click the *Display options for this project* pick list, select the *All New Projects* item, and then specify **the same settings** that you set in the previous step.

12. On the *Trust Center* page, click the *Trust Center Settings* button.

13. On the *Macro Settings* page of the *Trust Center* dialog, select the *Disable all macros except digitally signed macros* option.

14. On the *Legacy Formats* page of the *Trust Center* dialog, select the *Allow loading files with legacy or non-default file formats* option.

15. Click the *OK* button to close the *Trust Center* dialog.

16. Click the *OK* button to close the *Project Options* dialog as well.

17. Save but **do not** close the **Training Advisor 04.mpp** sample file.

Step #6 - Save the Project

The final step in the six-step definition process is to save the project file according to your organization's naming conventions. To save your project, complete the following steps:

1. Click the *File* tab and then click the *Save* item in the *Backstage* menu.

The software displays the *Save As* dialog shown in Figure 4 - 52. By default, the system selects the My Documents folder in the *Save As* dialog. You can change the default folder location by selecting a different folder in the *Default file location* field on the *Save* page of the *Project Options* dialog.

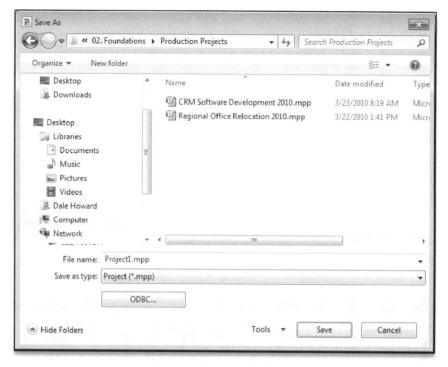

Figure 4 - 52: Save As dialog

2. In the *File name* field of the *Save As* dialog, enter a name for your project that conforms to your organization's naming convention.

3. Click the *Save* button.

Hands On Exercise

Exercise 4-13

Your organization's naming convention for project files includes the department name, the 3-letter initials of the project manager, and a brief description of the project in the file name. Save this project file using the company naming convention.

1. Return to the **Training Advisor 04.mpp** sample file.

2. Click the *File* tab and then click the *Save As* item in the *Backstage* menu.

3. In the *Save As* dialog, save your file using your department name, your own three-letter initials, and the words *Training Advisor*.

4. Click the *Save* button.

5. Close the **Training Advisor 04.mpp** sample file

Saving a Project as an Alternate File Type

Beyond saving a project using the default Microsoft Project 2010 file type, the system allows you to save your project using alternate file types. When you save a new project file for the first time, the system selects the *Project (*.mpp)* option as the default file type, which saves the project file in the native Microsoft Project 2010 file format. If you want to save all of your projects using a backwards compatible file type, remember that you can specify an alternate file type as the default file type on the *Save* page of the *Project Options* dialog. The file types available in Microsoft Project 2010 include the following:

 Warning: In order to work with some of the file types below, you must change the settings on the *Legacy Formats* page in the *Trust Center* as discussed in the previous topic.

- **Microsoft Project 2007** – This file type maintains backwards compatibility with Microsoft Project 2007 and with Microsoft Project 2003 with Service Pack 3 (SP3) applied.

- **Microsoft Project 2000-2003** – This file type maintains backwards compatibility with Microsoft Project 2000, 2002, and 2003.

- **Project Template (*.mpt)** – Only users with Microsoft Project 2010 can create a new project from project templates saved with this file type.

- **Microsoft Project 2007 Template (*.mpt)** – Users of both Microsoft Project 2007 and 2010 can create a new project from project templates saved with this file type.

- **PDF Files (*.pdf)** – Select this file type to save a project file as a Portable Document Format (PDF) file. Using the PDF file type allows you to share project information with users who do not have Microsoft Project 2010 installed on their workstations.

- **XPS Files (*.xps)** – Select this file type to save a project file as an XML Paper Specification file.

- **Excel Workbook (*.xlsx)** - Select this file type to save a project file as a Microsoft Excel workbook using a format that allows only Microsoft Excel 2007 and 2010 to open the workbook.

- **Excel Binary Workbook (*.xlsb)** – Select this file type to save the project file as a Macro-Enabled Excel workbook file stored in Binary format rather than XLSX format. Use this file format to save a very large Microsoft Project file quickly and efficiently. This file type is compatible with versions of Microsoft Excel earlier than the 2007 version; however, users must download and install a converter for their version of Microsoft Excel before they can open this file type.

- **Excel 97-2003 Workbook (*.xls)** – Select this file type to save a project file as a Microsoft Excel workbook using a format that allows Excel 97 through Excel 2003 to open the workbook directly without using a converter.

- **Text (Tab delimited) (*.txt)** and **CSV (Comma delimited) (*.csv)** – Select one of these two file types to save your project file as a text file.

- **XML Format** – Select this file type to save your project file as an Extensible Markup Language (XML) file.

To save a Microsoft Project 2010 file using an alternate file type, click the *File* tab and then click the *Save As* tab in the *Backstage*. In the *Save As* dialog, click the *Save as type* pick list and select an alternate file type, as shown in Figure 4 - 53.

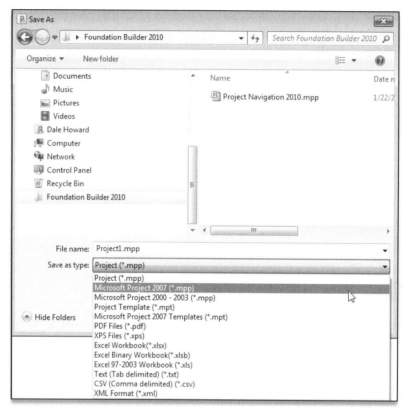

**Figure 4 - 53: Select an alternate file type
on the Save as type pick list**

Many of the alternate file types require you to use the *Import/Export Wizard* to save the file. Because the *Import/Export Wizard* is a very complex tool with many options, I devote an entire module to the import/export process in this book's companion volume, *Microsoft Project 2010 Ultimate Learning Guide: Advanced*. Therefore, in this module, I do not discuss how to save a project using most of the alternate file types.

Saving a Project File as a PDF or XPS Document

Before you save a Microsoft Project 2010 file as a PDF or XPS file, apply the view you want to display in the resulting file, such as the *Gantt Chart* view. Click the *File* tab and then click the *Save As* tab in the *Backstage*. In the *Save As* dialog, click the *Save as type* pick list, and then select either the *PDF Files* (*.pdf*) item or the *XPS Files* (*.xps*) item. Click the *Save* button and Microsoft Project 2010 displays the *Document Export Options* dialog shown in Figure 4 - 54.

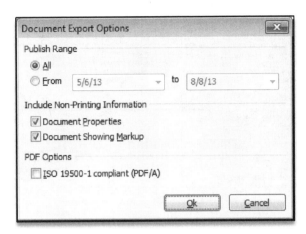

Figure 4 - 54: Document Export Options dialog

In the *Publish Range* section, select the *All* option to export all tasks in the project, along with the entire *Gantt Chart* timeline if you applied the *Gantt Chart with Timeline* view in the project. Select the *From* option and select a date range to print the task list on the left side with the date range specified for the Gantt chart.

In the *Include Non-Printing Information* section of the dialog, leave the *Document Properties* option and the *Document Showing Markup* option selected to include this information in the PDF or XPS file. Users can view this non-printing information in the PDF file by clicking File ➢ Properties in the Adobe Acrobat Reader software. Deselect **one or both of** these options to remove the non-printing information from the PDF or XPS file.

In the *PDF Options* section, select the *ISO 19500-1 Compliant (PDF/A)* option to save a PDF document in ISO compliant format. Do not select this option if you do not need an ISO compliant PDF file. Click the *OK* button to save the project file as a PDF file. Figure 4 - 55 shows a Microsoft Project 2010 project file saved as a PDF document and displayed in the Adobe Acrobat Reader software. Figure 4 - 56 shows the same project file saved as an XPS document and displayed in the Microsoft XPS Viewer application.

Companies use the PDF/A file format for the long-term archiving of electronic documents. This file format guarantees that users can reproduce the original document in exactly the same way years later.

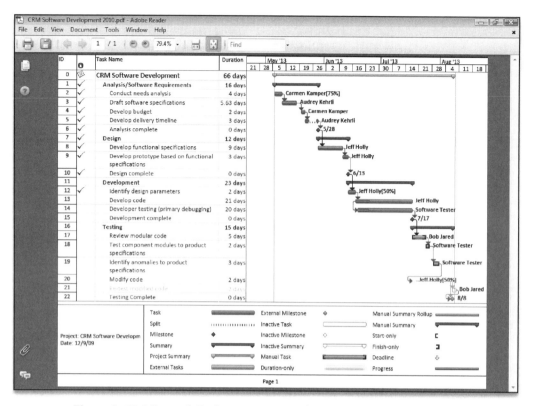

Figure 4 - 55: Microsoft Project 2010 project file saved as a PDF document

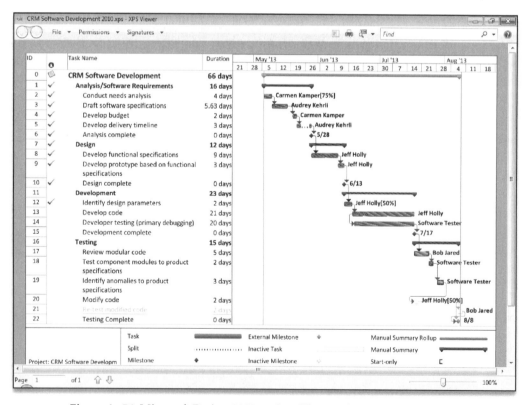

Figure 4 - 56: Microsoft Project 2010 project file saved as an XPS document

You can also save a Microsoft Project 2010 file as a PDF or XPS document by clicking the *File* tab and then clicking the *Save & Send* tab in the *Backstage*. On the *Save & Send* page, click the *Create PDF/XPS Document* menu item and then click the *Create a PDF/XPS* button. In the *Browse* dialog, browse to the location where you want to save the file and then click the *Save as type* pick list and choose your file type.

Understanding Reduced Functionality with Older Project File Formats

If you save a Microsoft Project 2010 file using the Microsoft Project 2007 file type, the system displays the *Saving to Previous Version – Compatibility Checker* warning dialog shown in Figure 4 - 57. The dialog warns you of Microsoft Project 2010 features not supported in the 2007 version of the software application. Notice that the warning dialog shown in Figure 4 - 57 warns about *Manually Scheduled Tasks* and *Manually Scheduled Summary Tasks* in the project, and reveals how the software converts these features to work with the 2007 version of the software.

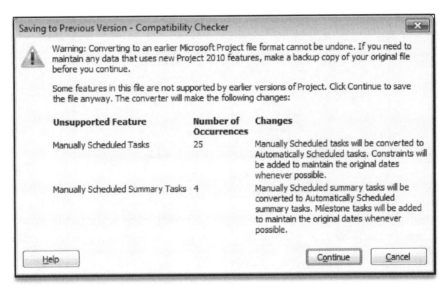

Figure 4 - 57: Saving to Previous Version – Compatibility Checker dialog

When you click the *Continue* button in the *Saving to Previous Version – Compatibility Checker* dialog, the system converts the data that relies on new features as follows:

- The system changes *Manually Scheduled* tasks to *Auto Scheduled* tasks, and adds Start No Earlier Than (SNET) constraints to the tasks to preserve current dates in the schedule.

- The system changes *Manually Scheduled* summary tasks to *Auto Scheduled* summary tasks.

- After converting *Manually Scheduled* summary tasks to *Auto Scheduled* summary tasks, the system adds two milestone tasks immediately after the summary task to indicate the original start date and finish date for the summary task. The system adds a Must Start On (MSO) constraint to these milestone tasks as well.

- The system deletes *Inactive* tasks.

- The system removes *Strikethrough* font formatting on any tasks manually formatted by the user.

- If you apply custom formatting to the *Team Planner* view, save the file as an earlier version, then close and re-open the file, you lose the custom formatting in the *Team Planner* view.

- The system converts 32-bit colors to the 16 colors used in all previous versions of Microsoft Project. These colors apply to font formatting, Gantt bar colors, and cell background formatting (Microsoft Project 2007 only).

- Previous versions of Microsoft Project do not display the *Timeline* view.

- The system applies AutoFilter to the data in the project.

If you save a Microsoft Project 2010 file using the Microsoft Project 2003 file type, the system displays the *Saving to Microsoft Project 2000-2003 format* dialog shown in Figure 4 - 58. The dialog warns you of Microsoft Project 2010 features not supported in the earlier version of the software application.

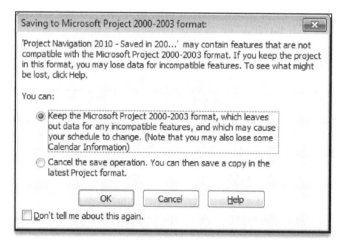

**Figure 4 - 58: Saving to Microsoft
Project 2000-2003 Format dialog**

When you save a Microsoft Project 2010 file in the Microsoft Project 2000-2003 file format, the system converts the data that relies on new features the same way as with the 2007 file format, and impacts your saved file as follows:

- You lose any information contained in *Budget* fields, such as in the *Budget Cost* field.

- The system converts each *Cost* resource to a same-named *Material* resource, but you do not lose information contained in the *Cost* fields for the *Cost* resources.

- The system removes cell background formatting applied to tasks, but you do not lose font formatting.

- The system removes information contained in the *Assignment Owner* field and other fields added to Project since the 2003 version.

- The system converts recurring calendar exceptions to a series of multiple individual exceptions.

- The system removes all information related to enterprise custom fields.

Opening a Project Created in an Older Version of Microsoft Project

In Microsoft Project 2010, when you open a project file created in an earlier version of the software, the system opens the file in *Compatibility Mode*, discussed previously in the *Save* options section in this module. The system displays this information to the right of the file name in the title bar of the application window as shown previously in Figure 4 - 41. While you have a project file open in *Compatibility Mode*, you cannot use any of the new features of the software, such as *Manually Scheduled* tasks or *Inactive* tasks. If you save the project file as a Microsoft Project 2010 file, the system enables all of the new features in the software, but handles existing tasks and new tasks as follows:

- The system sets existing tasks and new tasks to *Auto Scheduled*. You can then set any existing or new tasks to *Manually Scheduled*.

- The system does not display the *Task Mode* column automatically. To display this column, you must do so manually.

- The system does not display the *Gantt with Timeline* view automatically. To display this view, apply the *Gantt with Timeline* view manually.

Hands On Exercise

Exercise 4-14

Save your project using several alternate file types.

1. Open the **CRM Software Development 2010.mpp** sample file.

2. Click the *File* tab and then click the *Save As* item in the *Backstage* menu.

3. In the *Save As* dialog, click the *Save as type* pick list, select the *PDF Files (*.pdf)* item, and then click the *Save* button.

4. In the *Document Export Options* dialog, leave all of the default options selected and then click the *OK* button.

5. Click the *File* tab and then click the *Save As* item in the *Backstage* menu.

6. In the *Save As* dialog, change the file name to *CRM Software Development 2007*.

7. In the *Save As* dialog, click the *Save as type* pick list, select the *Microsoft Project 2007 (*.mpp)* item, and then click the *Save* button.

8. In the *Saving to Previous Version - Compatibility Checker* dialog, click the *Continue* button.

9. Notice the **[Compatibility Mode]** label appended to the file name on the title bar at the top of the Microsoft Project 2010 application window.

10. Notice how Microsoft Project 2010 placed constraints on most of the tasks in the Testing phase of the project.

11. Click the *Task* tab to display the *Task* ribbon, and notice that the system disables the *Inactivate*, *Manually Schedule*, and *Auto Schedule* buttons.

12. Close the **CRM Software Development 2007.mpp** sample file, and when prompted in a warning dialog, click the *No* button to close it without saving further changes.

Saving a Project to SharePoint

If your organization uses Microsoft SharePoint Foundation 2010 or Microsoft SharePoint Server (MSS) 2010, you can save your Microsoft Project 2010 project files to a SharePoint site in a document library. Before you can save your project file to a SharePoint site, however, your organization must meet the following requirements:

- Your SharePoint administrator must create a SharePoint site for you.

- Your SharePoint administrator must supply you with the URL of the site.

- Either you or your SharePoint administrator must create a document library for your project.

- You must navigate to the SharePoint site and copy the URL to your Windows clipboard.

 Warning: Your organization **must** use Microsoft SharePoint Foundation 2010 or Microsoft SharePoint Server 2010 before you can save your Microsoft Project 2010 files in a document library in SharePoint. You cannot use any previous version of SharePoint for this functionality.

Figure 4 - 59 shows a Microsoft SharePoint Server 2010 site containing a document library called Project 2010 Production Projects.

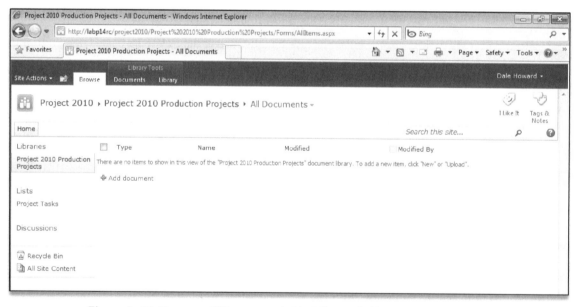

Figure 4 - 59: Document Library created in Microsoft SharePoint Server 2010

After meeting the previous set of conditions, you can save a Microsoft Project 2010 file to the SharePoint site by completing the following steps:

4. Click the *File* tab and then click the *Save & Send* tab.

5. On the *Save & Send* page, click the *Save to SharePoint* tab.

Microsoft Project 2010 displays the *Save & Send* page with the *Save to SharePoint* section shown in Figure 4 - 60.

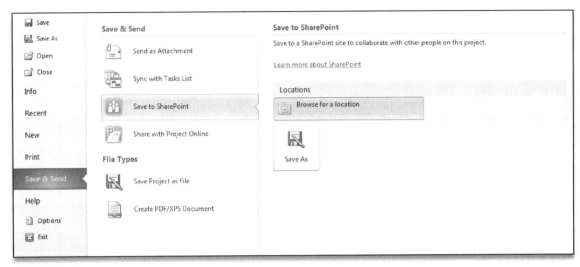

Figure 4 - 60: Save to SharePoint page in the Backstage

6. In the *Save to SharePoint* section, double-click the *Browse for a location* button. Microsoft Project 2010 displays the *Save As* dialog.

7. In the *Save As* dialog, paste the URL of the SharePoint site into the address field at the top of the dialog, as shown in Figure 4 - 61.

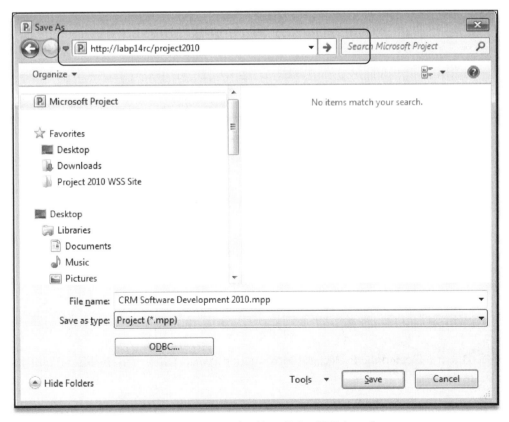

**Figure 4 - 61: Paste the SharePoint URL into the
address field at the top of the Save As dialog**

8. Press the *Enter* key on your computer keyboard and allow the *Save As* dialog to access the SharePoint site, as shown in Figure 4 - 62.

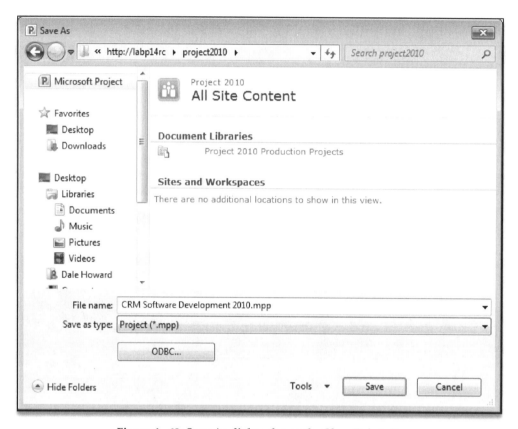

Figure 4 - 62: Save As dialog shows the SharePoint site

9. In the SharePoint site shown in the *Save As* dialog, double-click a library in the *Document Libraries* section in which you want to save your project.

Notice in Figure 4 - 63 that I selected the Project 2010 Production Projects library in the SharePoint site.

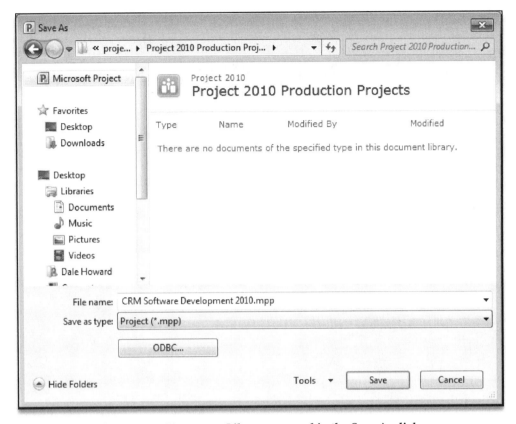

Figure 4 - 63: Document Library accessed in the Save As dialog

10. Click the *Save* button in the *Save As* dialog.

As Microsoft Project 2010 saves the project file to the SharePoint site, the system displays a progress meter in a *Saving* dialog as shown in Figure 4 - 64.

Figure 4 - 64: Saving dialog

Figure 4 - 65 shows a project file saved in the Project 2010 Production Projects document library in the SharePoint site shown previously in Figure 4 - 59.

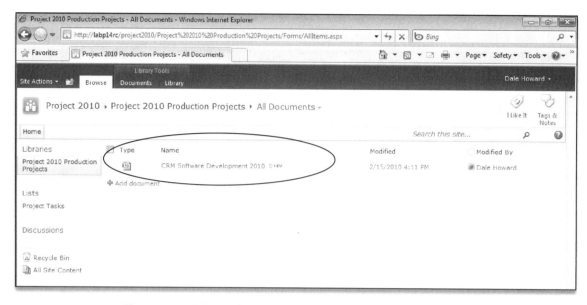

Figure 4 - 65: Microsoft Project 2010 file saved in a SharePoint site

Warning: After you save your project to a document library in SharePoint, Microsoft Project 2010 is designed to save the URL of the SharePoint site in the *Locations* section of the *Save to SharePoint* page in the *Backstage*. Because of a bug at release, the system does not work as designed and **does not** save the URL of the SharePoint site for you.

To open a project file saved in a SharePoint site, complete the following steps:

1. Click the *File* tab and then click the *Open* menu item in the *Backstage*.

2. In the *Open* dialog, enter or paste the URL of the SharePoint site into the address field at the top of the dialog and then press the *Enter* key.

3. In the *Document Library* section of the SharePoint site, double-click the name of the library containing the project, and then select the project, as shown in Figure 4 - 66.

4. Click the *Open* button in the *Open* dialog.

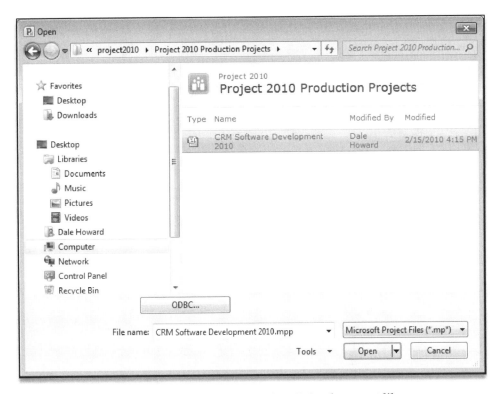

Figure 4 - 66: Open a project in a SharePoint document library

To provide you with faster access to the SharePoint site, save the URL in the *Favorites* list on the left side of the *Save As* dialog or the *Open* dialog.

Sharing a Project via E-Mail

Microsoft Project 2010 allows you to send a project file via e-mail to multiple users. Each user receives an individual copy of the project and can comment on the file. To send a file via e-mail, click the *File* tab and then click the *Save & Send* tab. On the *Save & Send* page, click the *Send as Attachment* button. The system opens a new blank e-mail message with the project file attached, as shown in Figure 4 - 67.

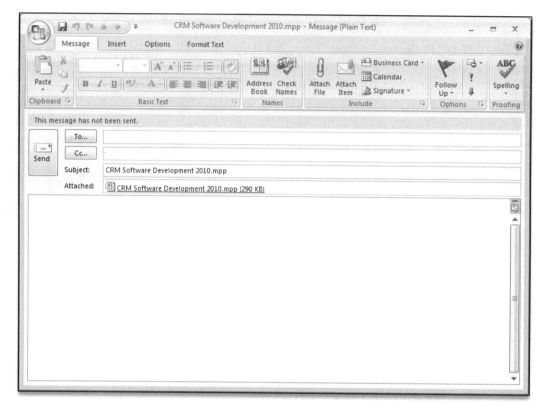

Figure 4 - 67: E-mail message with Microsoft Project 2010 file attached

Notice in Figure 4 - 67 that Microsoft Project 2010 enters the name of the attached project file in the *Subject* field of the outgoing e-mail message. Select one or more recipients and enter e-mail message text as needed. Click the *Send* button to send your email.

Warning: If you do not have your e-mail application running when you send the e-mail message with the attachment, your e-mail application does not send the outgoing e-mail message until the next time you launch the application.

Module 05

Project Task Planning

Learning Objectives

After completing this module, you will be able to:

- Understand the task planning process
- Understand change highlighting
- Use Manually Scheduled tasks and Auto Scheduled tasks
- Use basic task planning skills to create a project schedule
- Set task dependencies, constraints, and deadline dates
- Document the task list with appropriate task notes
- Use cell background formatting to display tasks of interest
- Estimate task Durations
- Determine task drivers
- Create recurring tasks
- Enter a Fixed Cost on a task

Inside Module 05

155

156

Understanding the Task Planning Process

After you define your project, the planning process begins. The first step in the planning process is task planning. If you do not create your project from a template, then you must manually complete a series of steps in Microsoft Project 2010 to complete the task planning process.

When you create a task list manually, you must thoughtfully analyze the activities required to complete the project. Depending on the size of your project, this may mean lots of typing! You can use either a "top down" or "bottom up" approach to create the initial task list. The "top down" approach begins by listing the major phases of the project, as well as the project deliverables under each phase. Under each deliverable you list the activities necessary to produce the deliverable. To help you with the process of "top down" planning, Microsoft Project 2010 includes a new feature that allows you to insert "top down" summary tasks. I discuss this new feature later in this module.

The "bottom up" approach works in the opposite direction. Using this approach, you list all of the activities in the project and then organize the activities into phase and deliverable summary sections. You can be effective in creating the task list for the project using either approach. Your organization may adhere to pre-defined project lifecycle standards, which obligate you to use a structured framework. Whenever you create a new project manually, it is a good idea to follow this methodology:

1. Create the task list.

2. Create summary tasks to generate the project's Work Breakdown Structure (WBS).

3. Create project milestones.

4. Set task dependencies and document unusual task dependencies with a task note.

5. Set task constraints and deadline dates, and document all task constraints with a task note.

6. Set task calendars for any task with an alternate working schedule and document the task calendars with a task note.

7. Estimate task effort or durations according to your preferred or required methodologies.

8. Create recurring tasks (optional).

9. Enter known fixed costs.

In successive topical sections in this module, I discuss each of the steps in the preceding task planning methodology.

Auto-Wrapping Task Names

During the task planning process, you see the new *Auto-Wrap Task Names* feature in Microsoft Project 2010 when you enter a task name that exceeds the width of the *Task Name* column. This feature increases the row height automatically and wraps the text inside the cell. In all previous versions of the tool, the only way to auto-wrap task names was to manually increase the height of the task row until the task name wrapped completely within the cell. In Microsoft Project 2010, the software auto-wraps task names in cells when one of several events occurs:

- You manually type a task name that exceeds the width of the *Task Name* column and then press the **Enter** key to complete the data entry. The software automatically increases the row height for that task to wrap the task name within the cell.

- You paste a task name that exceeds the width of the *Task Name* column. The software automatically increases the row height for that task to wrap the task name within the cell.

- You manually decrease the width of the *Task Name* column. The software automatically increases the row height for **every** task with a name exceeding the width of the *Task Name* column.

- You manually increase the width of the *Task Name* column. The software automatically decreases the row height for that task and un-wraps the text.

Warning: Microsoft Project 2010 **does not** decrease the row height of wrapped tasks automatically when you widen the *Task Name* column to "best fit" the longest task name. This means you must manually decrease the row height of every task row that includes a task name formerly wrapped using the new *Auto-Wrap Task Names* feature.

Understanding Change Highlighting

Whenever you make a change anywhere in a Microsoft Project 2010 schedule, the software uses change highlighting to graphically show you all tasks impacted by the change. This behavior begins the moment you enter the first task in the project and continues until you complete the project. For example, if you change the schedule of any task with successors, the software applies the light blue cell background color in the *Duration*, *Start*, and/or *Finish* columns for every impacted task. Figure 5 - 1 shows a project before I make revisions to the schedule. Figure 5 - 2 shows the same project after I change the duration of the Test task from 2 days to 4 days. Notice how Microsoft Project 2010 changes the cell formatting color for the *Duration* and *Finish* columns of the Test task, and changes the cell formatting color to the *Start* and/or *Finish* columns of each impacted task and summary task, including the Project Summary Task.

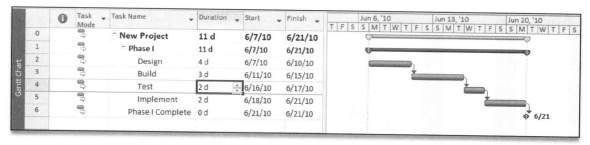

Figure 5 - 1: Project before schedule changes

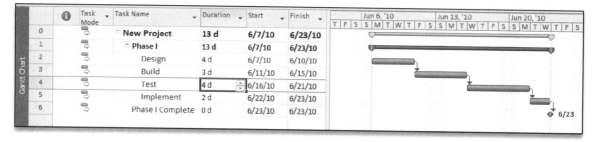

Figure 5 - 2: Project after making schedule changes

To change the cell background color used to indicate changed tasks, click the *Format* tab to display the *Format* ribbon. In the *Format* section of the *Format* ribbon, click the *Text Styles* button. In the *Text Styles* dialog, click the *Item to Change* pick list and select the *Changed Tasks* item on the list. Select a different color in the *Background Color* pick list and click the *OK* button.

Understanding Manually Scheduled vs. Auto Scheduled Tasks

By now you must be more than a little curious about how you actually use what is probably the most important change to Microsoft Project 2010 in many years, *Manually Scheduled* tasks. You may also be wondering why Microsoft chose to introduce manual scheduling, and if you are a dynamic scheduling purist, you might even be close to convulsions when you think about how uncontrollable a schedule can be using this feature.

One of Microsoft's goals in introducing *Manually Scheduled* tasks is to lower the barrier for entry-level users accustomed to managing their projects in Excel so that they can start to learn how to use a scheduling tool. The thinking is that this at least gets them into the correct environment. When a user sets a task to *Manually Scheduled* mode, entering task data into a project does not cause task dates to change unless the user specifies them. Users who are untrained in the behaviors of the Microsoft Project scheduling engine are typically put off by the scheduling engine's insistence on remaining in control of dates in all prior versions of Microsoft Project.

The new *Manually Scheduled* tasks feature also addresses another previously unmet Microsoft Project user need by providing a way to represent tasks where scheduling information is unavailable, such as during early phase planning. Additionally, this feature helps Microsoft Project work better with real-world scenarios, such as scheduling projects where agile methodologies are in use.

Manually Scheduled tasks do not require duration, start date, or finish date data, thereby providing complete flexibility. As you learned previously in Module 04, Project Definition, among your first steps in specifying options settings for a new project is to set the *Task Mode* setting to either the *Manually Scheduled* or *Auto Scheduled* option. Unless you specify otherwise, Microsoft Project 2010 sets the *Task Mode* to the *Manually Scheduled* option for all tasks in every new project. As you create your task list, the software sets each new task to the *Task Mode* setting you specified.

Using Basic Task Planning Skills

You should possess a variety of basic task skills to use Microsoft Project 2010 effectively. I discuss each of these basic task planning skills in the following topical sections.

Entering and Editing Tasks

Entering *Auto Scheduled* tasks and *Manually Scheduled* tasks in Microsoft Project 2010 is very similar to entering data in a Microsoft Excel spreadsheet. To enter a new task, complete the following steps:

1. Select a blank cell in the *Task Name* column of the task sheet.

2. Type the task name.

3. Press the **Enter** key or **Down-Arrow** key on the keyboard.

To edit the name of an existing task, select the task and then use any of the following methods:

- Double-click the task and edit the name in the *Task Information* dialog.

- Retype the task name.

- Press the **F2** function key on the keyboard and edit the task name.

- Select the name of the task and then click anywhere in the cell to enable in-cell editing.

Entering Manually Scheduled Tasks

During the task planning process, you can designate any task as either a *Manually Scheduled* task or an *Auto Scheduled* task. To specify the *Task Mode* setting for any task, complete the following steps:

1. Click the *Task* tab to display the *Task* ribbon.

2. Select the task(s) whose *Task Mode* setting you want to change.

3. Click the *Manually Schedule* button or the *Auto Schedule* button on the *Task* ribbon.

To specify the *Task Mode* setting for an individual task, you can also select a cell in the *Task Mode* column for the task, click the pick list in the *Task Mode* cell, and choose either *Manually Scheduled* or *Auto Scheduled* from the list.

Figure 5 - 3 shows a project in which I included four *Auto Scheduled* tasks (Design, Build, Test, and Implement) and two *Manually Scheduled* tasks (Rebuild and Retest). Notice the following about this project:

- Microsoft Project 2010 displays a unique indicator to the left of each task in the *Indicators* column to identify the *Task Mode* setting for each task.

- Every *Auto Scheduled* task includes a duration value in the *Duration* column, along with date values in the *Start* and *Finish* columns.

- The Rebuild and Retest tasks have no values in the *Duration*, *Start*, or *Finish* columns.

- The *Gantt Chart* view does not include Gantt bars for these two *Manually Scheduled* tasks.

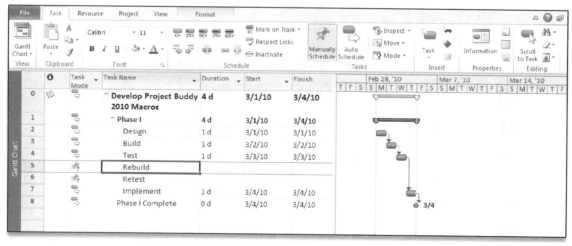

Figure 5 - 3: New project includes both Manually Scheduled tasks and *Auto Scheduled* tasks

When you specify any task as a *Manually Scheduled* task, Microsoft Project 2010 allows you to specify values in the *Duration*, *Start*, and *Finish* columns in a number of ways, including:

- Specify no duration, start, or finish values until you have an estimated duration, start, or finish date.

- Enter text information in the *Duration* column about an approximate duration, and enter text information in the *Start* and *Finish* columns about approximate start and finish dates.

- Enter an estimated duration (such as *5 days*) in the *Duration* column, and/or an estimated date (such as *12/21/2012*) in the *Start* and *Finish* columns.

 In addition to typing text to enter an approximate duration, start date, or finish date, you can enter other textual information, such as "TBD" or "Decision by 11/01/10."

In Figure 5 - 3 shown previously, you can see an example of two *Manually Scheduled* tasks with no duration, start, or finish date information. When you create a new *Manually Scheduled* task, Microsoft Project 2010 leaves the *Duration*, *Start*, and *Finish* columns blank. In Figure 5 - 4, you see an example of two *Manually Scheduled* tasks with approximate duration values (entered as "About 1w" and "About 2d") and approximate start dates (entered as "Late May" and "Early June").

4		Test	1 d	3/3/10	3/3/10
5		Rebuild	About 1w	Late May	
6		Retest	About 2d	Early June	
7		Implement	1 d	3/4/10	3/4/10

Figure 5 - 4: Approximate Duration and Start values for *Manually Scheduled* tasks

If you enter a valid duration value (such as *5 days*) for a *Manually Scheduled* task, Microsoft Project 2010 displays a "highlighted" Gantt bar for the task. If you also enter a valid date value (such as *12/21/2012*) in the *Start* or *Finish* columns, the software displays a silhouetted teal-colored Gantt bar for the task. In Figure 5 - 5, notice that I entered a valid duration value for the Rebuild and Retest tasks, and specified a valid date value in the *Start* column for only the Retest task. Notice the two different types of Gantt bars for these tasks. Notice also the different indicators shown in the *Indicators* column for the Rebuild and Retest tasks.

	ⓘ	Task Mode	Task Name	Duration	Start	Feb 28, '10 T F S S M T W T F S	Mar 7, '10 S M T W T
0			⁻ **Develop Project Buddy 2010 Macros**	7 d	3/1/10		
1			⁻ **Phase I**	7 d	3/1/10		
2			Design	1 d	3/1/10		
3			Build	1 d	3/2/10		
4			Test	1 d	3/3/10		
5			Rebuild	1 w	Late May		
6			Retest	2 d	3/8/10		
7			Implement	1 d	3/4/10		
8			Phase I Complete	0 d	3/4/10		◆ 3/4

Figure 5 - 5: *Manually Scheduled* tasks with Duration and Start date values specified

Hands On Exercise

Exercise 5-1

Use basic task planning skills to define the task list in the Training Advisor Rollout project.

1. Open the **Training Advisor 05a.mpp** sample file.

2. Scroll to the first blank row at the bottom of the existing task list and add the following new tasks:

    Create Training Schedule

    Provide End User Training

Notice that Microsoft Project 2010 creates these two new tasks as a *Manually Scheduled* task, controlled by the default *Task Mode* setting in the left end of the Status bar at the bottom of the application window.

3. Drag your split bar to the right edge of the *Finish* column.

4. For the *Create Training Schedule* task, enter *5 days* in the *Duration* column and enter *Late March* in the *Start* column.

5. For the *Provide Enter User Training* task, enter *10 days* in the *Duration* column and enter *By May* in the *Finish* column.

Notice the unusual Gantt bar displayed by Microsoft Project 2010 for these two *Manually Scheduled* tasks.

6. Select the *Conduct Skills Accessment* task, press the **F2** function key on your keyboard, and then change the spelling of "Accessment" to "Assessment."

7. Scroll to the top of the task list, and then double-click the right edge of the *Task Name* column header to "best fit" the column width.

Notice that Microsoft Project 2010 **does not** decrease the row height automatically for the *Determine Server Specifications* task, whose name the software auto-wrapped previously.

8. Double-click the bottom edge of the ID #2 row header to "best fit" the row height for the *Determine Server Specifications* task.

9. Drag the split bar on the right edge of the *Duration* column.

10. Save but **do not** close **Training Advisor 05a.mpp** sample file.

Moving Tasks

During the task planning process, you may create the task list with tasks in the wrong order. To move a task, complete the following steps:

1. Click the task ID number (row header) on the far left end of the task and release the mouse button.

2. Click and hold the task ID number to "grab" the task.

3. Move the mouse pointer up or down on the screen to move the task.

As you move the mouse pointer, you see a gray I-beam bar to indicate that you are moving the task, as shown in Figure 5 - 6.

		ℹ	Task Mode	Task Name	Duration	Start
	0			⁻ **New Project**	**1 d**	**6/7/10**
	1			Build	1 d	6/7/10
	2			Test	1 d	6/7/10
	3			Design	1 d	6/7/10
	4			Implement	1 d	6/7/10

Figure 5 - 6: Moving a task

4. Drag the task until you position the gray I-beam indicator where you want to place the task.

5. Release the mouse button to complete the move and "drop" the task in its new location.

You can also move a group of tasks as a block by first selecting the ID numbers of all of the tasks you want to move. When you click and hold any one of the selected ID number, you can drag the entire block of tasks to a new location in the project. Additionally, when you move a summary task, all of its subtasks move with it.

Hands On Exercise

Exercise 5-2

Drag and drop tasks into the correct order in a project.

1. Return to the **Training Advisor 05a.mpp** sample file.

2. Click the row header for ID #6, the *Load and Configure Software* task, and then release the mouse button.

3. Click and hold the row header for ID #6 and then drag and drop the task immediately above task ID #5, the *Perform Server Stress Test* task.

4. Click and drag the row headers for task ID #19 and #20 to select the tasks as a block, and then release the mouse button.

5. Click and hold the row header for either of the two selected tasks and then drag them as a block above task ID #18, the *Training Complete* task.

6. Save but **do not** close **Training Advisor 05a.mpp** sample file.

Inserting Tasks

While entering a task list, you may discover that you omitted one or more tasks. To insert new tasks in your project plan, select any cell in the row where you want to insert the new task and then use one of the following methods:

- On the *Task* ribbon, click the *Task* button in the *Insert* section of the *ribbon*.

- Press the **Insert** key on your computer keyboard.

- Right-click in the row and then select the *Insert Task* item on the shortcut menu.

Microsoft Project 2010 adds a new blank task row automatically above the selected task. If you add the new task using the **Insert** key on your keyboard, the system simply adds a new blank task. If you use the *Task* button on the *Task* ribbon or the *Insert Task* item on the shortcut menu, the system adds a new task named *<New Task>* with a default duration of 1 day. After using any of these three methods, you must still enter the name of the new task.

To add multiple new tasks simultaneously, select as many rows as the number of new tasks you would like to add, and use one of the preceding methods. For example, in Figure 5 - 7 I want to add two new tasks before the Implement task, so I select the Implement task and the following blank task as the location of the two new tasks.

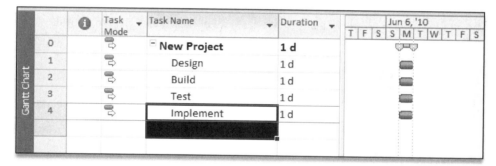

Figure 5 - 7: Preparing to insert two new tasks after the Test task

When I click the *Task* button on the *Task* ribbon, the software inserts two new tasks named <New Task> with a Duration of 1 day, as shown in Figure 5 - 8.

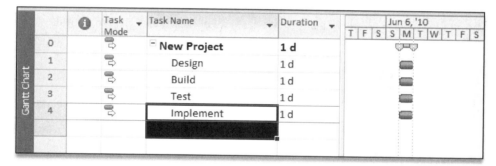

Figure 5 - 8: Two new tasks inserted before the Implement task

Hands On Exercise

Exercise 5-3

Members of the project team determined that your project is missing a necessary task in the Testing section of the project. Insert a new task called Resolve Connectivity Errors between the Verify Connectivity task and the Testing Complete task.

1. Return to the **Training Advisor 05a.mpp** sample file.

2. Select task ID #11, the *Testing Complete* task.

3. Click the *Task* button in the *Insert* section of the *Task* ribbon.

Because the default *Task Mode* setting for this project is *Manually Scheduled*, notice that Microsoft Project 2010 created a new *Manually Scheduled* task named <New Task>.

4. With the new unnamed task still selected, click the *Auto Schedule* button in the *Tasks* section of the *Task* ribbon.

5. Change the name of the new task to *Resolve Connectivity Errors* and then press the **Enter** key on your computer keyboard.

6. Save but **do not** close **Training Advisor 05a.mpp** sample file.

Deleting Tasks

While entering a task list, you may find that you no longer need one or more tasks in the project plan. To delete a task, complete the following steps, select the ID number of the task you want to delete and use one of the following methods:

*   Press the **Delete** key on your computer keyboard.

*   Right-click in the on the selected row and then select the *Delete Task* item on the shortcut menu.

If you select any cell in the *Task Name* column (rather than selecting the task ID number) and then press the **Delete** key on your computer keyboard, the software displays a Smart Tag to the left of the cell. When you float your mouse pointer over the Smart Tag, the system displays a pick list. Click the Smart Tag pick list and then select whether to clear the contents of only the *Task Name* cell or to delete the entire task. Figure 5 - 9 shows the Smart Tag for deleting a task after selecting only the name of the task, rather than the task ID number.

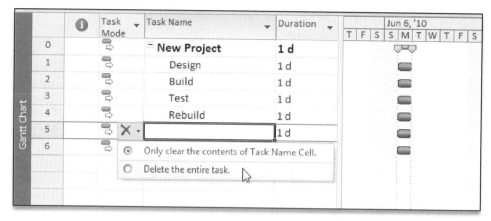

Figure 5 - 9: Smart Tag displayed after deleting a task

When you select a cell in the *Resource Name* column in any resource view and press the *Delete* key, the software also displays a Smart Tag to the left of the cell. The choices are similar to those offered while deleting a cell in any task view.

Hands On Exercise

Exercise 5-4

Members of the project team concluded that they already know the server specifications for this project. Therefore, you do not need the Determine Server Specifications task and need to delete it.

1. Return to the **Training Advisor 05a.mpp** sample file.

2. Select the row header for ID #2, the *Determine Server Specifications* task.

3. Press the **Delete** key on your computer keyboard.

4. Save but **do not** close **Training Advisor 05a.mpp** sample file.

Creating the Work Breakdown Structure (WBS)

The Work Breakdown Structure (WBS) divides the project tasks into meaningful and logical components. The WBS consists of summary tasks representing major aspects of the project, such as phase and deliverable sections, along with subtasks in each summary section. Figure 5 - 10 shows a simple generic Work Breakdown Structure comprised of phase and deliverable sections, with four subtasks in each deliverable section.

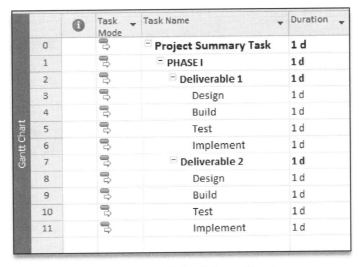

Figure 5 - 10: Work Breakdown Structure

To create a Work Breakdown Structure in a project, you must create a series of summary tasks and subtasks. The purpose of summary tasks is to summarize or "roll up" the data contained in the subtasks. Microsoft Project 2010 offers you several ways to create summary tasks and subtasks. As with all previous versions of the software, you can create summary tasks and subtasks by completing the following steps:

1. Type the names of a summary task and its subtasks.

2. Select the tasks that you want to make subtasks of the summary task.

3. Click the *Indent* button in the *Schedule* section of the *Task* ribbon.

In the project shown in Figure 5 - 11, I select from the Design task through the Implement task to prepare to make them subtasks of the PHASE I summary task.

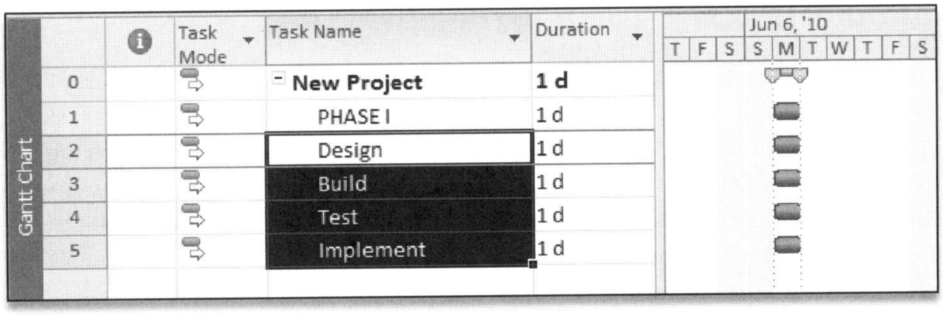

Figure 5 - 11: Prepare to make PHASE I a summary task

After I click the *Indent* button in the *Schedule* section of the *Task* ribbon, the software makes the four selected tasks sub-tasks of the PHASE I summary task. Figure 5 - 12 shows the result of this procedure.

	ⓘ	Task Mode ▾	Task Name ▾	Duration ▾	Jun 6, '10
					T F S S M T W T F S
0			⊟ **New Project**	**1 d**	
1			⊟ **PHASE I**	**1 d**	
2			Design	1 d	
3			Build	1 d	
4			Test	1 d	
5			Implement	1 d	

Figure 5 - 12: PHASE I summary task with four subtasks

Notice in Figure 5 - 12 how Microsoft Project 2010 displays summary tasks and subtasks:

- It formats PHASE I in bold.

- It shows an outline indicator (+ sign) in front of the PHASE I task name.

- It changes the Gantt bar shape for PHASE I.

- It indents the Design task through the Implement task one level to the right of PHASE I.

Converting an existing task to a summary task causes the system to roll up information from the subtasks to the summary task. This changes the behavior of the summary task, but it does not change any underlying data that you previously entered in the existing task before you converted it to a summary task. If you convert the summary task back to a regular task, any previously entered data reappears. Because this can cause surprising schedule changes, MSProjectExperts recommends that you create all of your summary tasks **from new tasks** rather than by converting tasks in which you previously entered work or duration values.

Inserting Summary Tasks

The other method for creating summary tasks is to use a new feature in Microsoft Project 2010. This new feature allows you to insert summary tasks into your project. Many organizations like to do "top down" task planning by creating summary tasks initially to represent phase and deliverable sections in the project, and then they add regular tasks to each summary section. In previous versions of Microsoft Project, "top down" task planning was difficult. In the 2010 version, however, Microsoft makes "top down" task planning easier by using the new *Insert Summary Task* feature, particularly in combination with *Manually Scheduled* tasks.

To perform "top down" task planning in Microsoft Project 2010, click the *Insert Summary Task* button 🐦 in the *Insert* section of the *Task* ribbon. The software inserts a new unnamed summary task and subtask, as shown in Figure 5 - 13.

	❶	Task Mode	Task Name		Duration	
1			⊟ **\<New Summary Task\>**		1 day	
2			\<New Task\>			

Figure 5 - 13: Newly Inserted Summary Task during
"top down" task planning process

After inserting the new summary task and subtask pair, you should edit the name of the summary task, replacing the default value with the name of the phase or deliverable section it represents. Similarly, you eventually edit the name of the subtask and add additional subtasks as needed. You can leave the name of the subtask with its original \<New Task\> name as a placeholder for a future subtask until you are ready to add detail tasks to the summary section.

If you insert a summary task below another summary task or a subtask, Microsoft Project 2010 automatically indents the new summary task at the same level of indenture as the task immediately preceding it. This is the default behavior of the tool, and you cannot change it. For example, Figure 5 - 14 shows a new summary task and subtask pair inserted after the Design task. Notice that the system indented the new summary task at the same level as the Design task preceding it. To resolve the indenting situation shown in Figure 5 - 14, select the new summary task and then click the *Outdent Task* button in the *Schedule* section of the *Task* ribbon.

	❶	Task Mode	Task Name		Duration	
1			⊟ **Phase I**		1 day	
2			Design			
3			⊟ **\<New Summary Task\>**		1 day	
4			\<New Task\>			

Figure 5 - 14: New summary task indented at same
level as the Design task preceding it

In addition to inserting summary tasks during "top down" task planning, Microsoft Project 2010 also makes it easier to insert a summary task for a selected group of subtasks. For example, consider the set of four tasks shown in Figure 5 - 15. I want to show that each of these four tasks is a subtask in the Phase I section of the project.

	❶	Task Mode	Task Name		Duration	
1			Design		1 day?	
2			Build		1 day?	
3			Test		1 day?	
4			Implement		1 day?	

Figure 5 - 15: Four tasks ready for inclusion
as subtasks of Phase I

To make these tasks a subtask in the Phase I section of the project, select the four tasks and then click the *Insert Summary Task* button on the *Task* ribbon. Microsoft Project 2010 automatically inserts a new unnamed summary task and indents the four tasks as subtasks of the summary section, as shown in Figure 5 - 16. You can then rename the new summary task as desired.

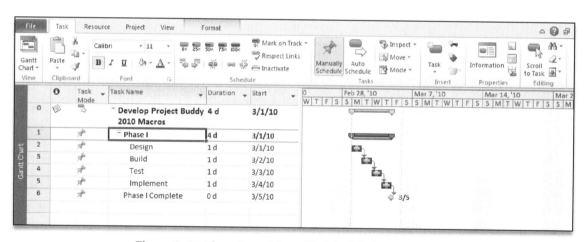

Figure 5 - 16: Four tasks inserted as subtasks
below the new unnamed summary task

Creating a Manually Scheduled Summary Task

In addition to creating *Manually Scheduled* tasks, Microsoft Project 2010 also allows you to create *Manually Scheduled* summary tasks. For example, Figure 5 - 17 shows a project with a *Manually Scheduled* summary task with *Manually Scheduled* subtasks. Notice in Figure 5 - 17 that the software displays a different type of summary Gantt bar for *Manually Scheduled* summary tasks than it does for *Auto Scheduled* summary tasks.

Figure 5 - 17: Phase I as a *Manually Scheduled* summary task

The behavior of *Manually Scheduled* summary tasks is similar to the behavior of *Manually Scheduled* tasks, but with a few differences, including:

- Microsoft Project 2010 formats the summary Gantt bar to show schedule *Warnings* about schedule conflicts.

- Microsoft Project 2010 shows a schedule *Warning* in the *Finish* column of every task causing the schedule conflict with the *Manually Scheduled* summary task.

Notice in Figure 5 - 18 that the software formats the summary Gantt bar for the Phase I summary task to show a schedule *Warning*, indicating that the duration of the subtasks now exceeds the duration of the *Manually Scheduled* summary task. The system also shows schedule *Warnings* in the *Finish* column for each subtask causing the schedule problem. To resolve the schedule problems, you can use the *Task Inspector* on the Phase I summary task, which offers the option to extend the duration of the *Manually Scheduled* summary task. I discuss the *Task Inspector* feature later in this module.

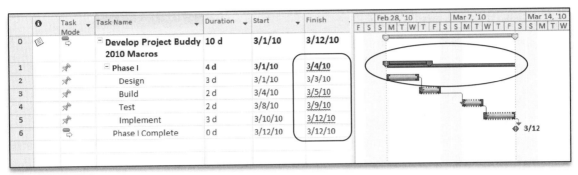

Figure 5 - 18: Schedule Warnings on a Manually Scheduled summary task and subtasks

Hands On Exercise

Exercise 5-5

Create the Work Breakdown Structure for the Training Advisor Rollout project creating summary tasks representing the phases of the project.

1. Return to the **Training Advisor 05a.mpp** sample file.

2. Select task IDs #8-10, from the *Install Training Advisor Clients* task to the *Resolve Connectivity Errors* task.

3. Click the *Indent* button in the *Schedule* section of the *Task* ribbon.

4. Leave the *Testing Complete* task at the same level as the *TESTING* summary task (**do not** indent this task).

5. Select task IDs #13-19, from the *Setup Test Training Server* task to the *Provide End User Training* task.

6. Click the *Indent* button in the *Schedule* section of the *Task* ribbon.

7. Leave the *Training Complete* task at the same level as the *TRAINING* summary task (**do not** indent this task).

8. Select task IDs #14-16, from the *Create Training Module 01* task to the *Create Training Module 03* task.

9. Click the *Insert Summary Task* button in the *Insert* section of the *Task* ribbon.

Notice how Microsoft Project 2010 inserted the new summary task and indented the selected tasks as subtasks automatically.

10. With the newly inserted summary task still selected, click the *Manually Schedule* button in the *Tasks* section of the *Task* ribbon.

Notice how Microsoft Project 2010 displays the unusual Gantt bar for the *Manually Scheduled* summary task.

11. Enter the name *Create Training Materials* for the new summary task you inserted.

12. Save but **do not** close **Training Advisor 05a.mpp** sample file.

Creating Milestones

In project management terms, we define a milestone as "a significant point in time" in a project that most typically indicates a point of completion. You may use a milestone to indicate the beginning point of a project, the ending point for a phase or a deliverable, or the ending point for an entire project. Most projects contain multiple milestones.

Microsoft Project 2010 offers you several ways to create milestone tasks. As with all previous versions of the software, you can create milestones by inserting a new task and then changing the value in the *Duration* column to *0 days*. Notice in Figure 5 - 19 that the *Gantt Chart* symbol for a milestone is a black diamond that displays the finish date of the milestone to the right of the black diamond.

		Task Mode	Task Name	Duration	Jun 6, '10
0			⁻ **New Project**	**1 d**	
1			⁻ **PHASE I**	**1 d**	
2			Design	1 d	
3			Build	1 d	
4			Test	1 d	
5			Implement	1 d	
6			Phase I Complete	0 d	◆ 6/7

Figure 5 - 19: Phase I Complete is a milestone task

In Figure 5 - 19, notice that indenture level for the Phase I Complete milestone task is the same as the PHASE I summary task. For ease of high-level reporting, msProjectExperts recommends that you always outdent milestone tasks to the same level as the summary tasks they represent. With this structure in place, when you show and print Outline Level 1 tasks (the phase sections of your project), you see each phase and its corresponding milestone. The milestones show the finish date of each phase.

Warning: When you outdent milestone tasks at the same level as summary tasks, as recommended in the previous Best Practice note, the milestone tasks no longer move with their summary tasks. Before you attempt to move the entire summary task section to another location in the project, you should temporarily indent the milestone to the task level.

Microsoft Project 2010 allows you to create a milestone for a task with a *Duration* value *greater than 0 days* by completing the following steps:

1. Double-click the task to open the *Task Information* dialog.
2. Click the *Advanced* tab.
3. Select the *Mark task as milestone* option and then click the *OK* button.

Inserting a Milestone Task

The other method for creating milestone tasks is to use a new feature in Microsoft Project 2010. This new feature allows you to insert milestone tasks into your project directly. To create a milestone task by inserting it, select the location for the new milestone task and then click the *Milestone* button in the *Insert* section of the *Task* ribbon. The software automatically inserts a new task named <New Milestone> with a value of 0 days in the *Duration* column, as shown in Figure 5 - 20.

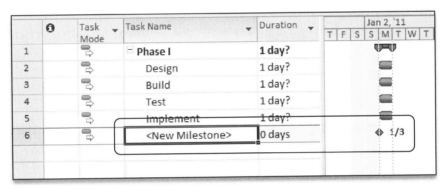

Figure 5 - 20: New inserted milestone task

After inserting a new milestone task, you should rename it. For the new milestone I inserted in the project shown Figure 5 - 20, I might rename the milestone task *Phase I Complete*, for example.

Hands On Exercise

Exercise 5-6

Create milestone tasks to denote the completion date of each phase and for project completion in the Training Advisor Rollout project.

1. Return to the **Training Advisor 05a.mpp** sample file.

2. Scroll down to the first blank line at the end of your project and add a new task named *Project Complete*.

3. Select the new *Project Complete* task and then click the *Auto Schedule* button in the *Tasks* section of the *Task* ribbon.

4. For the moment, leave the value in the *Duration* column as *1 day* for the *Project Complete* task.

5. For task ID #6, the *Installation Complete* task, change the value in the *Duration* column to *0 days*.

Notice that Microsoft Project 2010 converted this task to a milestone task automatically.

6. Using the **Control** key on your computer keyboard, simultaneously select the following tasks:

   - Task ID #11, the *Testing Complete* task
   - Task ID #21, the *Training Complete* task
   - Task ID #22, the *Project Complete* task

7. Click the *Information* button in the *Properties* section of the *Task* ribbon to display the *Multiple Task Information* dialog for the selected tasks.

8. In the *Multiple Task Information* dialog, set the *Duration* value to *0 days*, and then click the *OK* button.

Notice that Microsoft Project 2010 automatically converted all three selected tasks to milestone tasks as a group.

9. Select task ID #18, the *Conduct Skills Assessment* task.

10. Click the *Insert Milestone* button in the *Insert* section of the *Task* ribbon.

11. With the new milestone task still selected, click the *Auto Schedule* button in the *Tasks* section of the *Task* ribbon.

12. With the new milestone task still selected, click the *Outdent* button in the *Schedule* section of the *Task* ribbon.

Notice that this action outdents the new milestone task to the same level of indenture as the *Create Training Materials* summary task.

13. Change the name of the new milestone task to *Training Materials Created*.

14. Save but **do not** close **Training Advisor 05a.mpp** sample file.

Using Task Notes and Cell Background Formatting

Task notes are an important part of project documentation and are essential to understanding the historical information about any project. You can add notes to tasks at any time during the life of the project. To add a note to a task, use any of the following methods:

- Select the task and then click the *Task Notes* button in the *Properties* section of the *Task* ribbon.

- Double-click the task and then click the *Notes* tab.

- Right-click on the task and then select the *Notes* item on the shortcut menu.

Using any of the preceding methods, the system displays the *Notes* tab in the *Task Information* dialog shown in Figure 5 - 21. Type the text of the note, add formatting as needed, and then click the *OK* button.

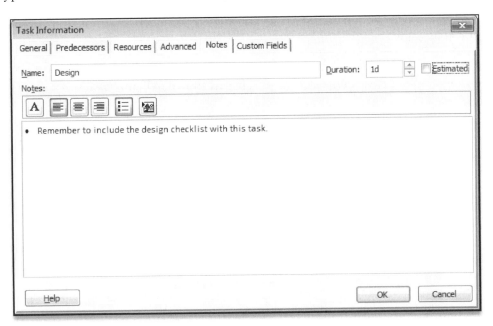

Figure 5 - 21: Task Information dialog, Notes Page

MsProjectExperts recommends that you use "bulleted list" formatting for the text of your notes, as shown in Figure 5-21. When a task contains multiple notes, the bulleted list formatting makes the individual notes easier to read in the *Task Information* dialog, and when you print the project and include a *Notes* page at the end.

After you add a note to a task, Microsoft Project 2010 displays a note indicator in the *Indicators* column to the left of the task, as shown in Figure 5 - 22. You can read the text of the note by floating your mouse pointer over the note indicator.

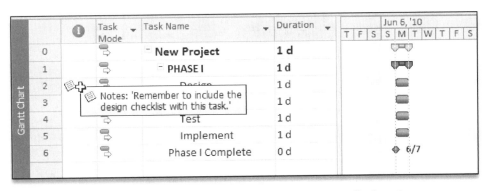

Figure 5 - 22: Notes indicator with screen tip text displayed

To easily identify tasks of interest, such as project milestones or slipping tasks, you can use cell background formatting in Microsoft Project 2010. This feature is similar to the cell background formatting feature in Microsoft Excel. You can manually set cell background formatting for one or more tasks, or you can set it automatically using a filter or a

VBA macro. To manually set cell background formatting on any task, select the ID numbers of the tasks whose cell background color you want to format, and then use one of the following methods:

- Click the *Background Color* button in the *Font* section of the *Task* ribbon for format the cell background using the default yellow color.

- Click the *Background Color* pick list button in the *Font* section of *the Task* ribbon and select a color in either the *Theme Color* or *Standard Colors* sections of the pick list, as shown in Figure 5 - 23.

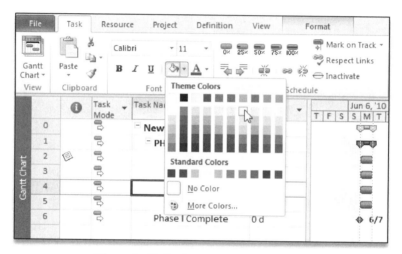

Figure 5 - 23: Background Color pick list

- Click the *Background Color* pick list button in the *Font* section of *the Task* ribbon and then click the *More Colors* item in the pick list. Select a color in the *Colors* dialog as shown in Figure 5 - 24 and then click the *OK* button.

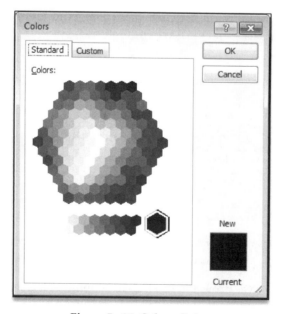

Figure 5 - 24: Colors dialog

- Click the *Font Dialog Launcher* icon in the lower right corner of the *Font* section of the *Task* ribbon. The system displays the *Font* dialog shown in Figure 5 - 25.

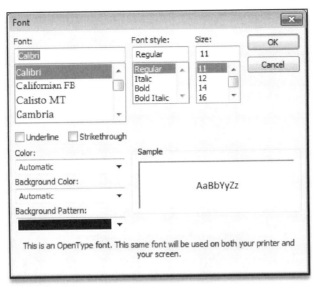

Figure 5 - 25: Font dialog

In the *Font* dialog, click the *Background Color* pick list and select the color of your background formatting. Click the *Background Pattern* pick list and select a pattern for the background color, if necessary. Click the *Color* pick list and select a different font color, if necessary. For example, if you select a dark color in the *Background Color* pick list, you should choose a lighter color in the *Color* pick list. Click the *OK* button when finished.

In the *Font* dialog shown in Figure 5 - 26, I selected the *Red, Darker 25%* color in the *Background Color* pick list and selected the *White* color in the *Color* pick list. Using contrasting colors between the *Color* pick list and the *Background Color* pick list helps users to more easily read the text of tasks with the cell background formatting applied.

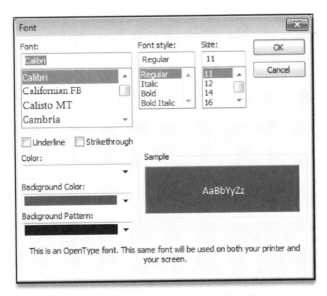

Figure 5 - 26: Font dialog with cell background formatting applied

Warning: In the *Font* dialog, **do not** select the first pattern on the *Background Pattern* pick list (the white pattern). If you select this pattern, the system **does not** display any cell background formatting for the selected tasks.

Figure 5 - 27 shows the background cell formatting for the Test task in a project.

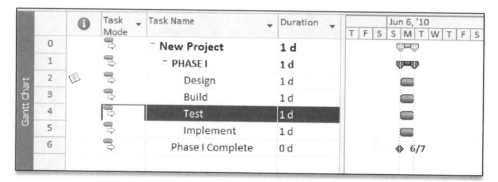

Figure 5 - 27: Cell background formatting for the Test task

Cell background formatting is an attribute of the view in which you apply the formatting. When you apply cell background formatting to a task, Microsoft Project 2010 applies formatting to the task for all tables in the current view only. For example, if you apply the yellow color to a task displayed in the *Gantt Chart* view, the software applies the background formatting to the task in every task table you apply in the *Gantt Chart* view (such as the *Cost* and *Work* tables). However, if you display the *Tracking Gantt* view, the system does not apply any cell background formatting to the task in this view. This means that you can apply cell background formatting to different tasks in different views.

Hands On Exercise

Exercise 5-7

Add task notes and apply cell background formatting to tasks in a project.

1. Return to the **Training Advisor 05a.mpp** sample file.

2. Select task ID #8, the *Install Training Advisor Clients* task.

3. Click the *Task Notes* button in the *Properties* section of the *Task* ribbon.

4. On the *Notes* tab of the *Task Information* dialog, click the *Bulleted List* button.

5. Enter the following text in the note field:

   Installation script location is \\corp\apps\training_advisor.

6. Click the *OK* button.

7. Float your cursor over the note indicator in the *Indicators* column to view the note on the *Install Training Advisor Clients* task.

8. Using the **Control** key on your computer keyboard, select the ID numbers for **all** of the milestone tasks in the project (task IDs #6, 11, 18, 22, and 23).

9. Click the *Font Dialog Launcher* icon in the lower right corner of the *Font* section of the *Task* ribbon to display the *Font* dialog.

10. In the *Font* dialog, click the *Background Color* pick list and choose the *Olive Green, Lighter 80%* color in the *Theme Color* section of the pick list (second color in the seventh column).

11. Click the *OK* button.

Notice how the cell background coloring calls attention to the milestone tasks and makes them easier to identify in the project.

12. Right-click on the *Select All* button (upper left corner of the task sheet) and select the *Cost* table.

Notice how the *Cost* table shows the cell background color for the milestone tasks. This is because the cell background formatting applies to all tables in the view in which you applied the formatting (in this case, the *Gantt Chart* view).

13. Right-click on the *Select All* button and select the *Entry* table.

14. Click the *Gantt Chart* pick list button in the *View* section of the *Task* ribbon and select the *Tracking Gantt* view on the list.

Notice that the milestone tasks do not show the cell background formatting seen previously. Because you applied the formatting in the *Gantt Chart* view, the formatting does not display in the *Tracking Gantt* view.

15. Click the *Gantt Chart* pick list button in the *View* section of the *Task* ribbon and reselect the *Gantt Chart* view.

16. Save and close the **Training Advisor 05a.mpp** sample file.

Using Task Dependencies

After completing the initial steps in the task planning process, your next step is to determine the order in which tasks occur. This process requires you to determine and set task dependencies between tasks in the project.

Understanding Task Dependencies

When you set a dependency relationship between two tasks, Microsoft Project 2010 designates the first task as the **predecessor task** and designates the second task as the **successor task** in the dependency relationship. The software offers you the following four default task dependency types:

- Finish-to-Start (abbreviated as FS)

- Start-to-Start (SS)

- Finish-to-Finish (FF)

- Start-to-Finish (SF)

Figure 5 - 28 shows each of these four default dependency types.

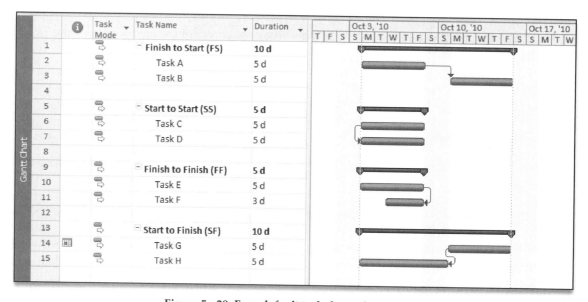

Figure 5 - 28: Four default task dependency types

A **Finish-to-Start (FS)** dependency means that the predecessor task must finish completely before the successor task can start. Figure 5 - 28 shows an FS dependency between Task A and Task B.

A **Start-to-Start (SS)** dependency means that the predecessor task must start before the successor task can start. Most people use this dependency to show that two tasks must start at the same time. Figure 5 - 28 shows an SS dependency between Task C and Task D.

 A Start-to-Start relationship does not mean that the predecessor and successor tasks **must** start at the same time. It simply means that successor task may start any time **after** the predecessor task starts.

A **Finish-to-Finish (FF)** dependency means that the predecessor task must finish before the successor task can finish. Most people use this dependency to show that two tasks must finish at the same time. Figure 5 - 28 shows an FF dependency between Task E and Task F.

A Finish-to-Finish relationship does not mean that the predecessor and successor tasks **must** finish at the same time. It simply means that the successor task may finish any time **after** the predecessor task finishes.

MsProjectExperts recommends that you be cautious with using the Finish-to-Finish (FF) dependency because it is extremely difficult to force two or more independent events to finish at precisely the same time. A best practice is to use an FF dependency as a predictive relationship to tell you when to start the successor task so that the linked tasks **might finish** at approximately the same time.

A **Start-to-Finish (SF)** dependency means that the predecessor task must start before the successor task can finish. You should use this dependency whenever the start date of one task triggers when another task must finish. Figure 5 - 28 shows an SF dependency between Task G and Task H.

Taking a test and studying for the test are two tasks that have a Start-to-Finish (SF) dependency. The start date of the test determines when you must finish your studying. Therefore, taking the test is the predecessor and studying for the task is the successor. The SF dependency states that you must finish your studying before the test begins.

Setting Task Dependencies

To set a dependency in Microsoft Project 2010, complete the following steps:

1. Select two or more tasks that are dependent on each other.

2. Click the *Link Tasks* button in the *Schedule* section of the *Task* ribbon.

When you complete these steps, Microsoft Project 2010 sets a Finish-to-Start (FS) dependency on the selected tasks by default. To change the dependency type to any of the other three, continue with the following steps:

3. Double-click the link line between two dependent tasks. The system displays the *Task Dependency* dialog shown in Figure 5 - 29.

Figure 5 - 29: Task Dependency dialog

4.   Click the *Type* pick list and select the desired dependency type.

5.   Click the *OK* button.

Warning: Set task dependencies **only** on regular tasks and milestone tasks. **Do not** set dependencies on summary tasks, as doing this can lead to circular reference errors any time in the future. Circular reference errors are very difficult to troubleshoot and resolve, so it is better to avoid them by not setting task dependencies on summary tasks.

Warning: Be very careful when you use the *Control* key to select multiple tasks to link them. After selecting one task initially, when you press the *Control* key, Microsoft Project 2010 assumes the first task you selected is the predecessor task and all other tasks you select are successor tasks. This means that when using the *Control* key to select multiple tasks, the order in which you select the tasks is very important in the dependency planning process!

Linking Manually Scheduled Tasks

If you specify task dependencies by linking *Manually Scheduled* tasks with predecessor and successor tasks, Microsoft Project 2010 **initially schedules** each *Manually Scheduled* task as follows:

*   If you do not enter duration, start, or finish values for a *Manually Scheduled* task, the software sets the duration of the task to the default value of *1d* and then calculates the start and finish dates accordingly, based on its dependency relationship with its predecessor task.

*   If you enter an approximate duration on a *Manually Scheduled* task (such as *About 5 days*, for example), the software maintains the approximate duration, but treats the task as if it has a duration value of *1 day*, and then calculates the start and finish dates accordingly.

*   If you enter a numerical duration value on a *Manually Scheduled* task, the software maintains the valid duration, and then calculates the start and finish dates accordingly.

*   If you enter an approximate start and/or finish date on a *Manually Scheduled* task (such as *Early October*, for example), the software replaces the approximate date values for calculated dates in the *Start* and *Finish* columns.

*   If you enter a valid start date on a *Manually Scheduled* task, the software **ignores** the start date and calculates the start date based on its dependency relationship with its predecessor task.

*   If you enter a valid finish date on a *Manually Scheduled* task, the software honors the finish date, calculates the duration of the task based on the scheduled start date and the valid finish date, and then schedules the task accordingly.

To understand how the system initially schedules *Manually Scheduled* tasks when you link them with predecessor and successor tasks, first examine the *Manually Scheduled* tasks shown in Figure 5 - 30. Notice that Task A contains no duration, start, or finish information. Notice that Task B has an approximate duration while Task C has a valid duration value. Notice that Task D has an approximate start date, while Task E has a valid start date value. Notice that Task F has an approximate finish date, while Task G has a valid finish date value. Also notice the unusual bracket-shaped Gantt bars for the two tasks that have a valid start or finish date.

Figure 5 - 30: Manually Scheduled tasks BEFORE setting task dependencies

Now examine the same set of *Manually Scheduled* tasks after I link them with Finish-to-Start (FS) dependencies in Figure 5 - 31. Notice that the software behaves exactly as I described in the previous bulleted list. Take special notice of how the software scheduled Task G. The software calculated the start date of the task, honored the finish date of the task, and calculated a 5-day duration between these two dates.

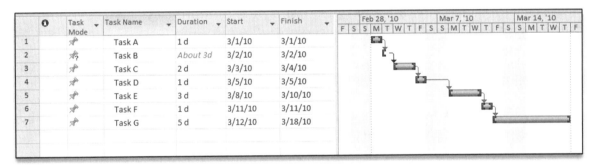

Figure 5 - 31: Manually Scheduled tasks AFTER setting task dependencies

 When you link *Manually Scheduled* tasks using task dependencies, the software calculates the **intial schedule** of each task. If you later change the duration, start, or finsh date of a *Manually Scheduled* task, Microsoft Project 2010 **does not** recalculate the schedule of the *Manually Scheduled* task. I discuss this behavior in the next section of this module.

Removing a Task Dependency

To remove a dependency relationship between two or more tasks, complete the following steps:

1. Select the tasks from which you wish to remove the dependencies.

2. Click the *Unlink Tasks* button on the *Standard* toolbar.

You can also remove a task dependency by double-clicking on the link line between the dependent tasks and then clicking the *Delete* button in the *Task Dependency* dialog.

Hands On Exercise

Exercise 5-8

Set each of the four types of task dependencies for *Auto Scheduled* and *Manually Scheduled* tasks.

1. Open the **Dependency Planning 2010.mpp** sample file.

You determine that Task A, Task B, Task C, and Task D are a "chain of events" that must occur sequentially. Link them with a Finish-to-Start (FS) dependency.

2. Select from *Task A* through *Task D* and then click the *Link Tasks* button in the *Schedule* section of the *Task* ribbon.

You determine that Task E and Task F must start at the same time, and that Task E is the "driving event" between these two tasks. Set a Start-to-Start (SS) dependency on these two tasks.

3. Select *Task E* and *Task F* and then click the *Link Tasks* button in the *Schedule* section of the *Task* ribbon.

4. In the *Gantt chart*, double-click the link line between the Gantt bars for *Task E* and *Task F* to display the *Task Dependency* dialog.

5. In the *Task Dependency* dialog, click the *Type* pick list, select the *Start-to-Start (SS)* item on the list, and then click the *OK* button.

You determine that Task G and Task H must finish at the same time, and that Task G is the "driving event" between these two tasks. Set a Finish-to-Finish (FF) dependency on these two tasks.

6. Select *Task G* and *Task H* and then click the *Link Tasks* button in the *Schedule* section of the *Task* ribbon.

7. In the *Gantt chart*, double-click the link line between the Gantt bars for *Task G* and *Task H* to display the *Task Dependency* dialog.

8. In the *Task Dependency* dialog, click the *Type* pick list, select the *Finish-to-Finish (FF)* item on the list, and then click the *OK* button.

Your professor scheduled a World History final examination for 8:00 AM on Friday, March 22. You believe you need two days to study for the exam. The date and time of the exam determines when you need to finish studying. Set a Start-to-Finish (SF) dependency between the *World History Final Exam* task and the *Study for the Exam* task.

9. Select the *World History Final Exam* and *Study for the Exam* tasks and then click the *Link Tasks* button in the *Schedule* section of the *Task* ribbon.

10. In the *Gantt chart*, double-click the link line between the Gantt bars for these two tasks to display the *Task Dependency* dialog.

11. In the *Task Dependency* dialog, click the *Type* pick list, select the *Start-to-Finish (SF)* item on the list, and then click the *OK* button.

12. Save but **do not** close the **Dependency Planning 2010.mpp** sample file.

Using Lag Time with Dependencies

Lag time is a delay in the start or finish date of a successor task. You can use *lag* time for a number of reasons, including situations such as the following:

- You need to plan for the delivery time delay between ordering equipment or supplies and receiving them in a FS dependency relationship.

- You require the completion of a portion (time or percentage) of the predecessor task before the successor task begins such as might be the case where you want to show that the painters can start painting after a portion of the dry wall work is complete in a SS dependency relationship.

You can enter *lag* time as either a time value, such as *5 days*, or as a percentage of the duration of the predecessor task, such as *50%*. To enter *lag* time on a dependency, complete the following steps:

1. Double-click the link line between two dependent tasks.

2. In the *Task Dependency* dialog, enter a **positive** value in the *Lag* field (either as a time unit, such as *days*, or as a percentage).

3. Click the *OK* button.

In the *Task Dependency* dialog shown in Figure 5 - 32, notice that I added *3d* of *lag* time to the FS dependency between the Design task and the Build task.

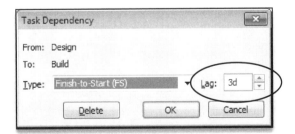

**Figure 5 - 32: Task Dependency dialog
with 3d lag time entered**

You can also add *lag time* in the *Predecessors* column of the *Task Entry* table in any task view, such as the *Gantt Chart* view. Using notation such as *1FS+3d* means that task ID #1 is a predecessor to the selected task, with a Finish-to-Start (FS) dependency, and with 3 days of *lag time*.

Figure 5 - 33 shows two different dependencies with *lag* time. To the FS dependency between Task A and Task B, I added *2 days* of *lag* time. This dependency means that Task B must start 2 days after Task A finishes, such as might be the case when cement needs to cure before additional building steps can begin. To the SS dependency between Task C and Task D, I added a *50% lag* time. This means that Task C starts, and when it is 50% completed, Task D starts.

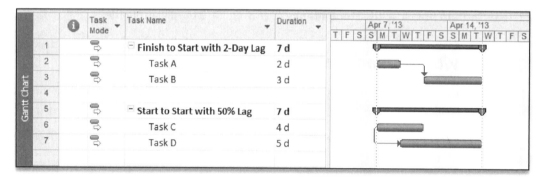

Figure 5 - 33: Lag time added to two different dependencies

Using Lead Time with Dependencies

Lead time is the opposite of *lag* time. Most people use *lead* time to create an overlap between two tasks linked with a Finish-to-Start (FS) dependency. To enter *lead* time on a task dependency, complete the following steps:

1. Double-click the link line between two dependent tasks.

2. In the *Task Dependency* dialog, enter a **negative** value in the *Lag* field (either as a time unit, such as *days*, or as a percentage).

3. Click the *OK* button.

In the *Task Dependency* dialog shown in Figure 5 - 34, notice that I added *2d* of *lag* time (-2d of *lead* time) to the FS dependency between the Test task and the Implement task.

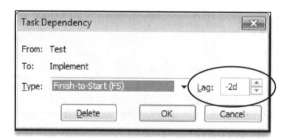

**Figure 5 - 34: Task Dependency dialog
with 2d lead time added**

In an FS dependency, *2 days* of *lead* time means the successor task can start 2 days **before** the finish date of the predecessor task. Adding 2 days of *lead* time on an FS dependency creates an overlap between the dependent tasks as shown in Figure 5 - 35.

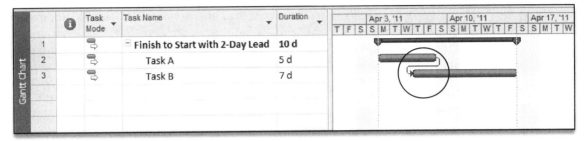

Figure 5 - 35: FS Dependency with 2 days of lead time

Warning: Project managers often use *lead time* to "fast track" a project by compressing the time it takes to complete a project schedule. Doing this is risky and can cause scheduling problems that result in an even later project finish date than originally scheduled. Because of this, msProjectExperts recommends that you be very careful when using *lead time* in your projects.

Hands On Exercise

Exercise 5-9

Add *lag* time and *lead* time on task dependencies.

1. Return to the **Dependency Planning 2010.mpp** sample file.

You determine that the Setup Equipment task cannot begin until 5 days after the Order Equipment task finishes. Set a Finish-to-Start (FS) dependency with *5 days* of *lag* time between the Order Equipment and Setup Equipment tasks.

2. Select the *Order Equipment* and *Setup Equipment* tasks and then click the *Link Tasks* button in the *Schedule* section of the *Task* ribbon.

3. In the *Gantt chart*, double-click the link line between the Gantt bars for these two tasks to display the *Task Dependency* dialog.

4. In the *Task Dependency* dialog, click the *Type* pick list, enter *5d* in the *Lag* field and then click the *OK* button.

5. Float your mouse pointer over the link line between these two tasks to see the screen tip indicating that the FS dependency includes 5 days of *lag* time.

You determine that the Decorate Rooms task cannot start until the Paint Rooms task reaches 50% completion. Set a Start-to-Start (SS) dependency with *50% lag* time on the Paint Rooms and Decorate Rooms tasks.

6. Select the *Paint Rooms* and *Decorate Rooms* tasks and then click the *Link Tasks* button in the *Schedule* section of the *Task* ribbon.

7. In the *Gantt chart*, double-click the link line between the Gantt bars for these two tasks to display the *Task Dependency* dialog.

8. In the *Task Dependency* dialog, manually type *50%* in the *Lag* field and then click the *OK* button.

9. Float your mouse pointer over the link line between these two tasks to see the screen tip indicating that the SS dependency includes 50% *lag* time.

You determine that Task J must start 2 days before Task I finishes. Set a Finish-to-Start (FS) dependency with *2 days lead* time between Task I and Task J.

10. Select *Task I* and *Task J* and then click the *Link Tasks* button in the *Schedule* section of the *Task* ribbon.

11. In the *Gantt chart*, double-click the link line between the Gantt bars for *Task I* and *Task J* to display the *Task Dependency* dialog.

12. In the *Task Dependency* dialog, enter *-2d* in the *Lag* field and then click the *OK* button.

13. Float your mouse pointer over the link line between these two tasks to see the screen tip indicating that the FS dependency includes 2 days of *lead* time.

You determine that your team must complete the Assemble Meeting Packets task 5 days before the Annual Shareholder Meeting task begins. Because the start date of the Annual Shareholder Meeting task drives the finish date of the Assemble Meeting Packets task, set a Start-to-Finish (SF) dependency between these two tasks with *5 days* of *lead* time.

14. Select the Annual Shareholder Meeting task and the Assemble Meeting Packets task, and then click the *Link Tasks* button in the *Schedule* section of the *Task* ribbon.

15. In the *Gantt chart*, double-click the link line between the Gantt bars for these two tasks to display the *Task Dependency* dialog.

16. In the *Task Dependency* dialog, enter *-5d* in the *Lag* field and then click the *OK* button.

17. Float your mouse pointer over the link line between these two tasks to see the screen tip indicating that the SF dependency includes 5 days of *lead* time.

18. Save but **do not** close the **Dependency Planning 2010.mpp** sample file.

Understanding Schedule Warnings and Suggestions

When you link *Manually Scheduled* tasks and then later change the project schedule, Microsoft Project 2010 recalculates the schedule for **only** *Auto Scheduled* tasks. It **does not** recalculate the schedule for *Manually Scheduled* tasks. Instead, the software calculates a likely start and finish date in the background, and then compares the current start and finish dates with the likely start and finish dates. If there is a schedule discrepancy, the software displays a *Warning* on that task by applying a red wavy underline to the date in the *Finish* column and by formatting the Gantt bar with a dotted outline. For example, in the schedule shown in Figure 5 - 36, I manually entered a duration value on the Design, Build, and Test tasks. This resulted in a schedule discrepancy on the Rebuild task, and the warnings from Microsoft Project 2010.

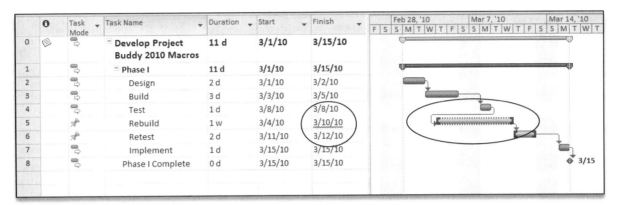

Figure 5 - 36: Schedule discrepancy Warning on a Manually Scheduled task

By default, Microsoft Project 2010 shows *Warnings* about schedule discrepancies on *Manually Scheduled* tasks; however, you can configure the software to show *Suggestions* about how to optimize your schedule as well. As I noted in Module 04, Project Definition, you can enable *Suggestions* by selecting the *Show task schedule suggestions* option on the *Schedule* page of the *Project Options* dialog. Remember that you can choose to apply this option only to the current project or for all new projects. If you did not select this option in the *Project Options* dialog, you can select this option for the current project by clicking the *Inspect* pick list button on the *Task* ribbon and then selecting the *Show Suggestions* item, as shown in Figure 5 - 37.

Figure 5 - 37: Enable optimization Suggestions
for Manually Scheduled tasks

When you enable optimization *Suggestions*, Microsoft Project 2010 examines the current start and finish date for each *Manually Scheduled* task and looks for opportunities to optimize the schedule with an earlier start or finish date. If the software finds an opportunity for you to improve your schedule, the system displays a *Suggestion* for that task by applying a green wavy underline to the date in the *Finish* column. For example, in the schedule shown in Figure 5 - 38, I manually entered a start date of Wednesday, March 10 on the Rebuild task. This caused a gap between the finish date of the Test task and the start date of the Rebuild task, and resulted in an optimization *Suggestion* from Microsoft Project 2010.

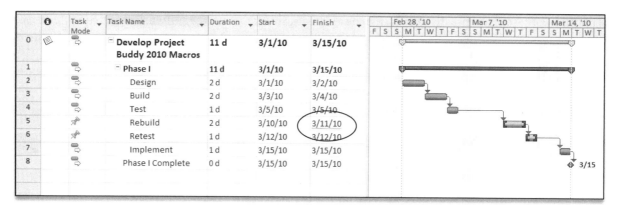

Figure 5 - 38: Optimization Suggestion on a Manually Scheduled task

When you float your mouse pointer over an optimization *Suggestion* in the *Finish* column, the system displays a tool tip with the words, *Potential scheduling optimization. Right-click to see options.* When you right-click in the *Finish* cell for the task with the optimization *Suggestion,* as suggested in the tool tip, the shortcut menu provides three options for acting on the *Suggestion,* including the *Fix in Task Inspector, Respect Links* and *Ignore Problems for this Task* items shown in Figure 5 - 39.

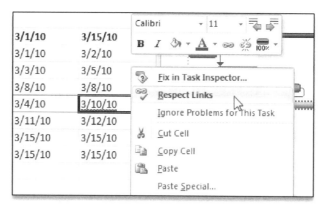

Figure 5 - 39: Respect Links item in
shortcut menu for a schedule Warning

Using the Respect Links Feature

Microsoft Project 2010 allows you to respond to schedule *Warnings* and optimization *Suggestions* using the new *Respect Links* feature. To use this feature, right click in any cell containing a *Warning* or a *Suggestion.* The system displays the shortcut menu shown previously in Figure 5 - 39.

When you click the *Respect Links* item on the shortcut menu for a schedule *Warning* or optimization *Suggestion,* Microsoft Project 2010 changes the start and finish dates of the task to the calculated start and finish dates, based on the task dependencies between the tasks, and then removes the schedule *Warning* or *Suggestion.* Keep in mind that this action might result in a new schedule *Warning* or optimization *Suggestion* on other *Manually Scheduled* tasks linked to the re-scheduled task!

Using the Task Inspector

The *Task Inspector* is a newly revamped feature of Microsoft Project 2010 evolving from the *Task Drivers Pane* found in Microsoft Project 2007. The *Task Inspector* offers more functionality than its 2007 predecessor. You can use the *Task In-*

spector to examine both *Manually Scheduled* tasks and *Auto Scheduled* tasks to resolve schedule problems and to determine the reason for the current scheduled start date of any task. To display the *Task Inspector*, click the *Inspect* button in the *Tasks* section of the *Task* ribbon. The system displays the *Task Inspector* on the left side of the application window.

Depending on the type of task you select, the *Task Inspector* includes either three sections or one section only. For example, Figure 5 - 40 shows the *Task Inspector* for a *Manually Scheduled* task with a schedule *Warning*. Notice that the first section displays the reason for the schedule *Warning* (the task needs to be delayed by 3 days). The *Repair Options* section offers the *Respect Links* button and the *Auto Schedule* button to resolve the schedule problem. The *Factors Affecting Task* section reveals the reason for the scheduled start date of the selected task.

Figure 5 - 41 shows the *Task Inspector* for a task with an optimization *Suggestion*. Notice that only the first section differs from the *Task Inspector* shown in Figure 5 - 40, and reveals the reason for the optimization *Suggestion* (the task can start 2 days earlier than currently scheduled). Figure 5 - 42 shows the *Task Inspector* for an *Auto Scheduled* task and contains only a single section, the *Factors Affecting Task* section. To close the *Task Inspector* click the *Close* (**X**) button in the upper right corner of the pane.

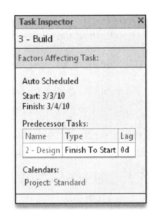

Figure 5 - 42: Task Inspector for an *Auto Scheduled* task

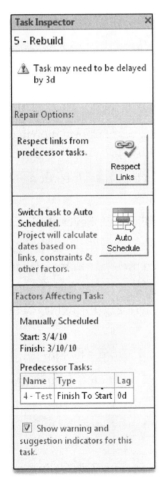

Figure 5 - 40: Task Inspector for a task with a Warning

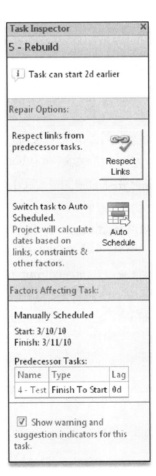

Figure 5 - 41: Task Inspector for a task with a Suggestion

191

For *Auto Scheduled* tasks, the *Task Inspector* tool reveals the reason for the current scheduled start date of any task. Possible reasons can include task dependencies, non-working time on a calendar, a task calendar applied to the task, constraints, and even leveling delays from leveling a resource overallocation.

Hands On Exercise

Exercise 5-10

Link *Manually Scheduled* tasks and then use the *Task Inspector* tool.

1. Return to the **Dependency Planning 2010.mpp** sample file.

2. Scroll down to the group of *Manually Scheduled* tasks and then drag the split bar to the right edge of the *Finish* column.

Notice that these seven *Manually Scheduled* tasks include a mix of different types of information in the *Duration*, *Start*, and *Finish* fields. Notice also the unusual Gantt bars for *Task M*, *Task O*, and *Task Q*.

3. Select from *Task K* to *Task Q* and then click the *Link Tasks* button in the *Schedule* section of the *Task* ribbon.

Notice how Microsoft Project 2010 calculates dates in the *Start* and *Finish* columns for every task, and calculates values in the *Duration* column for every task except *Task L*.

4. For *Task P,* change the value in the *Duration* column to *3d* and then press the **Enter** key on your computer keyboard.

 Notice that the system displays a schedule *Warning* in the *Finish* column for *Task Q* (the red wavy underline below the date) and changes the Gantt bar shape for the task as well.

5. Float your mouse pointer over the schedule *Warning* for *Task Q* and read the tool tip.

6. Right-click in the schedule *Warning* for *Task Q* and then select the *Respect Links* item in the short-cut menu.

7. For *Task Q,* change the date in the *Start* column to *April 8, 2013* and then press the **Enter** key on your computer keyboard.

Notice that the system displays an optimization *Suggestion* in the *Finish* column for *Task Q* (the green wavy underline below the date).

8. Select *Task Q* again, then click the *Inspect* pick list button in the *Tasks* section of the *Task* ribbon, and select the *Inspect Task* item on the pick list.

9. In the *Task Inspector* sidepane, click the *Respect Links* button.

Notice how Microsoft Project 2010 removes the gap between the Gantt bars for *Task P* and *Task Q* by scheduling *Task Q* to start immediately after *Task P* finishes.

10. Close the *Task Inspector* sidepane.

11. Save but **do not** close the **Dependency Planning 2010.mpp** sample file.

Using Alternate Methods to Set Dependencies

Microsoft Project 2010 offers you several other methods for setting task dependencies. One of the simplest is to apply the *Gantt Chart* view and then drag the split bar to the right until you see the *Predecessors* column, as shown in Figure 5 - 43.

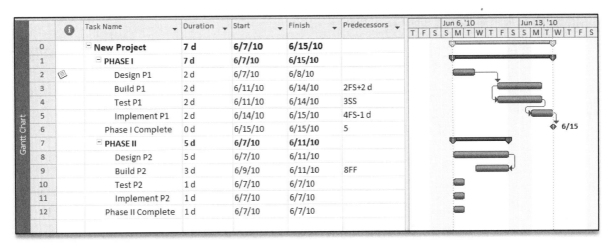

Figure 5 - 43: Predecessors column in the Gantt Chart view

In Figure 5 - 43, notice the "shorthand" Microsoft Project 2010 uses for dependencies in the *Predecessors* column. Since the predecessor for the Build P1 task is the Design P1 task (ID #2), the software displays the numeral "2" in the *Predecessors* column for the Build P1 task, indicating a Finish-to-Start dependency with the Design P1 task. Notice also that the FS dependency between the Design P1 and Build P1 tasks includes 2 days of *lag* time, indicated by the "+2d" text appended to the "2FS" text. Notice also in Figure 5 - 43 that the predecessor for the Test P1 task is the Build P1 task with a Start-to-Start dependency, indicated by the "3SS" text in the *Predecessors* column.

If you wish to enter dependencies for tasks using the *Predecessors* column, use the following approach:

- If the dependency is Finish-to-Start (FS), enter only the ID number of the predecessor task in the *Predecessors* column.

- If the dependency is Start-to-Start (SS), enter the ID number of the predecessor task along with the characters "SS" in the *Predecessors* column.

- If the dependency is Finish-to-Finish (FF), enter the ID number of the predecessor task along with the characters "FF" in the *Predecessors* column.

- If the dependency is Start-to-Finish (SF), enter the ID number of the predecessor task along with the characters "SF" in the *Predecessors* column.

- To add *lag* time to any dependency relationship, include a plus sign character (+) along with the amount of *lag* time.

- To add *lead* time to any dependency relationship, include a minus sign character (-) along with the amount of *lead* time.

Another way to set task dependencies is to use the *Task Entry* view following these steps:

1. Apply the *Gantt Chart* view.

2. Click the *View* tab to display the *View* ribbon.

3. In the *Split View* section of the *View* ribbon, select the *Details* option checkbox.

Remember that the *Task Entry* view is a combination view consisting of the *Gantt Chart* view in the top pane and the *Task Form* view in the bottom pane.

4. Right-click anywhere in the *Task Form* view (bottom pane) and select the *Predecessors & Successors* item on the shortcut menu.

5. Select any task in the *Gantt Chart* view (top pane).

Figure 5 - 44 shows the *Task Entry* view with the *Predecessors & Successors* details applied to the *Task Form*.

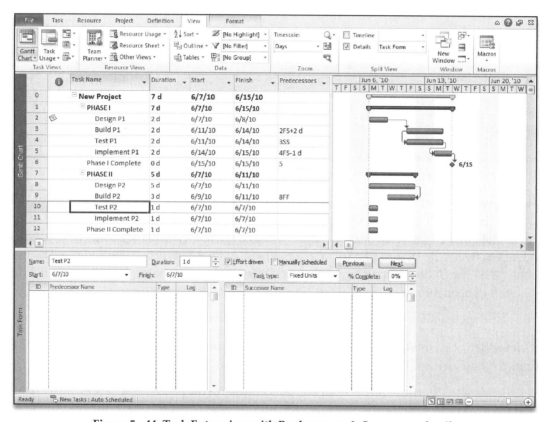

Figure 5 - 44: Task Entry view with Predecessors & Successors details

6. In the *Task Form*, click the first blank line in either the *Predecessor Name* column or the *Successor Name* column.

7. Click the pick list arrow button in the selected column and then select the name of the task from the list of tasks. Notice in Figure 5 - 45 that I am selecting the Build P2 task in the *Predecessor Name* column for the Test P2 task.

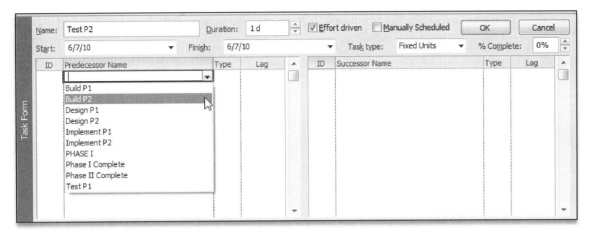

Figure 5 - 45: Select a task from the Predecessor Name column

8. Click the first blank line of the *Type* column, click the pick list arrow button, and then select a dependency type from the list of four possible dependencies.

9. Enter *lag* time or *lead* time in the *Lag* column, if needed.

10. Click the *OK* button.

The final method for setting dependencies is to use the *Task Information* dialog by completing the following steps:

1. Double-click any successor task in the project to display the *Task Information* dialog for the selected task.

2. Click the *Predecessors* tab.

3. Click the first blank line in the *Predecessors* column, click the pick list arrow button, and then select a task from the list, as shown in Figure 5 - 46.

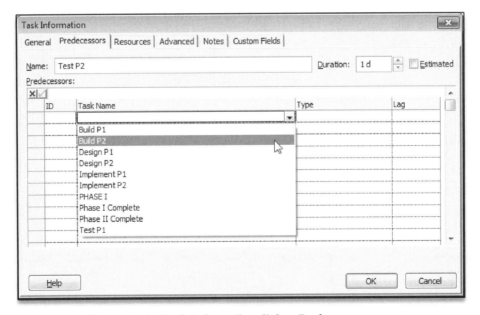

Figure 5 - 46: Task Information dialog, Predecessors page

When you select a task name in the *Task Name* column, the system automatically selects the Finish-to-Start (FS) dependency item in the *Type* column and enters *0d* of *lag time* in the *Lag* column.

4. Click the first blank line of the *Type* column, click the pick list arrow button, and then select a different dependency type from the list, if needed.

5. Enter *lag* time or *lead* time in the *Lag* column, if needed.

6. Click the *OK* button.

Hands On Exercise

Exercise 5-11

Edit task dependencies using alternate methods.

1. Return to the **Dependency Planning 2010.mpp** sample file.

Using the *Predecessors* column, add 2 days of *lag* time to the to the Start-to-Start (SS) dependency between Task E and Task F.

2. Drag the vertical split bar to the right side of the *Predecessors* column.

3. Select the *Predecessors* cell for *Task F*, press the **F2** function key on your computer keyboard, and then add the *+2d* text to the end of the *6SS* text. Press the **Enter** key to complete the editing.

4. Drag the vertical split bar back to the right side of the *Duration* column.

Using the *Task Entry* view, change the *lag* time to *10 days* for the dependency between the Order Equipment task and the Setup Equipment task.

5. Select the *Order Equipment* task in the *Gantt Chart* view (top pane).

6. Click the *View* tab and then select the *Details* option checkbox in the *Split View* section of the *View* ribbon.

7. Right-click anywhere in the *Task Form* (lower pane) and select the *Predecessors & Successors* item on the shortcut menu.

8. In the *Task Form*, change the value in the *Lag* column for the *Setup Equipment* successor task from *5d* to *10d* and then click the *OK* button.

9. **Deselect** the *Details* option checkbox in the *Split View* section of the *View* ribbon o close the *Task Form*.

Using the *Task Information* dialog, designate Task A as a predecessor to Task I using the default Finish-to-Start (FS) dependency.

10. Double-click *Task I* to display the *Task Information* dialog.

11. In the *Task Information* dialog, click the *Predecessors* tab and click the *Task Name* cell on the first blank row, click the pick list button, and select *Task A* on the pick list.

12. Click the *OK* button.

13. Save and close the **Dependency Planning 2010.mpp** sample file.

Exercise 5-12

Set task dependencies in your Training Advisor Rollout project using any of the previous methods.

1. Open to the **Training Advisor 05b.mpp** sample file.

2. Individually link each of the following task sequences with a Finish-to-Start (FS) dependency:

   - Task ID's #2-6

   - Task ID's #8-11

   - Task ID's #13 and #15 (use the **Control** key to select only these two tasks)

   - Task ID's #15-18

   - Task ID's #19-23

Historical records show that it normally takes the server vendor 8 days to deliver a server after we order it.

3. Add *8 days* of *lag* time to the FS dependency between task ID's #2 and #3.

The Conduct Skills Assessment task can begin once team members complete 90% of the Create Training Module #3 task.

4. Using the **Control** key, select task ID's #17 and #19, and then set a Start-to-Start (SS) dependency with a 90% *lag* time.

5. Notice the schedule *Warnings* shown in the Gantt bars for the Task IDs #14, 20, and 21.

Because of the time needed before training rooms become available, the Provide Training task cannot begin until 5 days after the Create Training Schedule task completes.

6. Add *5 days* of *lag* time to the FS dependency between task ID's #20 and #21.

7. Using the **Control** key, select task ID's #6 and #8, and then link them with a Finish-to-Start (FS) dependency.

The previous represents the best practice approach to linking phases or deliverables. Setting dependencies in this manner avoids the possibility of a circular reference error that could render you unable to open your project in the future!

8. Using the **Control** key, select task ID's #11 and #20, and then link them with a Finish-to-Start (FS) dependency.

9. Save but **do not** close the **Training Advisor 05b.mpp** sample file.

Exercise 5-13

Respond to schedule *Warnings* in your Training Advisor Rollout project.

1. Return to the **Training Advisor 05b.mpp** sample file, if necessary.

2. Drag the split bar to the right side of the *Finish* column.

3. Notice the schedule *Warning* in the *Finish* column for task ID #14, the *Create Training Materials* summary task, and in the Gantt bar for this task as well.

4. Right-click in the *Finish* cell for the *Create Training Materials* summary task and then select the *Switch to Auto Scheduled* item on the shortcut menu.

Completing the previous step converts the *Create Training Materials* summary task from a *Manually Scheduled* summary task to an *Auto Scheduled* summary task, and eliminates the possibility of any future schedule *Warnings* on this task.

5. Notice the schedule *Warning* in the *Finish* column for task ID #21, the *Provide End User Training* task, and in the Gantt bar for this task as well.

6. Right-click in the *Finish* cell for the *Provide End User Training* task and then select the *Fix in Task Inspector* item on the shortcut menu.

7. In the *Task Inspector* sidepane, click the *Respect Links* button to resolve the schedule *Warning* on the *Provide End User Training* task.

8. Close the *Task Inspector* sidepane.

9. Save and close **Training Advisor 05b.mpp** sample file.

Setting Task Constraints and Deadline Dates

Microsoft Project 2010 offers you two options to constrain tasks in the project schedule:

- Constraints

- Deadline dates

A constraint is a restriction that you set on the start date or finish date of a task. When you set a constraint on a task in Microsoft Project 2010, you limit the software's ability to automatically reschedule the task's start date or finish date when the schedule changes on predecessor tasks. You can use constraints for all types of schedule limitations, including the following:

- **Contractual dates for task completion** when you have an obligation to complete a certain task in your project by a certain date.

- **Delivery dates for equipment and supplies** when a vendor guarantees delivery of equipment by a certain date.

- **Resource availability restrictions** when a resource cannot begin work on a task until after a certain date due to other project commitments.

Using a deadline date is a way to set a "soft target date" for the completion of a task. Unlike constraints, deadline dates **do not** limit the Microsoft Project 2010 scheduling engine, but the system does show an indicator if the task's finish date slips past the deadline date.

Setting Constraints

To set a constraint on a task, complete the following steps:

1. Double-click the task whose start or finish date you need to restrict.

2. In the *Task Information* dialog, click the *Advanced* tab.

Figure 5 - 47 shows the *Advanced* page in the *Task Information* dialog.

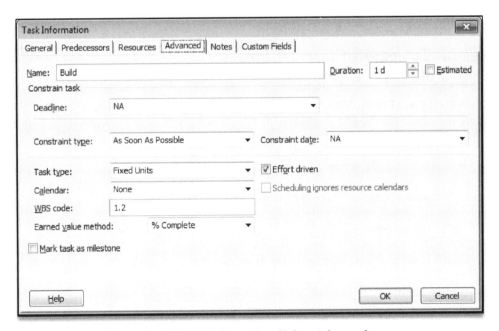

Figure 5 - 47: Task Information dialog, Advanced page

3. Click the *Constraint type* pick list and select a constraint.

4. Click the *Constraint date* pick list and select a date in the calendar date picker.

Notice in the *Task Information* dialog shown in Figure 5 - 48 that I selected the *Start No Earlier Than* constraint in the *Constraint type* pick list and selected the date *6/14/10* in the *Constraint date* field.

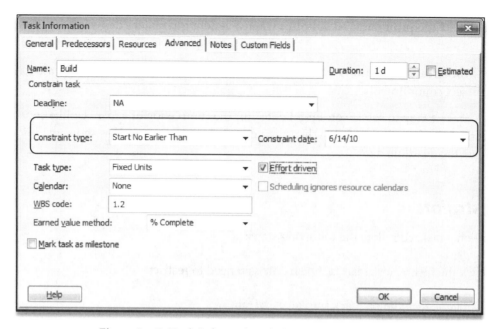

Figure 5 - 48: Task Information dialog with constraint set

5. Click the *OK* button to set the constraint.

Adding Notes on Tasks with Constraints

When you set a constraint on a task, it is wise to add a note to the task to document the reason for the constraint. Adding a note makes it easier for others to understand why you set the constraint originally, and you can use this information later to evaluate the historical data in your project. To add a constraint note to a task, complete the following steps:

1. Double-click the task with the constraint.

2. In the *Task Information* dialog, click the *Notes* tab.

3. Click the *Bulleted List* button.

4. Click in the *Notes* text field and enter the body of your note.

5. Click the *OK* button.

A good "shorthand" method for documenting a constraint is to include the following information in the body of the note:

- Abbreviation or acronym for the constraint type (such as *SNET*).

- The date of the constraint (such as *06/14/10*).

- The reason for setting the constraint (such as *Contractual delivery date for supplies*).

Figure 5 - 49 shows *Notes* page of the *Task Information* dialog, with the note documenting the reason for constraint shown previously in Figure 5 - 48.

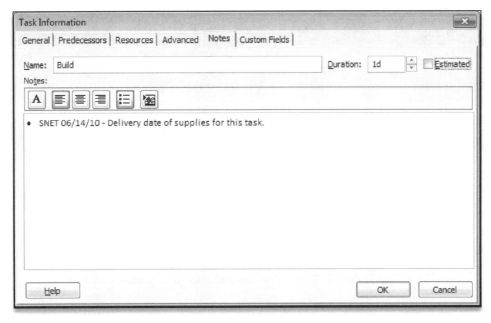

Figure 5 - 49: Task Information dialog, note documents a constraint

Understanding Flexible and Inflexible Constraints

In Microsoft Project 2010, constraints are either **flexible** or **inflexible**. A flexible constraint allows the software to re-schedule the task as required, while an inflexible constraint limits or even stops the tool from using its normal scheduling behavior. The information shown in Table 5 - 1 and Table 5 - 2 documents the behavior of Microsoft Project 2010 when you set a constraint in a project scheduled from a start date.

Flexible Constraints		
Constraint Name	**Indicator Color**	**Constraint Description**
As Soon As Possible	None	Default constraint on new tasks when the project is scheduled with a start date
As Late As Possible	None	Default constraint on new tasks when the project is scheduled with a finish date
Finish No Earlier Than	Blue	The task cannot finish earlier than the constraint date
Start No Earlier Than	Blue	The task cannot start earlier than the constraint date

Table 5 - 1: Flexible Constraints, project scheduled from a start date

Inflexible Constraints		
Constraint Name	**Indicator Color**	**Constraint Description**
Finish No Later Than	Red	The task cannot finish later than the constraint date
Must Finish On	Red	The task must finish on the constraint date
Must Start On	Red	The task must start on the constraint date
Start No Later Than	Red	The task cannot start later than the constraint date

Table 5 - 2: Inflexible Constraints, project scheduled from a start date

The *Project Information* dialog contains a special field known as the *Schedule from* field. To access the *Project Information* dialog, click the *Project Information* button in the *Properties* section of the *Project* ribbon. You use the *Schedule from* field to determine the scheduling direction for the Microsoft Project 2010 scheduling engine. The default option in the *Schedule from* field is *Project Start Date*, which means that the system schedules from the start date of your project **into the future** so that it can calculate the finish date of your project. You can reverse the direction of the scheduling engine, however, by selecting *Project Finish Date* in the *Schedule from* field. With this option selected, the system schedules from the finish date of your project **into the past** so that it can calculate the start date of your project.

I mention the *Schedule from* option because this option also determines whether a constraint is flexible or inflexible. Shown previously, the information in Table 5 - 1 and Table 5 - 2 documents the behavior of the tool when you set a constraint in a project scheduled from a **start** date. The information in Table 5 - 3 and Table 5 - 4 documents the behavior of the tool when you set a constraint in a project scheduled from a **finish** date.

Flexible Constraints		
Constraint Name	**Indicator Color**	**Constraint Description**
As Soon As Possible	None	Default constraint on new tasks when the project is scheduled with a start date
As Late As Possible	None	Default constraint on new tasks when the project is scheduled with a finish date
Finish No Later Than	Blue	The task cannot finish later than the constraint date
Start No Later Than	Blue	The task cannot start later than the constraint date

Table 5 - 3: Flexible Constraints, project scheduled from a finish date

Inflexible Constraints		
Constraint Name	**Indicator Color**	**Constraint Description**
Finish No Earlier Than	Red	The task cannot finish earlier than the constraint date
Must Finish On	Red	The task must finish on the constraint date
Must Start On	Red	The task must start on the constraint date
Start No Earlier Than	Red	The task cannot start earlier than the constraint date

Table 5 - 4: Inflexible Constraints, project scheduled from a finish date

Understanding Planning Wizard Messages about Constraints

When you set a task constraint in a project scheduled from a start date, Microsoft Project 2010 displays a *Planning Wizard* message when the resulting situation meets both of the following conditions:

- The constraint is *inflexible*, such as a *Finish No Later Than* constraint.

- The constrained task is a successor task, meaning that it has one or more predecessors.

 Microsoft Project 2010 also displays a *Planning Wizard* message that warns about a schedule conflict when you set either a *flexible* constraint or an *inflexible* constraint on a task that is a predecessor to one or more *Manually Scheduled* tasks. Because the system does not change the schedule of *Manually Scheduled* tasks automatically, it warns you of the potential scheduling conflict that may arise from this situation.

The *Planning Wizard* message, such as the one shown in Figure 5 - 50, is a warning that these two conditions can cause potential scheduling problems in your project.

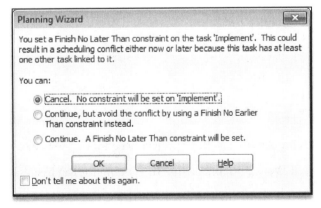

Figure 5 - 50: Planning Wizard message
warns about setting a constraint

The default response in this dialog is the first choice, which is to cancel setting the constraint. If you truly want to set an *inflexible* constraint and risk potential scheduling problems, the *Planning Wizard* requires you to pick the third choice, *Continue*. The second option, by the way, makes no sense at all since selecting this option allows the software to change the constraint to a *flexible* constraint, an outcome that defeats the purpose of setting the *inflexible* constraint in the first place!

msProjectExperts recommends that you **do not** select the *Don't tell me about this again* checkbox to disable *Planning Wizard* messages about scheduling issues. Seeing warning messages of this type is a good way to confirm you selected the constraint you desire, especially if it is an *inflexible* constraint on a task that has predecessor tasks.

Understanding Task Scheduling Changes

One of the major changes in Microsoft Project 2010 is the way the software responds when you manually enter a date in either the *Start* or *Finish* column for a task. In previous versions of the software, when you manually entered a start date for a task, the system added a *Start No Earlier Than (SNET)* constraint on the task, using the date you entered as the constraint date. When you manually entered a finish date on a task, the system added a *Finish No Earlier Than (FNET)* constraint, using the date you entered as the constraint date. If you manually entered **both** a start date and a finish date on a task, the software sets either a *SNET* constraint or a *FNET* constraint, depending on which date you entered last.

In Microsoft Project 2010, when you manually enter a start date only on a task, the system continues to add a *Start No Earlier Than (SNET)* constraint on the task, using the date you entered as the constraint date. Likewise, when you manually enter only a finish date on a task, the system continues to add a *Finish No Earlier Than (FNET)* constraint on the task, using the date you entered as the constraint date.

The major change in behavior occurs when you manually enter **both** a start date and a finish date on a task. In this situation, Microsoft Project 2010 **calculates the duration of the task**. This behavior is a radical change from all previous versions of the software. In addition, when you manually enter both a start date and a finish date on a task, the software sets either a *SNET* constraint or a *FNET* constraint, depending on which date you entered last.

Hands On Exercise

Exercise 5-14

Two issues with the Training Advisor Rollout project necessitate the use of constraints:

- In the Statement of Work, the contractual finish date for the Installation phase is February 7, 2014.

- Because of commitments to other projects, there are no testers available to verify client connectivity until February 10, 2014 or later.

In response to these issues, apply constraints to tasks in the Training Advisor Rollout project. In addition, re-schedule *Manually Scheduled* tasks, as needed.

1. Return to the **Training Advisor 05c.mpp** sample file.

2. Zoom the timescale to *Months over Weeks*.

3. Double-click task ID #6, the *Installation Complete* milestone task, to display the *Task Information* dialog.

4. Click the *Advanced* tab in the *Task Information* dialog.

5. On the *Advanced* page of the dialog, click the *Constraint type* pick list and select the *Finish No Later Than* constraint from the list.

6. Click the *Constraint date* pick list and select the date *February 7, 2014* in the calendar date picker.

7. Click the *Notes* tab, click the *Bulleted List* button, and then enter the following comment in the notes field:

   FNLT 2/7/14 – Contractual finish date for Installation phase.

8. Click the *OK* button.

9. If prompted by a *Planning Wizard* dialog, click the third choice, *Continue*, and then click the *OK* button

10. Double-click task ID #9, the *Verify Connectivity* task.

11. Click the *Advanced* tab, click the *Constraint type* pick list and select the *Start No Earlier Than* constraint from the list.

12. Click the *Constraint date* pick list and select the date *February 10, 2014* in the calendar date picker.

13. Click the *Notes* tab, click the *Bulleted List* button, and then enter the following comment in the notes field:

   SNET 2/10/14 – Resource availability issue.

14. Click the *OK* button to set the constraint.

15. If you see a *Planning Wizard* dialog, select the *Continue* option to set the constraint and then click the *OK* button.

Microsoft Project 2010 displays the *Planning Wizard* warning message because the *Verify Connectivity* task is a predecessor to several *Manually Scheduled* tasks in the *Training* phase of the project. After setting the constraint, notice how the system moves the Gantt bar for this task to the date you specified in the *Constraint date* field. Notice also that the system did not automatically reschedule the two *Manually Scheduled* tasks in the *Training* phase.

16. Drag the split bar to the right edge of the *Finish* column.

Notice the schedule *Warning* for the *Create Training Schedule* task in the *Testing* phase of the project.

17. Right-click in the *Finish* cell for the *Create Training Schedule* task and then select the *Respect Links* item in the shortcut menu.

Notice that this action creates a new schedule *Warning* on the *Provide End User Training* task as well.

18. Right-click in the *Finish* cell for *the Provide End User Training* task and then select the *Respect Links* item in the shortcut menu.

19. Select task IDs #20 and #21, the *Create Training Schedule* task and the *Create Training Schedule* task.

20. On the *Task* ribbon, click the *Auto Schedule* button in the *Tasks* section to convert these two *Manually Scheduled* tasks to *Auto Scheduled* tasks.

21. On the Status bar in the lower left corner of the Microsoft Project 2010 application window, click the default *Task Mode* selector and choose the *Auto Scheduled* option.

From this point forward, your Training Advisor Rollout project uses only *Auto Scheduled* tasks.

22. Drag the split bar to the right edge of the *Duration* column.

23. Save but **do not** close the **Training Advisor 05c.mpp** sample file.

Using Deadline Dates

In addition to constraints, Microsoft Project 2010 allows you to set deadline dates on tasks. Deadline dates are similar to constraints, but do not limit the scheduling engine. When you set a deadline date on a task, the software places a solid green arrow in the *Gantt chart* on the same line as the task's Gantt bar. To set a deadline date for any task, complete the following steps:

1. Double-click on the task.

2. In the Task Information dialog, click the *Advanced* tab.

3. Click the *Deadline* pick list and select a date in the calendar date picker.

4. Click the *OK* button.

Notice in Figure 5 - 51 that I set a deadline date of 6/23/10 on the Phase I Complete milestone task.

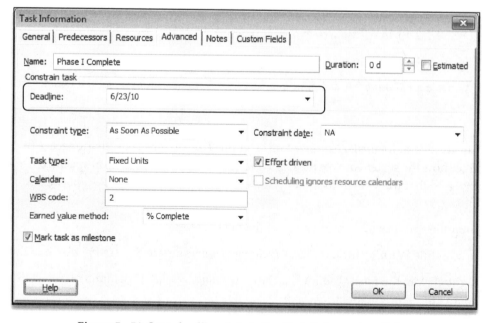

Figure 5 - 51: Set a deadline date in the Task Information dialog

Figure 5 - 52 shows how Microsoft Project 2010 displays the deadline date as a solid green arrow to the right of the milestone symbol in the *Gantt chart* for the Phase I Complete task.

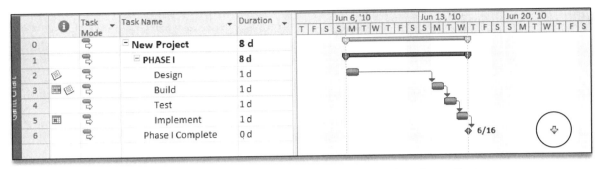

Figure 5 - 52: Deadline date indicator for the Phase I Complete milestone

Hands On Exercise

Exercise 5-15

The project manager set May 2, 2014 as the target finish date for the Training Advisor Rollout project. Set this date as the deadline date for the entire project.

1. Return to the **Training Advisor 05c.mpp** sample file.

2. Double-click task ID #23, the *Project Complete* milestone task.

3. Click the *Advanced* tab.

4. Click the *Deadline* pick list and select *May 2, 2014* in the calendar date picker.

5. Click the *OK* button to set the deadline date on the task.

Notice the solid green arrow for the deadline date in the *Gantt chart* to the far right of the milestone symbol for the *Project Complete* milestone task.

6. Save but **do not** close the **Training Advisor 05c.mpp** sample file.

Viewing Missed Constraints and Deadline Dates

Microsoft Project 2010 gives you a limited warning when you miss a constraint date or a deadline *date*. When the start or finish date of a task slips past the constraint date of an *inflexible* constraint, such as a *Finish No Later Than (FNLT)* constraint, Microsoft Project 2010 displays the *Planning Wizard* dialog shown in Figure 5 - 53. In this dialog, the software warns you of the schedule conflict, and gives you an opportunity to cancel the action or to allow the schedule conflict to occur.

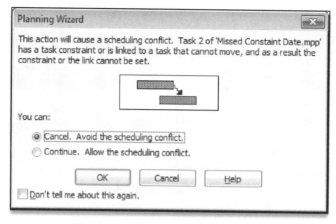

**Figure 5 - 53: Planning Wizard message
for a missed constraint date**

The default setting in this *Planning Wizard* dialog is to cancel the action that caused the scheduling conflict. If you select the second choice, *Continue*, Microsoft Project 2010 completes the scheduling change allowing the scheduling conflict; however it does not remove the constraint causing the scheduling conflict. Figure 5 - 54 shows the missed constraint date on the Phase I Complete milestone task. The slippage on the Design task delayed the finish date of all successor tasks, and pushed the milestone past its constraint date. Notice how the link line between the Implement task and the Phase I Complete milestone task "wraps back" in time, an indication of the missed constraint date.

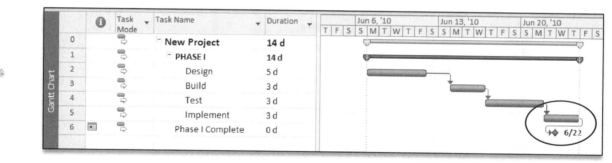

Figure 5 - 54: Missed constraint on the Phase I Complete milestone

When the finish date of a task slips past its deadline date, the software **does not** display a *Planning Wizard* warning dialog. Instead, it displays only a *Missed Deadline* indicator in the *Indicators* column. For example, Figure 5 - 55 shows the missed deadline date on the Phase I Complete milestone task with a *Missed Deadline* indicator in the *Indicators* column to the left of the task name.

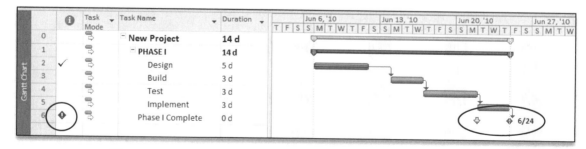

Figure 5 - 55: Missed deadline date on the Phase I Complete milestone

Assigning Task Calendars

Assign a task calendar when you want to manually override the current schedule for any task with a completely different schedule defined in a custom calendar. In Figure 5 - 56, Microsoft Project 2010 schedules the Build task on a Monday and Tuesday, must only occur on only a Thursday or Friday. Because of this requirement, I need to apply a task calendar override the schedule and let the Microsoft Project 201 scheduling engine reschedule the task only on Thursdays and Fridays.

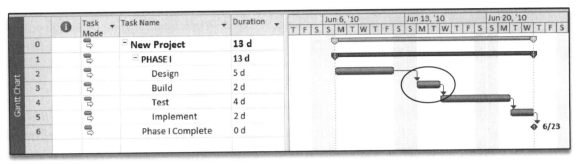

Figure 5 - 56: Build task scheduled for Monday and Tuesday

 Before you can assign a task calendar, you must create a new base calendar for this purpose. You learned how to create a new base calendar in Module 04, Project Definition.

To apply a task calendar to any task, complete the following steps:

1. Double-click the task you wish to manually reschedule.

2. In the *Task Information* dialog, click the *Advanced* tab.

3. Click the *Calendar* pick list and select a base calendar from the list, as shown in Figure 5 - 57.

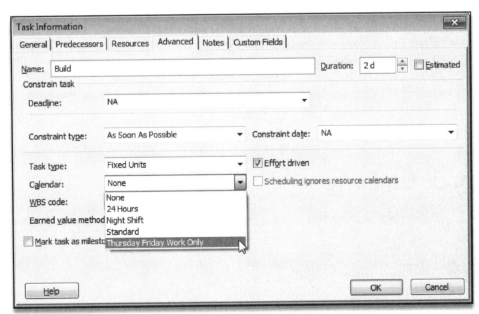

Figure 5 - 57: Select a task calendar in the Task Information dialog

4. Optionally, select the *Scheduling ignores resource calendars* option.

5. Click the *OK* button.

The *Scheduling ignores resource calendars* option forces the system to ignore resource calendars in the task scheduling process. With this option selected, the system schedules assigned resources to work even when their base calendars indicate that they are not available for work. If you leave the *Scheduling ignores resource calendars* option **deselected**, then the system schedules the task using the **common working time** between the project calendar (set in the *Project Information* dialog) and the base calendars of the resources assigned to the task. Selecting this option is useful when you need to schedule resources to work on days that are non-working time otherwise, such as on weekends and company holidays.

Figure 5 - 58 shows the same project after assigning the *Thursday Friday Work Only* task calendar on the Build task. Notice how the software rescheduled the Build task from Monday and Tuesday to the next available Thursday and Friday. Notice also how Microsoft Project 2010 displays a special task calendar indicator in the Indicators column for the task.

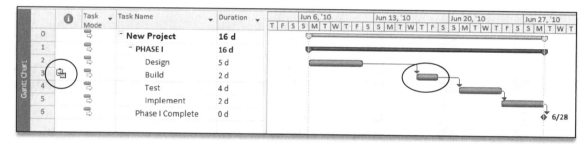

**Figure 5 - 58: Build task rescheduled
using a Task Calendar**

When you assign a task calendar to override the schedule of a task, MSProjectExperts recommends that you always add a note to the task to document the reason for using the task calendar. Think about how mysterious the scheduling gap might appear in Figure 5 - 58 without a task note to explain it!

Hands On Exercise

Exercise 5-16

The Perform Server Stress Test task must occur only on a Saturday or a Sunday; therefore, assign a task calendar to this in the Training Advisor Rollout project.

1. Return to the **Training Advisor 05c.mpp** sample file.

2. Zoom the timescale to *Weeks Over Days*.

3. Click the *Task* tab to display the *Task* ribbon, if necessary.

4. Select task ID #5, the *Perform Server Stress Test* task, and then click the *Scroll to Task* button in the *Editing* section of the *Task* ribbon.

5. Double-click the *Perform Server Stress Test* task.

6. In the *Task Information* dialog, click the *Advanced* tab.

7. On the *Advanced* page of the dialog, click the *Calendar* pick list and select the *Weekend Work Only* calendar.

8. Select the *Scheduling ignores resource calendars* checkbox option.

9. Click the *Notes* tab and add a task note documenting the reason for using the task calendar.

10. Click the *OK* button.

Notice how Microsoft Project 2010 schedules the task during the first available weekend because you over-rode the task schedule using a task calendar.

11. Save but **do not** close the **Training Advisor 05c.mpp** sample file.

Understanding Duration-Based and Effort-Based Planning

Microsoft Project 2010 allows you to drive your schedule based on effort or duration. Generally speaking, duration-based planning is easier for most novice schedulers and more instinctive to the average user. It is somewhat easier to manage as it requires less work to estimate and less work to track. The trade off is that you lose a significant degree of accuracy and, in the final analysis, you gain much less insight into what went right or what went wrong in your project.

When using duration-based planning, you typically use the *Percent Complete* method to track your project. When using effort-based planning, you typically use the *Actual Work and Remaining Work* method to track your project. In the first scenario, you estimate duration estimates to tasks and as you apply your resources, the system calculates the work values for you. Using the latter approach, you enter your work estimates and the system calculates the duration values for you.

Estimating duration is less accurate because when you ask a resource to estimate how long a task will take them to complete, they tend to factor in the non-project work they have on their plate. Typically, a resource will tell you that the task takes a day when the effort involved is as little as an hour. This is only human nature! On the other hand, when you carefully ask a resource if they had nothing else on their plate, how many hours the task will consume, you are very likely to get a fairly accurate work estimate unless the type of work is unfamiliar to the resource. You may need to assure the resource that you will take their non-project workload into account when you produce the schedule.

Duration-based planning is a top-down approach and, as such, it does not indicate how you derived the duration estimate. Further, when you look at a slipping schedule, you must go back to your resources and ask questions like, "Are you working on it or not?" or "Is it more work than you expected?" When you estimate effort and collect *Actual Work and Remaining Work* tracking data, the answers to these questions become self-evident in the system. Furthermore, for many projects labor is the primary cost factor. Because Microsoft Project 2010 calculates costs based on work, if you don't estimate and track work, you won't get very good cost data from the system.

By now you may be asking yourself if effort-based planning and tracking is much more accurate and insightful, and why anyone would use duration-based planning. The simple answer is that it is simple when compared to asking people to track their time for you. Unless your organization is already in the habit of collecting time from resources, your effort-driven efforts will meet with significant resistance from your resources.

Estimating Task Durations

After you create the task schedule, including setting task dependencies and constraints, you are ready to estimate task durations, wherever appropriate. According to Microsoft Project 2010, duration is "the total span of active working time for a task." Another way to think of duration is the "window of opportunity" during which the team members work on the task.

Many novice users of Microsoft Project 2010 wrongly assume that duration and work are interchangeable terms in a project. In some cases, this may be true, but in many cases, duration and work are two entirely different estimates. Consider the following examples:

- A resource must perform 40 hours of work during a 10-day time period. The duration of this task, therefore, is 10 days because it is the "window" during which the resource performs the work (40 hours).

- We allow an executive 5 days to approve a deliverable, but the executive will only perform 2 hours of actual work on the approval. The duration of this task, therefore, is 5 days because this is the "window" during which the executive performs the work (2 hours).

Notice in the two preceding examples that the duration or "window of opportunity" does not consider the amount of work performed on the task. The duration is simply the period of time during which team members perform the work, regardless of how much or how little work the task requires. There are several ways to determine a task duration estimate:

- Get the estimate from the team member who will actually perform the work on the task. This allows you to tap the skills, knowledge, and experience of the team member, and this is a Project Management Institute best practice.

- If you cannot get the duration estimate from a team member, then get an estimate from a team leader who has experience in this type of work.

- If you cannot get a duration estimate from a team leader, study your organization's repository of completed projects and get an estimate based on historical data for similar tasks.

- If you cannot use any of the previous methods, then set your own reasonable estimate, but validate your duration estimate later against the actual completion data for the task.

To enter duration values, simply type your estimate in the *Duration* column for each task. You may enter the duration value using any time unit, including hours, days, weeks, months, etc. By default, the system formats duration values in days.

Hands On Exercise

Exercise 5-17

Enter estimated task durations for some of the tasks in the Training Advisor Rollout project.

1. Return to the **Training Advisor 05c.mpp** sample file.

2. Zoom the timescale to *Months Over Weeks*.

3. Enter estimated duration values in the *Duration* column for tasks as follows:

ID	Task Name	Duration
2	Order Server	2 days
3	Setup Server and Load O/S	4 days
4	Load and Configure Software	5 days
5	Perform Server Stress Test	2 days
13	Setup Test Training Server	3 days
15	Create Training Module 01	5 days
16	Create Training Module 02	5 days
17	Create Training Module 03	5 days

4. Do not change the previously-entered duration values for task ID #20-21, the *Create Training Schedule* and *Provide Enter User Training* tasks.

5. Leave the default duration of *1 day* for every other task in the project.

6. Save but **do not** close the **Training Advisor 05c.mpp** sample file.

Using the Task Inspector to Determine Task Drivers

A **task driver** is any factor that determines the start date of a task. Task drivers can include any of the following factors:

- Task Mode setting, whether *Manually Scheduled* or *Auto Scheduled*

- Constraints, such as *Start No Earlier Than (SNET)* constraint

- Predecessor tasks (including *lag* time or *lead* time)

- Nonworking time on the project calendar and the base calendars resources assigned to the task

- Leveling delays caused by leveling resource overallocations

- An *Actual Start* date on the task

You can use the *Task Inspector* tool to determine the task drivers for any task by completing the following steps:

1. Click the *Task* tab to display the *Task* ribbon, if necessary.

2. In the *Tasks* section of the *Task* ribbon, click the *Inspect* pick list and select the *Inspect Task* item in the list.

3. Select the task whose drivers you wish to determine.

The software displays the task drivers for the selected task in the *Factors Affecting Task* section of the *Task Inspector* sidepane, as shown in Figure 5 - 59. Notice that the *Task Inspector* sidepane shows that the task drivers on the selected task include a predecessor task as well as the base calendar for the assigned resource, Bob Siclari.

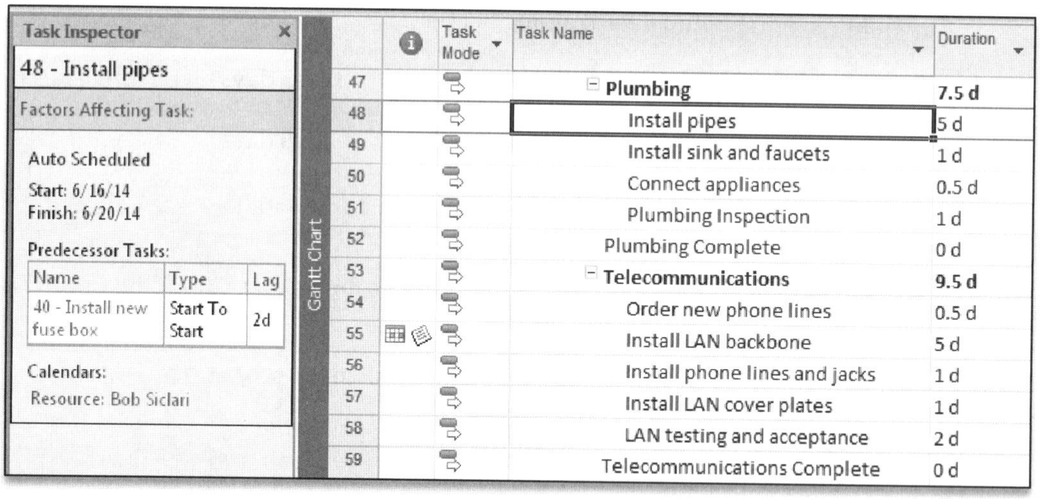

**Figure 5 - 59: Task drivers for
the selected task**

4. To view the base calendar for any resource assigned to the selected task, click the name of the resource in the *Task Inspector* sidepane. Microsoft Project 2010 displays the *Change Working Time* dialog for the selected resource, as shown for Bob Siclari in Figure 5 - 60.

214

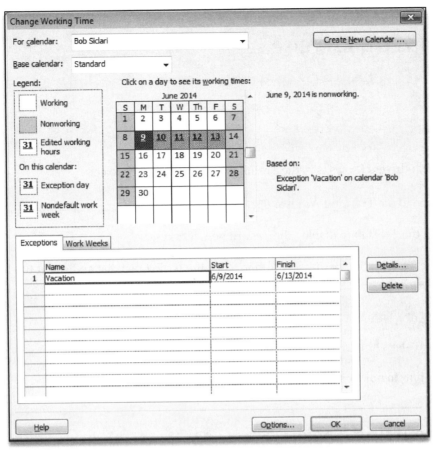

**Figure 5 - 60: Change Working Time
dialog for Bob Siclari**

Notice in Figure 5 - 60 that I scheduled Bob Siclari for a week of vacation from June 9-13, 2014. This period of non-working time affects the start dates and/or finish dates of any task to which I previously assigned Bob Siclari during the week that is now nonworking time.

 I discuss how to enter nonworking time on resource calendars in Module 06, Project Resource Planning.

5. Close the *Task Inspector* sidepane when finished.

Hands On Exercise

Exercise 5-18

Determine task drivers for tasks in the Training Advisor Rollout project.

1. Return to the **Training Advisor 05c.mpp** sample file.

2. Click the *Task* tab to display the *Task* ribbon, if necessary.

3. In the *Tasks* section of the *Task* ribbon, click the *Inspect* pick list and select the *Inspect Task* item in the list.

4. Select any task and then study the task driver for that task.

5. Repeat steps #2 and #3 for several different tasks in the project.

6. Save but **do not** close the **Training Advisor 05c.mpp** sample file.

Creating Recurring Tasks

In Microsoft Project 2010, a recurring task is any task that repeats on a regular cycle. Many project managers use a recurring task for project-related meetings, such as a project team meeting or a project status meeting. You can insert a recurring task anywhere in a project plan, although most people prefer to insert a recurring task at the beginning or the end of the task list.

Warning: Using a recurring task almost always creates resource overallocations in your project for every resource you assign to both the recurring task and regular tasks. Therefore, use recurring tasks cautiously, and prepare for the presence of resource overallocations as a result.

To insert a recurring task into a project plan, complete the following steps:

1. Select the location in the project where you want to insert the recurring task.

2. Click the *Task* tab to display the *Task* ribbon, if necessary.

3. In the *Insert* section of the *Task* ribbon, click the *Task* pick list button and select the *Recurring Task* item on the pick list. Microsoft Project 2010 displays the *Recurring Task Information* dialog shown in Figure 5 - 61.

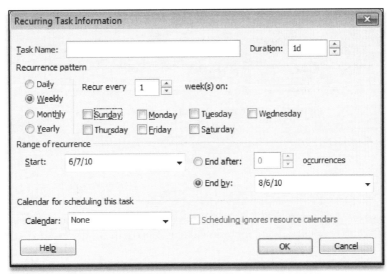

Figure 5 - 61: Recurring Task Information dialog

4. In the *Recurring Task Information* dialog, enter a name for the recurring task in the *Task Name* field.

5. In the *Duration* field, enter the duration of the recurring task (normally entered in hours).

6. In the *Recurrence pattern* section, select how often the task occurs and when it occurs.

Figure 5 - 62 through Figure 5 - 65 show the options available in the *Recurrence pattern* section with the *Daily*, *Weekly*, *Monthly*, and *Yearly* recurrence options selected. Notice in Figure 5 - 64, for example, that you can set a monthly recurring task to occur on a specific date each month, such as the 15th or the 30th, or you can set it to occur on a certain time of the month, such as on the last Friday of each month.

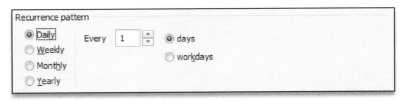

Figure 5 - 62: Daily recurrence pattern options

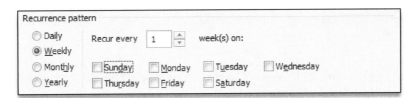

Figure 5 - 63: Weekly recurrence pattern options

Figure 5 - 64: Monthly recurrence pattern options

Figure 5 - 65: Yearly recurrence pattern options

To create a *recurring task* that occurs on a quarterly basis (every third month), select the *Monthly* option in the *Recurrence pattern* section of the dialog, and then set the task to occur every 3 months.

7. In the *Range of Recurrence* section, select the date of the first occurrence in the *Start* field if you do not want the first instance of the recurring task to occur during the first week of the project. If you do not select an alternate date in the *Start* field, the system enters the start date of the project in this field, and then calculates the date of the first occurrence of the recurring task from the start date of the project.

8. In the *Range of Recurrence* section, select the *End by* option, or select the *End after* option and then specify the number of occurrences in the *occurrences* field.

If you select the *End by* option in the *Recurring Task Information* dialog, Microsoft Project 2010 calculates the number of occurrences needed in the project based on the start date and finish date of the project.

9. Leave the *Calendar* field value set to *None*. You should only select a value in the *Calendar* field if you need to override the schedule of the recurring task with a custom task calendar.

10. Click the *OK* button.

In Figure 5 - 66, I created a recurring task called *Bi-Weekly Project Meeting*. Notice that this 4-hour meeting occurs every two weeks on Wednesday, and that Microsoft Project 2010 calculates 4 occurrences from 6/7/10 (the project start date) through 8/6/10 (the scheduled project finish date).

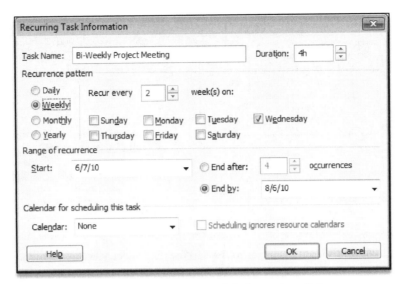

**Figure 5 - 66: Recurring Task Information dialog
set up to create the Bi-Weekly Meeting**

When you click the *OK* button, Microsoft Project 2010 creates the recurring task in your project. Figure 5 - 67 shows the first two instances of the Bi-Weekly Project Meeting, scheduled every two weeks on Wednesday.

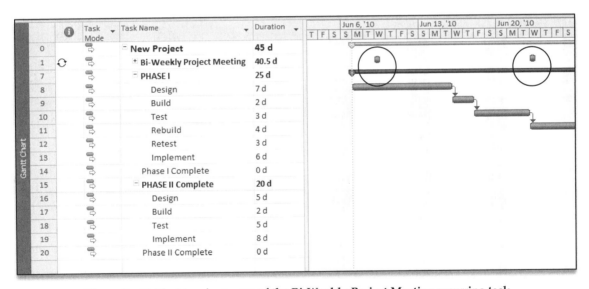

Figure 5 - 67: First two instances of the Bi-Weekly Project Meeting recurring task

In Figure 5 - 67, notice that the software displays a *recurring task* indicator (circular arrows) in the *Indicators* column, and shows an *outline* indicator (+ sign) in front of the name of the recurring task. Click the + sign and - sign to expand or collapse the instances of the recurring task. Figure 5 - 68 shows the expanded Bi-Weekly Project Meeting recurring task with the four individual instances of the meeting. Notice that the value in the *Duration* column reveals that each meeting is 4 hours.

If desirable, Microsoft Project 2010 allows you to edit the name of each instance of a recurring task, if needed. For example, some companies refer to the first project status meeting as the *Project Kick-Off* meeting, and refer to the last meeting as the *Project Closure* meeting.

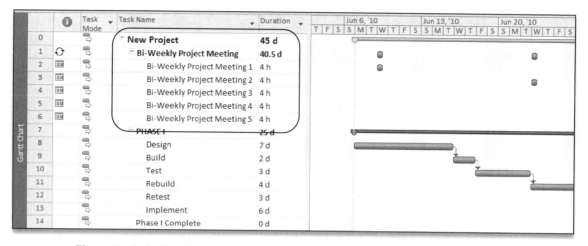

Figure 5 - 68: Individual instances of the Bi-Weekly Project Meeting recurring task

Hands On Exercise

Exercise 5-19

The team leaders from the project team must attend a 2-hour project status meeting every Monday, beginning the second week of the project. The project manager estimates approximately 14 meetings. Therefore, create a recurring task in the Training Advisor Rollout project to account for these project status meetings.

1. Return to the **Training Advisor 05c.mpp** sample file.

2. Select task ID #1, the INSTALLATION summary task.

3. In the *Insert* section of the *Task* ribbon, click the *Task* pick list button and select the *Recurring Task* item on the pick list.

4. In the *Recurring Task Information* dialog, create the recurring task using the following information:

   - **Name** – Project Status Meeting

   - **Duration** – 2h

   - **Recurrence Pattern** – Weekly, Every week on Monday

   - **Start** – 1/13/14

   - **End after** – 14 occurrences

   - **Calendar** – None

5. Click the *OK* button to create the recurring task.

6. Save but do not close the **Training Advisor 05c.mpp** sample file.

Planning for Known Fixed Costs

The final step in the task planning process is to plan for known fixed costs on tasks. Examples of fixed costs include the cost of a building permit, the cost of a piece of equipment or hardware, or the cost of room rental. Most tasks do not have a fixed cost associated with them, but if a task does have a known fixed cost associated with it, you can enter the fixed cost amount by completing the following steps:

1. Apply any task view, such as the *Gantt Chart* view.

2. Right-click on the *Select All* button and select the *Cost table* on the shortcut menu.

3. Drag the split bar to the right side of the *Fixed Cost Accrual* column.

4. Enter the known fixed cost for the task in the *Fixed Cost* column.

5. Click the *Fixed Cost Accrual* pick list for the task and select the accrual method you want to use to allocate the fixed cost amount on the task.

6. Double-click the task and then select the *Notes* tab in the *Task Information* dialog.

7. Enter a notes text documenting the reason for the fixed cost and then click the *OK* button.

Step #4 above mentions that you need to select a *Fixed Cost Accrual* method for the task. The method you select determines how the software assesses the amount of the fixed cost on the task. The *Fixed Cost Accrual* column offers you three methods for accruing a fixed cost on a task in Microsoft Project 2010:

• The *Start* method causes the software to assess the entire fixed cost amount at the beginning of the task.

• The *End* method causes the software to assess the entire fixed cost amount at the end of the task.

• The *Prorated* method causes the software to distribute the fixed cost amount evenly over the duration of the task.

Figure 5 - 69 shows the *Cost* table for a construction project that contains a task called *Obtain construction permits*. This task has a known fixed cost associated with it, which is the cost of all the required construction permits. To plan for this known fixed cost, I entered *$4,350* in the *Fixed Cost* column, and selected the *End* option in the *Fixed Cost Accrual* column as well.

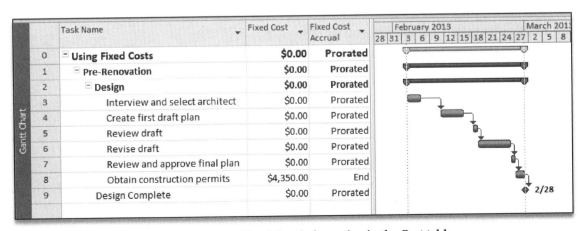

Figure 5 - 69: Enter Fixed Cost information in the Cost table

When you enter actual progress for tasks during the execution stage of the project, you can also use the *Fixed Cost* column to show **unplanned** fixed costs for tasks. Planned fixed costs do not show as variance to the project, while unplanned fixed costs do show as variance to the project.

Hands On Exercise

Exercise 5-20

Plan for a known fixed cost (the cost of a new server) in the Training Advisor Rollout project.

1. Return to the **Training Advisor 05c.mpp** sample file.

2. Right-click on the *Select All* button and select the *Cost* table on the shortcut menu.

3. Drag the split bar to the right side of the *Fixed Cost Accrual* column.

4. For task ID #17, the *Order Server* task, enter *$6,048* in the *Fixed Cost* column.

5. For the *Order Server* task, select the *End* option in the *Fixed Cost Accrual* column.

6. Double-click the *Order Server* task and then select the *Notes* tab in the *Task Information* dialog.

7. On the *Notes* page, click the *Bulleted List* button and then enter the following note text:

   Fixed Cost of $6,048 for a Dell PowerEdge T710 server for the Training Advisor enterprise software system.

8. Click the *OK* button to close the *Task Information* dialog.

9. Right-click on the *Select All* button and select the *Entry* table on the shortcut menu.

10. Save and close the **Training Advisor 05c.mpp** sample file.

Module 06

Project Resource Planning

Learning Objectives

After completing this module, you will be able to:

- Understand project resources
- Create a Work resource
- Create a Generic resource
- Create a Material resource
- Create Cost resources
- Enter basic and custom information for each type of resource
- Sort resources
- Insert a new resource

Inside Module 06

Defining Project Resources

Microsoft Project 2010 defines resources in a variety of ways and organizes them conceptually in the Resource Organization Chart shown in Figure 6 - 1.

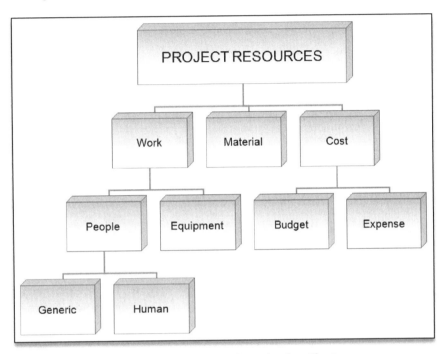

Figure 6 - 1: Resource Organization Chart

Microsoft Project 2010 allows you to define three basic resource types: *Work, Material*, and *Cost*. You use *Work* resources to model people and equipment while you use *Material* resources to represent the supplies consumed during the project lifecycle. You use *Cost* resources to track budget costs and project expenses unrelated to the *Work* resources assigned to tasks. *Work* resources affect both the schedule and the cost of the project, while *Material* and *Cost* resources affect only the project cost.

 Unfortunately, Microsoft Project 2010 does not recognize a formal type of resource called *Equipment*. Therefore, if you wish to use equipment resources in your projects, understand in advance that the software treats equipment resources the same as human resources in determining the project schedule.

Microsoft Project 2010 organizes people resources into two groups: generic and human resources. A human resource is a specific individual whom you can identify by name. A generic resource is a skill-based placeholder resource, such as a VB.Net Software Developer. Generic resources allow you to specify the skills required for a task assignment before you know which human resources are available to work on the task. You can later replace generic resources with human resources who possess the same skills.

You should identify all resources that you may eventually assign to tasks, and then enter the appropriate *Max. Units* availability for each resource into the *Resource Sheet* view to show their availability for project work. The software measures the *Max. Units* availability of *Work* resources as a percentage, where 100% represents a full-time worker and

50% represents a part-time worker such as a college intern. For a human resource, you should not enter a *Max. Units* value greater than 100%.

You cannot realistically expect that any of your *Work* resources are available at 100%, and even equipment has service downtime. People attend meetings, answer phone calls, make trips to the bathroom, and stop to chat with coworkers as a matter of course. To drive an accurate schedule, you should consider reducing resource availability based on your organization's reality. In some organizations, for example, resource availability for project work is as little as 25%.

The software also measures the *Max. Units* availability of generic resources as a percentage; however, this percentage may exceed 100%. For example, to show that I have four full-time software developers available for project work, I enter the *Max. Units* availability as 400% for a generic resource called Software Developer

In Microsoft Project 2010, you cannot enter *Max. Units* availability for *Material* or *Cost* resources. This is because *Material* and *Cost* resources affect only project costs and do not affect the project schedule.

Prior to assigning resources to tasks, you should enter a variety of basic and custom resource information for each resource in your project. You enter basic information in the *Resource Sheet* view in columns such as the *Resource Name*, *Group*, *Max. Units*, *Std. Rate*, and *Base Calendar* columns. You enter custom information, such as vacation time and alternate cost rates, in the *Resource Information* dialog for each resource.

Creating Work Resources

The first step in the resource planning process is to enter the basic resource information in the *Resource Sheet* view for the *Work* resources in your project team. To apply the *Resource Sheet* view, click the *Resource* tab to display the *Resource* ribbon. In the *View* section of the *Resource* ribbon, click the *Team Planner* pick list button and select the *Resource Sheet* view from the list. Figure 6 - 2 shows the *Resource Sheet* view with the resource *Entry* table applied.

Figure 6 - 2: Resource Sheet view with the Entry table applied

In the *Resource Sheet* view, enter information in the following columns for each project team member:

- In the *Resource Name* column, enter the first and last name of each human resource.

You may optionally enter the name of each human resource in "last name, first name" format; however, you **cannot** use the comma character to separate the last name from the first name because the comma character is reserved by the system. Instead, use the semi-colon character or a space character to separate the last name and first name of each resource.

- In the *Type* column, select the *Material* value if the resource is a *Material* resource or the *Cost* value if the resource is a *Cost* resource. Otherwise, leave the value set as the default *Work* value for a human resource or a generic resource.

- In the *Material Label* column, enter text to describe how you measure the consumption of the *Material* resource. For example, I measure the consumption of concrete in cubic yards. The software does not allow you to enter a *Material Label* value for *Work* or *Cost* resources.

- In the *Initials* column, enter the initials of each resource. By default, Microsoft Project 2010 auto-populates in the *Initials* column only the first initial of the first word from the *Resource Name* column.

- In the *Group* column, enter the skill, team, department, or some other name to use for grouping and filtering the resources in your project team.

- In the *Max. Units* column, enter a percentage representing the maximum amount of an average working day the resource is available for project work on this project. Enter 100% or your discounted availability only for resources that are available for full-time project work, and enter a value less than 100% for resources who are available to work less than full-time.

- In the *Std. Rate* column, enter the rate at which you cost the resource's work. The default measure is hourly cost, such as $50.00/hr, but you may also enter a cost using any other time units, such as $8,000/wk.

- In the *Ovt. Rate* column, enter the rate at which you cost overtime work. In Microsoft Project 2010, overtime work is any work you enter explicitly in the *Overtime Work* or *Actual Overtime Work* fields.

- In the *Cost/Use* column, enter the "flat rate" that accrues each time you use the resource in the project. The *Cost/Use* column is similar to the "trip charge" billed by a plumber to get the plumber to show up at your home.

Warning: msProjectExperts recommends that you **never** enter a resource's actual salary in any of the resource cost fields. Doing so may result in privacy issues with your company's HR department and could even cause dissension and morale problems with project staff. In fact, some European Union countries have laws prohibiting this practice. Instead, use "blended" or average rates for resources within a team, a department, a business unit, or even across your entire organization.

- In the *Accrue At* column, select a value that determines how Microsoft Project 2010 applies the timephased costs when you assign the selected resource to a task. You can apply the cost at the beginning of the task by selecting the *Start* value, or apply the cost at the end of the task by selecting the *End* value. The default value, *Prorated*, applies the cost evenly across the duration of the task.

- In the *Base Calendar* column, select the base calendar that Microsoft Project 2010 uses to set up the resource's personal calendar. If you entered your company holidays on the Standard calendar, and then specified this calendar as the resource's base calendar, then the resource's personal calendar automatically inherits all company holidays.

- The *Code* column is a free text field in which you may enter any type of additional information about the resource, such as the cost center code or work phone number for the resource.

Similar to Microsoft Excel, you can speed up the entry of resources by using the *Fill Handle* tool to fill data from one cell to consecutive cells above or below it. To do so, select the cell whose content you want to fill into other cells, click and hold the *Fill Handle* tool in the lower right corner of the selected cell, then drag up or down to fill as many cells as you want.

If your organization used Microsoft Project Server 21010, avoid using non-alphanumeric characters other than the underscore when entering resource names. Special characters can cause problems when you save your project to the Project Server database.

Hands On Exercise

Exercise 6-1

Enter *Work* resources in the project team for the Training Advisor Rollout project.

1. Open the **Training Advisor 06.mpp** sample file.

2. Click the *View* tab to display the *View* ribbon.

3. In the *Split View* section of the *View* ribbon, deselect the *Timeline* checkbox to hide the *Timeline* view temporarily.

4. Click the *Resource* tab to display the *Resource* ribbon.

5. In the *View* section of the *Resource* ribbon, click the *View* pick list button and select the *Resource Sheet* view from the list.

6. At the bottom of the list of resources already entered in the *Resource Sheet* view of the project, add a new *Work* resource using the basic resource information shown in Table 6 - 1.

Column	Value to Enter/Select
Resource Name	Vicky Joslyn
Type	Work
Material Label	
Initials	VJ
Group	Test
Max. Units	100%
Std. Rate	$50.00/h
Ovt. Rate	$75.00/h
Cost/Use	$0.00
Accrue At	Prorated
Base Calendar	Standard
Code	500

Table 6 - 1: Create a Work resource

7. Save but **do not** close the **Training Advisor 06.mpp** sample file.

Entering Custom Resource Information

The second step in the resource planning process is to enter custom resource information for each *Work* resource in your project team. Custom resource data includes information such as vacation time, alternate cost rates, or notes about the resource. To enter this information, display the *Resource Information* dialog using one of the following methods:

- Double-click the name of the resource.

- Select the resource and then click the *Information* button in the *Properties* section of the *Resource* ribbon.

- Right-click on the resource name and then select the *Information* item on the shortcut menu.

Figure 6 - 3 shows the *Resource Information* dialog for a resource named George Stewart. Notice a number of fields in the *General* page of the dialog show information I entered previously in the *Resource Sheet* view of the project.

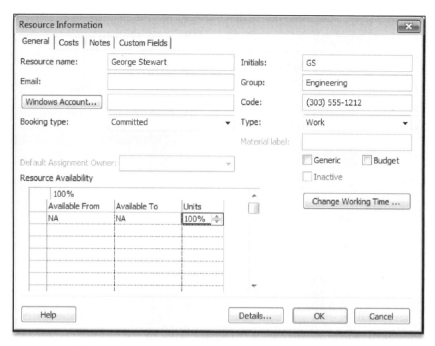

Figure 6 - 3: Resource Information dialog, General page

The *Resource Information* dialog includes four pages of information for each resource, including the *General, Costs, Notes,* and *Custom Fields* pages. I discuss each of these pages separately.

Entering General Information

The *General* page includes some of the information you already entered in the *Resource Sheet* view of the project in the *Resource Name, Type, Initials, Group,* and *Code* columns. This page in the dialog allows you to enter additional information, including the resource's e-mail address, Windows user account, and availability information. From this page, you can also designate a *Work* resource as a generic resource by selecting the *Generic* option.

Use the data grid in the *Resource Availability* section to enter changes in the availability of a resource, such as when a part-time employee becomes a full-time employee on a specific date. You can also use this section to indicate changes in the number of generic resources available, for example, to show that your organization will add two new network engineers on August 1 of the current year.

Figure 6 - 4 shows the changes in availability for the resource, George Stewart, who changes from full-time to part-time to attend graduate school during the 2011-2012 school year. Notice how his *Units* availability changes from *100%* (full-time) to *50%* (half-time) and then returns to *100%* (full-time) again. The software automatically updates these availability changes in the *Max. Units* field for the resource.

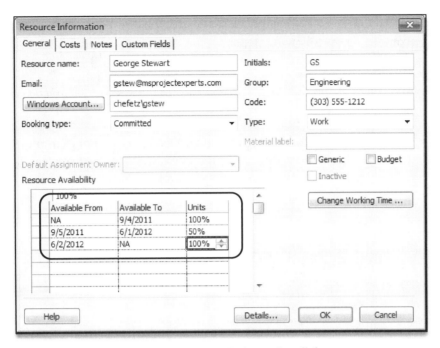

**Figure 6 - 4: Resource Information dialog,
changes to Resource Availability**

MsProjectExperts recommends that you always document changes in the *Resource Availability* section of
the *Resource Information* dialog by adding a note to the resource.

Changing Working Time

There are several situations that require you to change the working schedule for a resource, which are:

- The resource works a schedule different from the schedule specified on the Standard calendar.

- You need to add nonworking time for the resource, such as vacation or planned sick leave.

- You need to make minor modifications to the resource's working schedule, such as adding Saturday work for
a specific period of time.

I discuss how to configure each of these schedule needs separately.

Setting an Alternate Working Schedule

If you wish to create an alternate working schedule for a resource, and the schedule differs from the Standard calendar, there are two ways to accomplish this. To use the first method, you must create a custom base calendar in the project. Refer back to Module 04, if necessary, for the steps to create a custom base calendar. After you create the custom base calendar, simply select that new calendar as the *Base Calendar* column for the selected resource in the *Resource Sheet* view of the project.

If a base calendar with the schedule you wish does not exist already, you can specify the non-standard working schedule for the resource by completing the following steps:

1.   Click the *Change Working Time* button on the *General* page of the *Resource Information* dialog.

The software displays the *Change Working Time* dialog for the selected resource. For example, Figure 6 - 5 shows the *Change Working Time* dialog for George Stewart. By default, the software selects the *Exceptions* tab at the bottom of the dialog.

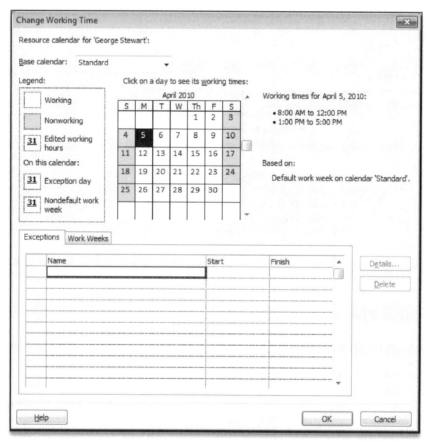

Figure 6 - 5: Change Working Time dialog, Exceptions tab

2.   In the bottom half of the dialog, click the *Work Weeks* tab. Figure 6 - 6 shows the *Work Weeks* tab in the *Change Working Time* dialog for George Stewart.

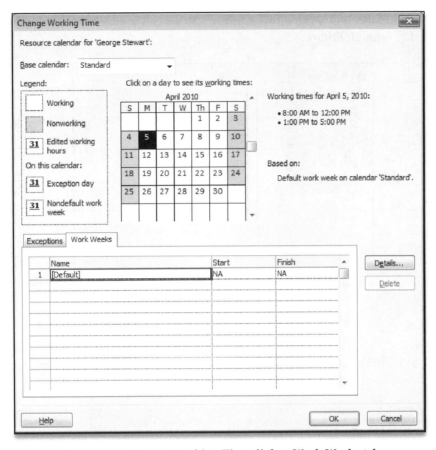

Figure 6 - 6: Change Working Time dialog, Work Weeks tab

3. Select the *[Default]* item in the *Work Weeks* data grid and then click the *Details* button. The system displays the *Details* dialog for the default working schedule shown in Figure 6 - 7.

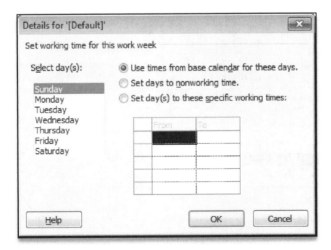

**Figure 6 - 7: Details dialog for the
default working schedule**

4. In the *Select day(s)* list, select the days whose schedule you wish to change.

5. Select the *Set days to nonworking time* option in the upper right corner of the dialog.

6. Enter the alternate working schedule in the *Working times* data grid.

Figure 6-9 shows the *Details* dialog for a working schedule where the resource works 9 hours per day from 8:00 AM to 6:00 PM each day Monday through Friday.

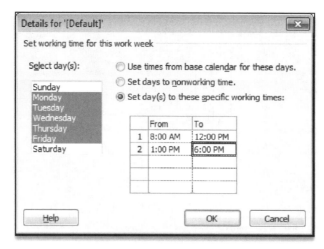

**Figure 6 - 8: Details dialog shows
alternate working schedule**

7.   Click the *OK* button to close the *Details* dialog. Figure 6 - 9 shows the *Change Working Time* dialog with the new alternate working schedule for George Stewart.

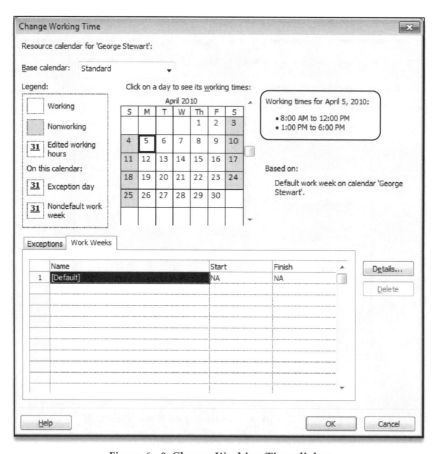

**Figure 6 - 9: Change Working Time dialog
with alternate working schedule**

Entering Nonworking Time

Microsoft Project 2010 allows you to enter nonworking time, such as vacations and planned medical leave, for each individual resource. To enter nonworking time for the resource, complete the following steps:

1. Click the *Change Working Time* button on the *General* page of the *Resource Information* dialog.

2. Click the *Exceptions* tab. The system displays the *Exceptions* tab of the *Change Working Time* dialog, shown previously in Figure 6 - 5.

3. In the calendar grid at the top of the page, select the days you want to set as nonworking time.

4. In the *Exceptions* data grid in the bottom half of the dialog, select the *Name* cell in the first blank line.

5. In the *Name* cell of the *Exceptions* data grid, enter a name for the nonworking time instance, such as *Vacation*.

6. Press the *Enter* key on your computer keyboard.

The software automatically sets the selected time period as nonworking time, such as the vacation time for George Stewart in June 2011 as shown in Figure 6 - 10.

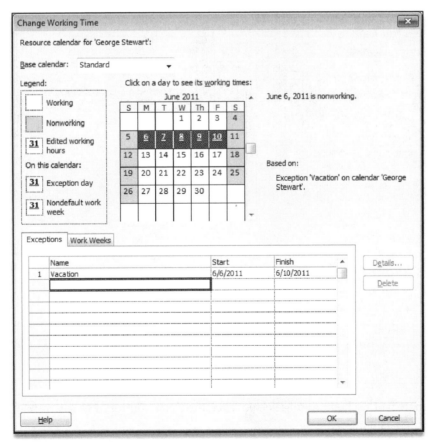

**Figure 6 - 10: Nonworking time
in June 2011 for George Stewart**

Setting Working Schedule Changes

At some point, you may need to set an alternate working schedule for a limited period of time, such as when a resource might work an extended work week during summer months. To set an alternate working schedule for a resource for a specific period of time, complete the following steps:

1. Click the *Change Working Time* button on the *General* page of the *Resource Information* dialog.

2. Click the *Work Weeks* tab.

3. In the *Work Weeks* data grid, select the first blank below the [Default] line.

4. In the *Name* cell, enter a name for the alternate working schedule and then press the **Right-Arrow** key on your computer keyboard. Make sure you leave selected the name of the alternate working schedule.

5. Enter the starting date of the schedule change in the *Start* field and enter the ending date in the *Finish* field for the alternate working schedule.

For example, Figure 6 - 11 shows the extended working schedule that I want to change for George Stewart during the month of August 2011 only.

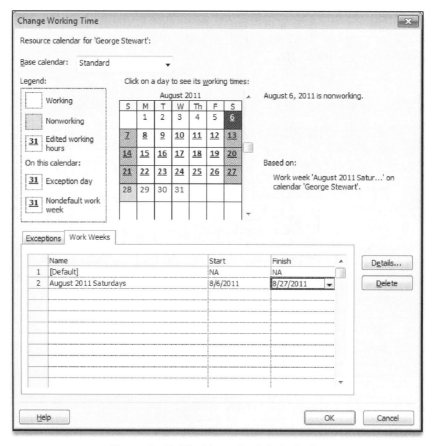

Figure 6 - 11: Working schedule includes
Saturdays for August 2011 only

6. With the alternate work schedule still selected, click the *Details* button. The software displays the *Details* dialog shown previously in Figure 6 - 8.

7. In the *Details* dialog for the alternate working schedule, set the working schedule for each day of the week, as needed.

The *Details* dialog shown in Figure 6 - 12 displays the Saturday work schedule for George Stewart during August 2011 only.

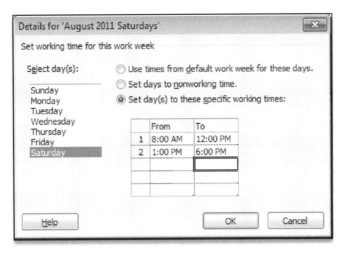

**Figure 6 - 12: Details dialog shows Saturdays
as work days in August 2011 only**

8.   Click the *OK* button to close the *Details* dialog. Figure 6 - 13 shows the *Change Working Time* dialog with the August 2011 schedule change for George Stewart.

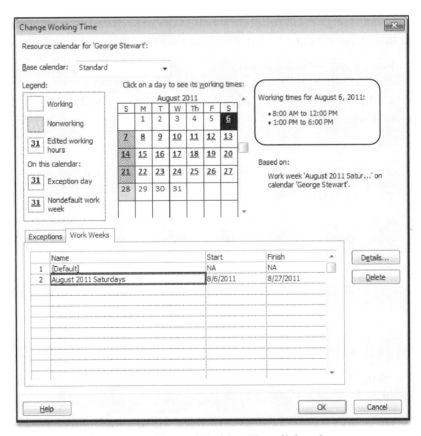

**Figure 6 - 13: Change Working Time dialog shows
Saturdays as work days in August 2011 only**

Hands On Exercise

Exercise 6-2

The functional manager for Mickey Cobb approved her vacation request for a week of vacation from March 17-21, 2014. The regular working schedule for Vicky Joslyn includes every Saturday morning from 8:00 AM – 12:00 PM. Specify working schedule information for these two members of the project team in the Training Advisor Rollout project.

1. Return to the **Training Advisor 06.mpp** sample file.

2. Double-click the resource named *Mickey Cobb*.

3. In the *Resource Information* dialog, click the *Change Working Time* button on the *General* page.

4. Click the *Exceptions* tab, if necessary.

5. In the top half of the *Change Working Time* dialog, scroll the calendar data grid to *March 2014*.

6. In the calendar data grid, select the dates *March 17-21, 2014*.

7. In the *Exceptions* data grid in the bottom half of the dialog, enter the name *Vacation* for the exception and then press the *Enter* key on your computer keyboard.

Notice how Microsoft Project 2010 marks March 17-21, 2014 as nonworking time in the calendar grid.

8. Click the *OK* button to close the *Change Working Time* dialog and then click the *OK* button again to close the *Resource Information* dialog.

9. Double-click the resource named Vicky Joslyn.

10. In the *Resource Information* dialog, click the *Change Working Time* button on the *General* page.

11. Click the *Work Weeks* tab.

12. In the *Work Weeks* data grid at the bottom of the dialog, select the *[Default]* item, if necessary.

13. Click the *Details* button.

14. In the *Details* dialog, select *Saturday* in the *Select days* list on the left side of the dialog.

15. Select the *Set day(s) to these specific working times* option.

16. Enter *8:00 AM* in the first *From* cell and enter *12:00 PM* in the first *To* cell.

17. Click the *OK* button to close the *Details* dialog.

18. Select any Saturday in the calendar grid and examine the working schedule shown in the upper right corner of the *Change Working Time* dialog.

19. Click the *OK* button to close the *Change Working Time* dialog and then click the *OK* button again to close the *Resource Information* dialog.

20. Save but **do not** close the **Training Advisor 06.mpp** sample file.

Entering Cost Information

To enter custom cost information for any resource, displays the *Resource Information* dialog for the resource and then click the *Costs* tab. The *Resource Information* dialog *Costs* page, shown in Figure 6 - 14, displays the *Standard Rate, Overtime Rate,* and *Per Use Cost* fields for the selected resource. In addition, the *Cost rate tables* section of the page also contains five cost rate tables labeled *A (Default)* through *E*. Cost rate table *A* contains the rates you entered in the *Resource Sheet* view in the *Std. Rate, Ovt. Rate,* and *Cost/Use* columns. You can use cost rate tables *B* through *E* to specify alternate cost rates. You can set the cost rates on any of the cost rate tables so that the rate changes on a given day automatically, such as when a resource receives a salary increase or when your organization increases the billing rate to clients.

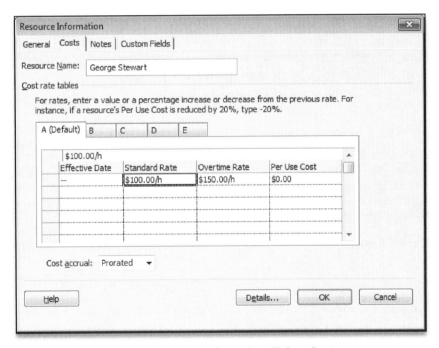

Figure 6 - 14: Resource Information dialog, Costs page

As a part of the cost model for your project, you may need to change cost rates on a specific date for a resource on the project team. For example, on April 1 of next year, a resource's *Standard Rate* increases by $20/hour and the resource's *Overtime Rate* increases by $30/hour. To define a new cost rate that begins on a specific date, select the *A (Default)* cost rate table tab and then enter the date in the *Effective Date* field on the first blank line of the data grid. Enter the new rates in the *Standard Rate* cell and *Overtime Rate* cell on that line, as shown in Figure 6 - 15.

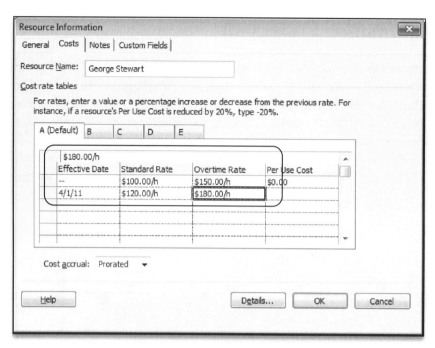

Figure 6 - 15: Resource Information dialog
Cost rate increase on 4/1/11

When you enter a cost rate change for a resource, Microsoft Project 2010 automatically costs all work for the resource at the new cost rate beginning with the date you enter in the *Effective Date* field. Using the example shown in Figure 6 - 15, the software costs all of George Stewart's task work at $100/hour before 4/1/11 and costs all work on and after 4/1/11 at $120/hour.

You might have a team member who plays multiple roles in a project, and whose cost depends on the team member's role in the project. For example, we cost George Stewart's work at $100/hour for engineering tasks but cost his work at $250/hour for tasks in which he must provide expert witness testimony before any governmental entity. To specify an alternate cost rate for a resource, select one of the alternate cost rate table tabs (*B* through *E*) in the *Cost rate tables* section of the *Cost* page and then enter the alternate rate(s) on the first line of the data grid on that tab, as shown in Figure 6 - 16.

msProjectExperts recommends that you always document your use of alternate cost rates with a resource note. The note should explain how to use the alternate rates shown on cost rate tables *B* through *E*. You **do not** need to use a note to document the rate shown on cost rate table *A (Default)* since this is the default cost rate for all tasks until you choose an alternate cost rate.

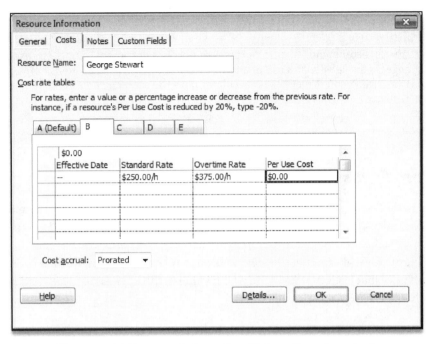

**Figure 6 - 16: Resource Information dialog, alternate cost rate
for expert witness testimony work on cost rate table B**

Entering Resource Notes

Use the *Notes* page in the *Resource Information* dialog to record additional information about the selected resource, such as changes in availability and notes about how to use alternate cost rates. Figure 6 - 17 shows the blank *Notes* page in the *Resource Information* dialog.

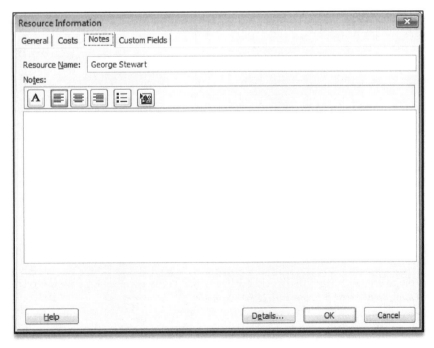

Figure 6 - 17: Resource Information dialog, Notes page

MSProjectExperts recommends the use of resource notes to document important resource information such as changes in availability and use of alternate cost rates. This makes it easier for others to understand how Microsoft Project 2010 calculates both the schedule and the cost of tasks to which you assign the resource.

Using the Custom Fields Page

The *Custom Fields* page in *the Resource Information* dialog shows any custom resource fields available in your project. If you created any local custom resource fields or outline codes, they appear on the *Custom Fields* page. If your organization uses Project Server 2010, then this page also displays any custom enterprise resource fields created by the Project Server administrator. Figure 6 - 18 shows the *Custom Fields* page with two custom outline codes named *Engineering Skill* and *Region Office*. Notice that I selected *Electrical* as the value in the *Engineering Skill* field and I am preparing to select *Denver* as the value in the *Region Office* field.

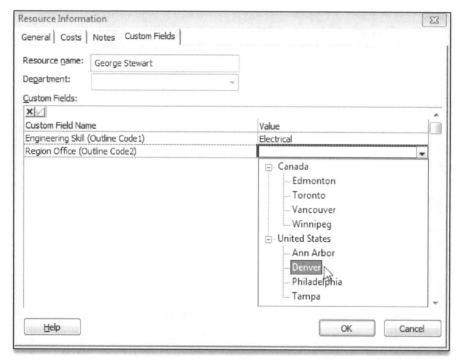

Figure 6 - 18: Resource Information dialog
Custom Fields page

I discuss how to create custom fields and outline codes in the companion volume to this book, *Ultimate Learning Guide to Microsoft Project 2010: Advanced*.

Hands On Exercise

Exercise 6-3

The cost rates for Ruth Andrews increase by 25% on April 1, 2014. Mike Andrews works on the Help Desk primarily, but does occasional testing work that you cost at the same rate as members of Test team. Enter custom cost information and notes for these two members of the project team in the Training Advisor Rollout project.

1. Return to the **Training Advisor 06.mpp** sample file.

2. Double-click the name *Ruth Andrews* and then click the *Cost* tab in the *Resource Information* dialog.

3. Select the cost rate table *A (Default)* page in the *Cost rate tables* section of the *Cost* page, if necessary.

4. On the first blank line of the data grid, enter *April 1, 2014* in the *Effective Date* column, enter *25%* in the *Standard Rate* column, and enter *25%* in the *Overtime Rate* column.

Notice how Microsoft Project 2010 calculated the correct Standard Rate and Overtime Rate values when you entered *25%* in each of these columns.

5. Click the *OK* button to close the *Resource Information* dialog.

6. Double-click the name *Mike Andrews* and then click the *Cost* tab in the *Resource Information* dialog.

7. Click the *B* tab in the *Cost rate tables* section of the *Cost* page.

8. On the first blank line of the data grid on the cost rate table *B* page, enter *$50/hour* in the *Standard Rate* column and *$75/hour* in the *Overtime Rate* column.

9. Click the *Notes* tab.

10. On the *Notes* page, click the *Bulleted List* button and then enter the following text in the *Notes* field:

Cost rate table B – Alternate cost rate for testing tasks.

11. Save but do close the **Training Advisor 06.mpp** sample file.

Creating Generic Resources

Generic resources are skill-based or placeholder resources that you can assign to tasks before you know the actual human resources to assign. You can also use generic resources to model project costs in the early stages of the project before you begin assigning any human resources. To create a generic resource, complete the following steps in the *Resource Sheet* view of your project:

1. Enter the name of the generic resource in the *Resource Name* column.

2. Enter all other basic information in the columns of the *Resource Sheet* view as you would for a non-generic resource.

3. Double-click the name of the generic resource.

4. On the *General* page in the *Resource Information* dialog, select the *Generic* checkbox in the right side of the dialog.

5. Specify cost information on the *Costs* page.

6. Specify custom field values on the *Custom Fields* page, if needed.

7. Click the *OK* button.

Figure 6 - 19 shows the *Resource Information* dialog for a generic resource named Electrical Engineer. Notice that I set the *Units* value in the *Resource Availability* section to 400% indicating that our organization has four full-time electrical engineers to perform project work.

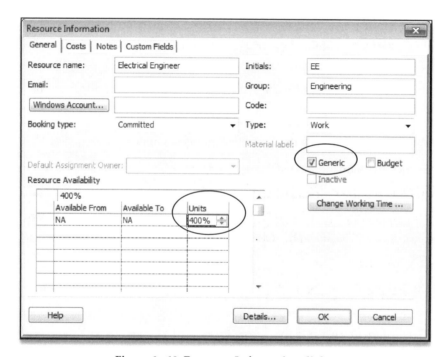

**Figure 6 - 19: Resource Information dialog
for a Generic resource**

 If you use the Standard version of Microsoft Project 2010, the *Generic* checkbox is not an available option in the *Resource Information* dialog. This feature is **only** available in the Professional version of Microsoft Project 2010.

Hands On Exercise

Exercise 6-4

Create a generic resource in the Training Advisor Rollout project.

1. Return to the **Training Advisor 06.mpp** sample file.

2. At the bottom of the resource list in the *Resource Sheet* view of the project, add a new generic resource using the basic resource information shown in Table 6 - 2.

Column	Value to Enter/Select
Resource Name	Training Developer
Type	Work
Material Label	
Initials	TD
Group	TechEd
Max. Units	500%
Std. Rate	$40.00/h
Ovt. Rate	$60.00/h
Cost/Use	$0.00
Accrue At	Prorated
Base Calendar	Standard
Code	401

Table 6 - 2: Create a generic resource

3. Double-click the name of the *Training Developer* resource and then click the *General* tab, if necessary.

4. In the *Resource Information* dialog, select the *Generic* checkbox and then click the *OK* button.

If you use the Standard version of Microsoft Project 2010, you **do not** have a *Generic* checkbox in the *Resource Information* dialog. Therefore, simply omit the preceding step.

5. Save but do not close the **Training Advisor 06.mpp** sample file.

Creating Material Resources

You use *Material* resources to represent the supplies consumed during the life of the project. To create a *Material* resource, complete the following steps in the *Resource Sheet* view of your project:

1. Enter the name of the *Material* resource in the *Resource Name* column.

2. Click the pick list button in the *Type* field for the *Material* resource and select the *Material* item on the list.

3. Enter a value in the *Material Label* column to indicate how you measure the consumption of the *Material* resource.

4. In the *Std. Rate* field, enter the cost for each unit consumed, as specified in the *Type* field.

The *Material label* field allows you to define your own consumption units corresponding with the costs that you set. For instance, concrete for a construction project might be labeled "cubic yards" while an electronic component might be labeled "each" or "assembly." The point is that you should make the label correspond to how you measure the consumption and cost of when you use the Material resource in your project. In Figure 6 - 20, notice that I entered a *Material* resource called *120V UPS Unit* whose consumption is *Each* and which we cost at *$549/each*.

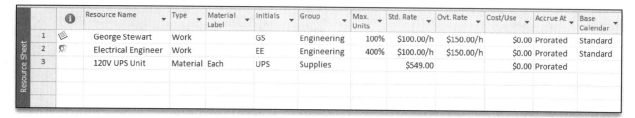

		Resource Name	Type	Material Label	Initials	Group	Max. Units	Std. Rate	Ovt. Rate	Cost/Use	Accrue At	Base Calendar
1		George Stewart	Work		GS	Engineering	100%	$100.00/h	$150.00/h	$0.00	Prorated	Standard
2		Electrical Engineer	Work		EE	Engineering	400%	$100.00/h	$150.00/h	$0.00	Prorated	Standard
3		120V UPS Unit	Material	Each	UPS	Supplies		$549.00		$0.00	Prorated	

Figure 6 - 20: 120V UPS Unit resource is a Material resource

Hands On Exercise

Exercise 6-5

Create a *Material* resource in the Training Advisor Rollout project.

1. Return to the **Training Advisor 06.mpp** sample file.

2. At the bottom of the resource list in the *Resource Sheet* view of the project, add a new *Material* resource using the basic resource information shown in Table 6 - 3.

Column	Value to Enter/Select
Resource Name	Student Materials
Type	Material
Material Label	Sets
Initials	SM
Group	Supplies
Max. Units	
Std. Rate	$50.00
Ovt. Rate	
Cost/Use	$0.00
Accrue At	Prorated
Base Calendar	
Code	900

Table 6 - 3: Create a Material resource

3. Save but do not close the **Training Advisor 06.mpp** sample file.

Creating Cost Resources

Microsoft added *Cost* resources as a new feature in Microsoft Project 2007 and continues to offer *Cost* resources in the 2010 version of the tool. You generally use *Cost* resources in several situations:

- You need to connect project data to a third-party financial system. For example, you need to export project costs to a Microsoft Dynamics ERP system on a monthly basis.

- You need to specify an overall monetary budget to your project. For example, your organization allocates $1,500,000 as the budget for your project and you need to enter this information in your project.

- You need to manually enter actual project costs in your project plan. For example, you do not use resource cost rates in the *Standard Rate* and *Overtime Rate* fields for each resource. Instead, you manually enter actual project costs from a monthly report generated in a Microsoft Dynamics ERP system.

- You need to track additional project costs and show the total extra expenditure as a line item in a resource view in your project. For example, you need to track travel expenses for the resources assigned to tasks in your project, and need to report on travel expenses as a line item expenditure in your project.

Microsoft Project 2010 provides you with two types of *Cost* resources: *Budget Cost* resources and *Expense Cost* resources. To use *Cost* resources effectively you may need to create at least one *Budget Cost* resource and at least one *Expense Cost* resource in your project.

Creating a Budget Cost Resource

To create a *Budget Cost* resource, complete the following steps in the *Resource Sheet* view of your project:

1. Enter the name of the *Budget Cost* resource in the *Resource Name* column.

2. Click the pick list button in the *Type* field for the *Cost* resource and select the *Cost* item on the list.

3. Enter additional information for the *Budget Cost* resource in the *Initials*, *Group*, *Accrue At*, and *Code* columns, as needed.

4. Double-click the name of the *Budget Cost* resource.

5. In the *General* page of the *Resource Information* dialog, select the *Budget* checkbox on the right side of the dialog, as shown in Figure 6 - 21.

6. Click the *OK* button.

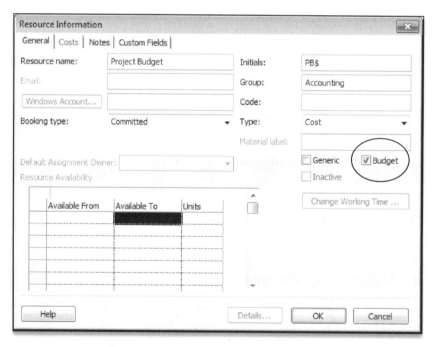

Figure 6 - 21: Create a Budget Cost resource

Creating an Expense Cost Resource

The steps needed to create an *Expense Cost* resource are nearly identical to those needed to create a *Budget Cost* resource. To create an *Expense Cost* resource, complete the following steps in the *Resource Sheet* view of your project:

1. Enter the name of the *Expense Cost* resource in the *Resource Name* column.

2. Click the pick list button in the *Type* field for the *Cost* resource and select the *Cost* item on the list.

3. Enter additional information for the *Expense Cost* resource in the *Initials, Group, Accrue At*, and *Code* columns, as needed.

Figure 6 - 22 shows two *Cost* resources in my project. I created a *Budget Cost* resource named Project Budget and I created an *Expense Cost* resource named Travel Expense.

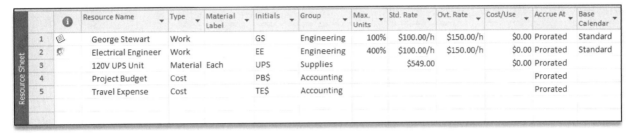

		Resource Name	Type	Material Label	Initials	Group	Max. Units	Std. Rate	Ovt. Rate	Cost/Use	Accrue At	Base Calendar
1		George Stewart	Work		GS	Engineering	100%	$100.00/h	$150.00/h	$0.00	Prorated	Standard
2		Electrical Engineer	Work		EE	Engineering	400%	$100.00/h	$150.00/h	$0.00	Prorated	Standard
3		120V UPS Unit	Material	Each	UPS	Supplies		$549.00		$0.00	Prorated	
4		Project Budget	Cost		PB$	Accounting					Prorated	
5		Travel Expense	Cost		TE$	Accounting					Prorated	

Figure 6 - 22: Two new Cost resources added to the project

Hands On Exercise

Exercise 6-6

In your Training Advisor Rollout project, you need to enter an overall budget for your project, and you need to track the amount of money spent on software licenses. Create a *Budget Cost* resource and an *Expense Cost* resource in your project.

1. Return to the **Training Advisor 06.mpp** sample file.

2. At the bottom of the resource list in the *Resource Sheet* view of the project, add a new *Cost* resource using the basic resource information shown in Table 6 - 4.

Column	Value to Enter/Select
Resource Name	Project Budget
Type	Cost
Material Label	
Initials	PB$
Group	Accounting
Max. Units	
Std. Rate	

Column	Value to Enter/Select
Ovt. Rate	
Cost/Use	
Accrue At	Prorated
Base Calendar	
Code	999

Table 6 - 4: **Create a Budget Cost resource**

3. Double-click the name of the *Project Budget* resource.

4. In the *General* page of the *Resource Information* dialog, select the *Budget* checkbox on the right side of the dialog.

5. Click the *OK* button.

6. At the bottom of the resource list in the *Resource Sheet* view of the project, add a second *Cost* resource using the basic resource information shown in Table 6 - 5.

Column	Value to Enter/Select
Resource Name	Software Licenses
Type	Cost
Material Label	
Initials	SL$
Group	Accounting
Max. Units	
Std. Rate	
Ovt. Rate	
Cost/Use	
Accrue At	Prorated
Base Calendar	
Code	999

Table 6 - 5: **Create an Expense Cost resource**

7. Save but do not close the **Training Advisor 06.mpp** sample file.

Sorting Resources in the Resource Sheet View

After you create all of the resources needed for your project team, you may want to sort the resources. To sort the resources in the *Resource Sheet* view, complete the following steps:

1. Click the *View* tab to display the *View* ribbon.

2. In the *Data* section of the *View* ribbon, click the *Sort* pick list and select the *Sort By* item on the list. Microsoft Project 2010 displays the *Sort* dialog shown in Figure 6 - 23.

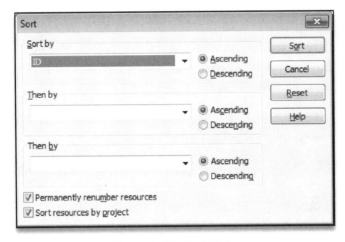

Figure 6 - 23: Sort dialog

3. Select the fields upon which you want to sort using the *Sort by* pick list and the two *Then by* pick lists.

4. Select either the *Ascending* or *Descending* option for the *Sort by* pick list and the two *Then by* pick lists.

5. Leave the Permanently renumber resources option selected.

6. Leave the *Sort resources by project* option selected as well.

7. Click the *Sort* button to sort the resources according to the sorting criteria you specify in the *Sort* dialog.

Hands On Exercise

Exercise 6-7

Sort the resources in your project team for the Training Advisor Rollout project. Apply a three-level sorting by the resource *Type* value, then by the *Group* value, and finally by the *Resource Name* value.

1. Return to the **Training Advisor 06.mpp** sample file.

2. Click the *View* tab to display the *View* ribbon.

3. In the *Data* section of the *View* ribbon, click the *Sort* pick list and select the *Sort By* item on the list.

4. In the *Sort* dialog, click the *Sort by* pick list and select the *Type* field.

5. Select the *Descending* option for the *Sort by* pick list.

6. Click the first *Then by* pick list and select the *Group* field.

7. Leave the *Ascending* option selected for the first *Then by* pick list.

8. Click the second *Then by* pick list and select the *Name* field.

Notice that the real name of the *Resource Name* column is actually the *Name* column. Microsoft applies the title *Resource Name* to the column for ease of use.

9. Leave the *Ascending* option selected for the second *Then by* pick list.

10. Select the *Permanently renumber resources* and *Sort resources by project* options, if not already selected.

11. Click the *Sort* button to sort the resources using this custom sorting order.

12. Study the unusual sorting order for the resources shown in the *Resource Sheet* view of your project.

13. Click the *Task* tab to apply the *Task* ribbon.

14. In the *View* section of the *Task* ribbon, click the *Gantt Chart* button to apply the *Gantt Chart* view.

15. Save and close the **Training Advisor 06.mpp** sample file.

Inserting New Resources in the Resource Sheet View

A new feature in Microsoft Project 2010 allows you to insert new resources in any resource view using the *Add Resources* pick list button in the *Resource* ribbon. To insert a new resource in your project using this feature, complete the following steps in the *Resource Sheet* view:

1. Click the *Resource* tab to display the *Resource* ribbon.

2. In the *View* section of the *Resource* ribbon, click the *View* pick list button and select the *Resource Sheet* view.

3. In the *Insert* section of the *Resource* ribbon, click the *Add Resources* pick list button shown in Figure 6 - 24.

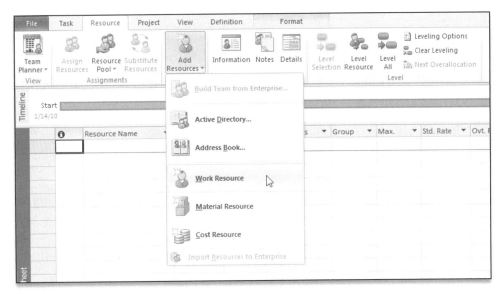

Figure 6 - 24: Add Resources pick list

4. On the *Add Resources* pick list, select the *Work Resource, Material Resource,* or *Cost Resource* item. Microsoft Project 2010 inserts a new resource based on the type you selected. Notice in Figure 6 - 25 that I created one new resource of each type (Work, Material, and Cost).

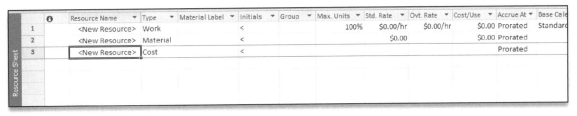

Figure 6 - 25: Work, Cost, and Material resources inserted in a project

When you insert a new resource using the *Add Resources* pick list, Microsoft Project 2010 creates the new resource by inserting the name *<New Resource>* in the *Resource Name* field, inserting the < symbol in the *Initials* field, and selecting the *Prorated* value in the *Accrue At* field for all three types of resources. For a *Work* resource, the system also selects the *Work* value in the *Type* field, defaults the *Max. Units* field value to *100%*, enters *$0.00/hr* in the *Std. Rate* and *Ovt. Rate* fields, enters *$0.00* in the *Cost/Use* field, and selects the *Standard* calendar in the *Base Calendar* field. For a *Material* resource, the system selects the *Material* value in the *Type* field and enters *$0.00* in the *Std. Rate* and *Cost/Use* fields. For a *Cost* resource, the system selects the *Cost* value in the *Type* field. After you insert any of the three types of resources, you must rename the resource and provide any other basic and custom resource information you want to record for the selected resource.

When you insert a new *Cost* resource, the system creates an *Expense Cost* resource automatically. If you need to create a new *Cost* resource as a *Budget Cost* resource, double-click on the name of the *Cost* resource and select the *Budget* option on the *General* page of the *Resource Information* dialog.

Module 07

Project Assignment Planning

Learning Objectives

After completing this module, you will be able to:

- Understand work estimation techniques
- Assign resources to tasks using the Task Entry view and the Assign Resources dialog
- Understand and use Task Types
- Change the Cost Rate Table for an assignment
- Use Effort-Driven scheduling to shorten task Duration
- Assign a Material resource to tasks
- Assign Budget Cost and Expense Cost resources to tasks
- Use filtering and graphing in the Assign Resources dialog
- Use the Team Planner view to analyze resource allocation
- Locate and level resource overallocations in Resource views and in Task views
- Understand how Manually Scheduled tasks interact with resource assignments

Inside Module 07

Understanding Assignments

After you complete task and resource planning, you are ready to make assignments. When you assign a resource to a task, Microsoft Project 2010 creates an assignment in the Microsoft Project Data Model, as shown in Figure 7 - 1. A good way to think of an assignment is "who does what, when, and how much on a task." When thinking about assignments, keep in mind that there may be many assignments related to one task. Each resource you assign to a task creates a new assignment.

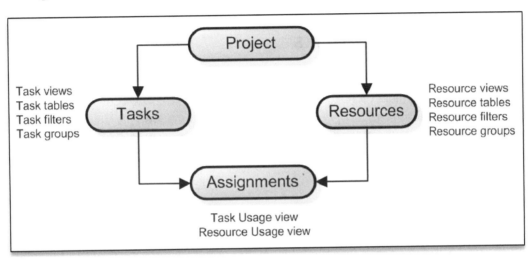

Figure 7 - 1: Complete Microsoft Project Data Model

Using a Work Estimation Methodology

In addition to the duration-based planning you performed in Module 05, Project Task Planning, you may also need to estimate work or effort prior to assigning resources to tasks. Determining a reasonable work estimate for a task assignment can be challenging, especially if the task is a new type never performed by any resource in your organization.

Some companies use specific rules or methodologies for work estimating. I describe these methodologies as the "4 and 40" rule or the "8 and 80" rule. In the "4 and 40" rule, for example, no resource may perform less than 4 hours of work on any task, nor perform more than 40 hours of work. If a task requires less than 4 hours of work, you should merge the task with another task. If a task requires more than 40 hours of work, then you should split the task into one or more tasks that require 40 hours of work or less. The "8 and 80" rule follows the same type of restrictions: no less than 8 hours of work for a resource on a task, and no more than 80 hours of work.

Assigning Resources Using a Best Practice

The Project Management Institute (PMI) recommends that you involve resources in the estimating process by asking them to propose work estimates on their task assignments. This is a best practice for the following reasons:

- Based on their skills, knowledge, and experience, your resources' work estimates are more accurate than "pulling a number out of thin air."

- Getting work estimates from your resources gives you their "buy in" and gives them a sense of ownership in the project.

- It is easier to hold a resource to a work estimate if the resource actually provided the estimate.

- Resources are more likely to give you accurate progress reports on tasks for which they provided the work estimates.

If it is not possible to involve the resources in the estimating process, get the work estimates from Subject Matter Experts (SME), such as team leaders, and then allow the resources to approve the estimates.

Assigning Resources to Tasks

After you enter project team members in the *Resource Sheet* view of your project, you are ready to assign team members to tasks. Like all previous versions of the tool, Microsoft Project 2010 offers two powerful tools for assigning resources to tasks, but the method you use to apply these tools is different than in all previous versions of the software. These two powerful resource assignment tools are:

- *Task Entry* view

- *Assign Resources* dialog

In addition to the *Task Entry* view and the *Assign Resources* dialog, Microsoft Project 2010 also includes a new *Team Planner* view that you can use to analyze resource assignments. In the remainder of this module, I present an in-depth treatment of how to use each of these tools for assignment planning and analysis, along with additional information on how to level resource overallocations.

Warning: During the resource assignment process, **do not** assign resources to summary tasks, as this greatly increases the work hours and costs for your project. Instead, if you need to show a resource as the responsible person for a summary section of the project, use the built-in *Contact* field, create a custom field and name it *Responsible Person*, or assign the resource to the milestone for the summary section of that project.

Using the Task Entry View

The *Task Entry* view is the most powerful way to assign resources to tasks because it gives you total control over all of the attributes in the Microsoft Project 2010 scheduling engine. Using the *Task Entry* view, you can do all of the following in a single location:

- Assign multiple resources simultaneously, and specify different *Units* and *Work* values for each resource.

- Enter the *Duration* of the task.

- Set the *Task Type* for the task to determine whether the software fixes or "locks" the *Units*, *Work*, or *Duration* value for the task.

- Specify the *Effort Driven* status of the task to determine what happens when you add or remove resources on the task.

- Set the *Task Mode* for the task as either *Manually Scheduled* or *Auto Scheduled.*

The only disadvantage of using the *Task Entry* view is that you cannot assign resources to multiple tasks simultaneously. This means that you cannot use the *Task Entry* view to assign resources to a *recurring* task, for example.

To apply the *Task Entry* view, complete the following steps:

1. Click the *Task* tab and then click the *Gantt Chart* button (if you do not have the *Gantt Chart* view displayed already).

2. Click the *View* tab to apply the *View* ribbon.

3. Select the *Details* checkbox in the *Split View* section of the *View* ribbon. Microsoft Project 2010 displays the *Task Entry* view, shown in Figure 7 - 2.

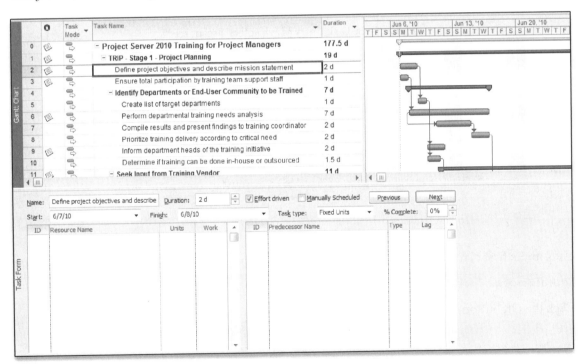

Figure 7 - 2: Task Entry view

If you have the *Timeline* view displayed along with the *Gantt Chart* view, Microsoft Project 2010 must close the *Timeline* view before it can display the *Task Entry* view.

The *Task Entry* view is a combination view consisting of two other views, each displayed in a separate pane. The *Task Entry* view includes the *Gantt Chart* view in the top pane and the *Task Form* view in the bottom pane. To assign a resource to a task using the *Task Entry* view, take the following steps:

1. Select a single task in the *Gantt Chart* pane.

2. In the *Task Form* pane, select the first blank cell in the *Resource Name* column and then click the pick list button in that cell. The software displays the list of resources you added to the *Resource Sheet* view, as shown in Figure 7 - 3.

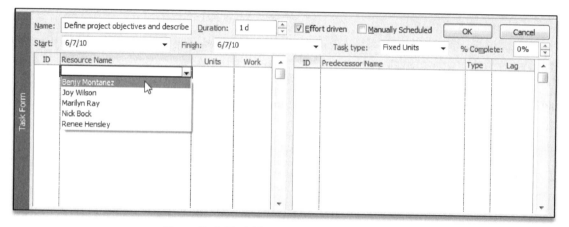

Figure 7 - 3: Task Entry view, select a resource

3. Click the first blank cell in the *Units* column and then select or enter a *Units* value for the selected resource.

In the *Units* column, you can use the spin control feature to select a value, but Microsoft Project 2010 displays only *Units* values in 50% increments (0%, 50%, 100%, etc.). For *Units* values you cannot select using the spin control feature, such as 25% or 75%, you must manually type the *Units* value you need.

4. Click in the first blank cell in the *Work* column and enter the estimated work hours for that resource.

5. Repeat steps #2-4 for each additional resource you wish to assign to the task.

6. Click the *OK* button.

Warning: Do not click the *OK* button in the *Task Form* pane until you finish selecting **all** of the resources you need and finish setting both the *Units* and *Work* values for each resource.

Microsoft Project 2010 assigns the resource to the task and then calculates the *Duration* value based on the *Units* and *Work* values you enter. Notice in Figure 7 - 4 that I assigned Benjy Montanez at *50%* Units and *16* hours of *Work*, and based on these two numbers, the software calculated a *Duration* value of *4 days* for the task. Notice also that the software changed the *OK* and *Cancel* buttons to the *Previous* and *Next* buttons. Using the *Previous* and *Next* buttons, you can navigate easily from task to task during the assignment process.

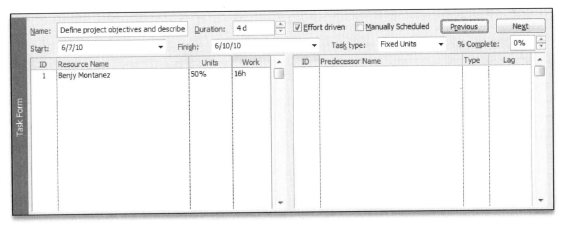

**Figure 7 - 4: Task Entry view, Duration calculated
after assigning a resource with Units and Work**

7.   Click the *Next* button to select the next task in the project and to continue assigning resources to tasks.

To assign resources to a task for which you already entered an estimated *Duration* value previously, complete the following steps:

1.   In the *Gantt Chart* pane, select the task with the estimated *Duration* value.

2.   In the *Task Form* pane, select the name of a resource from the list in the *Resource Name* column.

3.   Enter a *Units* value for the resource in the *Units* column.

4.   **Do not** enter a *Work* value.

5.   Repeat steps #2-4 for each additional resource you wish to assign to the task.

6.   Click the *OK* button.

Microsoft Project 2010 calculates the *Work* value for each resource assigned to the task. Notice in Figure 7 - 5 that I assigned three resources to work full-time on the task with a *Duration* value of *10 days*, so the software calculated *80 hours* in the *Work* column for each resource.

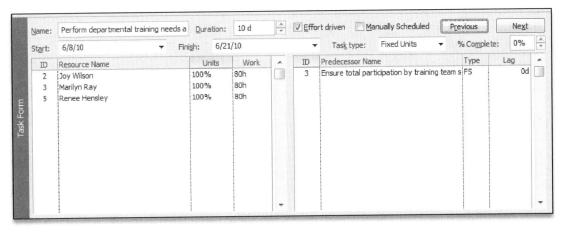

**Figure 7 - 5: Task Entry view, Work calculated after
assigning resources with Units and Duration**

Hands On Exercise

Exercise 7-1

The assignment process is already under way in the Training Advisor Rollout project, with resources assigned to all tasks in the *Installation* phase of the project. Apply the *Task Entry* view and then assign resources to the remaining tasks in the project.

1. Open the **Training Advisor 07.mpp** sample file.

2. Click the *View* tab to display the *View* ribbon.

3. In the *Split View* section of the *View* ribbon, select the *Details* checkbox to apply the *Task Entry* view.

Notice that the *Task Entry* view is a combination view, consisting of the *Gantt Chart* view in the top pane with the *Task Form* view in the bottom pane.

Testing phase: Members of the *NetOps* team have very limited availability to work in the Training Advisor Rollout project, but provided work estimates for the tasks they must perform in this project. Assign resources to tasks in the *Testing* phase of the project.

4. In the *Gantt Chart* pane, select task ID #23, the *Install Training Advisor Clients* task.

5. In the *Task Form* pane, click the pick list on the first blank line of the *Resource Name* column and select *Dave Harbaugh* from the list of project team members.

6. Set the *Units* value to *50%*, enter a *Work* value of *48 hours*, and then click the *OK* button to complete the assignment.

7. In the *Task Form*, click the *Next* button to select task ID #24, the *Verify Connectivity* task.

8. Assign *Mike Andrews* to the *Verify Connectivity* task at *50%* units and *40 hours* of work, and then click the *OK* button.

9. Click the *Next* button to select task ID #25, the *Resolve Connectivity Errors* task.

10. Assign *Bob Jared* to the *Resolve Connectivity Errors* task at *25%* units and *40 hours* of work, and then click the *OK* button.

For the last three tasks, notice how Microsoft Project 2010 calculated a *Duration* value for the task based on the values you entered in the *Units* and *Work* columns for the assignment.

Training phase: Continue assigning resources to tasks in the *Training* phase of the Training Advisor Rollout project.

11. In the *Gantt Chart* pane, select task ID #34, the *Conduct Skills Assessment* task.

12. Assign *Chuck Kirkpatrick* and *Kent Bergstrand* to the *Conduct Skills Assessment* task at *50%* units each and *40 hours* of work each, and then click the *OK* button.

13. Click the *Next* button to task ID #35, the *Create Training Schedule* task.

14. Assign *Kent Bergstrand* to the *Create Training Schedule* task at *25%* units and then click the *OK* button (**do not** enter a value in the *Work* column).

Since you previously estimated the *Duration* value of *5 days* for this task during the task planning process, notice how Microsoft Project 2010 calculates a *10 hour* value in the *Work* field automatically.

15. **Deselect** the *Details* checkbox in the *Split View* section of the *View* ribbon to close the *Task Form* pane.

16. Scroll back to the top of the task list in your Training Advisor Rollout project.

17. Save but **do not** close the **Training Advisor 07.mpp** sample file.

Using the Assign Resources Dialog

The *Assign Resources* dialog is a second tool you can use in the assignment process. The *Assign Resources* dialog is ideal for assigning resources to recurring tasks, such as meetings, because it allows you to select and assign multiple resources to the recurring task. The *Assign Resources* dialog is also ideal for assigning one or more resources to multiple tasks simultaneously, and for replacing one resource with another on multiple tasks simultaneously. Although the *Assign Resources* dialog offers you a simple interface to assign resources to tasks quickly, keep in mind that it does not have all of the options available in the *Task Entry* view.

Using the *Assign Resources* dialog, you have no control over most of the attributes of the scheduling engine. This means you cannot specify the *Duration*, the *Work*, the *Task Type*, the *Effort Driven* status, or the *Task Mode* for a task. Furthermore, you cannot assign multiple resources to a task and individually select different *Units* values for each resource. To display the *Assign Resources* dialog, use one of the following methods:

- Click the *Resource* tab and then click the *Assign Resources* button in the *Assignment* section of the *Resource* ribbon.

- Right-click on any task and then select the *Assign Resources* item on the shortcut menu.

Microsoft Project 2010 displays the *Assign Resources* dialog, as shown in Figure 7 - 6.

In the *Assign Resources* dialog, the system sorts the resources in ascending order by the *Resource Name* column , and **not** in the order they appear on the *Resource Sheet* view of your project.

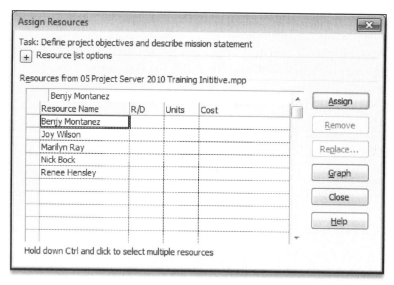

Figure 7 - 6: Assign Resources dialog

To assign a resource to tasks using the *Assign Resources* dialog, complete the following steps:

1. Select one or more tasks.

2. Select a single resource in the list of resources shown in the dialog.

3. Select or enter a *Units* value (if different than *100%* units).

4. Click the *Assign* button.

The *Assign Resources* dialog indicates that you assigned the resource to the selected tasks by moving the assigned resource to the beginning of the list, and by adding a checkmark indicator to the left of the resource's name. Notice in Figure 7 - 7, for example, that I assigned Nick Bock to work full time (*100%* units) on the selected task. If you previously entered cost rates for your resources in the *Std. Rate* column of the *Resource Sheet* view, Microsoft Project 2010 also calculates a cost value in the *Cost* column of the *Assign Resources* dialog for each assigned resource. Notice in Figure 7 - 7 that Nick Bock's assignment on the selected task costs the project *$800*, as indicated in the *Cost* column.

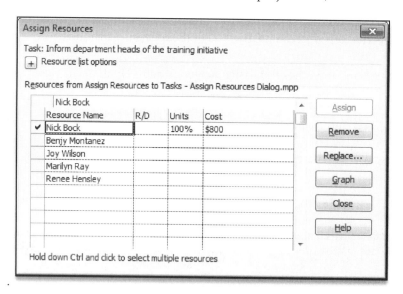

Figure 7 - 7: Assign Resources dialog
with one resource assigned to a task

To assign multiple resources to tasks using the *Assign Resources* dialog, complete the following steps:

1. Select one or more tasks.

2. In the *Assign Resources* dialog, select multiple resources using either the **Control** key or the **Shift** key on your computer keyboard.

3. **Do not** set a *Units* value for any resource.

4. Click the *Assign* button.

If you do not enter a *Units* value when assigning a resource in the *Assign Resources* dialog, Microsoft Project 2010 enters the *Max. Units* value for the resource from the *Resource Sheet* view of your project. This means that if the *Max. Units* value for a resource is *50%*, and you do not supply a *Units* value when assigning this resource, the *Assign Resources* dialog assigns the resource with a *Units* value of *50%* automatically. The exception to this rule is for generic resources that have a *Max. Units* value greater than 100%. In this case, if you do not supply a *Units* value for the generic resource, the *Assign Resources* dialog assigns the generic resource with a *Units* value of only *100%* automatically.

Warning: Do not use the *Assign Resources* dialog to assign multiple resources to a task that requires using a different *Units* value for each resource. The software assigns the first resource at the *Units* value you select and then adds each of the other resources as **helpers** on the task using *Effort Driven* scheduling, decreasing the *Duration* of the task accordingly. This behavior is one of the major reasons that new users find Microsoft Project 2010 so frustrating! Instead, use the *Task Entry* view when you need to assign multiple resources with different *Units* values.

Hands On Exercise

Exercise 7-2

Assign resources to tasks in the Training Advisor Rollout project using the *Assign Resources* dialog.

1. Return to the **Training Advisor 07.mpp** sample file.

2. Click the *Resource* tab and then click the *Assign Resources* button in the *Assignment* section of the *Resource* ribbon.

3. Select task ID #1, the *Project Status Meeting* recurring task.

4. In the *Assign Resources* dialog, use the **Control** key on your computer keyboard to select the following resources as a group:

   • Carolyn Fross – administrative assistant

   • Helen Howard – NetOps team leader

   • Melena Keeth – TechEd team leader

- Richard Sanders – project manager

- Vicky Joslyn – Test team leader

5. Click the *Assign* button to assign these five resources to the *Project Status Meeting* recurring task.

Notice how Microsoft Project 2010 assigned these five resources at a *Units* value of *100%* since you did not supply a *Units* value for any of them in the *Assign Resources* dialog.

6. Click the *expand* symbol (the **+** sign) to the left of the *Project Status Meeting* recurring task to expand the occurrences of this recurring task.

Notice that although you **do not** see the resources assigned to the *Project Status Meeting* recurring task itself, you **do see** the resources assigned to each of the individual occurrences of the recurring task.

7. Click the *collapse* symbol (the **-** sign) to the left of the *Project Status Meeting* recurring task to collapse the occurrences of this recurring task.

8. Select task ID #30-32, from the *Create Training Module 01* task to the *Create Training Module 03* task.

9. In the *Assign Resources* dialog, select the *Training Developer* resource, enter a *Units* value of *100%*, and click the *Assign* button.

After completing the training materials and setting the training schedule, the company plans to offer three sets of concurrent training classes at three different locations on the corporate campus.

10. Select task ID #36, the *Provide End User Training* task.

11. In the *Assign Resources* dialog, use the **Control** key on your computer keyboard to select the following resources as a group:

- Chuck Kirkpatrick

- Kent Bergstrand

- Ruth Andrews

12. Click the *Assign* button to assign these three resources to the *Provide End User Training* task.

13. Click the *Close* button to close the *Assign Resources* dialog.

14. Save but **do not** close the **Training Advisor 07.mpp** sample file.

Understanding the Duration Equation

When you assign a resource to a task using the *Task Entry* view, and you enter a *Units* value and a *Work* value for the resource, Microsoft Project 2010 calculates the *Duration* value for the task automatically. How does the software calculate duration? The software uses a simple formula known as the **Duration Equation**, written as follows:

$$\mathbf{Duration} = \mathbf{Work} \div (\mathbf{Hours\ Per\ Day} \times \mathbf{Units})$$

or

$$D = W \div (HPD \times U)$$

The default *Hours Per Day* value is 8 hours per day. You can locate this value by clicking the *File* tab and then clicking the *Options* item in the *Backstage* menu. In the *Project Options* dialog, click the *Schedule* tab. You find the *Hours per day* option in the *Calendar options for this project* section, as shown in Figure 7 - 8.

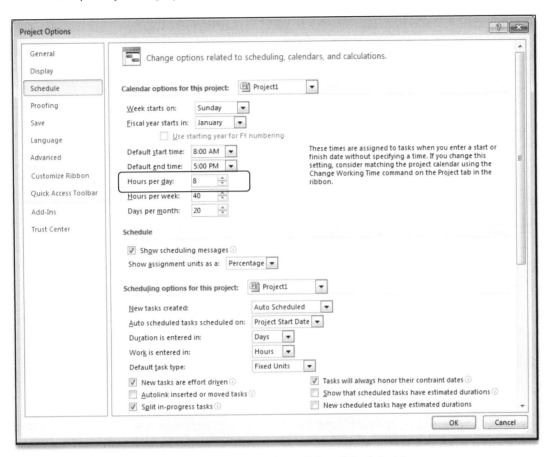

**Figure 7 - 8: Project Options dialog, Schedule tab
shows the Hours per day setting**

To demonstrate how the Duration Equation works, I assign a resource to a task at *50% Units* and *40 hours* of *Work*. Using the Duration Equation, Microsoft Project 2010 calculates the *Duration* value at *10 days* as follows:

$$D = W \div (HPD \times U)$$

$$D = 40 \div (8 \times 50\%)$$

$$D = 40 \div 4 = 10 \text{ days}$$

When you assign a resource to a task and enter *Duration* and *Units* values (rather than *Units* and *Work* values), Microsoft Project 2010 calculates the *Work* value. How does the software calculate work? The software uses a modified version of the Duration Equation, rewritten to solve for the *Work* variable as follows:

$$\textbf{W}ork = \textbf{D}uration \times \textbf{H}ours \textbf{ P}er \textbf{ D}ay \times \textbf{U}nits$$

or

$$W = D \times HPD \times U$$

For example, I assign a resource to work *50% Units* on a task with a *Duration* value of *10 days*, Microsoft Project 2010 calculates *40 hours* of *Work* as follows:

W = D × HPD × U

W = 10 × 8 × 50%

W = 10 × 4 = 40 hours

You can also rewrite the Duration Equation to solve for the *Units* variable as follows:

$$\text{Units} = \text{Work} \div (\text{Duration} \times \text{Hours per Day})$$

or

$$U = W \div (D \times HPD)$$

For example, I assign a resource *40 hours* of *Work* on a task with a *Duration* value of *10 days*, Microsoft Project 2010 calculates a *Units* value of 50% as follows:

U = W ÷ (D × HPD)

U = 40 ÷ (10 × 8)

U = 40 ÷ 80 = .5 or 50%

Understanding Task Types

You can specify the *Task Type* setting for any task to one of three types: *Fixed Units, Fixed Work,* or *Fixed Duration.* You can select **only one** *Task Type* setting for each task. The default *Task Type* setting for every task is *Fixed Units,* unless you specify otherwise in the *Project Options* dialog. To specify the *Task Type* setting for any task, select the task and then use one of the following methods:

- Apply the *Task Entry* view. In the *Task Form,* click the *Task Type* pick list and select the desired *Task Type* setting.

- Double-click the task and then click the *Advanced* tab in the *Task Information* dialog. Click the *Task Type* pick list and select the desired *Task Type* setting.

- Click the *Information* button in the *Properties* section of the *Task* ribbon and then click the *Advanced* tab in the *Task Information* dialog. Click the *Task Type* pick list and select the desired *Task Type* setting.

- Right-click on the task and then select the *Information* item on the shortcut menu. In the *Task Information* dialog, click the *Advanced* tab. Click the *Task Type* pick list and select the desired *Task Type* setting.

> You can also specify the *Task Type* setting for multiple tasks simultaneously by selecting a group of tasks first. Click the *Information* button in the *Properties* section of the *Task* ribbon and then click the *Advanced* tab in the *Multiple Task Information* dialog. Click the *Task Type* pick list and select the desired *Task Type* setting for the selected tasks.

Specify the *Task Type* setting for tasks using the following information as your guide:

- **Fixed Units** – Microsoft Project 2010 locks the *Units* value for all resources assigned to a *Fixed Units* task. Set the *Task Type* option to *Fixed Units* when a resource has a known availability to perform work on tasks in your project. For example, you assign a resource to work on a task at *50% Units* because the resource also works half time on the Help Desk. Use the *Fixed Units* task type on this task to guarantee that the software does not recalculate the *50% Units* value if you change either the *Work* or *Duration* values on the task.

- **Fixed Work** – The software locks the *Work* value for all resources assigned to a *Fixed Work* task. Set the *Task Type* option to *Fixed Work* when you are certain about the number of hours to complete a task. For example, you hire a consultant to work on a project task, and the work is set at 40 hours by contract. Use the *Fixed Work* task type on this task to guarantee that Microsoft Project 2010 does not recalculate the *40 hours* of *Work* if you change either the *Units* or *Duration* values on the task.

- **Fixed Duration** – The software locks the *Duration* value on a *Fixed Duration* task. Set the *Task Type* to *Fixed Duration* when you are certain of the *Duration* value for a task, such as when you have a known "window of opportunity" to complete the task. For example, you have a task called Shareholder Conference and the conference lasts 3 days. Use the *Fixed Duration* task type on this task to guarantee that the software does not recalculate the *Duration* value of *3 days* if you change either the *Units* or *Work* values on the task.

The *Task Type* setting you select fixes or "locks" one of the three variables in the Duration Equation for the selected task. When you change one of the two non-fixed variables, Microsoft Project 2010 calculates the other non-fixed variable automatically. Table 7 - 1 shows the behavior of all three Task Types when you change the non-fixed variable, and when you change the fixed variable as well.

Task Type	Fixed Variable	You Change	Recalculated Variable
Fixed Units	Units	Work	Duration
Fixed Units	Units	Duration	Work
Fixed Work	Work	Units	Duration
Fixed Work	Work	Duration	Units
Fixed Duration	Duration	Units	Work
Fixed Duration	Duration	Work	Units
Fixed Units	Units	Units	Duration
Fixed Work	Work	Work	Duration
Fixed Duration	Duration	Duration	Work

Table 7 - 1: Task Type behavior

The only exception to the Task Type behavior documented in Table 7 - 1 occurs when you initially assign a resource to a *Fixed Duration* task and enter a value in the *Work* field. In this situation, Microsoft Project 2010 does the following:

- In the *Units* field in the *Task Form* pane, the software enters the *Max. Units* value for the resource from the *Resource Sheet* view of your project.

- In the background, the software calculates the correct *Units* value, but does not display it in the *Units* field in the *Task Form* pane. Instead, the software stores this value in the *Peak* field, which you cannot see in the *Task Form* pane.

- The software assigns the resource using the correctly calculated *Units* value stored in the *Peak* field.

If you want to see the values in the *Units* and *Peak* fields, you can add the *Assignment Units* field and the *Peak* field to the *Task Usage* view of your project. At this point, however, do not despair. I provide an in-depth discussion of the behavior of the *Assignment Units* and *Peak* fields in the next section of this module.

When you change a non-fixed variable for any task type Microsoft Project 2010 automatically recalculates the other non-fixed variable. When you change the **fixed** variable, however, the software invokes one of the programming decisions implemented by the Microsoft Project software development team many years ago. For example, which variable should the software recalculate when you change the *Units* value on a *Fixed Units* task, or change the *Work* value on a *Fixed Work* task, or change the *Duration* value on a *Fixed Duration* task?

We refer to the decisions made by the software development team as the Microsoft Project programming biases. These programming biases are as follows:

- If you change the *Units* variable on a *Fixed Units* task, Microsoft Project 2010 **always** recalculates the *Duration* variable.

- If you change the *Work* variable on a *Fixed Work* task, Microsoft Project 2010 **always** recalculates the *Duration* variable.

- If you change the *Duration* variable on a *Fixed Duration* task, Microsoft Project 2010 **always** recalculates the *Work* variable.

As you can see, Microsoft Project 2010 has a bias to calculate changes in *Duration* rather than to *Work* or *Units*. If the software cannot change *Duration*, it has a bias to calculate changes in *Work* rather than *Units*.

Hands On Exercise

Exercise 7-3

Learn more about *Task Types* by changing the variables in the Duration Equation for tasks with different *Task Types*.

1. Open the **Understanding Task Types.mpp** sample file.

2. In the *Task Usage* pane, select the *Fixed Units 1* task.

3. Click the *Task* tab and then click the *Scroll to Task* button in the *Editing* section of the *Task* ribbon to show the timephased *Work* hours in the timephased grid (right side of the view).

4. In the *Task Form* pane, change the *Work* value to *48h* and then click the *OK* button.

5. Click the *Next* button in the *Task Form* pane to select the *Fixed Units 2* task.

6. In the *Task Form* pane, change the *Duration* value to *8d* and then click the *OK* button.

For this *Fixed Units* task, notice that when you change the *Work* variable, Microsoft Project 2010 recalculates the *Duration* variable, and when you change the *Duration* variable, the system recalculates the *Work* variable.

7. Click the *Next* button in the *Task Form* pane to select the *Fixed Units 3* task.

8. In the *Task Form* pane, change the *Units* value to *100%* and then click the *OK* button.

For this *Fixed Units* task, notice that when you change the *Units* variable, Microsoft Project 2010 recalculates the *Duration* variable. This behavior is the first of three programming biases I discussed in the previous topical subsection.

9. Click the *Next* button in the *Task Form* pane to select the *Fixed Work 1* task.

10. In the *Task Form* pane, change the *Units* value to *100%* and then click the *OK* button.

For this *Fixed Work* task, notice that when you change the *Units* variable, Microsoft Project 2010 recalculates the *Duration* variable.

11. Click the *Next* button in the *Task Form* pane to select the *Fixed Work 2* task.

12. In the *Task Form* pane, change the *Duration* value to *5d* and then click the *OK* button.

For this *Fixed Work* task, notice that when you change the *Duration* variable, Microsoft Project 2010 **did not** re-calculate the *Units* variable as expected. Or **did it** change the *Units* variable, but the system does not display the recalculated *Units* variable in the *Task Form* pane?

13. Drag the split bar to the right side of the *Peak* column.

14. Scroll down to view the assignment information for *Debbie Kirkpatrick* on the *Fixed Work 2* task, if necessary.

Notice in the *Task Usage* pane that Microsoft Project 2010 now includes **two fields** relating to the assignment units: the *Assignment Units* field and the *Peak* field. The *Units* value you see in the *Task Form* pane is actually the *Assignment Units* field, which shows the **original** *Units* value on the task (*50%*). The *Peak* field contains the **new** *Units* value after you changed the *Duration* value on the *Fixed Work* task. Notice that the *Peak* field shows the **correct** *Units* value of *100%*. Notice also in the timephased grid on the right side of the view that the system schedules the *Work* hours correctly at 8 hours per day based on the 100% *Units* value in the *Peak* field. Therefore, even though the *Units* value does not seem to be correct in the *Task Form* pane (*50%*), the software **does schedule the task correctly** using the value shown in the *Peak* field (*100%*).

Warning: If you are a previous user of any prior version of Microsoft Project, you undoubtedly find the new behavior of the *Units* field in the *Task Form* pane **confusing**, along with the interaction between the *Assignment Units* field and the *Peak* field. Because of this, I provide an in-depth treatment of the *Peak* field and the *Assignment Units* field in the next topical subsection of this module.

15. Click the *Next* button in the *Task Form* pane to select the *Fixed Work 3* task.

16. In the *Task Form* pane, change the *Work* value to *32h* and then click the *OK* button.

For this *Fixed Work* task, notice that when you change the *Work* variable, Microsoft Project 2010 recalculates the *Duration* variable. This behavior is the second of three programming biases I discussed in the previous topical subsection.

17. Click the *Next* button in the *Task Form* pane to select the *Fixed Duration 1* task.

18. In the *Task Form* pane, change the *Units* value to *100%* and then click the *OK* button.

For this *Fixed Duration* task, notice that when you change the *Units* variable, Microsoft Project 2010 recalculates the *Work* variable.

19. Click the *Next* button in the *Task Form* pane to select the *Fixed Duration 2* task.

20. In the *Task Form* pane, change the *Work* value to *60h* and then click the *OK* button.

For this *Fixed Duration* task, notice that when you change the *Work* variable, Microsoft Project 2010 **did not** recalculate the *Units* variable. Once again, examine the *Task Usage* pane and notice that the *Peak* field contains the expected value of *75%*. Notice also in the timephased grid that the system schedules the *Work* hours correctly at 6 hours per day based on the *75%* value in the *Peak* field.

21. Click the *Next* button in the *Task Form* pane to select the *Fixed Duration 3* task.

22. In the *Task Form* pane, change the *Duration* value to *6d* and then click the *OK* button.

For this *Fixed Duration* task, notice that when you change the *Duration* variable, Microsoft Project 2010 recalculates the *Work* variable. This behavior is the final of three programming biases I discussed in the previous topical subsection.

23. Click the *View* tab and then deselect the *Details* checkbox in the *Split View* section of the *View* ribbon.

24. Save but **do not** close the **Understanding Task Types.mpp** sample file.

Understanding the Peak and Assignment Units Fields

As you now know after completing the previous Hands On Exercise, Microsoft made a major change in how Microsoft Project 2010 uses the *Units* field in the *Task Form* pane. To gain a thorough understanding of this behavior, it helps to understand how the software works when you initially assign a resource to a task. Suppose that I assign Mickey Cobb to the Design task at *100% Units* and *40 hours* of *Work*, as shown in Figure 7 - 9. Notice that Microsoft Project 2010 calculates a *Duration* value of *5 days* for this *Fixed Work* task.

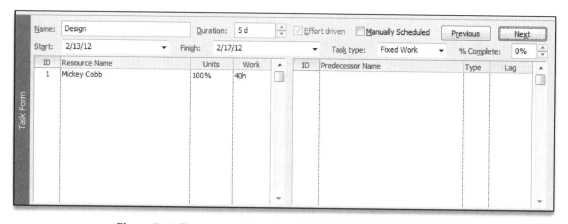

Figure 7 - 9: Resource assigned at 100% Units to the Design task

When I assign Mickey Cobb to the Design task at 100% *Units*, the system creates a resource assignment on the task and captures the original *Units* value of *100%*. You can see the resource assignment information in either the *Task Usage* view or *Resource Usage* view of a project. Figure 7 - 10 shows the initial assignment information for Mickey Cobb's resource assignment on the Design task in the *Task Usage* view of my project. Notice that the system assigns the 40 hours of work using a flat pattern of 8 hours/day over the 5-day duration of the task.

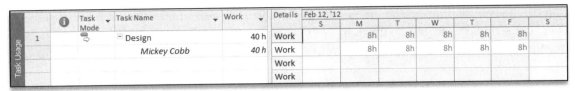

Figure 7 - 10: Task Usage view shows the resource assignment information

Although not displayed by default in either the *Task Usage* view or *Resource Usage* view, Microsoft Project 2010 offers several additional assignment fields you can use to understand how the software handles the original *Units* value on the resource assignment. These additional fields include:

- *Assignment Units* (an assignment field)

- *Peak* (an assignment field)

- *Percent Allocation* (a timephased assignment field)

- *Peak Units* (a timephased assignment field)

To add the *Assignment Units* field to the *Task Usage* view, right-click on the *Work* column header. The system displays the shortcut menu shown in Figure 7 - 11.

Figure 7 - 11: Shortcut menu to add a new field

Click the *Insert Column* item in the shortcut menu and then select the *Assignment Units* field from the lengthy pick list displayed by the system. Microsoft Project 2010 inserts the *Assignment Units* field to the left of the *Work* field, as shown in Figure 7 - 12.

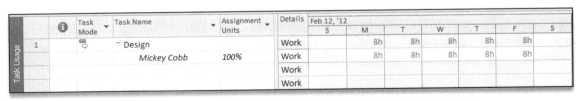

Figure 7 - 12: Assignment Units column added to the Task Usage view

After adding the *Assignment Units* field to the *Task Usage* view, you can also add the *Percent Allocation* timephased assignment field to the timephased grid on the right side of the view. To add the *Percent Allocation* field, right-click anywhere in the timephased grid. On the shortcut menu, select the *Detail Styles* item at the top of the menu, as shown in Figure 7 - 13.

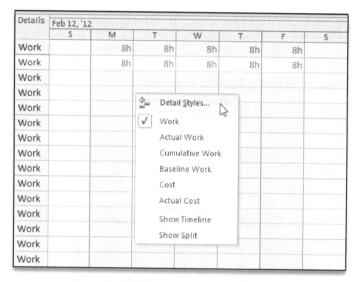

**Figure 7 - 13: Shortcut menu to add a new
timephased field to the timephased grid**

The system displays the *Detail Styles* dialog shown in Figure 7 - 14. The *Detail Styles* dialog shows you the list of all available timephased fields in the *Available Fields* list on the left side of the dialog.

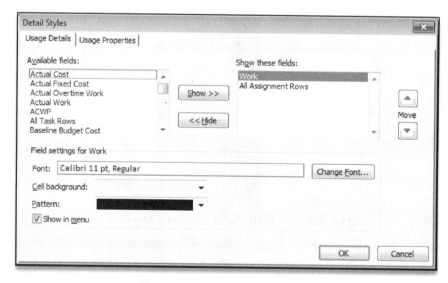

Figure 7 - 14: Detail Styles dialog

In the *Detail Styles* dialog, scroll to the bottom of the *Available Fields* list and select the *Percent Allocation* field. Click the *Show* button to add the *Percent Allocation* field to the *Show These Fields* list. Click the *OK* button to add the *Percent Allocation* timephased assignment field to the timephased grid, as shown in Figure 7 - 15.

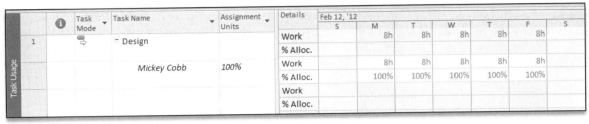

Figure 7 - 15: Percent Allocation field added to the timephased grid

When I assigned Mickey Cobb to the Design task, I assigned her at 100% *Units*, which represents the **original** *Units* value for her task assignment. Notice in Figure 7 - 15 shown previously that the *Percent Allocation* timephased field shows the **original** *Units* value of 100% for Mickey Cobb's assignment on the Design task.

To add the *Peak* field to the *Task Usage* view, drag the split bar to the right of the *Work* column and then right-click the *Work* column header. Click the *Insert Column* item in the shortcut menu and then select the *Peak* field from the pick list. The system displays the *Peak* field to the right of the *Assignment Units* field, as shown in Figure 7 - 16. Notice that both the *Peak* field and the *Assignment Units* field show the same *Units* value of 100%.

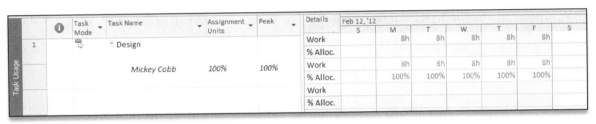

Figure 7 - 16: Peak field added to the Task Usage view

To add the *Peak Units* timephased assignment field to the *Task Usage* view, right-click in the timephased grid and select the *Detail Styles* item at the top of the shortcut menu. In the *Detail Styles* dialog, select the *Peak Units* field from the *Available Fields* list. Click the *Show* button to add the *Peak Units* field to the *Show These Fields* list and then click the *OK* button to add the *Peak Units* timephased field to the timephased grid, as shown in Figure 7 - 17.

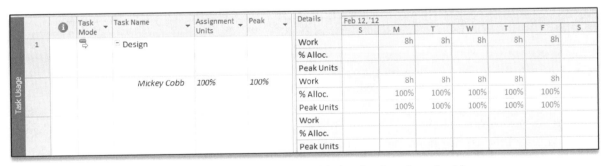

Figure 7 - 17: Peak Units field added to the timephased grid

When you make any change to the project that causes the Scheduling Engine to recalculate the *Units* value on the assignment, such as when you change the *Duration* value on a *Fixed Work* task, or you change the *Work* value on a *Fixed Duration* task, the system responds as follows:

- The system displays the **original** *Units* value in the *Assignment Units* field.

- The system captures the **recalculated** *Units* value in the *Peak* field.

- Using the **recalculated** *Units* value in the *Peak* field, the system reschedules the timephased work accordingly in the timephased grid.

For example, I change the value in the *Duration* field to *10 days*, as shown in Figure 7 - 18. Notice that Microsoft Project 2010 **does not** show the recalculated *Units* value in the *Task Form* pane.

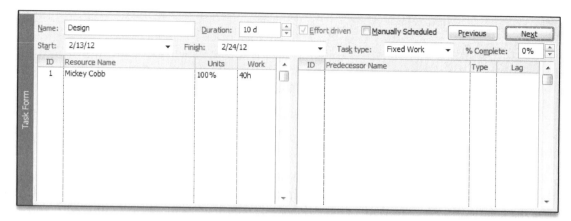

Figure 7 - 18: Change the Duration value to 10 days

Instead, Microsoft Project 2010 does the following in the *Task Usage* view shown in Figure 7 - 19:

- The system displays the **original** *Units* value of **100%** in the *Assignment Units* field.

- The system captures the **recalculated** *Units* value of **50%** in the *Peak* field.

- Using the new **50%** value in the *Peak* field, the system reschedules the timephased work at 4 hours per day in the timephased grid.

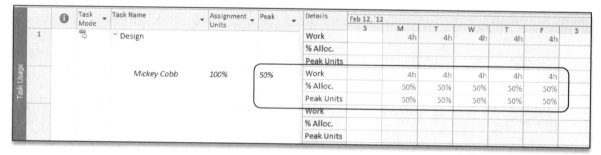

Figure 7 - 19: Peak field captures the recalculated Units value

Notice in Figure 7 - 19 shown previously that the timephased *Percent Allocation* field shows the correct assignment units value on Mickey Cobb's assignment in the timephased grid. Notice also that the system correctly schedules the timephased *Work* for this task at 4 hours per day using the 50% value.

Beyond the new behavior of the *Assignment Units* and *Peak* fields, as documented in this section of the module, you may see additional new behavior in Microsoft Project 2010 when you begin entering progress in your project. I provide thorough documentation about this additional new behavior in Module 08, Project Execution.

Hands On Exercise

Exercise 7-4

Study the *Assignment Units* and *Peak* fields in Microsoft Project 2010.

1. Return to the **Understanding Task Types.mpp** sample file.

2. Right-click anywhere in the timephased grid and select the *Detail Styles* item on the shortcut menu.

3. In the *Detail Styles* dialog, select the *Percent Allocation* field in the *Available fields* list and then click the *Show* button to add the field to the *Show these fields* list.

4. In the *Available fields* list, select the *Peak Units* field and then click the *Show* button.

5. Click the *OK* button.

6. In the timephased grid, double-click the right edge of the *Details* column header to "best fit" the column width.

7. Click the *Task* tab to display the *Task* ribbon.

8. Select the name of the assigned resource, *Debbie Kirkpatrick*, on the *Fixed Work 2* task and then click the *Scroll to Task* button in the *Editing* section of the *Task* ribbon.

9. Examine the values in the *Assignment Units* field (the **original** *Units* value) and the *Peak field* (**re-calculated** *Units* value) for *Debbie Kirkpatrick's* assignment on the *Fixed Work 2* task.

10. Examine the timephased *Work* and *Percent Allocation* fields in the timephased grid for *Debbie Kirkpatrick's* assignment as well.

11. Examine the values in the *Assignment Units* field and the *Peak* field for *Greg Owens'* assignment on the *Fixed Duration 2* task.

12. Examine the timephased *Work* and *Percent Allocation* fields in the timephased grid for *Greg Owens'* assignment as well.

13. Save and close the **Understanding Task Types.mpp** sample file.

Setting the Cost Rate Table

Microsoft Project 2010 offers you two special assignment views, the *Task Usage* and *Resource Usage* views, in which you can select the *Cost Rate Table* used to calculate the cost of an assignment. To apply the *Task Usage* view, use one of the following methods:

*   In the *View* section of the *Task* ribbon, click the *Gantt Chart* pick list button and select the *Task Usage* view from the list.

Module 07

- In the *Task Views* section of the *View* ribbon, click the *Task Usage* button.

Figure 7 - 20 shows the *Task Usage* view for a project. By default, the *Task Usage* view consists of the task *Usage* table on the left side and the timephased grid on the right side. The *Task Name* column shows a list of all project tasks, along with the resource assignments for each task. Below each task, the software indents the resource assignments one level, and formats them in italics to distinguish them from the tasks. The timephased grid displays the timephased *Work* field for each task and resource assignment, with the assigned work phased over time. Microsoft Project 2010 formats the timephased *Work* cells of each task using the gray cell background color and of each resource assignment using a white cell background color.

	ⓘ	Task Mode	Task Name	Work	Details	S	M	T	W	T	F	S
0			⁻ **Cost Rate Tables**	**480 h**	Work		8h	8h	8h	16h	16h	
1			⁻ **Phase I**	**240 h**	Work		8h	8h	8h	16h	16h	
2			⁻ Design P1	24 h	Work		8h	8h	8h			
			Cindy McNair	*24 h*	Work		8h	8h	8h			
3			⁻ Build P1	64 h	Work					16h	16h	
			Marcia Bickel	*32 h*	Work					8h	8h	
			Jerry King	*32 h*	Work					8h	8h	
4			⁻ Test P1	80 h	Work							
			Cindy McNair	*40 h*	Work							
			George Stewart	*40 h*	Work							
5			⁻ Implement P1	72 h	Work							
			George Stewart	*24 h*	Work							
			Steve Garcia	*24 h*	Work							
			Leanne Owens	*24 h*	Work							
6			Phase I Complete	0 h	Work							

Figure 7 - 20: Task Usage view

To apply the *Resource Usage* view, use one of the following methods:

- In the *View* section of the *Resource* ribbon, click the *Team Planner* pick list button and then select the *Resource Usage* view from the list.

- In the *Resource Views* section of the *View* ribbon, click the *Resource Usage* button.

Figure 7 - 21 shows the *Resource Usage* view. By default, the *Resource Usage* view consists of the resource *Usage* table on the left and the timephased grid on the right. The *Resource Name* column displays a list of all project resources, along with the task assignments for each resource. Below each resource, the software indents the task assignments one level, and formats them in italics to distinguish them from the resources. The timephased grid displays the timephased *Work* field for each resource and task assignment, with the assigned work phased over time. Microsoft Project 2010 formats the timephased *Work* cells of each resource using the gray cell background color and of each task assignment using a white cell background color.

In addition to the names of all resources in the project team, the *Resource Name* column includes an additional item named *Unassigned Resources*. This item displays tasks not yet assigned to any resource., such as milestone tasks. At the conclusion of the assignment planning process, the *Unassigned Resources* item should not include any regular tasks in your project, and should include only milestone tasks.

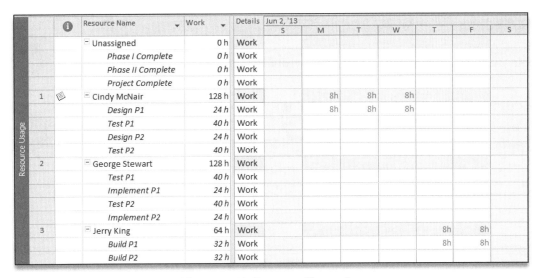

Figure 7 - 21: Resource Usage view

To see the cost of any assignment, complete the following steps:

1.   Apply either the *Task Usage* or *Resource Usage* view.

2.   Right-click on the *Select All* button and select the *Cost* table from the shortcut menu.

3.   Right-click anywhere in the timephased grid and then select the *Cost* details from the shortcut menu.

4.   Right-click anywhere in the timephased grid again and then deselect the *Work* details from the shortcut menu.

Figure 7 - 22 shows you the *Resource Usage* view with the *Cost* table applied, and with the timephased *Cost* field shown in the timephased grid.

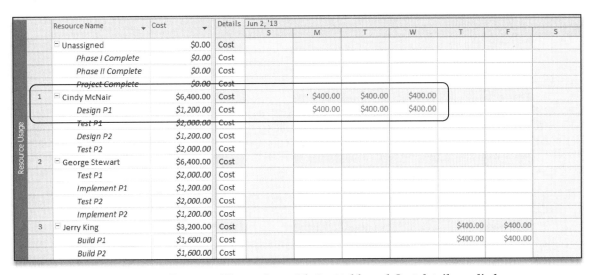

Figure 7 - 22: Resource Usage view with Cost table and Cost details applied

By default, Microsoft Project 2010 applies the *Standard Rate* value from *Cost Rate Table A* at the time you initially assign a resource to a task. After assigning the resource to a task, you can then modify the *Cost Rate Table* used to calculate the cost for that assignment. Notice in Figure 7 - 22 that cost for Cindy McNair's Design P1 task is $1,200, phased over time at $400.00 per day using her *Standard Rate* value of *$50/hour* on *Cost Rate Table A*. To change the *Cost Rate Table* for an assignment, complete the following steps:

1.   Apply either the *Task Usage* or *Resource Usage* view.

2.   Double-click the assignment for which you wish to change the *Cost Rate Table*.

The software displays the *Assignment Information* dialog shown in Figure 7 - 23.

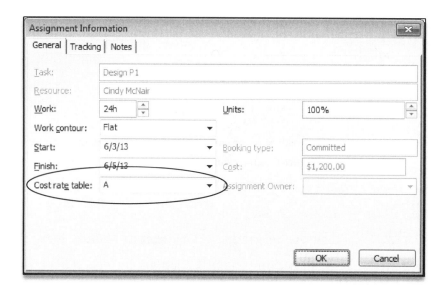

Figure 7 - 23: Assignment Information dialog

3.   Click the *Cost rate table* pick list button and then select an alternate *Cost Rate Table* value (*B* through *E*).

4.   Click the *OK* button.

> You can also display the *Assignment Information* dialog by right-clicking on an assignment and then selecting the *Information* item on the shortcut menu. If you select multiple assignments simultaneously, right-click on any of the selected assignments and select the *Information* item on the shortcut menu to display the *Multiple Assignment Information* dialog.

Microsoft Project 2010 automatically recalculates the cost for that assignment using the *Standard Rate* from the alternate *Cost Rate Table* you select. Figure 7 - 24 shows the *Resource Usage* view after selecting the *B* table in the *Cost rate table* field for Cindy McNair. Notice that the cost for Cindy McNair's Design P1 task is now $2,400, phased over time at $800.00 per day using her alternate rate of *$100/hour* on *Cost Rate Table B*.

Resource Name	Cost	Details	Jun 2, '13 S	M	T	W	T	F	S
⊟ Unassigned	$0.00	Cost							
Phase I Complete	$0.00	Cost							
Phase II Complete	$0.00	Cost							
Project Complete	$0.00	Cost							
⊟ Cindy McNair	$7,600.00	Cost		$800.00	$800.00	$800.00			
Design P1	$2,400.00	Cost		$800.00	$800.00	$800.00			
Test P1	$2,000.00	Cost							
Design P2	$1,200.00	Cost							
Test P2	$2,000.00	Cost							
⊟ George Stewart	$6,400.00	Cost							
Test P1	$2,000.00	Cost							
Implement P1	$1,200.00	Cost							
Test P2	$2,000.00	Cost							
Implement P2	$1,200.00	Cost							
⊟ Jerry King	$3,200.00	Cost					$400.00	$400.00	
Build P1	$1,600.00	Cost					$400.00	$400.00	
Build P2	$1,600.00	Cost							

Figure 7 - 24: Resource Usage view after selecting Cost Rate Table B rate

To change the *Cost Rate Table* for multiple assignments, the fastest method is to temporarily insert the *Cost Rate Table* column in either the *Task Usage* or *Resource Usage* view with the *Cost* table applied. To insert the *Cost Rate Table* column, right-click on the *Cost* column header, select the *Insert Column* item in the shortcut menu, and then select the *Cost Rate Table* field in the list of available fields. Figure 7 - 25 shows the *Resource Usage* view with the *Cost Rate Table* column inserted in the *Cost* table. Notice that the *Cost Rate Table* column shows that I selected *B* rate for Cindy McNair's Design P1 task. After inserting the *Cost Rate Table* column, you can use copy and paste or use the *Fill Handle* to copy the alternate *Cost Rate Table* selection to additional assignments.

Resource Name	Cost Rate Table	Cost	Details	Jun 2, '13 S	M	T	W	T	F
⊟ Unassigned		$0.00	Cost						
Phase I Complete	A	$0.00	Cost						
Phase II Complete	A	$0.00	Cost						
Project Complete	A	$0.00	Cost						
⊟ Cindy McNair		$7,600.00	Cost		$800.00	$800.00	$800.00		
Design P1	B	$2,400.00	Cost		$800.00	$800.00	$800.00		
Test P1	A	$2,000.00	Cost						
Design P2	A	$1,200.00	Cost						
Test P2	A	$2,000.00	Cost						
⊟ George Stewart		$6,400.00	Cost						
Test P1	A	$2,000.00	Cost						
Implement P1	A	$1,200.00	Cost						
Test P2	A	$2,000.00	Cost						
Implement P2	A	$1,200.00	Cost						
⊟ Jerry King		$3,200.00	Cost					$400.00	$400.00
Build P1	A	$1,600.00	Cost					$400.00	$400.00
Build P2	A	$1,600.00	Cost						

Figure 7 - 25: Resource Usage view with Cost Rate Table column inserted

Hands On Exercise

Exercise 7-5

Although Mike Andrews works primarily on the Help Desk, in the Training Advisor Rollout project he works on two tasks that involve testing work. For all testing tasks, you must cost Mike Andrews' assignments using the higher testing *Standard Rate* value specified on *Cost Rate Table B*.

1. Return to the **Training Advisor 07.mpp** sample file.

2. Click the *View* tab and then click the *Resource Usage* button in the *Resource Views* section of the *View* ribbon.

3. Click the *Task* tab to display the *Task* ribbon.

4. Right-click on the *Select All* button and select the *Cost* table on the shortcut menu.

5. Right-click anywhere in the timephased grid and select the *Cost* item in the shortcut menu.

6. Right-click again in the timephased grid and **deselect** the *Work* item in the shortcut menu.

7. Select resource ID #2, *Mike Andrews*, and then click the *Scroll to Task* button in the *Editing* section of the *Task* ribbon.

Notice the current cost information for Mike Andrews and for his task assignments in the *Cost* column of the *Cost* table and in the timephased *Cost* field shown in the timephased grid.

> Microsoft Project 2010 formats the name, Mike Andrews, in red because the system thinks that he is overallocated. This is because you assigned him to work on a task that occurs only on a Saturday and Sunday. Because these days are nonworking time, the system assumes he must be overallocated, which he is not! I discuss how to address this false overallocation in the last topical section of this module.

8. Double-click the *Perform Server Stress Test* task assignment for *Mike Andrews*.

9. In the *Assignment Information* dialog, click the *Cost rate table* pick list, select the *B* value, and then click the *OK* button.

Notice how Microsoft Project 2010 recalculates the cost of this task assignment using the *Standard Rate* value of *$50/hour* specified on *Cost Rate Table B*.

10. Select the *Verify Connectivity* task for *Mike Andrews* and then click the *Scroll to Task* button in the *Editing* section of the *Task* ribbon.

11. Right-click in the *Verify Connectivity* task for *Mike Andrews* and select the *Information* item on the shortcut menu.

12. In the *Assignment Information* dialog, click the *Cost rate table* pick list, select the *B* value, and then click the *OK* button.

13. Right-click anywhere in the timephased grid and select the *Work* item in the shortcut menu.

14. Right-click again in the timephased grid and **deselect** the *Cost* item in the shortcut menu.

15. Right-click on the *Select All* button and select the *Usage* table on the shortcut menu.

16. Save but **do not** close the **Training Advisor 07.mpp** sample file.

Assigning Material Resources

You use Material resources in a project to track project consumables. You can assign Material resources using either of two methods:

- Fixed consumption rate

- Variable consumption rate

You should assign a Material resource at a **fixed consumption rate** when the amount of the resource consumed does not depend upon the duration of the task. For example, when you assign the Material resource named Paper at "25 Reams" to a Project Administration task, this consumes 25 reams of paper, regardless of the duration of the task is 30 days or 12 months.

You should assign a Material resource at a **variable consumption rate** when the amount of the resource consumed depends directly on the duration of the task. For example, you assign the Material resource named Gasoline to the task Excavate Site at 100 gallons/day. You know that the excavation consumes 500 gallons in 5 days or 2,000 gallons in 20 days. When you assign a Material resource to a task, make sure that you pick the correct assignment method.

To assign Material resource to a task using either a fixed consumption rate or a variable consumption rate, complete the following steps:

1. Apply the *Gantt Chart* view.

2. In the *Split View* section of the *View* ribbon, select the *Details* checkbox to apply the *Task Entry* view.

3. Select a task in the *Gantt Chart* pane.

4. In the *Task Form* pane, select a Material resource from the pick list of resources in the *Resource Name* column.

5. Enter the consumption for the Material resource in the *Units* column.

To assign the Material resource using a fixed consumption rate, enter only a number in the *Units* field, such as **25** to the consumption of the resource at 25 units. To assign the Material resource using a variable consumption rate, enter a number plus a slash symbol plus a time period in the *Units* field, such as **100/d** to show the consumption of the resource at 100 units per day.

6. Click the *OK* button.

Microsoft Project 2010 shows the total consumption of the Material resource in the *Work* column of the *Task Form* pane. Figure 7 - 26 shows the fixed consumption assignment of the Paper resource to the Project Administration task. Figure 7 - 27 shows the assignment after I change the duration of the task from 30 days to 45 days. Notice the amount of the Paper resource consumed does not change on this task.

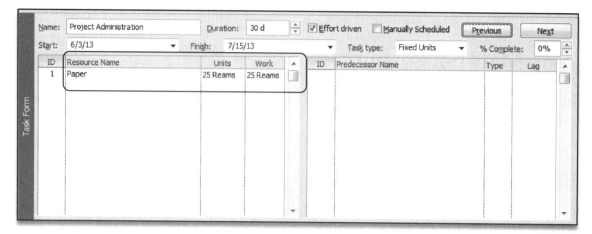

Figure 7 - 26: Material resource Paper assigned at a fixed consumption rate

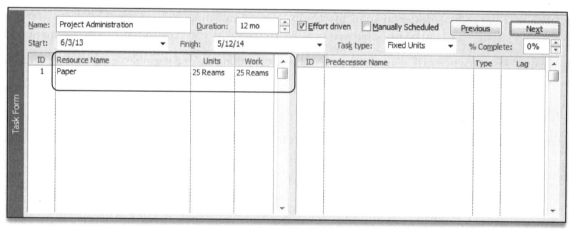

**Figure 7 - 27: No change in Paper consumption at a fixed
consumption rate assignment when the duration increases**

Figure 7 - 28 shows the variable consumption rate for the Gasoline resource assigned to the Excavate Site task. Figure 7 - 29 shows the consumption amount change after I increase the duration of the task from 5 days to 20 days. Notice that the amount of the Gasoline resource consumed **changes in proportion** to the duration change.

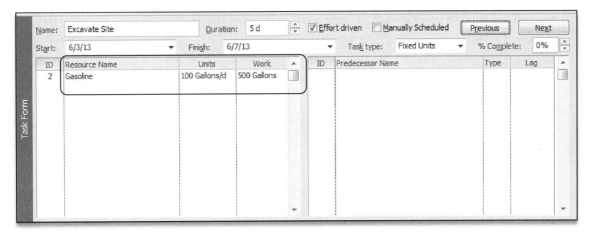

Figure 7 - 28: Material resource Gasoline assigned at a variable consumption rate

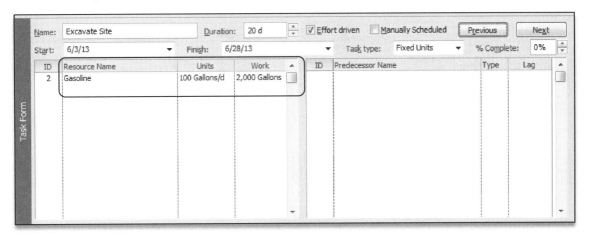

Figure 7 - 29: Consumption of the Gasoline resource changes as Duration changes

Hands On Exercise

Exercise 7-6

Assign a Material resource to a task in the Training Advisor Rollout project.

1. Return to the **Training Advisor 07.mpp** sample file.

2. Click the *View* tab and then click the *Gantt Chart* button in the *Task Views* section of the *View* ribbon to apply the *Gantt Chart* view.

3. In the *Split View* section of the *View* ribbon, select the *Details* checkbox to apply the *Task Entry* view.

4. In the *Gantt Chart* pane, select task ID #36, the *Provide End User Training* task.

5. In the *Task Form* pane, select the first blank cell below the name of the last resource in the *Resource Name* column.

6. Click the *Resource Name* pick list and select the *Student Materials* resource.

7. In the *Units* column for the *Student Materials* resource, enter **36/d** in the *Units* cell to set a variable consumption rate of 36 sets per day.

> I estimated the variable consumption rate for the student materials as 12 students per class multiplied by 3 concurrent classes each day, which means we consume 36 sets of student materials for each day of training. This value ensures that I order enough sets of student materials to supply all of the students in all of the sessions of the training classes.

8. Click the *OK* button.

Notice that Microsoft Project 2010 calculated the need for 360 sets of student materials during the 10 days of duration for this task.

9. In the *Split View* section of the *View* ribbon, **deselect** the *Details* checkbox to close the *Task Form* pane.

10. Click the *Task* tab to display the *Task* ribbon.

11. Save but **do not** close the **Training Advisor 07.mpp** sample file.

Assigning Cost Resources

When you use a Budget Cost resource in a project, Microsoft Project 2010 allows you to assign the resource to **only** the Project Summary Task (Row 0). This allows you to set a budget for the overall project as a whole, but it does not allow you to set a budget on phases, deliverables, or individual tasks. To specify an overall budget for your project, complete the following steps:

1. Click the *View* tab and then click the *Task Usage* button in the *Task Views* section of the *View* ribbon.

2. In your project, select the Project Summary Task (Row 0).

3. Click the *Resource* tab and then click the *Assign Resources* button in the *Assignments* section of the *Resource* ribbon.

4. In the *Assign Resources* dialog, select your Budget Cost resource and then click the *Assign* button.

5. Click the *Close* button to close the *Assign Resources* dialog.

Figure 7 - 30 shows that I assigned my Budget Cost resource to the Project Summary Task.

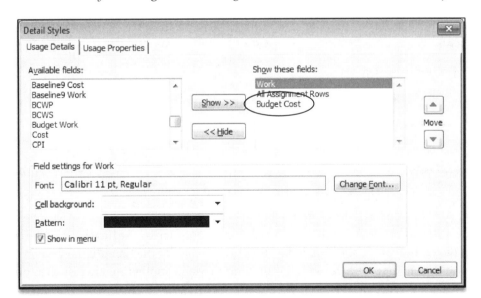

		Task Mode	Task Name	Work	Details	Apr 6, '14 S	M	T	W	T	F	S
0			− Office Renovation	1,114 h	Work		8h	8h	6h		6h	
			Project Budget		Work							
1			− Pre-Renovation	282 h	Work		8h	8h	6h		6h	
2			− Design	156 h	Work		4h	4h	2h		4h	
3			− Interview and select architect	10 h	Work		4h	4h	2h			
			Steve Garcia	10 h	Work		4h	4h	2h			
4			− Create first draft plan	52 h	Work						4h	
			Jerry King	52 h	Work						4h	
5			− Review draft	10 h	Work							
			Jerry King	4 h	Work							
			Steve Garcia	6 h	Work							
6			− Revise draft	20 h	Work							
			Jerry King	20 h	Work							
7			− Review and approve final plan	8 h	Work							
			Jerry King	4 h	Work							
			Steve Garcia	4 h	Work							

Figure 7 - 30: Budget Cost resource assigned to the Project Summary Task

6. Right-click on the *Select All* button and select the *Cost* table on the shortcut menu.

7. Right-click on the *Fixed Cost* column header, select the *Insert Column* item on the shortcut menu, and then select the *Budget Cost* column.

8. Right-click anywhere in the timephased grid and then select the *Detail Styles* item in the shortcut menu.

9. In the *Detail Styles* dialog, select the *Budget Cost* field and click the *Show* button to add the field to the *Show these fields* list.

Figure 7 - 31 shows the *Detail Styles* dialog with the *Budget Cost* field added to the *Show these fields* list.

Figure 7 - 31: Detail Styles dialog with Budget Cost field added

10. Click the OK button to close the *Details Styles* dialog and insert the *Budget Cost* timephased field.

11. In the timephased grid, double-click the right edge of the *Details* column header to "best fit" the column width.

Figure 7 - 32 shows the *Task Usage* view with the *Budget Cost* column displayed in the *Cost* table on the left and with the timephased *Budget Cost* field displayed in the timephased grid on the right.

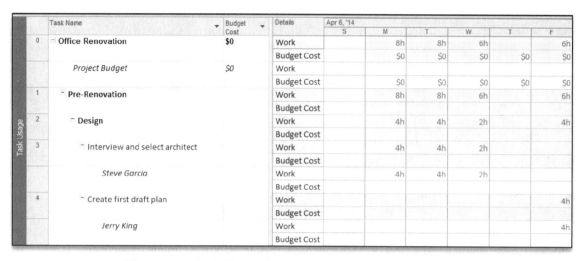

Figure 7 - 32: Task Usage view prepared to enter project budget

12. In the *Budget Cost* column for the Budget Cost resource assignment on the Project Summary Task, enter your planned budget for the entire project and then press the **Enter** key on your computer keyboard.

Figure 7 - 33 shows the *Budget Cost* value for my Project Budget resource assigned to the Project Summary Task.

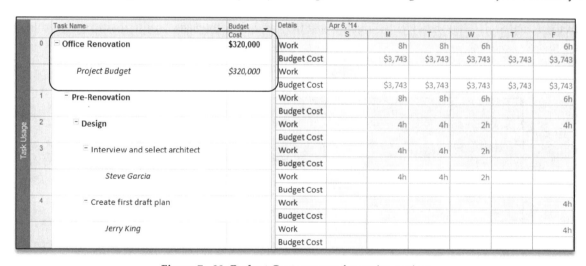

Figure 7 - 33: Budget Cost amount for entire project

If you set the *Accrue At* field value to *Prorated* for the Budget Cost resource in the *Resource Sheet* view of your project, then Microsoft Project 2010 apportions the *Budget Cost* amount evenly across the time span of the entire project. You see the timephased *Budget Cost* amounts in each day ($3,743 each day) of the timephased grid shown previously in Figure 7 - 33. If you wish to reapportion the *Budget Cost* information in another manner, such as on a monthly basis, then complete the following additional steps:

13. Click the *View* tab, click the *Zoom* button in the *Zoom* section of the *View* ribbon, and zoom the *Timescale* to the level of detail at which you wish to reapportion the *Budget Cost* amount.

14. In the timephased grid, enter your anticipated *Budget Cost* values in the *Budget Cost* cells for your Budget Cost resource assignment.

In Figure 7 - 34, notice that I entered my *Project Budget* values on a monthly basis, roughly timephased to correspond with the planned work hours for each month.

Task Name	Budget Cost	Details	Qtr 2, 2014			Qtr 3, 2014			
			Apr	May	Jun	Jul	Aug	Sep
0	Office Renovation	$320,000	Work	218h	304h	380h	176h	36h	
			Budget Cost	$40,000	$65,000	$120,000	$80,000	$15,000	
	Project Budget	$320,000	Work						
			Budget Cost	$40,000	$65,000	$120,000	$80,000	$15,000	
1	Pre-Renovation		Work	218h	64h				
			Budget Cost						
2	Design		Work	92h	64h				
			Budget Cost						
3	Interview and select architect		Work	10h					
			Budget Cost						
	Steve Garcia		Work	10h					
			Budget Cost						
4	Create first draft plan		Work	52h					
			Budget Cost						
	Jerry King		Work	52h					
			Budget Cost						

Figure 7 - 34: Project Budget information entered in timephased grid

In addition to the *Budget Cost* field, Microsoft Project 2010 includes an additional budget field called *Budget Work*. This field allows you to set a budget for working hours for your project in addition to a cost budget.

Using Expense Cost Resources

After you enter your project budget using a Budget Cost resource, you can assign Expense Cost resources to your project so that you can track additional project expenses. Microsoft Project 2010 allows you to assign Expense Cost resources to any type of task in the project, including summary tasks, subtasks, and milestone tasks. The software **does not** allow you to assign an Expense Cost resource to the Project Summary Task, however. To assign an Expense Cost resource to tasks in your project, complete the following steps:

1. Using the customized *Task Usage* view documented in the previous topical section, select any task in the project, including a regular task, a summary task, or a milestone task.

2. Click the *Resource* tab and then click the *Assign Resources* button in the *Assignments* section of the *Resource* ribbon.

3. In the *Assign Resources* dialog, select your Expense Cost resource and then click the *Assign* button.

Figure 7 - 35 shows the *Assign Resources* dialog after assigning an Expense Cost resource named *Travel Expense*. I want to use this resource to capture the travel expenses for my project so that I can report this amount as a line item expenditure.

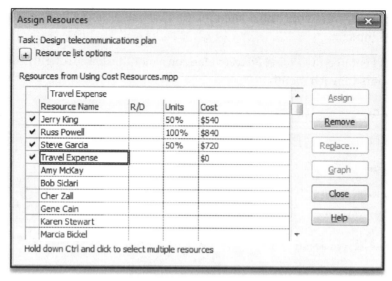

**Figure 7 - 35: Assign Resources dialog after
assigning an Expense Cost resource**

4. In the *Cost* column for the Expense Cost resource in the *Assign Resources* dialog, enter the amount of **antic-ipated expenditure** and then press the **Enter** key on your computer keyboard.

Figure 7 - 36 shows the *Assign Resources* dialog after entering my estimated expenditure for travel expenses on the selected task. Notice that I anticipate the travel expenses at $1,525 for this task.

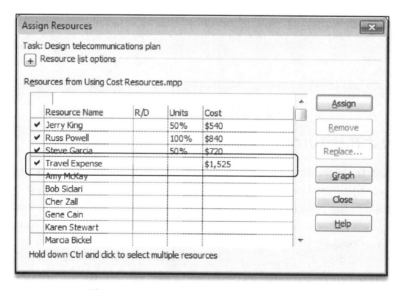

**Figure 7 - 36: Assign Resources dialog after
assigning an Expense Cost resource**

5. Continue selecting tasks, assigning the Expense Cost resources, and entering anticipated expenditures until you finish.

6. Click the *Close* button to close the *Assign Resources* dialog.

Hands On Exercise

Exercise 7-7

Your organization assigns a $225,000 overall budget for your Training Advisor Rollout project. The Training Advisor software vendor charges $75,000 for the license for the server software, plus $50,000 for the number of client software licenses needed by your organization. Using this additional cost information, assign a Budget Cost resource and an Expense Cost resource to tasks in your project.

To limit the amount of time you must spend on this Hands On Exercise, the **Training Advisor 07.mpp** sample file contains a custom view used to assign a Cost resource to tasks in the project. If you want to use this custom view for your own projects, the final steps of this Hands On Exercise show you how to copy the custom view to your own Global.mpt file, which makes the custom view available for all of the current and future projects you manage.

1. Return to the **Training Advisor 07.mpp** sample file.

2. Click the *Gantt Chart* pick list button in the *View* section of the *Task* ribbon and select the *_Cost Resources* view in the *Custom* section of the pick list.

3. Select the Project Summary Task (Row 0) and then click the *Scroll to Task* button in the *Editing* section of the *Task* ribbon to bring the cost information into view in the timephased grid.

4. Click the *Resource* tab to display the *Resource* ribbon.

5. Click the *Assign Resources* button to display the *Assign Resources* dialog.

6. In the *Assign Resources* dialog, select the *Project Budget* resource and then click the *Assign* button.

Notice how Microsoft Project 2010 allows you to assign this Budget Cost resource to the Project Summary Task (Row 0).

7. In the *Assign Resources* dialog, click the *Close* button to close the dialog.

8. In the left side of the view, enter *$225,000* in the *Budget Cost* column for the *Project Budget* resource and then press the **Enter** key on your computer keyboard.

9. Click the *View* tab to display the *View* ribbon.

10. Click the *Timescale* pick list in the *Zoom* section of the *View* ribbon and then select the *Quarters* item in the pick list.

11. In the timephased grid on the right side of the view, select the *Qtr 1* cell for the *Budget Cost* row for the *Project Budget* assignment, enter *$175,000* in the cell, and then press the **Enter** key on your computer keyboard.

12. Select the *Qtr 2* cell for the *Budget Cost* row for the *Project Budget* assignment, enter *$50,000* in the cell, and then press the **Enter** key on your computer keyboard.

13. Select task ID #19, the *Load and Configure Software* task.

14. Click the *Resource* tab to display the *Resource* ribbon.

15. Click the *Assign Resources* button to display the *Assign Resources* dialog.

16. In the *Assign Resources* dialog, select the *Software Licenses* resource and then click the *Assign* button.

17. In the *Cost* field for the *Software Licenses* resource in the *Assign Resources* dialog, enter *$75,000* and then press the **Enter** key on your computer keyboard.

18. Scroll down and select task ID #23, the *Install Training Advisor Clients* task.

19. In the *Assign Resources* dialog, select the *Software Licenses* resource and then click the *Assign* button.

20. In the *Cost* field for the *Software Licenses* resource in the *Assign Resources* dialog, enter *$50,000* and then press the **Enter** key on your computer keyboard.

21. In the *Assign Resources* dialog, click the *Close* button to close the dialog.

Notice how Microsoft Project 2010 applied your planned costs for software licenses in the *Cost* column on the left side of the view for each assignment of the *Software Licenses* resource.

22. Click the *Task* tab to display the *Task* ribbon.

23. Click the *Gantt Chart* button in the *View* section of the *Task* ribbon to reapply the *Gantt Chart* view.

24. Save but **do not** close the **Training Advisor 07.mpp** sample file.

Using Effort Driven Scheduling

In Microsoft Project 2010, you can designate each task individually as either an *Effort Driven* task or a *non-Effort Driven* task. The *Effort Driven* status of any task determines how the software responds when you add or remove resources from a task to which you previously assigned one or more resources. The default setting for every task in Microsoft Project 2010 is *Effort Driven*.

To assign additional resources as helpers to a task using *Effort Driven* scheduling, complete the following steps:

1. Select a task to which you previously assigned at least one resource.

2. Apply the *Task Entry* view.

3. In *Task Form* pane, select the *Effort driven* option, if not already selected.

4. Select one or more additional resources in the *Resource Name* column, and set a *Units* value for each additional resource.

5. **Do not** enter a *Work* value for any of the additional resources.

6. Click the *OK* button.

When you add a resource to an *Effort Driven* task, the software keeps the *Remaining Work* value constant and allocates the *Remaining Work* proportionately to each resource based on each resource's *Units* value. Consider the following examples of how Microsoft Project 2010 distributes the *Remaining Work* based on the *Units* values of each resource:

- I assign Ann Dyer to the Design task at 100% units and 80 hours of work, and the software calculates a duration of 10 days for the task. Using *Effort Driven* scheduling, I add Kevin Holthaus to the task at 100% units. Microsoft Project 2010 shortens the duration to 5 days and allocates the 80 hours of *Remaining Work* evenly between the two resources (40 hours each to Ann Dyer and to Kevin Holthaus), as shown in Figure 7 - 37.

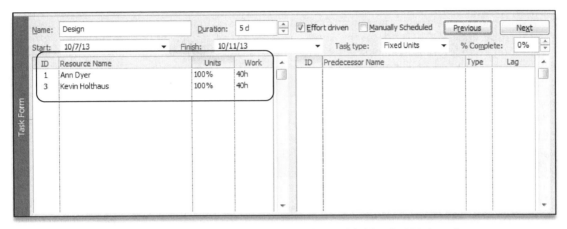

Figure 7 - 37: Using Effort Driven scheduling with identical Units values

- I assign Ann Dyer to the Design task at 100% units and 80 hours of work, and the software calculates a duration of 10 days for the task. Using *Effort Driven* scheduling, I add Kevin Holthaus to the task at **50% units**. In this situation, Microsoft Project 2010 shortens the duration to 6.67 days and allocates the 80 hours of *Remaining Work* **proportionately** between the two resources (53.33 hours to Ann Dyer and 26.67 hours to Kevin Holthaus), as shown in Figure 7 - 38.

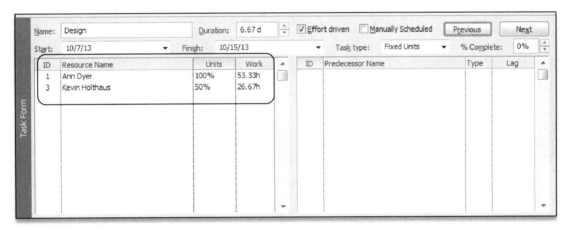

Figure 7 - 38: Effort Driven scheduling with different Units values

How does Microsoft Project 2010 actually determine the proportionate split of the original 80 hours of work? Ann Dyer's *Units* value of *100%* is two-thirds of the total units of *150%* for both resources (100/150 = 2/3), so the system allocates Ann Dyer two-thirds of the total work, which is 53.33 hours (80 x 2/3 – 53.33). Kevin Holthaus' *Units* value of *50%* is one-third of the total units value (50/150 = 1/3), so the system allocates Kevin Holthaus one-third of the total *Work*, which is 26.67 hours (80 x 1/3 = 26.67).

When you assign additional resources to an *Effort Driven* task, msProjectExperts recommends that you also increase the *Work* hours for each resource in the range of **10% to 20%** to account for the increased communications overhead between the resources.

When you remove a resource from an *Effort Driven* task with multiple resources already assigned, Microsoft Project 2010 **increases** the *Duration* of the task and **increases** the *Remaining Work* value proportionately for each remaining resource. This behavior is also known as *Effort Driven* scheduling, although most people do not realize this.

Remember that when you assign additional resources to an *Effort Driven* task, Microsoft Project 2010 allocates the **Remaining Work** proportionately between all of the assigned resources. So how does the software respond when you add a helper to a task that already contains some completed work? Consider the following example:

- I assign Brian Harry to the Build task at 100% units and 80 hours of work, and the software calculates a duration of 10 days for the task. Brian completed 40 hours of actual work, which leaves 40 hours of remaining work. Using *Effort Driven* scheduling, I add Lisa Roach to the task at 100% units. Microsoft Project 2010 shortens the duration to 7.5 days and allocates the 40 hours of **remaining work** evenly between the two resources (20 hours each to Brian Harry and Lisa Roach), as shown in Figure 7 - 39.

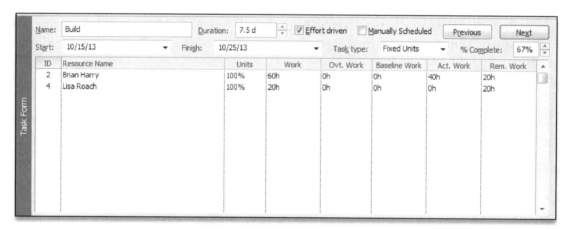

Figure 7 - 39: Using Effort Driven scheduling with completed work
Microsoft Project 2010 allocates Remaining Work

Figure 7 - 39 shows the *Task Form* view with the *Work* details applied. To view the *Work* details, right-click anywhere in the *Task Form* pane and then select *Work* on the shortcut menu. Notice in Figure 7 - 39 that the software holds the 40 hours of remaining work constant, which gives Brian Harry 60 hours of total work (40 hours of actual work .+ 20 hours of remaining work) and gives Lisa Roach 20 hours of total work (0 hours of actual work + 20 hours of remaining work).

On *Fixed Units* or *Fixed Work* tasks, assigning additional resources using *Effort Driven* scheduling **shortens the Duration** of the task. On a *Fixed Duration* task, however, assigning additional resources using *Effort Driven* scheduling **decreases the Units** for each assigned resource.

Using Non-Effort Driven Scheduling

In the real world, not all tasks are *Effort Driven* in nature, meaning that no matter how many helpers you add to the task, the duration remains unchanged. The classic example is adding additional drivers to drive the school bus along its route; this task takes 2 hours to complete regardless of how many drivers you add. When you add additional resources to a *non-Effort Driven* task, Microsoft Project 2010 increases the total work on the task, and does not reduce the duration of the task. Conversely, when you remove a resource from a *non-Effort Driven* task, the software decreases the total work on the task, and does not increase the duration.

To specify a task as *non-Effort Driven* and then assign additional resources to the task, complete the following steps:

1. Select the task you wish to make *non-Effort Driven*.

2. Apply the *Task Entry* view.

3. In the *Task Form* pane, **deselect** the *Effort driven* checkbox option.

4. Click the *OK* button.

5. Select one or more additional resource in the *Resource Name* column, and set a *Units* value for each additional resource.

6. **Do not** enter a *Work* value for any of the additional resources.

7. Click the *OK* button.

Figure 7 - 40 shows the same example I used previously in Figure 7 - 37 and Figure 7 - 38, except that I changed the task to *non-Effort Driven*. Notice how the duration remained the same while the software increased the total amount of work instead.

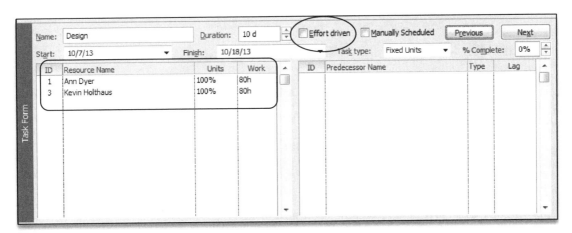

Figure 7 - 40: Using non-Effort Driven scheduling
Microsoft Project 2010 increases total work

Hands On Exercise

Exercise 7-8

After reviewing the project schedule, senior management in your organization made a decision to shorten the duration of the Resolve Connectivity Errors task by assigning an additional resource to assist with the work. Use *Effort Driven* scheduling to shorten the duration of this task.

1. Return to the **Training Advisor 07.mpp** sample file.

2. Click the *View* tab and then select the *Details* checkbox in the *Split View* section of the *View* ribbon to apply the *Task Entry* view.

3. In the *Gantt Chart* pane, select ID # 25, the *Resolve Connectivity Errors* task.

4. In the *Task Form* pane, make sure the *Effort driven* checkbox is selected (if not, select it and then click the *OK* button).

5. In the *Task Form* pane, add *Terry Uland* to the task at *25% Units* (**do not** type a *Work* value) and then click the *OK* button.

Notice how Microsoft Project 2010 decreases the duration of the task to only 10 days.

6. To account for the increased communication needs between the assigned resources, increase the *Work* value for each resource to **24 hours** and then click the *OK* button.

Notice now how the software increased the duration to 12 days, which probably represents a more "realistic" duration for this task.

7. **Deselect** the *Details* checkbox in the *Split View* section of the *View* ribbon to close the *Task Form* pane and reapply the *Gantt Chart* view.

8. Save but **do not** close the **Training Advisor 07.mpp** sample file.

Exercise 7-9

Learn more about *Effort Driven* scheduling by adding a resource to a task where the existing resource has completed some actual work on the task.

1. Open the **Using Effort Driven Scheduling.mpp** sample file.

2. Click the *View* tab and then select the *Details* checkbox in the *Split View* section of the *View* ribbon to apply the *Task Entry* view.

3. In the *Gantt Chart* pane, select the *Implement* task.

4. Right-click anywhere in the *Task Form* pane and then select the *Work* details on the shortcut menu.

Notice in the *Actual Work* column of the *Task Form* pane that Greg Owens previously completed 24 hours of work on this task. Notice in the *Remaining Work* column that he has 40 hours of work left to complete on this task.

    5.   In the *Task Form* pane, add *Cindy McNair* at *100% Units* and then click the *OK* button.

Notice that Microsoft Project 2010 distributed the 40 hours of remaining work evenly between the two resources. This means that Greg Owens now has 24 hours of actual work plus 20 hours of remaining work (44 hours of total work), while Cindy McNair has only 20 hours of remaining work.

    6.   Save and close the **Using Effort Driven Scheduling.mpp** sample file.

Replacing Resources Assigned to Tasks

After assigning generic or skill-based resources to tasks, you may eventually need to replace these generic resources with human resources. The *Assign Resources* dialog allows you to locate the right type of human resources with the necessary availability and then to perform the resource replacement. This dialog contains a number of filtering options that you access by clicking the *Resource list options* button (+ button) at the top of the dialog. Figure 7 - 41 shows the *Assign Resources* dialog with the *Resource list options* section expanded.

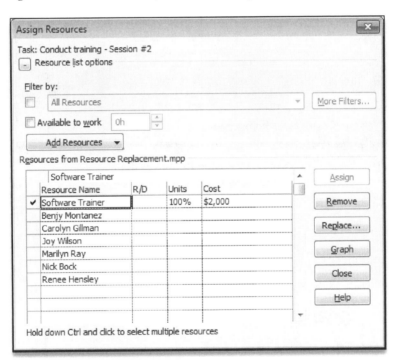

**Figure 7 - 41: Assign Resources dialog
with Resource list options expanded**

The options in the *Resource list options* section of the dialog allow you to apply a filter to locate the right type of human resource to replace an assigned resource. Before you can apply any filter, however, you must make sure you populated the *Resource Sheet* view with some type of data upon which you can filter. For example, you might populate the *Group* column with data used to identify the skills or role for each resource in your project. Once done, you can filter for a value in this column using the default *Group…* filter. To apply a filter to the resources shown in the *Assign Resources* dialog, select the *Filter by* checkbox option, click the *Filter by* pick list, and select any default or custom filter. The *Assign Resources* dialog displays only those resources that meet your filtering criteria.

After you apply a filter, you can also filter further to identify resources with the necessary availability during the scheduled time frame for the selected task. Select the *Available to work* option and enter the number of hours of work required for the selected task in the *Available to work* field. For example, in Figure 7 - 42, I selected the *Group...* filter and used this filter to locate members of the Training group. Then I refined the filter to locate trainers who have at least 40 hours of availability to work on the *Conduct training – Session #2* selected task. Notice also in Figure 7 - 42 that the *Assign Resources* dialog reveals there are only two trainers who have at least 40 hours of availability to work on this task, Joy Wilson and Renee Hensley.

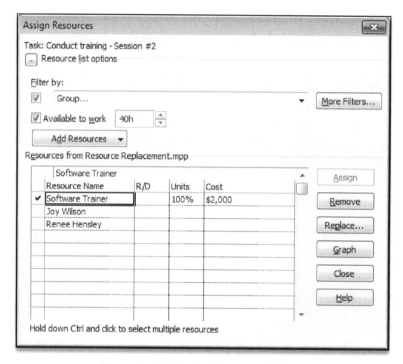

Figure 7 - 42: Assign Resources dialog,
Filter for an available resource

After filtering, you can replace the assigned resource with another resource by completing the following steps:

1. In the *Assign Resources* dialog, select the resource currently assigned to the task.

2. Click the *Replace* button.

The software displays the *Replace Resource* dialog shown in Figure 7 - 43.

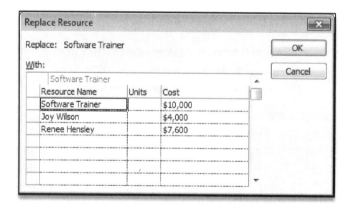

Figure 7 - 43: Replace Resource dialog

3. Select the new resource and then click the *OK* button.

When a team member leaves your project team before you complete the project, you can use the *Assign Resources* dialog to reassign all of the departing resource's uncompleted work. Microsoft Project 2010 leaves the actual work with the departing resource, and transfers only the remaining work to the new resource. This preserves the historical record of the work performed by the departing resource.

Beyond the filter capabilities in the *Resource list options* section of the *Assign Resources* dialog, Microsoft Project 2010 also allows you to display a resource graph for any project team member. To use this feature, select one or more tasks and then click the *Graphs* button in the *Assign Resources* dialog. The system displays a combination view with the *Gantt Chart* view in the top pane and the *Resource Graph* view in the bottom pane, as shown in Figure 7 - 44. The system leaves the *Assign Resources* dialog open, so before you study this custom combination view, you may want to click the *Close* button to close the *Assign Resources* dialog.

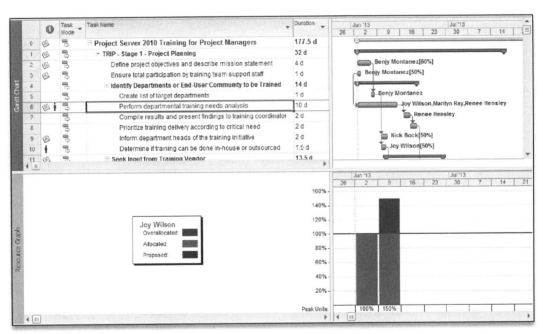

Figure 7 - 44: Combination view with Gantt Chart pane and Resource Graph pane

This custom combination view shows you a graph with allocation and overallocation information for each of the resources assigned to the selected tasks. By default, the *Resource Graph* pane initially displays the first resource assigned to the first selected task in the left side of the pane. In Figure 7 - 44, notice that I assigned three resources to the selected task, but the *Resource Graph* pane shows the first resource assigned, Joy Wilson.

The default information displayed in *Resource Graph* pane is a graph with *Peak Units* information for each resource assigned to the selected tasks. *Peak Units*, by the way, represents the maximum *Units* value assigned to each resource in each time period. The graph shows allocation information with blue columns, and shows overallocation information with red columns, for all tasks to which I assignd the current resource in the project.

If you see the resource's name formatted in red, and see red columns anywhere in the graph for a selected resource, then this resource is overallocated. Notice in the graph shown in the *Resource Graph* pane in Figure 7 - 44 that I accidentally overallocated Joy Wilson at *150% Units* during the week of June 9, indicated by the red bar extending above the *100% Max. Units* line (thick black horizontal line in the graph). When a resource's *Peak Units* value exceeds the resource's *Max. Units* value in any time period, Microsoft Project 2010 considers the resource overallocated.

 If you use the **Professional** version of Microsoft Project 2010, you may also see a third type of information about *Proposed* resource assignments, indicated by purple columns. You can only use this feature, however, if you use Project Server 2010. If your organization does not use Project Server 2010, you **do not** see any purple columns in the *Resource Graph* pane.

In the left side of the *Resource Graph* pane, you can scroll using the horizontal scroll bar at the bottom to individually display each of the resources assigned to the selected tasks. In the right side of the *Resource Graph* pane, you can scroll using the horizontal scroll bar to display allocation information in past or in future time periods for all tasks to which you assigned the resource. The timescale at the top of the *Resource Graph* pane displays the same time units displayed in the timescale at the top of the *Gantt Chart* pane. Using the options in the *Zoom* section of the *View* ribbon, you can zoom the timescales to show more or less detailed allocation information in both the *Gantt Chart* pane and the *Resource Graph* pane.

The *Resource Graph* pane allows you to display other assignment information beyond the *Peak Units* data by right-clicking anywhere in the graph side of the *Resource Graph* pane. Microsoft Project 2010 displays a shortcut menu with other sets of assignments details shown below the *Peak Units* item, as shown in Figure 7 - 45.

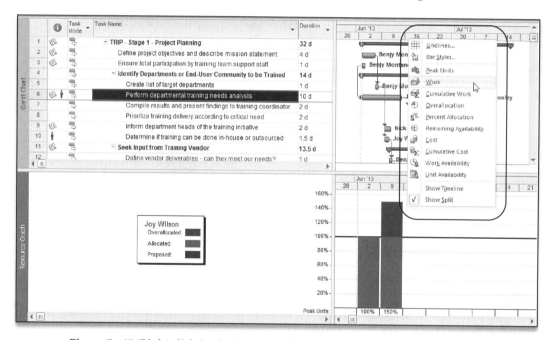

Figure 7 - 45: Right-click in the Resource Graph to view other allocation details

The *Resource Graph* pane allows you to display the following sets of assignment details in the graph:

- **Peak Units** – The graph displays *Peak Units* information as a percentage, and shows allocation data with blue columns and overallocation data with red columns. The combined stacked columns value represents the total *Peak Units* field value in any time period.

- **Work** – The graph displays *Work* information in hours, and allocation data with blue columns and overallocation data with red columns. The combined stacked columns value represents the total number of hours of assigned work in any time period

- **Cumulative Work** – The graph displays blue columns representing the resource's *Cumulative Work* in hours during each time period.

- **Overallocation** – The graph displays only *Overallocation* information in hours using red columns.

- **Allocation** – The graph shows the percentage of work allocated (the *Percent Allocation* field) for each time period. Microsoft Project 2010 uses the formula Percent Allocation = Assigned Work / Work Capacity x 100 to calculate the *Percent Allocation* value for each time period. For example, if you assign a resource to work full-time on a task with a duration of 1 day, the system calculates the *Percent Allocation* value as *100%* **for that one day**. However, if you do not assign any other tasks to the resource during that week, then the system also calculates *Percent Allocation* value **for that entire week** is only *20%* (8/40 x 100%).

- **Remaining Availability** – The graph displays only *Remaining Availability* information in hours using blue columns. The system uses the formula Remaining Availability = Availability – Assignment Work to calculate the *Remaining Availability* value for each time period. For example, if a resource is available to work 8 hours/day (Max. Units = 100%), and you assign a resource to work *50% Units* on a 5-day duration task, the system calculates the *Remaining Availability* for the resource as 4 hours/day and 20 hours for the entire week.

- **Cost** – The graph displays blue columns representing the cost over time using the currency you specify in the *Display* page of the *Project Options* dialog. The system uses the formula Cost = Standard Rate x Work to calculate the *Cost* value in each time period.

- **Cumulative Cost** – The graph displays blue columns representing the resource's *Cumulative Cost* in each time period using your selected currency option.

- **Work Availability** – The graph displays *Work Availability* information in hours using blue columns. The system uses the value in the *Max. Units* field plus the resource's working schedule to calculate the resource's *Work Availability* value in each time period.

- **Unit Availability** – The graph displays *Unit Availability* information as a percentage using blue columns. The system uses the value in the *Max. Units* field plus the resource's working schedule to calculate the resource's *Unit Availability* value in each time period.

To close the *Resource Graph* pane, use one of the following methods:

- Double-click anywhere in the split bar between the *Gantt Chart* pane and the *Resource Graph* pane.

- Click the *View* tab and then deselect the *Details* checkbox in the *Split View* section of the *View* ribbon.

Hands On Exercise

Exercise 7-10

Locate an available human resource with the right skills to replace the generic resource assigned to the Create Training Materials section of the Training Advisor Rollout project.

1. Return to the **Training Advisor 07.mpp** sample file.

2. Simultaneously select task IDs #30-32, the *Create Training Module 01*, *Create Training Module 02*, and *Create Training Module 03* tasks.

3. Click the *Resource* tab and then click the *Assign Resources* button in the *Assignments* section of the *Resource* ribbon.

4. In the *Assign Resources* dialog, click the *Resource list options* button (the + button) to expand the filtering options.

5. Select the *Filter by* checkbox, click the *Filter by* pick list button, and then select the *Group…* filter.

6. In the *Group* dialog, type *TechEd* in the *Group name* field, and then click the *OK* button.

Notice how Microsoft Project 2010 shows you only the resources who are members of the TechEd team, specified previously in the *Group* column in the *Resource Sheet* view.

7. In the *Assign Resources* dialog, select the *Available to work* checkbox and then enter *120 hours* in the *Available to work* field.

When you set the *Available to work* option to *120 hours*, it guarantees that the filtered resource list contains only those resources that are available to work full-time on the three selected tasks. Notice that Marilyn Ray and Ruth Andrews are the only resources with the right skills **and** with 120 hours of availability to work on these tasks.

Exercise 7-11

Substitute an available human resource for a generic resource.

1. Return to the **Training Advisor 07.mpp** sample file, if necessary.

2. In the *Assign Resources* dialog, select the *Training Developer* resource and then click the *Replace* button.

3. In the *Replace Resource* dialog, select *Ruth Andrews* and then click the *OK* button.

4. Click the *Close* button to close the *Assign Resources* dialog.

5. Save but **do not** close the **Training Advisor 07.mpp** sample file.

Using the Team Planner View

 Warning: Only the **Professional** version of Microsoft Project 2010 includes the *Team Planner* view. If you use the Standard version of the software, the *Team Planner* view **is not** an available view.

At any point during the assignment planning process, you may want to display the new *Team Planner* view in Microsoft Project 2010. This new view allows you to analyze the current state of resource assignments in your project using a friendly graphical display. To apply the *Team Planner* view, click the *Resource* tab and then click the *Team Planner* button in the *View* section of the *Resource* ribbon. The system displays the *Team Planner* view for your project, as shown in Figure 7 - 46.

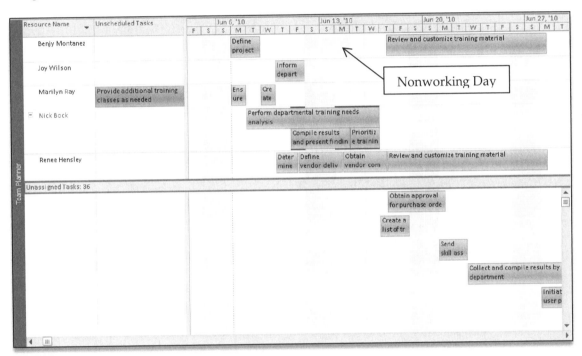

Figure 7 - 46: Team Planner view

 Warning: The first time you apply the *Team Planner* view in a project, the software always scrolls to the **current date** in the *Gantt Chart* area on the right side of the view. If you schedule your project to start in the future, you may not see any tasks in the *Unassigned Tasks* pane. To see tasks in the *Unassigned Tasks* pane, you must scroll the *Gantt Chart* to the start date of your project.

The *Team Planner* view displays resource and assignment information in two panes. The top pane is the *Resource* pane and shows resources from the *Resource Sheet* view of your project, sorted by ID number. Assigned tasks appear in the *Gantt Chart* area on the right side of the pane for each resource. Unlike the *Gantt Chart* view, however, the *Team Plan-*

ner view displays the Gantt bars arranged horizontally on a single line for each resource. *Unscheduled Tasks* (*Manually Scheduled* tasks with no *Duration, Start,* or *Finish* date) already assigned to a resource appear in the *Unscheduled Tasks* column to the right of the resource name.

The *Gantt Chart* area of the *Resource* pane also shows nonworking time for each resource, displayed as a gray shaded band for each time period. Nonworking time includes weekends and company holidays for all resources, plus vacation and planned sick leave for each resource individually. In the *Gantt Chart* area of the *Resource* pane shown previously in Figure 7 - 46, you can also see that Benjy Montanez has one day of nonworking time scheduled on Monday, June 14, indicated by the gray shaded band in the *Gantt Chart* area for this resource. To learn more about any person's nonworking time for any time period, double-click the gray shaded band for that time period. Microsoft Project 2010 displays the *Change Working Time* dialog shown in Figure 7 - 47. Notice in the *Change Working Time* dialog shown in Figure 7 - 47 that Benjy Montanez scheduled a Personal Day Off on June 14. Click the *Cancel* button to close the *Change Working Time* dialog for the selected resource.

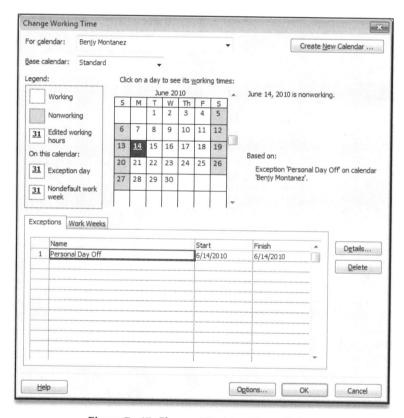

**Figure 7 - 47: Change Working Time dialog,
Personal Day Off for Benjy Montanez**

The bottom pane of the *Team Planner* view is the *Unassigned Tasks* pane and shows the list of tasks not yet assigned to any resource, sorted by task ID number. The *Gantt Chart* area on the right side of the *Unassigned Tasks* pane shows the current schedule for each unassigned task, based on the schedule specified in the *Gantt Chart* view of the project. The system zooms the *Gantt Chart* area to the *Weeks Over Days* level of zoom by default.

In the *Team Planner* view shown previously in Figure 7 - 46, notice that I already assigned tasks to each team member in the project, including one *Unscheduled Task* assigned to Marilyn Ray. To view additional information about any task, float your mouse pointer over the Gantt bar of the task. Microsoft Project 2010 displays a screen tip for the selected Gantt bar, as shown in Figure 7 - 48.

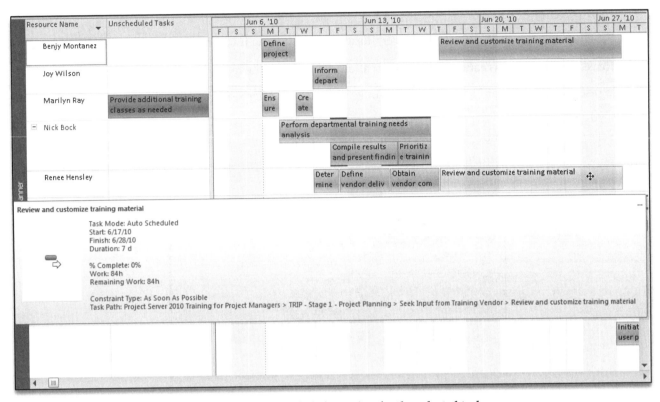

Figure 7 - 48: Schedule information for the selected task

The *Team Planner* view uses special colors and formatting to display task information for each assigned and unassigned task. The key to understanding the color formatting is as follows:

- Light blue Gantt bars represent unstarted *Auto Scheduled* tasks.

- Teal (turquoise) Gantt bars represent *Manually Scheduled* tasks.

- Dark blue in a Gantt bar represents task progress for both *Auto Scheduled* tasks and *Manually Scheduled* tasks.

- Gray Gantt bars represent external tasks in another project.

- Black Gantt bars with white text represent late tasks (tasks where the current *% Complete* progress does not extend to the *Status Date* of the project).

- Resource names formatted in red represent overallocated resources.

- Red borders on a Gantt bar represent the overallocated time periods for a resource.

For example, in Figure 7 - 46 and Figure 7 - 48 shown previously, the system formats Nick Bock's name in red, and displays red borders on his three assigned tasks. This indicates that Nick Bock is overallocated on these three tasks. In fact, he is overallocated specifically on June 11, 14, 15, and 16 on these three tasks.

Leveling an Overallocated Resource in the Team Planner View

While in the *Team Planner* view, Microsoft Project 2010 allows you to resolve resource overallocations using several different methods, including the following:

- Level the resource overallocation using the built-in leveling tool in the software.

- Reschedule a task that is causing an overallocation by dragging it to a different time period.

- Reassign a task that is causing an overallocation by dragging the task to a different resource.

To level a resource overallocation using the built-in leveling tool in Microsoft Project 2010, complete the following steps:

1. Select the name of an overallocated resource in the *Resource* pane.

2. In the *Level* section of the *Resource* ribbon, click the *Leveling Options* button. The system displays the *Resource Leveling* dialog shown in Figure 7 - 49.

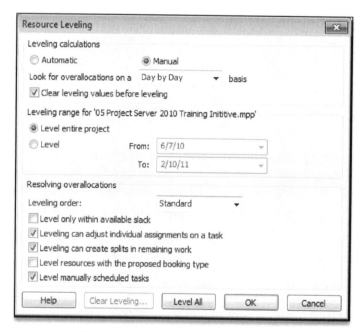

Figure 7 - 49: Resource Leveling dialog

3. In the *Resource Leveling* dialog, select the options you want to use for leveling the selected resource and then click the *OK* button.

The *Resource Leveling* dialog in Microsoft Project 2010 contains all of the leveling options available in the 2007 version of the software, plus one new option: the *Level Manually Scheduled Tasks* option. The system selects this option by default, and you must deselect it if you do not want the leveling operation to level *Manually Scheduled* tasks.

Warning: Do not click the *Level All* button in the *Resource Leveling* dialog. If you click the *Level All* button, you lose control over the leveling process because the software levels **all** of the overallocated resources in your project in a single operation.

4. Click the *Level Resource* button in the *Level* section of the *Resource* ribbon.

When you use the built-in leveling tool to level an overallocated resource, Microsoft Project 2010 resolves the overallocation using one or both of the following methods:

- The software delays tasks or assignments.

- The software splits tasks or assignments.

Figure 7 - 50 shows the *Team Planner* view after leveling the resource overallocations for Nick Bock using the built-in leveling tool in Microsoft Project 2010. Notice that the software delayed several of the tasks assigned to Nick Bock to resolve the overallocation.

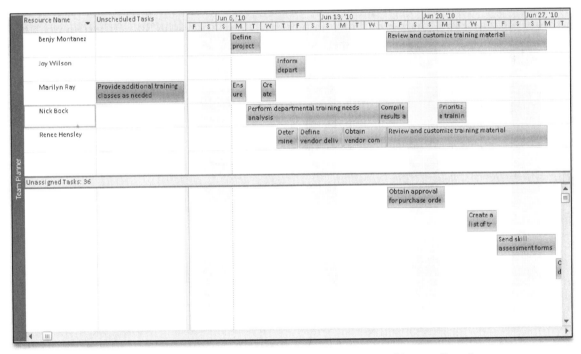

Figure 7 - 50: Team Planner view after leveling Nick Bock's overallocations

If you prefer to use a manual approach to level a resource overallocation, Microsoft Project 2010 allows you to reschedule a task by dragging it to a different time period, or dragging tasks to a different resource.

Dragging Tasks in the Team Planner View

You can use the "drag and drop" functionality of the *Team Planner* view to do any of the following:

- Drag an assigned task to a different time period to reschedule the task.

- Drag an assigned task to a different resource.

- Drag an unassigned task to a resource.

To reschedule a task to a different time period, simply drag the task's Gantt bar to the new time period. Keep in mind, however, that when you reschedule a task by dragging it to a new time period, Microsoft Project 2010 sets a *Start No Earlier Than* (SNET) constraint on the task automatically. If you drag a task beyond the right edge of the *Team Planner* view, the system scrolls the view automatically so that you do not need to release the mouse button and scroll manually.

 Warning: Microsoft Project's use of SNET constraints in the *Team Planner* view may be contrary to the best interests of your scheduling model if you want to maintain a fully dynamic model. SNET constraints prevent a task from moving to an earlier start date if an earlier start becomes available. You can easily clear delays added by the built-in leveling tool with a press of a button, but you must manually remove constraints added by the *Team Planner*.

To reassign a task to another resource, simply drag the task's Gantt bar from the assigned resource to the new resource and drop it on the desired time period. For example, Figure 7 - 51 shows the *Team Planner* view after I dragged two tasks assigned to Nick Bock and reassigned them to Marilyn Ray. These two tasks were the tasks causing the resource overallocation for Nick Bock.

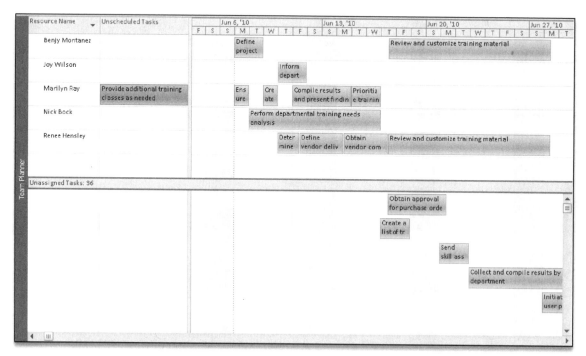

Figure 7 - 51: Resolve a resource overallocation by dragging tasks to another resource

You can also reassign a task to another resource by right-clicking on the Gantt bar for the task, choosing the *Reassign To* item on the shortcut menu, and then selecting the name of the new resource.

To assign an *Unassigned Task* to any resource using the *Team Planner* view, drag the task's Gantt bar from the bottom pane to the top pane and drop it in the time period during which you want to schedule the task for the selected resource. Keep in mind that when you assign a task to a resource using this method, Microsoft Project 2010 assigns the task to the resource at **100% Units** automatically, indicating full-time work on the task.

To reassign or reschedule multiple tasks simultaneously, press and hold the *Control* key to select multiple tasks, and then drag and drop the block of selected tasks. Microsoft Project 2010 **does not** allow you to drag and drop multiple **unassigned** tasks simultaneously in the *Team Planner* view, however.

Changing Schedule Information in the Team Planner View

As you analyze assignment information in the *Team Planner* view, at some point you may need to revise schedule information. Microsoft Project 2010 allows you to revise your project as follows in the *Team Planner* view:

- You can change the *Task Mode* option for a task by right-clicking on the Gantt bar for the task and choosing either the *Auto Schedule* or *Manually Schedule* item on the shortcut menu.

- You can set a task to *Inactive* status by right-clicking on the Gantt bar for the task and choosing the *Inactivate Task* item on the shortcut menu.

- You can change information for any task (such as setting a constraint or applying a task calendar) by double-clicking the Gantt bar for the task and entering the information in the *Task Information* dialog. You can also right-click on the Gantt bar for the task and choose the *Information* item on the shortcut menu.

- You can apply the *Task Details Form* in a split view arrangement with the *Team Planner* view by clicking the *Task* tab and then clicking the *Display Task Details* button in the *Properties* section of the *Task* ribbon. When you select the Gantt bar for any assigned task in the top pane, the *Task Details Form* in the bottom pane displays relevant information about the task and its assigned resources. Notice in Figure 7 - 52 that the *Task Details Form* displays information about the Perform Departmental Training Needs Analysis task whose Gantt bar I selected in the top pane. To close the *Task Details Form*, click the *Display Task Details* button again in the *Task* ribbon.

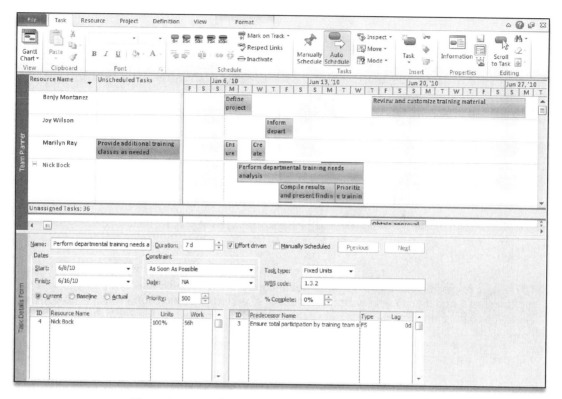

Figure 7 - 52: Task Details Form applied in a split-screen arrangement with the Team Planner view

- You can prevent resource overallocations in your project by clicking the *Format* tab and then clicking the *Prevent Overallocations* button in the *Format* ribbon. With this option selected, the software levels all existing overallocations in the project immediately, and levels any future resource overallocation when it occurs, such as when you drag a task or assign a task that causes a resource overallocation. Microsoft Project 2010 indicates in the *Team Planner* view that you selected this option by highlighting the *Prevent Overallocations* button and by displaying a *Prevent Overallocations: On* indicator at the left end of the Status bar at the bottom of the application window, as shown in Figure 7 - 53.

During the execution stage of your project, you can also enter progress against a task by right-clicking on the task's Gantt bar and selecting a *% Complete* value on the *Mini Toolbar* section of the shortcut menu. The *Mini Toolbar* offers you the *0%, 25%, 50%, 75%,* and *100%* buttons with which to enter the progress on a task quickly.

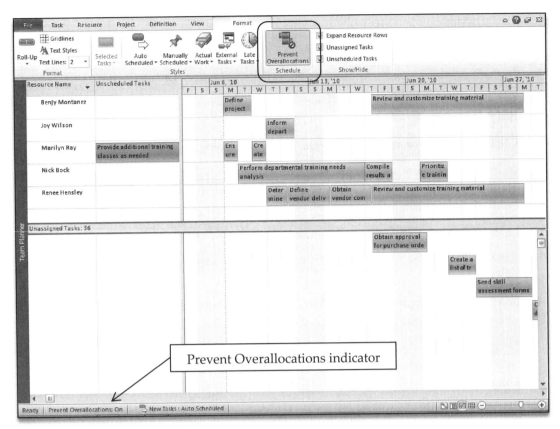

Figure 7 - 53: Prevent Overallocations option selected

Hands On Exercise

Exercise 7-12

Use the *Team Planner* view to analyze resource assignments and to level resource overallocations.

1. Open the **Using the Team Planner View.mpp** sample file.

2. Click the *Resource* tab and then click the *Team Planner* button in *View* section of the *Resource* ribbon.

3. Examine the tasks currently assigned to each resource. **Note:** Scroll to the right, as needed, to view task assignments for each resource and unassigned tasks as well.

4. Scroll to the week of September 22, 2013 for *Dan Morton* and look for the week of nonworking time in the *Gantt Chart* area (gray shaded cells).

5. Double-click in the gray shaded cells during the week of nonworking time for *Dan Morton* to display the *Change Working Time* dialog and reveal the reason for the nonworking time.

Notice that Dan Morton has a week of educational leave scheduled for the week of September 13, 2013.

6. Click the *Cancel* button to close the *Change Working Time* dialog.

7. In the *Level* section of the *Resource* ribbon, click the *Leveling Options* button.

8. In the *Resource Leveling* dialog, click the *Leveling Order* pick list and select the *Priority, Standard* order.

9. Click the *OK* button to close the *Resource Leveling* dialog.

10. In the *Resource* pane, scroll to the week of September 8, 2013 and notice the red borders on the Gantt bars for the three tasks assigned to *Dan Morton*, indicating he is an overallocated resource on these three tasks.

11. Select *Dan Morton* and then click the *Level Resource* button in the *Resource* ribbon

Notice that Microsoft Project 2010 delayed two of the three tasks assigned to Dan Morton to resolve the overallocation.

12. Select the overallocated resource, *Marilyn Ray*, and then scroll to the right to locate her resource overallocation beginning the week of September 29, 2013.

13. Drag the Gantt bar for the *Initiate End-User Placement Matrix* task from *Marilyn Ray* to *Cassie Endicott*. **Note:** Be sure to keep the **same time schedule** for the task when you drag the Gantt bar to *Cassie Endicott*.

14. Select the overallocated resource, *Renee Hensley*, and then scroll to the week of September 15, 2013 to locate her resource overallocation.

15. Click the *Level Resource* button in the *Resource* ribbon.

Notice that Microsoft Project 2010 delayed a task assigned to Renee Hensley to resolve the overallocation.

16. Scroll to the week of October 13, 2013 and locate tasks not yet assigned to any resource in the *Unassigned Tasks* pane.

17. Drag the Gantt bar for the *Determine course dates, start and end times, and locations* task to *Dan Morton*. **Note:** Be sure to keep the **same time schedule** for the task when you drag the Gantt bar to Dan Morton.

18. Click the *Task* tab and then click the *Gantt Chart* button to apply the *Gantt Chart* view.

19. Locate task ID #25, the *Determine course dates, start and end times, and locations* task you assigned to Dan Morton.

In the *Indicators* column, notice that Microsoft Project 2010 applied a *Start No Earlier Than (SNET)* constraint on this task after you assigned it to Dan Morton. This is the consequence of dragging and dropping task Gantt bars in the *Team Planner* view.

20. Save and close the **Using the Team Planner View.mpp** sample file.

Understanding Resource Overallocation

During the resource assignment process, you may accidentally overallocate one or more resources in the project. An overallocation occurs when you assign more work to a resource than the resource can do during the working time available, resulting in a *Units* value that exceeds the *Max. Units* value for the resource. Each of the following situations results in an overallocated resource:

- You assign a resource to work 32 hours in a single day.

- You assign a resource to work 160 hours in a single week.

- You assign a resource to work 30 minutes in a 15-minute time period.

Leveling is the process you use to resolve resource overallocations so that your project resources are no longer overallocated. The third bullet point reveals an important truth about leveling overallocated resources:

Not all overallocations are worth leveling.

You should definitely level the overallocations I describe in the first two bulleted items above, because either situation would likely cause your project finish date to slip. The third situation is not worth leveling, however, as the amount of time spent leveling this overallocation is not worth the bother.

In addition to the three previous examples, you can also overallocate a resource by assigning the resource to a task at a *Units* value of *200%* when the *Max. Units* value for the resource is *100%*. You cannot resolve this type of overallocation using the built-in leveling tool in Microsoft Project 2010. Instead, you must manually resolve this type of overallocation by reducing the *Units* value for the resource's assignment on the task.

Locating Resource Overallocations

The easiest way to locate overallocated resources is to use the *Resource Usage* view. To apply this view, click the *Resource* tab to display the *Resource* ribbon, click the *Team Planner* pick list button, and then select the *Resource Usage* view from the list. Because Microsoft Project 2010 formats overallocated resources with red text, look for any resource names formatted in red. To determine the time periods during which a resource is overallocated, select an overallocated resource and then click the *Next Overallocation* button in the *Level* section of the *Resource* ribbon. When you click the *Next Overallocation* button, Microsoft Project 2010 scrolls the timephased grid and selects the start of the first resource overallocation, as shown in Figure 7 - 54.

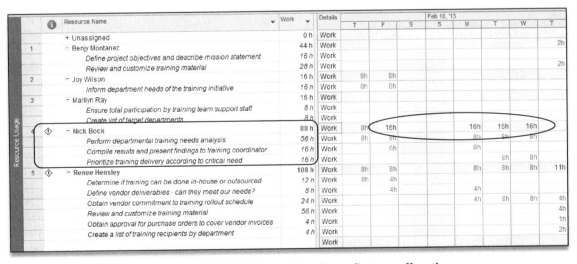

Figure 7 - 54: Resource Usage view shows first overallocation

In Figure 7 - 54, notice that I assigned Nick Bock to work 16 hours each day in a four-day period during the weeks of February 3 and 10, 2013. I accidentally caused this overallocation when I assigned Nick to work on three overlapping tasks, each of which requires full-time work. In addition, notice that I also overallocated Renee Hensley. In Figure 7 - 54, you can see the start of one of her overallocations on the right side of the timephased grid.

As you continue to click the *Next Overallocation* button, Microsoft Project 2010 selects the start of each successive over-allocation. When the software cannot locate any more resource overallocations, it displays the dialog shown in Figure 7 - 55.

Figure 7 - 55: No more resource overallocations

Leveling Overallocated Resources

As I previously stated, leveling is the process you use to resolve resource overallocations. There are many ways to level overallocated resources, including each of the following:

- Substitute an available resource for the overallocated resource.

- Increase the availability of overallocated resources.

- Schedule overtime for the overallocated resource.

- Manually delay tasks with overallocated resources.

- Delay the start of a resource assignment on a task.

- Adjust the project schedule using task constraints to eliminate resource assignment conflicts.

- Split tasks by interrupting the work on a task to make resources available for other assignments.

- Adjust dependencies and add *Lag* time.

- Add resources to an *Effort Driven* task to shorten the duration of the task.

- Look for potential overlapping work opportunities, such as Finish to Start dependencies that do not have a true "finish to start" relationship.

- Negotiate with your project sponsor or customer to delay the finish date of the project.

- Negotiate with your project sponsor or customer to reduce the feature set (scope) of the project.

- Use the built-in leveling tool in Microsoft Project 2010.

Notice that using the built-in leveling tool in Microsoft Project 2010 appears last on the preceding list! Each of the preceding leveling methods is powerful and useful for leveling overallocated resources; however, most users assume the only way to level is to use the built-in leveling tool found in Microsoft Project 2010. Given the complexity of using the software's leveling capabilities, the average user of Microsoft Project 2010 is far better off using any of the other manual leveling methods. The key to using any method for resource leveling is to remember that you must take **complete control** of all leveling decisions.

Using a Leveling Methodology

Many Microsoft Project 2010 users attempt to level all of their overallocated resources simultaneously in the *Gantt Chart* view using the built-in leveling tool. Although this approach can work in some situations, most often it leads to frustration. This approach does not give you insight into how the software leveled the overallocations, and can lead to failure because you did not take control over the leveling process. A much better approach is to level overallocated resources using the following methodology:

1. Level each overallocated resource individually in the *Resource Usage* view.

2. Study the results of the leveling process in the *Leveling Gantt* view.

3. Clear unacceptable leveling results and then level the overallocated resource using any other method.

4. Repeat steps #1-3 for each overallocated resource.

Setting Leveling Options

Before you begin the process of leveling overallocated resources in the *Resource Usage* view, you should specify your leveling options by clicking the *Leveling Options* button in the *Level* section of the *Resource* ribbon. The system displays the *Resource Leveling* dialog shown in Figure 7 - 56. This dialog, by the way, is the same *Resource Leveling* dialog shown previously in Figure 7 - 49 when leveling overallocations in the new *Team Planner* view.

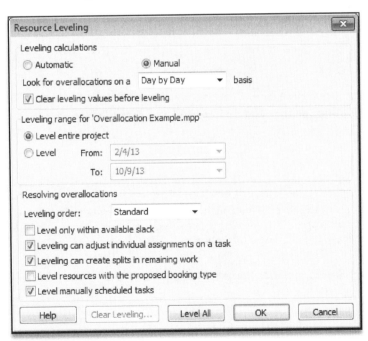

Figure 7 - 56: Resource Leveling dialog

In the *Resource Leveling* dialog, there are several options in the *Resource overallocations* section of the dialog that you may want to change from their default setting. These options include:

- Set the *Leveling order* option to the *Priority, Standard* value. By selecting this option, you force the software to consider first the *Priority* number of each task in the software's algorithm of five leveling factors. The other factors include predecessor task relationships, the start date of each task, the *Total Slack* value for each task, and whether the task has an inflexible constraint.

- Select the *Level only within available slack* option to guarantee that the leveling operation does not change the finish date of your project. With this option selected, Microsoft Project 2010 levels overallocations until it reaches the point where it must delay the finish date of your project. At this point, the system discontinues the leveling process and displays a warning dialog. From this point forward, you must select an alternate method for leveling remaining overallocations.

- If your project contains *Manually Scheduled* tasks with overallocated resources, and you want to manually reschedule the tasks to resolve these overallocations, then you should **deselect** the *Level manually scheduled tasks* option. If you leave this option selected, Microsoft Project 2010 delays or splits any *Manually Scheduled* tasks with overallocated resources assigned to them.

Warning: MSProjectExperts recommends that you **never** select the *Automatic* option in the *Leveling Calculations* section of the *Resource Leveling* dialog. When applied, the *Automatic* leveling option causes Microsoft Project 2010 to level all overallocated resources automatically in all open projects without asking your permission!

After you select your leveling options in the *Resource Leveling* dialog, click the *OK* button. Microsoft Project 2010 saves your option selections in this dialog so that you do not need to reselect them every time you want to level resource overallocations.

Warning: Do not click the *Level All* button in the *Resource Leveling* dialog. If you click the *Level All* button, you lose control over the leveling process because the software levels **all** of the overallocated resources in your project in a single operation.

Leveling an Overallocated Resource

To start the process of leveling overallocated resources, select the most critical resource in the project. Your most critical resource is the one whose skills and availability are the most limited in your organization. After selecting this resource, click the *Level Resource* button in the *Level* section of the *Resource* ribbon. Microsoft Project 2010 displays the *Level Resources* dialog shown in Figure 7 - 57.

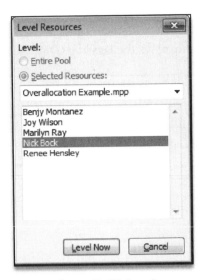

**Figure 7 - 57: Level
Resources dialog**

The *Level Resources* dialog selects the same resource you selected in the *Resource Usage* view. Click the *Level Now* button in the dialog to level the overallocations for the first selected resource using the leveling options you set in the *Resource Leveling* dialog. When you use the built-in leveling tool to level an overallocated resource, Microsoft Project 2010 resolves the overallocation using one or both of the following methods:

- The software delays tasks or assignments.

- The software splits tasks or assignments.

To see the results of leveling the first overallocated resource, you must apply the *Leveling Gantt* view.

Viewing Leveling Results

The best way to apply the *Leveling Gantt* view is to open a new window containing this view by completing the following steps:

1. Click the *View* tab to display the *View* ribbon.

2. Click the *New Window* button in the *Window* section of the *View* ribbon. Microsoft Project 2010 displays the *New Window* dialog shown in Figure 7 - 58.

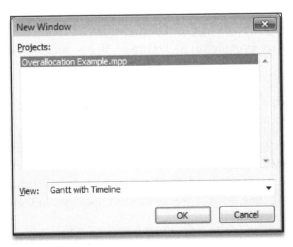

Figure 7 - 58: New Window dialog

3. Click the *View* pick list button and select the *Leveling Gantt* item on the list.

4. Click the *OK* button. The software displays the *Leveling Gantt* view shown in Figure 7 - 59.

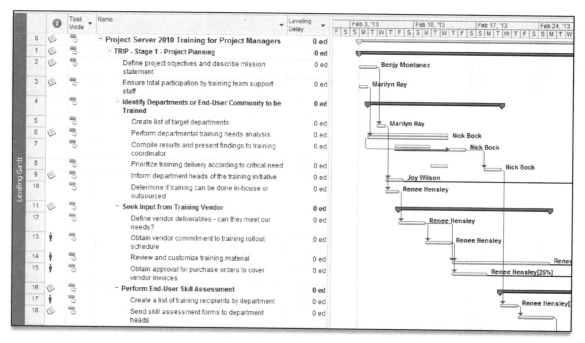

Figure 7 - 59: Leveling Gantt view

The *Leveling Gantt* view includes the *Delay* table on the left and the *Leveling Gantt* chart on the right. The symbols used in the *Leveling Gantt* view are as follows:

- The **tan Gantt bars** represent the pre-leveled schedule for each task you assigned to the overallocated resource . Figure 7 - 59 shows that I created the resource overallocation for Nick Bock accidentally by assigning him to work full-time on three parallel tasks (task ID numbers #6, 7, and 8).

- The **light blue Gantt bars** represent the schedule of the tasks after the software levels the resource overallocation. Figure 7 - 59 shows that Microsoft Project 2010 delayed task ID #7 (which then delayed task ID #8 due to a Finish-to-Start dependency relationship with task ID #7), which resolved Nick Bock's resource overallocation.

- The **brown underscore** to the left of any Gantt bar represents the amount of delay applied to the task schedule to level the resource overallocation. Figure 7 - 59 shows the delay symbol to the left of the Gantt bar for task ID #7.

- The **teal underscore** to the right of any Gantt bar represents the amount of time you can delay the task without delaying the finish date of the entire project.

The *Delay* table contains the *Leveling Delay* column to the right of the *Task Name* column. This column shows the amount of delay the software applies to a task to level a resource overallocation. By default, Microsoft Project 2010 measures the amount of *Leveling Delay* in **elapsed days** (displayed as **edays** or **ed**). Each elapsed day is a 24-hour calendar day that ignores nonworking time, such as weekends and holidays. In Figure 7 - 59, notice that the software delayed task ID #7 six elapsed days (6 ed).

Clearing Leveling Results

As you study the results of leveling an overallocated resource, you may find that Microsoft Project 2010 did not level the overallocation as you wished. In these situations, you must clear the unacceptable leveling and then level using another method. To clear an unacceptable overallocation, complete the following steps:

1. Click the *Resource* tab to display the *Resource* ribbon.

2. Select any tasks leveled in an unacceptable manner.

3. Click the *Clear Leveling* button in the *Level* section of the *Resource* ribbon. Microsoft Project 2010 displays the *Clear Leveling* dialog shown in Figure 7 - 60.

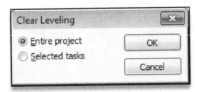

Figure 7 - 60: Clear Leveling dialog

4. In the *Clear Leveling* dialog, select the *Selected tasks* option and then click the *OK* button.

The software sets the *Leveling Delay* value back to the default value to *0d* for each selected task. At this point, you must level the resource overallocation using another method. You have many options available to you, including using one of the manual leveling methods I previously discussed. Another option is to set a *Priority* number on tasks showing the relative importance of each task, and then re-level the overallocations in the *Resource Usage* view.

Setting Task Priority Numbers

When you set a task *Priority* number, Microsoft Project 2010 levels the resource overallocation based on the task *Priority* numbers you assign. The software delays tasks with lower *Priority* numbers while maintaining the original schedule of the task with the highest *Priority* number. To set a *Priority* number on tasks with overallocated resources, complete the following steps:

1. Double-click a task assigned to an overallocated resource. Microsoft Project 2010 displays the *Task Information* dialog shown in Figure 7 - 61.

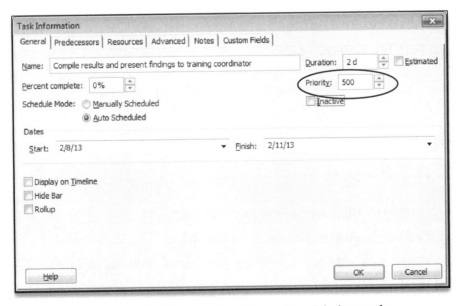

Figure 7 - 61: Task Information dialog – Set a Priority number

2. Click the *General* tab, if necessary.

3. Set a value between 0 and 1000 in the *Priority* field.

Remember that 0 signifies the lowest priority and 1000 signifies the highest priority for any task.

4. Click the *OK* button.

5. Repeat steps #1-4 for each task to which you assigned the overallocated resource.

When setting *Priority* numbers on multiple tasks, be sure to specify a **different** priority number on each task.

An alternate method for setting *Priority* numbers to tasks is to insert the *Priority* field temporarily in the *Leveling Gantt* view by completing the following steps:

1. Right-click on the *Leveling Delay* column header.
2. Select the *Insert Column* item on the shortcut menu.
3. In the pick list of available fields, select the *Priority* field.
4. Enter values in the *Priority* column for each task with an overallocated resource assigned.

After setting task *Priority* numbers, return to the *Resource Usage* window and then level the overallocated resource again.

For the sake of simplicity, I offer only a brief presentation on resource leveling. For an in-depth treatment of resource leveling, refer to the *Advanced Resoure Leveling* section of the companion volume to this book, *Ultimate Microsoft Project 2010: Advanced*.

Hands On Exercise

Exercise 7-13

Locate resource overallocations and then level overallocated resources.

1. Return to the **Training Advisor 07.mpp** sample file.

2. Click the *Resource* tab to display the *Resource* ribbon.

3. In the *View* section of the *Resource* ribbon, click the *Team Planner* pick list button and select the *Resource Usage* view.

4. Scroll the timephased grid to the week of January 5, 2014.

5.   Click the *Next Overallocation* button in the *Level* section of the *Resource* ribbon.

Notice that Mickey Cobb is overallocated during the first two days of week of January 5, 2014.

6.   Click the *Next Overallocation* button again.

Notice that Mike Andrews is overallocated during the weekend of February 1-2, 2014. The system indicates he is overallocated because you assigned him to work on a weekend. This is not a true overallocation, however, since the task work must occur on a weekend. In a situation like this, you should ignore this overallocation.

7.   Scroll the timephased grid back to the week of January 5, 2014.

8.   Scroll down the list of resources and select *Mickey Cobb*.

9.   Click the *Level Resource* button in the *Level* section of the *Resource* ribbon.

10. Click the *Level Now* button in the *Level Resources* dialog.

Notice that Mickey Cobb's name is no longer formatted in red, indicating that Microsoft Project 2010 leveled her overallocation successfully.

11. Click the *View* tab and then click the *New Window* button in the *Window* section of the *View* ribbon.

12. In the *New Window* dialog, click the *View* pick list and select the *Leveling Gantt* view, and then click the *OK* button.

Notice that Microsoft Project 2010 leveled Mickey Cobb's resource overallocation by setting a *Leveling Delay* value of *2 elapsed days* on task ID #28, the *Setup Test Training Server* task.

13. Click the *Close Window* button (**X** button) in the upper right corner of the *Leveling Gantt* window to close the window.

14. Click the *Task* tab and then click the *Gantt Chart* button in the *View* section of the *Task* ribbon.

15. Save but **do not** close the **Training Advisor 07.mpp** sample file.

Leveling Resource Overallocations in a Task View

Another powerful new feature in Microsoft Project 2010 helps you to detect and level resource overallocations on a task-by-task basis in any task view, such as the *Gantt Chart* view. Previous versions of the software did not allow you to detect resource overallocations in a task view, displaying overallocation information and indicators only in a resource view, such as the *Resource Usage* view. In all previous versions of the software, the system allowed you to level resource overallocations in a task view, but it leveled the overallocations for all resources and all tasks simultaneously, which meant you lost control over the leveling process.

To detect a resource overallocation in a task view using Microsoft Project 2010, apply any task view, such as the *Gantt Chart* view. Look in the *Indicators* column for any task with a "burning man" indicator, as this indicator identifies the task as assigned to an overallocated resource. For example, Figure 7 - 62 shows the *Gantt Chart* view of my project. Notice the special indicator in the *Indicators* column for task IDs #6, #7, and #8, indicating that I have an overallocated resource assigned to these three tasks. In this situation, the overallocated resource is Nick Bock. The overallocation is a consequence of assigning Nick Bock at *100% Units* on three tasks that run in parallel. Because he cannot work full-time on three tasks simultaneously, the system shows that Nick Bock is an overallocated resource on these three tasks.

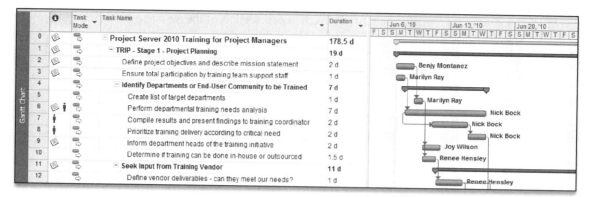

Figure 7 - 62: Three tasks with an overallocated resource assigned

As with previous versions of the software, Microsoft Project 2010 continues to allow you to level resource overallocations in the *Resource Usage* view for each resource individually. This method continues to offer you the most control over the leveling process. However, the 2010 version of the software does allow you to effectively level on a task-by-task basis in the *Gantt Chart* view, providing you with more control over the leveling process than in any other version. To level on a task-by-task basis, right-click in the *Indicators* column on any cell containing a "burning man" indicator. The system displays the shortcut menu shown in Figure 7 - 63, and offers three methods for dealing with the overallocation.

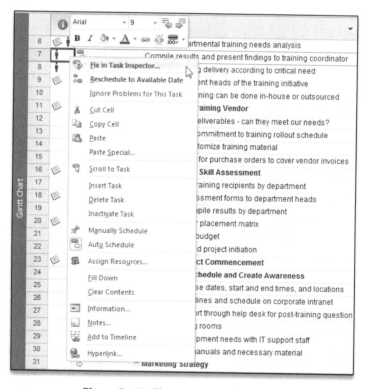

**Figure 7 - 63: Shortcut menu for a task
assigned to an overallocated resource**

The first option in the shortcut menu is the *Fix in Task Inspector* option. If you select this option, the system opens the *Task Inspector* sidepane on the left side of the *Gantt Chart* view, as shown in Figure 7 - 64.

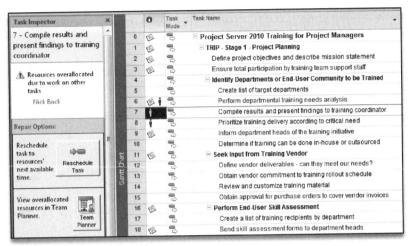

Figure 7 - 64: Task Inspector for a task assigned to an overallocated resource

The *Task Inspector* sidepane offers two options in the *Repair Options* section for resolving the resource overallocation. Click the *Reschedule Task* button to delay the task to the first available time period that resolves the overallocation. Click the *Team Planner* button to apply the *Team Planner* view, in which you can level the resource using any of the methods I discussed in the previous section of this module.

The second option in the shortcut menu is the *Reschedule to Available Date* option. If you select this option, Microsoft Project 2010 delays the task to the first available time period that resolves the overallocation. Selecting this option is the same as clicking the *Reschedule* button in the *Task Inspector* sidepane.

Lastly, you can use the third option on the shortcut menu, *Ignore Problems for This Task*. If you select this option, the system hides the "burning man" indicator for that task in the *Indicators* column, but does nothing to resolve the resource overallocation.

Hands On Exercise

Exercise 7-14

Locate and resolve resource overallocations in the *Gantt Chart* view.

1. Open the **Level Overallocations in a Task View.mpp** sample file.

2. Scroll down through the list of tasks and look for any task that shows the "burning man" indicator in the *Indicators* column, indicating the task has an overallocated resource assigned to it.

Note: You should see that task IDs #6, 7, 8, 13, 14, 15, 19, and 20 have an overallocated resource assigned to them.

3. Float your mouse pointer over the overallocation indicator for task ID #7, the *Compile Results and Present Findings to Training Coordinator* task, and read the text in the ScreenTip.

4. Right-click in the *Indicators* cell for task ID #7 and then select the *Fix in Task Inspector* item on the shortcut menu.

5. In the *Task Inspector* sidepane, read the available information about the resource overallocation on this task.

6. Click the *Reschedule Task* button in the *Task Inspector* sidepane to resolve the resource overallocation on this task.

Notice that this action resolved the resource overallocation on task IDs #6 and #8 as well.

7. Select task ID #14, the *Review and Customize Training Material* task, and then click the *Reschedule Task* button in the *Task Inspector* sidepane.

8. Close the *Task Inspector* sidepane.

9. Right-click in the *Indicators* column for task ID #20, the *Initiate End-User Placement Matrix* task, and then select the *Reschedule To Available Date* item on the shortcut menu.

Without using the *Task Inspector* sidepane, notice that you resolved the resource overallocation on task IDs #19 and #20.

10. Save and close the **Resource and Assignment Planning 3.mpp** sample file.

Exercise 7-15

Disable overallocation warning messages for a task assigned to an overallocated resource.

1. Return to the **Training Advisor 07.mpp** sample file.

Notice that task ID #20, the *Perform Server Stress Test* task, displays the "burning man" indicator in the *Indicators* column. As I stated earlier in this module, the "burning man" indicator reveals that Microsoft Project 2010 believes the assigned resource is overallocated because the task occurs during nonworking time on a Saturday and Sunday. In reality, the assigned resource is **not overallocated** because you intentionally scheduled this task to occur on a weekend due to unique scheduling requirements for this type of work.

2. Right-click in the *Indicators* cell for task ID #20 and select the *Fix in Task Inspector* item on the shortcut menu.

3. Scroll to the bottom of the *Task Inspector* sidepane and **deselect** the *Show warnings and suggestion indicators for this task* checkbox.

Notice that Microsoft Project 2010 no longer displays a "burning man" indicator for this task.

4. Close the *Task Inspector* sidepane.

5. Save and close the **Training Advisor 07.mpp** sample file.

Understanding the Intricacies of Manually Scheduled Tasks

If you choose to use the new *Manually Scheduled* tasks feature in Microsoft Project 2010, it is important that you understand how they work during the resource assignment process, especially in regard to calendar exceptions. During the assignment planning process, you will undoubtedly encounter some unexpected design limitations and quirks that underlie the functionality of *Manually Scheduled* tasks. Most important is that you understand how *Manually Scheduled* tasks differ from *Auto Scheduled* tasks in feature support and work calculations when tasks start of finish on a non-working time period.

Understanding Unsupported Task Features

When you work with *Manually Scheduled* tasks, you cannot use task constraints or work contours, which the software reserves for *Auto Scheduled* tasks only. Furthermore, *Manually Scheduled* tasks do not allow you to enter values in the *Overtime Work*, *Actual Overtime Work*, and *Remaining Overtime Work* fields. In essence, Microsoft did not design *Manually Scheduled* tasks to support effort-based planning and tracking. In fact, *Manually Scheduled* tasks **distort** the planned work values in your schedule when they span calendar exceptions in either the *Project calendar* or the calendars of the resources assigned to the *Manually Scheduled* tasks.

Understanding Work Value Calculations for Calendar Exceptions

For the most part, *Manually Scheduled* tasks behave the way *Fixed Duration* tasks behave in Microsoft Project 2010. In fact, when you schedule a *Manually Scheduled* task to occur on normal working days where the resource assigned to the task works the same schedule as the task schedule, you would be hard pressed to see a difference. Perhaps the most perplexing oddity in the way Microsoft implements *Manually Scheduled* tasks is what happens to work values when *Manually Scheduled* tasks begin or end on non-working days, and when the start date and time or the finish date and time do not fully align with working time on the effective task calendar. To better understand these oddities, I define some terminology and concepts for you:

- Microsoft Project 2010 always honors the start date and time and finish date and time that you specify for a *Manually Scheduled* task, even if the task starts or finishes on a non-working day. In order to accomplish this, the system creates work values to anchor the task, if necessary.

- The **effective calendar** for a *Manually Scheduled* task assignment is the resource calendar unless the task has a task calendar. If the task has a task calendar, then the effective calendar is the intersection of the task calendar and the resource calendar unless one of the following is true: 1) you assign a task calendar and you enable the *Scheduling ignores resource calendars* option in the *Task Information* dialog, or 2) the intersection of the task calendar and resource calendar contains no working time.

- The system creates a **Default Day** exception when a *Manually Scheduled* task starts or ends on a day with no working time on the effective calendar. For example, you set a *Manually Scheduled* task to start on a Sunday and the resource calendar does not have working time on Sunday, and you do not assign a task calendar to override the resource calendar. In this situation, the system creates working time for that day based on the effective calendar provided that the **Default Day** exception encompasses the start time or end time of the task.

- When you set a *Manually Scheduled* task to begin on a day where the effective calendar has working time, the system creates an **Elapsed Time** exception to close the gap between the start time of a *Manually Scheduled* task and the start time of the effective calendar or until the end of the day if the system finds no working time after the start time of the task.

- When you set a *Manually Scheduled* task to begin on a day where the effective calendar has no working time, and a **Default Day** exception does not encompass the start time of the task, the system creates an **Elapsed Time** exception counting backwards from the start time of the task until either working time or the beginning of the day 00:00 hours is reached.

- When you set a *Manually Scheduled* task to end on a day where the effective calendar has working time, and the task end time occurs before the start of the working time on the effective calendar, the system creates an **Elapsed Time** exception counting backward from the end time of the task until the beginning of the day at 00:00 hours.

 When you assign resources to *Manually Scheduled* tasks where the system must create either a **Default Day** or **Elapsed Time** exception, resources appear as overallocated.

 When you apply a resource to a *Manually Scheduled* task, the system first fills the available working time on the effective calendar and then determines how to handle the start and end times if these do not align with the start and end times of the effective calendar.

Figure 7 - 65 shows a *Manually Scheduled* task where I set the duration to five days and the start date as Saturday, August 3. The *Project calendar* is the default *Standard* calendar, with working hours set at 8 hours per day Monday through Friday from 8:00 AM - 12:00 PM. and 1:00 - 5:00 PM. After creating this *Manually Scheduled* task, I assigned a part-time resource (Mickey Cobb) whose calendar schedule is only 4 hours per day Monday through Friday from 8:00 AM – 12:00 PM. The system calculates the work for this assignment at **25 hours**, rather than the 20 hours you might expect! If I applied the same resource to an *Auto Scheduled* task, the system would calculate 20 hours of work and push the task start date to the first available working time period on the resource calendar (Monday), unless I previously set a task calendar to override the resource calendar.

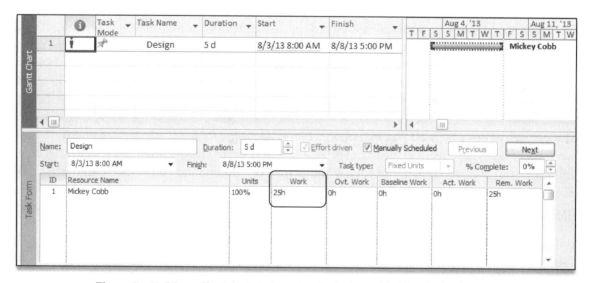

Figure 7 - 65: Manually Scheduled work calculation with identical calendars

When I apply the *Task Usage* view shown in Figure 7 - 66, you can see how Microsoft Project 2010 calculated the 25 hours of work and then applied the work to the resource assignment. Notice the following:

- The system applied 4 hours of planned work on Saturday, August 3.

- The system applied **no work** on Sunday, August 4.

- The system applied 4 hours of work per day from Monday through Wednesday, August 5-7.

- The system applied **9 hours** of work on Thursday, August 8.

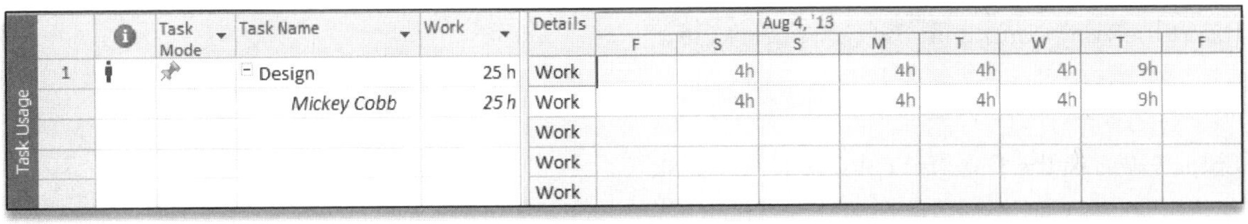

			Task Mode	Task Name	Work	Details		Aug 4, '13						
		ⓘ					F	S	S	M	T	W	T	F
1	ⅰ		📌	⁻ Design	25 h	Work		4h		4h	4h	4h	9h	
				Mickey Cobb	25 h	Work		4h		4h	4h	4h	9h	
						Work								
						Work								
						Work								

Figure 7 - 66: Work distribution shown in the Task Usage view

What happened here? In order to honor a start date that occurs on a nonworking day, Microsoft Project 2010 applied 4 hours of planned work on the first day of the task to anchor the start date of the task. Furthermore, the system applied the amount of hours the resource would normally work during a working day, creating a **Default Day** exception. In this case, the calendars for the resource and the *Project calendar* are in agreement as all time is nonworking time. The system does not create an **Elapsed Time** exception for Saturday because there is no working time on that day. The system schedules no planned work on Sunday, honoring the non-working time exception on Sunday because it is not the planned start or planned finish date of the task. As expected, the system applies 4 hours of work to the next three working days for the assigned resource.

Why did Microsoft Project 2010 calculate and apply 9 hours on Thursday? Here is the first oddity you may face when using *Manually Scheduled* tasks. The system calculated 9 hours of work to span the gap between the working times specified on the resource calendar and the finish time of the task. The resource works from 8:00 AM – 12:00 PM, but the task does not end until 5:00 PM. Because the resource stops working at noon, the system creates a 9-hour **Elapsed Time** exception to honor the finish time of the task. Figure 7 - 67 shows the *Task Usage* view with the timephased grid for Thursday zoomed to the *Days Over Hours* level of zoom. You can see how the system calculated 9 hours of work, applying 1 hour of work for each one-hour time period from 8:00 AM – 5:00 PM, including the non-working time period from 12:00 – 1:00 PM.

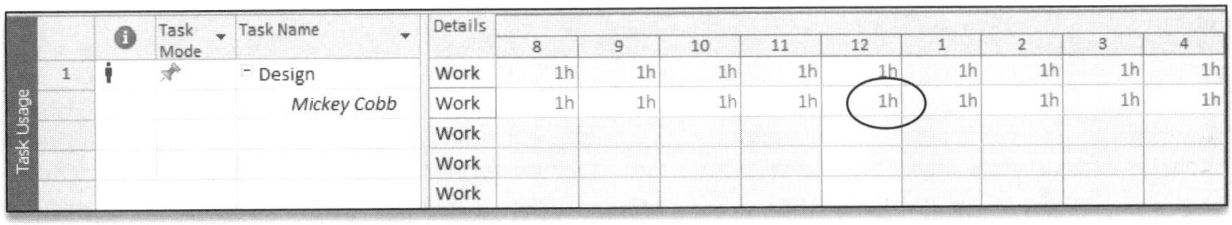

			Task Mode	Task Name	Details	8	9	10	11	12	1	2	3	4
		ⓘ												
1	ⅰ		📌	⁻ Design	Work	1h	1h	1h	1h	1h	1h	1h	1h	1h
				Mickey Cobb	Work	1h	1h	1h	1h	1h	1h	1h	1h	1h
					Work									
					Work									
					Work									

Figure 7 - 67: Work distribution for Thursday shown in the Task Usage view with the timephased grid zoomed to Days Over Hours

Next, consider a more complex scenario where I set the schedule as half days from 8:00 AM - 12:00 PM on the *Project calendar*, and where I set the *Default start time* to *8:00 AM* and the *Default end time* to *12:00 PM* in the *Project Options* dialog. In this case, I also assign a resource whose calendar used a working schedule of 1:00 – 5:00 PM. In other words, there is no overlap in the working schedule between the resource's calendar and the *Project calendar*.

Warning: Make sure that your *Calendar Settings* agree with your working time settings in the *Project* base calendar or your duration calculation may become confusing.

To set up this special scenario, I completed the following steps in Microsoft Project 2010:

1. Create a new *Manually Scheduled* task.

2. Insert the *Work* column in the *Gantt Chart* view.

3. Enter *20 hours* of estimated work in the *Work* column for the task.

4. Enter *5 days* in the *Duration* column for the task.

Given that the *Project calendar* shows only four hours of work per day, I calculate in my head that the software should apply the 20 hours of work at 4 hours/day over the 5 days of the task duration.

5. Enter a start date of Monday, August 5th, 2013 in the *Start* column for the task.

Figure 7 - 68 shows the result in Microsoft Project 2010. Notice that the system assumed a *Start* time of *8:00 AM* for the task and calculated a *Finish* date and time *August 9, 2013* at *12:00 PM*. At this point, the behavior of the *Manually Scheduled* task seems consistent and predictable.

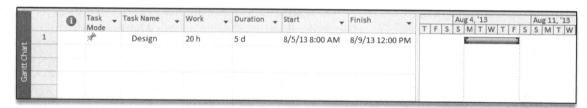

Figure 7 - 68: Manually Scheduled task, no resource assigned

When I apply the *Task Usage* view shown in Figure 7 - 69, you can see that the system applies the work evenly at 4 hours per day across 5 days of duration, as you might expect it to do for an *Auto Scheduled* task.

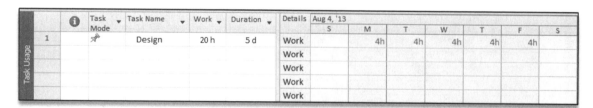

Figure 7 - 69: Work distribution for a Manually Scheduled task without a resource

6. I assign a resource to the *Manually Scheduled* task at a *Units* value of *100%*.

Remember that the working schedule on the resource's calendar is Monday through Friday, from 1:00 – 5:00 PM. In other words, there is absolutely **no overlap** between the working schedules shown on the resource's calendar and on the *Project calendar*. The system calculates *33 hours* in the *Work* field, as shown in Figure 7 - 70.

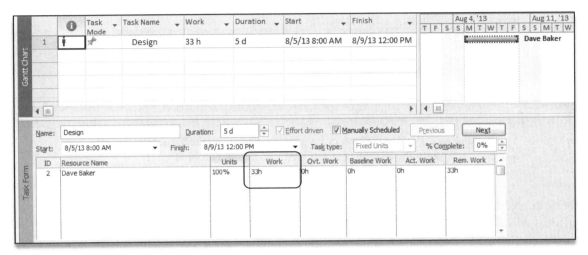

Figure 7 - 70: Manually Scheduled work calculation with differing calendars

When I apply the *Task Usage* view shown in Figure 7 - 71, you can see how Microsoft Project 2010 calculated the 33 hours of work and then applied the work to the resource assignment. Notice the following:

- The system applied **9 hours** of planned time on Monday, August 5.

- The system applied 4 hours of work per day from Tuesday through Thursday, August 6-8.

- The system applied **12 hours** of work on Friday, August 9.

	i	Task Mode	Task Name	Work	Duration	Details	Aug 4, '13 S	M	T	W	T	F	S
1	i	📌	⊟ Design	33 h	5 d	Work		9h	4h	4h	4h	12h	
			Dave Baker	33 h		Work		9h	4h	4h	4h	12h	
						Work							
						Work							
						Work							

Figure 7 - 71: Work distribution shown in the Task Usage view

How did Microsoft Project 2010 calculate and apply 9 hours of work on Monday? Here is the second oddity you may face when using *Manually Scheduled* tasks. Because the resource works from 1:00 - 5:00 PM, the system applies 4 hours of work during this time span. Remember that the task schedule is 8:00 AM – 12:00 PM. Because of this, the system creates an **Elapsed Time** exception to fill the gap between the start time of the task and the start time of the resource on Monday, adding 5 hours of work value to honor the task start time. This includes the 1-hour time period from 12:00 – 1:00 PM, and yields a total of 9 hours of work on Monday. As expected, the system applies 4 hours of work to the next three working days for the assigned resource.

Figure 7 - 72 shows the *Task Usage* view with the timephased grid for Monday zoomed to the *Days Over Hours* level of zoom. You can see how the system calculated 9 hours of work, applying 1 hour of work for each one-hour time period from 8:00 AM – 5:00 PM, including the non-working time period from 12:00 – 1:00 PM.

Figure 7 - 72: Work distribution for Monday shown in the Task Usage view with the timephased grid zoomed to Days Over Hours

How did Microsoft Project 2010 calculate and apply 12 hours of work on Friday? Here is the third oddity you may face when using *Manually Scheduled* tasks. On Friday, the task finish time (12:00 PM) is earlier than the start time of the assigned resource (1:00 PM). Because the resource has working time, but no working time that intersects with the task, the system creates an **Elapsed Time** exception by counting backwards from the end time of the task until it encounters either available working time or the beginning of the day. In this case, there is no available working time between 12:00 noon (when the task finishes) and 12:00 midnight (the beginning of the day), so the system adds 12 hours of working time to the task starting at 12:00 midnight to honor the finish time.

Figure 7 - 73 shows the *Task Usage* view with the timephased grid for Friday zoomed to the *Days Over 2-Hour Time Periods* level of zoom. You can see how the system calculated 12 hours of work, applying the work from 12:00 midnight to 12:00 noon that day.

Figure 7 - 73: Work distribution for Friday shown in the Task Usage view with the timephased grid zoomed to Days Over 2-Hour time periods

Understand that when you see these odd work values in your schedule for *Manually Scheduled* tasks, you must expose both the date and the time in the *Start* and *Finish* fields and you must be aware of the start and end times on the resource calendar to make sense of the calculations. When you assign multiple resources to tasks, the system applies the same set of rules to each resource when calculating work values. Remember that the system may need to create **Elapsed Time** exceptions that count forward or backwards to a working time period or the end of the day in order to anchor the tasks and honor start and end times.

Warning: In the release version (RTM) of Microsoft Project 2010, the built-in leveling tool does not recognize work for a resource on any day that includes an **Elapsed Time** exception. This may affect how the system levels resource overcalculations in your projects if you use *Manually Scheduled* tasks.

As referenced in the previous *Warning* note, you must be aware of the default behavior of Microsoft Project 2010 when leveling resource overallocations on *Manually Scheduled* tasks. Keep in mind that when you have *Manually Scheduled* tasks that contain **Elapsed Time** exceptions included in your work paths, the built-in leveling tool does not recognize work values on these days. Instead, you must look for these exceptions and add additional leveling delays to correct for this manually. Also note that Microsoft is aware of this problem and hopes to fix it in a future service pack for Microsoft Project 2010 or n the next version of Microsoft Project.

MSProjectExperts recommends that you do not use *Manually Scheduled* tasks that span non-working days and times if an accurate work value calculation is critical to your project planning. Use *Manually Scheduled* tasks only if you are fully familiar with the method the system uses to calculate **Default Day** and **Elapsed Time** exceptions, and you compensate for the additonal work values when you encounter them.

Hands On Exercise

Exercise 7-16

Examine the working schedule on the *Standard* calendar and a resource calendar. Set up Microsoft Project 2010 to view the **dates and times** for the start and finish of each task in a project.

1. Open the **Digging Deeper into Manually Scheduled Tasks.mpp** sample file.

2. Closely examine the **dates and times** for each task in the *Start* and *Finish* columns.

3. On the *Project* ribbon, click the *Change Working Time* button.

4. In the calendar grid at the top of the *Change Working Time* dialog, select any working day from Monday through Friday.

5. In the upper right corner of the *Change Working Time* dialog, examine the working schedule for the *Standard* calendar.

Notice that the working time for the *Standard* calendar is Monday through Friday from 8:00 AM – 12:00 PM.

6. At the top of the *Change Working Time* dialog, click the *For calendar* pick list and select *Chuck Kirkpatrick* on the list.

Notice that the working time on the calendar for Chuck Kirkpatrick is Monday through Friday from 1:00 – 5:00 PM. Keep in mind that there is **no common working time** between the *Standard* calendar and the resource calendar for Chuck Kirkpatrick.

7. Click the *Cancel* button to close the *Change Working Time* dialog.

8. Click the *File* tab and then click the *Options* item in the *Backstage* menu.

9. On the *General* page of the *Project Options* dialog, click the *Date Format* pick list and select the *1/28/09 12:33 PM* item.

Completing the previous step allows you to see both the **date and time** in the *Start* and *Finish* columns for any task.

10. Click the *OK* button to close the *Project Options* dialog.

11. Drag the split bar to the right edge of the *Finish* column.

Exercise 7-17

Study the behavior of **Default Day** and **Elapsed Time** exceptions on scheduling.

1. In the *Gantt Chart* pane, select the *Design* task, if necessary.

2. In the *Task Form* pane, assign *Chuck Kirkpatrick* at *100% Units* and then click the *OK* button.

Notice in the *Task Form* pane that Microsoft Project 2010 calculates **33 hours** of work, rather than the 20 hours of work you might expect. Notice also that the system displays the "burning man" icon to the left of the *Design* and *Build* tasks, indicating that Chuck Kirkpatrick is overallocated on these two tasks.

3. In the *View* section of the *Task* ribbon, click the *Gantt Chart* pick list button and select the *Task Usage* view on the list.

4. In the *Task Usage* pane, select the *Design* task and then click the *Scroll to Task* button in the *Editing* section of the *Task* ribbon to bring the planned work hours into view in the timephased grid.

Notice that the system calculates 9 hours of work on Monday May 5, by applying 4 hours of normal working time to the resource and then calculating an **Elapsed Time** exception to close the gap between the start of the task at 8:00 AM and the start time for the resource at 1:00 PM, adding an additional 5 hours of work.

Notice that Microsoft Project 2010 calculates 12 hours of work on Friday, May 9. Because the day contains working time it does not create a **Default Day** exception. However, there is no working time available on the effective calendar before the end time of the task so the system creates an **Elapsed Time** exception counting backwards from the end time of the task at 12:00 PM until it reaches the beginning of the day at 12:00 AM.

5. In the *Task* ribbon, click the *Gantt Chart* button to reapply the *Gantt Chart* view in the upper pane.

6. In the *Gantt Chart* pane, select the *Test* task.

7. In the *Task Form* pane, assign *Chuck Kirkpatrick* to this task at *100% Units* and then click the *OK* button.

8. In the *View* section of the *Task* ribbon, click the *Gantt Chart* pick list button and select the *Task Usage* view on the list.

9. In the *Task Usage* pane, select the *Test* task and then click the *Scroll to Task* button to bring the planned work hours into view in the timephased grid.

Notice that the system calculates **33 hours** of work for this task as well. Notice also that the system creates the same **Elapsed Time** exceptions as it did for the *Design* task, but it respects the non-working time for Saturday and Sunday and schedules no work on those two weekend days.

10. In the *Task* ribbon, click the *Gantt Chart* button to reapply the *Gantt Chart* view in the upper pane.

11. In the *Gantt Chart* pane, select the *Rebuild* task.

12. In the *Task Form* pane, assign *Chuck Kirkpatrick* to this task at *100% Units* and then click the *OK* button.

Notice that Microsoft Project 2010 calculates **8 hours** of work for this task. Because the start time of the task is 1:00 PM, which matches the start time of the resource calendar, the system does not need to create any exceptions to calculate and schedule the work for this task. Notice also that the Gantt bar for this 2-day task does not span two calendar days. This is because the start time of the task on Thursday, May 22 (1:00 PM) does not match the start time on the *Standard* calendar (8:00 AM). To compensate, Microsoft Project 2010 displays the start of the Gantt bar on Friday, May 23, at 8:00 AM.

13. In the *Gantt Chart* pane, select the *Implement* task.

14. In the *Task Form* pane, assign *Chuck Kirkpatrick* to this task at *100% Units* and then click the *OK* button.

15. In the *View* section of the *Task* ribbon, click the *Gantt Chart* pick list button and select the *Task Usage* view on the list.

16. In the *Task Usage* pane, select the *Implement* task and then click the *Scroll to Task* button to bring the planned work hours into view in the timephased grid.

Notice that the system calculates **24 hours** of work for this task. Even though the task starts at 1:00 PM on Monday, May 26 (which is the Memorial Day holiday), the system still schedules 4 hours of work on that day. Even though the task finishes at 5:00 PM on Saturday, May 31 (which is a nonworking day), the system still schedules 4 hours of work on that day. The system does this by creating a **Default Day** exception for each of these days. For each of the working days from Tuesday through Friday, the system schedules 4 hours of work per day.

17. In the *Task* ribbon, click the *Gantt Chart* button to reapply the *Gantt Chart* view in the upper pane.

18. Click the *View* tab to display the *View* ribbon.

19. Deselect the *Details* checkbox to close the *Task Form* pane.

20. Click the *Task* tab to display the *Task* ribbon again.

Exercise 7-18

Study the effect of **Elapsed Time** exceptions on resource leveling.

1. Select the *Build* task and then click the *Scroll to Task* button in the *Editing* section of the *Task* ribbon.

2. To level the resource overallocation on the *Build* task, right-click anywhere in the task and then click the *Reschedule to Available Date* item on the shortcut menu.

To resolve the resource overallocation, notice that Microsoft Project 2010 applies a leveling delay to the task. The system reschedules the task to start on Friday, May 9, at 1:00 PM and finish on Thursday, May 15 at 5:00 PM. The system does this **in spite** of the fact that the resource is already fully booked on these two days on the *Design* task and the *Test* task! Remember that in the release version (RTM) of Microsoft Project 2010, the built-in leveling tool does not recognize work for a resource on any day that includes an **Elapsed Time** exception.

3. Click the *File* tab and then click the *Options* item in the *Backstage* menu.

4. On the *General* page of the *Project Options* dialog, click the *Date Format* pick list and select **your preferred format** for date display.

5. Click the *OK* button to close the *Project Options* dialog.

6. Save and close the **Digging Deeper into Manually Scheduled Tasks.mpp** sample file.

Module 08

Project Execution

Learning Objectives

After completing this module, you will be able to:

- Reschedule an unstarted project to a new start date
- View the Critical Path for a project
- Save an original baseline for a project
- Understand the proper use of the multiple Baseline fields in Microsoft Project 2010
- Understand the three primary methods for entering project progress
- Enter progress for a Cost resource
- Reschedule uncompleted work from past reporting periods into the current reporting period
- Reschedule a task to a future time period
- Set a task to Inactive status
- Synchronize a project with a SharePoint Tasks list

Inside Module 08

Understanding the Execution Process

Project execution is the process of doing the actual work described in the project plan. During the execution stage of each project, you typically perform each of the following actions:

- View the Critical Path.

- Save an original project baseline.

- Track project progress.

- Analyze project variance.

- Revise the project.

- Manage project changes.

- Report on project progress.

In this module, I discuss the topics shown in the first three bulleted list items, plus I discuss additional topics relevant to the execution stage of a project. In succeeding modules, I discuss the other actions you need to perform in Microsoft Project 2010 during the execution stage of your project.

Rescheduling an Unstarted Project

Many project managers face the problem of rescheduling the start date of an unstarted project. Common reasons for rescheduling an unstarted project include budget shortfalls and lack of resources. For example, consider the unstarted project shown in Figure 8 - 1. When I planned the project originally, I did the following:

- I scheduled the project to start on April 16.

- I set a *Finish No Later Than* constraint of May 5 on the Phase I Complete milestone task.

- I set a *Start No Earlier Than* constraint of June 18 on the Test Beta Classes task.

- I set a *deadline date* of June 12 on the Phase II Complete milestone to signify the target finish date of Phase II.

- I set a *deadline date* of July 20 on the Project Complete milestone to signify the target finish date of the entire project.

To make it easier for you to see the *deadline date* symbols in the Gantt chart shown in Figure 8 - 1, I removed the dates that Microsoft Project 2010 usually displays to the right of each milestone symbol. This way you can easily see both the *Milestone* symbols and the *deadline date* symbols on the Phase II Complete and Project Complete milestone tasks.

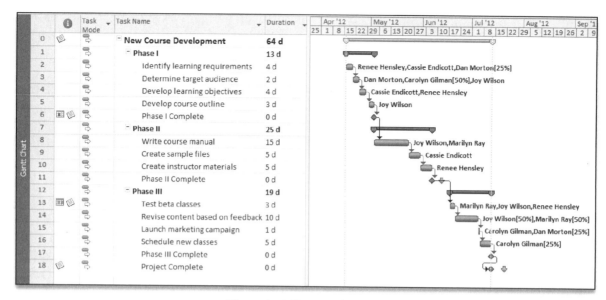

Figure 8 - 1: Unstarted project

Shortly before team members began work on this project, company management announced a 4-week delay to allow the project team members to work on a higher priority project. In previous versions of Microsoft Project, project managers can reschedule the project by clicking the *Adjust Dates* button on the *Analysis* toolbar. The limitation of the *Adjust Dates* dialog in previous versions of the software is that the tool does not reschedule *Deadline* dates, thus forcing the project manager to manually change *Deadline* dates after rescheduling the project *Start* date.

In Microsoft Project 2010, you can reschedule the *Start* date of an unstarted project by clicking the *Project* tab and then clicking the *Move Project* button in the *Schedule* section of the *Project* ribbon. When you click the *Move Project* button, the system displays the *Move Project* dialog shown in Figure 8 - 2.

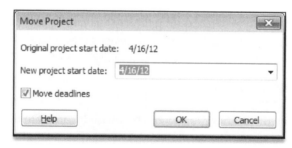

Figure 8 - 2: Move Project dialog

In the *Move Project* dialog, the system displays the current project *Start* date in the *Original project start date* field. To reschedule the project, enter or select a new project *Start* date in the *New project start date* field. If you want the system to reschedule *Deadline* dates, leave the *Move deadlines* option selected. When you click the *OK* button, Microsoft Project 2010 reschedules your project using the following actions:

- The system enters your new project *Start* date in the *Start date* field of the *Project Information* dialog.

- The system reschedules the dates of constraints, based on the duration difference measured in working days between the original *Start* date and the new *Start* date of the project.

- The system reschedules *Deadline* dates, based on the duration difference measured in working days between the original *Start* date and the new *Start* date of the project.

Figure 8 - 3 shows the unstarted project rescheduled to start 4 weeks (20 working days) later than originally planned. After entering the new project *Start* date of May 14 in the *Move Project* dialog, Microsoft Project 2010 did the following:

- The system entered May 14 in the *Start date* field of the *Project Information* dialog.

- The system changed the *Finish No Later Than* constraint date on the Phase I Complete milestone task from May 5 to June 2 (20 working days).

- The system changed the *Start No Earlier Than* constraint date on the Test Beta Classes task from June 18 to July 16 (20 working days).

- The system changed the *Deadline* date on the Phase II Complete milestone task from June 12 to July 11 (20 working days).

- The system changed the *Deadline* date on the Project Complete milestone task from July 20 to August 18 (20 working days).

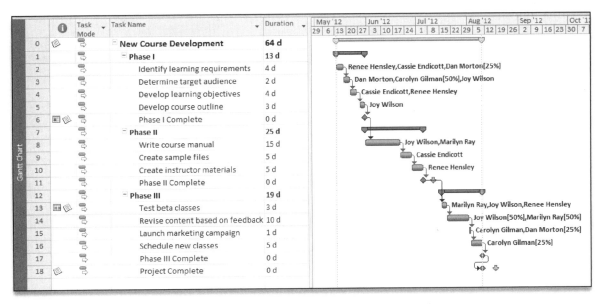

Figure 8 - 3: Unstarted project rescheduled 20 days later

Keep in mind that when you use the *Move Project* dialog to reschedule your project, Microsoft Project 2010 assumes that you want to move *Constraint* dates and *Deadline* dates exactly the same number of days that you moved the project *Start* date. In reality, this may not be true, and you may need to change the *Constraint* dates and *Deadline* dates manually. In addition, if you set a *Baseline* for the unstarted project before rescheduling it, you may want to set a new *Baseline* for the project to capture the new schedule information.

Hands On Exercise

Exercise 8-1

Reschedule the *Start* date of an unstarted project to a date four months in the future due to a shortage of resources to work in the project.

1. Open the **Reschedule an Unstarted Project.mpp** sample file.

Notice that three tasks in the project contain constraints and the *Project Complete* milestone tasks includes a *Deadline* date.

2. Float your mouse pointer over the constraint indicators in the *Indicators* column and examine the *Constraint* dates for the three tasks with constraints.

3. Examine the *Deadline* date on the *Project Complete* milestone task.

4. Click the *Project* tab and then click the *Move Project* button in the *Schedule* section of the *Project* ribbon.

5. In the *Move Project* dialog, enter the date **October 7, 2013** in the *New project start date* field.

6. In the *Move Project* dialog, leave the *Move deadlines* option selected.

7. Click the *OK* button to reschedule the project.

Notice that Microsoft Project 2010 displays *Change Highlighting* on the duration values of the *Project Summary Task* (Row 0) and on the *Training* summary task. This indicates a change in duration due to the Thanksgiving weekend company holidays after rescheduling the project *Start* date.

8. Float your mouse pointer over the constraint indicators in the *Indicators* column and examine the **new** *Constraint* dates on the three tasks with constraints.

9. Examine the **new** *Deadline* date on the *Project Complete* milestone task.

10. Save and close the **Reschedule an Unstarted Project.mpp** sample file.

Viewing the Critical Path

Microsoft Project 2010 defines the **Critical Path** as "The series of tasks that must be completed on schedule for a project to finish on schedule." Every task on the Critical Path is a **Critical task**. By default, all tasks on the Critical Path have a Total Slack of 0 days, which means they cannot slip without delaying the project *Finish* date. If the *Finish* date of any Critical task slips by even 1 day, the projects *Finish* date slips as well.

Microsoft Project 2010 defines a **non-Critical task** as any task that is 100% complete or any task with a Total Slack greater than 0 days. A non-Critical task can slip by its amount of Total Slack before it impacts the *Finish* date of the project. For example, if a task has 5 days of Total Slack, the task can finish 5 days late before the resulting slippage would change the project *Finish* date. To manage your project well, you should be aware of the non-Critical tasks in your project, but you should focus your energies on managing the tasks on the Critical Path.

Microsoft Project 2010 automatically calculates the *Total Slack* field value for each task to determine the Critical Path of the project. To view the Total Slack for any task, apply the *View* ribbon, click the *Tables* button in the *Data* section of the *View* ribbon, and then select the *Schedule* table. The *Total Slack* column is the last column on the right side of the *Schedule* table.

In Microsoft Project 2010, the Critical Path may run from the *Start* date to the *Finish* date of the project, or it may begin anywhere in the project and run to the *Finish* date of the project. This behavior is a key difference from the traditional Critical Path Method (CPM) definition of the Critical Path.

If you make changes to your project, either by entering actual progress or by making plan revisions, keep in mind that the Critical Path may change.

There are a number of ways to determine the Critical Path in any project in Microsoft Project 2010. The simplest method is to format the *Gantt Chart* view to display red Gantt bars for Critical tasks. To format the *Gantt Chart* view, complete the following steps:

1. Click the *View* tab and then click the *Gantt Chart* button in the *Task Views* section of the *View* ribbon.

2. Click the *Format* tab to display the *Format* ribbon.

3. Select the *Critical Tasks* checkbox in the *Bar Styles* section of the *Format* ribbon.

4. Optionally select the *Slack* checkbox as well.

In the formatted *Gantt Chart* view shown in Figure 8 - 4, notice that Microsoft Project 2010 displays the following:

- **Red bars** represent Critical tasks on the Critical Path. These tasks have a Total Slack of 0 days.

- **Blue bars** represent non-Critical tasks. These tasks are completed tasks or have a Total Slack greater than 0 days.

- A **black stripe** to the right of any Gantt bar represents the amount of Total Slack for the task.

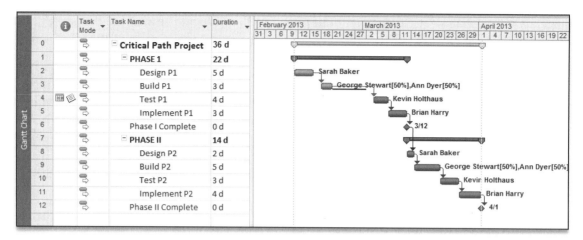

Figure 8 - 4: Gantt Chart formatted to show the Critical Path and Total Slack

Warning: Because of an unfixed bug in the release (RTM) version of Microsoft Project 2010, when you select the *Critical Tasks* checkbox on the *Format* ribbon, the system **removes** the names of assigned resources displayed to the right of Gantt bars for Critical tasks. To display the names of your assigned resources, double-click anywhere in the white part of the Gantt chart to display the *Bar Styles* dialog. Scroll to the bottom of the list, select the *Critcal* item, and then select the *Text* tab. On the *Text* tab, click the *Right* pick list and select the *Resource Names* field. Click the *OK* button when finished.

You can also view the Critical Path in any project by applying the *Tracking Gantt* view. Be aware, however, that the *Tracking Gantt* view displays Gantt bars for both the Critical Path and for the baseline schedule of the project. Remember that red Gantt bars show Critical tasks, blue Gantt bars show non-Critical tasks, and gray Gantt bars show the original baseline schedule of each task.

In Microsoft Project 2010, you can change the software's definition of a Critical task by clicking the *File* tab and then clicking the *Options* item in the *Backstage* menu. In the *Project Options* dialog, select the *Advanced* tab and then scroll down to the *Calculation options for this project* section of the dialog. To change the software's definition of a Critical task, change the *Tasks are critical if slack is less than or equal to* option to a value greater than 0 days, and then click the *OK* button.

Using this technique is a helpful way to see the "nearly Critical tasks" in your project. "Nearly Critical tasks" are those tasks that are not on the true Critical Path, but are close enough to impact the *Finish* date of the project if they slip by an amount greater than their *Total Slack* value. For example, I have a task with only 1 day of Total Slack, so this task is not a true Critical task since it has a *Total Slack* value greater than 0 days. However, if this task slips only 2 days, the *Finish* date of the project slips as well. Therefore, it is not a bad idea to identify the "nearly Critical tasks" in any project.

Hands On Exercise

Exercise 8-2

Display the Critical Path and Total Slack in your Training Advisor Rollout project. View the Total Slack for each task, and then display "nearly Critical tasks" as well.

1. Open the **Training Advisor 08.mpp** sample file.

2. Click the *Format* tab and then select the *Critical Tasks* and *Slack* checkboxes in the *Bar Styles* section of the *Format* ribbon.

Notice that Microsoft Project 2010 displays Critical tasks with red Gantt bars, non-Critical tasks with blue Gantt bars, and Total Slack with a black stripe to the right of several blue Gantt bars. Because of a bug in the release (RTM) version of the software, notice also that the resource names no longer appear to the right of the red Gantt bars.

3. In the *Bar Styles* section of the *Format* ribbon, click the *Format* pick list button and select the *Bar Styles* item on the list.

4. In the *Bar Styles* dialog, scroll down to the bottom of the list and select the *Critical* item.

5. In the lower left corner of the *Bar Styles* dialog, click the *Text* tab.

6. Click the *Right* pick list and select the *Resource Names* field.

7. Click the *OK* button.

8. Right-click on the *Select All* button (upper left corner of the task sheet) and select the *Schedule* table.

9. Pull the split bar to the right so that you can view the *Total Slack* column on the far right side of the *Schedule* table.

Notice that the *Total Slack* value for every Critical task is *0 days*, indicating that these tasks cannot slip without delaying the project *Finish* date. Notice also that the first three tasks in the *Installation* phase have only 1 day of Total Slack.

10. In the *Data* section of the *View* ribbon, click the *Tables* pick list button and select the *Entry* table.

11. Dock the split bar on the right edge of the *Duration* column.

12. Click the *File* tab and then click the *Options* item in the *Backstage* menu.

13. In the *Project Options* dialog, select the *Advanced* tab and then scroll down to the *Calculation options for this project* section of the dialog.

14. Change the *Tasks are critical if slack is less than or equal to* option value to *2 days*, and then click the *OK* button.

Notice that Microsoft Project 2010 displays red Gantt bars for the first three tasks in the *Installation* phase. The software now shows the true Critical Path, along with "nearly Critical tasks" as well. You can use this technique at any time to see "nearly Critical tasks" in any project.

15. Click the *Undo* button in your *Quick Access Toolbar* to redisplay only the true Critical Path in the project.

16. Save but **do not** close the **Training Advisor 08.mpp** sample file.

Working with Project Baselines

Prior to executing a project, you should save a baseline for your project. All of the variance measurements that Microsoft Project 2010 calculates for you are dependent on the existence of a baseline. A baseline represents a snapshot of the work, cost, and schedule estimates as represented in your initial project plan. Your baseline should represent the schedule your stakeholders approved before you begin tracking progress. Saving a project baseline provides you with a way to analyze project variance by comparing the current state of the project against the original planned state of the project (the baseline).

When you save a baseline in Microsoft Project 2010, the software captures the current values for five important task fields and two important resource fields, and then saves these values in a corresponding set of Baseline fields. Table 8 - 1 shows the original fields and their corresponding Baseline fields.

Data Type	Field	Baseline Field
Task	Duration	Baseline Duration
Task	Start	Baseline Start
Task	Finish	Baseline Finish
Task	Work	Baseline Work
Task	Cost	Baseline Cost
Resource	Work	Baseline Work
Resource	Cost	Baseline Cost

Table 8 - 1: Baseline information

In addition to the five important task fields captured in the baseline, Microsoft Project 2010 also captures the information in several other task fields as well. The software captures the extra cost information in the *Fixed Cost* and *Fixed Cost Accrual* fields, saving this information in the *Baseline Fixed Cost* and *Baseline Fixed Cost Accrual* fields respectively. The software also captures the estimated task schedule information in the *Scheduled Duration, Scheduled Start,* and *Scheduled Finish* fields, saving this information in the *Baseline Estimated Duration, Baseline Estimated Start,* and *Baseline Estimated Finish* fields respectively. Remember that Microsoft Project 2010 uses these estimated schedule fields primarily with the new *Manually Scheduled* tasks feature. If you use *Budget Cost* resources in your project, Microsoft Project 2010 also captures budget information in the *Budget Cost* and *Budget Work* fields, saving this information in the *Baseline Budget Cost* and *Baseline Budget Work* fields respectively.

Microsoft Project 2010 also saves the timephased values for both tasks and resources in the timephased *Baseline Work* and *Baseline Cost* fields as well. You can view these timephased values in the timephased grid portion of either the *Task Usage* and *Resource Usage* views.

Saving a Project Baseline

To save a baseline for the entire project in Microsoft Project 2010, complete the following steps:

1. Click the *Project* tab to display the *Project* ribbon.

2. In the *Schedule* section of the *Project* ribbon, click the *Set Baseline* pick list button and select the *Set Baseline* item on the list. The system displays the *Set Baseline* dialog shown in Figure 8 - 5.

Figure 8 - 5: Set Baseline dialog

3. Select the *Set Baseline* option.

4. Leave the *Baseline* item selected in the *Set Baseline* pick list.

5. In the *For:* section, leave the *Entire project* option selected.

6. Click the *OK* button.

MSProjectExperts recommends that you save an original baseline for the entire project only once during the life of the project. After a change control procedure that adds new tasks to your project, you may save a baseline for only the new tasks. This maintains the integrity of your original project baseline.

Saving a "Rolling Baseline"

Some project managers must begin the execution stage for a project that they have not completely planned, but they still need to save a baseline for the portion they have completely planned. To understand this unique baseline need, consider the following example:

- Your project consists of three consecutive phases, named Phase I, Phase II, and Phase III.

- You must completely plan the tasks in Phase I, but do only "skeleton planning" for the tasks in Phase II and Phase III.

- You must baseline the Phase I tasks and then begin the execution of the Phase I tasks.

- As the work progresses in Phase I, you do the detailed planning for the tasks in Phase II and then baseline only those tasks.

- As the work begins in Phase II, you do the detailed planning for tasks in Phase III and then baseline only those tasks.

The preceding description characterizes the need for saving a "rolling baseline" to capture the baseline information in a series of rolling waves. The "rolling baseline" captures the original values in Phase I, then later appends the baseline information from Phase II, and finally appends the baseline information from Phase III as well. To save a "rolling baseline" for each set of selected tasks in a project, complete the following steps:

1. Select the tasks you are ready to baseline.

2. In the *Schedule* section of the *Project* ribbon, click the *Set Baseline* pick list button and select the *Set Baseline* item on the list.

3. Select the *Set Baseline* option.

4. Leave the *Baseline* item selected in the *Set Baseline* pick list.

5. In the *For:* section, choose the *Selected Tasks* option.

6. In the *Roll Up Baselines* section, select the *To all summary tasks* option, as shown in Figure 8-7.

**Figure 8 - 6: Set Baseline dialog,
ready to baseline selected tasks**

7. Click the *Set as Default* button.

8. Click the *OK* button.

9. When you baseline the Phase II and Phase III tasks, click the *Yes* button in the warning dialog about overwriting the baseline.

Saving Over a Previous Baseline

To determine whether you previously saved an original baseline in a project, simply click Tools ➤ Tracking ➤ Set Baseline. Microsoft Project 2010 indicates whether you previously saved a baseline displaying the date on which you saved it, as displayed in Figure 8 - 7.

**Figure 8 - 7: Last saved on date
in the Set Baseline dialog**

If you attempt to save baseline information over your original baseline, Microsoft Project 2010 warns you with the message in the dialog shown in Figure 8 - 8.

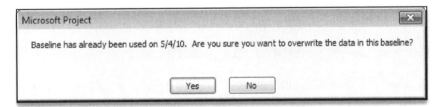

**Figure 8 - 8: Warning dialog
Overwrite original baseline**

If you are saving additional baseline information in the "rolling baseline" process, then click the *Yes* button in the warning dialog shown in Figure 8 - 9. The software **does not** overwrite your original baseline information as indicated in the dialog, but simply appends the new information to the original baseline.

Viewing the Project Baseline

When you save a project baseline, Microsoft Project 2010 copies the current values from one set of fields into the corresponding set of Baseline fields. You can view the baseline data for your project tasks by completing the following steps:

1. Display any task view, such as the *Gantt Chart* or *Task Sheet* view.

2. Right-click the *Select All* button and then select the *More Tables* item on the shortcut menu.

3. In the *More Tables* dialog, select the *Baseline* table and click the *Apply* button.

Figure 8 - 9 shows the task *Baseline* table applied to the *Gantt Chart* view.

		Task Name	Baseline Dur.	Baseline Start	Baseline Finish	Baseline Work	Baseline Cost
	0	**Critical Path Project**	36 d	2/11/13	4/1/13	232 h	$14,600.00
	1	**PHASE 1**	22 d	2/11/13	3/12/13	120 h	$7,000.00
	2	Design P1	5 d	2/11/13	2/15/13	40 h	$2,000.00
	3	Build P1	3 d	2/18/13	2/20/13	24 h	$1,800.00
	4	Test P1	4 d	3/4/13	3/7/13	32 h	$800.00
	5	Implement P1	3 d	3/8/13	3/12/13	24 h	$2,400.00
	6	Phase I Complete	0 d	3/12/13	3/12/13	0 h	$0.00
	7	**PHASE II**	14 d	3/13/13	4/1/13	112 h	$7,600.00
	8	Design P2	2 d	3/13/13	3/14/13	16 h	$800.00
	9	Build P2	5 d	3/15/13	3/21/13	40 h	$3,000.00
	10	Test P2	3 d	3/22/13	3/26/13	24 h	$600.00
	11	Implement P2	4 d	3/27/13	4/1/13	32 h	$3,200.00
	12	Phase II Complete	0 d	4/1/13	4/1/13	0 h	$0.00

Figure 8 - 9: Gantt Chart view, Baseline table applied

In all previous versions of Microsoft Project, the *Baseline* table includes the *Baseline Duration* column to the right of the *Task Name* column. In Microsoft Project 2010, the *Baseline* table includes the *Baseline Estimated Duration* column in place of the *Baseline Duration* column. Do not be confused by the column header of the *Baseline Estimated Duration* column, however. Microsoft added a *Title* to the column so that *Baseline Duration* appears in the column header instead of *Baseline Estimated Duration*.

Unlike the default task *Baseline* table, Microsoft Project 2010 **does not** contain a default resource *Baseline* table that shows only the baseline values for each resource. To display the *Baseline Work* and *Baseline Cost* values for each resource, complete the following steps:

1. Apply the *Resource Sheet* view.

2. Right-click on the *Type* column header and then select *Insert Column* from the shortcut menu.

3. In the pick list of available fields, select the *Baseline Work* field.

4. Right-click on the *Type* column header again and then select *Insert Column* from the shortcut menu.

5. In the pick list of available fields, select the *Baseline Cost* field.

Figure 8 - 10 shows the *Resource Sheet* view with the *Baseline Work* and *Baseline Cost* inserted temporarily in the resource *Entry* table.

Figure 8 - 10: Resource Sheet view with baseline fields

To remove the *Baseline Work* and *Baseline Cost* fields from the *Resource Sheet* view, do the following:

1. Select the column headers of both *Baseline* fields.

2. Right-click on the selected column headers and then click the *Hide Column* menu item.

Clearing the Project Baseline

You may need to clear the baseline information for a project, such as when management decides to delay the start of your project indefinitely. In a situation like this, your baseline information is invalid when your executives finally determine a new project start date. To clear the baseline values for your project complete the following steps:

1. In the *Schedule* section of the *Project* ribbon, click the *Set Baseline* pick list button and select the *Clear Baseline* item on the list. Microsoft Project 2010 displays the *Clear Baseline* dialog shown in Figure 8 - 11.

Figure 8 - 11: Clear Baseline dialog

2. Select the *Clear baseline plan* option.

3. On the *Clear baseline plan* pick list, leave the *Baseline* item selected.

4. Select the *Entire project* option.

5. Click the *OK* button.

You can clear the baseline for selected tasks only by choosing the *Selected tasks* option in the *Clear Baseline* dialog.

Using Additional Baselines

Beyond the original project baseline that you save in the *Baseline* set of fields, Microsoft Project 2010 allows you to save baseline information in up to ten additional sets of baseline fields, numbered *Baseline 1* through *Baseline 10*. You can select one by clicking the *Set baseline* pick list in the *Set Baseline* dialog shown in Figure 8 - 12.

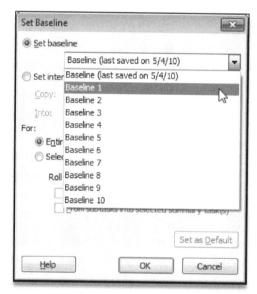

**Figure 8 - 12: Set Baseline dialog
with additional baseline fields**

There are several serious limitations to saving baseline information in one of the additional sets of baseline fields. For example, none of the additional baseline fields (such as the *Baseline 5 Duration* field) appears in any default tables in Microsoft Project 2010. This means that you must create one or more custom tables to view the additional baseline information. Beyond this, Microsoft Project 2010 calculates all task variance using the *Baseline* set of fields. This means that if you want to calculate variance using any other set of baseline fields (such as the *Baseline 5* set of fields), you must create your own custom fields containing custom formulas for this purpose.

MSProjectExperts recommends that you use the additional sets of *Baseline* fields to save historic baseline states. After you save your original baseline initially in the *Baseline* set of fields, save the baseline information a second time to *Baseline 1* set of fields. When you need to rebaseline your project, such as after a major change control procedure, save the new baseline information in the *Baseline* set of fields, and then save it a second time in the *Baseline 2* set of fields. By doing this each time you make a significant baseline change, you capture the historical data about the baseline before you rebaselined the project.

Beyond the primary baseline fields and additional sets of baseline fields, Microsoft Project 2010 allows you to save a partial set of baseline information as an *Interim Plan*. When you save an *Interim Plan*, the system saves the *Scheduled Start* date in the *Start1* field and the *Scheduled Finish* date in the *Finish1* field for each task in the project, but saves no information about the duration, cost, or work for each task. Because of this, *Interim Plan* information is limited in its usefulness. To save an *Interim Plan*, select the *Set interim plan* option in the *Set Baseline* dialog, as shown in Figure 8 - 13.

Figure 8 - 13: Save Interim Plan

The *Scheduled Start* and *Scheduled Finish* fields are new fields added in Microsoft Project 2010. The system uses these two fileds primarily with the new *Manually Scheduled* tasks feature. For *Auto Scheduled* Tasks, the *Scheduled Start* field always contains the same date as the *Start* field, and the *Scheduled Finish* field always contains the same date in the *Finish* field.

Hands On Exercise

Exercise 8-3

Now that you have completed your project planning, you are ready to save a baseline for the Training Advisor Rollout project.

1.   Return to the **Training Advisor 08.mpp** sample file.

2.   Right-click on the *Select All* button and select the *More Tables* item on the shortcut menu.

3. In the *More Tables* dialog, select the *Baseline* table and click the *Apply* button.

4. Drag the vertical split bar all the way to the right so that you can see all of the columns in the *Baseline* table.

5. In the *Schedule* section of the *Project* ribbon, click the *Set Baseline* pick list button and select the *Set Baseline* item on the list.

6. Select the *Set Baseline* option.

7. Leave the *Baseline* item selected in the *Set Baseline* pick list.

8. In the *For:* section, leave the *Entire project* option selected.

9. Click the *OK* button.

Notice the software saved baseline values for every task in the project in the five *Baseline* columns shown in the *Baseline* table.

10. Right-click on the *Select All* button again and reapply the *Entry* table.

11. Drag the vertical split bar back to the right edge of the *Duration* column.

12. In the *Schedule* section of the *Project* ribbon, click the *Set Baseline* pick list button and select the *Set Baseline* item on the list again.

Notice that the *Set Baseline* pick list displays the date you saved the baseline for this project.

13. Click the *Cancel* button to exit the *Set Baseline* dialog.

14. Save and close the **Training Advisor 08.mpp** sample file.

Tracking Project Progress

After your project team members begin working on tasks in your project, your next step is to begin collecting actual progress from your team members so that you can track project progress. You must stress the importance of tracking actual data to your team members and confirm that they are delivering accurate information to you in a timely manner. Collecting actual project data is the first step toward a clear understanding of the current state of the project.

There are three general methods for tracking project progress in Microsoft Project 2010:

- Percent Complete

- Actual Work + Remaining Work

- Daily Timesheet + Remaining Work

Each of these methods for tracking project progress offers advantages and disadvantages.

The three preceding progress-tracking methods match up with the three default progress tracking methods in Microsoft Project Server 2010. If you use Microsoft Project 2010 **without** Project Server, then you must enter actual progress from your team members manually. For example, you might print paper timesheets or create Excel spreadsheets in which your team members can report their actual progress.

Entering Progress Using Percent Complete

The simplest method of tracking progress is to ask your team members to estimate the percentage of the work that they have completed on each task during the reporting period. This method works better for construction projects, where it is more common to estimate the amount of work completed. This method is much less reliable in other environments, such as with software development projects.

The chief limitation of the Percent Complete tracking method is that it is not date-sensitive. In fact, when you enter a *Percent Complete* value for a task in Microsoft Project 2010, the software assumes that the task **started and finished as scheduled**. If you wish to use the Percent Complete method for tracking project progress, you can address this date limitation by gathering the following progress information from each team member for each task assignment:

- Actual Start date

- Percent Complete

- Actual Finish date

During each reporting period, your team members should report the actual date they began work on a task, along with their estimate of the percentage of work completed on the task. When the task is complete, your team members should report the actual date that they completed work on the task. Based on the information your team members provide for you, you can manually enter actual progress using the Percent Complete method by completing the following steps:

1. Apply the *Gantt Chart* view.

2. Right-click on the *Select All* button and select the *Tracking* table.

3. Widen the *Task Name* column, if necessary.

4. Drag the vertical split bar to the right of the *% Complete* column.

5. "Drag and drop" the *% Complete* column between the *Actual Start* and *Actual Finish* columns.

6. Enter the actual start date of each resource assignment in the *Actual Start* column.

7. Enter an estimated percent complete in the *% Complete* column.

8. When the assigned resources complete a task, enter the actual completion date in the *Actual Finish* column.

Figure 8 - 14 shows the *Tracking* table set up for the Percent Complete method of tracking progress. Notice that the Design P1 task is 100% complete with both an actual start date and an actual finish date. The Build P1 task is only 50% complete with an actual start date but with no actual finish date.

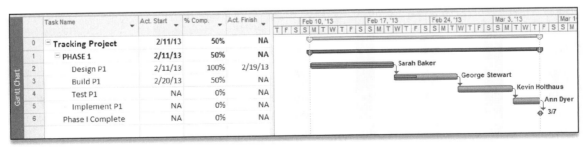

Figure 8 - 14: Tracking table set up to enter Percent Complete

Hands On Exercise

Exercise 8-4

Enter project progress for the first two weeks of the Training Advisor Rollout project using the Percent Complete method.

1. Open the **Training Advisor 08a.mpp** sample file.

2. Right-click on the *Select All* button and select the *Tracking* table from the shortcut menu.

3. Widen the *Task Name* column, if necessary.

4. "Drag and drop" the *% Complete* column between the *Actual Start* and *Actual Finish* column.

5. For task ID #17, the *Order Server* task, enter *01/06/14* in the *Actual Start* column and enter *01/07/14* in the *Actual Finish* column.

Notice that Microsoft Project 2010 marks the task as 100% complete by entering *100%* in the *% Complete* column and by displaying a black progress line in the Gantt bar for the task.

6. For task ID #28, the *Setup Test Training Server* task, enter *100%* in the *% Complete* column.

Notice that Microsoft Project 2010 enters the current start date of the task in the *Actual Start* column and enters the current finish date of the task in the *Actual Finish* column.

7. For task ID #30, the *Create Training Module 01* task, enter *01/15/14* in the *Actual Start* field.

Notice that Microsoft Project 2010 delays the Gantt bar for this task to a date two days later than the original start date. The reason for the late start date is because Ruth Andrews, the assigned resource, was sick on Monday and Tuesday of that week.

8. For the *Create Training Module 01* task, enter *60%* in the *% Complete* column.

9. Expand the occurrences of the *Project Status Meeting* recurring task.

10. Enter *100%* in the *% Complete* column for the *Project Status Meeting 1* task.

11. Collapse the occurrences of the *Project Status Meeting* recurring task.

12. Save and close the **Training Advisor 08a.mpp** sample file.

Entering Progress Using Actual Work and Remaining Work

Another tracking method requires your team members to report the total amount of actual work hours they performed to date for each task, and to provide their estimate on the amount of remaining work for each task as well. For example, a designer reports 20 hours of actual work to date on a 40-hour task, but estimates 30 hours of remaining work (rather than 20 hours) because the original 40-hour estimate of work was too low.

This tracking method allows you to see date slippage, based on any increased remaining work estimates submitted by your team members. However, this method may not present a true picture of task progress, especially if a task started late. When using this method for tracking project progress, Microsoft Project 2010 once again assumes that each task **started and finished as currently scheduled**.

If you wish to use the Actual Work and Remaining Work method of tracking project progress, you can address the date limitation issue by obtaining the following progress information from each team member for each task assignment:

- Actual Start date

- Actual Work

- Remaining Work estimate

- Actual Finish date

During each reporting period, team members report the actual date they began work on a task, the number of hours of actual work completed to date, and their estimate on the amount of remaining work hours. When a task is complete, team members report the actual date that they completed the work. Based on the information your team members provide, you can manually enter actual progress using the Actual Work and Remaining Work method by completing the following steps:

1. Apply the *Gantt Chart* view.

2. Right-click on the *Select All* button and select the *Tracking* table.

3. Widen the *Task Name* column, if necessary.

4. "Drag and drop" the *Actual Work* column between the *Actual Start* and *Actual Finish* columns.

5. Right-click on the *Actual Finish* column header and select *Insert Column* from the shortcut menu.

6. In the list of available columns, select the *Remaining Work* column.

7. Drag the vertical split bar to the right edge of the *Actual Finish* column.

8. Enter the actual start date of the task in the *Actual Start* column.

9. Enter the actual work completed to date in the *Actual Work* column.

10. Enter a revised remaining work estimate in the *Remaining Work* column, if necessary.

11. When the assigned resource completes a task, enter the actual completion date in the *Actual Finish* column.

Figure 8 - 15 shows the *Tracking* table set up for the Actual Work and Remaining Work method of tracking progress. The project manager originally scheduled 24 work hours on the Build P1 task. The assigned team member performed 24 hours of actual work on the task, but increased the remaining work estimate by 16 hours. This means the task will probably finish late, based on the increased remaining work estimate.

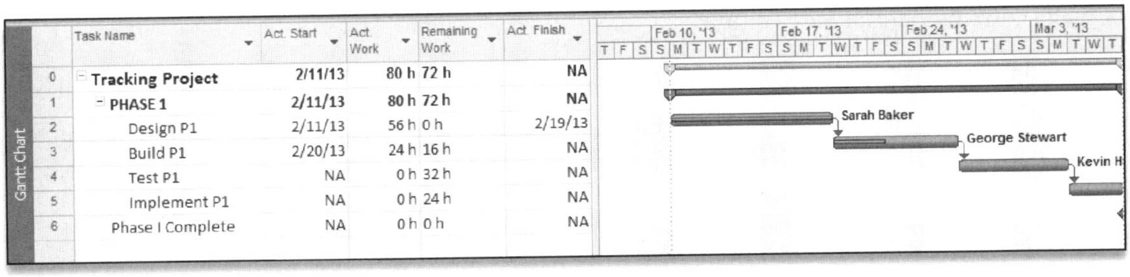

Figure 8 - 15: Tracking table set up to enter Actual Work and Remaining Work

When a team member increases their *Remaining Work* estimate, MSProjectExperts recommends that you add a task note to document the reason for changes in *Remaining Work* value. Doing so may assist in the estimating process in future projects.

Hands On Exercise

Exercise 8-5

Enter project progress for the first two weeks of the Training Advisor Rollout project using the Actual Work and Remaining Work method.

1. Open the **Training Advisor 08b.mpp** sample file.

2. Right-click on the *Select All* button and select the *Tracking* table.

3. Widen the *Task Name* column, if necessary.

4. "Drag and drop" the *Actual Work* column between the *Actual Start* and *Actual Finish* columns.

5. Right-click on the *Actual Finish* column header and select *Insert Column* from the shortcut menu.

6. In the list of available columns, select the *Remaining Work* column.

7. Drag the vertical split bar to the right edge of the *Actual Finish* column.

8. For task ID #17, the *Order Server* task, enter *1/6/14* in the *Actual Start* column and enter *01/07/14* in the *Actual Finish* column.

Notice that Microsoft Project 2010 marks the task as 100% complete. Notice also that the software calculates the actual work as 12 hours and sets the remaining work to 0 hours as well.

9. For task ID #28, the *Setup Test Training Server* task, enter *24h* in the *Actual Work* column.

Notice that Microsoft Project 2010 marks the task as 100% complete by setting the *Remaining Work* value to *0h*, by entering the current start date of the task in the *Actual Start* column, and by entering the current finish date of the task in the *Actual Finish* column.

10. For task ID #30, the *Create Training Module 01* task, enter *01/15/14* in the *Actual Start* field.

Notice that Microsoft Project 2010 delays the Gantt bar for this task to a date two days later than the original start date. The reason for the late start date is because Ruth Andrews, the assigned resource, was sick on Monday and Tuesday of that week.

11. For the *Create Training Module 01* task, enter *24h* in the *Actual Work* column.

12. For the *Create Training Module 01* task, enter *32h* in the *Remaining Work* column.

After Ruth Andrews began work on the *Create Training Module 01* task, she discovered her original work estimate of 40 hours was too low, which is why she increased the remaining work estimate by 16 hours. Because of the late start and the increased remaining work estimate, this task is seriously behind schedule.

13. Add a task note to the Creating Training Module 01 task to document the reason for the schedule slippage.

14. Expand the occurrences of the *Project Status Meeting* recurring task.

15. Enter *10h* in the *Actual Work* column for the *Project Status Meeting 1* task.

16. Collapse the occurrences of the *Project Status Meeting* recurring task.

17. Save and close the **Training Advisor 08b.mpp** sample file.

Entering Progress Using a Daily Timesheet

The most challenging method of tracking project progress requires your team members to enter their actual work hours in a daily timesheet. In addition, your team members must also give their estimate of the remaining work hours on each task at the end of the week. To use this method of tracking progress, you must manually create some type of form in which your team members can record progress, such as a paper timesheet you print for them or an electronic timesheet in Microsoft Excel you create for them.

This daily time method of tracking progress is date sensitive because your team members report their actual work on a day by day basis, and you enter their Actual Work values in Microsoft Project 2010 on a daily basis as well. The system infers the *Actual Start* date based on the first day on which you enter actual progress on the task. Likewise, the system infers the *Actual Finish* date of the task as the date that completes the total work on the task.

 MsProjectExperts recommends that project team members record actual project progress on a daily basis, and submit their progress to the project manager on a weekly basis. Even though team members may protest, studies show that it takes an average of only 5 minutes per day to collect and record project progress, even if you use a paper timesheet.

Based on the information your team members provide for you in their paper or electronic timesheets, you can manually enter actual progress using the Daily Timesheet method by completing the following steps:

1. Click the *View* tab and then click the *Resource Usage* button in the *Resource Views* section of the *View* ribbon.

2. In the *Zoom* section of the *View* ribbon, click the *Timescale* pick list and select the *Days* item on the list.

3. Right-click anywhere in the timephased grid (gray/white timesheet) and then select the *Actual Work* item on the shortcut menu.

4. Widen the *Details* column in the timephased grid, if necessary.

5. In the *Split View* section of the *View* ribbon, select the *Details* option checkbox to display the *Resource Form* view in the lower pane.

6. Right-click anywhere in the *Resource Form* pane (bottom pane) and select the *Work* item on the shortcut menu.

7. In the *Resource Usage* pane (top pane), click the *Select All* button to select all of the resources and their assignments in the column.

8. In the *Data* section of the *View* ribbon, click the *Outline* pick list button and select the *Hide Subtasks* item in the list to collapse all of the task assignments for every resource.

9. Expand the task assignments for the first resource for which you want to enter actual progress using the Daily Timesheet method.

Figure 8 - 16 shows the *Resource Usage* view, set up to enter progress for the tasks assigned to Sarah Baker using the Daily Timesheet method.

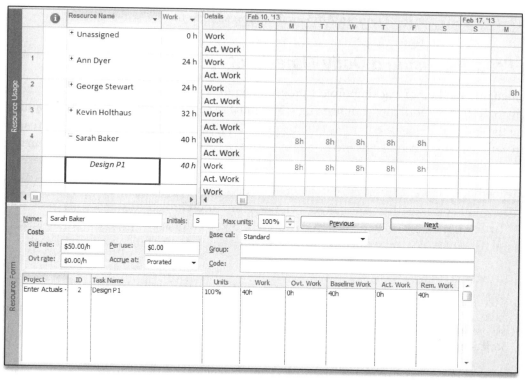

Figure 8 - 16: Ready to enter progress using the Daily Timesheet method

 After you expand the task assignments for a resource, click the *Task* tab to display the *Task* ribbon. Select any task assignment and then click the *Scroll to Task* button in the *Editing* section of the *Task* ribbon to scroll the planned work hours into view in the timephased grid.

 In the timephased grid, gray cells are for timephased values for resources, and white cells are for timephased values for task assignments. When you enter progress in the timephased grid, be sure to enter your *Actual Work* hours in the white cells and not the gray cells.

To enter *Actual Work* values and adjust the *Remaining Work* value for any resource's task assignment, complete the following steps:

1. Select the desired resource, then expand the resource's task assignments by clicking the minus sign (-) symbol in front of the resource's name.

2. Select the *Actual Work* assignment cell in the timephased grid for the selected resource assignment.

3. Type the actual work values in the *Actual Work* assignment cell for each day of the week, as reported by the resource.

4. In the *Resource Form* pane, select the *Remaining Work* value for the correct resource assignment.

5. Increase or decrease the selected *Remaining Work* value, as needed.

6. Click the *OK* button in the *Resource Form* pane when finished.

Figure 8 - 17 shows that I entered actual progress for Sarah Baker on her Design P1 task assignment during the week of February 10, 2013. Notice that I entered 0 hours of actual work on Wednesday, indicating the resource performed no work that day. I also increased the *Remaining Work* estimate from 16 to 24 hours for the Design P1 task assignment.

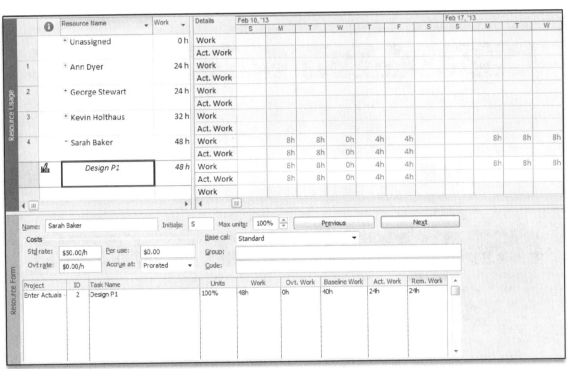

Figure 8 - 17: Actual Work entered and Remaining Work revised

 If a resource performs no *Actual Work* for one or more days on an in-progress task, enter a zero value (0) on the days the resource performed no work on the task. Microsoft Project 2010 reschedules the uncompleted work to the end of the task and delays the task *Finish* date accordingly.

Hands On Exercise

Exercise 8-6

Enter project progress using the daily timesheet method in the Training Advisor Rollout project.

1. Open the **Training Advisor Rollout 08c.mpp** sample file.

2. Use the directions in this topical section to set up the *Resource Usage* view to enter actual progress and to adjust the remaining work estimate.

3. Using the following paper timesheets from the first two weeks of the project, enter *Actual Work* values in the timephased grid and then adjust the *Remaining Work* value in the *Resource Form* pane:

Name: Mickey Cobb	Week Of: 1/5/14					
Task Name	**M**	**T**	**W**	**Th**	**F**	**Rem. Work**
Order Server	8	2				0
Setup Test Training Server			8	8	6	0

Name: Ruth Andrews	Week Of: 1/12/14					
Task Name	**M**	**T**	**W**	**Th**	**F**	**Rem. Work**
Create Training Module 01	8	8				24
Task Notes	Resource worked Monday and Tuesday but called in sick the rest of the week.					

To add a task note while entering actual progress in this special view, double-click the name of the task assignment in the *Resource Form* pane to open the *Task Information* dialog. Click the *Notes* tab and then enter the text of the note.

Name: Jeff Holly		Week Of: 01/19/14				
Task Name	M	T	W	Th	F	Rem. Work
Setup Server and Load O/S			2	2	4	12

4. Display the *View* ribbon, if necessary, and then deselect the *Details* option checkbox to close the *Resource Form* pane.

5. Click the *Gantt Chart* button in the *Task Views* section of the *View* ribbon to reapply the *Gantt Chart* view.

6. In the *Zoom* section of the *View* ribbon, click the *Timescale* pick list and select the *Days* item on the list to zoom to *Weeks Over Days* in the *Gantt Chart* view.

7. Click the *Task* tab to display the *Task* ribbon.

8. Select task ID #21, the *Installation Complete* milestone task, and then click the *Scroll to Task* button in the *Editing* section of the *Task* ribbon to bring this milestone task's Gantt bar into view.

Notice that Microsoft Project 2010 **does not** reschedule the Installation Complete milestone task to 2/10/14 as you might expect, based on the FS dependency with its predecessor task. This is because the milestone task has a *Finish No Later Than* constraint set for 2/7/14. Due to the schedule slippage on Jeff Holly's task, you cannot meet the contractual obligation on this milestone task, so you re-negotiated with the project sponsor for a 2/11/14 *Finish* date for the *Installation Complete* phase.

9. Double-click task ID #21, the *Installation Complete* milestone task, and then click the *Advanced* tab in the *Task Information* dialog.

10. Click the *Constraint Date* pick list and select the *2/11/14* constraint date.

11. Click the *Notes* tab and then add a note stating that you could not meet the original contractual *Finish* date for the phase, and then state the new contractual *Finish* date.

12. Click the *OK* button to close the *Task Information* dialog.

13. Save but do not close the **Training Advisor Rollout 08c.mpp** sample file.

Exercise 8-7

You receive an e-mail message from Jeff Holly stating, "The server was delivered two days later than scheduled. After starting the server setup, I encountered an unanticipated database software upgrade that cost $995. Because of this, I must redo 4 hours of work that I did previously." Add this additional status information to the Training Advisor Rollout project.

1. Double-click task ID #18, the *Setup Server and Load O/S* task, and then click the *Notes* tab in the *Task Information* dialog.

2. Add the following bulleted note to the task: "Server delivered two days late. $995 Fixed Cost for unanticipated DB software upgrade. Resource must redo 4 hours of work done previously."

3. Click the *OK* button when finished.

4. Right-click on the *Select All* button and select the *Cost* table on the shortcut menu.

Notice the planned *Fixed Cost* value of *$6,048* you entered during task planning on the *Order Server* task.

5. In the *Fixed Cost* column for the *Setup Server and Load O/S* task, enter *$995* for the price of the unanticipated database software upgrade.

6. Right-click on the *Select All* button and select the *Entry* table on the shortcut menu.

7. Save but do not close the **Training Advisor Rollout 08c.mpp** sample file.

Exercise 8-8

Enter project progress for the first two Project Status Meeting occurrences.

1. Expand the occurrences of the *Project Status Meeting* recurring task, and then select the *Project Status Meeting 1* task.

2. Click the *Scroll to Task* button in the *Editing* section of the *Task* ribbon to bring the Gantt bar into view for the meeting.

3. Click the *100%* button in the *Schedule* section of the *Task* ribbon.

The fastest and most reliable way to mark a meeting completed is to select it and then click the *100%* button in the *Task* ribbon.

4. Select the *Project Status Meeting 2* task and then click the *100%* button again.

5. Collapse all of the occurrences of the *Project Status Meeting* recurring task.

6. Save but do not close the **Training Advisor Rollout 08c.mpp** sample file.

Warning: If you attempt to enter *Actual Work* hours for a recurring task in the timephased grid on a daily basis , Microsoft Project 2010 time phases the *Actual Work* value you enter **over the entire day**. This means that a 2-hour meeting now spans a 1-day duration rather than the original 2 hour planned duration. Because of this behavior, I strongly recommend that you **do not** enter *Actual Work* values in the timephased grid for a recurring task. Instead, use the *100% Complete* button on the *Task* ribbon, as you did in Exercise 8-8.

Entering Progress for an Expense Cost Resource

To enter actual cost information for an Expense Cost resource, display the *Task Usage* view and then apply the *Cost* table. Right-click anywhere in the timephased grid and select the *Cost* details, then right-click again in the timephased grid and select the *Actual Cost* details as well. Enter the actual expenditure in the *Actual Cost* column for the Expense Cost resource assignment. Microsoft Project 2010 evenly distributes the actual cost expenditure across the duration of the task in the timephased grid. If you wish to time phase the actual cost expenditure to show how you actually spend the money, re-type the *Actual Cost* values in the timephased grid.

Figure 8 - 18 shows a slightly-modified *Task Usage* view after I entered $1,472 of actual expense in the *Actual Cost* column for the Travel Expense cost resource assigned to the Design Telecommunications Plan task. Figure 8 - 19 shows the same *Task Usage* view after I manually entered $1,472 of actual expense data in the timephased grid on the last day of the Design Telecommunications Plan task for the Travel Expense cost resource.

Task Name	Total Cost	Actual Cost	Details	May 4, '14 S	M	T	W	T
8 ⊟ Design telecommunications plan	$3,625	$3,572	Work		16h	16h	16h	
			Cost		$1,208	$1,208	$1,208	
			Act. Cost		$1,208	$1,208	$1,155	
Jerry King	$540	$540	Work		4h	4h	4h	
			Cost		$180	$180	$180	
			Act. Cost		$180	$180	$180	
Russ Powell	$840	$840	Work		8h	8h	8h	
			Cost		$280	$280	$280	
			Act. Cost		$280	$280	$280	
Steve Garcia	$720	$720	Work		4h	4h	4h	
			Cost		$240	$240	$240	
			Act. Cost		$240	$240	$240	
Travel Expense	$1,525	$1,472	Work					
			Cost		$508	$508	$508	
			Act. Cost		$508	$508	$455	

Figure 8 - 18: Task Usage view after entering Actual Cost expenditure for a Cost resource

Notice in Figure 8 - 18 that the amount of actual cost ($1,472) is less than the original estimated cost ($1,525) for the Travel Expense resource. If you do not use all of the money allocated for an Expense Cost resource assignment, as in Figure 8 - 18, drag the split bar to the right to expose the *Remaining Cost* column. In the *Remaining Cost* column, set the value to *$0.00* for the Expense Cost resource assignment. This shows the expenditure came in "under budget" for the assignment.

Task Name	Total Cost	Actual Cost	Details	May 4, '14 S	M	T	W	T
8 ⊟ Design telecommunications plan	$3,572	$3,572	Work		16h	16h	16h	
			Cost		$700	$700	$2,172	
			Act. Cost		$700	$700	$2,172	
Jerry King	$540	$540	Work		4h	4h	4h	
			Cost		$180	$180	$180	
			Act. Cost		$180	$180	$180	
Russ Powell	$840	$840	Work		8h	8h	8h	
			Cost		$280	$280	$280	
			Act. Cost		$280	$280	$280	
Steve Garcia	$720	$720	Work		4h	4h	4h	
			Cost		$240	$240	$240	
			Act. Cost		$240	$240	$240	
Travel Expense	$1,472	$1,472	Work					
			Cost		$0	$0	$1,472	
			Act. Cost		$0	$0	$1,472	

Figure 8 - 19: Task Usage view after time phasing the Actual Cost expenditure

Hands On Exercise

Exercise 8-9

In preparing for loading and configuring the Training Advisor software, Carmen Kamper purchased the necessary software licenses from the software vendor. Enter actual expense information for an Expense Cost resource in your Training Advisor Rollout project.

1. Return to the **Training Advisor Rollout 08c.mpp** sample file.

2. In the *View* section of the *Task* ribbon, click the *Gantt Chart* pick list button and select the *_Cost Resources* view in the *Custom* section at the top of the pick list.

3. Scroll down and then select task ID #19, the *Load and Configure Software* task assigned to Carmen Kamper.

4. Click the *Scroll to Task* button in the *Editing* section of the *Task* ribbon to bring the timephased *Cost* hours into view for the task.

5. Drag the split bar to the right to expose the *Actual Cost* column.

6. Enter *$84,000* in the *Actual Cost* column for the *Software Licenses* resource assignment.

The extra $9,000 of actual cost for software licenses is due to the additional users your organization plans to hire for a new regional office in Irvine, California later this year.

7. Double-click the *Load and Configure Software* task and then select the *Notes* tab.

8. Add the following bulleted note to the task: "$9,000 of additional cost for extra software licenses needed for new staff in the planned regional office in Irvine, CA."

9. Click the *OK* button when finished.

10. Click the *Gantt Chart* button in the *View* section of the *Task* ribbon to reapply the *Gantt Chart* view.

11. Save and close the **Training Advisor Rollout 08c.mpp** sample file.

Rescheduling Uncompleted Work

Regardless of which method of tracking progress you use, after entering actual progress in your project plan in Microsoft Project 2010 you must also locate and reschedule uncompleted tasks that remain in a past reporting period. Uncompleted tasks usually fall into one of the following situations:

- The resource(s) assigned to the task reported no actual progress on the task during the last reporting period (no progress).

- The resource(s) assigned to the task reported progress on the task, but reported no progress on one or more of the final days of the last reporting period (interrupted partial progress).

Figure 8 - 20 shows a project that contains both completed and uncompleted work during the first reporting period of the project. In the sample project, today is Monday, April 22nd, represented by the red line in the Gantt chart in the right side of the project. Notice in the Phase I section that Myrta Hansen completed all of her scheduled work during the 4/14/13 reporting period. Notice in the Phase II section that Nick Bock completed only part of his scheduled work during that reporting period. Notice in the Phase III section that Lisa Glause did not complete any of her scheduled work during that reporting period. Because both Nick Bock and Lisa Glause failed to complete their scheduled work during the 4/14/13 reporting period, the current project schedule is **no longer accurate** because of uncompleted work scheduled in the past prior to April 22, 2013.

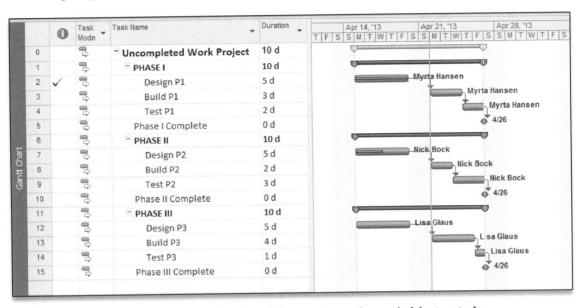

Figure 8 - 20: Uncompleted work in a past reporting period for two tasks

To address situations such as the one shown in Figure 8 - 20, you must reschedule uncompleted work from the past reporting period into the current reporting period by completing the following steps:

1. Select all tasks with uncompleted work in past reporting periods.

2. Click the *Project* tab to display the *Project* ribbon.

3. In the *Status* section of the *Project* ribbon, click the *Update Project* button. Microsoft Project 2010 displays the *Update Project* dialog shown in Figure 8 - 21.

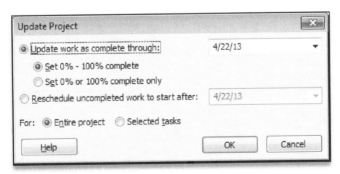

Figure 8 - 21: Update Project dialog

4. Select the *Reschedule uncompleted work to start after* option.

5. Click the *Reschedule uncompleted work to start after* pick list and select a date **one day before** which the work resumes on the uncompleted tasks.

6. Select the *Selected tasks* option.

Figure 8 - 22 shows the *Update Project* dialog with the correct options selected to reschedule uncompleted work for only selected tasks.

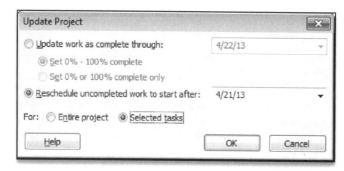

Figure 8 - 22: Update Project dialog set up to reschedule uncompleted work for selected tasks

7. Click the *OK* button.

 The *Update Project* dialog also offers the *Entire project* option as well. When selected, this option allows Microsoft Project 2010 to reschedule **every** uncompleted task in the past automatically. Although this approach can certainly be faster, experienced project managers do not like the loss of control of the rescheduling process.

Microsoft Project 2010 reschedules uncompleted work from past reporting periods by splitting in-progress tasks and by setting a *Start No Earlier Than (SNET)* constraint on unstarted tasks. Figure 8 - 23 shows the new project schedule after rescheduling uncompleted work for two tasks. Notice that the software splits the in-progress Design P2 task assigned to Nick Bock, as indicated by the split indicator (…) in the middle of the Gantt bar. Notice that software rescheduled the entire unstarted Design P3 task assigned to Lisa Glause using a *Start No Earlier Than (SNET)* constraint.

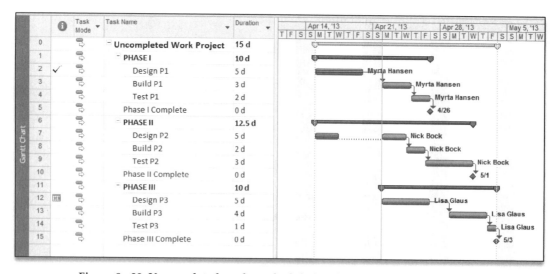

Figure 8 - 23: Uncompleted work rescheduled to the current reporting period

An alternate approach for rescheduling uncompleted work in the past is to use the options on the *Move* pick list in the *Tasks* section of the *Task* ribbon. The options on the *Move* button allow to to move selected tasks by a time period you select, such as 1 day, 1 week, or 4 weeks.

Hands On Exercise

Exercise 8-10

Reschedule uncompleted work from the past reporting period into the current reporting period.

1. Open the **Training Advisor Rollout 08d.mpp** sample file.

2. Click the *Project* tab to display the *Project* ribbon.

3. Select task ID #30, the *Create Training Module 01* task, and then click the *Update Project* button in the *Status* section of the *Project* ribbon.

4. In the *Update Project* dialog, Select the *Reschedule uncompleted work to start after* option.

5. Click the *Reschedule uncompleted work to start after* pick list and select *1/19/14* on the calendar date picker.

6. Choose the *Selected tasks* option and then click the *OK* button.

Notice how Microsoft Project 2010 splits this in-progress task to reschedule uncompleted work to the third week of the project.

7. Save and close the **Training Advisor Rollout 08d.mpp** sample file.

If you specify a *Status Date* for your project **before** you reschedule uncompleted work, Microsoft Project 2010 automatically enters the *Status Date* value in the *Reschedule uncompleted work to start after* field. The *Status Date* of your project should be the last day of the previous reporting period. To set a *Status Date* for your project, click the *Project Information* button in the *Properties* section of the *Project* ribbon and select a date in the *Status date* field.

Rescheduling a Task

Project managers occasionally need to reschedule one or more tasks in a project to show a delay in an in-progress project. Common reasons for rescheduling a task can include team members failing to start and/or complete a task in a previous reporting period or lack of resources to work on the task as currently scheduled. For example, consider the project shown in Figure 8 - 24. After team members completed all of the tasks in Phase I of the project, I learned that I must put the remainder of the project "on hold" for a month (4 weeks or 20 working days). Therefore, I must reschedule the tasks in the project beginning with the Write Course Manual task.

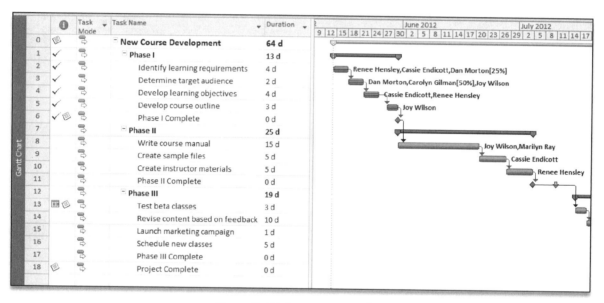

Figure 8 - 24: In-progress project

In previous versions of Microsoft Project, a project manager must reschedule tasks manually using one of two methods:

- On the *Advanced* tab of the *Task Information* dialog, set a *Start No Earlier Than* (SNET) constraint with the new *Start* date of the task as the *Constraint Date*.

- Use the *Reschedule Uncompleted Work* feature in the *Update Project* dialog.

A new method for rescheduling one or more tasks in Microsoft Project 2010 allows you to select the tasks you want to reschedule and then click the *Move* pick list button in the *Tasks* section of the *Task* ribbon, as shown in Figure 8 - 25. The *Move* pick list includes three sections that allow you to reschedule the selected tasks.

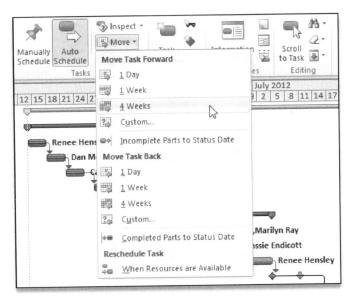

Figure 8 - 25: Move pick list

The *Move Task Forward* section offers options that allow you to reschedule the selected tasks into the future by 1 day, by 1 week, by 4 weeks, by a specific amount of time you specify, or by rescheduling uncompleted work forward past the *Status Date* of the project. The *Move Task Back* section offers you options that allow you to reschedule the selected tasks into the past by 1 day, by 1 week, by 4 weeks, by a specific amount of time you specify, or by rescheduling completed work back to the *Status Date* of the project. The *Reschedule Task* section includes a single option that allows you to delay the task until the assigned resource is available. This final option allows you to manually level an overallocated resource assigned to the selected tasks.

To reschedule the tasks in the project shown previously in Figure 8 - 24, I selected the Write Course Manual task (the first task in Phase II), and then I selected the *4 Weeks* item on the *Move* pick list. Microsoft Project 2010 reschedules this task and all successor tasks 4 weeks into the future by setting a *Start No Earlier Than* (SNET) constraint on the task with a constraint date of June 28, as shown in Figure 8 - 26. June 28 is four weeks (20 working days) later than the original start date for the Write Course Manual task.

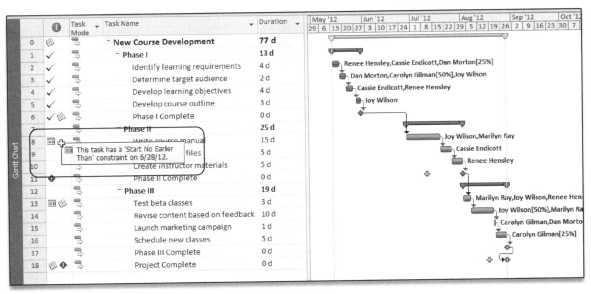

**Figure 8 - 26: Start No Earlier Than constraint on the Write Course
Manual task delays Phase II and Phase III by four weeks**

Notice the special indicators displayed in the *Indicators* column for the Phase II Complete milestone task and the Project Complete milestone task, as shown in Figure 8 - 26. These indicators show that these two milestone tasks slipped past the *Deadline* dates I specified on these tasks. Because the project is slipping, this indicates that I will miss the original *Deadline* dates on these tasks, which is a natural consequence of a slipping project.

Hands On Exercise

Exercise 8-11

Due to a lack of resources, put a project "on hold" by rescheduling tasks in the project to a start date one week in the future.

1. Open the **Reschedule Tasks.mpp** sample file.

2. Select task ID #4, the *Load and Configure Software* task.

3. Press and hold the **Control** key on your keyboard, and then select task ID #15, the *Create Training Module 01* task.

4. Release the **Control** key on your computer keyboard and then click the *Task* tab.

5. Click the *Move* pick list button in the *Tasks* section of the *Task* ribbon and then select the *1 Week* item on the pick list.

Notice how Microsoft Project 2010 splits the *Create Training Module 01* task and delays the entire *Load and Configure Software* task by setting a *Start No Earlier Than (SNET)* constraint on the task.

6. Save and close the **Reschedule Tasks.mpp** sample file.

Setting Tasks to Inactive

After you baseline a project and begin tracking progress, you may discover that you no longer need some tasks in the project. Best practices with Microsoft Project dictate that you should never delete a task with a baseline, because in deleting the task you lose the baseline data on the task, thereby losing the ability to track variance on the deleted task. Instead, best practice dictates that you should **cancel** the unneeded task, rather than delete it. To cancel an unneeded task using the 2007 version of Microsoft Project, for example, I recommend the following Best Practice approach:

1. Set the *Remaining Work* value to 0h on the task in the task *Work* table. When you complete this step, Microsoft Project 2007 changes the Gantt bar to the *Milestone* symbol (a black diamond).

2. Double-click the *Milestone* symbol for the task and choose another symbol that you want to use to represent a cancelled task.

3. Change the *Cell Background Color* of the task to a color representing a cancelled task (I personally like the lime green color).

4. Add a note to the task to document the reason for cancelling it.

Warning: The Inactivate Task feature is available **only** in the Professional version of Microsoft Project 2010. You **cannot** use this feature if you have the Standard version of the software. If you have the Standard version of the software, use the four-step method documented previously for Microsoft Project 2007 users.

Cancelling an unneeded task in Microsoft Project 2010 is much simpler; to cancel a task you simply set the task to *Inactive* status. Consider the project shown in Figure 8 - 27. After the project team completed all tasks in Phase II and the first two tasks in Phase III, management cancelled the remainder of the project due to budgetary restrictions. Therefore, I can close out the project by setting the last four tasks in Phase III to *Inactive* status.

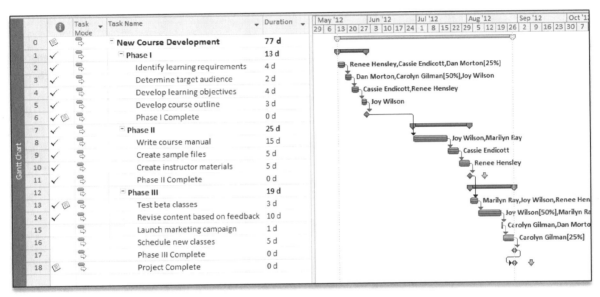

Figure 8 - 27: Project cancelled before completing Phase III

To set unneeded tasks to *Inactive* status in Microsoft Project 2010, select one or more tasks and then click the *Inactivate* button in the *Schedule* section of the *Task* ribbon. Figure 8 - 28 shows the *Inactivate* button on the *Task* ribbon, along with its floating Tooltip.

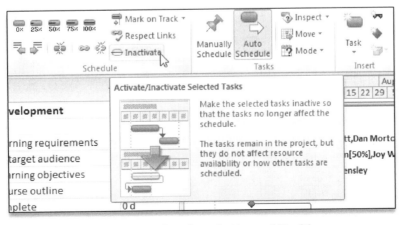

Figure 8 - 28: Inactivate button and Tooltip

Figure 8 - 29 shows the project after setting the last four tasks in Phase III to *Inactive* status. When you cancel a task using the *Inactivate* button, Microsoft Project 2010 does the following:

- The system formats the text of the *Inactive* task using the strikethrough font effect and the gray font color.

- The system formats the Gantt bar of the *Inactive* task using a hollow (unfilled) pattern.

- The system treats the *Inactive* task as if it has 0h of remaining work. This means the *Inactive* task no longer affects resource availability for resources assigned to it, as indicated in the Tooltip shown previously in Figure 8 - 28.

- Although the system continues to show link lines for the *Inactive* task, the system schedules successor tasks as if they are not linked to the *Inactive* task. This means that the duration of the *Inactive* task no longer affects the schedule of successor tasks, as indicated also in the Tooltip shown previously in Figure 8 - 28.

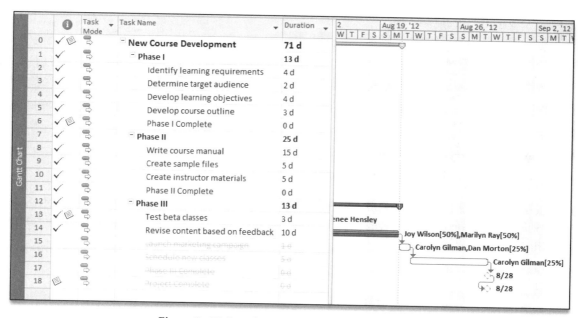

Figure 8 - 29: Last four tasks cancelled in Phase III

Figure 8 - 30 shows the four *Inactive* tasks with the *Work* table applied in the *Gantt Chart* view. Notice that the system did not set the *Remaining Work* to 0h. Notice also that the system shows -20h of Work Variance (in the *Variance* column) on the Phase III summary task and on the *Project Summary Task,* caused by inactivating two tasks with 10h of work assigned to each task.

		Task Name	Work	Baseline	Variance	Actual	Remaining	% W. Comp.
0		New Course Development	672 h	692 h	-20 h	672 h	0 h	100%
1		Phase I	200 h	200 h	0 h	200 h	0 h	100%
2		Identify learning requirements	72 h	72 h	0 h	72 h	0 h	100%
3		Determine target audience	40 h	40 h	0 h	40 h	0 h	100%
4		Develop learning objectives	64 h	64 h	0 h	64 h	0 h	100%
5		Develop course outline	24 h	24 h	0 h	24 h	0 h	100%
6		Phase I Complete	0 h	0 h	0 h	0 h	0 h	100%
7		Phase II	320 h	320 h	0 h	320 h	0 h	100%
8		Write course manual	240 h	240 h	0 h	240 h	0 h	100%
9		Create sample files	40 h	40 h	0 h	40 h	0 h	100%
10		Create instructor materials	40 h	40 h	0 h	40 h	0 h	100%
11		Phase II Complete	0 h	0 h	0 h	0 h	0 h	100%
12		Phase III	152 h	172 h	-20 h	152 h	0 h	100%
13		Test beta classes	72 h	72 h	0 h	72 h	0 h	100%
14		Revise content based on feedback	80 h	80 h	0 h	80 h	0 h	100%
15		Launch marketing campaign	10 h	10 h	0 h	0 h	10 h	0%
16		Schedule new classes	10 h	10 h	0 h	0 h	10 h	0%
17		Phase III Complete	0 h	0 h	0 h	0 h	0 h	0%
18		Project Complete	0 h	0 h	0 h	0 h	0 h	0%

Figure 8 - 30: Work table shows cancelled tasks

Remember that when you set a task to *Inactive* status, Microsoft Project 2010 schedules successor tasks as if they are not linked to the *Inactive* task. For example, Figure 8 - 31 is the same schedule shown previously in Figure 8 - 29, except that I did not set the Phase III Complete and Project Complete milestone tasks to *Inactive* status. Notice that the system schedules these two milestone tasks as if they are not linked to the two *Inactive* tasks by scheduling them on the *Start* date of the project. Because of this behavior, you should link successor tasks to the nearest *Active* predecessor task to reset the project schedule from that point forward.

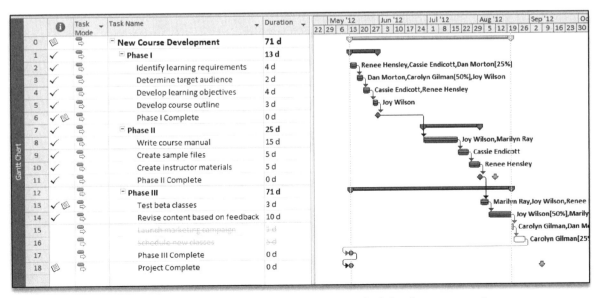

Figure 8 - 31: Inactive tasks do not control the schedule of successor tasks

Warning: Microsoft Project 2010 does not allow you to cancel a completed task or an in-progress task by setting it to *Inactive* status. To cancel the uncompleted work in an in-progress task, apply the task *Work* table and then set the *Remaining Work* value to *0h* for the task.

If you set a task status to *Inactive* using the *Inactivate* button, and later find you need the task after all, you can reset the task to *Active* status by selecting it and then clicking the *Inactivate* button again.

Hands On Exercise

Exercise 8-12

Cancel an unneeded task by setting its status to *Inactive*.

1. Open the **Inactivate a Task.mpp** sample file.

2. Select task ID #18, the *Rewrite Training Module 03* task, which team members report is no longer needed in the project.

3. Click the *Task* tab and then click the *Inactivate* button in the *Schedule* section.

4. Select the *Create Training Module 03* task, press and hold the **Control** key on your keyboard, and then select the *Training Materials Created* milestone task.

5. Click the *Link Tasks* button in the *Schedule* section of the *Task* ribbon.

6. Double-click the *Rewrite Training Module 03* task and then click the *Notes* tab in the *Task Information* dialog.

7. Click to the right of the existing text in the *Notes* field and then press the **Enter** key on your keyboard to add a new blank line.

8. In the *Notes* field, add a note to document the reason for setting the task to *Inactive* status (team members believe they no longer need the task) and then click the *OK* button.

9. Save and close the **Inactivate a Task.mpp** sample file.

Synchronizing with a SharePoint Tasks List

If your organization uses Microsoft SharePoint Foundation 2010 or Microsoft SharePoint Server (MSS) 2010, but does not use the enterprise tool Microsoft Project Server 2010, you can leverage the power of SharePoint by publishing your project file to a SharePoint site as a *Tasks* list, and then synchronizing your project tasks with the SharePoint tasks list. This feature enables two-way communication between you and your project team members. It allows you to display the current task schedule to all team members, and allows your team members to submit task updates for their assigned tasks. Before you can use this feature, you must meet a number of requirements for both SharePoint and your Microsoft Project 2010 file. The requirements for SharePoint include:

- Your SharePoint administrator must create a SharePoint site for you.

- Your SharePoint administrator must create user accounts on the SharePoint site for all of the resources you intend to use in your projects.

- Your SharePoint administrator must supply you with the URL for the site.

Warning: The *Synchronize with a SharePoint Tasks List* feature is available **only** in the Professional version of Microsoft Project 2010. You **cannot** use this feature if you have the Standard version of the software.

Warning: Your organization **must** use either Microsoft SharePoint Foundation 2010 or Microsoft SharePoint Server 2010 before you can publish and synchronize your Microsoft Project 2010 tasks with a *Tasks* list in SharePoint. You **cannot** use any previous version of Windows SharePoint Services for this functionality.

The requirements for your Microsoft Project 2010 file include:

- You can save the project file in any location, including the SharePoint site, a network share, or even a folder on your workstation's hard drive.

- The name of each resource you enter in the *Resource Sheet* view of your project **must** match the resource's User Name in the SharePoint site exactly.

- You **must** use the *Manually Scheduled* task mode for **all tasks** in your project, including summary tasks.

- No two summary tasks at the same level of indenture can have the same name.

- You must use **only** *Finish-to-Start (FS)* dependencies to link tasks in your project. You **must not** use any other dependency relationship and you **must not** use *Lag* time or *Lead* time on the FS dependencies.

- You **must not** use any type of constraints in your project, other than the default *As Soon As Possible (ASAP)* constraint.

- You **cannot** assign generic resources to tasks in your project.

- You **must not** use any special characters in the names of summary tasks. Special characters include the following:

  ~ " # % : * & < > ? / { } |

 Despite the many restrictions shown in the preceding list of bulleted items, you **can** use *Deadline* dates in your project!

Figure 8 - 32 shows a project that meets all of the requirements in the preceding list of bulleted items. Notice in particular that I set all tasks to *Manually Scheduled*, including summary tasks, and assigned only one resource per task.

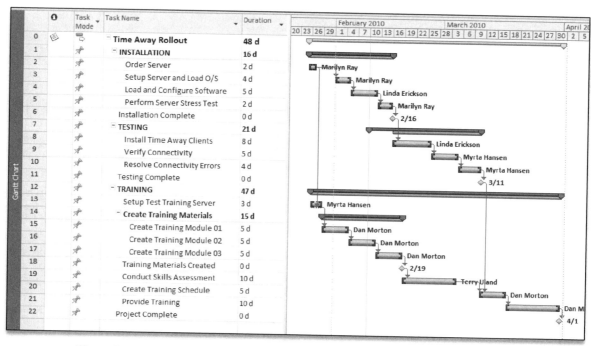

Figure 8 - 32: New project ready for synchronization with a Tasks list in SharePoint

To kick off the task synchronization with the SharePoint feature in Microsoft Project 2010, you must publish your project to SharePoint by completing the following steps:

1. Click the *File* tab and then click the *Save & Send* tab in the *Backstage*.

2. On the *Save & Send* page, click the *Sync with Tasks List* tab.

3. In the *Sync with Tasks List* section on the *Save & Send* page, enter or paste the URL of the SharePoint site in the *Site URL* field, as shown in Figure 8 - 33.

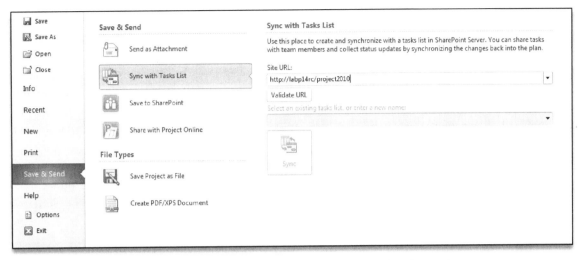

Figure 8 - 33: Enter Site URL in the Sync with Tasks List section

4.   Click the *Validate URL* button to confirm the URL you entered.

If you enter an incorrect URL for the SharePoint site, or if you do not have a user account in the SharePoint site, the system displays the dialog shown in Figure 8 - 34. To resolve this problem, you may need to confirm the URL of the SharePoint site with your SharePoint administrator, and confirm that you do have a user account in the SharePoint site.

Figure 8 - 34: Error message in accessing SharePoint site

If you enter a valid URL and you do have a user account on the SharePoint site, the system redisplays the *Sync with Tasks List* section on the *Save & Send* page. On this page, the system activates the *Select an existing tasks list or enter a new name* field and the *Sync* button, as shown in Figure 8 - 35.

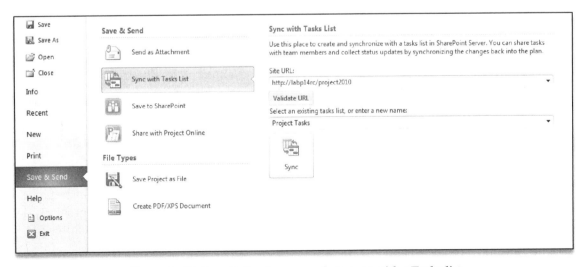

Figure 8 - 35: Save & Send page, ready to sync with a Tasks list

If a *Tasks* list already exists in the SharePoint site, for instance as a result of someone publishing a project to Share-Point, then you should see the name of that *Tasks* list in the *Select an existing tasks list or enter a new name* field. For example, notice in Figure 8 - 35 shown previously that the *Select an existing tasks list or enter a new name* field contains the name of the *Project Tasks* list. This is the *Tasks* list shown previously in Module 03 that project managers use to create new projects in Microsoft Project 2010. If the SharePoint site does not contain an existing *Tasks* list, then the *Select an existing tasks list or enter a new name* field is blank. When you initially publish your project to a SharePoint *Tasks* list, you should manually enter the name of a new *Tasks* list in the *Select an existing tasks list or enter a new name* field.

To minimize confusion in the minds of your team members about *Task* lists for multiple projects, msProjectExperts recommends that you name your *Task* list using the same name of the project containing the tasks you want to sync with SharePoint.

After you enter the name of a new *Tasks* list in the *Select an existing tasks list or enter a new name* field, click the *Sync* button. As Microsoft Project 2010 publishes your project to the SharePoint *Tasks* list, the system displays the *SharePoint Synchronization* dialog shown in Figure 8 - 36. This dialog shows the status of the synchronization process with the SharePoint *Tasks* list and reports progress as it creates the *Tasks* list, reads the *Properties* of the *Tasks* list, downloads the *Tasks* list from SharePoint, compares the *Tasks* list in SharePoint with the tasks in your Microsoft Project 2010 plan, and then writes the *Tasks* list data to SharePoint and your project file.

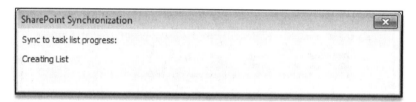

Figure 8 - 36: SharePoint Synchronization dialog

During the publishing process, if the system encounters an error of any type, such as if you fail to meet the requirements specified for a project, then Microsoft Project 2010 displays an error dialog to document the error and suggest a solution. For example, the error dialog shown in Figure 8 - 37 warns you if you fail to set the *Task Mode* value to *Manually Scheduled* for each task in your project.

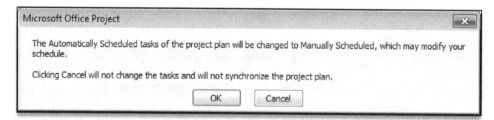

Figure 8 - 37: Error dialog about Automatically Scheduled tasks

After you publish your project successfully to a SharePoint *Tasks* list, users can see the *Tasks* list in the SharePoint site. For example, Figure 8 - 38 shows a new *Tasks* list called Time Away Deployment in the SharePoint site. By default, the *Tasks* list shows only first-level tasks initially. This means I see only the Phase summary tasks (INSTALLATION, TESTING, and TRAINING) plus their corresponding milestone tasks.

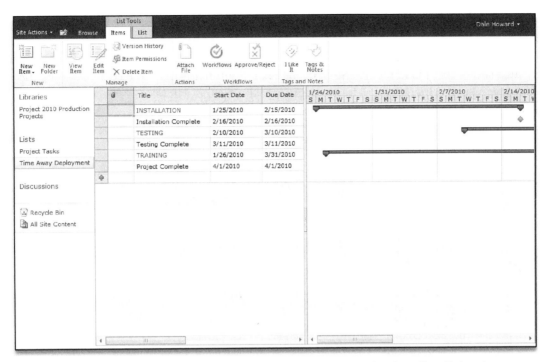

Figure 8 - 38: Tasks list for the Time Away Deployment project in a SharePoint site

To view the subtasks for any summary task, click the name of the summary task. For example, Figure 8 - 39 shows the four subtasks of the INSTALLATION summary task. It is on this SharePoint page that team members can collaborate with you by submitting task updates for their assigned tasks, or even submitting new tasks for the project.

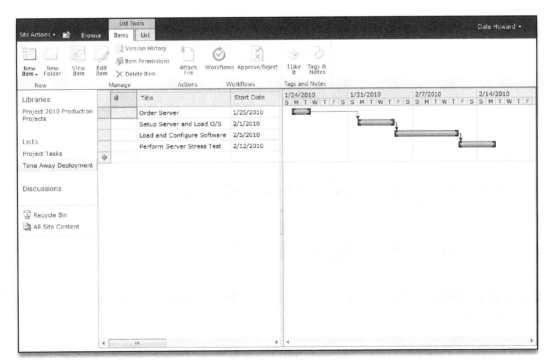

Figure 8 - 39: Subtasks of the INSTALLATION summary task

Adding Fields to the Task Synchronization Process

When you initially publish your project to a SharePoint *Tasks* list, Microsoft Project 2010 uses the information in the project to create a series of fields in the list. Most of the SharePoint fields map to a corresponding *Task* field in the project file, but several of the SharePoint fields do not map to any field in Microsoft Project 2010. Table 8 - 2 shows the list of SharePoint fields and the corresponding fields in Microsoft Project 2010.

SharePoint Tasks Field	Microsoft Project 2010 Field
Title	Name (Task Name)
Start Date	Start
Due Date	Finish
% Complete	% Complete
Assigned To	Resource Names
Predecessors	Predecessors
Priority	No corresponding field
Task Status	No corresponding field

Table 8 - 2: Fields in a SharePoint tasks list and
their corresponding fields in Microsoft Project 2010

In addition to the standard fields included in the task synchronization process, Microsoft Project 2010 allows you to add other fields, including both standard fields and custom fields, for reporting purposes or to give team members additional information about their task assignments. To add other fields to the task synchronization process, complete the following steps:

1. Click the *File* tab and then click the *Save & Send* tab in the *Backstage*.

2. On the *Save & Send* page, click the *Manage Fields* button in the *Manage Fields* section of the page.

 After you publish your project tasks to SharePoint initially, you can also access the *Manage Fields* button and the *Synch* button on the *Info* page in the *Backstage;* however you cannot perform your initial publish from the *Info* page.

The system displays the *Manage Fields* dialog shown in Figure 8 - 40. Notice that the *Manage Fields* dialog confirms the field mapping I documented previously in Table 8 - 2.

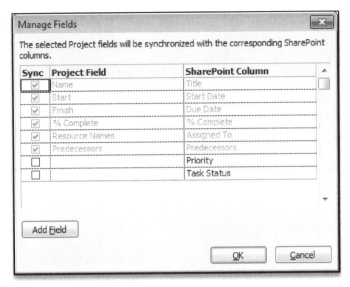

Figure 8 - 40: Manage Fields dialog

 Microsoft Project 2010 does not allow you to select the *Sync* checkbox for the *Priority* and *Task Status* fields in SharePoint because there are no fields in Microsoft Project 2010 that correpond to these two SharePoint fields. You may not find them useful. If this is the case, you or your SharePoint administrator can remove these two fields from the *Project Tasks* view for your project in SharePoint. I discuss how to modify the *Project Tasks* view a little later in this section of the module.

3. In the *Manage Fields* dialog, click the *Add Field* button. The system displays the *Add Field* dialog shown in Figure 8 - 41.

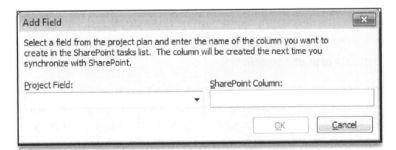

Figure 8 - 41: Add Field dialog

4. In the *Add Field* dialog, click the *Project Field* pick list and select a default or custom field in Microsoft Project 2010. The system enters the name of the field in the *SharePoint Column* field automatically.

5. In the *Add Field* dialog, optionally, enter an alternate name in the *SharePoint Column* field and then click the *OK* button.

The system displays the new field in the *Manage Fields* dialog, as shown in Figure 8 - 42. Notice in the *Manage Fields* dialog that I added the *Actual Start* field and the *Actual Finish* field. The next time I click the *Sync* button, Microsoft Project 2010 will create these two corresponding fields in the SharePoint tasks list.

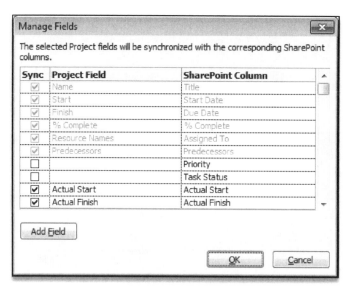

**Figure 8 - 42: Manage Fields dialog shows
two new fields added**

6.   Click the *OK* button to close the *Manage Fields* dialog.

> The *Actual Start* and *Actual Finish* fields, shown in the *Manage Fields* dialog in the previous figure are
> two excellent examples of useful fields you can add to the SharePoint tasks list for your project. These
> two fields allow team members to report when they **actually** started and finished a task, which allows
> you to see schedule variance if a team member starts or finishes a task on a different day than its
> baseline dates. Because of this, msProjectExperts recommends as a best practice that you add the
> *Actual Start* and *Actual Finish* fields in the *Manage Fields* dialog for each project you publish to a
> SharePoint tasks list.

7.   Click the *Sync* button to create the new field(s) in the SharePoint tasks list.

Modifying the Project Tasks View in SharePoint

After you sync your project tasks with the SharePoint tasks list, the system creates a new SharePoint field for each
new Microsoft Project 2010 field you selected in the *Manage Fields* dialog. However, the system **does not** add the new
fields to the default *Project Tasks* view for your project's SharePoint tasks list. This means that either you or your
SharePoint administrator must add the new fields manually to the *Project Tasks* view in SharePoint. Before you can
edit the *Project Tasks* view in SharePoint, your SharePoint administrator must make sure you are a member of the
Project 2010 Owners group in SharePoint.

If you have the proper permissions in SharePoint, you can edit the default *Project Tasks* view for your project tasks list
by completing the following steps:

1.   Navigate to the SharePoint site where your organization stores projects and tasks lists.

2.   Click the name of your project's tasks list in the *Lists* section of the Quick Launch Menu on the left side of the
page. The system displays the first-level *Tasks for your project* view, shown previously in Figure 8 - 38.

3.   At the top of the SharePoint page, click the *List* item on *the List Tools* tab. The system displays the *List* ribbon
shown in Figure 8 - 43.

Figure 8 - 43: List ribbon at the top of a SharePoint tasks page

4. In the *List* ribbon, click the *List Settings* button in the *Settings* section of the ribbon. SharePoint displays the *List Settings* page shown in Figure 8 - 44 and Figure 8 - 45. Because of the length of the *List Settings* page, I need to break the screenshot into two separate figures.

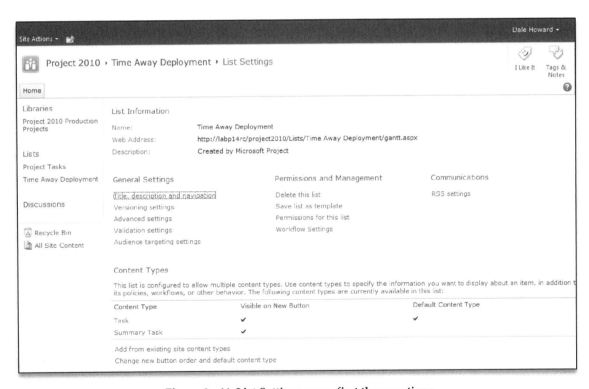

Figure 8 - 44: List Settings page, first three sections

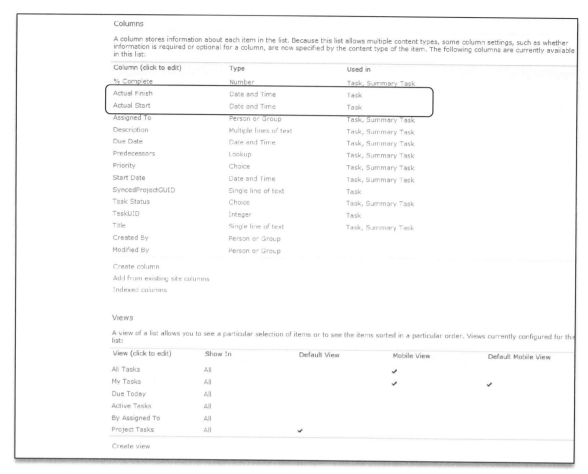

Figure 8 - 45: List Settings page, last two sections

Notice in the *Columns* section of the *List Settings* page shown in Figure 8 - 45 that the system created the *Actual Start* and *Actual Finish* fields in the SharePoint tasks list, as expected.

5. In the *Views* section of the *List Settings* page, click the name of the *Project Tasks* view to open this View for editing. The system displays the *Edit View* page shown in Figure 8 - 46.

When you navigate to the *Edit View* page, the system expands the *Gantt Columns*, *Sort*, and *Filter* sections by default. For the sake of brevity, however, I collapsed these three sections, as shown in Figure 8 - 46. You do not need to change any settings in these three sections to modify the *Project Tasks* view to include the *Actual Start* and *Actual Finish* fields.

6. In the *Columns* section of the *Edit View* page, select the checkbox for the *Actual Start* field and the *Actual Finish* field.

7. In the *Columns* section of the *Edit View* page, select a value in the *Position from Left* pick list for the *Actual Start* field and the *Actual Finish* field to control the order of the columns displayed in the View.

8. Click the *OK* button to save the changes to the *Project Tasks* view.

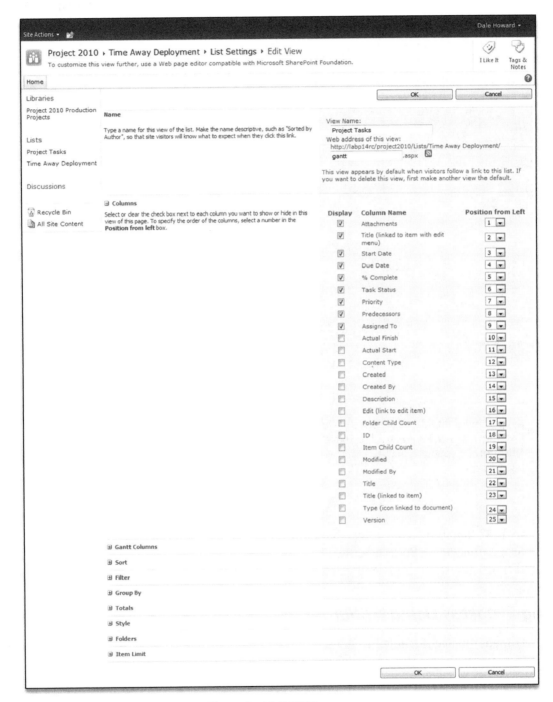

Figure 8 - 46: Edit View page

Figure 8 - 47 shows the edited *Project Tasks* view applied to the tasks in the INSTALLATION phase of the project.

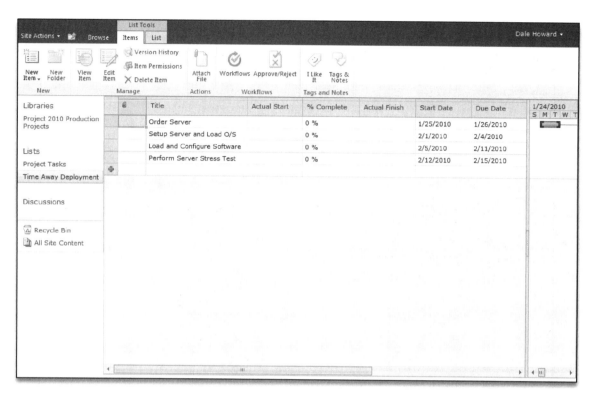

Figure 8 - 47: Project Tasks view shows new display order of columns

Keep in mind that the *Project Tasks* view is the default view for the SharePoint page that displays first-level summary tasks **and** for the SharePoint page that shows subtasks for these summary tasks. Therefore, if you modify the default *Project Tasks* view, you see the same columns in the same order on **both pages**.

Notice in Figure 8 - 47 that the display order of columns in my edited *Project Tasks* view is as follows: Title, Actual Start, % Complete, Actual Finish, Start Date, and Due Date. To take maximum advantage of using the Sync to Share-Point Tasks List functionality, I recommend you use these columns in the order I specified for my project.

Reporting Progress Using a SharePoint Tasks List

In the *Tasks* list for your project, SharePoint allows your project team members to collaborate with you using each of the following features:

- Enter task progress.

- Adjust the planned Start date or Finish date of a task.

- Create a new task.

If you use the column order shown previously in Figure 8 - 47, I recommend you teach your team members to report task progress on their SharePoint tasks using the following methodology:

1. When you start work on a new task, enter the date you began work on the task in the *Actual Start* field.

2. Enter your estimate of the percentage of work completed to date on the task in the *% Complete* field.

3. When you complete work on a task, enter the date you finished work on the task in the *Actual Finish* field.

4. Attach a document to the task, if needed, to provide supporting information.

5. Use the date in the *Start Date* field to determine when you **should** begin work on a task.

6. Use the date in the *Due Date* field to determine when you **should** finish work on a task.

MSProjectExperts recommends as a best practice that you use the display order of columns shown in Figure 8 - 47 and that you use the progress reporting methodology documented above. Doing so allows you to truly "harness the power" of the Syc with SharePoint Tasks List functionality!

Warning: If you use the *Actual Start* and *Actual Finish* fields in the synchronization process, keep in mind that SharePoint assumes **12:00 AM** as the time for any date entered by a team member in both of these fields. To make the best use of these two fields in SharePoint, team members should enter both the **date and time** they started or finished a task. For example, the team member might enter "1/25/2010 8:00 AM" in the *Actual Start* field or enter "1/26/2010 5:00 PM" in the *Actual Finish* field. If you lack team member cooperation for this process, you may wish to omit using the *Actual Start* and *Actual Finish* fields and use only the *% Complete* field for SharePoint synchronization.

To enter progress on a task, at a minimum the team member needs to enter a value in the *% Complete* field for the task. If you follow the methodology I recommend above, the team member should also enter or select a date in the *Actual Start* field and/or *Actual Finish* field as per best practice. When finished, the team member should also press the **Enter** key on the keyboard to save the data in the SharePoint database. For example, notice in Figure 8 - 48 that Mickey Cobb entered data in the *Actual Start*, *% Complete,* and *Actual Finish* fields to indicate that she started and finished work on the task during the same week. Notice the icon to the left of the task indicates that she has not yet pressed the **Enter** key to save the data.

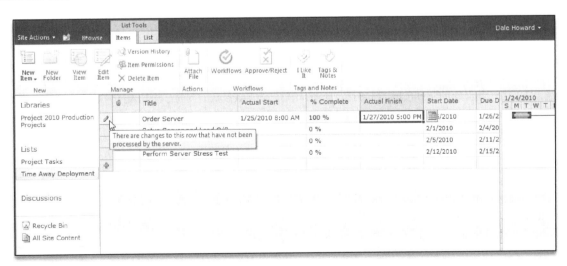

**Figure 8 - 48: Progress entered on the Order Server task
but not yet saved to the SharePoint database**

387

Notice in Figure 8 - 48 that the team member entered both a date and a time in the *Actual Start* and *Actual Finish* fields for the Order Server task. Remember that if a team member does not enter a time value with the date value, SharePoint sets the time value to 12:00 AM (midnight) for the date entered.

After the team member presses the **Enter** key to save the data to the SharePoint database, the system briefly displays another indicator for the progress of the save, and then removes the indicator. To update the progress entered by your team members, open the project and then click the *Sync* button on the *Save & Send* page in the *Backstage*. After Microsoft Project 2010 synchronizes the task progress data from the SharePoint tasks list, you may see a *Conflict Resolution* dialog such as the one shown in Figure 8 - 49.

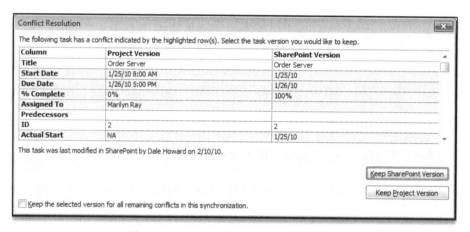

Figure 8 - 49: Conflict Resolution dialog

The *Conflict Resolution* dialog shows you the differences between the tasks in SharePoint and the tasks in your Microsoft Project 2010 project file. To accept the task updates from your team members, click the *Keep SharePoint Version* button. To reject the task updates from your team members, and reset the SharePoint tasks to the schedule in the Microsoft Project 2010 file, click the *Keep Project Version* button. If you have multiple pending task updates from your team members, you can also select the *Keep the selected version for all remaining conflicts in this synchronization* option before you click either button to auto-accept or auto-reject all pending task updates.

If you click the *Keep SharePoint Version* button in the *Conflict Resolution* dialog, you see the progress applied to the tasks in your project file. For example, Figure 8 - 50 shows the project file after accepting task progress submitted by Marilyn Ray and Myrta Hansen during the first week of the project.

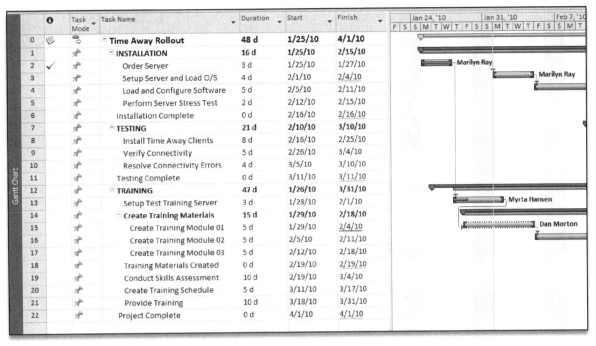

**Figure 8 - 50: Microsoft Project 2010 file after
synchronizing task progress on two tasks**

Notice in the project shown in Figure 8 - 50 that Microsoft Project 2010 displays a schedule *Warning* on the *Finish* date of the Create Training Module 01 task. To maintain an accurate project schedule, I need to respond to all schedule *Warnings* and then synchronize this project again.

To adjust the planned *Start* date or planned *Finish* date of any task, a team member needs only to enter or select a new date in the *Start Date* field or the *Due Date* field. When you synchronize your project file with the SharePoint tasks list, Microsoft Project 2010 adjusts the *Start* and *Finish* date of the task according to the new schedule estimated by the team member.

To add a new task to the Microsoft Project 2010 project, a team member must enter the new task information in the last line of the SharePoint task list, indicated by a green plus sign (+)symbol at the left end of the row. At a minimum, the team member should enter a task name in the *Title* field; but can optionally enter a planned *Start* date or *Finish* date in the *Start Date* and *Due Date* fields, can also select a predecessor for the new task in the *Predecessors* field, and can even select an assigned resource in the *Assigned To* field. For example, Figure 8 - 51 shows a team member entering a new task named Tune Server.

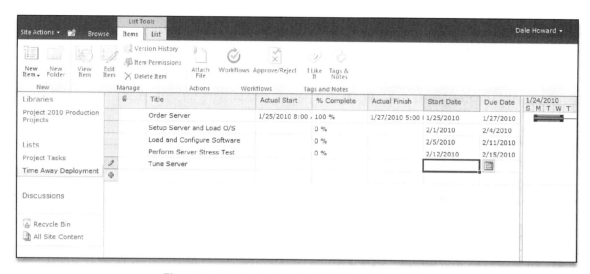

Figure 8 - 51: New task submitted from SharePoint

When you accept a new task update from SharePoint, Microsoft Project 2010 adds the new task at the beginning of the summary section in which the team member created it. If the team member specified information in the *Start Date, Due Date, Predecessors,* or *Assigned To* fields, Microsoft Project 2010 accepts this information and schedules the task accordingly. Keep in mind that when the system adds the new task to the Microsoft Project 2010 project file, this can result in schedule *Warnings* and resource overallocations, such as those shown in the project in Figure 8 - 52. After accepting the new task, you must move the task manually into its correct position in the project file and then synchronize with SharePoint again.

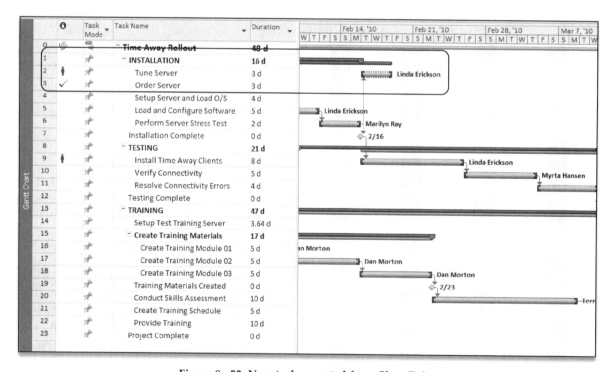

Figure 8 - 52: New task accepted from SharePoint into the Microsoft Project 2010 project file

Figure 8 - 53 shows the Microsoft Project 2010 project file after accepting two progress updates and a new task from SharePoint after the first week of the project. Because you must use *Manually Scheduled* tasks in your project, you must continuously deal with schedule *Warnings* and resource overallocations.

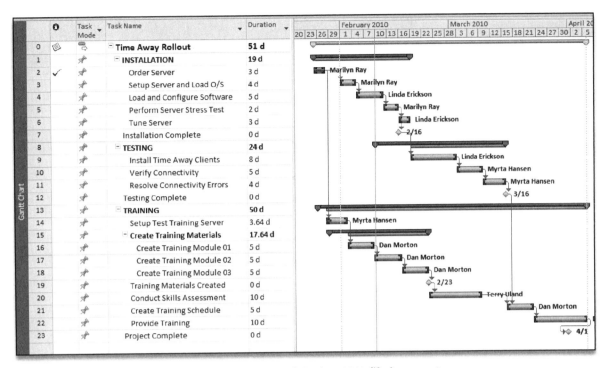

	0	Task Mode	Task Name	Duration
0	📋	🔁	Time Away Rollout	51 d
1		📌	INSTALLATION	19 d
2	✓	📌	Order Server	3 d
3		📌	Setup Server and Load O/S	4 d
4		📌	Load and Configure Software	5 d
5		📌	Perform Server Stress Test	2 d
6		📌	Tune Server	3 d
7		📌	Installation Complete	0 d
8		📌	TESTING	24 d
9		📌	Install Time Away Clients	8 d
10		📌	Verify Connectivity	5 d
11		📌	Resolve Connectivity Errors	4 d
12		📌	Testing Complete	0 d
13		📌	TRAINING	50 d
14		📌	Setup Test Training Server	3.64 d
15		📌	Create Training Materials	17.64 d
16		📌	Create Training Module 01	5 d
17		📌	Create Training Module 02	5 d
18		📌	Create Training Module 03	5 d
19		📌	Training Materials Created	0 d
20		📌	Conduct Skills Assessment	10 d
21		📌	Create Training Schedule	5 d
22		📌	Provide Training	10 d
23		📌	Project Complete	0 d

Figure 8 - 53: Microsoft Project 2010 file is current
after task updates during the first week of the project

Warning: If you set a task to *Inactive* status at any point in the life of the project, the system sets the task to *Inactive* status in your Microsoft Project 2010 plan, but SharePoint continues to show the task as an *Active* task. Because of this, you may want to cancel the task by setting its *Remaining Work* value to *0h* instead of setting it to *Inactive* status.

Module 09

Variance Analysis, Plan Revision, and Change Control

Learning Objectives

After completing this module, you will be able to:

- Understand the different types of project variance

- Understand the difference between "estimated" variance and "actual" variance

- Create a custom view to analyze Duration variance

- Create custom views, tables, filters, and groups

- Use the Organizer to manage default and custom views, tables, filters, and groups

- Define plan revision and change control

- Revise a project plan to bring it back on schedule

- Understand how the Autolink feature works when you insert a new task between two other tasks with dependencies

- Use change control procedures to add a new task to a project

- Baseline a project after adding new tasks

- View the schedule of multiple baselines in a project

Inside Module 09

Understanding Variance

At the end of every reporting period, you should analyze project variance by comparing actual progress and remaining estimates against the original project baseline. This is the way you determine schedule slippage and overruns, as well as identifying existing and/or potential problems with your project schedule. Analyzing variance is the first step in revising the project plan to bring it back on track with its original goals and objectives.

Understanding Variance Types

In Module 08, I documented that when you save a baseline in Microsoft Project 2010, the software baselines the current values for five important task fields. These fields include the *Duration, Start, Finish, Work,* and *Cost.* Because the system saves five task values in a project baseline, the system calculates five types of task variance:

- Duration variance

- Start variance

- Finish variance

- Work variance

- Cost variance

About Those Extra Task Baseline Fields

In Module 08, I noted that in addition to the five important task fields captured in the baseline, Microsoft Project 2010 also captures extra baseline information in several other task fields as well. The software captures the extra baseline information in the following fields: the *Baseline Fixed Cost* and *Baseline Fixed Cost Accrual* fields; the *Baseline Estimated Duration, Baseline Estimated Start,* and *Baseline Estimated Finish* fields; and the *Baseline Budget Cost* and *Baseline Budget Work* fields.

Even though Microsoft Project 2010 captures the extra task baseline information in these seven fields, the software **does not** include any corresponding variance fields for these fields. This means that if you want to analyze Fixed Cost variance, for example, there is no default field called *Fixed Cost Variance.* So, if you want to analyze Fixed Cost variance, you must create a custom task field containing a formula to calculate this variance. The same is true for the other six extra baseline fields as well.

Calculating Variance

To calculate variance, Microsoft Project 2010 uses the following formula:

Variance = (Actual Progress + Remaining Estimates) - Baseline

In Microsoft Project 2010, a positive variance is unfavorable to the project, and means that the project schedule is late, or that work and/or cost are over budget. Negative variance is favorable to the project, and means that the project is ahead of schedule, or that work and/or cost are under budget.

For example, suppose that the actual work for a task is 60 hours, the remaining work estimate is 40 hours, and the baseline work for the task is 80 hours. Using the formula above, Microsoft Project 2010 calculates the work variance as:

Work Variance = (Actual Work + Remaining Work) – Baseline Work

Work Variance = (60 hours + 40 hours) – 80 hours

Work Variance = 100 hours - 80 hours

Work Variance = 20 hours

The resulting 20-hour work variance is unfavorable to the project because the total work hours exceed the original baseline work budget.

Understanding Actual vs. Estimated Variance

Microsoft Project 2010 measures two types of variance in any project: **Actual Variance** and **Estimated Variance**. It is important that you understand the distinction between the two. Actual variance occurs when an actual value, such as actual work, exceeds its original baseline. For example, suppose that a task has a baseline work of 40 hours, but the task is complete and the actual work on the task is 50 hours. Using the formula for variance, Microsoft Project 2010 calculates the variance as follows:

Work Variance = (Actual Work + Remaining Work) – Baseline Work

Work Variance = (50 hours + 0 hours) – 40 hours

Work Variance = 10 hours

Because the task is complete and the actual work exceeds the baseline work by 10 hours, this type of variance is actual variance. In other words, the task went over its baseline budget on work and it is now too late for the project manager to do anything about it.

On the other hand, estimated variance is variance that "might" occur, based on the estimates submitted by the project team members. Estimated variance occurs when actual progress plus remaining estimates (such as actual work + remaining work) exceeds the baseline. For example, a task has a baseline work of 40 hours. At the end of the first week of work on the task, the resource reports 25 hours of actual work, plus a remaining work estimate of 30 hours. Using the formula for variance, Microsoft Project 2010 calculates the variance as follows:

Work Variance = (Actual Work + Remaining Work) – Baseline Work

Work Variance = (25 hours + 30 hours) – 40 hours

Work Variance = 55 hours – 40 hours

Work Variance = 15 hours

The 15 hours of work variance is only an "estimate" at this point, which is caused by the resource "estimating" 15 hours more work than originally scheduled. Estimated variance is very important to you because it is variance that "might" occur and which gives you time to mitigate the possible slippage or overrun.

Analyzing Project Variance

Microsoft Project 2010 offers you the following locations from which to analyze project variance:

- *Tracking Gantt* view

- *Variance* table

- *Work* table

- *Cost* table

The *Tracking Gantt* view and the *Variance* table allow you to analyze start and finish variance for tasks. The *Work* and *Cost* tables allow you to analyze work and cost variance respectively.

 Microsoft Project 2010 does not offer a default table from which to analyze Duration variance. If you want to see Duration variance, you must create your own custom table for this purpose. In Module 10, I teach you how to create a custom view that you can use to analyze Duration variance.

Analyzing Date Variance

Date variance is a major concern for every project manager because many projects have an inflexible project finish date. You can analyze date variance graphically by applying the *Tracking Gantt* view. To apply the *Tracking Gantt* view, use one of the following methods:

- On the *Task* ribbon, click the *Gantt Chart* pick list button and select the *Tracking Gantt* view from the list.

- On the *Resource* ribbon, click the *Team Planner* pick list button and select the *Tracking Gantt* view from the list.

- On the *View* ribbon, click the *Gantt Chart* pick list button and select the *Tracking Gantt* view from the list.

Microsoft Project 2010 applies the *Tracking Gantt* view shown in Figure 9 - 1.

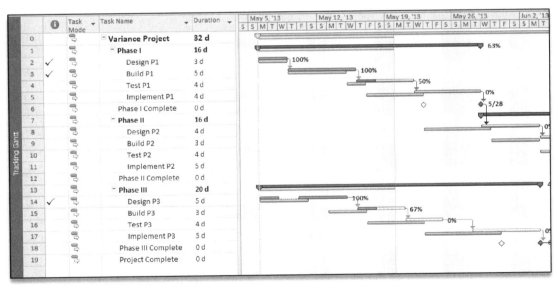

Figure 9 - 1: Tracking Gantt view

Following is a description of the symbols shown in the *Gantt Chart* screen on the right side of the *Tracking Gantt* view:

- Light red Gantt bars represent planned work for tasks on the Critical Path.

- Light blue Gantt bars represent planned work for tasks not on the Critical Path.

397

- Light teal Gantt bars represent planned work for *Manually Scheduled* tasks not on the Critical Path.

- Dark red Gantt bars represent completed work for tasks on the Critical Path.

- Dark blue Gantt bars represent completed work for tasks not on the Critical Path.

- Dark teal Gantt bars represent completed work for *Manually Scheduled* tasks not on the Critical Path.

- Gray Gantt bars represent the baseline schedule for each task.

- Black solid diamonds represent the current schedule for each milestone task.

- Teal solid diamonds represent the current schedule for *Manually Scheduled* tasks.

- Hollow diamonds represent the baseline schedule for each milestone task.

- The percentage value at the right end of each Gantt bar represents the *% Complete* field value for each task.

- The tan bar on the bottom half of each summary task Gantt bar represents the cumulative *% Complete* field value for all of the subtasks for the summary task.

To see every possible symbol that Microsoft Project 2010 can display in the *Tracking Gantt* view, double-click anywhere in the white part of the *Gantt Chart* screen on the right side of the view. The system displays the *Bar Styles* dialog, which shows you the definition for every symbol used in the *Tracking Gantt* view.

The *Tracking Gantt* view allows you to see slippage graphically in your project by comparing blue, red, and teal Gantt bars with their accompanying gray Gantt bars (the baseline schedule for each task). If a blue, red, or teal Gantt bar slips to the right of its gray Gantt bar, then the task is slipping. Additionally, if a black or teal diamond slips to the right of its hollow diamond, then the milestone task is slipping. Using the *Tracking Gantt* view to analyze date variance, it is easy to see the slippage in all phases of the project, as well as the overall slippage for the final project finish date.

Use the *Variance* table to view the date variance in a numerical format, such as in days. To apply the *Variance* table, display any task view (such as the *Tracking Gantt* view) and then use either of the following methods:

- Right-click on the *Select All* button and then select the *Variance* table in the shortcut menu.

- In the *View* ribbon, click the *Tables* pick list and select the *Variance* table in the list.

Microsoft Project 2010 displays the *Variance* table shown in Figure 9 - 2.

	Task Mode	Task Name	Start	Finish	Baseline Start	Baseline Finish	Start Var.	Finish Var.
0		**Variance Project**	**5/6/13**	**6/19/13**	**5/6/13**	**6/14/13**	**0 d**	**3 d**
1		**Phase I**	**5/6/13**	**5/28/13**	**5/6/13**	**5/22/13**	**0 d**	**3 d**
2		Design P1	5/6/13	5/8/13	5/6/13	5/8/13	0 d	0 d
3		Build P1	5/9/13	5/15/13	5/9/13	5/14/13	0 d	1 d
4		Test P1	5/16/13	5/21/13	5/15/13	5/16/13	1 d	3 d
5		Implement P1	5/22/13	5/28/13	5/17/13	5/22/13	3 d	3 d
6		Phase I Complete	5/28/13	5/28/13	5/22/13	5/22/13	3 d	3 d
7		**Phase II**	**5/29/13**	**6/19/13**	**5/23/13**	**6/14/13**	**3 d**	**3 d**
8		Design P2	5/29/13	6/3/13	5/23/13	5/29/13	3 d	3 d
9		Build P2	6/4/13	6/6/13	5/30/13	6/3/13	3 d	3 d
10		Test P2	6/7/13	6/12/13	6/4/13	6/7/13	3 d	3 d
11		Implement P2	6/13/13	6/19/13	6/10/13	6/14/13	3 d	3 d
12		Phase II Complete	6/19/13	6/19/13	6/14/13	6/14/13	3 d	3 d
13		**Phase III**	**5/6/13**	**6/3/13**	**5/6/13**	**5/30/13**	**0 d**	**2 d**
14		Design P3	5/6/13	5/14/13	5/6/13	5/10/13	0 d	2 d
15		Build P3	5/16/13	5/20/13	5/13/13	5/16/13	3 d	2 d
16		Test P3	5/21/13	5/24/13	5/17/13	5/22/13	2 d	2 d
17		Implement P3	5/28/13	6/3/13	5/23/13	5/30/13	2 d	2 d
18		Phase III Complete	6/3/13	6/3/13	5/30/13	5/30/13	2 d	2 d
19		Project Complete	6/19/13	6/19/13	6/14/13	6/14/13	3 d	3 d

Figure 9 - 2: Variance table applied in the Tracking Gantt view

To analyze date variance, examine each value in the *Start Variance* and *Finish Variance* columns. Figure 9 - 2 shows that the *Finish Variance* value for the Project Summary Task (Row 0) equals 3 days, revealing that this project is 3 days late on its finish date, caused by the late finish for the tasks in Phase I. Because of the 3 days of *Finish Variance* in Phase I, all of the tasks in Phase II are 3 days late as well. Notice also that the tasks in Phase III are each 2 days late on their finish date due to the late finish of the Design P3 task.

Analyzing Work Variance

Use the *Work* table to analyze work variance and to determine when project work exceeds its original planned work budget. To apply the *Work* table, display any task view (such as the *Tracking Gantt* view) and then use either of the following methods:

- Right-click on the *Select All* button and then select the *Work* table in the shortcut menu.
- In the *View* ribbon, click the *Tables* pick list and select the *Work* table in the list.

Microsoft Project 2010 displays the *Work* table shown in Figure 9 - 3.

		Task Name	Work	Baseline	Variance	Actual	Remaining	% W. Comp.
	0	⁻ **Variance Project**	**456 h**	**432 h**	**24 h**	**176 h**	**280 h**	**39%**
	1	⁻ **Phase I**	**168 h**	**136 h**	**32 h**	**120 h**	**48 h**	**71%**
	2	Design P1	24 h	24 h	0 h	24 h	0 h	100%
	3	Build P1	80 h	64 h	16 h	80 h	0 h	100%
	4	Test P1	32 h	16 h	16 h	16 h	16 h	50%
	5	Implement P1	32 h	32 h	0 h	0 h	32 h	0%
	6	Phase I Complete	0 h	0 h	0 h	0 h	0 h	0%
	7	⁻ **Phase II**	**152 h**	**152 h**	**0 h**	**0 h**	**152 h**	**0%**
	8	Design P2	32 h	32 h	0 h	0 h	32 h	0%
	9	Build P2	48 h	48 h	0 h	0 h	48 h	0%
	10	Test P2	32 h	32 h	0 h	0 h	32 h	0%
	11	Implement P2	40 h	40 h	0 h	0 h	40 h	0%
	12	Phase II Complete	0 h	0 h	0 h	0 h	0 h	0%
	13	⁻ **Phase III**	**136 h**	**144 h**	**-8 h**	**56 h**	**80 h**	**41%**
	14	Design P3	40 h	40 h	0 h	40 h	0 h	100%
	15	Build P3	24 h	32 h	-8 h	16 h	8 h	67%
	16	Test P3	32 h	32 h	0 h	0 h	32 h	0%
	17	Implement P3	40 h	40 h	0 h	0 h	40 h	0%
	18	Phase III Complete	0 h	0 h	0 h	0 h	0 h	0%
	19	Project Complete	0 h	0 h	0 h	0 h	0 h	0%

Figure 9 - 3: Work table applied in the Tracking Gantt view

To analyze work variance, examine each value in the *Variance* column. In Figure 9 - 3, the *Variance* value for the Project Summary Task (Row 0) reveals that this project is currently 24 hours over budget. Phase I is currently 32 hours over its work budget. Build P1 is 16 hours over budget, and the task is complete; therefore, Build P1 shows actual variance. Test P1 is also 16 hours over budget, but the task is only 50% complete; therefore, Test P1 shows estimated variance. Phase III is 8 hours **under** its work budget, indicated by the negative value in the *Variance* column.

> In the *Work* table, the real name of the *Variance* column is *Work Variance*. Microsoft uses the shorter name as the title of this column for display purposes only. You can see the real name of the column by floating your mouse pointer over the *Variance* column header. The system displays a tooltip that shows the title of the column, followed by the real name of the column in parentheses.

Analyzing Cost Variance

Use the *Cost* table to analyze cost variance and to determine when project costs exceed its original planned cost budget. To apply the *Cost* table, display any task view (such as the *Tracking Gantt* view) and then use either of the following methods:

- Right-click on the *Select All* button and then select the *Cost* table in the shortcut menu.

- In the *View* ribbon, click the *Tables* pick list and select the *Cost* table in the list.

Microsoft Project 2010 displays the *Cost* table shown in Figure 9 - 4.

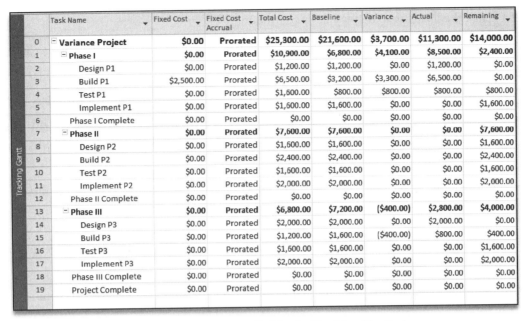

	Task Name	Fixed Cost	Fixed Cost Accrual	Total Cost	Baseline	Variance	Actual	Remaining
0	⊟ **Variance Project**	**$0.00**	**Prorated**	**$25,300.00**	**$21,600.00**	**$3,700.00**	**$11,300.00**	**$14,000.00**
1	⊟ **Phase I**	**$0.00**	**Prorated**	**$10,900.00**	**$6,800.00**	**$4,100.00**	**$8,500.00**	**$2,400.00**
2	Design P1	$0.00	Prorated	$1,200.00	$1,200.00	$0.00	$1,200.00	$0.00
3	Build P1	$2,500.00	Prorated	$6,500.00	$3,200.00	$3,300.00	$6,500.00	$0.00
4	Test P1	$0.00	Prorated	$1,600.00	$800.00	$800.00	$800.00	$800.00
5	Implement P1	$0.00	Prorated	$1,600.00	$1,600.00	$0.00	$0.00	$1,600.00
6	Phase I Complete	$0.00	Prorated	$0.00	$0.00	$0.00	$0.00	$0.00
7	⊟ **Phase II**	**$0.00**	**Prorated**	**$7,600.00**	**$7,600.00**	**$0.00**	**$0.00**	**$7,600.00**
8	Design P2	$0.00	Prorated	$1,600.00	$1,600.00	$0.00	$0.00	$1,600.00
9	Build P2	$0.00	Prorated	$2,400.00	$2,400.00	$0.00	$0.00	$2,400.00
10	Test P2	$0.00	Prorated	$1,600.00	$1,600.00	$0.00	$0.00	$1,600.00
11	Implement P2	$0.00	Prorated	$2,000.00	$2,000.00	$0.00	$0.00	$2,000.00
12	Phase II Complete	$0.00	Prorated	$0.00	$0.00	$0.00	$0.00	$0.00
13	⊟ **Phase III**	**$0.00**	**Prorated**	**$6,800.00**	**$7,200.00**	**($400.00)**	**$2,800.00**	**$4,000.00**
14	Design P3	$0.00	Prorated	$2,000.00	$2,000.00	$0.00	$2,000.00	$0.00
15	Build P3	$0.00	Prorated	$1,200.00	$1,600.00	($400.00)	$800.00	$400.00
16	Test P3	$0.00	Prorated	$1,600.00	$1,600.00	$0.00	$0.00	$1,600.00
17	Implement P3	$0.00	Prorated	$2,000.00	$2,000.00	$0.00	$0.00	$2,000.00
18	Phase III Complete	$0.00	Prorated	$0.00	$0.00	$0.00	$0.00	$0.00
19	Project Complete	$0.00	Prorated	$0.00	$0.00	$0.00	$0.00	$0.00

Figure 9 - 4: Cost table applied in the Tracking Gantt view

To analyze cost variance, examine each value in the *Variance* column. In Figure 9 - 4, the *Variance* value for the Project Summary Task (Row 0) reveals that the project is currently $3,700 over budget. This variance is because Phase I is currently $4,100 over budget while Phase III is currently $400 **under** budget. Notice that a significant part of the cost variance in Phase I arises from the $2,500 in the *Fixed Cost* column for the Build P1 task. Remember that you can use the *Fixed Cost* column to track unanticipated task costs.

In the *Cost* table, the real name of the *Variance* column is *Cost Variance*. Microsoft uses the shorter name as the title of this column for display purposes only. You can see the real name of the column by floating your mouse pointer over the *Variance* column header. The system displays a tooltip that shows the title of the column, followed by the real name of the column in parentheses.

Hands On Exercise

Exercise 9-1

Actual progress is current through Friday, February 7, 2014 in your Training Advisor Rollout project. The red dashed line in the *Gantt Chart* view indicates that the "current" date is Monday, February 10, 2014. Analyze schedule, date, work, and cost variance in your project.

1. Open the **Training Advisor 09.mpp** sample file.

2. Click the *View* tab to display the *View* ribbon.

3. On the *View* ribbon, click the *Gantt Chart* pick list button and select the *Tracking Gantt* view from the list.

4. Scroll through the *Tracking Gantt* chart to analyze schedule slippage for each task in the project.

5. In the *Indicators* column, float your mouse pointer over the notes indicator for any task with a note (the notes indicator looks like a yellow sticky note) and try to determine why this project is slipping.

6. Right-click on the *Select All* button and select the *Variance* table in the shortcut menu.

7. Drag the split bar to the right edge of the *Finish Variance* column.

8. In the *Start Variance* and *Finish Variance* columns, analyze the schedule slippage data for every task in the project

9. Right-click on the *Select All* button and select the *Work* table in the shortcut menu.

10. Examine the data in the *Variance* column and analyze work variance for every task in the project.

11. Right-click on the *Select All* button and select the *Cost* table in the shortcut menu.

12. Examine the data in the *Variance* column and analyze cost variance for every task in the project.

13. Right-click on the *Select All* button and select the *Entry* table in the shortcut menu.

14. Drag the split bar back to the right edge of the *Duration* column.

15. Save but **do not** close the **Training Advisor 09.mpp** sample file.

Understanding Custom Views

An experienced project manager once said to me, "Microsoft Project is like a black hole. It takes, but it won't give back." He was describing his frustration with gathering meaningful information about his projects. He knew the information was "in there somewhere" but he just could not find it! Using custom views, you can quickly locate pertinent project information, including project variance.

What Is A View?

Most of us think of a View as a "way of looking at our data." However, Microsoft Project 2010 formally defines a View as follows:

View = Table + Filter + Group + Screen

In order to extract meaningful information from your projects, such as duration variance information, you may need to create your own custom views so that you can see:

- Columns of data you want to see (the table)

- Only the rows of data you want to see (the filter)

- Rows grouped the way you want to see them (the group)

- Your data displayed on the screen using your desired layout (the screen)

Creating a New Custom View Using a Four-Step Method

A "best practice" approach for creating custom views is to apply a four-step method. These four steps are:

1. Select an existing table or create a new custom table.

2. Select an existing filter or create a new custom filter.

3. Select an existing group or create a new custom group.

4. Create the new view using the desired table, filter, group, and screen.

Creating a Custom Table

The first step requires you to select an existing table or to create a new custom table if no existing table meets your reporting needs. Because a table is a collection of columns, a key question to ask during this step is, "What columns of data do I want to see in my new view?" The answer to this question determines whether you select an existing table or create a new custom table.

The easiest way to create a new table is to copy an existing table and then modify the copy. To create a new table using this method, complete the following steps:

1. In the *Data* section of the *View* ribbon, click the *Tables* pick list and select the *More Tables* item on the list. Microsoft Project 2010 displays the *More Tables* dialog shown in Figure 9 - 5.

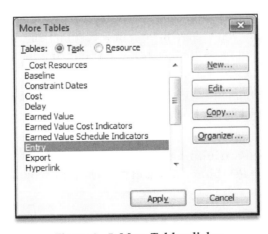

Figure 9 - 5: More Tables dialog

2. From the list of default and custom tables, select a table and then click the *Copy* button. Microsoft Project 2010 displays the *Table Definition* dialog shown in Figure 9 - 6.

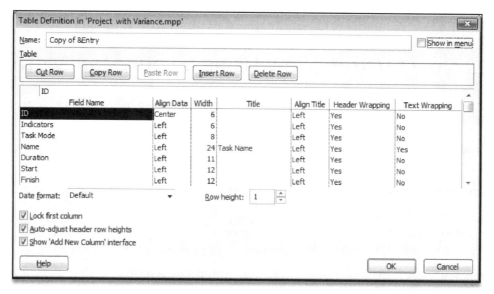

Figure 9 - 6: Table Definition dialog

3. In the *Name* field, enter an original name for the new custom table.

In Figure 9 - 6, the ampersand character (**&**) in the name of the table precedes the hotkey character associated with the table. To access the *Entry* table using hotkeys, type the following sequence in your computer keyboard: **Alt + W**, **TA**, **E**. Alt+ W selects the *View* ribbon, TA expands the *Table* pick list, and E selects the *Entry* table.

4. Select the *Show in menu* option if you wish to see the table displayed on *Tables* pick list in the *View* ribbon.

5. To delete any field you do not want to see in your new custom table, select the field and then click the *Delete Row* button in the dialog or press the **Delete** key on your computer keyboard.

6. To add a new field at the bottom of the list of fields, click in the *Field Name* column in the blank row below the last field, click the pick list button and then select the name of your field from the list.

7. To insert a new field between two other fields in the list, select the row where you want to insert the new field and then click the *Insert Row* button. Click in the *Field Name* column in the blank row, click the pick list button and then select the name of your field from the list.

8. For each field you add to the *Table Definition* dialog, enter or select a value in the *Align Data, Width, Align Title, Header Wrapping,* and *Text Wrapping* columns.

The *Text Wrapping* column is a new feature in Microsoft Project 2010 that allows you to specify whether the system wraps text in the field automatically when the length of the text string exceeds the width of the column. The software wraps text in the *Name* field (*Task Name* column) by default. When you add new fields to the table, the system sets the *Text Wrapping* value to *No* for each new field, but you can change the value to *Yes* as needed.

9.   If you want to display alternate text in the column header for any field, enter the alternate text in the *Title* field.

10. If desirable, click the *Date format* pick list and select the display format for dates shown in your custom table.

The *Date* format pick list is a little-known feature of Microsoft Project 2010 that allows you to select a unique date format for dates shown only in your custom table. The software applies the selected date format to **only** the custom table, while applying the default date format to every standard table.

The *Table Definition* dialog also contains the new *Show 'Add New Column' Interface* option in the lower left corner of the dialog. The system enables this option by default. When selected, this option displays the *Add New Column* virtual column as the last column on the right side of the table. If you do not want to see the *Add New Column* virtual column in your new table, deselect this option.

Figure 9 - 7 shows the *Table Definition* dialog for a new custom table I created to show the differences between the *% Complete* field values and the *% Work Complete* field values for every task. Notice in the dialog that I included a title for the *% Complete* field to show that this field actually represents the *% Duration Complete* value for each task. Notice that I also deselected the new *Show 'Add New Column' Interface* option to hide the *Add New Column* virtual column in my new custom table.

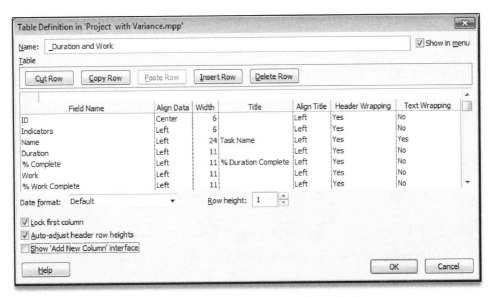

Figure 9 - 7: Completed custom table definition

11. Click the *OK* button to close the *Table Definition* dialog.

12. Click the *Apply* button to display your new table.

Figure 9 - 8 shows the new custom *_Duration and Work* table I created using the previous steps, applied in the *Gantt Chart* view.

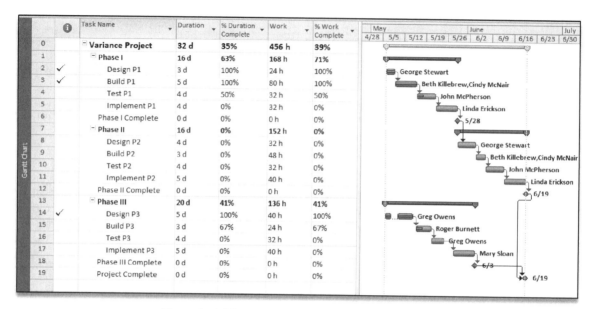

Figure 9 - 8: New custom _Duration and Work table

When you use the *More Tables* dialog to create a new table, Microsoft Project 2010 copies the new table automatically to your Global.mpt file. This makes the new custom table available for all of your current and future projects.

Hands On Exercise

Exercise 9-2

Create a new custom table to show Duration variance data.

1. Return the **Training Advisor 09.mpp** sample file.

2. In the *Data* section of the *View* ribbon, click the *Tables* pick list and select the *More Tables* item on the list.

3. In the *More Tables* dialog, select the *Work* table and then click the *Copy* button.

4. In the *Table Definition* dialog, enter *_Duration* in the *Name* field and then select the *Show in menu* option.

The underscore character preceding the table name forces the table to the top of the menu and indicates it is a custom table rather than a default table.

MSProjectExperts recommends that you use a unique naming convention, such as preceding the name with an underscore character, when creating custom objects such as views, tables, filters, or groups. Using a naming convention separates your customization objects from the default objects included in Microsoft Project 2010.

5. Select the *Name* field in the *Field Name* column and then click the *Insert Row* button.

6. In the *Field Name* column, click the pick list for the new blank row and select the *Indicators* field.

7. For the *Indictors* field, specify each of the column values as follows:

Align Data	Width	Title	Align Title	Header Wrapping	Text Wrapping
Left	9		Left	Yes	No

8. Modify the existing fields in the data grid to show the information in the following table.

Original Field	New Field
ID	ID
Indicators	Indicators
Name	Name
Work	Duration
Baseline Work	Baseline Duration
Work Variance	Duration Variance
Actual Work	Actual Duration
Remaining Work	Remaining Duration
% Work Complete	% Complete

9. Use the **Backspace** key on your keyboard to remove the value in the *Title* column for every field **except** the *Task Name* field.

 Warning: To delete the text in the *Title* column, you must select the text and then press the **Backspace** key on your keyboard. If you press the *Delete* key, Microsoft Project 2010 removes the entire field rather than deleting the text.

10. Select the *Duration Variance* field and then click the *Cut Row* button.

11. Select the *Duration* field and then click the *Paste Row* button.

By completing the two preceding steps, you moved the most important column in the table (the *Duration Variance* column) to the immediate right of the *Task Name* column. Arranging the columns in this order makes it easier to spot tasks with duration slippage.

12. Click the *OK* button.

13. Select your new custom table and then click the *Apply* button to view and study the table.

14. "Best fit" the *Task Name* column, if necessary.

15. Save but do not close the **Training Advisor 09.mpp** sample file.

Creating a Custom Filter

The second step for creating a new view is to select an existing filter, or to create a new filter if no existing filter meets your reporting requirements. The filter extracts the exact rows of data you wish to see in your view. A key question to ask before completing this step is, "What rows of data do I want to see in my new view?" The answer to this question determines whether you select an existing filter or create a new custom filter. If you need to create a new filter, complete the following steps:

1. Click the *View* tab to display the *View* ribbon.

2. In the *Data* section of the *View* ribbon, click the *Filter* pick list and select the *More Filters* item on the list. Alternately, you can also click the *Highlight Filter* pick list and select the *More Highlight Filters* item. Microsoft Project 2010 displays the *More Filters* dialog shown in Figure 9 - 9.

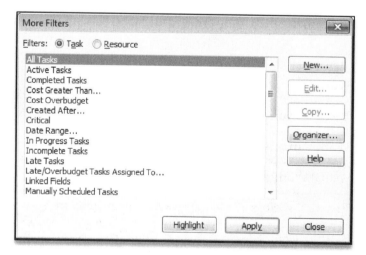

Figure 9 - 9: More Filters dialog

3. Click the *New* button in the *More Filters* dialog. Microsoft Project 2010 displays the *Filter Definition* dialog shown in Figure 9 - 10.

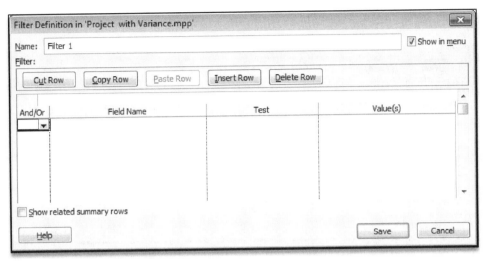

Figure 9 - 10: Filter Definition dialog for a new custom filter

4. Enter a name for the new filter in the *Name* field.

5. Select the *Show in menu* option if you want your new filter to display in *Filter* and *Highlight Filter* pick lists in the *View* ribbon.

6. In the data grid, enter your desired filter criteria in the *Field Name*, *Test*, *Value(s)*, and *And/Or* columns.

 To create a compound filter with multiple lines of filtering criteria, you must select an *And* value or an *Or* value for each line after the first line.

7. Select the *Show related summary rows* option if you wish to see all summary tasks for every task that meets your filter criteria, regardless of whether the summary task meets the filter criteria.

 Selecting the *Show related summary rows* option guarantees that the filter shows you the Work Breakdown Structure (WBS) for each task displayed by the filter. This helps you to identify the phase and/or deliverable section of the project for each task the filter displays.

Figure 9 - 11 shows the *Filter Definition* dialog with criteria for a new custom filter to display all tasks that exceed their original budget of work hours specified in the *Baseline Work* field.

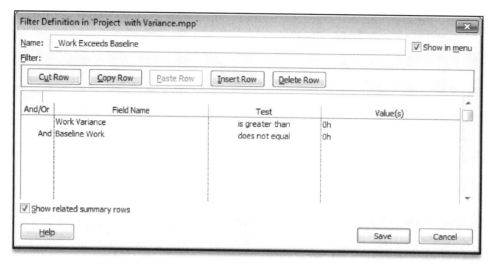

Figure 9 - 11: Filter criteria in the Filter Definition dialog

The *_Work Exceeds Baseline* filter shown in Figure 9 - 11 displays every task that is over its original budget of work hours specified in the *Baseline Work* field. The filter displays completed, in-progress, and unstarted tasks that are over budget on work. This differs from the behavior of the default *Work Overbudget* filter that displays **only** completed and in-progress tasks in which the *Actual Work* value exceeds the *Baseline Work* value.

8.   Click the *Save* button to close the *Filter Definition* dialog.

9.   In the *More Filters* dialog, select your new custom filter, if necessary, and then click the *Apply* button to test the filter.

Figure 9 - 12 shows the *_Work Exceeds Baseline* filter applied in the *Gantt Chart* view with the *Work* table displayed. Notice that this custom filter displays all types of tasks that are over budget on work. This includes a completed task (Build P1), two in-progress tasks (Test P1 and Build P3), and an unstarted task (Implement P1).

	Task Name	Work	Baseline	Variance	
0	Variance Project	480 h	432 h	48 h	
1	Phase I	176 h	136 h	40 h	
3	Build P1	80 h	64 h	16 h	Beth Killebrew,Cindy McNair
4	Test P1	32 h	16 h	16 h	John McPherson
5	Implement P1	40 h	32 h	8 h	Linda Erickson
13	Phase III	152 h	144 h	8 h	
15	Build P3	40 h	32 h	8 h	Roger Burnett

Figure 9 - 12: _Work Exceeds Baseline filter applied in the Gantt Chart view

When you create a new filter, Microsoft Project 2010 copies the new filter automatically into your Global.mpt file. This makes the new custom filter available for all of your current and future projects.

Hands On Exercise

Exercise 9-3

Create a custom filter to locate tasks whose Duration exceeds their Baseline Duration.

1. Return the **Training Advisor 09.mpp** sample file.

2. Right-click on the *Select All* button and select the new custom *_Duration* table, if necessary.

3. Click the *View* tab to display the *View* ribbon.

4. In the *Data* section of the *View* ribbon, click the *Filter* pick list and select the *More Filters* item on the list.

5. In the *More Filters* dialog, click the *New* button.

6. In the *Filter Definition* dialog, enter or select the following information:

Name	_Duration Variance > 0d		
Show in menu	Selected		
And/Or	**Field Name**	**Test**	**Value(s)s**
	Duration Variance	is greater than	0d
Show related summary rows		Selected	

7. Click the *Save* button to save the new filter.

8. In the *More Filters* dialog, select your new filter, if necessary, and then click the *Apply* button to test the filter.

9. After you confirm the filter works correctly as designed, press the **F3** function key to reapply the *[No Filter]* filter.

10. Save but do not close the **Training Advisor 09.mpp** sample file.

Creating a Custom Group

The third step in creating a new view is to select an existing group or create a new group if no existing group meets your reporting needs. In Microsoft Project 2010, groups allow you to categorize, sort, and summarize your project data. Because very few default groups exist in Microsoft Project 2010, it is likely that you will need to create a new group as a part of any new custom view to which you want to apply grouping. To create a new custom group, complete the following steps:

1. Click the *View* tab to display the *View* ribbon.

2. In the *Data* section of the *View* ribbon, click the *Group By* pick list and select the *More Groups* item on the list. Microsoft Project 2010 displays the *More Groups* dialog shown in Figure 9 - 13.

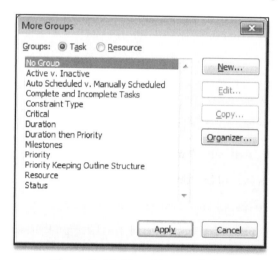

Figure 9 - 13: More Groups dialog

3. In the *More Groups* dialog, click the *New* button. Microsoft Project 2010 displays the *Group Definition* dialog shown in Figure 9 - 14.

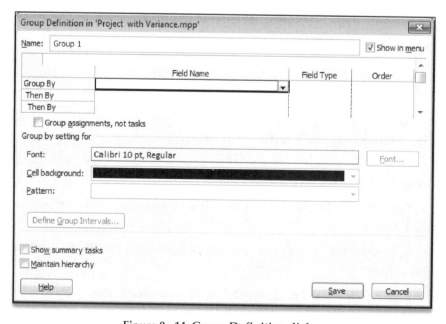

Figure 9 - 14: Group Definition dialog

4. Enter a name for the new custom group in the *Name* field and then select the *Show in menu* option if you want the new custom group to display in the *Group by* pick list in the *View* ribbon.

5. In the data grid, enter the desired grouping information on the *Group By* line in the *Field Name, Field Type,* and *Order* columns.

6. To create multi-level grouping, enter additional grouping information in one or more of the *Then By* lines in the data grid.

> You can create a custom group that applies grouping on assignments in any assignment view. This means that a task group can apply grouping to resource assignments in the *Task Usage* view, and a resource group can apply grouping to the task assignments in the *Resource Usage* view. To create a group that applies grouping on assignments, select the *Group assignments, not tasks* option. Alternately, you can also click the *Field Type* pick list for the field upon which you want to group and then select the *Assignments* value on the list.

7. If you want to specify grouping intervals, click the *Define Group Intervals* button. Microsoft Project 2010 displays the *Define Group Interval* dialog shown in Figure 9 - 15.

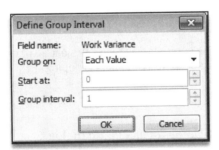

**Figure 9 - 15: Define Group
Interval dialog**

You use the options in the *Define Group Interval* dialog to set up grouping with specific interval ranges. Based on the type of field you select, Microsoft Project 2010 offers the appropriate interval options in the *Group on* pick list. For example, notice in Figure 9 - 15 that I selected the *Work Variance* field. Because the *Work Variance* field contains time data, the *Group on* pick list contains group interval options for *Minutes, Hours, Days, Weeks,* and *Months.* For my reporting criteria, I want to group tasks by their *Work Variance* value, grouped in 8-hour intervals, generating groups from 0-8h, 8-16h, 16-24h, etc.

In addition, the *Define Group Interval* dialog also includes a *Start at* field. You can use this field to specify the starting value of your first group interval. For example, if you set the *Group on* value to *Hours,* set the *Group interval* value to *8,* and leave the *Start at* value to *0,* the system creates the first group interval as **0h - < 8h**. If you change the *Start at* value to *2,* the system creates the first group interval as **2h - < 10h**. If you want to specify a value in the *Start at* field, the value you select **must be less than** the value you specify in the Group interval field; otherwise, the *Start at* value you specify has no effect on the group intervals created when you apply the group.

When you specify a value in the *Start at* field, the system **may not** create the group intervals you expect. This is because Microsoft Project 2010 must create a group interval for every task in the project. Using the preceding example, I have a number of tasks in the project that have a *0h* value in the *Work Variance* field. If I set the *Start at* value to *2*, the system **does not** create the first group interval as **2h - < 10h**. Instead, the system creates the first group interval as **-6h - < 2h** to so that there is a group interval for tasks with *0h* value in the *Work Variance* column.

8. In the *Define Group Interval* dialog, select your desired interval values in the *Group on, Start at,* and *Group interval* fields. Figure 9 - 16 shows the completed *Define Group Interval* dialog with grouping set in 8-hour intervals.

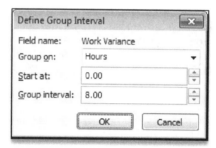

**Figure 9 - 16: Define Group Interval
dialog with 8-hour intervals**

If you do not specify grouping intervals, Microsoft Project 2010 creates a separate group interval for each set of values in the field on which you apply grouping.

9. Click the *OK* button to close the *Define Group Interval* dialog.

10. Click the *Cell background* pick list and select an alternate color other than the default tan color, if necessary.

11. Click the *Pattern* pick list and select an alternate pattern other than the default solid pattern, if necessary.

12. Click the *Font* button and select alternate font settings, if necessary.

By changing the values in the *Cell Background* and *Pattern* fields, you can create your own color scheme for each grouping level in your custom group

13. Select the *Show summary tasks* option if you wish to see summary tasks included in the grouping intervals.

Warning: If you select the *Show summary tasks* option, Microsoft Project 2010 **does not** maintain the Work Breakdown Structure (WBS) for your project when you apply the group. This means that the software might list a summary task in one grouping interval and one of its subtasks in a different grouping interval. If you want to see the WBS for each task, a better option is **not** to select the *Show summary tasks* option and to select the *Maintain hierarchy* option instead.

14. If you want to show the WBS of summary tasks for each task with the group applied, select the *Maintain hierarchy* option.

Figure 9 - 17 shows the completed *Group Definition* dialog for the custom *_Work Variance* group. Notice that I selected the *Maintain hierarchy* option since I want to see the WBS for every task.

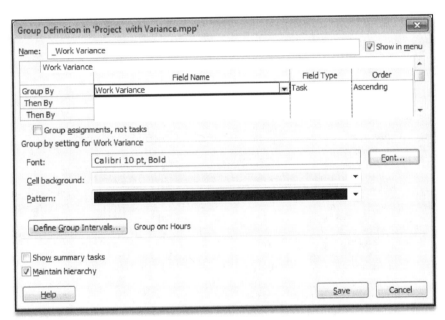

**Figure 9 - 17: Completed _Work Variance group
definition in the Group Definition**

15. Click the *Save* button to close the *Group Definition* dialog.

16. In the *More Groups* dialog, select your new custom group, if necessary, and then click the *Apply* button to test it.

Warning: When applying a task group, do not apply the group in any view containing a Gantt Chart screen, as this action generates a "tangled spaghetti" pattern with the link lines between Gantt bars. Instead, for better results, always apply task groups after displaying the *Task Sheet* view first.

Figure 9 - 18 shows the custom *_Work Variance* group applied to the *Task Sheet* view with the *Work* table displayed. Because I set the *Group interval* value to *8* in the *Define Group Interval* dialog, the system creates groups in intervals of 8 hours each, from 0-8h, 8-16h, and 16-24h, as I expected. Because I also selected the *Maintain hierarchy* option in the *Group Definition* dialog, notice that Microsoft Project 2010 displays the WBS for each task in each group interval as well.

	Task Name	Work	Baseline	Variance	Actual	Remaining	% W. Comp.
	⊟ Work Variance: 0 h - <8 h	288 h	288 h	0 h	64 h	224 h	22%
	⊟ 1 Phase I	24 h	24 h	0 h	24 h	0 h	100%
2	Design P1	24 h	24 h	0 h	24 h	0 h	100%
	⊟ 2 Phase I Complete	0 h	0 h	0 h	0 h	0 h	0%
6	Phase I Complete	0 h	0 h	0 h	0 h	0 h	0%
	⊟ 3 Phase II	152 h	152 h	0 h	0 h	152 h	0%
8	Design P2	32 h	32 h	0 h	0 h	32 h	0%
9	Build P2	48 h	48 h	0 h	0 h	48 h	0%
10	Test P2	32 h	32 h	0 h	0 h	32 h	0%
11	Implement P2	40 h	40 h	0 h	0 h	40 h	0%
	⊟ 4 Phase II Complete	0 h	0 h	0 h	0 h	0 h	0%
12	Phase II Complete	0 h	0 h	0 h	0 h	0 h	0%
	⊟ 5 Phase III	112 h	112 h	0 h	40 h	72 h	35%
14	Design P3	40 h	40 h	0 h	40 h	0 h	100%
16	Test P3	32 h	32 h	0 h	0 h	32 h	0%
17	Implement P3	40 h	40 h	0 h	0 h	40 h	0%
	⊟ 6 Phase III Complete	0 h	0 h	0 h	0 h	0 h	0%
18	Phase III Complete	0 h	0 h	0 h	0 h	0 h	0%
	⊟ 7 Project Complete	0 h	0 h	0 h	0 h	0 h	0%
19	Project Complete	0 h	0 h	0 h	0 h	0 h	0%
	⊟ Work Variance: 8 h - <16 h	80 h	64 h	16 h	16 h	64 h	20%
	⊟ 1 Phase I	40 h	32 h	8 h	0 h	40 h	0%
5	Implement P1	40 h	32 h	8 h	0 h	40 h	0%
	⊟ 5 Phase III	40 h	32 h	8 h	16 h	24 h	40%
15	Build P3	40 h	32 h	8 h	16 h	24 h	40%
	⊟ Work Variance: 16 h - <24 h	112 h	80 h	32 h	96 h	16 h	85%
	⊟ 1 Phase I	112 h	80 h	32 h	96 h	16 h	85%
3	Build P1	80 h	64 h	16 h	80 h	0 h	100%
4	Test P1	32 h	16 h	16 h	16 h	16 h	50%

Figure 9 - 18: _Work Variance group applied in the Task Sheet view

When you create a new group, Microsoft Project 2010 copies the new group automatically into your Global.mpt file. This makes the new custom group available for all of your current and future projects.

Hands On Exercise

Exercise 9-4

Create a new custom group to apply grouping tasks by Duration Variance in descending order in 1-day intervals.

1. Return to the **Training Advisor 09.mpp** sample file.

2. Click the *View* tab to display the *View* ribbon.

3. In the *Task Views* section of the *View* ribbon, click the *Timeline* pick list button and then select the *Task Sheet* view from the list.

4. Right-click on the *Select All* button and select the new custom *_Duration* table.

5. In the *Data* section of the *View* ribbon, click the *Group By* pick list and select the *More Groups* item on the list.

6. In the *More Groups* dialog, click the *New* button.

7. In the *Group Definition* dialog, set up the group criteria shown as follows:

Name	_Duration Variance
Show in menu	Selected
Field Name	Duration Variance
Field Type	Task
Order	Descending
Group assignments not tasks	Not selected
Show summary tasks	Not selected
Maintain hierarchy	Selected

8. Click the *Define Group Intervals* button and set up group intervals in the *Define Group Interval* dialog as follows:

Group on	Days
Start at	0.00
Group interval	1.00

9.   Click the *OK* button to close the *Define Group Interval* dialog.

10. Click the *Save* button to close the *Group Definition* dialog.

11. Select your new custom group, if necessary, and then click the *Apply* button to test the group.

12. Collapse the *Duration Variance: 0d - <1d* section to hide tasks with a *Duration Variance* value less than 1 day.

13. Press **Shift + F3** as the shortcut key to reapply the *No Group* group.

14. In the *Task Views* section of the *View* ribbon, click the *Gantt Chart* button to reapply the *Gantt Chart* view.

15. Right-click on the *Select All* button and select the customized *Entry* table.

16. Save but do not close the **Training Advisor 09.mpp** sample file.

Creating a New Custom View

The final step in the view creation process is to combine your desired screen, table, filter, and group into a new custom view. The screen selection is a very important component of any custom view, as it controls what appears on the right side of the new custom view. For example, when choosing a screen, you determine whether the right side of the view displays a *Gantt Chart* screen of some type (such as in the *Tracking Gantt* view), a timephased grid screen (such as in the *Resource Usage* view), or no screen at all (such as in the *Task Sheet* view).

 Warning: Carefully select your *Screen* option because you cannot change the screen selection after you complete the process of creating your new custom view. If you accidentally select the wrong screen, you must delete the new view using the *Organizer* dialog and then create the new view again from scratch.

To create your new custom view, complete the following steps:

1.   Click the *View* tab to display the *View* ribbon.

2.   In the *Task Views* section of the *View* ribbon, click the *Gantt Chart* pick list and select the *More Views* item on the list. Microsoft Project 2010 displays the *More Views* dialog shown in Figure 9 - 19.

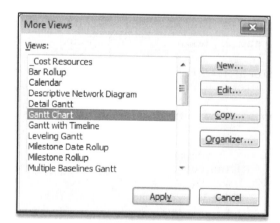

Figure 9 - 19: More Views dialog

3. In the *More Views* dialog, click the *New* button. Microsoft Project 2010 displays the *Define New View* dialog shown in Figure 9 - 20.

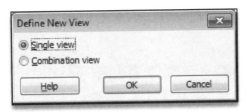

Figure 9 - 20: Define New View dialog

4. To create a custom single pane view, leave the default *Single view* option selected and click the *OK* button. Microsoft Project 2010 displays the *View Definition* dialog shown in Figure 9 - 21.

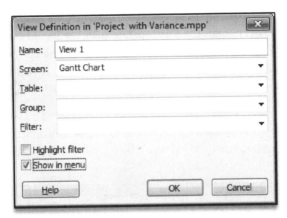

Figure 9 - 21: View Definition dialog

 You can also start the process of creating a new custom view by selecting any existing view in the *More Views* dialog and then clicking the *Copy* button. The limitation of using this method is that Microsoft Project 2010 **does not** allow you to change the *Screen* value when creating a single pane view.

5. In the *View Definition* dialog, enter a name for the new custom view in the *Name* field.

6. Click the *Screen* pick list and select the screen you want to appear on the right side of the view. Microsoft Project 2010 offers you a list of sixteen screen choices, each of which matches up with one of the default views you see in the software.

7. Click the *Table* pick list and select the table you want to use in your custom view. You can select any default table or any custom table you created previously.

8. Click the *Group* pick list and select the group you want to use in your custom view. You can select any default group or any custom group you created previously.

9. Click the *Filter* pick list and select the filter you want to use in your custom view. You can select any default filter or any custom filter you created previously.

10. Select the *Highlight filter* option is you wish to apply the selected filter as a highlight filter.

Remember that a highlight filter displays all tasks in your project, but highlights only those tasks that meet your filter criteria. By default, Microsoft Project 2010 highlights the tasks using the yellow cell background color.

11. Select the *Show in menu* option if you wish to see the new custom view on a view menu.

When you select the *Show in menu* option, Microsoft Project 2010 adds the new custom view in the *Custom Views* section at the top of the *Gantt Chart* pick list in the *View* section of the *Tasks* ribbon. The system also displays the new custom view in the *Custom Views* section at the top of the appropriate pick list in either the *Task Views* or *Resource Views* section of the *View* ribbon. The system chooses the appropriate pick list based on the *Screen* option you select in the *View Definition* dialog. For example, if you select the *Gantt Chart* item on the *Screen* pick list, the system adds the custom view to the *Gantt Chart* pick list in the *Task Views* section of the ribbon. If you select the *Resource Usage* item on the *Screen* pick list, the system adds the custom view to the *Resource Usage* pick list in the *Resource Views* section of the ribbon.

Figure 9 - 22 shows the completed *View Definition* dialog. I intend to use this new custom view to display tasks that are over budget on work, compared against the original work budget specified in the *Baseline Work* field.

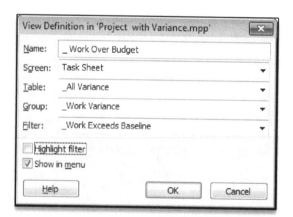

**Figure 9 - 22: Completed custom view criteria
in the View Definition dialog**

12. Click the *OK* button to close the *View Definition* dialog.

13. In the *More Views* dialog, select your new custom view, if necessary, and then click the *Apply* button to test your new view.

Figure 9 - 23 shows the new custom *_Work Over Budget* view, as defined in the *View Definition* dialog shown previously in Figure 9 - 22. Notice that the view displays only those tasks with a value greater than 0 hours in the *Work Variance* column. Notice also that I can see the WBS for each task because I selected the *Maintain hierarchy* option when I created the custom group included in this view.

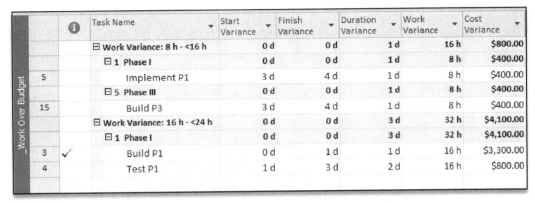

Figure 9 - 23: New custom _Work Over Budget view

When you create a new view, Microsoft Project 2010 copies the new view automatically into your Global.mpt file. This makes the new custom view available for all of your current and future projects.

Hands On Exercise

Exercise 9-5

Make a copy of the *Tracking Gantt* view and then modify the copy to create a custom view that shows all tasks with a *Duration Variance* value greater than *0 days*. Apply the filter as a highlight filter.

1. Return to the **Training Advisor 09.mpp** sample file.

2. Click the *View* tab to display the *View* ribbon.

3. In the *Task Views* section of the *View* ribbon, click the *Gantt Chart* pick list and select the *More Views* item on the list.

4. In the *More Views* dialog, select the *Tracking Gantt* view and then click the *Copy* button.

5. In the *View Definition* dialog, enter or select the following information:

Name	_Duration Slippage
Table	_Duration
Group	No Group
Filter	_Duration Variance > 0d
Highlight filter	Selected
Show in menu	Selected

When creating a new custom view, you must select a *Group* value in the *View Definition* dialog, even if you **do not** want to use a group in your view. If you fail to select a group when creating your new view, Microsoft Project 2010 displays an error message when you click the *OK* button to complete the view.

6. Click the *OK* button to close the *View Definition* dialog.

7. Select your new custom view, if necessary, and then click the *Apply* button.

8. In the *Zoom* section of the *View* ribbon, click the *Zoom* pick list and then click the *Zoom Out* button. Repeat this action a second time to zoom to the *Months Over Weeks* level of zoom.

9. After confirming the new view works as planned, click the *Gantt Chart* pick list button in the *Task Views* section of the *View* ribbon and select the *Gantt Chart* view.

10. Save but **do not** close to the **Training Advisor 09.mpp** sample file.

Creating a Combination View

Remember that a combination view consists of two views, each tiled in its own pane. Because of this, the steps needed to create a combination view are much different than the steps needed to create a single-screen view. As documented in the previous topical section, you use the four-step method to create a single-screen view. To create a combination view, however, complete the following steps:

1. Click the *View* tab to display the *View* ribbon.

2. In the *Task Views* section of the *View* ribbon, click the *Gantt Chart* pick list and select the *More Views* item on the list. Microsoft Project 2010 displays the *More Views* dialog shown previously in Figure 9 - 19.

3. In the *More Views* dialog, click the *New* button. Microsoft Project 2010 displays the *Define New View* dialog shown previously in Figure 9 - 20.

4. Select the *Combination view* option and click the *OK* button. Microsoft Project 2010 displays the *View Definition* dialog shown in Figure 9 - 24.

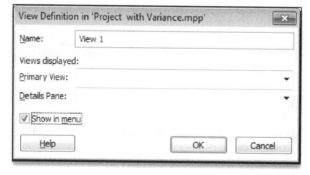

**Figure 9 - 24: View Definition dialog, ready to
create for a new combination view**

5. Enter a name for your new combination view in the *Name* field.

6. Select your desired views in the *Primary View* and *Details Pane* pick lists.

 The view you select in the *Primary View* field appears in the top pane of the combination view. The view you select in the *Details Pane* pick list appears in the bottom pane of the combination view.

7. Select the *Show in menu* option if you wish to see the new custom view in the appropriate view menu.

Figure 9 - 25 shows the *View Definition* dialog with the definition of a new combination view I intend to use to analyze resource overallocation data. When I apply this new view, I can select any overallocated resource in the *Resource Usage* pane (top pane) and see immediately the severity of overallocation in the *Resource Graph* pane (bottom pane).

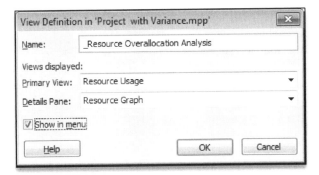

**Figure 9 - 25: View Definition dialog
with a new combination view**

8. Click the *OK* button to close the *View Definition* dialog.

9. Select your new custom view, if necessary, and then click the *Apply* button.

Figure 9 - 26 shows my new custom *_Resource Overallocation Analysis* combination view. Notice the view reveals that I assigned Linda Erickson accidentally to two parallel tasks. Because of this, I now assign her at 200% units from Thursday through Tuesday of the following week, which means she is overallocated. Facing an overallocation of this nature, I can level this resource overallocation using one of the techniques I discussed previously in Module 07, Project Assignment Planning.

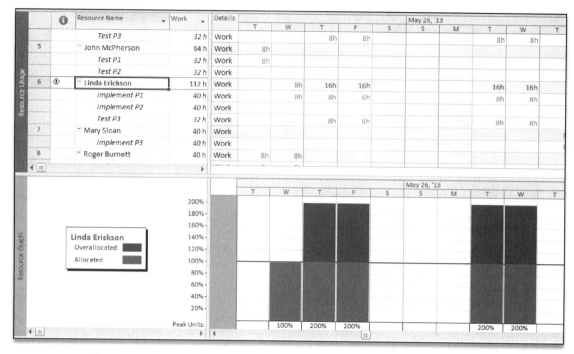

Figure 9 - 26: Custom _Resource Overallocation Analysis combination view

Hands On Exercise

Exercise 9-6

Create a custom combination view that you can use to troubleshoot task dependency problems.

1. Return to the **Training Advisor 09.mpp** sample file.

2. Click the *View* tab to display the *View* ribbon.

3. In the *Task Views* section of the *View* ribbon, click the *Gantt Chart* pick list and select the *More Views* item on the list.

4. In the *More Views* dialog, click the *New* button.

5. In the *Define New View* dialog, select the *Combination view* option and then click the *OK* button.

6. In the *View Definition* dialog, enter or select the following information:

Name	_Dependency Analysis
Primary View	Gantt Chart
Details Pane	Relationship Diagram
Show in menu	Selected

7. Click the *OK* button to close the *View Definition* dialog.

8. Select your new custom view, if necessary, and then click the *Apply* button.

9. Scroll down in the *Gantt Chart* pane and select task ID #35, the *Create Training Schedule* task.

10. In the *Relationship Diagram* pane, notice that the selected task has two predecessors and only one successor.

11. Select several other tasks in the *Gantt Chart* pane and experiment with using this new custom combination view.

12. Double-click anywhere in the split bar between the top pane and the bottom to close the bottom pane and return to the *Gantt Chart* view.

13. Save but **do not** close the **Training Advisor 09.mpp** sample file.

Using the Organizer

Every time you launch Microsoft Project 2010, the system opens the Global.mpt file in the background. The Global.mpt file is your "library" of default objects that ship with the software, including default views, tables, filters, groups, reports, etc. The Global.mpt file also serves as the "library" of the personal objects you create as well.

As I stated previously, when you create a custom view, table, filter, and/or group in Microsoft Project 2010, the system creates these objects in the project file and then adds them to the Global.mpt file automatically. By adding these objects to the Global.mpt file automatically, the system makes the view, table, filter, and/or group available to every current and future project you manage.

> If you do not want Microsoft Project 2010 to add custom views, tables, filters, and/or groups to the Global.mpt file automatically, you can disable this option. With this option disabled, you must manually add new custom views, tables, filters, and/or groups to the Global.mpt file using the *Organizer* dialog. To disable the automatic functionality, click the *File* tab and then click the *Options* tab in the *Backstage*. In the *Project Options* dialog, click the *Advanced* tab and **deselect** the *Automatically add new views, tables, filters, and groups to the global* option in the *Display* section of the dialog. Click the *OK* button when finished.

If you edit an existing view, table, filter, or group, keep in mind that Microsoft Project 2010 changes the object in the project only, but **does not** change the object in the Global.mpt file. This means you must copy the edited object from the project to the Global.mpt file to make the new version of the object available to every current and future project.

To manage the objects in the Global.mpt file, you must use the *Organizer* dialog. To access this dialog, click the *File* tab, click the *Info* tab, and then click the *Organizer* button on the *Info* page of the *Backstage*. The system displays the *Organizer* dialog shown in Figure 9 - 27.

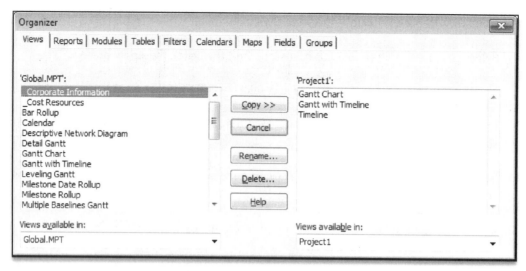

Figure 9 - 27: Organizer dialog

You can use the *Organizer* dialog to manage any of the custom objects you create in a project and/or in the Global.mpt file. Notice also in Figure 9 - 27 that the *Organizer* dialog shows two custom views in the list on the left side of the dialog (in the Global.mpt file), but shows only three default views in the list on the right side of the dialog (in the project file).

The *Organizer* dialog includes nine tabs that allow you to manage all of the default and custom objects available in Microsoft Project 2010. These objects include views, tables, filters, groups, reports, fields, calendars, maps, and modules.

 Missing from the *Organizer* dialog are two tabs found in previous versions of Microsoft Project. In the 2010 version of the software, Microsoft removed the *Toolbars* tab, since the new ribbons replace the toolbars found in previous versions. Microsoft also eliminated the *Forms* tab since the 2010 version of the software no longer includes a set of default forms to speed up data entry. Truthfully, forms were a little used feature in previous versions of the software, so most users will not even notice that Microsoft removed the default set of forms!

When you create a new custom object in a project file and/or in the Global.mpt file, you can use the Organizer to do any of the following:

• Copy custom objects from one file to another.

• Rename a custom object.

• Delete a custom object.

Copying Custom Objects

To copy a custom object to the Global.mpt file, complete the following steps:

1. Click the *File* tab, click the *Info* tab, and then click the *Organizer* button on the *Info* page of the *Backstage*.

2. Select the appropriate tab in the *Organizer* dialog for the type of object you want to manage (such as a filter or a view).

3. Select one or more objects on one side of the dialog.

4. Click the *Copy* button to copy the selected object(s) to the other side of the dialog.

5. Click the *Close* button when finished.

Using this technique, you can copy custom objects between the Global.mpt file and a project file, or between two project files. By default, Microsoft Project 2010 always displays objects from the Global.mpt file in the list on the left side of the *Organizer* dialog, and displays the objects from the active project in the list on the right side of the dialog. Using this default arrangement, you can copy objects back and forth between the Global.mpt file and the active project file. Notice in Figure 9 - 28 that I copied the *_Cost Resources* custom view from the Global.mpt file to a Project1 project.

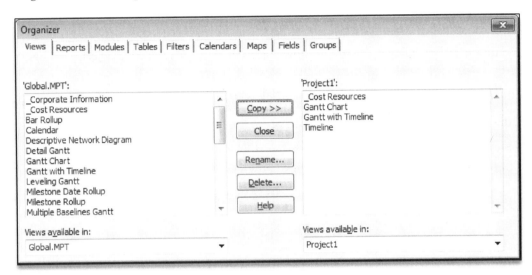

Figure 9 - 28: Copy a custom view from the Global.mpt file to a project file

 Warning: When you use the Organizer to manually copy a new custom view to the Global.mpt file, do not forget to copy any new tables, filters, and/or groups you created that are part of the custom view. If you neglect to copy all objects included in the new custom view, Microsoft Project 2010 displays an error message when you attempt to apply the new view in any project.

 When you use the *Organizer* dialog to copy an object to the Global.mpt file, Microsoft Project 2010 copies the object to the Global.mpt **loaded in memory**. When you exit the software, the system saves the changes to the Global.mpt file on your hard drive.

You can also use the *Organizer* dialog to copy objects from one project file to another. To perform this copy operation, complete the following steps:

1. Open each project.

2. Click the *File* tab, click the *Info* tab, and then click the *Organizer* button on the *Info* page of the *Backstage*.

3. Select the appropriate tab in the *Organizer* dialog for the type of object you want to manage.

4. Click the pick list in the **lower left corner** of the dialog (called the *Views available in* pick list when you have the *Views* tab selected), and select one of the open projects.

5. Click the pick list in the **lower right corner** of the dialog and select the second project.

6. Select one or more objects in the list on one side of the dialog and then click the *Copy* button to copy the selected objects to the list on the other side of the dialog.

7. Click the *Close* button when finished.

Renaming and Deleting Custom Objects

You can also use the *Organizer* dialog to rename existing objects or to delete unneeded objects in either the Global.mpt file or in a project. To rename an object, complete the following steps:

1. Click the *File* tab, click the *Info* tab, and then click the *Organizer* button on the *Info* page of the *Backstage*.

2. Select the appropriate tab in the *Organizer* dialog for the type of object you want to manage.

3. Select the object on either the right side or the left side of the dialog and then click the *Rename* button. Microsoft Project 2010 displays the *Rename* dialog shown in Figure 9 - 29.

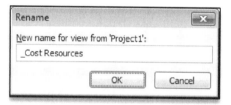

Figure 9 - 29: Rename dialog

4. Enter the new name for the object.

5. Click the *OK* button.

6. Click the *Close* button when finished.

To delete a custom object that you no longer need, complete the following steps:

7. Click the *File* tab, click the *Info* tab, and then click the *Organizer* button on the *Info* page of the *Backstage*.

8. Select the appropriate tab in the *Organizer* dialog for the type of object you want to manage.

9. Select the object on either the right side or the left side of the dialog and then click the *Delete* button. Microsoft Project 2010 displays the confirmation dialog shown in Figure 9 - 30.

Figure 9 - 30: Deletion confirmation dialog

10. Click the *Yes* button to delete the object.

11. Click the *Close* button when finished.

Warning: When you delete or rename a custom object, there is no *Undo* command to reverse your action. If you accidentally delete or rename a custom object, the only way to recover the original is to open a project containing the original object (if such a project even exists), and use the *Organizer* dialog to copy the object back to the Global.mpt file.

Hands On Exercise

Exercise 9-7

Use the Organizer dialog to view the new custom objects created in Exercises 9-2 through 9-6.

1. Click the *File* tab, click the *Info* tab, and then click the *Organizer* button on the *Info* page of the *Backstage*.

2. Notice the new *_Dependency Analysis* and *_Duration Slippage* views in the list on the **left side** of the *Organizer* dialog (in the Global.mpt file).

3. Notice the two new views in the list on the in the list on the **right side** of the dialog (in the Training Advisor 09.mpp file).

4. Click the *Tables* tab in the *Organizer* dialog.

5. Notice the new *_Duration* table in the lists on both sides of the dialog.

6. Click the *Filters* tab in the *Organizer* dialog.

7. Notice the new *_Duration Variance >0d* filter in the lists on both sides of the dialog.

8. Click the *Groups* tab in the *Organizer* dialog.

9. Notice the new *_Duration Variance* group in the lists on both sides of the dialog.

10. Click the *View* tab again in the *Organizer* dialog.

11. In the list of views on the **left side** (in the Global.mpt file) of the dialog, select the *_Dependency Analysis* view and then click the *Rename* button.

12. Enter the new name *_Dependency Relationships* in the *Rename* dialog and click the *OK* button.

13. In the list of views on the **right side** (in the Training Advisor 09.mpp file), select the *Copy of Gantt Chart* view, and then click the *Delete* button.

14. Click the *Yes* button in the confirmation dialog to confirm the deletion.

15. Click the *Close* button to close the *Organizer* dialog.

16. Click the *File* tab again to exit the *Backstage*.

17. Save but **do not** close the **Training Advisor 09.mpp** sample file.

Revising a Project Plan

After completing variance analysis, you may need to revise your project plan to bring it "back on track" against its original goals, objectives, and schedule. There are a number of strategies for revising a project plan, but each one requires careful consideration before you make the revision. You should perform a "what-if" analysis before making plan revisions, especially if you need formal approval to make the revisions.

Microsoft Project 2010 offers a number of methods for revising a project plan. These methods include:

- Add resources to *Effort Driven* tasks.

- Ask project team members to work overtime or on weekends.

- Increase project team availability for your project.

- Modify mandatory dependencies, including reducing or removing *Lag* time, or adding *Lead* time.

- Reduce the scope of the project.

- Renegotiate the project finish date.

Potential Problems with Revising a Plan

Prior to employing any of the preceding techniques, you should be aware of potential problems that may arise when you implement the revisions. Some of the potential problems include:

- Adding resources to an *Effort Driven* task can increase the total work on the task due to increased communication needs between the team members.

- Asking team members to work overtime on a regular basis can increase your employee turnover rate.

- Increasing team member availability for your project reduces their availability for projects managed by other project managers, causing those projects to slip.

- Reducing *Lag* time on task dependencies can create an overly optimistic project schedule.

- Adding *Lead* time on task dependencies can create a scheduling crisis when the predecessor task must finish completely, thus negating the intent of adding the *Lead* time.

- The scope of your project may be non-negotiable.

- The finish date of your project may be non-negotiable.

Hands On Exercise

Exercise 9-8

Revise the Training Advisor Rollout project by adding resources and adjusting resource availability to bring it "back on track" against its original baseline schedule.

1. Return to the **Training Advisor 09.mpp** sample file.

2. Click the *View* tab to display the *View* ribbon.

3. In the *Task Views* section of the *View* ribbon, click the *Gantt Chart* pick list button and select the *Tracking Gantt* item on the menu.

4. In the *Split View* section of the *View* ribbon, select the *Details* checkbox.

5. In the *Zoom* section of the *View* ribbon, click the *Timescale* pick list and select the *Weeks* item on the pick list.

6. In the *Tracking Gantt* pane, select task ID #23, the *Install Training Advisor Clients* task.

7. Scroll your *Tracking Gantt Chart* to the right so that you can see the Gantt bar for the selected task.

The temporary combination view you just created (*Tracking Gantt* view in the top pane and *Task Form* view in the bottom pane) is an excellent view to use when revising your project. This view shows you the immediate result of each revision compared against the original project baseline schedule.

8. In the *Task Form* pane, add Terry Uland with a *Units* value of *100%* (**do not** enter a value in the *Work* field) and click the *OK* button.

9. To account for the increased communication needs, add *4h* of extra work in the *Work* field for each *Work* resource and then click the *OK* button.

Due to commitments on another project, Mike Andrews is only able to work part-time (50% units) on the Verify Connectivity task. You negotiate with the other project manager to "borrow" Mike Andrews for a little extra time on this task to complete it sooner.

10. Select task ID #24, the *Verify Connectivity* task, increase the *Units* value for Mike Andrews to *75%*, and then click the *OK* button.

11. In the *Split View* section of the *View* ribbon, deselect the *Details* checkbox to close the *Task Form* pane and return to a single-pane *Tracking Gantt* view.

If you compare the project's current schedule (red Gantt bars and blue Gantt bars) to its original baseline schedule (gray Gantt bars), your project should appear slightly ahead of schedule.

12. In the *Task Views* section of the *View* ribbon, click the *Gantt Chart* pick list button and select the *Gantt Chart* item on the menu.

13. Save but **do not** close the **Training Advisor 09.mpp** sample file.

Using a Change Control Process

Change control is the process of managing requested changes in your project. Change requests can arise from a variety of sources, including your customer, your project sponsor, your project stakeholders, your company's executives, your fellow project managers, and even from your project team members. Because each change can result in schedule slippage and cost overruns, it is important that you manage all changes in your project. Remember the old project management saying, "Either you manage change, or change manages you!"

Your change control process should identify and maximize the benefits of change, and should avoid all changes that offer no benefit to the project or that impact the project negatively. Document your change management process in both the Statement of Work document and in the "rules of engagement" with your project sponsor and/or client. Following is an example of a change management process:

- Use a paper or electronic change request form to initiate the change request.

- Perform an impact analysis to assess the impact of the change on the project. Determine who does the impact analysis and how they report the results.

- Calculate the cost of the impact analysis and determine who pays for it. Remember that an impact analysis is never free!

- Enlist the support of an executive in your organization with the authority to accept or reject the change request.

- Apply a procedure for implementing an approved change request.

- In your project plan, indicate the tasks you changed or added because of the change request.

Inserting New Tasks in a Project

The most common change request is to add new tasks to a project. When you insert a new task between two dependent tasks, the *Autolink* feature of Microsoft Project 2010 determines whether the software automatically adds dependency links to the new task. If you disabled the *Autolink* feature in the *Project Options* dialog, per my directions in Module 04 (Project Definition), the software **does not** automatically link the new task to the existing tasks in the project. However, if you did not disable the *Autolink* feature, then Microsoft Project 2010 handles the task linking operation as follows:

- If the dependent tasks have a Finish-to-Start (FS) dependency, the software automatically links the new task to the existing tasks using the Finish-to-Start FS dependency.

- If the dependent tasks have any other type of dependency (SS, FF, or SF), then Microsoft Project 2010 **does not** automatically link the new task to the existing tasks. Instead, the software leaves the new task unlinked.

Because you should always make task dependency decisions, and not the software, msProjectExperts recommends that you either disable the *Autolink* feature or break the task dependency links between tasks in the section where you intend to insert new tasks. After inserting the new tasks, establish appropriate task dependencies for tasks in that section of your project plan.

Reminder: To disable the *Autolink* feature of Microsoft Project 2010, click the *File* tab and then click the *Options* item in the *Backstage*. In the *Project Options* dialog, click the *Schedule* tab. In the *Scheduling options for this project* section, deselect the *Autolink inserted or moved tasks* option, and then click the *OK* button.

When you add new tasks to a project through a change control process, msProjectExperts recommends that you format the new tasks with a unique color. You can format the font, the cell background color, and/or the Gantt bar color, as needed. Keep in mind that these formatting changes are visible only in the view in which you apply the formatting.

Hands On Exercise

Exercise 9-9

After preliminary analysis, members of the NetOps team are concerned about possible unfavorable results from stress testing the server. After completing the *Perform Server Stress Test* task, they request you add a new task called *Tune Server* with a 1-day window to perform the work. After reviewing the change request and its impact to the project, you approve the change request.

1. Return to the **Training Advisor 09.mpp** sample file.

2. Click the *Task* tab to display the *Task* ribbon.

3. Select task ID #21, the *Installation Complete* milestone task, and then press the **Insert** key on your computer keyboard.

4. In the new blank row, add a task named *Tune Server* and enter a *Duration* value of *1 day*.

5. Select task IDs #20-22 and then click the *Unlink Tasks* button in the *Schedule* section of the *Task* ribbon.

6. With task IDs #20-22 still selected, click the *Link Tasks* button to link the three selected tasks with a Finish-to-Start (FS) dependency.

7. Click the *View* tab to display the *View* ribbon.

8. In the *Split View* section of the *View* ribbon, select the *Details* checkbox.

9. In the *Gantt Chart* pane, select task ID #21, the new *Tune Server* task.

10. In the *Task Form* pane, select *Carmen Kamper*, enter a *Units* value of *100%*, and then click the *OK* button to complete the assignment.

11. In the *Split View* section of the *View* ribbon, deselect the *Details* checkbox.

12. Double-click task ID #21, the new *Tune Server* task, and then select the *Notes* tab in the *Task Information* dialog.

13. Add a note to the selected task, stating that the reason you added the task to the plan is because of a change request from the NetOps team, and then click the *OK* button.

14. Click the gray row header for task ID #21 to select the entire task, and then click the *Task* tab to display the *Task* ribbon.

15. In the *Font* section of the *Task* ribbon, click the *Background Color* pick list and select the *Red, Lighter 80%* item in the *Theme Colors* section of the pick list.

16. Click any other task to see the cell background color applied to the new task.

17. Save but **do not** close the **Training Advisor 09.mpp** sample file.

Rebaselining Your Project

After you add new tasks to your project through change control, you must rebaseline your project. There are a number of methodologies for rebaselining a project, including the following:

- Rebaseline all tasks in the project using the default *Baseline* set of fields. This method destroys all variance that existed in the project before you added the new tasks, and makes the project appear perfectly on schedule.

- Backup your current baseline into one of the ten additional sets of baseline fields (the *Baseline 1* through *Baseline 10* sets of fields), and then rebaseline your entire project using the default *Baseline* set of fields. This approach maintains the historical record shown in the original baseline for the project, but destroys all previous variance.

- Backup your current baseline into one of the ten additional sets of baseline fields, and then baseline only the new tasks in the project using the default *Baseline* set of fields. Microsoft Project 2010 offers you the option to baseline only the new tasks without rolling up the baseline data to summary tasks, or to baseline the new tasks and roll up the baseline values to each summary task to which the new tasks are subtasks, including the Project Summary Task (Row 0).

- Backup your original baseline into one of the ten additional sets of baseline fields, and then rebaseline only unstarted tasks using the default *Baseline* set of fields. This approach maintains the historical record shown in the original baseline for the project and maintains the variance recorded on all completed and in-progress tasks.

- Baseline all tasks in the project using one of the ten additional sets of baseline fields (the *Baseline 1* through *Baseline 10* sets of fields). If you want to use this technique, you must change the baseline Microsoft Project 2010 uses to calculate variance. You must also change how the system displays the baseline schedule, shown by gray Gantt bars, in the *Tracking Gantt* view of your project.

I discuss each of these rebaselining methodologies separately.

The default *Baseline* set of fields includes the following: *Baseline Start, Baseline Finish, Baseline Duration, Baseline Work,* and *Baseline Cost.* The ten additional sets of baselines, named *Baseline 1* through *Baseline 10,* include a corresponding set of fields. For example, the *Baseline1* set of fields includes the following: *Baseline 1 Start, Baseline 1 Finish, Baseline 1 Duration, Baseline 1 Work,* and *Baseline 1 Cost.*

Backing Up an Original Baseline

Before you rebaseline your project after a change control procedure, it is wise to backup the current baseline data stored in the default *Baseline* set of fields. This is true, regardless of whether you rebaseline the entire project, only selected tasks, or only unstarted tasks. As you know by now, Microsoft Project 2010 offers you 11 sets of fields in which to save baseline data. These sets of fields include the default *Baseline* set of fields, plus the *Baseline 1* through *Baseline 10* sets. You can use any of these ten sets of alternate baseline fields to backup the current baseline before you rebaseline your project. To backup your current baseline values, use the *Interim Plan* feature of Microsoft Project 2010 by completing the following steps:

1. Click the *Project* tab to display the *Project* ribbon.

2. In the *Schedule* section of the *Project* ribbon, click the *Set Baseline* pick list button and then click the *Set Baseline* item on the menu. Microsoft Project 2010 displays the *Set Baseline* dialog shown in Figure 9 - 31.

3. In the *Set Baseline* dialog, select the *Set interim plan* option.

4. Click the *Copy* pick list and select the *Baseline* item.

Figure 9 - 31: Set Baseline dialog

5. Click the *Into* pick list and select the next available set of baseline fields into which you want to backup the current baseline of the project, as shown in Figure 9 - 32.

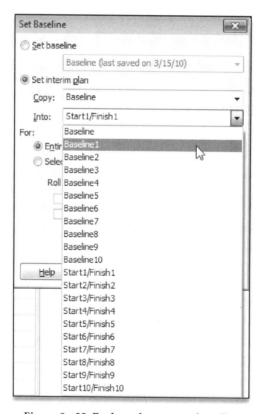

Figure 9 - 32: Backup the current baseline
into the Baseline 1 set of fields

6. In the *For:* section, select the *Entire project* option.

7. Click the *OK* button.

When you use this procedure, Microsoft Project 2010 copies all baseline information from the *Baseline* set of fields to the set of fields for the alternate baseline. If you select the *Baseline 1* set of fields in the *Into* pick list, the system copies the values for every task in the *Baseline Start* field to the *Baseline 1 Start* field, the *Baseline Finish* field to the *Baseline 1 Finish* field, etc. This is a useful way to preserve your original project baseline for historical purposes before you rebaseline your project. You can use this process for up to ten change control procedures, at which point you run out of alternate sets of baseline fields.

Rebaselining the Entire Project

To rebaseline an entire project using the default *Baseline* set of fields, complete the following steps:

1. Click the *Project* tab to display the *Project* ribbon.

2. In the *Schedule* section of the *Project* ribbon, click the *Set Baseline* pick list button and then click the *Set Baseline* item on the menu. Microsoft Project 2010 displays the *Set Baseline* dialog shown previously in Figure 9 - 31.

3. Select the *Set baseline* option and select the *Baseline* value in the *Set baseline* pick list.

4. In the *For:* section, select the *Entire project* option.

5. Click the *OK* button.

Microsoft Project 2010 displays the confirmation dialog shown in Figure 9 - 33.

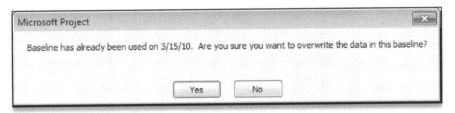

Figure 9 - 33: Overwrite Baseline confirmation dialog

6. In the confirmation dialog, click the *Yes* button.

Warning: Using this methodology, you lose all of your project's previous variance information because the procedure sets the variance values back to 0 in the *Start Variance*, *Finish Variance*, *Duration Variance*, *Work Variance*, and *Cost Variance* fields. Because of this, msProjectExperts strongly recommends that you **do not** use this methodology for rebaselining your project, unless this is the preferred methodology of your organization.

Baselining Only Selected Tasks

An ideal method for rebaselining a project after adding new tasks through a change control procedure is to baseline **only** the new tasks you added to the project. Microsoft Project 2010 offers you two methods for baselining only selected tasks, which are:

- Baseline only the selected tasks, but do not roll up the baseline values to any summary tasks in the project. Using this technique, new tasks show as variance against the original project baseline.

- Baseline only the selected tasks, but roll up the baseline values to all summary tasks in the project. When you choose this option, the baseline data rolls up to all summary tasks for which the selected tasks are subtasks, including the Project Summary Task (Row 0). Using this technique, new tasks do not show as variance against the original project baseline.

To baseline only selected tasks, complete the following steps:

1. Select the tasks you want to baseline.

2. Click the *Project* tab to display the *Project* ribbon.

3. In the *Schedule* section of the *Project* ribbon, click the *Set Baseline* pick list button and then click the *Set Baseline* item on the menu. Microsoft Project 2010 displays the *Set Baseline* dialog.

4. Select the *Set baseline* option and select the *Baseline* value in the *Set baseline* pick list.

5. In the *For:* section, choose the *Selected tasks* option, as shown in Figure 9 - 34.

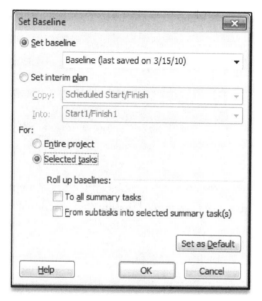

**Figure 9 - 34: Set Baseline dialog
to baseline selected tasks**

6. If you wish to roll up the baseline values to summary tasks, choose one of the following options in the *Roll up baselines* section:

- Select the *To all summary tasks* option if you want the software to roll up the baseline values to all summary tasks for which the selected tasks are subtasks and to the Project Summary Task as well.

- Select the *From subtasks into selected summary tasks* option if you want the software to roll up the baseline values to only the summary tasks currently selected (you must select these summary tasks before you begin the baselining process).

If you do not want to roll up the baseline values to any summary tasks, **do not** select either of the checkboxes in the *Roll up baselines* section of the dialog. This means that the selected tasks continue to show as variance against the current project baseline.

7. To save the current options in the *Roll up baselines* section of the dialog, click the *Set as Default* button.

8. Click the *OK* button. Microsoft Project 2010 warns you about overwriting the baseline data in the warning dialog shown in Figure 9 - 35.

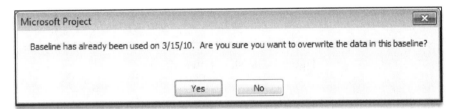

Figure 9 - 35: Warning dialog about overwriting baseline data

9. When warned about overwriting the original baseline, click the *Yes* button in the warning dialog.

In spite of the warning in the dialog, using this procedure does not actually "overwrite" the data in your original baseline. Instead, this procedure "appends" the baseline data from the new tasks to the current project baseline.

Rebaselining Only Unstarted Tasks

One final method for rebaselining a project after a change control procedure is to rebaseline only unstarted tasks. Using this method yields the following results:

- Your project continues to use the original baseline values on all completed and in-progress tasks, preserving current project variance on these tasks.

- The system rebaselines all unstarted tasks and resets their variance values to 0.

To rebaseline only unstarted tasks, complete the following steps:

1. Click the *View* tab to display the *View* ribbon.

2. In the *Data* section of the *View* ribbon, click the *Filter* pick list button and select the *More Filters* item. Microsoft Project 2010 displays the *More Filters* dialog shown in Figure 9 - 36.

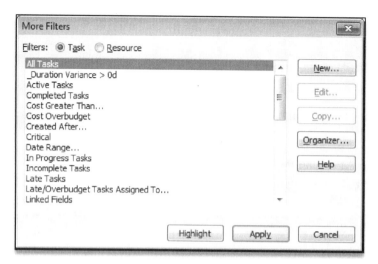

Figure 9 - 36: More Filters dialog

3. In the *More Filters* dialog, select the *Unstarted Tasks* item and then click the *Apply* button. Microsoft Project 2010 hides both completed tasks and in-progress tasks, displaying only unstarted tasks.

4. Click the *Select All* button to select all tasks in the project, including summary tasks and the Project Summary Task (Row 0).

5. Click the *Project* tab to display the *Project* ribbon.

6. In the *Schedule* section of the *Project* ribbon, click the *Set Baseline* pick list button and then click the *Set Baseline* item on the menu. Microsoft Project 2010 displays the *Set Baseline* dialog.

7. Select the *Set baseline* option and select the *Baseline* value in the *Set baseline* pick list.

8. In the *For:* section, choose the *Selected tasks* option.

9. **Do not** select either checkbox in the *Roll up baselines* section of the dialog.

10. Click the *OK* button.

11. When the system warns you about overwriting the original baseline, click the *Yes* button in the warning dialog.

12. Press the **F3** function key on your computer keyboard to reapply the *[No Filter]* filter.

Hands On Exercise

Exercise 9-10

Backup the original project baseline information in the *Baseline 1* set of fields for the Training Advisor Rollout project.

1. Return to the **Training Advisor 09.mpp** sample file.

2. Click the *Project* tab to display the *Project* ribbon.

3. In the *Schedule* section of the *Project* ribbon, click the *Set Baseline* pick list button and then click the *Set Baseline* item on the menu.

4. In the *Set Baseline* dialog, select the *Set interim plan* option.

5. Click the *Copy* pick list and select the *Baseline* item.

6. Click the *Into* pick list and select the *Baseline 1* value.

7. Select the *Entire project* option and then click the *OK* button.

8. Save but **do not** close the **Training Advisor 09.mpp** sample file.

Exercise 9-11

Baseline only selected tasks in the Training Advisor Rollout project.

1. Return to the **Training Advisor 09.mpp** sample file.

2. Select task ID #21, the new *Tune Server* task you created in Exercise 9-3.

3. In the *Schedule* section of the *Project* ribbon, click the *Set Baseline* pick list button and then click the *Set Baseline* item on the menu.

4. In the *Set Baseline* dialog, select the *Set baseline* option and select the *Baseline* value in the *Set baseline* pick list.

5. In the *For:* section, choose the *Selected tasks* option.

6. In the *Roll up baselines* section, select the *To all summary tasks* option.

7. Click the *OK* button.

8. When the system warns you about overwriting the current baseline, click the *Yes* button in the warning dialog.

9. Save but **do not** close the **Training Advisor 09.mpp** sample file.

Exercise 9-12

View the new project baseline in the Training Advisor Rollout project.

1. Return to the **Training Advisor 09.mpp** sample file.

2. Click the *View* tab to display the *View* ribbon.

3. In the *Task Views* section of the *View* ribbon, click the *Gantt Chart* pick list button and select the *Tracking Gantt* view.

4. Study the current schedule slippage for the project.

5. Click the *Gantt Chart* pick list button again and select the *Gantt Chart* view.

6. Save and close the **Training Advisor 09.mpp** sample file.

Rebaselining the Entire Project Using an Alternate Baseline

To rebaseline an entire project using one of the ten alternate sets of baseline fields, such as the *Baseline 1* set of fields, complete the following steps:

1. Click the *Project* tab to display the *Project* ribbon.

2. In the *Schedule* section of the *Project* ribbon, click the *Set Baseline* pick list button and then click the *Set Baseline* item on the menu. Microsoft Project 2010 displays the *Set Baseline* dialog.

3. In the *Set Baseline* dialog, click the *Set baseline* pick list and choose one of the ten alternate sets of baseline fields, such as the *Baseline 1* item shown in Figure 9 - 37.

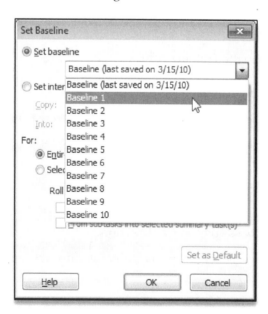

**Figure 9 - 37: Set Baseline dialog,
select the Baseline 1 set of fields**

4. In the *For:* section, select the *Entire project* option.

5. Click the *OK* button.

After you rebaseline your project using one of alternate sets of baseline fields, you must change the baseline Microsoft Project 2010 uses to calculate variance. To make this change, complete the following steps:

1. Click the *File* tab and then click the *Options* item in the *Backstage*.

2. In the *Project Options* dialog, click the *Advanced* tab.

3. In the *Earned Value options for this project* section of the dialog, click the *Baseline for Earned Value Calculation* pick list and select the alternate set of baselines used during the rebaselining process, as shown in Figure 9 - 38.

4. Click the *OK* button.

When you change the *Baseline for Earned Value Calculation* option in the *Project Options* dialog, you change how Microsoft Project 2010 calculates variance in your project. When you change this option, the system now uses the new set of baseline fields to calculate all variance in the project. This affects the *Start Variance, Finish Variance, Duration Variance, Work Variance,* and *Cost Variance* fields, and you see the results in the task *Work, Cost,* and *Variance* tables. For example, if you selected the *Baseline 1* set of fields in step #3 above, the system calculates the values in the *Work Variance* field for every task using the following formula: **Work Variance = Work – Baseline 1 Work**.

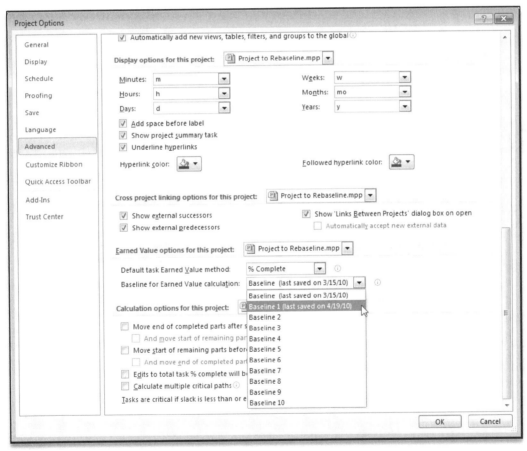

Figure 9 - 38: Select an alternate set of baseline fields

In addition to changing the set of baseline fields used to calculate variance in Microsoft Project 2010, you must also change the baseline schedule shown in the *Tracking Gantt* view. To change this view, complete the following additional set of steps:

1. Using the *Gantt Chart* pick list button on either the *Task* ribbon or the *View* ribbon, apply the *Tracking Gantt* view.

2. Click the *Format* tab to display the *Format* ribbon.

3. In the *Bar Styles* section of the *Format* ribbon, click the *Baseline* pick list button, and then select the alternate set of baseline fields, as shown in Figure 9 - 39.

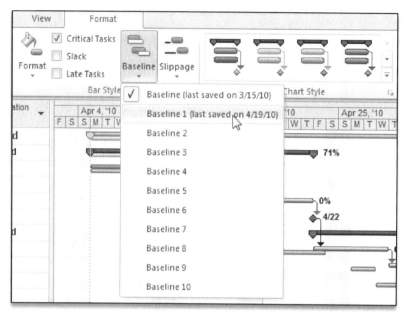

Figure 9 - 39: Select the alternate set of baseline fields for the Tracking Gantt view

For example, Figure 9 - 40 shows the default *Tracking Gantt* view for a project after a change control procedure added a new task to the project, and after the project manager rebaselined the project using the *Baseline 1* set of fields. Because the *Tracking Gantt* view uses the default *Baseline* set of fields to create the gray Gantt bars, the baseline schedule shown with the gray Gantt bars is not correct.

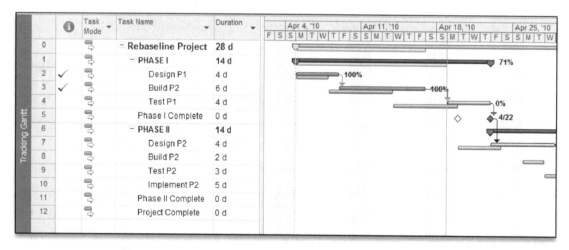

Figure 9 - 40: Tracking Gantt view using the Baseline schedule

Figure 9 - 41 shows the *Tracking Gantt* view after the project manager selected the *Baseline 1* set of fields in the *Baseline* pick list on the *Formatting* ribbon. The *Tracking Gantt* view now uses the *Baseline 1* set of fields to show the baseline schedule, which results in an accurate baseline schedule.

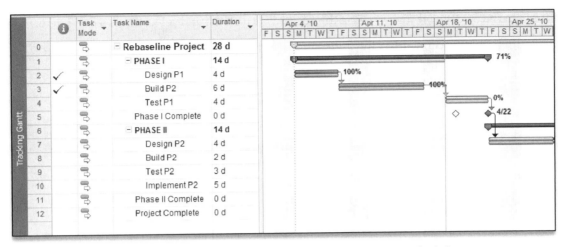

Figure 9 - 41: Tracking Gantt view using the Baseline 1 schedule

Warning: If you want to use this methodology for rebaselining a project after a change control procedure, you **must always** complete the steps to change the baseline used to calculate variance **and** the set of steps to show the correct baseline schedule in the *Tracking Gantt* view. If you fail to complete these two extra sets of steps, you cannot analyze project variance accurately, and you do not see the accurate baseline schedule in the *Tracking Gantt* view.

Hands On Exercise

Exercise 9-13

Due to a fire at the warehouse, the company required the project manager to move the stored furniture and equipment to a different storage facility. This resulted in the first change control procedure, which added task IDs #16 and #17 to the project. The project manager formatted the two new tasks using a light red cell background color, and then rebaselined the entire project using the *Baseline 1* set of fields.

As a result of finding asbestos in the ceiling, governmental regulations require the company to remove the asbestos properly. This resulted in the second change control procedure, which added task IDs #24, #26, and #27 to the project. The project manager formatted the three new tasks using a light green cell background color. After this second major change control procedure, rebaseline a project using the *Baseline 2* set of fields.

1. Open the **Rebaseline a Project.mpp** sample file.

2. Click the *Project* tab to display the *Project* ribbon.

3. In the *Schedule* section of the *Project* ribbon, click the *Set Baseline* pick list button and then click the *Set Baseline* item on the menu.

4. In the *Set Baseline* dialog, select the *Set baseline* pick list and select the *Baseline 2* item.

5. In the *For:* section, select the *Entire project* option.

6. Click the *OK* button.

Exercise 9-14

Configure Microsoft Project 2010 using the *Baseline 2* set of fields to calculate variance.

1. Return the **Rebaseline a Project.mpp** sample file.

2. Click the *File* tab and then click the *Options* item in the *Backstage*.

3. In the *Project Options* dialog, click the *Advanced* tab.

4. In the *Earned Value options for this project* section of the dialog, click the *Baseline for Earned Value Calculation* pick list and select the *Baseline 2* set of fields.

5. Click the *OK* button.

Exercise 9-15

Set up the *Tracking Gantt* view in Microsoft Project 2010 to show the *Baseline 2* schedule as gray Gantt bars.

1. Return to the **Rebaseline a Project.mpp** sample file.

2. Click the *Task* tab to display the *Task* ribbon.

3. Click the *Gantt Chart* pick list button and then select the *Tracking Gantt* view on the list.

4. Select task ID #24, the *Obtain asbestos removal permit* task, and then click the *Scroll to Task* button in the *Editing* section of the *Task* ribbon.

Notice that the *Tracking Gantt* chart shows no baseline schedule (no gray bars) for task IDs #24, #26, and #28. This is because the *Tracking Gantt* view currently shows the *Baseline 1* schedule for all tasks, and the *Baseline 1* schedule does not include these three tasks.

5. Click the *Format* tab to display the *Format* ribbon.

6. In the *Bar Styles* section of the *Format* ribbon, click the *Baseline* pick list button, and then select the *Baseline 2* schedule.

After the second change control procedure, which resulted in a second rebaselining of the project, Microsoft Project 2010 reset all variance to 0. You can see this reflected in the *Tracking Gantt* view, where the gray Gantt bars (the baseline schedule) now match the schedule of their accompanying blue or red Gantt bars (the current schedule of all tasks in the project).

7. Save but **do not** close the **Rebaseline a Project.mpp** sample file.

Viewing Multiple Baselines

When you use multiple baselines in a project, you can use the *Multiple Baselines Gantt* view to view up to three baselines at once. To apply this special view, complete the following steps:

1. On either the *Task* ribbon or the *View* ribbon, click the *Gantt Chart* pick list button and select the *More Views* item on the list.

2. In the *More Views* dialog, select the *Multiple Baselines Gantt* view and then click the *Apply* button.

In the *Multiple Baselines Gantt* view, Microsoft Project 2010 displays the baseline schedule for only the *Baseline, Baseline 1,* and *Baseline 2* sets of fields. For each task, the software displays a blue Gantt symbol for the *Baseline* schedule, a red Gantt symbol for the *Baseline 1* schedule, and green Gantt symbol for the *Baseline 2* schedule.

Hands On Exercise

Exercise 9-16

View alternate baseline schedule information in a project.

1. Return the **Rebaseline a Project.mpp** sample file.

2. Click the *View* tab to display the *View* ribbon.

3. In the *Task Views* section of the *View* ribbon, click the *Gantt Chart* pick list button and select the *More Views* item on the list.

4. In the *More Views* dialog, select the *Multiple Baselines Gantt* view and then click the *Apply* button.

5. In the *Zoom* section of the *View* ribbon, click the *Timescale* pick list and select the *Weeks* item.

6. Beginning with task ID #20, compare the schedule of the three different baselines in the *Construction deliverable* section of the project.

Notice how the baseline schedule for each task slips over time in the *Construction deliverable* section of the project, as evidenced by the schedule of the blue, red, and green Gantt symbols.

7. Save and close the **Rebaseline a Project.mpp** sample file.

Module 10

Project Reporting

Learning Objectives

After completing this module, you will be able to:

- Understand reporting features in Microsoft Project 2010

- Use enhanced copy and paste between Microsoft Office applications

- Use and format the Timeline view

- Create a custom view and table by modifying an existing view and table

- Use the Organizer in Microsoft Project 2010

- Format the Gantt Chart view using multiple methods

- Format the Team Planner view and the Task Usage view

Inside Module 10

Reporting in Microsoft Project 2010

During project execution, you must report project progress to one or more stakeholder groups. These typically include your project sponsor, your customer, your company executives, and even your project team. Microsoft Project 2010 offers you a number of ways to report about your project:

- Copy and paste Microsoft Project 2010 data to another Microsoft Office application.

- Use the new *Timeline* view in combination with the *Gantt Chart* view.

- Create custom views.

- Modify existing views.

I discuss each of these reporting options separately.

Using Enhanced Copy and Paste

As part of your reporting process during the execution stage of a project, you may need to copy and paste project data to another application. When you copy data from Microsoft Project 2010 and paste the data into another application in the Microsoft Office family, the paste operation works as follows:

- The Microsoft Office application pastes the Microsoft Project 2010 data in a table format that you can modify as needed.

- The Microsoft Office application indents tasks to reflect their hierarchy in the project.

- The Microsoft Office application retains field names as column headers for each column of data.

- The Microsoft Office application maintains complete text formatting and cell background color formatting. The text formatting includes the fonts, font sizes, font styles, and font colors, as well as other formatting such as bold, italic, underline, strikethrough, etc.

For example, Figure 10 - 1 shows a task list in a project. Notice the work breakdown structure in my project, along with the tasks highlighted using cell background formatting. I select the task information from the *Task Name* column through the *Finish* column, and from the *Project Summary Task* (Row 0) to the *Project Complete* milestone task, and then copy the information to the Windows clipboard.

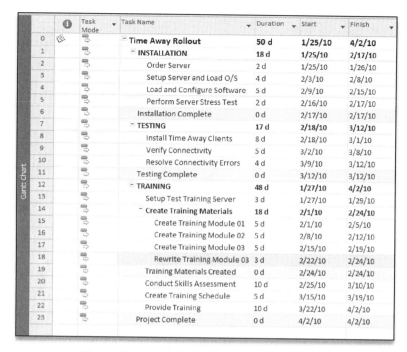

Figure 10 - 1: Task list in Microsoft Project 2007

After opening a new blank document in Microsoft Word 2007, I paste the contents of the Windows clipboard directly into the document shown in Figure 10 - 2. Notice how Microsoft Word 2007 pastes the project data into a table with the correct column headers at the top of each column. Notice also how Microsoft Word 2007 maintains the level of indenture for each task, along with the cell background formatting.

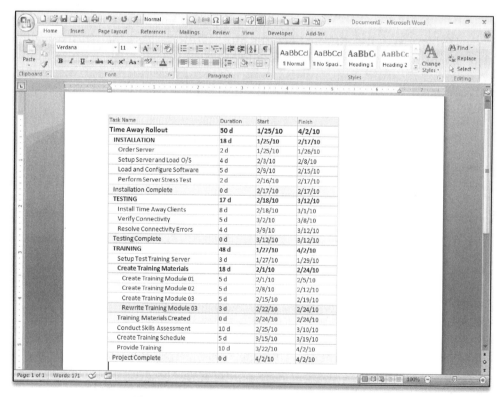

Figure 10 - 2: Microsoft Project 2010 task data pasted into a Microsoft Word 2007 document

When you copy data in an application in the Microsoft Office family, and paste the data into Microsoft Project 2010, the paste operation retains custom text formatting and cell background color formatting. Depending on the Office application, the paste operation may also retain other information as well. For example, if you paste a bulleted list from Microsoft Word into the *Task Name* field in Microsoft Project 2010, the paste operation converts the bulleted tasks into subtasks of the first task, making it a summary task.

> **Warning:** Be very wary about pasting data from Microsoft PowerPoint into your Microsoft Project 2010 project files. Keep in mind that the paste operation retains **complete** text formatting information, including bullets and the very large font sizes used in PowerPoint.

Figure 10 - 3 shows a project task list created in Microsoft Word 2007. Notice that I use several levels of bulleted text to indicate phase and deliverable summary tasks. Notice that I also use the text highlight feature in the application to highlight the Deliverable 1 Complete and Deliverable 2 Complete tasks. I select and copy the entire task list to the Windows clipboard.

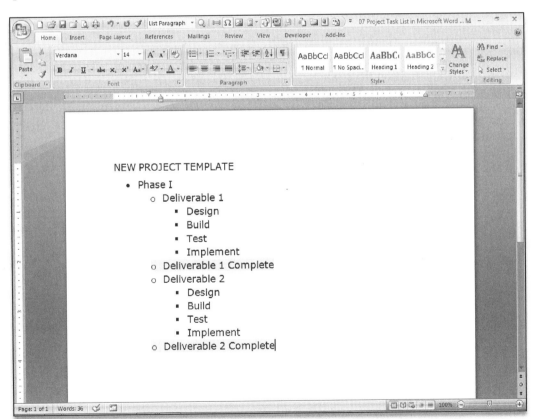

Figure 10 - 3: Task list created in Microsoft Word 2007

After opening a new blank project in Microsoft Project 2010, I paste the contents of the Windows clipboard directly into the first blank line of the project, as shown in Figure 10 - 4. Notice how Microsoft Project 2010 uses the various levels of the bulleted text to create summary tasks and subtasks, and that the software applies cell background formatting to the Deliverable 1 Complete and Deliverable 2 Complete tasks. Notice also that Microsoft Project 2010 uses the font and font size settings from Microsoft Word. After pasting text from another Office application, you may need to change the font and font size settings on the tasks in your Microsoft Project 2010 plan.

	ⓘ	Task Mode	▾	Task Name	▾	Duration	▾
1				⌐NEW PROJECT TEMPLATE		1 d	
2				⌐Phase I		1 d	
3				⌐Deliverable 1		1 d	
4				Design		1 d	
5				Build		1 d	
6				Test		1 d	
7				Implement		1 d	
8				Deliverable 1 Complete		1 d	
9				⌐Deliverable 2		1 d	
10				Design		1 d	
11				Build		1 d	
12				Test		1 d	
13				Implement		1 d	
14				Deliverable 2 Complete		1 d	

Figure 10 - 4: Task list from Microsoft Word 2007
pasted into a blank Microsoft Project 2010 project

The fastest way to set the default *Font*, *Font Style*, and *Font Size* settings for tasks in your Microsoft Project 2010 file is to click the *Gantt Chart* pick list button on the *Task* ribbon and to select the *Reset to Default* item on the pick list. In the confirmation dialog, click the *Yes* button to reset all default settings for task fonts, including the *Font*, *Font Style*, and *Font Size* settings. After completing these two steps, you lose the cell background formatting applied to any tasks, and you must reapply it if you want to retain the formatting.

Hands On Exercise

Exercise 10-1

Copy and paste task data from Microsoft Project 2010 to another Microsoft Office application.

1. Navigate to your student folder and open the **Project Navigation 2010.mpp** sample file.

2. Click the *Task* tab to display the *Task* ribbon.

3. Pull the split bar to the right to display the *Start* and *Finish* columns.

4. For all of the tasks in the *Pre-Renovation* section of the project (task IDs #1-17), select the information in the *Task Name*, *Duration*, *Start*, and *Finish* columns.

5. Click the *Copy* button in the *Clipboard* section of the *Task* ribbon.

6. Launch Microsoft Word.

7. In a new blank Word document, click the *Paste* button.

Notice how Microsoft Word pastes the Microsoft Project 2010 data into a table, correctly labels each column, and maintains the levels of indenture for every task.

8. Close the Microsoft Word document without saving it.

9. In Microsoft Project 2010, close but **do not** save the **Project Navigation 2010.mpp** sample file.

Exercise 10-2

Copy and paste task data from a Microsoft Office application to Microsoft Project 2010.

1. Return to your Microsoft Word application window.

2. Open the **Task List for Phases I and II.doc** sample document.

3. Select all of the tasks shown in the sample document and then click the *Copy* button.

4. Return to your Microsoft Project 2010 application window.

5. Click the *File* tab and then click the *New* menu item in the *Backstage*.

6. In the *Available Templates* page, double-click the *Blank Project* template to create a new blank project.

7. In the first blank row, click the cell in the *Task Name* column.

8. Click the *Paste* button in the *Clipboard* section of the *Task* ribbon.

Notice how Microsoft Project 2010 pastes the Word data into the project, creating summary tasks and sub-tasks, while maintaining the font formatting for each task.

9. In the *View* section of the *Task* ribbon, click the *Gantt Chart* pick list button and click the *Reset to Default* item on the menu.

10. When prompted in a warning dialog, click the *Yes* button to reset the task list to the default settings for the *Gantt Chart* view.

11. Close the new project without saving it.

12. Return to your Microsoft Word application window.

13. Close the **Task List for Phases I and II.doc** sample document without saving it.

14. Exit Microsoft Word.

Using the Timeline with the Gantt Chart View

Microsoft Project 2010 includes the new *Timeline* view that displays the current project schedule using a timeline presentation similar to what you see in Microsoft Visio or in any other timeline software application. You can modify the default *Timeline* view to show your current project schedule according to your reporting requirements. You can also export the *Timeline* view to other Microsoft Office applications, such as Microsoft PowerPoint.

The *Gantt with Timeline* view is the default view for every new project you create in Microsoft Project 2010. In fact, you see this view every time you launch the software, because the system always creates a new blank project on application launch. The *Gantt with Timeline* view is a split view that shows the *Timeline* view in the top pane and the *Gantt Chart* view in the bottom pane. Figure 10 - 5 shows the *Gantt with Timeline* view applied to an in-progress project.

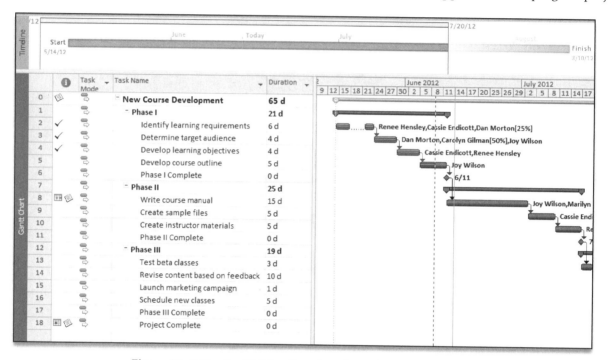

Figure 10 - 5: Gantt with Timeline view for an in-progress project

If you do not see the *Gantt with Timeline* view when you open a project, apply the *Gantt Chart* view and then click the *View* tab. In the *Split View* section of the *View* ribbon, select the *Timeline* option.

Depending on your level of zoom applied in your project, the *Timeline* view shows the following information by default:

- The gray *Timeline* bar represents the time span of the entire project, with the project *Start* date on the left end of the bar and the project *Finish* date on the right end of the bar. Notice in Figure 10 - 5 that the project runs from 5/14/12 to 8/10/12, indicated by the dates to the left and right of the gray *Timeline* bar.

- The system divides the *Timeline* bar into one-month segments using light blue tick marks, and displays the name of the month above each segment. Figure 10 - 5 shows that the project spans a partial month of May (not shown as a month name), plus the months of June, July, and August.

- The system indicates the current date with the word *Today* formatted with orange text above the *Timeline* bar and with an orange dashed line in the *Timeline* bar.

- The light blue *Pan and Zoom* bar above the *Timeline* bar represents the time span of the project currently visible in the *Gantt Chart* view. At the ends of the *Pan and Zoom* bar, the system displays the beginning and ending dates of the time span currently visible in the *Gantt Chart* view. Notice in Figure 10 - 5 that the gray *Timeline* bar extends only to 7/20/12, indicated by the date on the right end of the *Pan and Zoom* bar.

- The system uses light gray shading for the portion of the *Timeline* bar not visible in the *Gantt Chart* view. Figure 10 - 5 shows that project information is not visible past 7/20/12 in the *Gantt Chart* view, indicated by the light gray shading in the gray *Timeline* bar after that date.

As you scroll right or left in the *Gantt Chart* view, the *Pan and Zoom* bar scrolls with you to indicate the portion of the timeline currently visible in the Gantt Chart.

Adding a Task to the Timeline

To add any task to the *Timeline* view, right-click on the name of the task in the *Task Sheet* part of the *Gantt Chart* view and then click the *Add to Timeline* item on the shortcut menu. To add multiple tasks to the *Timeline* view, select a block of tasks, right-click anywhere in the selected block of tasks, and then click the *Add to Timeline* item on the shortcut menu. Microsoft Project 2010 adds the selected tasks to the *Timeline* view as shown in Figure 10 - 6. Notice that I added the Phase I and Phase II tasks to the *Timeline* view, along with the first three subtasks in the Phase II section of the project.

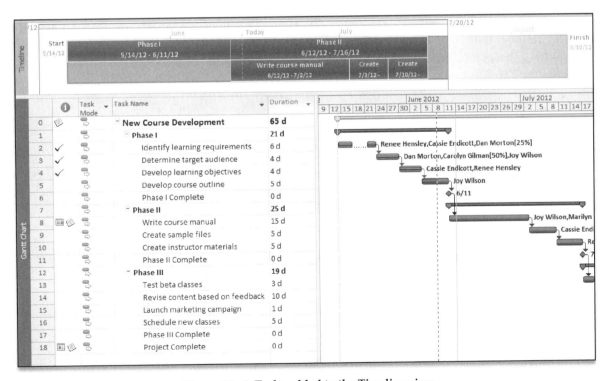

Figure 10 - 6: Tasks added to the Timeline view

You can also add a task in the *Timeline* view by double-clicking the task and then selecting the *Display on Timeline* option in the *General* page of the *Task Information* dialog. If you select multiple tasks, you can add a task in the *Timeline* view by selecting the *Task* ribbon and then clicking the *Information* button in the *Properties* section of the *Task* Ribbon. In the *Multiple Task Information* dialog, select the the *Display on Timeline* option in the *General* page.

After you add tasks to the *Timeline* view, you can rearrange the tasks on the *Timeline* bar using any of the following techniques:

- Drag a task to a new row above or below its current position in the *Timeline* bar.

- Drag a task above or below the *Timeline* bar to display the task as a callout.

- Drag a block of tasks by selecting them while pressing and holding the **Control** key on your keyboard, and then dragging the block of the selected tasks to a new position.

- Right-click on any task in the *Timeline* bar and select the *Display as Callout* item on the shortcut menu.

- Drag a new callout from the top of the *Timeline* bar to a position below the *Timeline* bar.

- Convert a callout to a task bar by right-clicking on the callout and then clicking the *Display as Bar* item on the shortcut menu.

When you drag tasks into a new position in the *Timeline* bar, or create callouts above or below the *Timeline* bar, Microsoft Project 2010 adjusts the height of the *Timeline* view automatically to accommodate the new information. For example, Figure 10 - 7 shows my *Timeline* view after I created two callouts and dragged the Phase II task and its subtask to a new row in the *Timeline* bar.

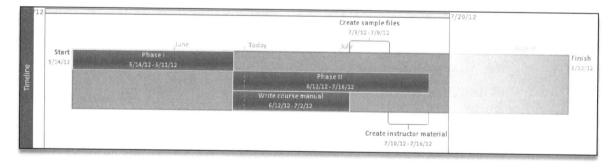

Figure 10 - 7: Rearranged tasks in the Timeline view

To remove a task or a callout from the *Timeline* view, right-click the task or the callout and then click the *Remove from Timeline* item on the shortcut menu.

Formatting the Timeline View

To format the *Timeline* view, click anywhere in the *Timeline* view to select it and then click the *Format* tab. The system displays the contextual *Format* ribbon with the *Timeline Tools* applied, shown in Figure 10 - 8. The process for formatting the *Timeline* view is similar to the process of formatting the *Gantt Chart* view that you learned earlier in this module.

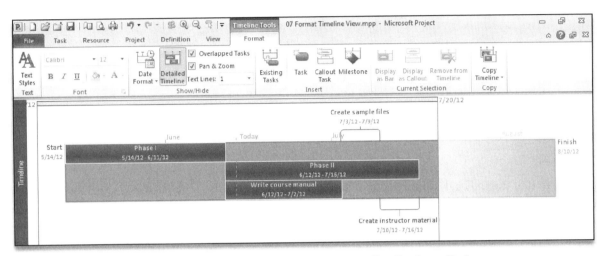

Figure 10 - 8: Format ribbon with the Timeline Tools applied

Using the Text Tools

To format the text for any set of objects shown in the *Timeline* view, click the *Text Styles* button in the *Text* section of the contextual *Format* ribbon. Microsoft Project 2010 displays the *Text Styles* dialog. Although this *Text Styles* dialog is similar to the same-named dialog shown previously in Figure 10 - 35, the *Item to Change* pick list includes a completely different list of items available for formatting, as shown in Figure 10 - 9.

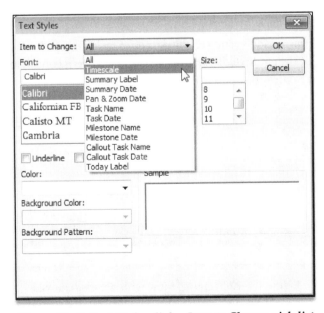

Figure 10 - 9: Text Styles dialog Item to Change pick list

Notice in Figure 10 - 9 that Microsoft Project 2010 does not allow you to change the *Background Color* or *Background Pattern* options in the *Text Styles* dialog for the *Timeline* view. The system limits you to changing only text formatting options such as the *Font* and *Color* items, for example.

 You can also display the *Text Styles* dialog by right-clicking anywhere in the white part of the *Timeline* view and then clicking the *Text Styles* item on the shortcut menu.

Using Font Tools

To change the font or the cell background color of an individual object in the *Timeline* view, select the object and then change the formatting options in the *Font* section of the contextual *Format* ribbon. To display the *Font* dialog, click the *Font* dialog launcher icon in the lower right corner of the *Font* section of the ribbon. To change the background color of a task, for example, select the task and choose a new color on the *Background Color* pick list.

Using Show/Hide Tools

To change the date format of the dates shown in the *Timeline* view, click the *Date Format* pick list button in the *Show/Hide* section and select a new date format. By default, the *Timeline* view uses the date format specified in the *Date Format* field on the *General* page of the *Project Options* dialog. On the *Date Format* pick list, Microsoft Project 2010 also allows you to hide some of the dates shown by default on the *Timeline* view. To hide the dates shown for each task, click the *Date Format* pick list and deselect the *Task Dates* option. To hide the current date, deselect the *Current Date* option on the *Date Format* pick list. To hide the dates shown above the *Timeline* bar, deselect the *Timescale* option on the *Date Format* pick list.

To remove the details from the *Timeline* view, such as the names of tasks and task dates, deselect the *Detailed Timeline* option in the *Show/Hide* section of the contextual *Format* ribbon. The system completely removes all details from the *Timeline* view. As you can see in Figure 10 - 10, without the details, the *Timeline* view is probably not very useful to you.

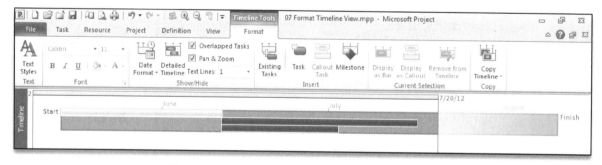

Figure 10 - 10: Timeline view with details removed

If your project contains parallel task sections, and you display overlapping tasks from these parallel sections in the *Timeline* view, the *Overlapped Tasks* option in the *Show/Hide* section works to your advantage. When selected, the *Overlapped Tasks* option displays each overlapping task on its own row in the *Timeline* view. For example, Figure 10 - 11 shows a different project with multiple parallel task sections and with each summary task section displayed on the *Timeline* view. Notice how Microsoft Project 2010 displays each overlapping section on its own task row in the *Timeline* view.

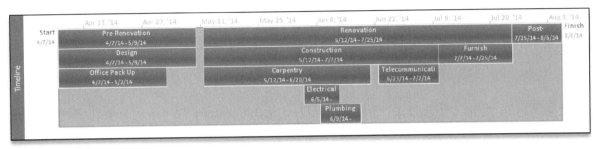

Figure 10 - 11: Timeline with Overlapped Tasks option selected

Figure 10 - 12 shows the same *Timeline* view with the *Overlapped Tasks* option deselected. Notice how the system displays all tasks on a single task row in the *Timeline* view, rendering the information all but impossible to read. For this reason, I recommend you leave the *Overlapped Tasks* option selected for the *Timeline* view when you build a timeline presentation containing numerous overlapping tasks.

Figure 10 - 12: Timeline with Overlapped Tasks option deselected

In the *Show/Hide* section of the contextual *Format* ribbon, the *Pan & Zoom* option allows you to display or hide the light blue *Pan and Zoom* bar shown at the top of the *Timeline* view. If you select the *Pan & Zoom* option, the system displays the *Pan and Zoom* bar; if you deselect this option, the system hides the *Pan and Zoom* bar.

The final option in the *Show/Hide* section is the *Text Lines* option, which allows you to determine how many lines of text to display for every task shown in the *Timeline* view. By default, the system sets the *Text Lines* value to *1 line*. Because of this, the system truncates long task names when displayed in the *Timeline* view. For example, consider the *Timeline* view shown previously in Figure 10 - 6. Notice how the system truncates the names of the three subtasks shown in the Phase II section with the *Text Lines* value set to the default *1 line* value. Compare the same *Timeline* view shown in Figure 10 - 13 with the *Text Lines* value set to *3 lines*.

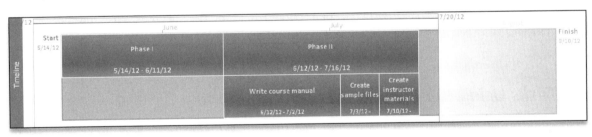

Figure 10 - 13: Timeline view with the Text Lines option set to 3 lines

Figure 10 - 14 shows the completed *Timeline* view after I formatted it using methods I documented in this section of the module. To format the *Timeline* view, I did the following:

- I added the Phase III task to the *Timeline* view.

- I changed the Create Instructor Materials task to a callout.

461

- I dragged the new callout to a position below the *Timeline* bar.

- I changed the *Date Format* option to the *Jan 28* format.

- I changed the *Background Color* setting for each task individually.

- Using the *Text Styles* dialog, I changed the *Font Color* setting to *Red* for the names of all callout items.

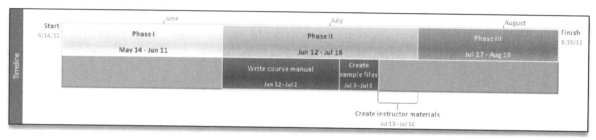

Figure 10 - 14: Timeline view after applying custom formatting

 Notice in Figure 10 - 14 that the *Timeline* view no longer includes the light blue *Pan and Zoom* bar at the top of the view. This is because I zoomed the *Gantt Chart* view to show the complete time span of the project. When you zoom the *Gantt Chart* view to show the Gantt bars for all tasks in the project, Microsoft Project 2010 removes the *Pan and Zoom* bar from the *Timeline* view automatically.

To change the type of object displayed in the *Timeline* view, or to remove an object from the *Timeline* view, use the buttons in the *Current Selection* section of the contextual *Format* ribbon. For example, to change a callout to a task bar, select the callout and then click the *Display as Bar* button. To change a task bar to a callout, select the task bar and then click the *Display as Callout* button. To remove a task or a callout from the *Timeline* view, select the task or callout and then click the *Remote from Timeline* button.

Adding Tasks Using the Contextual Format Ribbon

In addition to the formatting options available on the contextual *Format* ribbon for the *Timeline* view, this ribbon also offers options for adding or removing tasks in the *Timeline* view. In the *Insert* section, Microsoft Project 2010 includes four buttons that allow you to add new tasks to the *Timeline* view. To add a new existing task to the *Timeline* view, click the *Existing Tasks* button. The system displays the *Add Tasks to Timeline* dialog shown in Figure 10 - 15. Select the checkbox to the left of the task name and then click the *OK* button.

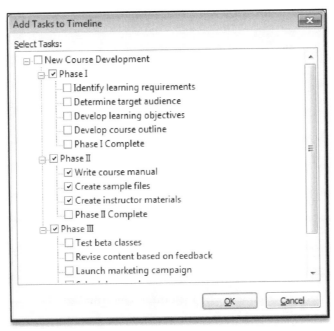

Figure 10 - 15: Add Tasks to Timeline dialog

The system adds the selected task(s) to the *Timeline* view. For example, notice in Figure 10 - 16 that I added the *Project Complete* milestone task to the *Timeline* view.

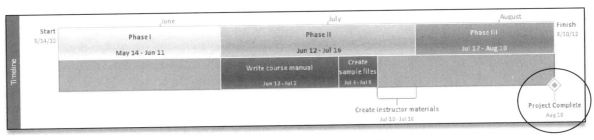

Figure 10 - 16: Milestone task added to the Timeline view

To add a completely new task to your project and add the new task to the *Timeline* view, click the *Task* button, the *Callout Task* button, or the *Milestone* button in the *Insert* section of the contextual *Format* ribbon. When you click any of these three buttons, Microsoft Project 2010 displays the *Task Information* dialog shown in Figure 10 - 17.

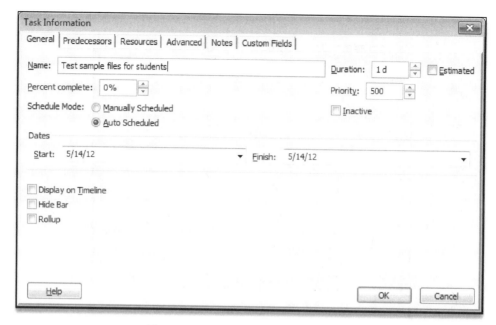

Figure 10 - 17: Task Information dialog

In the *Task Information* dialog, enter complete information about the new task, including information in the *Name* and *Duration* fields, and select the desired *Schedule Mode* option. Assuming you want to display the new task in the *Timeline* view, be sure to select the *Display on Timeline* option. If necessary, select predecessor tasks on the *Predecessors* page and assign resources to the new task on the *Resources* page. Click the *OK* button to finish. Microsoft Project 2010 creates the new task as the last task in the task list, and adds the new task to the *Timeline* view. Figure 10 - 18 shows a new task I added, Test Student Sample Files. After creating the new task, you must drag the task to the correct place in the project and set additional dependencies.

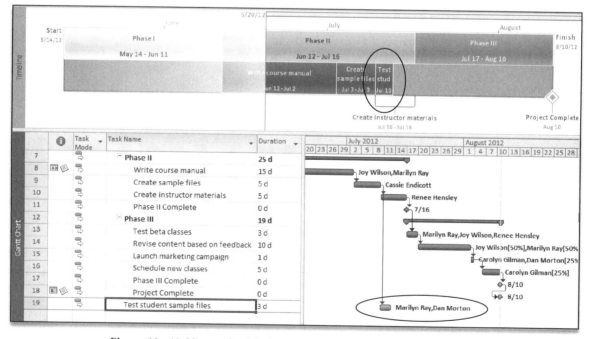

Figure 10 - 18: New task added to the project and to the Timeline view

You can also insert a new task in the project and add it to the *Timeline* view by right-clicking anywhere in the white part of the *Timeline* view, selecting the *Insert Task* menu item, and then clicking the *Callout Task*, *Task*, or *Milestone* item on the flyout menu.

Hands On Exercise

Exercise 10-3

Add tasks to the *Timeline* view.

1. Navigate to your student folder and open the **Format the Timeline View.mpp** sample file.

2. Click the *View* tab and then select the *Timeline* option in the *Split View* section of the *View* ribbon.

3. Grab the split bar along the bottom edge of the *Timeline* view and drag it down to approximately **triple** the height of the *Timeline* view.

4. Right-click on the name of the *Pre-Renovation* summary task and then click the *Add to Timeline* item on the shortcut menu.

Notice how Microsoft Project 2010 adds a bar to the *Timeline* view representing the *Pre-Renovation* summary task.

5. Using the **Control** key on your keyboard, select and highlight the following summary tasks as a group:

    *   Renovation

    *   Construction

    *   Furnish

    *   Post Renovation

6. Release the **Control** key, then right-click anywhere in one of the selected tasks and click the *Add to Timeline* item on the shortcut menu.

7. Using the **Control** key on your keyboard, select the three tasks highlighted with *Lime* as their cell background color (task IDs #22, 24, and 25).

8. Release the **Control** key, then right-click anywhere in one of the selected tasks and then click the *Add to Timeline* item on the shortcut menu.

9. In the *Timeline* view, right-click on the *Obtain asbestos removal permit* task bar (the left-most item in the third row) and click the *Display as Callout* item on the shortcut menu.

10. In the *Timeline* view, right-click on the task bar for the *Asbestos removal inspection* task bar (the right-most item in the third row) and click the *Display as Callout* item on the shortcut menu.

11. Grab the split bar along the bottom edge of the *Timeline* view and drag it down to add approximately one inch to the height of the *Timeline* view.

12. In the *Timeline* view, drag the *Remote asbestos in ceiling* task bar **below** the *Timeline* bar to display this task as a *Callout* below the timeline.

13. Using the **Control** key on your keyboard, select the task bars for the *Renovation, Construction,* and *Furnish* tasks in the *Timeline* view.

14. Release the **Control** key, and then drag the block of three selected task bars **one row below** their current position in the *Timeline* view.

15. Save but do not close the **Format the Timeline View.mpp** sample file.

Exercise 10-4

Customize the *Timeline* view.

1. Click anywhere in the *Timeline* view to select the view.

2. Click the *Format* tab to display the contextual *Format* ribbon with the *Timeline Tools* applied.

3. Click the *Text Styles* button in the *Text* section of the *Format* ribbon.

4. In the *Text Styles* dialog, click the *Item to Change* pick list and select the *Callout Task Name* item.

5. Click the *Color* pick list and select the *Red* color in the *Standard Colors* section of the dialog.

6. Click the *OK* button.

7. In the *Timeline* view, click the task bar for the *Construction* summary task.

8. In the *Font* section of the *Format* ribbon, click the *Background Color* pick list button and select the *Red* color in the first row of the *Theme Colors* section.

9. In the *Font* section of the *Format* ribbon, click the *Color* pick list button and select the *Yellow* color in the *Standard Colors* section.

10. In the *Show/Hide* section of the *Format* ribbon, click the *Date Format* pick list button and then **deselect** the *Timescale* item at the bottom of the pick list.

11. In the *Show/Hide* section of the *Format* ribbon, **deselect** the *Pan & Zoom* option.

12. Click the *Existing Tasks* button in the *Insert* section of the *Format* ribbon.

13. In the *Add Tasks to Timeline* dialog, select the checkbox for the *Project Complete* milestone task and then click the *OK* button.

14. Save but do not close the **Format the Timeline View.mpp** sample file.

Exporting the Timeline View

One additional feature of the new *Timeline* view allows you to export the entire *Timeline* view to any Microsoft Office application, such as Microsoft PowerPoint or Microsoft Visio. To copy the *Timeline* view, click the *Copy Timeline* pick list button in the *Copy* section of the contextual *Format* ribbon. The *Copy Timeline* pick list contains three choices, including *For E-Mail*, *For Presentation*, and *Full Size*.

If you select the *Full Size* item on the *Copy Timeline* pick list, Microsoft Project 2010 copies the full-size image of the *Timeline* view to your Windows clipboard. If you select the *For Presentation* item, the system optimizes the image for use in Microsoft PowerPoint by reducing the image size to approximately 90% of full size. If you select the *For E-Mail* item, the system optimizes the image for use in Microsoft Outlook by reducing the image size to approximately 60% of full size.

After copying the *Timeline* view to your clipboard, paste the image in one of the Microsoft Office applications. If you use an application that has image editing capabilities, such as Microsoft Word or Microsoft PowerPoint, you can continue to refine your *Timeline* view presentation. For example, Figure 10 - 19 shows the *Timeline* view after I pasted the image into a Microsoft PowerPoint presentation and applied additional formatting. Notice that I used the *Bevel* feature to give the tasks a 3-D appearance, and I used the *Glow* feature to alter the appearance of the *Project Complete* milestone task.

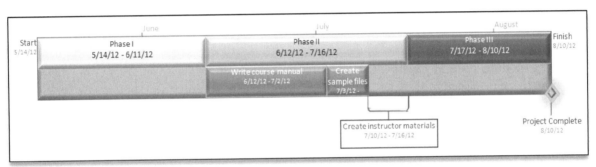

Figure 10 - 19: Timeline view formatted in Microsoft PowerPoint

You can also copy the *Timeline* view by right-clicking anywhere in the white part of the *Timeline* view, selecting the *Copy Timeline* item from the shortcut menu, and then clicking the *For E-Mail*, *For Presentation*, or *Full Size* item on the flyout menu.

Exercise 10-5

Export the *Timeline* view to another Microsoft Office application.

1. Return to the **Format the Timeline View.mpp** sample file.

2. Click anywhere in the *Timeline* view to select it.

3. Click the *Copy Timeline* pick list button in the *Copy* section of the *Format* ribbon and then select the *For Presentation* item on the pick list.

4. Launch Microsoft PowerPoint and create a new blank slide with no placeholder information.

5. Click the *Paste* button in Microsoft PowerPoint.

6. Zoom your PowerPoint slide to the *100%* level of zoom.

7. Double-click one of the task bars in the timeline image to launch the *Drawing Tools* feature in Microsoft PowerPoint.

8. Using the **Control** key on your computer keyboard, select each of the task bars in the Timeline image, and then release the **Control** key.

9. Use any of the object formatting features in Microsoft PowerPoint to format the selected task bars in the timeline image. For example, if you have Microsoft PowerPoint 2007, format the task bars using one of the *Bevel* items in the *Shape Effects* pick list.

10. Exit your Microsoft PowerPoint application and then return to your Microsoft Project 2010 application window.

11. Save and close the **Format the Timeline View.mpp** sample file.

Creating a New Table by Customizing an Existing Table

In the preceding module, I taught you how to create a custom view using a 4-step method. Using this method, you now know how to create a custom view by creating a custom table, filter, and group before you create the custom view. This 4-step method is not the only way to create a custom view. An alternate method for creating a new table is to use some new functionality included in Microsoft Project 2010. This new functionality includes the following:

- Customize an existing table and then save it as a new table.

- Use the *Add New Column* virtual column to customize the existing table.

- Reset a customized table back to its original default settings.

If your custom view does not need to use any default/custom filter or group, you can use this alternate method to create a new custom view and table quickly.

Customizing an Existing Table and Creating a New Table

A new feature in Microsoft Project 2010 allows you to temporarily customize any existing table and then save the customized table as an entirely new table. After you save the new custom table, the system then allows you to reset the original table back to its default settings. To customize any existing table, complete the following steps:

1. Right-click on the *Select All* button and select any default table for temporary customization.

2. Drag the split bar to the right to expose the columns in the selected table.

3. Right-click on the column header of any column you want to remove and then select the *Hide Column* item on the shortcut menu.

4. To add a new column to the table, right-click on the column header where you want to insert the column, and then select the *Insert Column* item in the shortcut menu.

5. From the list of available columns, select the new column you want to add and press the **Enter** key on your keyboard.

You can also insert a new column in the table by clicking the pick list button in the *Add New Column* virtual column and selecting the column from the list of available columns.

6. To change the settings for any column, such as the title displayed in the column header, right-click on the column you want to change and select the *Field Settings* item on the shortcut menu. Microsoft Project 2010 displays the *Field Settings* dialog shown in Figure 10 - 20.

Figure 10 - 20: Field Settings dialog

The *Field Settings* dialog allows you to enter text in the *Title* field to specify an alternate name for the column. In addition, you can specify a value in the *Align title* field and the *Align data* field to specify whether to align the column and its data on the left, on the right, or centered. Finally, you can set the width of the column in the *Width* field and you can specify whether to use the *Header Text Wrapping* feature by selecting this option as well.

7. In the *Field Settings* dialog, specify the column options you want and click the *OK* button.

If you click the *Best Fit* button in the *Field Settings* dialog, Microsoft Project 2010 sets the column width automatically to the width of the longest entry in the column.

If you do not include the custom table as part of a new custom view, then you are ready to save the customized table as a new table, and then to reset the customized table to its original default settings. To save the customized table as a new table, complete the following steps:

1. Click the *View* tab to display the *View* ribbon.

2. In the *Data* section of the *View* ribbon, click the *Tables* pick list and select the *Save Fields as a New Table* item on the list. Microsoft Project 2010 displays the *Save Table* dialog shown in Figure 10 - 21.

Figure 10 - 21: Save Table dialog

3. In the *Save Table* dialog, enter a name for the new custom table in the *Name* field and then click the *OK* button.

To reset the customized table back to its original default settings, complete these additional steps:

1. Right-click on the *Select All* button and select the **original table** you temporarily customized to create the new table.

2. In the *Data* section of the *View* ribbon, click the *Tables* pick list and select the *Reset to Default* item on the list.

Microsoft Project 2010 resets the customized table back to its original default settings. This action includes resetting the original list of columns, plus all formatting for the data in each column, and adding the *Add New Column* virtual column as well.

If you intend to save the customized table as a part of a customized view, you **do not** need to save the customized table **at this time**. Instead, after you customize the table, then customize the view and save the customized view as a new view. When you do this, Microsoft Project 2010 **also saves** the customized table as a new table automatically. When you reset the customized view back to its default settings, the system also resets the customized table back to its default settings as well.

Customizing a Table Using the Add New Column Feature

As I noted previously in this book, every default table in Microsoft Project 2010 includes the new *Add New Column* virtual column on the far right side of the table. You can use this feature as an alternate method of adding columns in a new custom table. The system offers you several ways to insert a new column using the *Add New Column* virtual column:

*   Click the column header at the top of the *Add New Column* virtual column and select a field from the list of available fields.

*   Click the column header at the top of the *Add New Column* virtual column and then enter the name of a new custom field in the blank column header.

*   Type data in any cell in the *Add New Column* virtual column.

When you type the name of a new custom field in the *Add New Column* virtual column header, the system creates a new custom *Text* field automatically, using the next available unused *Text* field. The system then redisplays the *Add New Column* virtual column to the right of the new custom column. For example, Figure 10 - 22 shows the new *Schedule Risk* column I added to a custom table using the *Add New Column* virtual column.

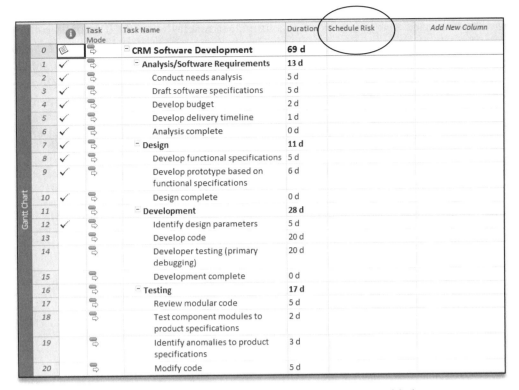

Figure 10 - 22: New custom Schedule Risk column added

When you create a new custom column using this method, keep in mind that Microsoft Project 2010 offers **only 30** custom *Text* fields. If you attempt to exceed this number by creating the thirty-first custom column, the system displays the *Delete Custom Fields* dialog shown in Figure 10 - 23. Because of the limit of 30 custom *Text* fields, you must delete an existing custom *Text* field by selecting the option checkbox for one or more fields and then clicking the *Delete Custom Fields* button in the dialog. When prompted in a confirmation dialog, click the *Yes* button to delete the selected fields.

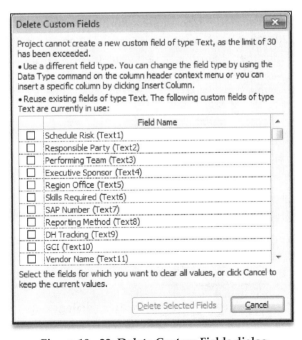

Figure 10 - 23: Delete Custom Fields dialog

When you type data in the *Add New Column* virtual column, Microsoft Project 2010 automatically selects the next available custom field using the data type you entered. For example, if you type *$500* in the *Add New Column* field, the software selects and inserts the next unused custom *Cost* field. If you enter *5d* in the *Add New Column* field, the software selects and inserts the next unused custom *Duration* field. For example, Figure 10 - 24 shows the new *Number1* column that the system added automatically after I typed a number in the *Add New Column* virtual column.

		Task Mode	Task Name	Duration	Schedule Risk	Number1	Add New Column
0			⁻ **CRM Software Development**	**69 d**		0	
1	✓		⁻ **Analysis/Software Requirements**	**13 d**		0	
2	✓		Conduct needs analysis	5 d		12357	
3	✓		Draft software specifications	5 d		0	
4	✓		Develop budget	2 d		0	
5	✓		Develop delivery timeline	1 d		0	
6	✓		Analysis complete	0 d		0	
7	✓		⁻ **Design**	**11 d**		0	
8	✓		Develop functional specifications	5 d		0	
9	✓		Develop prototype based on functional specifications	6 d		0	
10	✓		Design complete	0 d		0	
11			⁻ **Development**	**28 d**		0	
12	✓		Identify design parameters	5 d		0	
13			Develop code	20 d		0	
14			Developer testing (primary debugging)	20 d		0	
15			Development complete	0 d		0	
16			⁻ **Testing**	**17 d**		0	
17			Review modular code	5 d		0	
18			Test component modules to product specifications	2 d		0	
19			Identify anomalies to product specifications	3 d		0	
20			Modify code	5 d		0	

Figure 10 - 24: New custom Number column

If you create a new custom column by typing a value in the *Add New Column* virtual column, I strongly recommend that you either change the *Title* of the column or rename the field to display relevant information that identifies the column. To change the *Title* of a column, right-click on the column header and select the *Field Settings* item on the shortcut menu. Microsoft Project 2010 displays the *Field Settings* dialog shown in Figure 10 - 25. Enter a name for the column in the *Title* field and then click the *OK* button. When you enter a *Title* for a column, the column continues to retain its original name, such as *Number1*, but the column header displays the *Title* information instead of the column name. I like to think of the column *Title* as the "nickname" of the column.

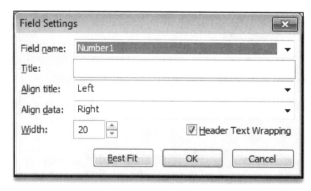

Figure 10 - 25: Field Settings dialog

472

To rename a column and give it a completely new name, right-click on its column header and select the *Custom Fields* item on the shortcut menu. The system displays the *Custom Fields* dialog shown in Figure 10 - 26. Click the *Rename* button, enter a new name for the field, and then click the *OK* button. Click the *OK* button to close the *Custom Fields* dialog as well.

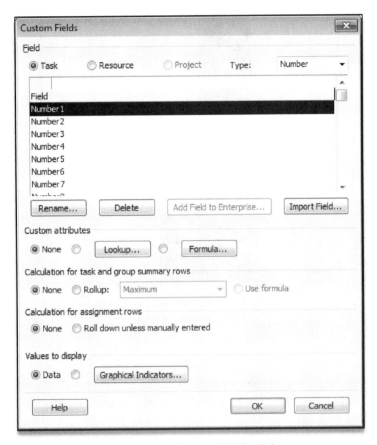

Figure 10 - 26: Custom Fields dialog

 The *Custom Fields* dialog also allows you to create all types of custom fields. I provide an in-depth presentation about how to create custom fields in this book's companion volume, which is the *Ultimate Learning Guide to Microsoft Project 2010: Advanced* book. In the companion volume, you learn how to create custom fields containing a lookup table or a fomula, and that display graphical indicators instead of data.

After creating a new custom column using either of the two previous methods, Microsoft Project 2010 also allows you to change the *Data Type* used for the column. For example, after I typed a number in the *Add New Column* virtual column, the system added the *Number1* field automatically. However, if for example I need to enter alphanumeric data in this column, I need to convert the *Data Type* from *Number* to *Text* instead. To change the *Data Type* for any custom column, right-click on the column header, select the *Data Type* item on the shortcut menu, and then select the desired *Data Type* item on the fly out menu as shown in Figure 10 - 27. Notice that I renamed the custom *Number1* column to *SAP Number* instead. Notice also that the fly out menu shows the original *Data Type* value for this column, the *Number* type.

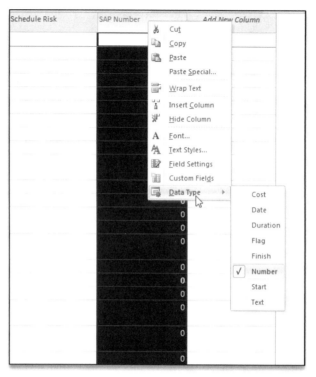

**Figure 10 - 27: Change the Data Type
for a custom column**

When you change the *Data Type* for a custom column, Microsoft Project 2010 selects the next available unused column with that *Data Type*. In my project, after converting the *SAP Number* column from a *Number* field to a *Text* field, the system selected the *Text2* field, applied the *SAP Number* name to the *Text2* field, and then removed the *SAP Number* name from the *Number1* field.

If you attempt to convert the *Data Type* for a column to an invalid type based on the data already in the column, Microsoft Project 2010 displays a warning dialog such as the one shown in Figure 10 - 28. For example, the system displays this dialog when I attempt to change the *SAP Number* column to the *Flag* data type. Notice in the dialog that if I click the *Yes* button to continue with the conversion operation, the system will delete all of the existing data in this column. In my situation, I must click the *No* button because I do not want to delete the data in this column.

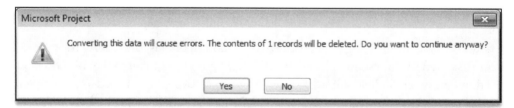

Figure 10 - 28: Warning dialog after changing to an invalid Data Type

Warning: When you add columns to any default table, remember that this action changes the definition of the table from this point forward. Because a number of views share common tables between them, adding columns to the table in one view causes the columns to appear in other views. For example, if you add columns to the *Entry* table in the *Gantt Chart* view, you see these additional columns in the *Tracking Gantt* view and the *Task Sheet* view because all three views use the *Entry* table by default.

Hands On Exercise

Exercise 10-6

Add several new custom columns using the *Add New Column* virtual column.

1. Open the **Customize an Existing View.mpp** sample file.

2. Pull the split bar to the far right side of the *Gantt Chart* view to expose all of the columns in the *Entry* table.

3. Click and drag across the column headers of the *Duration, Start, Finish, Predecessors,* and *Resource Names* columns to select these five columns.

4. Right-click anywhere in the column headers of the five selected columns, then click the *Hide Column* item on the shortcut menu to hide the five selected columns.

5. Click the column header of the *Add New Column* virtual column and select the *Responsible Person (Text1)* column.

6. Click the column header of the *Add New Column* virtual column and select the *Cost Center ID (Text2)* column.

> **Note:** The *Responsible Person* and *Cost Center ID* columns are **custom columns** I created specifically for this Hands On Exercise. These two columns **are not** default columns included in Microsoft Project 2010.

7. In the *Add New Column* virtual column, select the cell for task ID #17, the *Pre-Renovation Complete* milestone task.

8. Type a *Yes* value in the selected cell in the *Add New Column* virtual column.

Notice how Microsoft Project 2010 adds the new *Flag1* column to the left of the *Add New Column* virtual column.

In the *Flag1* column, select a *Yes* value for the following tasks:

- Task ID #69, the *Renovation Complete* milestone task

- Task ID #76, the *Post-Renovation Complete* milestone task

- Task ID #77, the *PROJECT COMPLETE* milestone task

9. Right-click in the *Flag1* column header and click the *Custom Fields* item on the shortcut menu.

10. In the *Custom Fields* dialog, select the *Flag1* field and then click the *Rename* button.

11. In the *Rename Field* dialog, enter the name *Major Milestone* in the *New name for Flag1* field and then click the *OK* button.

12. Click the *OK* button to close the *Custom Fields* dialog.

13. Right-click in the *Major Milestone* column header and click the *Field Settings* item on the shortcut menu.

14. In the *Field Settings* dialog, select the *Center* value in the *Align Title* and *Align Data* fields.

15. Set the *Width* field value to *14* and then click the *OK* button.

16. Save but **do not** close the **Customize an Existing View.mpp** sample file.

Creating a New View by Customizing an Existing View

In Module 08, Project Execution, I showed you how to format the *Gantt Chart* view using the *Format* ribbon to display the Critical Path in your project, and to optionally show the slack for each task as well. In the previous topical section of this module, I showed you how to customize an existing table using several methods. After you customize any default view and table, another new feature in Microsoft Project 2010 allows you to save **both** the customized view and customized table as an entirely new custom view and table in a single action. After you save the customized view and table, you can also reset the original view and table back to their default settings in a single action.

Figure 10 - 29 shows a customized *Gantt Chart* view with a customized *Entry* table applied as well. To customize the default *Gantt Chart* view and *Entry* table, I completed the following steps:

- I removed the *Task Mode* column.

- I created two new columns called *Schedule Risk* and *SAP Number*, and then populated a value in each of these fields for every task in the project.

- I formatted the *Gantt Chart* view by selecting the *Critical Path* and *Slack* options in the *Bar Styles* section of the *Format* ribbon.

- I changed the color scheme of the *Gantt Chart* view using one of the color schemes in the *Gantt Chart Style* section of the *Format* ribbon.

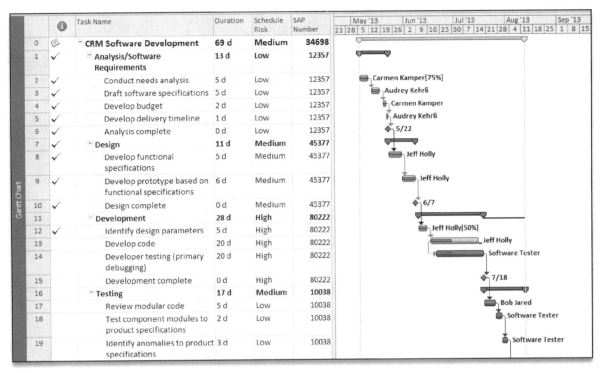

Figure 10 - 29: Customized Gantt Chart view

After customizing a default view and table, you can save them as a new custom view and table by completing the following steps:

1. Display the customized view, including the table to which you added the custom columns.

2. Click the *Task* tab to display the *Task* ribbon.

3. In the *View* section of the *Task* ribbon, click the *Gantt Chart* pick list button and then click the *Save View* item on the pick list menu. Microsoft Project 2010 displays the *Save View* dialog shown in Figure 10 - 30.

Figure 10 - 30: Save View dialog

4. In the *Save View* dialog, enter an original name for the custom view in the *Name* field and then click the *OK* button.

You can also save a customized view as a new view using several other ribbons. For example, on the *Resource* ribbon, click the *Team Planner* pick list button and then select the *Save View* item on the menu. On the *View* ribbon, click **any** pick list button in either the *Task Views* or *Resource Views* section of the ribbon and then click the *Save View* item on the menu.

After completing the previous set of steps, Microsoft Project 2010 adds your new view and table to your current project and to your Global.mpt file automatically. By adding the view and table to the Global.mpt file, the system makes them available in all current and future projects. To see your new view and table in the Global.mpt file, click the *File* tab and then click the *Organizer* button in the *Info* tab of the *Backstage*. The system displays the *Views* page of the *Organizer* dialog shown in Figure 10 - 31. Notice that the system added the new custom view named *_Company Tracking* to the list on the left side of the dialog (in the Global.mpt file) and to the list on the right side of the dialog (in the active project).

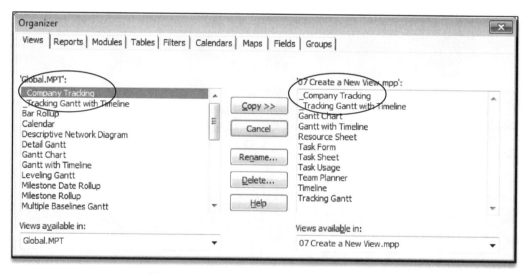

Figure 10 - 31: Organizer dialog, Views page

If you click the *Tables* tab, you can see your new custom table on the left side of the dialog (in the Global.mpt file) and in the right side of the dialog (in the active project). Notice in Figure 10 - 32 that the system named my new custom table by using the name of the view and by appending *Table 1* to the name of the table. In this case, the system named my new custom table *_Company Tracking Table 1*.

At this point, you have the option to edit the name of the table, if necessary. To edit the table name, select the table on the left side of the dialog and then click the *Rename* button. In the *Rename* dialog, enter a new name for the table (such as removing the *Table 1* text from the table name) and then click the *OK* button. Repeat this process for the name of the table on the right side of the dialog. Click the *Close* button to close the *Organizer* dialog and then click the *File* tab to exit the *Backstage*.

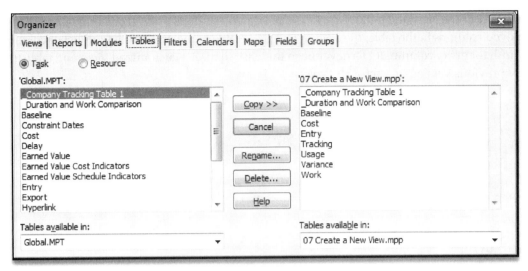

Figure 10 - 32: Organizer dialog, Tables page

Resetting a Default View and Table after Customization

After you create a new custom view and table by customizing a default view and table, I strongly recommend that you reset the customized default view and table to their original default settings before customization. To do this, complete the following steps:

1. Display the default view and table you customized previously.

2. Click the *Task* tab to display the *Task* ribbon.

3. In the *View* section of the *Task* ribbon, click the *Gantt Chart* pick list button and then click the *Reset to Default* item on the pick list menu. Microsoft Project 2010 displays the confirmation dialog shown in Figure 10 - 33.

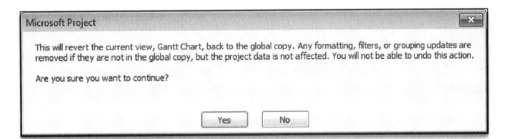

Figure 10 - 33: Confirmation dialog to reset a view to its default settings

4. In the confirmation dialog, click the *Yes* button.

As noted in the previous topical section, you can reset a view to its default settings by clicking any view pick list button on either the *Resource* ribbon or the *View* ribbon.

The system resets both the view and table to their original default settings prior to customization. This means if you added or removed columns in the table, the system resets the table to the original default list of columns and resets the column width for every column. It has never been this easy to reset a customized view and table to their default settings in any previous version of Microsoft Project!

Hands On Exercise

Exercise 10-7

Create a new custom view by saving a customized default view.

1. Return to the **Customize an Existing View.mpp** sample file, if necessary.

2. Double-click the right edge of the *Cost Center ID* column header to "best fit" the width of this column.

3. Pull the split bar to the right edge of the *Responsible Person* column.

4. Click the *Format* tab to display the contextual *Format* ribbon with the *Gantt Chart Tools* applied.

5. In the *Bar Styles* section of the *Format* ribbon, select the *Critical Tasks* option and the *Slack* option.

6. Select any color scheme in the *Gantt Chart Style* section of the *Format* ribbon.

7. Click the *Task* tab to display the *Task* ribbon.

8. Click the *Gantt Chart* pick list button and then click the *Save View* item on the list.

9. In the *Save View* dialog, enter the name _PMO Information in the *Name* field and then click the *OK* button.

10. Click the *Gantt Chart* pick list button and select the *Gantt Chart* view.

11. Click the *Gantt Chart* pick list button again and select the *Reset to Default* item on the list.

12. In the confirmation dialog, click the *Yes* button to reset the *Gantt Chart* view and the *Entry* table to their default configuration settings.

13. Pull the split bar to the right so that you can confirm that Microsoft Project 2010 did reset the *Entry* table to its default list of columns.

14. Click the *File* tab and then click the *Organizer* button in the *Info* tab of the *Backstage*.

Notice the new _PMO Information view in the *Global.MPT* section of the *Organizer* dialog.

15. Click the *Cancel* button to close the *Organizer* dialog.

16. Click the *File* tab again to exit the *Backstage*.

17. Save but **do not** close the **Customize an Existing View.mpp** sample file.

Exercise 10-8

Rename and delete objects using the *Organizer* dialog.

1. Return to the **Customize an Existing View.mpp** sample file.

2. Click the *File* tab, click the *Info* tab, and then click the *Organizer* button on the *Info* page of the *Backstage*.

3. Select the *Tables* tab in the *Organizer* dialog.

4. Select the *_PMO Information Table 1* item in the **left side** of the *Organizer* dialog (in the Global.mpt file) and then click the *Rename* button.

5. Enter the new name *_PMO Tracking Info* in the *Rename* dialog and click the *OK* button.

6. Select the *_PMO Information Table 1* item in the **right side** of the *Organizer* dialog (in the sample project file) and then click the *Delete* button.

7. Click the *Yes* button in the confirmation dialog to confirm the deletion.

8. Click the *Fields* tab.

9. Select the three custom fields on the right side of the dialog and then click the *Copy* button to copy them to your Global.mpt file.

10. Click the *Close* button to close the *Organizer* dialog.

11. Click the *File* tab again to exit the *Backstage*.

12. Save and close the **Customize an Existing View.mpp** sample file.

With the completion of this exercise, you now have a new custom view, a new custom table, and three custom fields for tracking project information. If you want to use the *Responsible Person* and *Cost Center ID* fields in your own organization, you **must** edit the items in the lookup table for each of these fields. To edit these two fields, use the *Custom Fields* dialog (click the *Custom Fields* button in the *Properties* section of the *Project* ribbon). If you do not want to use the custom view, table, and fields, then use the *Organizer* dialog to delete all of these custom objects from your Global.mpt file.

Formatting the Gantt Chart

As part of your project communication process, you may need to format the *Gantt chart* portion of the *Gantt Chart* view for printing or display purposes. In Module 08, Project Execution, I taught you how to format the Gantt chart to display Critical tasks and to display the Slack for each task as well. I repeated this information again earlier in this module to teach you how to create a new view by customizing a default view. In these two situations, I only "scratched the surface" of the view formatting capabilities available in Microsoft Project 2010. Now I want to show you the complete view formatting capabilities of the tool, which allow you to format the *Gantt Chart* view or any other default or custom view.

To format the Gantt chart, apply the *Gantt Chart* view and then click the *Format* tab. The system displays the contextual *Format* ribbon with the *Gantt Chart Tools* applied, indicated by the purple area above the *Format* tab shown in Figure 10 - 34.

Figure 10 - 34: Format ribbon with the Gantt Chart Tools applied

Using the Format Tools

The *Format* section of the contextual *Format* ribbon contains three buttons which allow you to format a number of items that appear in Microsoft Project 2010. Use these buttons to format text styles, gridlines, and progress lines, and to control the layout of Gantt bars in any *Gantt* view. I discuss each of these items separately.

Formatting Text Styles

When you click the *Text Styles* button in the *Format* section of the contextual *Format* ribbon, the system displays the *Text Styles* dialog. This dialog offers you the automatic formatting capabilities for both text and cell background formatting. For example, you can use this dialog to apply a cell background color to every milestone task and to apply a different cell background color to every summary task. When you click the *Item to Change* pick list, you see the list of every object to which you can apply the automatic formatting. A new feature in this dialog in Microsoft Project 2010 is the *Inactive Tasks* item shown in Figure 10 - 35.

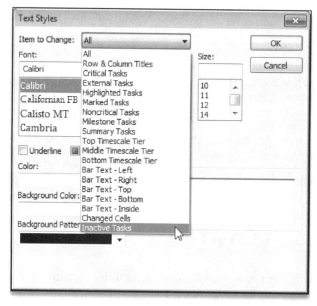

Figure 10 - 35: Text Styles dialog
Item to Change pick list

To apply automatic formatting to any object in a project, complete the following steps in the *Text Styles* dialog:

1. Click the *Item to Change* pick list and select an object.

2. Select the desired font formatting options in the *Font*, *Font Style*, and *Size* fields.

3. Select the *Underline* or *Strikethrough* checkboxes as needed.

4. Select a color formatting item in the *Color*, *Background Color*, and *Background Pattern* pick lists as needed.

5. Repeat steps #1-4 for each object you want to format automatically.

6. Click the *OK* button when finished.

The *Strikethrough* checkbox is another new feature in this dialog in Microsoft Project 2010. The system uses the *Strikethrough* font formatting by default on *Inactive* tasks, as shown in Figure 10 - 36. Notice in the *Text Styles* dialog that the system disables the *Background Color* and *Background Pattern* pick lists, as the system does not allow any kind of cell background formatting on *Inactive* tasks.

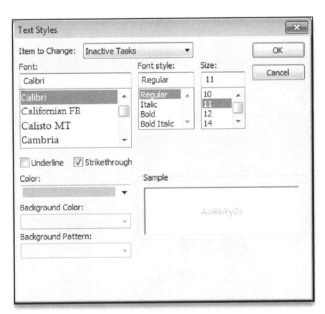

Figure 10 - 36: Text Styles dialog
Strikethrough font formatting option

If you want to change the values in either the *Color* pick list or *Background Color* pick list, you see the third new feature in this dialog: the expanded color palette. In all previous versions of the software, the system offered a small color palette with only sixteen standard colors. Microsoft Project 2010 now offers an expanded color palette with thousands of colors, available for font colors, cell background colors, Gantt bar colors, hyperlink colors, and grouping colors. For example, Figure 10 - 37 shows the expanded color palette in the *Color* pick list with the *Critical Tasks* item selected on the *Item to Change* pick list.

483

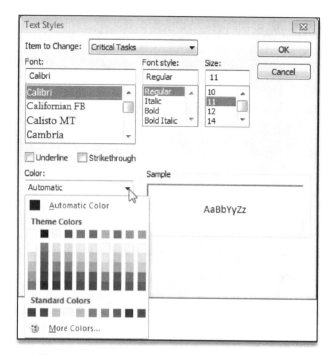

**Figure 10 - 37: Text Styles dialog, expanded color
palette on the Color pick list**

When you click the *Color* pick list or the *Background Color* pick list, the color palette offers a set of 60 colors in the *Theme Colors* section and a set of 10 colors in the *Standard Colors* section. In addition, if you select the *More Colors* item in the pick list, the system displays the *Colors* dialog shown in Figure 10 - 38. This dialog allows you to select a color from among the 142 colors on the *Standard* tab or the thousands of colors on the *Custom* tab.

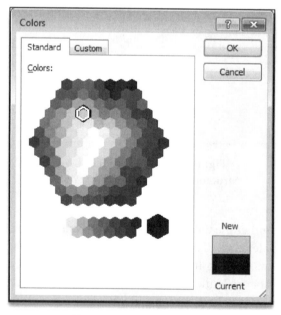

Figure 10 - 38: Color dialog

Formatting Gridlines

When you click the *Gridlines* pick list button in the *Format* section of the *Format* ribbon, the system displays two options on the list: the *Gridlines* item and the *Progress Lines* item. If you click the *Gridlines* item, Microsoft Project 2010 displays the *Gridlines* dialog shown in Figure 10 - 39. In the 2010 version of the software, Microsoft changed the default formatting for several types of gridlines shown in the *Line to Change* list. Gridlines with new formatting include the *Current Date*, *Project Start*, and *Project Finish* gridlines. Figure 10 - 39 shows the formatting for the *Current Date* gridline in the *Gridlines* dialog, for example.

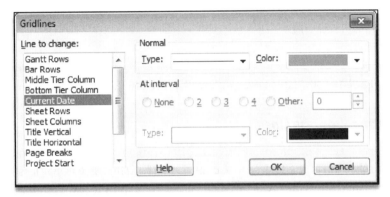

Figure 10 - 39: Gridlines dialog, Current Date formatting

As a part of your project reporting process, if you select a date in the *Status Date* field in the *Project Information* dialog, MsProjectExperts recommends that you also apply formatting to the *Status Date* gridline. This makes the *Status Date* gridline visible in the *Gantt Chart* view. For example, in the *Gridlines* dialog, you might select the last item on the *Type* pick list (the -- - -- - -- item) and the red color on the *Color* pick list. This creates a very visible reminder of the date currently entered in the *Status Date* field for your project.

Figure 10 - 40 shows a project in which I formatted the *Status Date* gridline using the preceding best practice recommendation. In this project, April 15th (Friday) is the *Status Date* of the project, representing the last day of the previous reporting period. The red dashed line is the *Status Date* gridline, which represents the date for which all task progress must be current or else the task is behind schedule. The solid orange gridline on April 19th is the current date for the project, by the way.

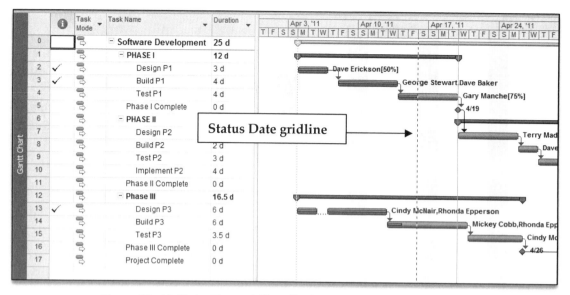

Figure 10 - 40: Status Date gridline displayed in the Gantt Chart view

Displaying and Formatting Progress Lines

You can use the *Progress Lines* feature in Microsoft Project 2010 to quickly locate tasks whose progress is behind schedule. A task that is behind schedule is any task whose cumulative *% Complete* value is less than the expected *% Complete* value, as of the *Status Date* value you specify in the project. For example, by the *Status Date* of my project, a task is only 25% complete when it should be 50% complete; therefore, this task is behind schedule.

When you click the *Gridlines* pick list button and then click the *Progress Lines* item, the system displays the *Progress Lines* dialog with the *Dates and Intervals* tab selected, shown in Figure 10 - 41. On the *Dates and Intervals* page of the dialog, Microsoft Project 2010 allows you to select the type of progress line(s) you want to display.

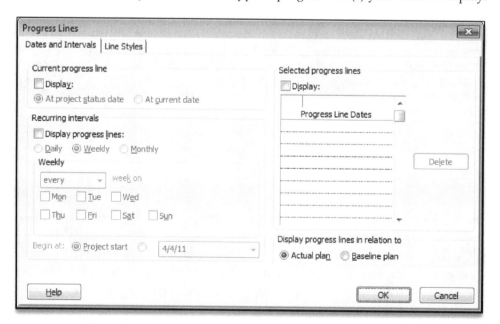

Figure 10 - 41: Progress Lines dialog, Dates and Intervals page

To display the most commonly used progress line, select the *Display* checkbox in the *Current progress line* section of the dialog, and then select the *At project status date* option. Selecting this option assumes you entered a date value in the

Status Date field in the *Project Information* dialog, of course. You have the option to select the *At current date* option if you wish. Click the *OK* button to display the progress line in your project.

Figure 10 - 42 shows the same project shown previously in Figure 10 - 40, but with a progress line displayed instead of the *Status Date* gridline. The progress line connects with the current progress point on any in-progress task, but does not connect with completed tasks or future unstarted tasks. If the progress line "spikes" to the left, the task is behind schedule, as of the *Status Date* value you specified for the project. If the progress line "spikes" to the right, the task is ahead of schedule. Most of the time, you should focus your attention on any task whose progress line spikes to the left. Notice in Figure 10 - 42 that the progress line "spikes" to the left for the Design P3 task and the Phase III summary task, indicating that these two tasks are behind schedule.

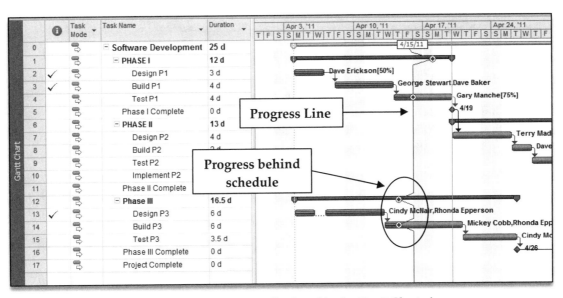

Figure 10 - 42: Progress Line displayed in the Gantt Chart view

In the *Progress Lines* dialog, the system offers you several other progress line options. For example, if you select the *Display progress lines* option in the *Recurring intervals* section of the dialog, Microsoft Project 2010 allows you to set up recurring progress lines on a daily, weekly, or monthly basis, as shown in Figure 10 - 43. If you select this option, you must also select other relevant information in this section of the dialog. For example, if you select the *Weekly* option, you must select an item in the *Weekly* pick list, and then select the checkbox for at least one day of the week. Beyond this, you must select a *Begin at* option to determine whether the recurring progress line begins on the project start date or on a day you specify manually.

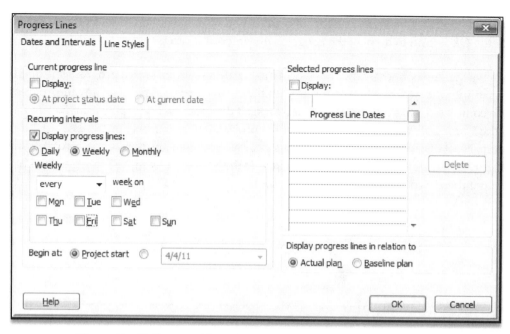

Figure 10 - 43: Progress Lines dialog, select a recurring progress line

Another progress line option in the *Progress Lines* dialog allows you to specify progress lines on **specific dates** in your project, such as on the dates of key milestones. To use this feature, select the *Display* checkbox in the *Selected progress lines* section of the dialog. For each line in the *Progress Line Dates* data grid, select or enter a date for a progress line you want to display in the project. For example, in Figure 10 - 44 notice that I specified a progress line previously on 4/8/11 and I am currently selecting another progress line on 4/15/11.

Because of the visual confusion you may create in a project by displaying multiple progress lines, you may want to delete progress lines that you no longer need. To delete a progress line, select its date in the *Progress Line Dates* data grid and then click the *Delete* button.

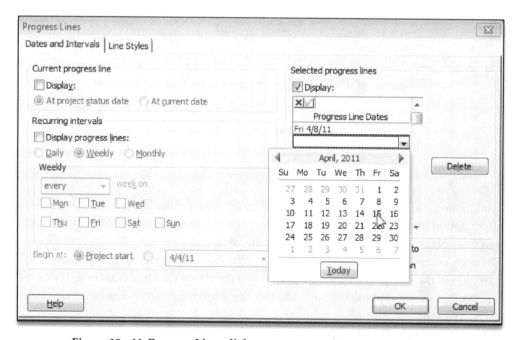

Figure 10 - 44: Progress Lines dialog, set progress lines on specific dates

The final progress lines option you can select on the *Dates and Intervals* page is whether to display progress lines based on current progress or on the baseline schedule of the project. You see these options in the *Display progress lines in relation to* section of the dialog. By default, the system selects the *Actual plan* option, but you may select the *Baseline plan* option instead. With the *Actual plan* option selected, Microsoft Project 2010 displays the progress line(s) based on the current schedule of the project, based on the *Actual Start* and *Actual Finish* dates for each task. If you select the *Baseline plan* option, the system displays the progress line(s) based on the baseline schedule of the project, based on the *Baseline Start* and *Baseline Finish* dates for each task.

After you specify the type of progress line you want to see, click the *Line Styles* tab in the *Progress Lines* dialog to format the display of the progress line. The system displays the *Line Styles* page of the dialog shown in Figure 10 - 45. Using the options on the *Line Styles* page, the system allows you to control the types, shapes, colors, and date display for the progress line as follows:

- In the *Progress line type* section of the dialog, select one of four display types. By default, the system selects the item in the upper left corner of the section.

- In the *Line Style* section of the dialog, select values in the *Line type*, *Line color*, *Progress point shape*, and *Progress point color* pick lists. The system allows you to format the shape and color for the current progress line and for all other progress lines as well.

- In the *Date display* section of the dialog, select the *Show date for each progress line* option to show the date for the progress line at the top of the progress line, directly below the *Timescale* bar. In the *Date display* section, you can also click the *Format* pick list and choose the formatting for the date. Additionally, you can click the *Font* pick list and select the font used for the date displayed on the progress line.

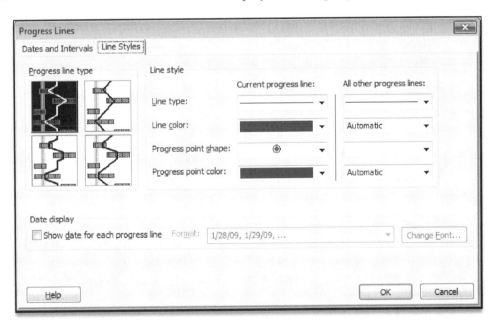

Figure 10 - 45: Progress Lines dialog, Line Styles page

Formatting the Display of Gantt Bars

When you click the *Layout* button, the system displays the *Layout* dialog shown in Figure 10 - 46. You use the options in this dialog to control how Microsoft Project 2010 lays out Gantt bars in any task view, such as in the *Gantt Chart* view.

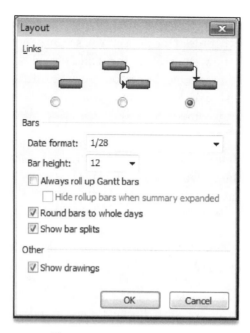

Figure 10 - 46: Layout dialog

The *Layout* dialog contains three sections in which you control how the system displays Gantt bars. In the *Links* section, select one of three options that control how the system displays the link lines between dependent tasks. By default, Microsoft Project 2010 selects the third option (straight link lines), but you can select the second option to display curving link lines, or the first option to display no link lines at all.

The *Bars* section contains a number of available options, including:

- Click the *Date Format* pick list and select the format for dates shown with Gantt bars. For example, the system displays dates to the right of milestone tasks by default.

- Click the *Bar Height* pick list and select a value for the height of each Gantt bar. By default, the system selects a *12* value in the *Bar Height* pick list (medium height). You can increase the value in the *Bar Height* field if you increased the font size for the names of tasks in the task list, or you can decrease the value in the *Bar Height* field if you decrease the font size for tasks.

- Select the *Always roll up Gantt bars* checkbox if you want Microsoft Project 2010 to roll up the Gantt bar symbols on their respective summary task Gantt bars. Figure 10 - 47 shows the Gantt chart for a project with this option selected.

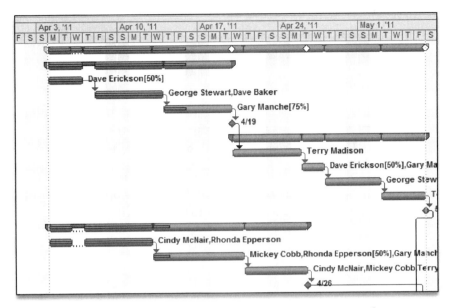

Figure 10 - 47: Gantt bars rolled up to their summary tasks

- If you select the *Always roll up Gantt bars* checkbox, the system activates a second checkbox as well. If you select the *Hide rollup bars when summary expanded* checkbox, the system hides summary Gantt bars when you collapse a summary task, and displays only the rolled up Gantt bars from its subtasks. If you expand a summary task, the system displays only the summary Gantt bar for the summary task. Keep in mind that this behavior is the opposite of how you might expect it to work!

- Use the *Round bars to whole days* option to determine how Microsoft Project 2010 displays the length of the Gantt bar for any task whose duration is not a whole number, for example, a task has a duration of 3.25 days. If you select this option, the system sets the length of the Gantt bar to a rounded duration of 3 days. If you deselect this option, the system sets the length of the Gantt bar to the exact duration value. Keep in mind that this option **does not** affect values in the *Duration*, *Start*, and *Finish* fields for any task; this option only affects how the system displays Gantt bars.

- Select the *Show bar splits* checkbox if you want the system to display the split symbol (...) in the Gantt bars of tasks containing a task split. Task splits usually occur when you enter an *Actual Work* value of *0h* in the timephased grid of either the *Task Usage* or *Resource Usage* view. Entering 0h of actual work indicates that the resource performed no work during the specified time period, such as on a day when the resource called in sick. If you deselect the *Show bar splits* checkbox, Microsoft Project 2010 displays every Gantt bar as a solid bar, even if the task contains a task split. Figure 10 - 48 shows the Gantt bar for a task containing a task split. With the *Show bar splits* checkbox selected, the system displays the task split symbol in the Gantt bar. Figure 10 - 49 shows the same Gantt bar, except with the *Show bar splits* option **deselected**. Notice that you cannot see the task split symbol since the system shows the Gantt bar as a solid bar.

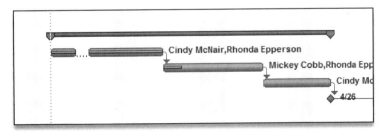

Figure 10 - 48: Show bar splits option selected

491

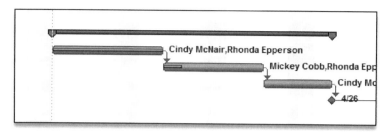

Figure 10 - 49: Show bar splits option deselected

- Select *Show drawings* checkbox if you want to add drawing objects to your Gantt chart using the *Drawing* button in the *Drawings* section of the *Format* ribbon. If you deselect this option, Microsoft Project 2010 disables the *Drawing* button so that you cannot add drawings to the Gantt chart.

When finished, click the *OK* button to close the *Layout* dialog and apply the selected layout options to the *Gantt Chart* view of your project.

Hands On Exercise

Exercise 10-9

Format the text styles, gridlines, and the layout of Gantt bars in the *Gantt Chart* view of a project.

1. Open the **Formatting Views.mpp** sample file.

2. Click the *Format* tab to display the contextual *Format* ribbon with the *Gantt Chart Tools* applied.

3. Click the *Text Styles* button in the *Format* section of the *Format* ribbon.

4. In the *Text Styles* dialog, click the *Item to Change* pick list and select the *Milestone Tasks* item.

5. Click the *Background Color* pick list and select the *Orange, Lighter 80%* color (lightest orange color) in the *Theme Colors* section of the dialog.

6. Click the *OK* button.

Notice how Microsoft Project 2010 formats the cell background color of every milestone task with the light orange color.

7. Click the *Gridlines* pick list button and then click the *Gridlines* item on the list.

8. In the *Gridlines* dialog, select the *Status Date* item at the bottom of the *Line to Change* list.

9. Click the *Type* pick list and select the last item on the list (the -- - -- -- - item).

10. Click the *Color* pick list and select the *Red* color in the *Standard Colors* section of the dialog.

11. Click the *OK* button.

Notice how Microsoft Project 2010 displays the *Status Date* of the project using a red dashed vertical line in the Gantt chart.

12. Click the *Layout* pick list button.

13. In the *Layout* dialog, select the second item in the *Links* section and then click the *OK* button.

Notice how Microsoft Project 2010 changes the straight link lines to the curving link lines for all tasks with dependencies.

14. Save but **do not** close the **Formatting Views.mpp** sample file.

Using the Columns Tools

Earlier in this module, I taught you a number of different ways to insert columns in a default table and view in Microsoft Project 2010. The *Columns* section of the contextual *Format* ribbon provides one more way to insert columns in a table and view. To insert a new column in the *Gantt Chart* view, for example, select the column where you want to insert the new column, and then click the *Insert Column* button. Microsoft Project 2010 inserts a new column to the left of the selected column and displays the list of available task fields, as shown in Figure 10 - 50. To complete the insertion process, scroll the list and select the column you want to insert.

Alternately, you can also type the name of the column you want to insert. When you type the name of a column, the system creates a new custom *Text* field using the name you enter. Because I discussed creating fields previously in this module, I do not discuss this topic again. If necessary, refer back to the *Customizing a Table Using the Add New Column Feature* topical section of this module and review the process for creating custom fields.

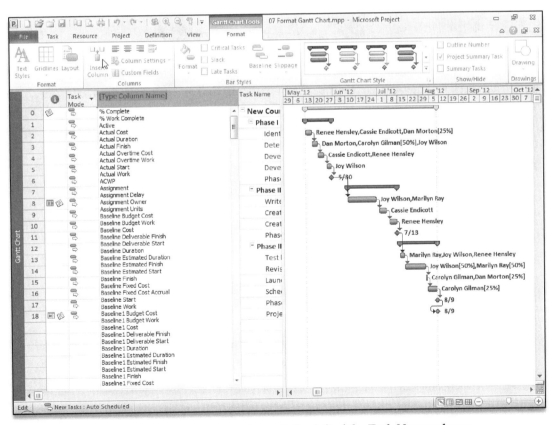

Figure 10 - 50: Insert a new column to the left of the Task Name column

To align the data in any column, select anywhere in a column and then click the *Align Text Left*, *Center*, or *Align Text Right* button. The system changes the alignment of the data in the column, but does not change the alignment of the text in the column header.

To control text wrapping for any column, select anywhere in the column you want to change and then select or deselect the *Wrap Text* button. By default, Microsoft Project 2010 enables the *Wrap Text* feature for only the *Task Names* column in task views and the *Resource Names* column in resource views. With the *Text Wrapping* feature enabled, the system increases the row height of tasks automatically for task names that are longer than the new width of the *Task Name* column.

Before you attempt to use the *Column Settings* pick list button, be certain to select a column in your Microsoft Project 2010 project file. When you click the *Column Settings* pick list button, the system displays the pick list menu shown in Figure 10 - 51.

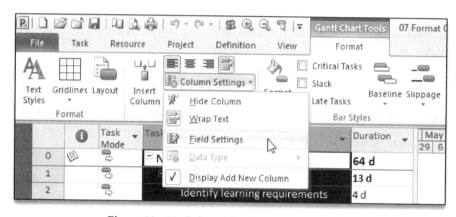

Figure 10 - 51: Column Settings pick list menu

In the *Column Settings* pick list menu, click the *Hide Column* item to hide the selected column. Select or deselect the *Wrap Text* item to enable or disable automatic text wrapping in the selected column. Click the *Field Settings* item to display the *Field Settings* dialog shown in Figure 10 - 52. Because I discussed the *Field Settings* dialog previously in this module, I do not discuss this topic again. If necessary, refer back to the *Customizing a Table Using the Add New Column Feature* topical section of this module and review the information about the *Field Settings* dialog.

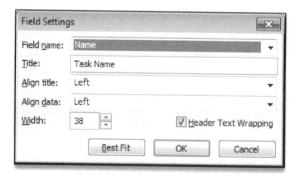

Figure 10 - 52: Field Settings dialog

In the *Column Settings* pick list menu, deselect the *Display Add New Column* item if you do not want to display the *Add New Column* virtual column on the far right side of the current table. You can display or hide the *Add New Column* virtual column for each table individually; however, the system displays the *Add New Column* virtual column in every default table included in Microsoft Project 2010.

Hands On Exercise

Exercise 10-10

Format the columns in the *Gantt Chart* view of a project.

1. Return to the **Formatting Views.mpp** sample file.

2. Click the *Task Mode* column header to select the entire column.

3. Click the *Insert Column* button in the *Columns* section of the *Format* ribbon, and then select the *% Complete* field from the list of available fields.

4. Double-click on the right edge of the *% Complete* column header to "best fit" the column automatically.

5. With the *% Complete* column still selected, click the *Center* button to center the data in the *% Complete* column.

6. With the *% Complete* column still selected, click the *Column Settings* pick list button and then click the *Field Settings* item.

7. In the *Field Settings* dialog, click the *Align Title* pick list and select the *Center* item.

8. Click the *OK* button.

9. Click the *Task Mode* column header to select the entire column.

10. Click the *Column Settings* pick list button and select the *Hide Column* item on the pick list.

11. Save but **do not** close the **Formatting Views.mpp** sample file.

Using the Bar Styles Tools

The *Bar Styles* section of the contextual *Format* ribbon contains a number of powerful tools that allow you to customize the *Gantt Chart* view to show exactly the type of information you want to see. When you click the *Format* pick list button, the system displays two options on the pick list menu: the *Bar* item and the *Bar Styles* item. If you want to format the appearance of individual bars in the *Gantt Chart* view, select the tasks you want to format, then click the *Format* pick list button and select the *Bar* item on the list. Microsoft Project 2010 displays the *Format Bar* dialog shown in Figure 10 - 53.

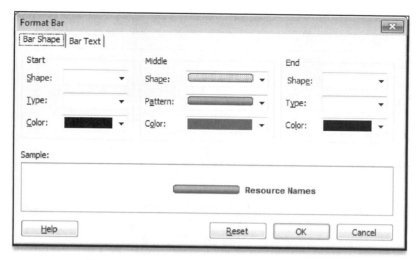

Figure 10 - 53: Format Bar dialog, Bar Shape tab

On the *Bar Shape* tab of the *Format Bar* dialog, the system offers three sections of fields that you use to format the shape and color of the selected Gantt bars. Use the *Shape, Type,* and *Color* pick lists in the *Start* and *End* sections to control the shapes used to draw the start and end of each selected Gantt bar. Use the *Shape, Pattern,* and *Color* pick lists in the *Middle* section to format the middle of the selected Gantt bars. Notice in Figure 10 - 53 shown previously that the Gantt bars for the selected tasks do not contain any start or end shape information. Figure 10 - 54 shows the *Bar Styles* dialog with custom information in the *Start, Middle,* and *End* sections of the dialog.

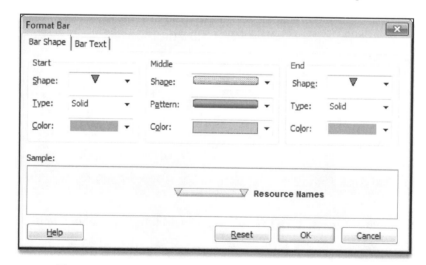

Figure 10 - 54: Format Bar dialog, Bar Shape tab with custom information in the Start, Middle, and End sections

Beyond formatting the shape and color of selected Gantt bars, you can use the *Bar Text* tab in the *Format Bar* dialog to display text information with the selected Gantt bars as well. Figure 10 - 55 shows the *Format Bar* dialog with the *Bar Text* tab selected. By default, Microsoft Project 2010 selects the *Resource Names* field in the *Right* pick list. This causes the system to display the names of assigned resources to the right of Gantt bars for regular tasks. You have the option to remove the *Resource Names* field from the *Right* pick list, if you like, and to select any field in the *Left, Right, Top, Bottom,* and *Inside* fields. For example, to display the *% Complete* field to the left of the selected Gantt bars, click the *Left*

496

pick list and select the *% Complete* field. When finished, click the *OK* button to apply the new formatting to the Gantt bars for the selected tasks.

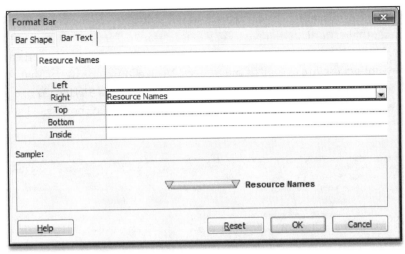

Figure 10 - 55: Format Bar dialog, Bar Text tab

If you want to format all of the Gantt bars in a project in a single action, click the *Format* pick list and select the *Bar Styles* item on the list. The system displays the *Bar Styles* dialog shown in Figure 10 - 56 with the *Manual Task* item selected. This dialog contains the definition of every object shown in the *Gantt Chart* view, including items like Gantt bars for regular tasks and the symbols for milestone tasks and summary tasks. You can change the appearance of an object by selecting its definition row in the *Bar Styles* dialog and then editing the information in the *Start*, *Middle*, and *End* sections of the *Bars* tab at the bottom of the dialog. If you click the *Text* tab in the bottom of the dialog, you see a data grid identical to the one shown on the *Bar Text* tab of the *Format Bar* dialog shown previously in Figure 10 - 55. To change the text displayed with any object, first select the object in the top part of the dialog, and then select the *Text* tab to configure the text information you want to show with the selected object. Click the *OK* button when finished.

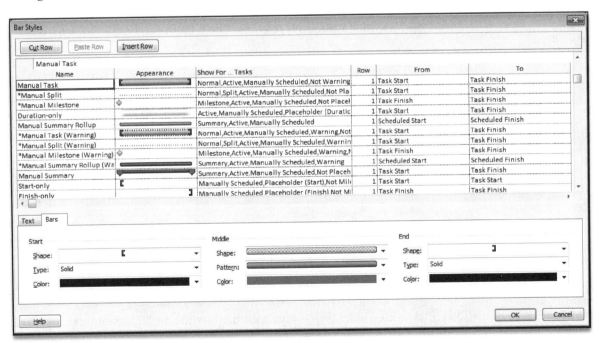

Figure 10 - 56: Bar Styles dialog with Manual Task item selected

As noted previously in Module 08, Project Execution, you can use the checkbox options in the *Bar Styles* section of the contextual *Format* ribbon to display the *Critical Path* in your project. To display the *Critical Path* in your project, select the *Critical Tasks* checkbox in the *Bar Styles* section of the contextual *Format* ribbon. Microsoft Project 2010 formats the *Gantt Chart* view with red bars representing critical tasks, and with blue bars representing non-critical tasks, as shown in Figure 10 - 57. Remember that critical tasks have a *Total Slack* value of *0 days* and cannot slip without changing the finish date of the project. Non-critical tasks have a *Total Slack* value *greater than 0 days* and can slip by the amount of the *Total Slack* before they impact the finish date of the project. Notice in Figure 10 - 57 that the critical path does not begin until the first task in the Phase II section of the plan. This is because of a *Start No Earlier Than* (SNET) constraint on that task, which creates *Total Slack* value *greater than 0 days* for the tasks in the Phase I section of the plan.

		Task Mode	Task Name	Duration
0			− **New Course Development**	**64 d**
1			− **Phase I**	**13 d**
2			Identify learning requirements	4 d
3			Determine target audience	2 d
4			Develop learning objectives	4 d
5			Develop course outline	3 d
6			Phase I Complete	0 d
7			− **Phase II**	**25 d**
8			Write course manual	15 d
9			Create sample files	5 d
10			Create instructor materials	5 d
11			Phase II Complete	0 d
12			− **Phase III**	**19 d**
13			Test beta classes	3 d
14			Revise content based on feedback	10 d
15			Launch marketing campaign	1 d
16			Schedule new classes	5 d
17			Phase III Complete	0 d
18			Project Complete	0 d

Figure 10 - 57: Critical Path displayed in the Gantt Chart view

Warning: Because of an unfixed bug in the release (RTM) version of Microsoft Project 2010, when you select the *Critical Tasks* checkbox on the *Format* ribbon, the system **removes** the names of assigned resources displayed to the right of Gantt bars for critical tasks. To display the names of your assigned resources, double-click anywhere in the white part of the Gantt chart to display the *Bar Styles* dialog. Scroll to the bottom of the list, select the *Critcal* item, and then select the *Text* tab. On the *Text* tab, click the *Right* pick list and select the *Resource Names* field. Click the *OK* button when finished.

To display the *Total Slack* in your project, select the *Slack* checkbox in the *Bar Styles* section of the contextual *Format* ribbon. Microsoft Project 2010 displays a dark blue underscore stripe to the right of the Gantt bar of every task with a *Total Slack* value *greater than 0 days*. Notice in Figure 10 - 58 that both the Phase I summary task and the Phase I Complete milestone task have a *Total Slack* value *greater than 0 days*, indicated by the dark blue underscore stripe to the right of their Gantt bars.

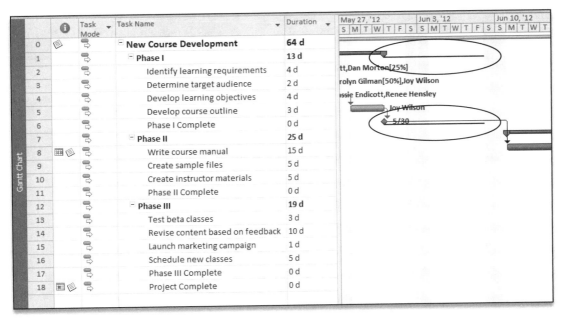

Figure 10 - 58: Total Slack displayed in the Gantt Chart view

In Microsoft Project 2010, a late task is any task whose current *% Complete* value is less than the expected *% Complete* value, as of the *Status Date* value you specify in the project. For example, Figure 10 - 59 shows the project after entering progress for the first week of the project. Notice that the assigned resources did not complete work on the Identify Learning Requirements task as expected. Because the task is not complete by the *Status Date*, indicated by the red dashed line on May 18, the system considers this task a late task.

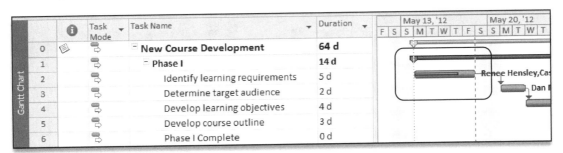

Figure 10 - 59: Progress entered for the first week

To display the *Late* tasks in your project, select the *Late Tasks* checkbox in the *Bar Styles* section of the contextual *Format* ribbon. Microsoft Project 2010 displays *Late* tasks using black Gantt bars, as shown in Figure 10 - 60.

Because the black color used for *Late* tasks make it difficult to see the progress bar (black stripe) in the Gantt bars, MsProjectExperts recommends you change the Gantt bar color to a color other than black. Click the *Format* pick list button and select the *Bar Styles* item on the list. In the *Bar Styles* dialog, scroll down and select the *Late* item in the data grid in the top half of the dialog. Select an alternate color in the *Color* field in the *Middle* section of the *Bars* tab, and click the *OK* button.

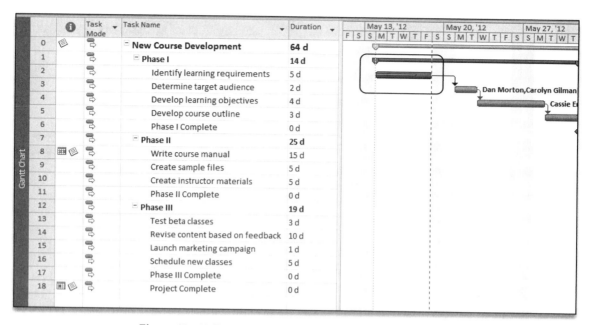

Figure 10 - 60: Late tasks displayed in the Gantt Chart view

As noted previously in Module 08, Project Execution, you can display your operating baseline in the *Gantt Chart* view by clicking the *Baseline* pick list button in the *Bar Styles* section of the contextual *Format* ribbon. The *Baseline* pick list displays a list of eleven available sets of *Baseline* fields, and indicates the save date for each set of *Baseline* fields, as shown in Figure 10 - 61.

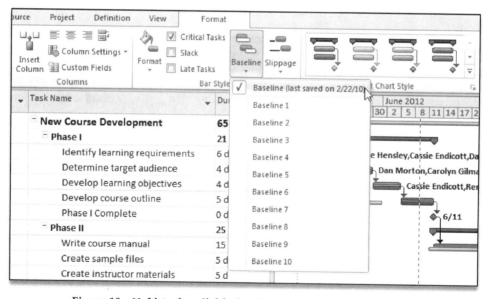

Figure 10 - 61: List of available Baselines on the Baseline pick list

On the *Baseline* pick list, select the baseline you want to show in the *Gantt Chart* view. Microsoft Project 2010 displays the selected baseline information using a gray bar for each task to represent the original baseline schedule for the task, as shown in Figure 10 - 62. After you apply the baseline information to your *Gantt Chart* view, compare the current schedule of each task with its baseline schedule. If the current schedule for any task is to the right of its accompanying gray Gantt bar, then the task is slipping. Notice in Figure 10 - 62 that my project is slipping after entering task progress for the first four weeks of the project.

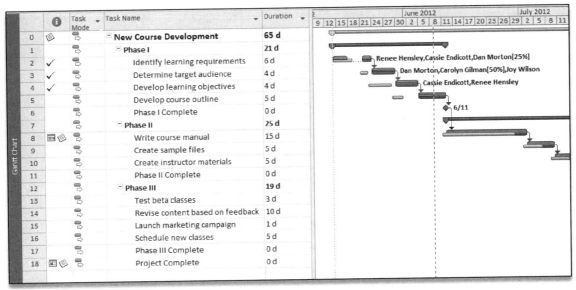

Figure 10 - 62: Baseline schedule applied to the Gantt Chart

To view the current amount of schedule slippage in your *Gantt Chart* view, click the *Slippage* pick list button in the *Bar Styles* section of the contextual *Format* ribbon. The *Slippage* pick list includes the same list of *Baseline* fields as on the *Baseline* pick list shown previously in Figure 10 - 61. Select one of the available sets of *Baseline* fields on the *Slippage* pick list. Microsoft Project 2010 displays a gray underscore stripe to the left of the Gantt bar for every slipping task, as shown in Figure 10 - 63. The length of the *Slippage* indicator represents the amount of slippage for each task.

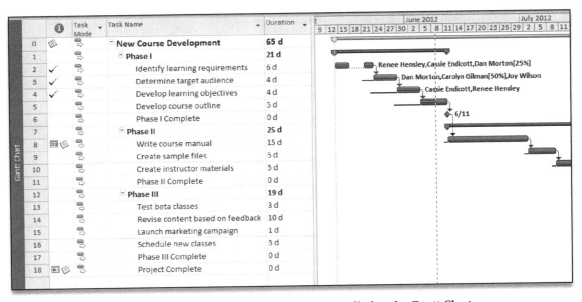

Figure 10 - 63: Slipping task information applied to the Gantt Chart

Using the Gantt Chart Style Tools

The single option in the *Gantt Chart Style* section of the contextual *Format* ribbon allows you to customize the color scheme and appearance of all of the symbols shown in the Gantt chart, including the symbols for regular tasks, summary tasks, milestone tasks, deadline date indicators, and more. To change the color scheme used for every symbol in the Gantt chart, click either the *up-arrow* or *down-arrow* buttons in the *Gantt Chart Style* section to view the list of available color schemes, and then select a color scheme. Alternately, you can click the *More* button directly below the *down-arrow* button to display a list of all available color schemes, as shown in Figure 10 - 64.

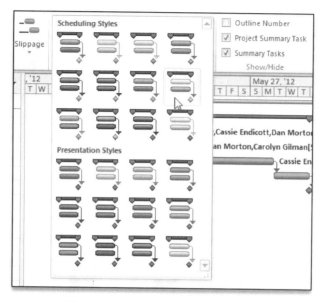

**Figure 10 - 64: Available color styles
in the Gantt Chart Styles pick list**

Notice that the *Gantt Chart Styles* pick list organizes the available color schemes into two sections. Use a color scheme in the *Scheduling Styles* section to format your *Gantt Chart* view for day-to-day project management work. Use a color scheme in the *Presentation Styles* section to format your *Gantt Chart* view for a presentation.

After you select a color scheme on the *Gantt Chart Styles* pick list, you can also click the *Format Bar Styles* dialog launcher icon in the lower right corner of the section, as shown in Figure 10 - 65. The system launches the *Bar Styles* dialog shown previously in Figure 10 - 56, with the selected color scheme applied to objects in the dialog.

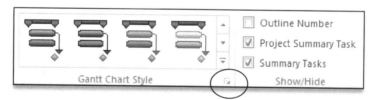

Figure 10 - 65: Format Bar Styles dialog launcher icon

Using the Show/Hide Tools

The *Show/Hide* section of the contextual *Format* ribbon contains three option checkboxes that allow you to show extra detail in the *Task Sheet* part of your *Gantt Chart* view. Unless you specify otherwise in the *Project Options* dialog, the system selects only the *Summary Tasks* option by default in each new project you create. Deselect the *Summary Tasks* option to hide summary tasks in your project temporarily, and to show only regular tasks and milestone tasks in your project, as shown in Figure 10 - 66.

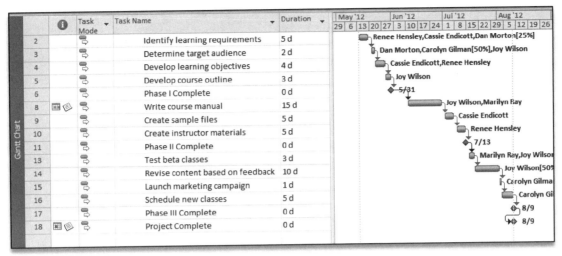

Figure 10 - 66: Summary Tasks option deselected in the Show/Hide section

With the *Summary Tasks* option selected, you can also select the *Project Summary Task* option to display the Project Summary Task (Row 0 or Task 0) in your project. Remember that the Project Summary Task is the highest level summary task in your project, and summarizes all of the information in the project. It shows you the current start date and the current calculated finish date of the project, the current duration of the project, the current amount of work and cost for the project, and shows you all variance for the project as well. Because of this, I strongly recommend you include the Project Summary Task in the *Gantt Chart* view of every project you manage! Figure 10 - 67 shows the Project Summary Task in a project.

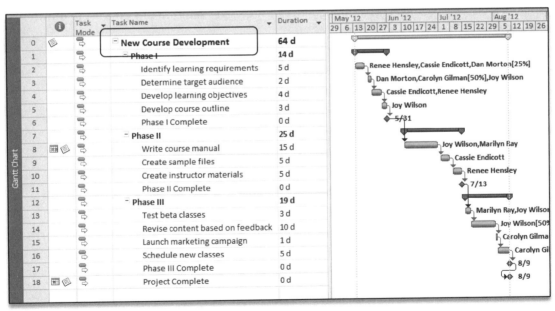

Figure 10 - 67: Project Summary Task option selected in the Show/Hide section

The final option you can select in the *Show/Hide* section of the contextual *Format* ribbon is the *Outline Number* option. When you select this option, Microsoft Project 2010 displays an outline number to the left of each task in the *Task Sheet* part of the *Gantt Chart* view, as shown in Figure 10 - 68.

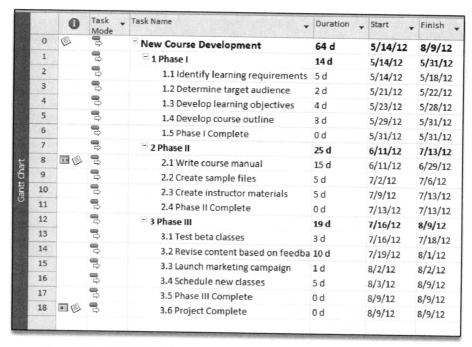

Figure 10 - 68: Outline Number option selected in the Show/Hide section

Using the Drawing Tools

The *Drawing* section of the contextual *Format* ribbon contains a single option. When you click the *Drawing* pick list button, the system displays the pick list shown in Figure 10 - 69. Use the items on this pick list to draw objects in your *Gantt Chart* view.

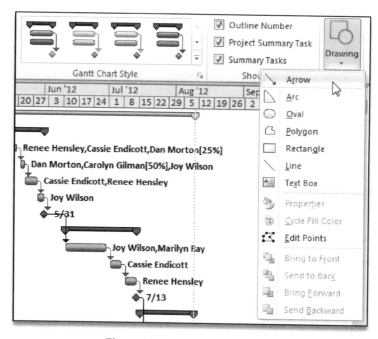

Figure 10 - 69: Drawing pick list

To add a text box drawing to your *Gantt Chart* view, for example, complete the following steps:

1. Click the *Drawing* pick list button and select the *Text Box* item.

Microsoft Project 2010 changes your mouse pointer arrow to a thin crosshair pointer with which to draw the object.

2. Click and hold your mouse button anywhere in the Gantt chart and then drag the crosshair away from the original location, such as dragging down and to the right.

3. Release the mouse button.

The system displays the new text box drawing object in the Gantt chart. The drawing object includes "grab handles" around the outer edge of the drawing object. You can use the "grab handles" to resize the object, if necessary.

4. Click in the center of the text box and type the text you want to display.

5. Resize the text box drawing, if necessary.

6. To move the text box drawing, click and hold on the outer edge of the text box drawing to "grab" it, and then drag and drop it a new location.

7. With the text box drawing selected, click the *Drawing* pick list button and select the *Properties* item on the list.

Microsoft Project 2010 displays the *Format Drawing* dialog with the *Line & Fill* tab selected, as shown in Figure 10 - 70. Use the options in the *Line* and *Fill* sections of the *Line & Fill* tab to change the appearance of the text box drawing. For example, you might click the *Line* pick list in the *Line* section and select a thicker line. You might click the *Color* pick list in the *Fill* section and select a background color such as yellow.

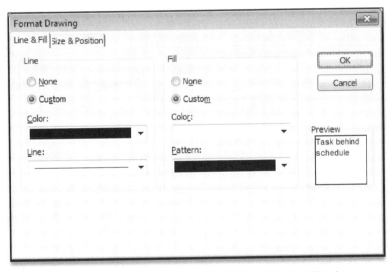

Figure 10 - 70: Format Drawing dialog, Line & Fill tab

If you click the *Size & Position* tab in the *Format Drawing* dialog, the system displays the *Size & Position* options shown in Figure 10 - 71. The options on the *Size & Position* tab allow you to "anchor" the text box drawing in the Gantt chart by attaching the drawing to a date on the timescale, or by attaching the drawing to a specific task. If you attach the drawing to the timescale, the system allows you to specify the distance of the drawing from the timescale by entering a value in the *Vertical* field. If you select the *Attach to task* option, you must manually enter the ID number of the task in the *ID* field, and specify an *Attachment point* option to determine whether to attach the drawing at the left or right end of the Gantt bar. The system also allows you to enter values in the *Horizontal* and *Vertical* fields to determine the distance of the drawing from the selected Gantt bar. Additionally, you can also enter values in the *Height* and *Width* fields in the *Size* section of the dialog to manually control the size of the drawing. Click the *OK* button when finished to format the new text box drawing according to your specifications.

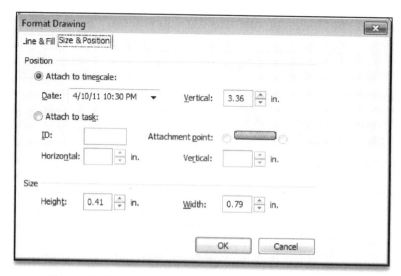

Figure 10 - 71: Format Drawing dialog, Size & Position tab

Figure 10 - 72 shows the *Gantt Chart* view of a project after I created a text box drawing and an arrow drawing. Together, these two drawing objects point to a task whose progress is currently behind schedule. Notice in the project that I also displayed the *Status Date* gridline using a red dashed line.

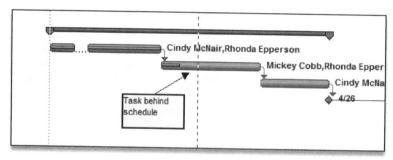

Figure 10 - 72: Text box drawing and arrow drawing
point to a task whose progress is behind schedule

Hands On Exercise

Exercise 10-11

Format the objects displayed in the *Gantt Chart* view of a project.

1. Return to the **Formatting Views.mpp** sample file.

2. In the *Bar Styles* section of the *Format* ribbon, select the *Critical Tasks* option.

3. Scroll through the Gantt chart and look for critical tasks (tasks with red Gantt bars).

4. Leave the *Critical Tasks* option selected and then select the *Slack* option.

5. Scroll through the Gantt chart and look for tasks with slack (tasks with a dark blue underscore stripe to the right of the Gantt bar).

6. Click the *Baseline* pick list button and select the *Baseline* item (the first baseline item listed).

7. Scroll through the Gantt chart and look for the baseline schedule of each task (gray Gantt bars).

8. Click the *Slippage* pick list button and select the *Baseline* item (the first Baseline listed).

9. Scroll through the Gantt chart and look for slipping tasks (tasks with a dark blue underscore stripe to the left of the Gantt bar).

10. In the *Gantt Chart Style* section of the *Format* ribbon, click the *More* button to see the complete list of styles available.

11. In the *Presentation Styles* section of the menu, select the second style in the first row (light blue Gantt bars).

12. In the *Bar Styles* section of the *Format* ribbon, click the *Format* pick list button and select the *Bar Styles* item to open the *Bar Styles* dialog.

13. In the *Bar Styles* dialog, select the *Critical* item and then click the *Text* tab in the bottom of the dialog.

14. Click the *Right* pick list and select the *Resource Names* field.

15. Click the *OK* button.

Note: As a result of an unfixed bug in the release (RTM) version of Microsoft Project 2010, you must complete steps #13-15 to display the assigned resources to the right of each red Gantt bar.

16. In the *Show/Hide* section of the *Format* ribbon, select the *Outline Number* option.

Notice how Microsoft Project 2010 displays the *Outline Number* value to the left of each task in the *Task Name* field.

17. Save but **do not** close the **Formatting Views.mpp** sample file.

Customizing the Team Planner View

In Module 07, Project Assignment Planning, I taught you how to use the new *Team Planner* view in Microsoft Project 2010. To customize this view, apply the *Team Planner* view and then click the *Format* tab. The system displays the contextual *Format* ribbon with the *Team Planner Tools* applied, as shown in Figure 10 - 73.

Figure 10 - 73: Format ribbon with the Team Planner Tools applied

507

Click the *Roll-Up* pick list button and select the level of WBS information to display for each Gantt bar shown in the *Team Planner* view. By default, the system selects the *All Subtasks* item on the *Roll-Up* pick list. When I created my project, I set it up so that summary tasks at *Outline Level 1* represent phases and summary tasks at *Outline Level 2* represent deliverables. Figure 10 - 74 shows the *Team Planner* view after selecting the *Outline Level 1* item on the *Roll-Up* pick list. Notice that Microsoft Project 2010 displays the name of each *Outline Level 1* summary task (the phases) as Gantt bars in the *Team Planner* view. Notice also that the software displays the selected outline level for the *Team Planner* view with an indicator at the left end of the *Status* bar at the bottom of the application window.

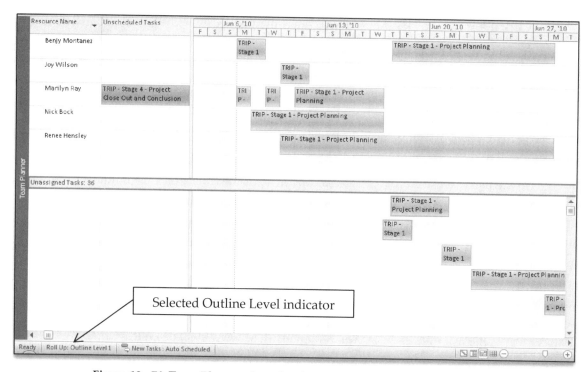

Figure 10 - 74: Team Planner view showing Outline Level 1 task information

Microsoft Project 2010 allows you to customize the display of gridlines and text in the *Team Planner* view. To change the gridline display, click the *Gridlines* button in the *Format* ribbon. The system displays the *Gridlines* dialog shown in Figure 10 - 75. In the *Gridlines* dialog, select an item in the *Line to Change* list and select the formatting on the *Type* and *Color* pick lists. When finished, click the *OK* button to apply the gridline formatting.

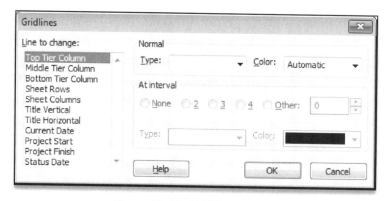

Figure 10 - 75: Gridlines dialog

To display the *Status Date* as a red dashed line in the *Team Planner* view, select the *Status Date* item in the *Line to Change* list, select the last item on the *Type* pick list, and choose the *Red* color on the *Color* pick list.

To customize how the software displays text in the *Team Planner* view, click the *Text Styles* button on the *Format* ribbon. The system displays the *Text Styles* dialog shown in Figure 10 - 76. In the *Text Styles* dialog, click the *Item to Change* pick list and choose a text style to format, and then select your desired formatting information for the selected text style in the other fields in the dialog. Click the *OK* button when finished.

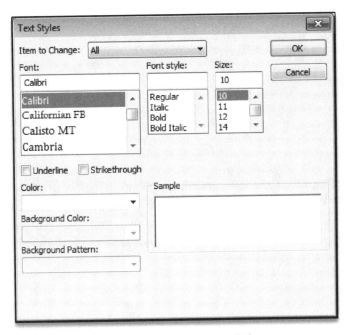

Figure 10 - 76: Text Styles dialog

Microsoft Project 2010 also allows you to format the colors of the Gantt bars shown in the *Team Planner* view. Notice in the *Format* ribbon shown previously in Figure 10 - 73 that the *Styles* section includes the *Selected Tasks*, *Auto Scheduled*, *Manually Scheduled*, *Actual Work*, *External Tasks*, and *Late Tasks* pick list buttons. To change the formatting of an individual Gantt bar or group of Gantt bars, select the Gantt bars you want to format and then click the *Selected Tasks* pick list button. To change the Gantt bars for a particular type of tasks, such as *Manually Scheduled* tasks, click the pick list button for the type of task whose Gantt bar you want to format. When you click the pick list button, the system displays a pick list of available formatting items. Notice in Figure 10 - 77, for example, that I want to change the *Fill Color* value for all *Manually Scheduled* tasks.

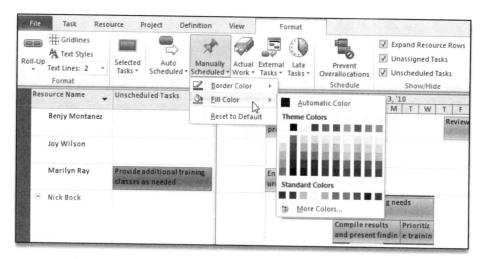

Figure 10 - 77: Format the Fill Color for Manually Scheduled tasks

To change the formatting for Gantt bars, the software allows you to specify both a *Border Color* value and a *Fill Color* value from a palette of values. With the exception of the *Selected Tasks* pick list, all of the other pick lists in the *Styles* section of the *Format* ribbon contain a *Reset to Default* item as well. If you change the color of any type of Gantt bar, and want to restore the original default value, simply select the *Reset to Default* item on the appropriate pick list.

As you format the *Team Planner* view for your project, Microsoft Project 2010 also allows you to determine which items to display in this view. The *Show/Hide* section of the *Format* ribbon offers three option checkboxes that control the items you see in the *Team Planner* view. By default, the software selects the *Expand Resource Rows* option so that you see the Gantt bars for parallel tasks on separate rows for each resource. For example, in the *Team Planner* view shown previously in Figure 10 - 77, the system shows two rows of tasks for Nick Bock, indicating parallel tasks occurring during the same time periods. If you deselect the *Expand Resource Rows* option, the system displays all tasks on a single row for each resource, and "stacks" Gantt bars on top of each other, as shown in Figure 10 - 78. Although deselecting this option may save vertical screen space, you may find it difficult to read the text contained in Gantt bars stacked on top of each other.

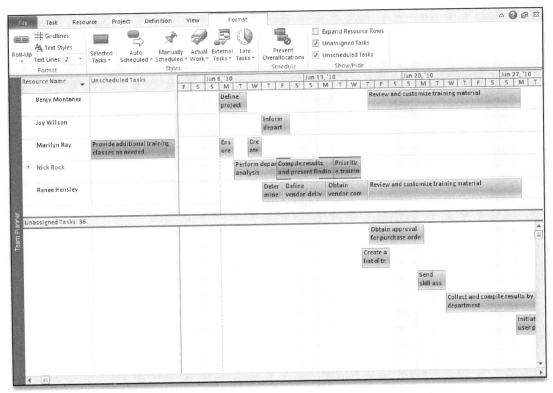

**Figure 10 - 78: Expand Resource Names option deselected,
Gantt bars stacked on a single row for each resource**

You can also collapse parallel tasks onto one row for any resource by clicking the *Expand/Collapse* indicator to the left of the resource's name. For example, notice the *Expand/Collapse* indicator to the left of Nick Bock's name in Figure 10 - 78.

Microsoft Project 2010 also allows you to determine which type of tasks to display. By default, the software selects the *Unassigned Tasks* and *Unscheduled Tasks* options in the *Show/Hide* section of the *Format* ribbon. If you do not want to see the *Unassigned Tasks* pane in the bottom half of the *Team Planner* view, deselect the *Unassigned Tasks* option. If you do not want to see the *Unscheduled Tasks* column in the *Team Planner* view, deselect the *Unscheduled Tasks* option. Figure 10 - 79 shows the *Team Planner* view with the *Unassigned Tasks* and *Unscheduled Tasks* options deselected in the *Show/Hide* section of the *Format* ribbon.

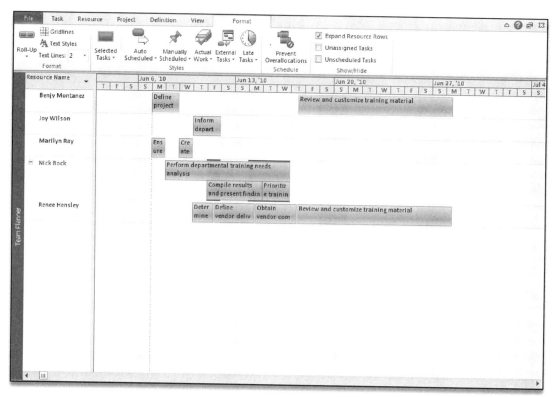

**Figure 10 - 79: Team Planner view with
Unassigned Tasks and Unscheduled Tasks hidden**

A final formatting option in the *Team Planner* view is not obvious: zooming the Timescale in the Gantt chart portion of the view. As I stated earlier in this section, Microsoft Project 2010 zooms the *Timescale* to the *Weeks Over Days* level of zoom. You can display any level of zoom you wish. Click the *View* tab and then click the *Zoom* pick list button in the *Zoom* section of the *View* ribbon to zoom in or zoom out as needed.

Hands On Exercise

Exercise 10-12

Customize the *Team Planner* view.

1. Open the **Using the Team Planner View.mpp** sample file.

2. Click the *Resource* tab to display the *Resource* ribbon and then click the *Team Planner* button in the *View* section of the ribbon.

3. Click the *Format* tab to display the contextual *Format* ribbon with the *Team Planner Tools* applied.

4. In the Gantt chart part of the *Team Planner* view, scroll to the week of September 8, 2013.

5. In the *Format* section of the *Format* ribbon, click the *Roll Up* pick list and select the *Outline Level 1* item on the list.

Notice how Microsoft Project 2010 displays the first-level summary tasks (Phases) for each resource in the *Team Planner* view.

6. Click the *Roll Up* pick list again and select the *All Subtasks* item on the list.

7. In the *Styles* section of the *Format* ribbon, click the *Manually Scheduled* pick list, select the *Fill Color* item, and then select a light green color on the color palette.

Notice how Microsoft Project 2010 changed the fill color for the *Manually Scheduled* task assigned to Marilyn Ray.

8. Click the *Manually Scheduled* pick list again and select the *Reset to Default* item on the list.

9. In the *Schedule* section of the *Format* ribbon, click the *Prevent Overallocations* button.

10. Scroll to the week of October 6, 2013 and locate the *Determine course dates, start and end times, and locations* task, currently assigned to Dan Morton.

11. Select the *Determine course dates, start and end times, and locations* task, then drag and drop the Gantt bar to George Stewart. **Note:** Be sure to keep the same time schedule for the task and drop the Gantt bar **on top of** the Gantt bar of George Stewart's existing task.

With the *Prevent Overallocations* button selected, notice how Microsoft Project 2010 immediately leveled the new resource overallocation for George Stewart.

12. In the *Show/Hide* section of the *Format* ribbon, deselect the *Unscheduled Tasks* checkbox.

Notice that Microsoft Project 2010 hides the *Unscheduled Tasks* column in the *Resources* pane.

13. Save and close the **Using the Team Planner View.mpp** sample file.

Formatting Other Views

As I noted in Module 02, Microsoft Project 2010 offers a contextual *Format* ribbon for every view in the system. When you select any view and click the contextual *Format* ribbon, the ribbon contains a set of options unique to the selected view. For example, if you select the *Task Usage* view, the system displays the contextual *Format* ribbon with the *Task Usage Tools* applied, as shown in Figure 10 - 80. With the *Task Usage* view displayed, the contextual *Format* ribbon contains several of the same sections shown for the *Gantt Chart* view, and contains two additional sections as well.

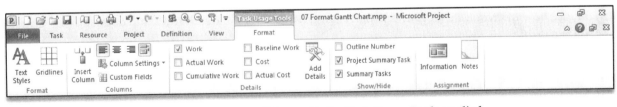

Figure 10 - 80: Format ribbon with the Task Usage Tools applied

The *Details* section contains six option checkboxes that control the details (rows) displayed in the timephased grid on the right side of the view (gray and white timesheet-like grid). By default, Microsoft Project 2010 selects only the *Work* option, which displays only the *Work* details in the timephased grid. Select additional checkboxes in the *Details* section as you require. To choose from a complete list of details available for the timephased grid, click the *Add Details* button in the *Details* section. The system displays the *Detail Styles* dialog, in which you can select from a complete list of rows for the timephased grid. Because the *Detail Styles* dialog is the same dialog found in previous versions of Microsoft Project, I do not discuss this feature.

When you select a resource assignment (italicized resource name below a task) in the *Task Usage* view, the system activates the two buttons in the *Assignment* section of the contextual *Format* tab. Click the *Information* button to display the *Assignment Information* dialog for the selected resource assignment. To add a note to a resource assignment, click the *Notes* button to display the *Assignment Information* dialog with the *Notes* tab selected. Because these dialogs are the same as in previous versions of Microsoft Project, I do not discuss these two features.

> The contextual *Format* ribbon for the *Resource* view is identical to the ribbon shown for the *Task Usage* view. This is because both of these views are assignment views that display assignment information, along with a timephased grid on the right side of the view.

I do not discuss the contextual *Format* ribbon for every view in Microsoft Project 2010. However, the information in this module can serve as an effective guide for you to format any view in the software.

Hands On Exercise

Exercise 10-13

Format the *Task Usage* view of a project.

1.   Return to the **Formatting Views.mpp** sample file, if necessary.

2.   Click the *View* tab and then click the *Task Usage* button in the *Task Views* section of the *View* ribbon.

3.   Click the *Format* tab to display the contextual *Format* ribbon with the *Task Usage Tools* applied.

4.   In the *Details* section of the *Format* ribbon, select the *Actual Work* and *Baseline Work* details.

Notice how Microsoft Project 2010 displays these two additional detail rows in the timephased grid on the right side of the *Task Usage* view.

5.   Double-click on the right edge of the *Details* column header in the timephased grid to "best fit" the column automatically.

6.   Click the *Add Details* button in the *Details* section of the *Format* ribbon.

7.   In the *Detail Styles* dialog, select the *Actual Work* item in the *Show these fields* list and then click the *Hide* button.

8.   In the *Available fields* list, select the *Cost* field, click the *Show* button, and then click the *OK* button.

9.   Save and close the **Formatting Views.mpp** sample file.

Module 11

Printing Views, Reports, and Visual Reports

Learning Objectives

After completing this module, you will be able to:

- Print default views and reports
- Create custom reports
- View and modify Visual Reports
- Create custom Visual Reports

Inside Module 11

More about Project Reporting

In Module 10, Reporting, I presented a number of methods for reporting project progress in Microsoft Project 2010. This module presents several additional methods for reporting, including the following:

- Printing default and custom views

- Printing default and custom reports

- Creating custom reports

- Creating Visual Reports in either Microsoft Excel or Microsoft Visio

I discuss each of these topics individually.

Printing Views

In Microsoft Project 2010, you can print any default or custom view by clicking the *File* tab and then clicking the *Print* tab in the *Backstage* menu. The system displays the *Print* page of the *Backstage* as shown in Figure 11 - 1. The system divides the *Print* page into two panes. In the left pane, you can set printing options; in the right pane you see a print preview of the project.

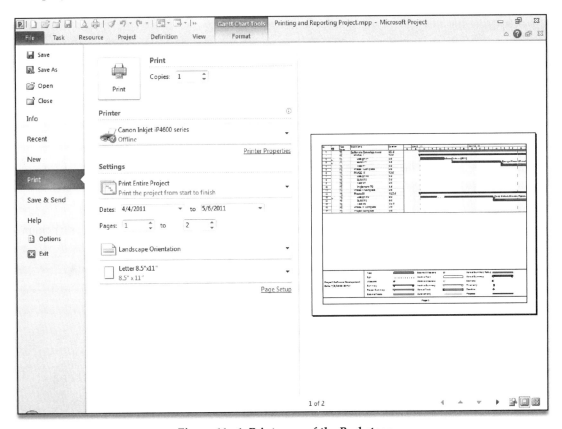

Figure 11 - 1: Print page of the Backstage

On the *Print* page, you can control any of the following printing options:

- Specify the number of copies to print in the *Copies* field.

- Select an available printer in the *Printer* pick list.

- Set printer options by clicking the *Printer Properties* link.

- Specify the date range for printing project information by clicking the *Settings* pick list and choosing a pre-defined date range.

- Manually enter a date range in the *Dates* and *To* fields.

- Specify the number of pages to print by selecting a value in the *Pages* and *To* fields.

- Specify the orientation of the printout on the *Print Orientation* pick list.

- Specify the paper size on the *Paper Size* pick list.

- Display the *Page Setup* dialog by clicking the *Page Setup* link.

- View the print preview of the project on the right side of the page.

- Navigate in the print preview using the buttons in the lower right corner of the page.

Warning: In the print preview pane, you may notice that you do not see all of the columns that you expect the software to print. One of the issues you may face when printing a view is that Microsoft Project 2010 prints only those columns that are **completely visible** in the *Task Sheet* portion of the view. Therefore, before printing any view, confirm that all of the columns you want to print are completely visible. This means you may need to drag the split bar to the right to expose a column completely for printing.

Using Page Setup

To customize the printout of your view, you may want to specify additional settings in the *Page Setup* dialog. To access the *Page Setup* dialog, click the *Page Setup* link in the *Print* page of the *Backstage*. Microsoft Project 2010 displays the *Page Setup* dialog with the *Page* tab selected, as shown in Figure 11 - 2.

Figure 11 - 2: Page Setup dialog, Page options

Table 11 - 1 through Table 11 - 6 display and describe the options available on each tab of the *Page Setup* dialog. Figures 11-3 to 11-8 show each page of the *Page Setup* dialog.

Page options	
Orientation	Select the *Portrait* or *Landscape* option.
Scaling	Use the *Adjust to* option to reduce or enlarge the printed image. Use the *Fit to* option to scale the printed view to a specific number of pages.
Other	Set the *Paper Size* option. Set the *First page number* option.

Table 11 - 1: Page options

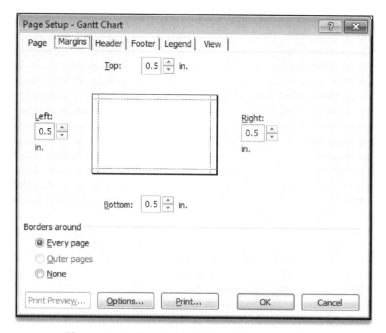

Figure 11 - 3: Page Setup dialog, Margins options

Margins options	
Margins	Set the top, bottom, left, and right margins.
Borders around	Place borders around every page, outer pages only, or no pages.

Table 11 - 2: Margins options

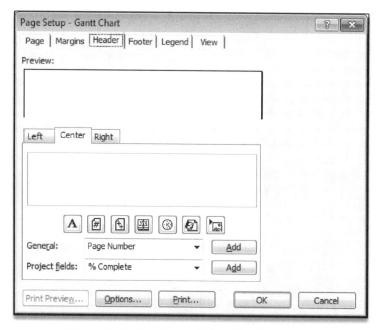

Figure 11 - 4: Page Setup dialog, Header options

Header options	
Preview	Displays a print preview of the completed header (the preview is not to scale).
Alignment	Enter up to five lines of text, field codes, or project information in the *Left*, *Center*, and *Right* tab sections using the *General* and *Project fields* pick lists.
	Click the buttons to format text or to add information such as page number, total number of pages, date and time stamps, file name, or clipart images.

Table 11 - 3: Header options

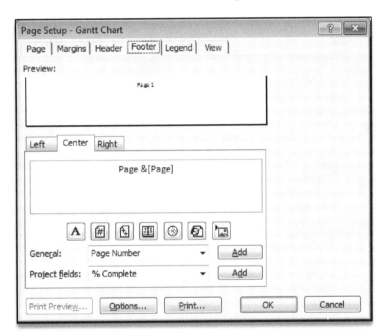

Figure 11 - 5: Page Setup dialog, Footer options

Footer options	
Preview	Displays a print preview of the completed footer (the preview is not to scale).
Alignment	Enter up to three lines of text, field codes, or project information in the *Left*, *Center*, and *Right* tab sections using the *General* and *Project fields* pick lists.
	Click the buttons to format text or to add information such as page number, total number of pages, date and time stamps, file name, or clipart images.

Table 11 - 4: Footer options

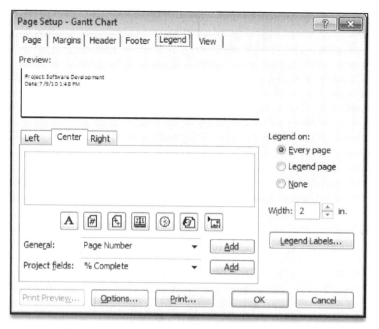

Figure 11 - 6: Page Setup dialog, Legend options

Legend options	
Preview	Displays a print preview of the completed legend text (the preview is not to scale).
Alignment	Enter up to three lines of text, field codes, or project information in the *Left*, *Center*, and *Right* tab sections using the *General* and *Project fields* pick lists.
	Click the buttons to format text or to add information such as page number, total number of pages, date and time stamps, file name, or clipart images.
Legend on	Print the legend on every page, on a separate legend page, or select the *None* option to prevent the legend from printing.
	Specify a value up to *5 inches* in the *Width* field to control the width of the text section on the left side of the legend.
Legend Labels	Click the *Legend Labels* button to change the font for the legend text.

Table 11 - 5: Legend options

You see the legend at the bottom of the printed page when printing the *Network Diagram* view or any view that includes a Gantt chart, such as the *Tracking Gantt* view. The legend includes a text section on the left side where you can include custom information.

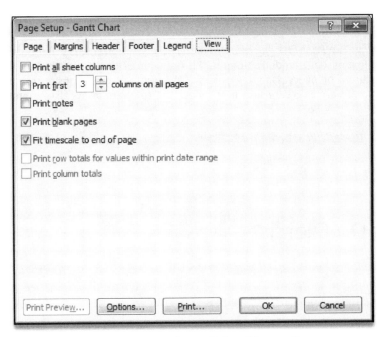

Figure 11 - 7: Page Setup dialog, View options

Microsoft Project 2010 enables the last two options on the *View* page when printing either the *Task Usage* view or the *Resource Usage* view. For all other views, the software disables these two options.

View options	
Print all sheet columns	Print all columns in the table regardless of how many are currently visible in the view.
Print first ___ columns on all pages	Print a specific number of columns on every page.
Print notes	Print all task notes on a separate page at the end of the printout.
Print blank pages	Print the blank pages in large *Network Diagram* view.
Fit timescale to end of page	Fit the timescale in the available space on each page.
Print row total for values within print date range	Print a total value at the right end of each row for only the selected date range.
Print column totals	Print a total at the bottom of each column.

Table 11 - 6: View options

Important Note: The *Print first ___ columns on all pages* option solves the problem of Microsoft Project 2010 not printing partially-hidden columns. This option guarantees that the software prints the selected number of columns on **every page**, regardless of the number of columns presently visible in the view. If additional columns are entirely visible in the view, the software prints all of them, but only on the first page.

Hands On Exercise

Exercise 11-1

Use the *Page Setup* dialog to print a specific number of columns in a view in the Training Advisor Rollout project.

1. Open the **Training Advisor 11.mpp** sample file.

2. Drag the vertical split bar slightly to the left to cover up half of the *Duration* column.

3. Click the *File* tab and then click the *Print* tab in the *Backstage* menu.

Notice that Microsoft Project 2010 does not display the *Duration* column in the *Print Preview* pane. Remember that this is because you hid half of the column.

4. In the *Print* page of the *Backstage*, click the *Page Setup* link to display the *Page Setup* dialog.

5. Click the *View* tab in the *Page Setup* dialog.

6. Select the *Print first __ columns on all pages* option and then set this option to *5 columns*.

7. Click the *OK* button to return to the *Print* page of the *Backstage*.

Notice in the print preview pane that the software displays the *Duration* column. This is because you selected the *Print first 5 columns* option on the *View* tab of the *Page Setup* dialog.

Exercise 11-2

Use the *Page Setup* dialog to add one or more notes pages when you print the *Gantt Chart* view.

1. In the *Print* page of the *Backstage,* click the *Page Setup* link to display the *Page Setup* dialog.

2. Click the *View* tab in the *Page Setup* dialog.

3. Select the *Print notes* option.

4. Click the *OK* button to return to the *Print* page of the *Backstage*.

5. In the print preview pane, click the *Page Right* button 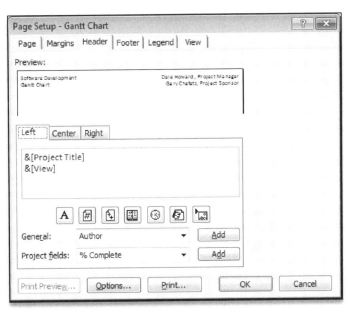 until you see the notes page.

6. Click anywhere in the notes page to zoom in and see larger text in the print preview pane.

Notice that the notes page displays every task with a note, and displays the full text of each note, including bullets.

7. Scroll left and right in the print preview pane, as needed, to ready the text of the notes.

8. Click the *File* tab to close the *Print* page in the *Backstage*.

9. Save but **do not** close the **Training Advisor 11.mpp** sample file.

Creating a Header or Footer

Creating a header or footer in a printed view is similar to the process for creating a header or footer in Microsoft Excel. To create a header or footer, complete the following steps:

1. Display the *Page Setup* dialog.

2. Select either the *Header* or the *Footer* tab.

3. Click the *Left*, *Center*, or *Right* tab in the page.

4. Click the *General* pick list, select a field, and then click the *Add* button.

5. Click the *Project fields* pick list, select a field, and then click the *Add* button.

6. Click one of the buttons at the bottom of the *Alignment* section to insert additional information, such as page numbers or the current date.

Figure 11 - 8 and Figure 11 - 9 show a custom header I set up for the *Gantt Chart* view. Figure 11 - 8 shows the left-aligned header information, while Figure 11 - 9 shows the right-aligned header information. Notice that the left-aligned header includes the project title and the current view, while the right-aligned header contains the name of the project manager (indicated by the *[Author]* field) and the project sponsor (indicated by the *[Manager]* field).

Figure 11 - 8: Page Setup dialog
Left section of Header page

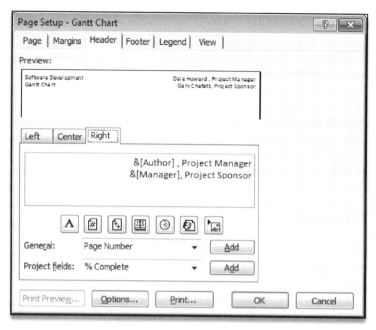

Figure 11 - 9: Page Setup dialog
Right section of Header page

Use exactly the same process to enter custom legend information on the *Legend* page of the *Page Setup* dialog.

Hands On Exercise

Exercise 11-3

Use the *Page Setup* dialog to create a custom header for the *Gantt Chart* view.

1. Return to the **Training Advisor 11.mpp** sample file.

2. Click the *File* tab and then click the *Print* tab in the *Backstage* menu.

3. In the *Print* page of the *Backstage*, click the *Page Setup* link to display the *Page Setup* dialog.

4. Click the *Header* tab in the *Page Setup* dialog and then click the *Center* tab, if necessary.

5. Click the *General* pick list, select the *Project Title* item, and then click the *Add* button.

6. Click in the text area to the right of the *& [Project Title]* field and then press the **Enter** key on the keyboard.

7. Click the *General* pick list, select the *Author* item, and then click the *Add* button.

8. Click in the text area to the right of the *& [Author]* field and then press the **Enter** key on the keyboard.

9. Click the *Insert Current Date* button ⊞ to insert the *Date* field.

10. Click the *OK* button to view the new header in the print preview pane.

11. In the print preview pane, click in the header area of the print preview to zoom in and read the text of the new custom header.

12. Click the *File* tab to close the *Print* page in the *Backstage*.

13. Save but **do not** close the **Training Advisor 11.mpp** sample file.

Setting Print Options

After you select your desired options in the *Page Setup* dialog, you are ready to set up print options. To set up your print options and then print your view, complete the following steps:

1. Click the *File* tab and then click the *Print* tab in the *Backstage* menu.

2. In the left side of the *Print* page, select your desired printing options as follows:

   • Click the *Printer* pick list and select the desired printer.

   • Click the *Printer Properties* link and set up the printer to print your view.

   • Click the *Date Range* pick list button and select a pre-defined date range. The pre-defined date range options include *Print Entire Project*, *Print Specific Dates*, *Print Specific Pages*, and *Print Custom Dates and Pages*. The *Settings* pick list includes additional options to include a notes page, to print all columns in the current table, and to print the left columns of each page.

   • If you do not select a pre-defined date range, you can manually enter a date range in the *Dates* and *To* fields.

   • Specify the number of pages to print by entering values in the *Pages* and *To* fields.

   • Specify the orientation of the printout on the *Print Orientation* pick list button.

   • Specify the paper size on the *Paper Size* pick list button.

3. Click the *Print* button.

Hands On Exercise

Exercise 11-4

Remove the legend section from the bottom of the page and then print a selected date range for the *Gantt Chart* view.

1. Return to the **Training Advisor 11.mpp** sample file.

2. Click the *File* tab and then click the *Print* tab in the *Backstage* menu.

3. Click the *Page Setup* link to display the *Page Setup* dialog.

4. In the *Page Setup* dialog, click the *Legend* tab.

5. On the *Legend* page of the dialog, select the *None* option in the *Legend on* section on the right side of the dialog, and then click the *OK* button.

6. In the *Print* page of the *Backstage*, click the *Date Range* pick list button and select the *Print Specific Dates* item on the list.

7. Click the *Dates* pick list and select the *1/6/2014* date.

8. Click the *To* pick list and select the *1/31/14* date.

Notice that the print preview pane displays only that portion of the *Gantt Chart* view between your two selected dates.

9. If you have a printer available, click the *Print* button to print the customized *Gantt Chart* view of your project.

10. Save but **do not** close the **Training Advisor 11**.mpp sample file.

The changes you make in the *Page Setup* dialog and the *Print* page become part of the view currently applied. If you want these changes to apply to every current and future project, click the *Organizer* button on the *Info* page of the *Backstage* and then copy the current view from the active project (on the right side of the dialog) to your Global.mpt file (on the left side of the dialog).

Printing Reports

Besides printing default and custom views, Microsoft Project 2010 also allows you to print default and custom reports. The system includes six categories of default reports, with the option to create additional custom reports as needed. To print a report, complete the following steps:

1. Click the *Project* tab to display the *Project* ribbon.

2. Click the *Reports* button in the *Reports* section of the *Project* ribbon. The system displays the *Reports* dialog shown in Figure 11 - 10.

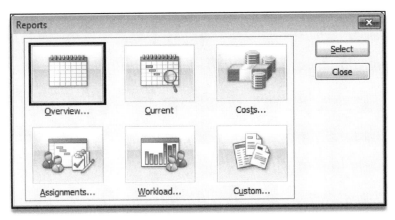

Figure 11 - 10: Reports dialog

3. Select a report category, such as the *Overview* category, and then click the *Select* button. You can also double-click the report category icon to select your desired category. If you selected the *Overview* category, Microsoft Project 2010 displays the *Overview Reports* dialog shown in Figure 11 - 11.

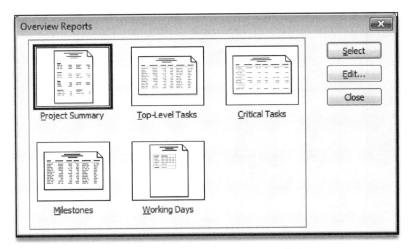

Figure 11 - 11: Overview Reports dialog

4. Select one of the *Overview* reports, such as the *Project Summary* report, and then click the *Select* button. You can also double-click the report icon to select your desired report. The system displays the *Print* page in the *Backstage*, with the report shown in the print preview pane, as shown in Figure 11 - 12.

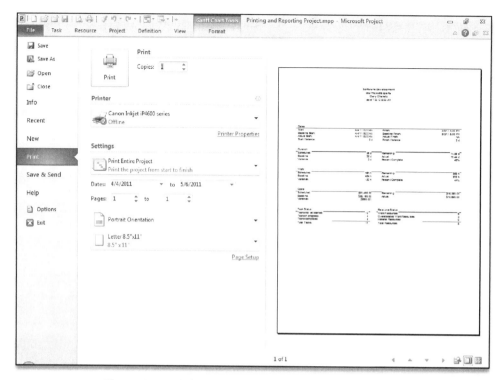

**Figure 11 - 12: Print page in the Backstage, print preview
pane shows the Project Summary Report**

5. Click anywhere in the print preview pane to zoom into that area of the report. Figure 11 - 13 shows the print preview pane after zooming into the top area of the *Project Summary* report.

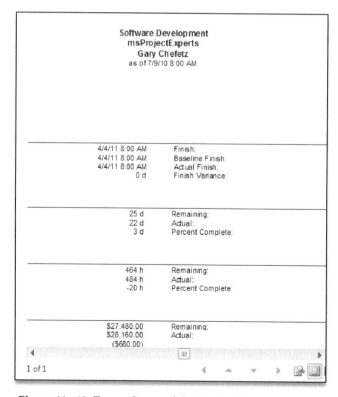

Figure 11 - 13: Zoomed area of the Project Summary report

6. Click anywhere in the print preview pane again to zoom out.

7. In the *Print* page, specify additional printing options, if needed.

8. Click the *Print* button at the top of the *Print* page to print the report.

Table 11 - 7 through Table 11 - 12 describe the reports found in each report category.

Overview Reports	
Project Summary	Displays an overview of dates, duration, work, costs, tasks, and resources.
Top-Level Tasks	Displays tasks at *Outline Level 1*.
Critical Tasks	Displays *Critical* tasks.
Milestones	Displays milestone tasks.
Working Days	Displays the daily working schedule and exceptions (nonworking time) on the *Standard* calendar.

Table 11 - 7: Overview Reports

Current Reports	
Unstarted Tasks	Uses the task *Entry* table to display tasks that have not started yet.
Tasks Starting Soon	Uses the task *Entry* table to display tasks starting within a date range you specify.
Task in Progress	Uses the task *Entry* table to display tasks that have started but have not finished yet, grouped by month.
Completed Tasks	Uses the task *Summary* table to display tasks, grouped by month, where both the *% Complete* and *% Work Complete* fields equal *100%*.
Should Have Started Tasks	Uses the task *Variance* table to display tasks that should start by a date you specify.
Slipping Tasks	Uses the task *Variance* table to display tasks where the current estimated *Finish* date is later than the *Baseline Finish* date (includes task notes as well).

Table 11 - 8: Current Activities Reports

Cost Reports	
Cash Flow	Uses a crosstab report to display task cost information in a timephased layout over one-week time periods (does not include resource assignments by default).
Budget	Uses the task *Cost* table to display cost information for all tasks, sorted in descending order on the *Cost* field.
Overbudget Tasks	Uses the task *Cost* table to display tasks where *Cost* value is greater than the *Baseline Cost* value, sorted in descending order by the *Cost Variance* field.
Overbudget Resources	Uses the resource *Cost* table to display resources whose *Cost* value is greater than the *Baseline Cost* value, sorted in descending order by the *Cost Variance* field.
Earned Value	Uses the task *Earned Value* table to display tasks Earned Value Analysis (EVA) information for every task.

Table 11 - 9: Cost Reports

Assignment Reports	
Who Does What	Uses the resource *Usage* table to display the task assignments for each resource.
Who Does What When	Uses a crosstab report to display resource work information in a timephased layout across daily time periods (shows *Work* resources only, but does include task assignments for each resource).
To-do List	Uses the task *Entry* table to display tasks for a specific resource you select, grouped by weeks.
Overallocated Resources	Uses the resource *Usage* table to display overallocated resources.

Table 11 - 10: Assignment Reports

The *To-do List* report is a great way to print a task list for each resource's reporting period. Be aware, however, that you must print one report for each team member assigned to tasks in the project. You **cannot** print a batch of *To-Do List* reports in a single operation.

Workload Reports	
Task Usage	Uses a crosstab report to display task work in a time-phased layout over one-week time periods (includes resource assignments by default).
Resource Usage	Uses a crosstab report to display resource work in a timephased layout over one-week time periods (includes task assignments by default).

Table 11 - 11: Workload Reports

The *Custom Reports* section includes all of the reports shown in the previous five sections, plus several additional reports. Table 11 - 12 describes the reports not listed in any other section.

Custom Reports	
Crosstab	Displays task cost information in a timephased layout over one-week time periods.
Resource	Uses the resource *Entry* table to display resource information for each resource.
Resource (material)	Uses the resource *Entry* table to display resource information for each *Material* resource.
Resource (work)	Uses the resource *Entry* table to display resource information for each *Work* resource (does not display *Cost* and *Material* resources).
Resource Usage (material)	Displays resource cost information in a timephased layout over one-week time periods for each *Material* resource (includes task assignments by default).
Resource Usage (work)	Displays resource cost information in a timephased layout over one-week time periods for each *Work* resource (includes task assignments by default).
Task	Displays basic task information for all tasks and includes the columns in the *Entry* table.

Table 11 - 12: Custom reports not listed in any other report section

You can use each of the custom reports as a starting point from which you can copy a default report and then quickly create your own custom report.

Hands On Exercise

Exercise 11-5

Examine the various default reports included in Microsoft Project 2010.

1. Return to the **Training Advisor 11.mpp** sample file.

2. Click the *Project* tab to display the *Project* ribbon.

3. Click the *Reports* button in the *Reports* section of the *Project* ribbon.

4. Display the print preview for each of the following default reports:

Report Section	Report Name
Overview	Project Summary
Current	Completed Tasks
Costs	Budget
Assignments	To-Do List (for Mickey Cobb)
Workload	Task Usage

5. Click the *Project* tab to close the *Print* page in the *Backstage*.

6. Save but **do not** close the **Training Advisor 11.mpp** sample file.

Understanding Report and View Interaction

When you print reports in Microsoft Project 2010, remember that the software produces reports based on views, including a table and a filter. When a view and report share the same table and filter, information expanded in the view is expanded in the report, so the information is visible in the report. Likewise, information collapsed in the view is collapsed in the report, so the information **is not** visible in the report.

Keep the following points in mind when printing any of the default Reports in Microsoft Project 2010:

- Most task reports use the task list that is visible in the *Task Sheet* view. Tasks collapsed in their respective summary tasks in the *Task Sheet* view do not display in most task reports. This is true of all six reports in the *Current* section.

- Most resource reports use the resource list visible in the *Resource Sheet* view. The *Overbudget Resources* and *Overallocated Resources* reports use the exact resource list in the *Resource Sheet* view.

- The software bases the *Cash Flow* report on the *Task Usage* view. Tasks collapsed to their respective summary tasks in the *Task Usage* view do not display in the *Cash Flow* report.

- The software bases the *Who Does What When* report on the *Resource Usage* view. Task assignments collapsed to their respective resources in the *Resource Usage* view do not display in the *Who Does What When* report.

- The software bases the *Task Usage* and *Resource Usage* reports on the *Task Usage* and *Resource Usage* views respectively.

Hands On Exercise

Exercise 11-6

Troubleshoot printing problems with the *Cash Flow* report.

1. Return to the **Training Advisor 11.mpp** sample file.

2. Click the *Project* tab to display the *Project* ribbon.

3. Click the *Reports* button in the *Reports* section of the *Project* ribbon.

4. In the *Reports* dialog, double-click the *Costs* section and then double-click the *Cash Flow* report.

5. Click twice in the print preview of the *Cash Flow* report to view the columns for the first two weeks of the project.

Notice that the *Project Status Meeting* recurring task displays no cost information, in spite of the fact that this task **does have** cost information associated with it.

6. Click the *Task* ribbon to close the *Print* page of the *Backstage*.

7. Expand the *Project Status Meeting* recurring task to view each individual task occurrence.

8. Click the *Project* tab and then click the *Reports* button in the *Reports* section of the *Project* ribbon.

9. In the *Reports* dialog, double-click the *Costs* section and then double-click the *Cash Flow* report.

Notice that the *Project Status Meeting* recurring task now displays cost information, beginning with the second week of the project. Remember, what is not visible in a view is not visible in any report based on that view.

10. Click the *Task* ribbon to close the *Print* page of the *Backstage*.

11. Collapse the *Project Status Meeting* recurring task to hide the individual task occurrences.

12. Save but **do not** close the **Training Advisor 11.mpp** sample file.

Exercise 11-7

Troubleshoot printing problems with the *Who Does What When* report.

1. Click the *Project* tab and then click the *Reports* button in the *Reports* section of the *Project* ribbon.

2. In the *Reports* dialog, double-click the *Assignments* section and then double-click the *Who Does What When* report.

3. Click anywhere in the first page of the report in the print preview window to zoom into the report.

Notice the *Who Does What When* report shows task assignments for **only three resources** (Jeff Holly, Mickey Cobb, and Bob Jared), in spite of the fact that you assigned every resource to at least one task.

4. Click the *Task* tab to close the *Print* page of the *Backstage*.

5. Click the *Gantt Chart* pick list button and select the *Resource Usage* view on the list.

Notice that I expanded the task assignments for **only** Jeff Holly, Mickey Cobb, and Bob Jared.

6. Click the *View* tab to display the *View* ribbon.

7. In the *Data* section of the *View* ribbon, click the *Outline* pick list button and select the *All Subtasks* item on the list. This step expands the task assignments for every resource.

8. Click the *Project* tab and then click the *Reports* button in the *Reports* section of the *Project* ribbon.

9. In the *Reports* dialog, double-click the *Assignments* section and then double-click the *Who Does What When* report.

10. Click anywhere in the first page of the report in the print preview window to zoom into the report.

Notice that you can now see **all** of the task assignments for **all** resources in the project team. Remember, what is not visible in the view is not visible in any report based on that view.

11. Click the *Task* tab to close the *Print* page of the *Backstage*.

12. Click the *Gantt Chart* button to reapply the *Gantt Chart* view.

13. Save but **do not** close the **Training Advisor 11.mpp** sample file.

Understanding Report Definition

Microsoft Project 2010 offers four types of custom reports: task, resource, crosstab, and monthly calendar. Task reports produce a printout similar to printing the *Task Sheet* view. Resource reports produce a printout similar to printing the *Resource Sheet* view. Crosstab reports produce a printout similar to printing either the *Task Usage* view or *Resource Usage* view. Monthly calendar reports produce a printout similar to printing the *Calendar* view. Microsoft Project 2010 formally defines task reports and resource reports as follows:

Report = Table + Filter + Report Details

Not surprisingly, this report definition is very similar to the view definition. The table determines the columns of data to display, while the filter extracts the rows of data you wish to see. The report details include additional information you wish to see, such as task notes or column totals.

The easiest way to understand report definition is to look at the definition of an existing report, such as the *Unstarted Tasks* report. To view this report, complete the following steps:

1. Click the *Project* tab and then click the *Reports* button in the *Reports* section of the *Project* ribbon.

2. In the *Reports* dialog, double-click the *Custom* icon. Microsoft Project 2010 displays the *Custom Reports* dialog shown in Figure 11 - 14.

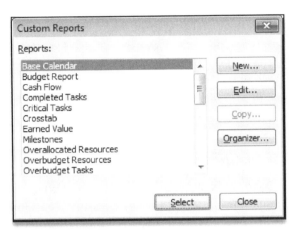

Figure 11 - 14: Custom Reports dialog

3. Select the *Unstarted Tasks* report and click the *Edit* button.

The software displays the *Task Report* dialog shown in Figure 11 - 15. Notice that the dialog includes three sections: the *Definition*, *Details*, and *Sort* sections. The dialog also includes a *Text* button you can use to change the text formatting in the report.

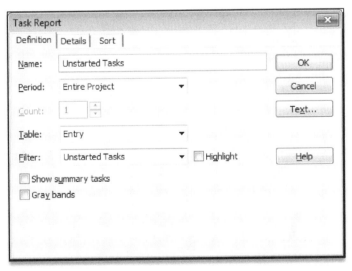

**Figure 11 - 15: Task Report dialog for the
Unstarted Tasks report, Definition page**

Notice in Figure 11 - 15 that the *Unstarted Tasks* report uses the *Entry* table and the *Unstarted Tasks* filter. On the *Definition* page of the dialog, you can also see other details available for the report, including:

- Select the *Highlight* option to apply the filter as a highlight filter.

- Select an item on the *Period* pick list to group tasks by time period.

- Select the *Show summary tasks* option to display summary tasks in the report.

- Select the *Gray bands* option to separate data sections in the report.

 When you select the *Highlight* option in a task report, Microsoft Project 2010 prints all tasks in your report , but uses a gray shaded band to highlight any task that meets the filter criteria. I recommend you try experimenting with this option before using it in a real report, as you may not like the results.

4. Click the *Details* tab in the *Task Report* dialog.

Microsoft Project 2010 displays the *Details* page shown in Figure 11 - 16. You can select additional details to print in the report, such as task notes, assignment information, borders, gridlines, and totals for the values in your report.

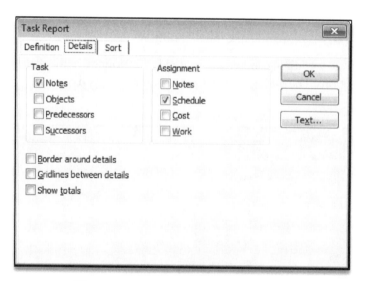

**Figure 11 - 16: Task Report dialog for the
Unstarted Tasks report, Details page**

Notice in Figure 11 - 16 that the default details for the *Unstarted Tasks* report include task notes and assignment schedule information. When you print the report, these two additional details appear in the *Unstarted Tasks* report shown in Figure 11 - 17. To capture the screenshot used in Figure 11 - 17, by the way, I printed the report to an XPS file and captured the resulting screenshot in the XPS file.

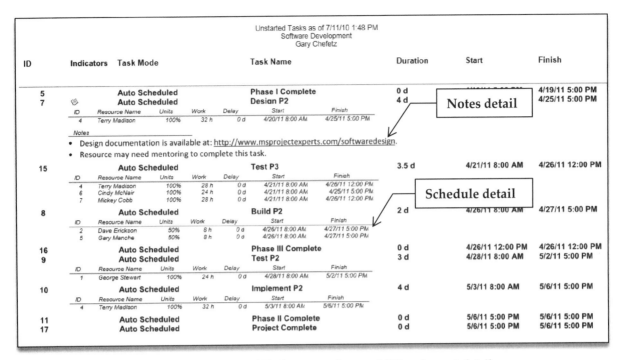

Figure 11 - 17: Unstarted Tasks report shows additional report details

 Selecting the *Notes* option adds a useful detail to any custom report definition. For reports that display project variance, adding the notes detail adds project annotation which may explain the reasons for the variance.

5.   Click the *Sort* tab in the *Task Report* dialog.

Microsoft Project 2010 displays the *Sort* page shown in Figure 11 - 18. The software allows you to sort by up to three fields, and to sort in ascending or descending order. Notice in Figure 11 - 18 that the *Unstarted Tasks* report displays tasks sorted by the *Scheduled Start* field and then by the *ID* field, both in *Ascending* order.

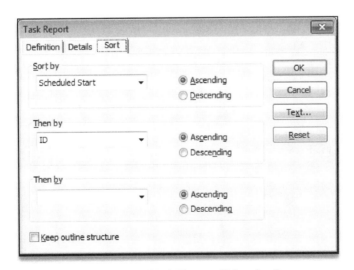

**Figure 11 - 18: Task Report dialog for the
Unstarted Tasks report, Sort page**

6. Click the *Text* button on any of the pages of the *Task Report* dialog.

Microsoft Project 2010 displays the *Text Styles* dialog shown in Figure 11 - 19. The settings in this dialog define the text formatting and background color formatting for every text object in the *Unstarted Task* report. These text objects include: critical tasks, noncritical tasks, milestone tasks, summary tasks, marked tasks, highlighted tasks, external tasks, task details, column titles, and totals.

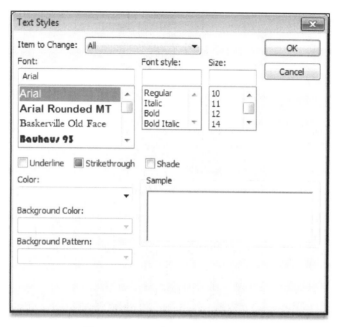

Figure 11 - 19: Text Styles dialog

7. Click the *Item to Change* pick list and select an item, such as the *Summary Tasks* item.

Figure 11 - 20 shows the formatting for summary tasks in the *Unstarted Tasks* report, as defined in the *Text Styles* dialog. Notice that the formatting includes the *Arial* font formatted in *Bold* at an *8 point* font size.

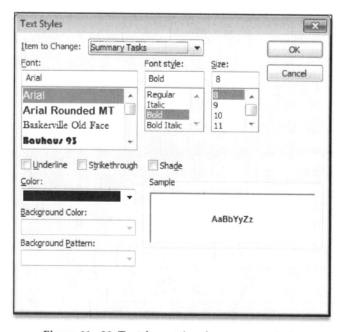

Figure 11 - 20: Text formatting for summary tasks

Hands On Exercise

Exercise 11-8

View the definition of a task report and a resource report.

1. Return to the **Training Advisor 11.mpp** sample file.

2. Click the *Project* tab and then click the *Reports* button in the *Reports* section of the *Project* ribbon.

3. Double-click the *Custom* icon to display the *Custom Reports* dialog.

4. Select the *Overallocated Resources* report and then click the *Edit* button.

5. In the *Resource Report* dialog, examine the report definition information shown on the *Definition*, *Details*, and *Sort* pages.

6. Click the *Cancel* button when finished.

7. In the *Custom Reports* dialog, select the *Slipping Tasks* report and then click the *Edit* button.

8. In the *Task Report* dialog, examine the report definition information shown on the *Definition*, *Details*, and *Sort* pages.

9. Click the *Cancel* button to close the *Task Report* dialog.

10. Click the *Cancel* button to close the *Custom Reports* dialog.

11. Save but **do not** close the **Training Advisor 11.mpp** sample file.

Creating Custom Reports

Once you understand the definition of reports, you are ready to create custom reports to meet your project reporting criteria. Remember that Microsoft Project 2010 defines task reports and resource reports as follows:

Report = Table + Filter + Report Details

Because reports and views are closely related, you can use a 3-step method to create a report in much the same way as you use the 4-step method to create a view. These three steps are:

1. Select an existing table or create a new table.

2. Select an existing filter or create a new filter.

3. Create the new report using your table and filter, and apply your desired report details and sorting.

In many cases, you can create a custom report using the same table and filter you used to create a custom view. When you know you want to both view and print particular information in your project, you should create the custom report immediately after creating the custom view while the table and filter you used in the view are fresh in your memory. To create either a custom resource report or a custom task report, complete the following steps:

1. Click the *Project* tab and then click the *Reports* button in the *Reports* section of the *Project* ribbon.

2. Double-click the *Custom* icon to display the *Custom Reports* dialog.

3. In the *Custom Reports* dialog, click the *New* button. Microsoft Project 2010 displays the *Define New Report* dialog shown in Figure 11 - 21.

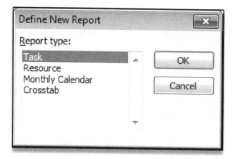

**Figure 11 - 21: Define New
Report dialog**

4. Select the desired *Report type* value and then click the *OK* button.

5. Enter a name for the custom report in the *Name* field.

6. Select your table in the *Table* pick list and select your filter in the *Filter* pick list.

7. Select other report details to meet your requirements on the definition, details, and sort pages.

8. Optionally, click the *Text* button to format the report text.

9. Click the *OK* button and then click the *Select* button to see a print preview of your new custom report.

Warning: An unfixed bug in the release version (RTM) of Microsoft Project 2010 prevents you from previewing or printing any default or custom report using the *Custom Reports* dialog. If you attempt to use this dialog to print either a default or custom report, the system prints the current view instead of the report.

msProjectExperts recommends that you copy an existing task or resource report, then rename and modify the copy. This is the fastest way to create a new custom report.

When you create custom views, tables, filters, or groups, Microsoft Project 2010 copies the new objects automatically to the Global.mpt file so that they are available for use in all current and future projects. When you create new custom reports, however, the system **does not** copy the new report to the Global.mpt file. Therefore, after you create your new report, remember to copy it to your Global.mpt file manually using the *Organizer* dialog to make it available in all current and future projects. You can access the *Organizer* dialog quickly by clicking the *Organizer* button in the *Custom Reports* dialog.

Hands On Exercise

Exercise 11-9

Create a custom task report based on the new table and filter used in the custom *_Duration Slippage* view.

1. Return to the **Training Advisor 11.mpp** sample file.

2. Click the *Project* tab and then click the *Reports* button in the *Reports* section of the *Project* ribbon.

3. Double-click the *Custom* icon to display the *Custom Reports* dialog.

4. In the *Custom Reports* dialog, click the *New* button.

5. In the *Define New Report* dialog, select the *Task* item in the *Report type* list and then click the *OK* button to create a new task report.

6. Enter or select the following information for the new report:

Definition Page	
Name	_Duration Slippage
Table	_Duration
Filter	_Duration Variance > 0d
Show summary tasks	Selected
Details Page	
Notes (Task)	Selected
Sort Page	
Sort by	Duration Variance (descending)

7. Click the *OK* button to close the *Task Report* dialog.

8. Click the *Organizer* button in the *Custom Reports* dialog to display the *Organizer* dialog.

9. In the *Organizer* dialog, select the *_Duration Slippage* report in the right side of the dialog and click the *Copy* button to copy it to the left side of the dialog (to the Global.mpt file).

10. Click the *Close* button to close the *Organizer* dialog.

11. Click the *Select* button in the *Custom Reports* dialog to see a print preview of your new *_Duration Slippage* report.

12. If you have a printer available, print a paper copy of your new report.

13. If you do not have a printer available, click the *Project* tab to close the *Print* page in the *Backstage*.

14. Save but **do not** close the **Training Advisor 11.mpp** sample file.

Creating Custom Monthly Calendar Reports

Microsoft Project 2010 does not ship with any default monthly calendar reports, so if you want use a calendar report, you must create your own. These monthly calendar reports resemble the default *Calendar* view that displays project tasks in a monthly or weekly calendar as shown in Figure 11 - 22.

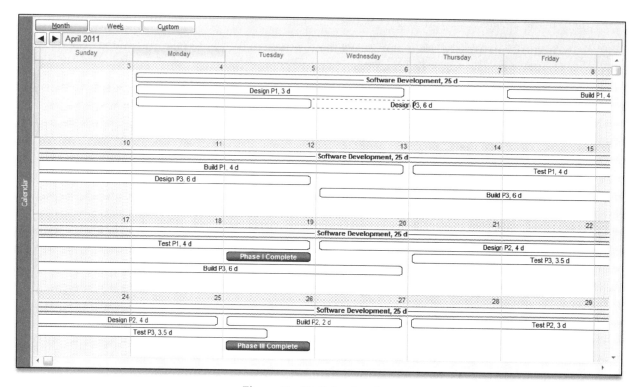

Figure 11 - 22: Calendar view

Notice the *Month*, *Week* and *Custom* buttons at the top of the *Calendar* view shown in Figure 11 - 22. These buttons allow you to define the precise time periods shown in the view.

To create a custom monthly calendar report, complete the following steps:

1. Click the *Project* tab and then click the *Reports* button in the *Reports* section of the *Project* ribbon.

2. Double-click the *Custom* icon to display the *Custom Reports* dialog.

3. In the *Custom Reports* dialog, click the *New* button.

4. In the *Define New Report* dialog, select the *Monthly Calendar* item in the *Report type* list and then click the *OK* button. Microsoft Project 2010 displays the *Monthly Calendar Report Definition* dialog shown in Figure 11 - 23.

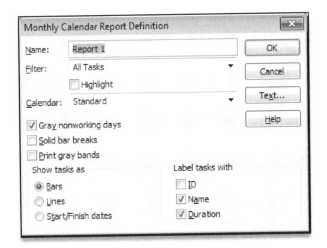

**Figure 11 - 23: Monthly Calendar
Report Definition dialog**

5. Enter a name for the custom report in the *Name* field.

6. If required, click the *Filter* pick list and select a filter other than the *All Tasks* filter.

7. Select all other details for your report, as needed. The additional options in the top and middle of the dialog include:

   • The *Highlight* option applies the selected filter as a highlight filter.

- The *Calendar* pick list offers a list of all base calendars and all resource calendars as shown in Figure 11 - 24. If needed for scheduling purposes, select a calendar other than the *Standard* calendar on the *Calendar* pick list.

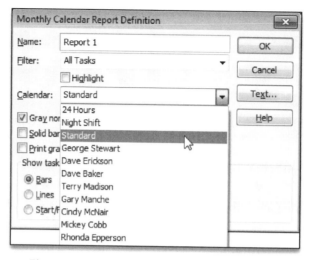

**Figure 11 - 24: Calendar pick list in the Monthly
Calendar Report Definition dialog**

- The *Gray nonworking days* option shows nonworking days as gray shaded cells in the printed monthly calendar report. If you deselect this option, Microsoft Project 2010 does not format any cells in gray, removing indications of nonworking days.

- When you select the *Solid bar breaks* option, the software shows a solid line at the end of a bar when a task continues into the next week. When you deselect this option, the bar does not include the solid line when the task continues into the next week.

- The monthly calendar report displays only six tasks per day in a vertical stack. When you exceed more than six tasks in a day, Microsoft Project 2010 adds the extra tasks on a separate sheet at the end of the printout. When you select the *Print gray bands* option, the system adds a gray band between each extra task. Deselecting this option causes the report to print the extra tasks without the gray bands.

- The *Show tasks as* section offers three options for how you want to display the tasks in the monthly calendar report. These options are:

  ○ If you select the *Bars* option, the system prints tasks as bars spanning the duration of each task.

  ○ If you select the *Lines* option, the system prints tasks as lines spanning the duration of each task.

  ○ If you select the *Start/Finish dates* option, the system prints only the start and finish dates for each task. The system indicates the start date of a task by prefixing S: to the task name, and indicates the finish date of a task by prefixing F: to the task name.

- The *Label tasks with* section offers three options for how you want to display the tasks in the monthly calendar report. These options are:

    ○ Select the *ID* option to include the ID number of each task.

    ○ Select the *Name* option to include the name of each task.

    ○ Select the *Duration* option to include the duration of each task.

8. You can click the *Text* button to format the report text.

9. Click the *OK* button to close the *Monthly Calendar Report Definition* dialog.

10. Click the *Select* button to see a print preview of your new custom monthly calendar report.

Warning: An unfixed bug in the release version (RTM) of Microsoft Project 2010 prevents you from previewing or printing any default or custom report using the *Custom Reports* dialog. If you attempt to use this dialog to print either a default or custom report, the system prints the current view instead of the report.

After you create your new monthly calendar report, remember to copy it to your Global.mpt file using the *Organizer* dialog to make it available in all current and future projects.

Hands On Exercise

Exercise 11-10

Create a custom monthly calendar report to show the tasks assigned to any resource.

1. Return to the **Training Advisor 11.mpp** sample file.

2. Click the *Project* tab and then click the *Reports* button in the *Reports* section of the *Project* ribbon.

3. Double-click the *Custom* icon to display the *Custom Reports* dialog.

4. In the *Custom Reports* dialog, click the *New* button.

5. In the *Define New Report* dialog, select the *Monthly Calendar* item in the *Report type* list and then click the *OK* button.

6. In the *Monthly Calendar Report Definition* dialog, enter or select the following details for the new report:

Name	_Monthly Task Assignments
Filter	Using Resource…
Calendar	Standard
Gray nonworking days	Selected
Show Tasks As	
Bars	Selected
Label Tasks With	
Name	Selected
Duration	Selected

7. Click the *OK* button to close the *Monthly Calendar Report Definition* dialog.

8. Click the *Organizer* button in the *Custom Reports* dialog to display the *Organizer* dialog.

9. In the *Organizer* dialog, select the *_Monthly Task Assignments* report in the right side of the dialog and click the *Copy* button to copy it to the left side of the dialog (to the Global.mpt file).

10. Click the *Close* button to close the *Organizer* dialog.

11. Click the *Select* button to see a print preview of your new custom monthly calendar report.

12. In the *Using Resource* dialog, select *Mike Andrews* from the *Show tasks using* pick list and then click the *OK* button.

13. If you have a printer available, print a paper copy of your new report.

14. If you do not have a printer available, click the *Project* tab to close the *Print* page in the *Backstage*.

15. Save but **do not** close the **Training Advisor 11.mpp** sample file.

Creating Custom Crosstab Reports

In Microsoft Project 2010, a crosstab report displays task or resource data in a timephased grid of rows and columns, with time period labels at the top of each column. For example, you can report on the work performed by each resource in a project on a weekly or monthly basis using a crosstab report. To create a custom crosstab report in Microsoft Project 2010, complete the following steps:

1. Click the *Project* tab and then click the *Reports* button in the *Reports* section of the *Project* ribbon.

2. Double-click the *Custom* icon to display the *Custom Reports* dialog.

3. In the *Custom Reports* dialog, click the *New* button.

4. In the *Define New Report* dialog, select the *Crosstab* item in the *Report type* pick list and then click the *OK* button. Microsoft Project 2010 displays the *Crosstab Report* dialog shown in Figure 11 - 25.

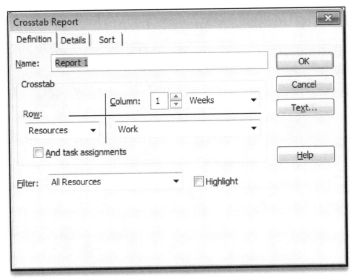

Figure 11 - 25: Crosstab Report dialog, Definition page

5. Select or enter the following information on the *Definition* page:

  • Enter a name for the custom report in the *Name* field.

  • Set the *Column* fields to the time periods you want to display in each column of the report.

  • Click the first *Row* pick list and select either the *Task* or *Resource* option to determine the type of information to display in the report.

  • Click the second *Row* pick list and select the field you want to display in each column of the report, such as the *Actual Work* field or *Actual Cost* field.

 Microsoft Project 2010 limits you to only one field in a cross tab report. This means that you cannot display both the *Work* and the *Actual Work* fields in the same crosstab report.

  • Select the *And resource assignments* option (or the *And task assignments* option) if you wish to see assignment information in addition to task or resource information included in the report.

  • If necessary, select a filter from the *Filter* pick list if you want to filter the data displayed in the report.

  • Select the *Highlight* option if you want the filter to highlight all tasks or resources that meet your filter criteria.

6. Click the *Details* tab and select additional details to include in the report.

Figure 11 - 26 shows the *Details* page in the *Crosstab Definition* dialog. This page includes additional details to print in the crosstab report, such as summary tasks, row and column totals, or gridlines. You specify the date format for the headers of each column using the *Date format* field at the bottom of the dialog.

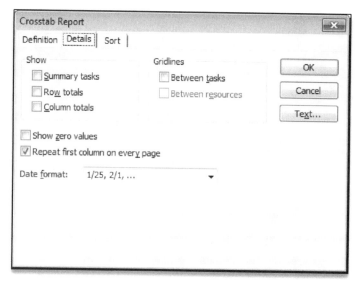

Figure 11 - 26: Crosstab Report dialog, Details page

The date format you select in the *Date format* pick list determines the width of every column in the crosstab report. For example, selecting the *Jan 25, Feb 1, ...* date format produces wider columns than the *1/25, 2/1, ...* date format. When you display a print preview of your crosstab report, if you see pound signs (#####) in any columns, you can resolve this display issue simply by selecting a date format that creates wider columns.

To make your crosstab report easier to read when the report spans multiple pages, MSProjectExperts recommends that you select the *Repeat first column on every page* option.

7. Click the *Sort* tab and set the sorting options for the data displayed in the crosstab report.

Figure 11 - 27 shows the *Sort* page of the *Crosstab Report* dialog. Notice that the sorting options are identical to those available in custom task and resource reports.

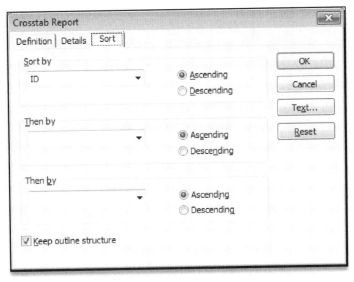

Figure 11 - 27: Crosstab Report dialog, Sort page

8. Click the *Text* button if you want to format the crosstab report text.

9. Click the *OK* button to close the *Crosstab Report* dialog.

After you create your new crosstab report, remember to copy it to your Global.mpt file using the *Organizer* dialog to make it available in all current and future projects.

10. Click the *Select* button to see a print preview of your new custom crosstab report.

Warning: An unfixed bug in the release version (RTM) of Microsoft Project 2010 prevents you from previewing or printing any default or custom report using the *Custom Reports* dialog. If you attempt to use this dialog to print either a default or custom report, the system prints the current view instead of the report.

MsProjectExperts recommends that you copy an existing crosstab report, then rename and modify the copy. This is the fastest way to create any new custom report.

Hands On Exercise

Exercise 11-11

Create a monthly version of the *Cash Flow* report that displays both tasks and assignments.

1. Return to the **Training Advisor 11.mpp** sample file.

2. Click the *Project* tab and then click the *Reports* button in the *Reports* section of the *Project* ribbon.

3. Double-click the *Custom* icon to display the *Custom Reports* dialog.

4. In the *Custom Reports* dialog, select the *Cash Flow Report* item and click the *Copy* button.

5. In the *Crosstab Report* dialog, enter or select the following details for the new crosstab report:

Name	_Monthly Cash Flow
Column	1 Months
And resource assignments	Selected

6. Leave all other report details set to their default values.

7. Click the *OK* button to close the *Crosstab Report* dialog.

8. Click the *Organizer* button in the *Custom Reports* dialog to display the *Organizer* dialog.

9. In the *Organizer* dialog, select the *_Monthly Cash Flow* report in the right side of the dialog and click the *Copy* button to copy it to the left side of the dialog (to the Global.mpt file).

10. Click the *Close* button to close the *Organizer* dialog.

11. Click the *Select* button to see a print preview of your new crosstab report.

12. If you have a printer available, print a paper copy of your new report.

13. If you do not have a printer available, click the *Project* tab to close the *Print* page in the *Backstage*.

14. Save but **do not** close the **Training Advisor 11.mpp** sample file.

Using Visual Reports

Microsoft introduced visual reports as a new feature in Microsoft Project 2007, and continues to offer improved visual report functionality in Microsoft Project 2010. Visual reports allow you to see your project data in a *PivotChart* and *PivotTable* in Microsoft Excel or in a *PivotDiagram* in Microsoft Visio. The software creates the visual report by building local OLAP (<u>O</u>n <u>L</u>ine <u>A</u>nalytical <u>P</u>rogramming) cubes directly on your computer's hard drive. These local OLAP cubes provide a multi-dimensional summary of task and resource data in your project.

 You can use the Excel Visual Reports with Microsoft Excel 2003, 2007, or 2010. To use the Visio Visual Reports, however, you must have Microsoft Visio **Professional** 2007 or 2010.

If you are a previous user of Microsoft Project 2007 and upgraded to the 2010 version, you might be interested in knowing the improvements to visual reports. Although these improvements are relatively minor, they include the following:

* You can add custom fields to the OLAP cubes used for the *Assignment Usage* and *Assignment Summary* visual reports.

* Visual reports now support custom field names of up to 100 characters, increased from 25 characters in Microsoft Project 2007.

Microsoft Project 2010 allows you to choose the fields to display in the visual report while viewing it and to make ad hoc modifications to the visual report without regenerating the underlying data. With this type of flexibility, visual reports offer you much greater flexibility than the default Reports that ship with the software.

To access visual reports, click the *Project* tab and then click the *Visual Reports* button in the *Reports* section of the *Project* ribbon. The system displays the *Visual Reports – Create Report* dialog shown in Figure 11 - 28.

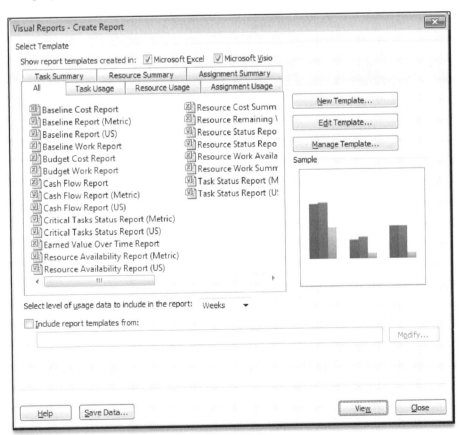

Figure 11 - 28: Visual Reports – Create Report dialog

The *Visual Reports – Create Report* dialog provides you with six categories of default visual reports for both Microsoft Excel and Microsoft Visio. The *Task Usage, Resource Usage,* and *Assignment Usage* categories display timephased task, resource, and assignment data respectively. The *Task Summary, Resource Summary,* and *Assignment Summary* categories display task, resource, and assignment data without timephased data. Table 11 - 13 through Table 11 - 18 describe the default visual reports included in each category.

Task Usage		
Report Name	**Type**	**Description**
Cash Flow	Excel	Combination column chart/line chart shows Cost (columns) and cumulative cost (lines) over time.

Table 11 - 13: Task Usage visual reports

Task Summary		
Report Name	**Type**	**Description**
Critical Tasks Status	Visio	Diagram shows Work, Remaining Work, and % Work Complete for both critical and non-critical tasks, with a progress bar representing the % Work Complete for each task.

Table 11 - 14: Task Summary visual reports

Resource Usage		
Report Name	**Type**	**Description**
Cash Flow	Visio	Diagram shows Cost and Actual Cost over time and broken down by resource type (Work, Material, and Cost). Diagram shows an orange triangle symbol when the Cost exceeds the Baseline Cost.
Resource Availability	Visio	Diagram shows Work and Remaining Availability for each resource, broken down by resource type (Work, Material, and Cost).
Resource Cost Summary	Excel	Pie chart shows project costs.
Resource Work Availability	Excel	Column chart shows Work Availability, Work, and Remaining Availability for all resources over time.
Resource Work Summary	Excel	Column chart shows Work Availability, Work, Remaining Availability, and Actual Work for all resources.

Table 11 - 15: Resource Usage visual reports

Resource Summary		
Report Name	**Type**	**Description**
Resource Remaining Work	Excel	Stacked column chart shows Actual Work and Remaining Work for all resources.

Table 11 - 16: Resource Summary visual reports

Assignment Usage		
Report Name	**Type**	**Description**
Baseline Cost	Excel	Column chart shows Baseline Cost, Cost, and Actual Cost for all tasks.
Baseline	Visio	Diagram compares Work and Cost with Baseline Work and Baseline Cost over time for all tasks. Displays a red stoplight when Work exceeds Baseline Work. Displays a yellow flag when Cost exceeds Baseline Cost.
Baseline Work	Excel	Column chart shows Baseline Work, Work, and Actual Work for all tasks.
Budget Cost	Excel	Column chart shows Budget Cost, Baseline Cost, Cost, and Actual Cost over time.
Budget Work	Excel	Column chart shows Budget Work, Baseline Work, Work, and Actual Work over time.
Earned Value Over Time	Excel	Line chart shows Earned Value (EV), Planned Value (BCWP), and Actual Cost (ACWP) over time through the *Status Date* of the project.

Table 11 - 17: Assignment Usage visual reports

Assignment Summary		
Report Name	**Type**	**Description**
Resource Status	Visio	Diagram shows Work and Cost for each resource with color shading in each box representing % Work Complete. White shading represents 100% Work complete, dark purple represents 0% Work complete, and light purple represents % Work Complete greater than 0% and less than 100%.
Task Status	Visio	Diagram displays Work and Cost for all tasks. Diagram displays an orange progress bar representing %

Assignment Summary		
Report Name	**Type**	**Description**
		Work Complete for each task and also shows a yellow "unhappy face" when Work exceeds Baseline Work. The system shows a yellow "neutral face" when Work is equal to or less than Baseline Work.

Table 11 - 18: Assignment Summary visual reports

Each Visio visual report is available in either a metric version or US version. The versions refer to the measurement units applied to the horizontal and vertical ruler bars in the PivotDiagram. When you select the metric version, the software applies the **millimeter** measurement to the ruler bar. When you select the US version, the software applies the **inches** measurement.

If you used Microsoft Project 2007 previously before upgrading to the 2010 version, you see some changes to the default data displayed in most of the Excel visual reports. These changes include:

- The **Baseline Cost Report** no longer includes the *Tasks* dimension in the *Row Labels* drop area of the *PivotTable*.

- The **Baseline Work Report** no longer includes the *Tasks* dimension in the *Row Labels* drop area of the *PivotTable*.

- The **Earned Value Over Time Report** shows Earned Value data only through the *Status Date* of the project. In Microsoft Project 2007, the report showed Earned Value data over the entire time span of the project, but the Earned Value dropped to 0 for every time period after the *Status Date* of the project.

- The **Resource Cost Summary Report** no longer includes the *Type* dimension in the *Row Labels* drop area of the *PivotTable*.

- The **Resource Remaining Work Report** no longer includes the *Type* and *Resources* dimensions in the *Row Labels* drop area of the *PivotTable*.

- The **Resource Work Summary Report** no longer includes the *Type* and *Resources* dimensions in the *Row Labels* drop area of the *PivotTable*.

For the Visio visual reports, Microsoft made only one minor change to the default data shown in the **Resource Status Report,** which displays information for a new default resource named *Task's Fixed Cost*. This new resource displays any extra task costs you add to the *Fixed Cost* column.

Viewing a Visual Report

To view a visual report, complete the following steps:

1. Click the *Project* tab and then click the *Visual Reports* button in the *Reports* section of the *Project* ribbon.

2. In the *Visual Reports – Create Report* dialog, click the tab containing the visual report you want to view.

3. In the selected report section, select a visual report from the list.

4. Click the *Select level of usage data to include in this report* pick list and select the data granularity you want to use in the report, as shown in Figure 11 - 29.

Microsoft Project 2010 generates the data in the local OLAP cubes using the granularity you select and then transfers the data to the visual report.

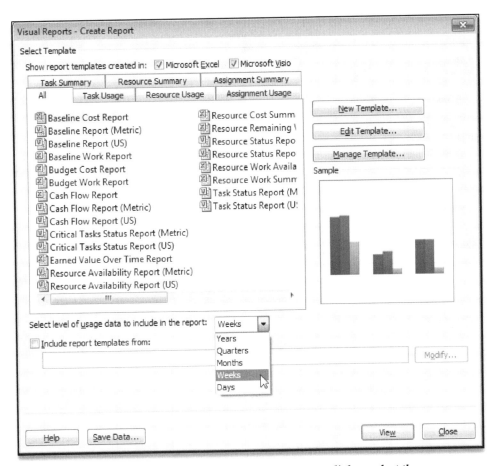

Figure 11 - 29: Visual Reports – Create Report dialog, select the granularity for the Resource Work Availability Report

Based on the size of your project, Microsoft Project 2010 sets a recommended value in the *Select level of usage data to include in this report* pick list. For most projects, the recommended value is *Weeks*. For very large projects, the recommended value might be *Months*, *Quarters*, or even *Years*.

5. If you want to supplement the standard list of task and resource details included with the local OLAP cube, click the *Edit Template* button.

557

Microsoft Project 2010 displays the *Visual Reports – Field Picker* dialog shown in Figure 11 - 30. In the *Selected Fields* list on the right, you see the standard list of detail fields added to the local OLAP cube automatically. This list includes fields like *Task WBS* and *Task Percent Complete*, for example. If you want to supplement this list with additional fields, select one or more fields in the *Available Fields* list and click the *Add* button.

The *Available Custom Fields* list shows the list of custom fields available for inclusion in the local OLAP cube, and includes any custom fields you created in the project. For example, notice in Figure 11 - 30 that the list includes two custom fields I created in this project: the *Accountable Person Task (dimension)* field and the *Cost Center ID Task (dimension)* field. To add any custom field to the local OLAP cube, select one or more fields in the *Available Custom Fields* list and click the *Add* button. Click the *Edit Template* button when finished.

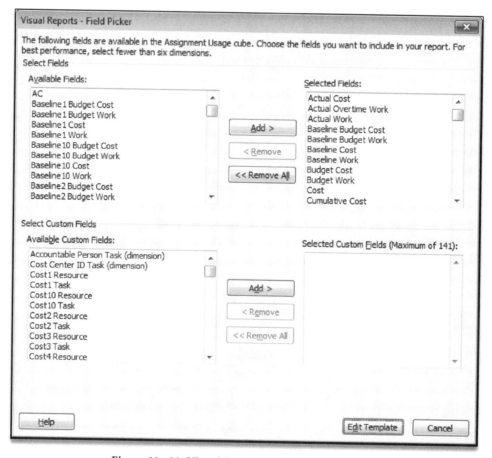

Figure 11 - 30: Visual Reports – Field Picker dialog

6. If you did not need to use step #5, click the *View* button to create the visual report.

Microsoft Project 2010 displays a progress indicator at the bottom of the dialog in which it indicates that it is gathering data for the report, building the local OLAP cubes, and then opening the visual report template for viewing. Figure 11 - 31 shows the completed *Baseline Cost* visual report in Microsoft Excel. Notice that the legend at the top of the chart explains the meaning of each column color.

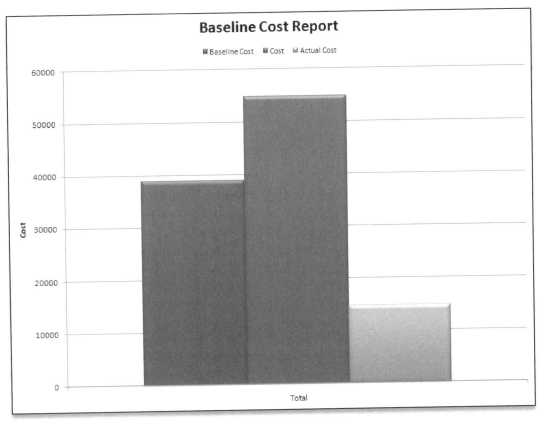

Figure 11 - 31: Baseline Cost visual report

7. Click the *Zoom Out* or *Zoom In* buttons to set the desired level of zoom.

In Microsoft Excel 2007 and 2010, the system sets the default level of zoom for each visual report to 125%. Depending on your monitor size and screen resolution, you may need to zoom out for every visual report you view.

The visual report in Microsoft Excel consists of two parts: the graphical *PivotChart*, shown previously in Figure 11 – 31, and the *PivotTable* containing the underlying data. To view the *PivotTable* data, click the *Task Usage*, *Resource Usage*, or *Assignment Usage* worksheet tab in the lower left corner of the application window. Figure 11 - 32 shows the *PivotTable* data on the *Assignment Usage* worksheet for the *Baseline Cost* visual report.

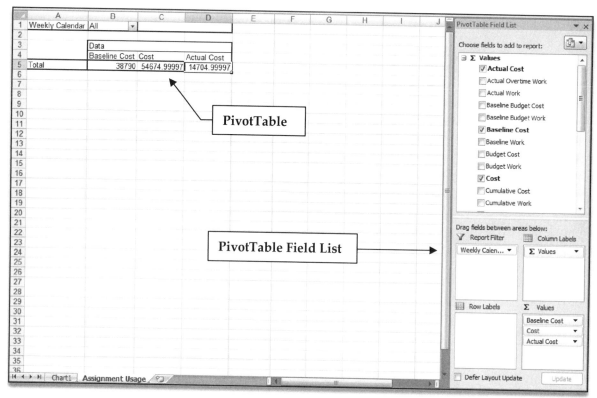

Figure 11 - 32: PivotTable data for the Baseline Cost visual report

The *Assignment Usage* worksheet consists of two parts. The worksheet displays the *PivotTable* in the upper left corner of the page, as shown in Figure 11 - 32. The *PivotTable* includes data areas for row fields, column fields, project filter fields, and total fields. The worksheet displays the *PivotTable Field List* sidepane on the right side of the page.

Figure 11 - 33 shows the *Task Status* visual report in Microsoft Visio. Because the default zoom level is set to display the entire page, you probably need to zoom in to see your visual report data clearly. Notice in Figure 11 - 33 that a visual report in Microsoft Visio consists of three parts: the *PivotDiagram*, the *PivotDiagram* sidepane on the left, and the floating *PivotDiagram* toolbar.

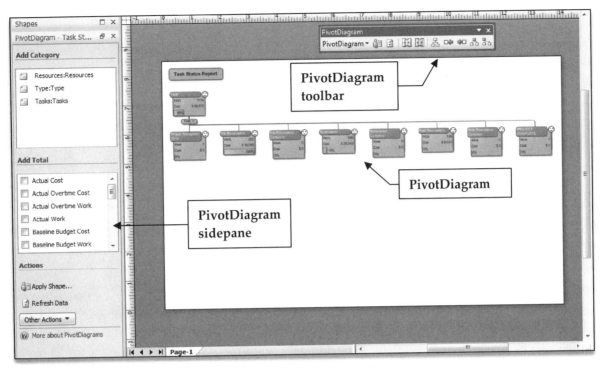

Figure 11 - 33: Task Status visual report

Hands On Exercise

Exercise 11-12

View visual reports in Microsoft Project 2010.

1. Return to the **Training Advisor 11.mpp** sample file.

2. Click the *Project* tab and then click the *Visual Reports* button in the *Reports* section of the *Project* ribbon.

3. Click the *Assignment Usage* tab and select the *Baseline Work Report* item.

4. Click the *Select level of usage data to include in this report* pick list and select the *Days* level of data granularity.

5. Click the *View* button.

6. Examine the *PivotChart* shown on the *Chart1* worksheet and the *PivotTable* data shown on the *Assignment Usage* worksheet.

7. Close and **do not** save the Microsoft Excel workbook, but leave the Excel application running.

8. Return to the Microsoft Project 2010 application window.

9. In the *Visual Reports – Create Report* dialog, click the *Resource Usage* tab.

10. Select the *Cash Flow Report (US)* item and then click the *View* button.

11. Zoom to the *100%* level of zoom and examine the information shown in this Visio visual report.

12. Close and **do not** save the Microsoft Visio diagram, and then close the Visio application.

13. Return to your Microsoft Project 2010 application window.

Customizing a Microsoft Excel Visual Report

You can customize any Microsoft Excel visual report by changing the *PivotTable* data on the *Task Usage*, *Resource Usage* or *Assignment Usage* worksheet. For example, you can use any of the following methods to customize the *PivotTable* data in the *Baseline Cost* visual report:

*   In the *PivotTable Field List* sidepane, deselect any fields you do not want to display, and select the fields you do want to display. The software adds the newly selected field(s) to the appropriate area in the sidepane. For example, notice in Figure 11 - 34 that I **deselected** the *Actual Cost* field in the *PivotTable Field List* sidepane, removing this field from both the *PivotTable* and the *PivotChart* as a consequence. Though not visible in Figure 11 - 34, I also selected the *Tasks* field for inclusion in the Excel visual report.

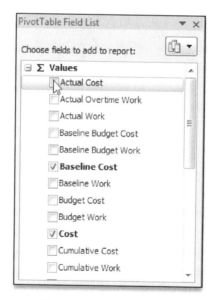

**Figure 11 - 34: Deselect the
Actual Cost field**

*   In the *PivotTable Field List* sidepane, drag and drop fields from the field list to the drop areas at the bottom of the pane. For example, I dragged the *Weekly Calendar* field from the *Report Filter* area to the *Row Labels* area, as shown in Figure 11 - 35. You can see the *Tasks* field in the *Row Labels* area as well.

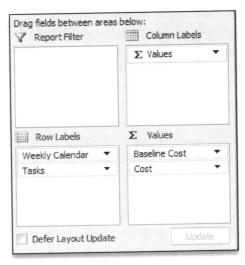

**Figure 11 - 35: Move the Weekly Calendar
field to the Row Labels area**

- In the *PivotTable*, click the *Expand* (+) or *Collapse* (-) buttons in any section on the left side to show the level details you want to see in the visual report. Notice in Figure 11 - 36 that I expanded the *Year* section to show *Quarters*, and I expanded the *Project Navigation 2010* task to show first-level tasks in the *Task 1* section.

	A	B	C	D	E	F	G
1			Drop Page Fields Here				
2							
3					Data		
4	Year	Quarter	Task	Task 1	Baseline Cost	Cost	
5	⊟2014	⊞Q2	Project Navigation 2010	Project Navigation 2010	0	0	
6				⊞Pre-Renovation	11030	16095	
7				Pre-Renovation Complete	0	0	
8				⊞Renovation	24120	26800	
9				Renovation Complete	0	0	
10			Project Navigation 2010 Total		35150	42895	
11		Q2 Total			35150	42895	
12		⊞Q3	⊟Project Navigation 2010	Project Navigation 2010	0	0	
13				⊞Pre-Renovation	0	0	
14				Pre-Renovation Complete	0	0	
15				⊞Renovation	0	2740	
16				Renovation Complete	0	0	
17				⊞Post-Renovation	3640	9040	
18				Post-Renovation Complete	0	0	
19				PROJECT COMPLETE	0	0	
20			Project Navigation 2010 Total		3640	11780	
21		Q3 Total			3640	11780	
22	2014 Total				38790	54675	
23	Grand Total				38790	54675	
24							

Figure 11 - 36: PivotTable with Year and Task sections expanded

- Select the details you want to see for any field in the *Row Labels* area by clicking the pick list arrow button in the field name. For example, to edit the details for the *Task* field, click the *Task* pick list. The system displays the *Select field* dialog shown in Figure 11 - 37. Using this dialog, you can select the specific task items you want to see in the *PivotTable*, such as first-level summary tasks that represent phases of the project.

Figure 11 - 37: Select field dialog

- Display properties fields in the *PivotTable*, if needed. If you add the *Task* field or the *Resource* field to the *Row Labels* area in any visual report, right-click on the *Task* or *Resource* field. In the shortcut menu, select the *Show Properties in Report* menu item, and then use the fly out menu to select the details you want to see in the report, as shown in Figure 11 - 38.

For this example, I do not include any properties fields in the *PivotTable*. In your own projects, be judicious with adding properties fields to your visual reports. Keep in mind that Microsoft Excel limits how much number formatting you can apply to properties fields, or prevents number formatting entirely. Beyond this, adding properties fields to your *PivotTable* can negatively impact the appearance of your *PivotChart* as well.

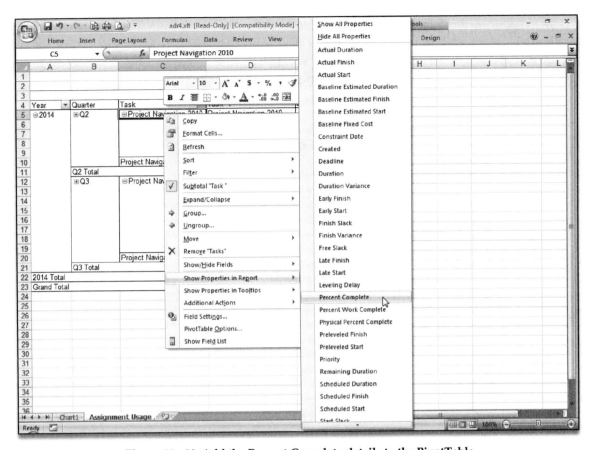

Figure 11 - 38: Add the Percent Complete details to the PivotTable

- Apply numeric formatting to the numbers in the *PivotTable*. For example, in Figure 11 - 39, I applied the *Accounting Number Format* numeric formatting to the data shown in the *PivotTable*, and then I clicked the *Decrease Decimal* button to reduce to *zero* the number of digits to the right of the decimal.

	A	B	C	D	E	F	G
1			Drop Page Fields Here				
2							
3					Data		
4	Year	Quarter	Task	Task 1	Baseline Cost	Cost	
5	2014	Q2	Project Navigation 2010	Pre-Renovation	$ 11,030	$ 16,095	
6				Renovation	$ 24,120	$ 26,800	
7			Project Navigation 2010 Total		$ 35,150	$ 42,895	
8		Q2 Total			$ 35,150	$ 42,895	
9		Q3	Project Navigation 2010	Pre-Renovation	$ -	$ -	
10				Renovation	$ -	$ 2,740	
11				Post-Renovation	$ 3,640	$ 9,040	
12			Project Navigation 2010 Total		$ 3,640	$ 11,780	
13		Q3 Total			$ 3,640	$ 11,780	
14	2014 Total				$ 38,790	$ 54,675	
15	Grand Total				$ 38,790	$ 54,675	
16							

Figure 11 - 39: PivotTable with numeric formatting applied

When you make changes to the data shown in the *PivotTable*, Microsoft Excel updates the changes immediately in the *PivotChart*. Figure 11 - 40 shows the updated *PivotChart* after making changes to the underlying data in the *PivotTable*. If you compare this updated *Baseline Cost* report with the original *Baseline Cost* report shown previously in Figure 11 - 31, you see dramatic changes in appearance after making only a few simple changes in the *PivotTable*.

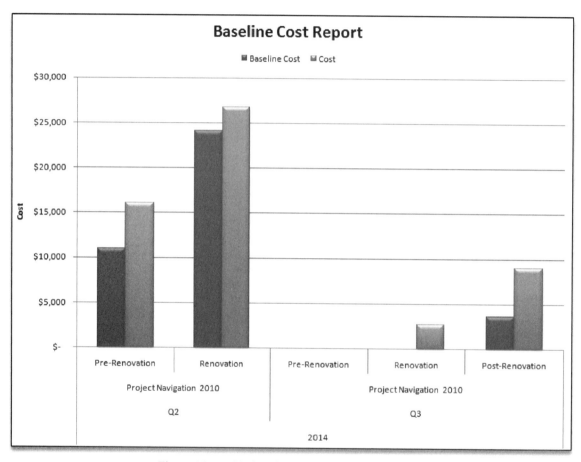

Figure 11 - 40: Updated Baseline Cost visual report

You can also modify the *PivotChart* by right-clicking anywhere in the area of the chart you want to change. When you right-click in the *Chart Area* of the *PivotChart*, Microsoft Excel displays the shortcut menu shown in Figure 11 - 41. Using the options on this shortcut menu, you can use any of the built-in chart formatting capabilities available in Microsoft Excel.

In Microsoft Excel 2007 and 2010, you can also double-click anywhere in the *PivotChart*. The system displays the contextual *Design* ribbon with the *PivotChart Tools* applied. Using the features on the *Design* ribbon, you can apply many different types of formatting to the *PivotChart*.

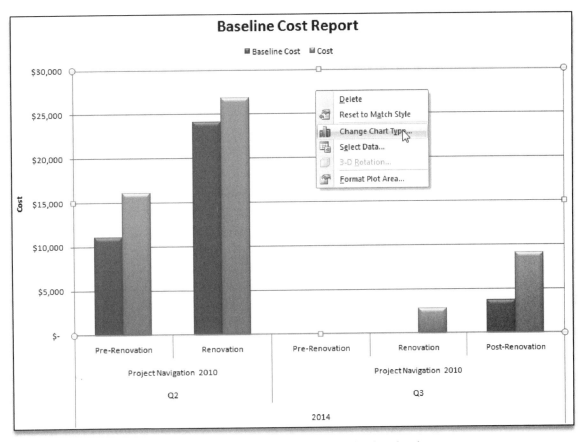

Figure 11 - 41: Right-click in the PivotChart to display the shortcut menu

If you select the *Change Chart Type* item on the shortcut menu, Microsoft Excel displays the *Change Chart Type* dialog shown in Figure 11 - 42. Select an alternate chart type in this dialog and then click the *OK* button.

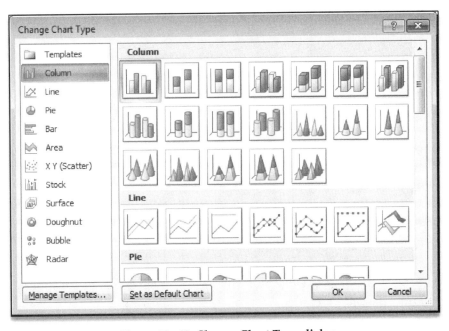

Figure 11 - 42: Change Chart Type dialog

Figure 11 - 43 shows the *PivotChart* after I applied the *Clustered Cylinder* chart type in the *Change Chart Type* dialog.

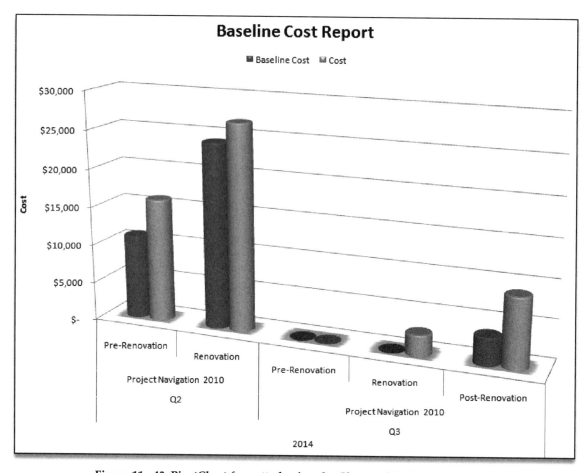

Figure 11 - 43: PivotChart formatted using the Clustered Cylinder chart type

 Because this is not a course on Microsoft Excel, I do not provide an exhaustive discussion about how to format either the *PivotTable* or the *PivotChart* in an Excel visual report.

Within Microsoft Excel, you can also do the following after viewing a visual report:

- Save the workbook by clicking the *Save* button.

- Print the workbook by clicking the *Office* button in the upper left corner of the application window, and then click *Print* from the *Office* menu.

- Close the workbook without saving it and then exit the application.

Customizing a Microsoft Visio Visual Report

You can customize a Microsoft Visio visual report by using any of the following methods

- Select one or more objects in the *PivotDiagram* and then change the options in the sidepane or on the floating toolbar.

- Manually delete objects in the *PivotDiagram*.

- Change the layout of objects in the *PivotDiagram*.

Notice in the *Task Status* visual report, shown previously in Figure 11 - 33, that the report displays only the first-level tasks representing the phases in the project. In this visual report, I want to show the second-level summary tasks for the *Renovation* phase to view the deliverables for that phase. To accomplish this, I must do the following:

1. Click the *Renovation* object to select it.

2. Click the *Tasks* pick list in the *Add Category* section of the sidepane and then select the *Task 2* item on the list, as shown in Figure 11 - 44.

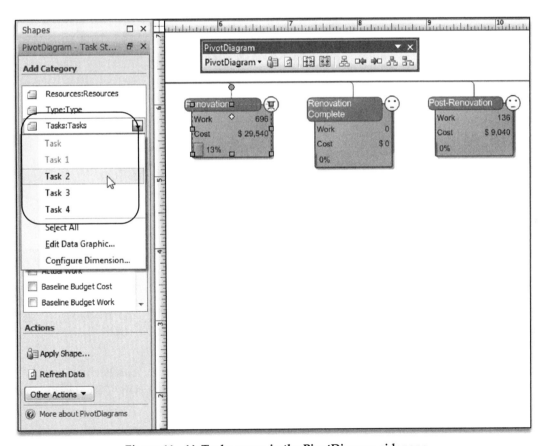

Figure 11 - 44: Tasks menu in the PivotDiagram sidepane

Figure 11 - 45 shows the *Task Status* visual report after adding the second-level summary task objects to the report.

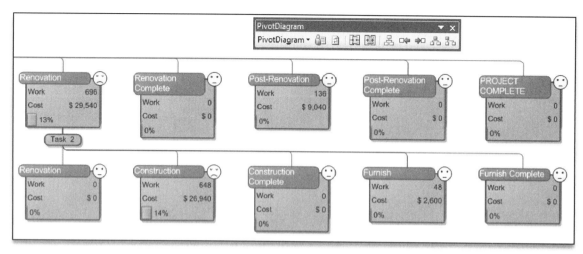

**Figure 11 - 45: Task Status visual report with second-level
summary tasks for the Renovation phase**

In the *Task Status* visual report shown in Figure 11 - 45, I want to remove the objects representing the Project Summary Task and all of the milestones. To delete an object, click the object to select it and then press the **Delete** key on the keyboard. Figure 11 - 46 shows my *Task Status* visual report after selecting and deleting these objects.

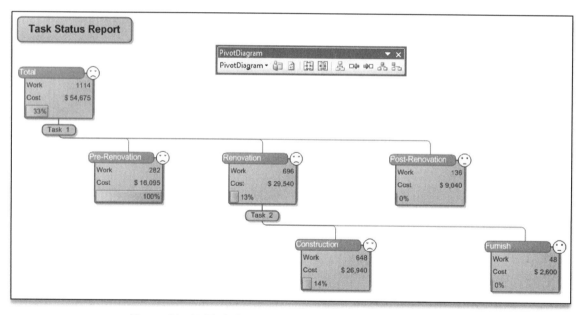

Figure 11 - 46: Task Status visual report after deleting objects

To change the layout of the objects, click the *Re-layout All* button on the floating *PivotDiagram* toolbar. You can also manually drag and drop objects anywhere on the *PivotDiagram*. Figure 11 - 47 shows the *Task Status* visual report after changing the layout of the *PivotDiagram* objects using the *Re-layout All* button.

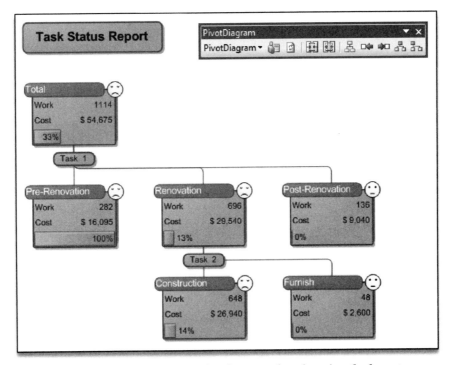

Figure 11 - 47: Task Status visual report after changing the layout

 Because this is not a course on Microsoft Visio, I do not provide an exhaustive discussion about how to format a *PivotDiagram*.

You can also do the following after viewing a visual report within Microsoft Visio:

- Save the visual report as a Drawing file.

- Print the visual report.

- Close the visual report without saving and then exit the application.

 ## Hands On Exercise

Exercise 11-13

Customize the *PivotTable* in an Excel visual report.

1. Return to the **Training Advisor 11.mpp** sample file.

2. Click the *Project* tab and then click the *Visual Reports* button in the *Reports* section of the *Project* ribbon.

3. Click the *Assignment Usage* tab and select the *Baseline Work Report* item.

4. Click the *View* button.

5. In your Microsoft Excel application window, click the *Assignment Usage* worksheet tab to view the *PivotTable* data.

6. Click anywhere in the *PivotTable* to display the *PivotTable Field List* sidepane on the right side of the page.

7. In the *PivotTable Field List* sidepane, **deselect** the *Actual Work* item in the *Choose fields to add to report* section.

8. In the *Choose fields to add to report* section of the *PivotTable Field List* sidepane, scroll down so that you can see the last two sections on the list (*Time* and *Type*).

9. Select the *Tasks* item in the *Tasks* section, and then **deselect** the *Weekly Calendar* item in the *Time* section.

10. In the *PivotTable*, expand the *Training Advisor Rollout* item in the *Task* section.

11. In the *PivotTable*, click the *Task* pick list.

12. In the *Select field* dialog, expand the *Training Advisor Rollout* item to view summary tasks and milestone tasks.

13. In the *Select field* dialog, **deselect** the *(Select All)* option and then select only the following task items:

    - INSTALLATION
    - TESTING
    - TRAINING

14. Click the *OK* button to close the *Select field* dialog.

15. Select all of the numbers in the *Baseline Work* and *Work* columns of the *PivotTable* and then format the numbers with the following number styles:

    - Comma Style
    - Zero digits to the right of the decimal point

16. Click the *Chart1* worksheet tab and study the new information shown in the *PivotChart*.

Exercise 11-14

Customize the *PivotChart* in an Excel visual report.

1. In the *Baseline Work* visual report, click anywhere in the *Chart Area* of the *PivotChart* and then close the *PivotTable Field List* sidepane that appears automatically on the right side of the screen.

2. Click and hold the right border of the *Chart Area* and then drag it over to the right edge of the *PivotChart*.

3. Right-click anywhere in the *Chart Area* of the *PivotChart* and select the *Change Chart Type* item on the shortcut menu.

4. In the *Change Chart Type* dialog, select the *Clustered Pyramid* option (second icon in the third row of the *Column* charts) and then click the *OK* button.

5. Save the *Baseline Work* visual report as an Excel workbook file in your student folder and name it *Custom Baseline Work Report.xls*.

6. Close the *Baseline Work* visual report file, but leave Microsoft Excel open.

7. Return to your Microsoft Project 2010 application window.

Saving Local OLAP Cube Data

After you view the visual report and return to Microsoft Project 2010, you can save the local OLAP cube data by clicking the *Save Data* button at the bottom of the *Visual Reports – Create Report* dialog. The system displays the *Visual Reports – Save Reporting Data* dialog shown in Figure 11 - 48.

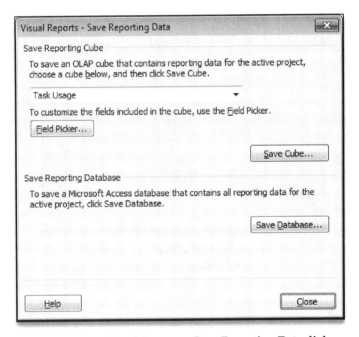

Figure 11 - 48: Visual Reports – Save Reporting Data dialog

Click the pick list *Save Reporting Cube* section of the dialog and select the local OLAP cube you wish to save. The pick list includes the following OLAP cubes: *Task Usage, Resource Usage, Assignment Usage, Task Summary, Resource Summary*, and *Assignment Summary*.

Click the *Field Picker* button to select the fields you want to include when you save the local OLAP cube. Microsoft Project 2010 displays the *Visual Reports – Field Picker* dialog shown previously in Figure 11 - 30. In this dialog, select the standard and custom fields you want to include in the OLAP cube and then click the *OK* button.

Click the *Save Cube* button when you are ready to save the local OLAP cube. In the *Save As* dialog, select a folder in which to save the cube file, enter a name for the cube file in the *File name* field, and then click the *Save* button. The system saves a file with the **.cub** file extension.

You also have the option to save all of the local OLAP cube information in a Microsoft Access Database (***.mdb**) file by clicking the *Save Database* button in the *Save Reporting Database* section of the dialog. Click the *Close* button when you complete the operation.

Creating Visual Report Templates

Microsoft Project 2010 allows you to create your own custom visual report templates or to edit any of the default visual report templates. The process is very similar whether creating or editing a visual report template. To create a new visual report template, click the *New Template* button in the *Visual Reports – Create Report* dialog. The software displays the *Visual Reports – New Template* dialog shown in Figure 11 - 49.

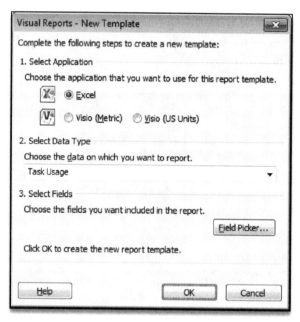

**Figure 11 - 49: Visual Reports –
New Template dialog**

In the *Select Application* section, select the *Excel*, the *Visio (Metric)*, or the *Visio (US Units)* option. In the *Select Data Type* section, click the pick list and select one of the following types of data: *Task Usage, Resource Usage, Assignment Usage, Task Summary, Resource Summary,* or *Assignment Summary*. In the *Select Fields* section, click the *Field Picker* button to select any additional fields to include in the report template in the *Visual Reports – Field Picker* dialog, shown previously in Figure 11 - 30.

In the *Visual Reports – Field Picker* dialog, the *Available Fields* list contains several fields denoted as dimension fields. Dimensions are project fields containing values at which the system totals fact data, such as work and availability. For example, the *Type* field represents the three types of resources available in Microsoft Project 2010: *Work, Material,* and *Cost* resources.

Warning: Be cautious when selecting dimensions for your new visual report template. Including more than five dimension fields can seriously degrade the performance of your visual report.

In the *Visual Reports – New Template* dialog, click the *OK* button. If you selected the *Excel* option in the *Select application* section of the dialog, the system launches Microsoft Excel and creates a new workbook with three worksheet tabs. The *Sheet1* worksheet contains an empty *PivotTable* shown in Figure 11 - 50. The system leaves the *Sheet2* and *Sheet3* worksheets blank.

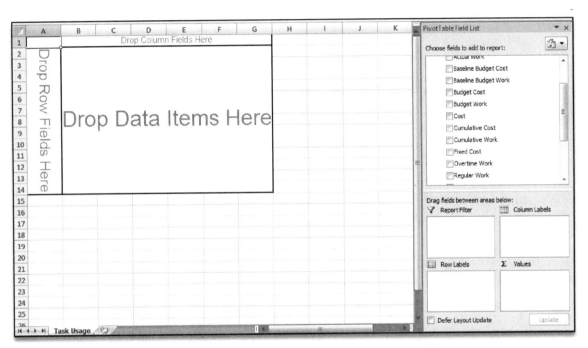

Figure 11 - 50: Sheet1 worksheet with empty PivotTable

Right-click the *Sheet1* tab and select the *Rename* option on the shortcut menu to rename the worksheet consistent with the type of visual report you wish to create. Because I want to create a *Work Flow* report similar to the *Cash Flow* report, I renamed the tab *Task Usage*. Right-click on the *Sheet2* tab and delete the worksheet. Repeat this action for the *Sheet3* tab as well.

Populate the *PivotTable* by selecting fields in the *Choose fields to add to report* section of the *PivotTable Field List* sidepane. Move the fields into the *Report Filter, Column Labels, Row Labels,* and *Values* areas at the bottom of the sidepane, as needed. To populate the *PivotTable* for the *Work Flow* report shown in Figure 11 - 51, I did the following:

- I selected the *Tasks* field and then dragged it from the *Row Labels* area to the *Report Filter* area.

- I selected the *Time Weekly Calendar* field and then dragged it from the *Column Labels* area to the *Row Labels* area.

- I selected the *Work* and *Cumulative Work* fields and the system added them to the *Values* area.

- I dragged the Σ *Values* field from the *Row Labels* drop area (where it appeared automatically) to the *Column Labels* drop area.

575

- I expanded the *Year* field in the *PivotTable* to show *Quarters*.

- I applied the *Accounting Number Format* numeric formatting to the numeric data in the *PivotTable*, and then reduced to *zero* the number of digits to the right of the decimal.

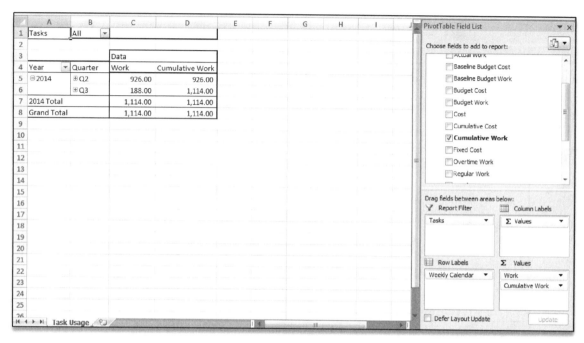

Figure 11 - 51: Task Usage page with populated PivotTable

Right-click on the worksheet tab at the bottom of the page, and then select the *Insert* item on the shortcut menu. Microsoft Excel displays the *Insert* dialog shown in Figure 11 - 52.

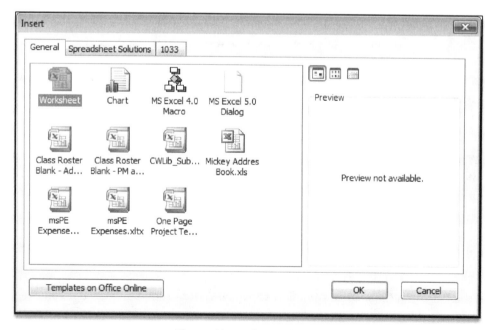

Figure 11 - 52: Insert dialog

In the *Insert* dialog, select the *Chart* icon and then click the *OK* button to insert a generic column chart based on the fields in the *PivotTable*. Figure 11 - 53 shows the generic *PivotChart*. Close both the *PivotTable Field List* sidepane and the *PivotChart Filter Pane* dialog.

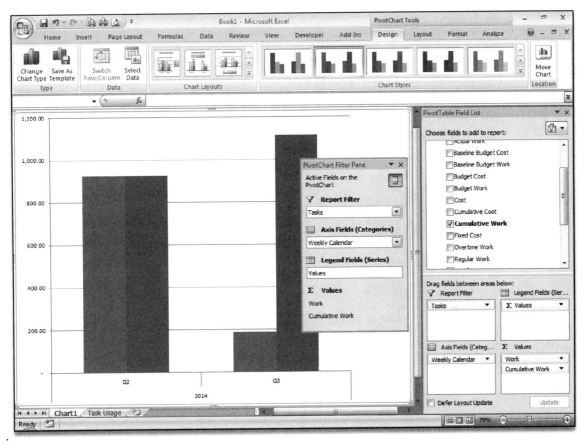

Figure 11 - 53: Generic PivotChart based on PivotTable data

Click anywhere in the *PivotChart* to select it and then click the *Layout* tab to display options on the *Layout* ribbon. Using these options, select your settings for one or more of the following:

- Chart Title

- Axis Titles

- Legend

- Data Labels

- Axes

- Gridlines

Click the *Design* tab to display the *Design* ribbon. Change the *Chart Style* option to meet your requirements. Format any of the *PivotChart* components to meet your reporting needs. Figure 11 - 54 shows my completed *PivotChart*, and I am now ready to save the visual report as a new template.

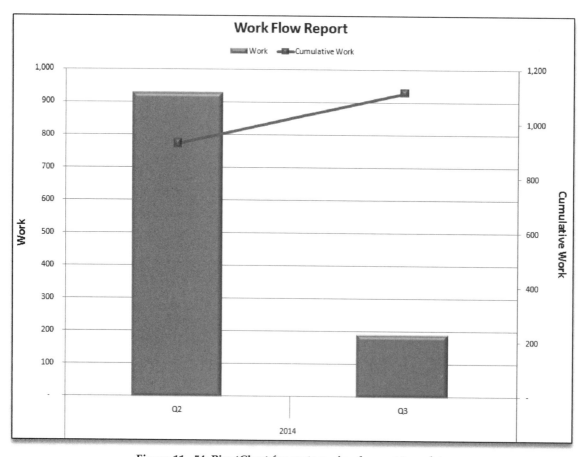

Figure 11 - 54: PivotChart for custom visual report template

When finished, click the *Save* button. Microsoft Excel displays the *Save As* dialog and selects the default template location, as shown in Figure 11 - 55. Click the *Save as type* pick list and select the *Excel template (*.xltx)* option. In the *File name* field, enter your template name using the name you want to appear in the *Visual Reports – Create Template* dialog, such as the *Work Flow Report*. Click the *Save* button when finished.

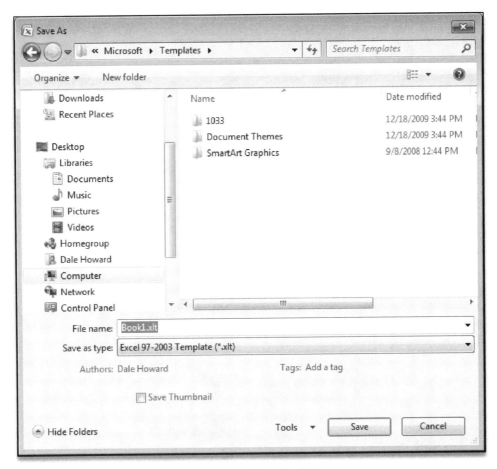

Figure 11 - 55: Save As dialog

Microsoft Project 2010 displays the warning dialog about external data in the workbook shown in Figure 11 - 56. Click the *Yes* button to save the new visual report template.

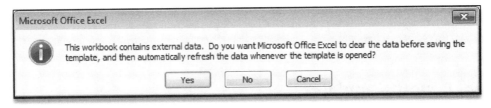

Figure 11 - 56: External data warning dialog

When you return to Microsoft Project 2010, your new visual report template appears on the appropriate tab in the *Visual Reports – Create Report* dialog. Figure 11 - 57 shows my new *Work Flow Report* template on the *Task Usage* tab in the *Visual Reports – Create Report* dialog.

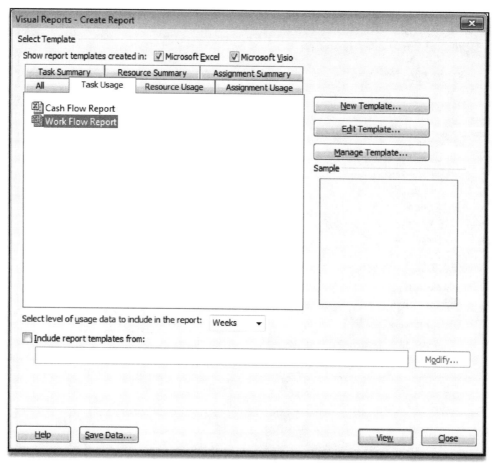

**Figure 11 - 57: Work Flow Report appears on the Task Usage tab
in the Visual Reports – Create Report dialog**

All visual report templates saved in the default templates folder appear automatically in the *Visual Reports – Create Report* dialog. If you save your visual report templates in any other folder, however, you **cannot** see them in the *Visual Reports - Create Report* dialog unless you select the *Include report templates from* option, click the *Modify* button, and then navigate to the folder containing your custom visual report templates.

Editing Visual Report Templates

As I stated earlier, the process of editing a visual report template is very similar to the process used to create a visual report template. To edit a visual report template, select a template and then click the *Edit Template* button in the *Visual Reports – Create Report* dialog. Microsoft Project 2010 displays the *Visual Reports – Field Picker* dialog. Select the fields you want included in the visual report template and then click the *Edit Template* button.

The system launches Microsoft Excel and opens the visual report template for editing. Modify the *PivotTable* and/or *PivotChart* as desired, and then click the *Save* button to save the modified visual report template.

Hands On Exercise

Exercise 11-15

Create a new visual report template.

1. In the *Visual Reports – Create Report* dialog in Microsoft Project 2010, click the *New Template* button.

2. In the *Visual Reports – New Template* dialog, select the *Excel* option in the *Select Application* section and select the *Task Summary* option in the *Select Data Type* section, and then click the *OK* button.

3. In Microsoft Excel, use the **Shift** key to select the *Sheet2* and *Sheet3* worksheet tabs as a group.

4. Right-click on the selected worksheet tabs, and then select the *Delete* item on the shortcut menu to remove these extra worksheets.

5. Right-click on the *Sheet1* worksheet tab, click the *Rename* item on the shortcut menu, and name the worksheet as *Task Summary*.

6. Drag the following fields to the following areas in the *PivotTable Field List* sidepane:

Field Name	Drop Area
Tasks	Report Filter
Actual Work Remaining Work	Values
Σ Values	Row Labels

7. Select the numbers in the *Totals* column and then format them as follows:

- Apply the *Comma Style* number formatting.

- Click the *Decrease Decimal* button twice to reduce to *zero* the number of digits to the right of the decimal.

8. Right-click on the *Task Summary* worksheet tab, click the *Insert* item on the shortcut menu.

9. In the *Insert* dialog, select the *Chart* item and click the *OK* button.

10. Close the *PivotTable Field List* sidepane and the *PivotChart Filter Pane* dialog.

Exercise 11-16

Format the *PivotChart* section of a new visual report template.

1. In Microsoft Excel, customize the *PivotChart* as follows:

    - Click the *Design* tab and then click the *Change Chart Type* button on the *Design* ribbon.

    - In the *Change Chart Type* dialog, select the *Exploded pie in 3-D* option (second from the right in the *Pie* section) and then click the *OK* button.

    - Right-click in the chart title and select the *Edit Text* item on the shortcut menu.

    - Rename the title as *Actual Work vs. Remaining Work*.

    - Click the *Layout* tab, click the *Legend* pick list button on the *Layout* ribbon, and then select the *Show Legend at Top* option.

    - Right-click in either slice of the pie chart and select the *3-D Rotation* item on the shortcut menu.

    - In the *Format Chart Area* dialog, set the *X Rotation* to *90 degrees*, set the *Y Rotation* to *30 degrees*, and then click the *Close* button.

    - Right-click in either slice of the pie chart and select the *Add Data Labels* item from the shortcut menu.

    - Right-click in either of the *Data Labels* in the pie chart, select the *Bold* item in the *Font Style* field and then select *14 points* in the *Size* field. Click on the *Font color* pick list button and choose the *White* color.

2. Save this workbook as an Excel template (*.xltx) in the default templates folder and name the template *Actual and Remaining Work Report*.

3. When the system warns you about external data, click the *Yes* button.

4. Close the *Actual and Remaining Work* workbook file then close the Excel application as well.

5. In the *Visual Reports – Create Report* dialog in Microsoft Project 2010, click the *Task Summary* tab.

You should now see your new visual report on the *Task Summary* page of the dialog.

6. Click the *Close* button to close the *Visual Reports – Create Report* dialog.

7. Save and close your **Training Advisor 11.mpp** project file.

Managing Your Visual Report Templates

To manage your visual report templates, select any visual report template in the *Visual Reports – Create Report* dialog and then click the *Manage Template* button. The system opens the default templates folder in a Windows Explorer window as shown in Figure 11 - 58 and selects the template you want to manage. From this location, you can rename or delete visual report templates as you wish.

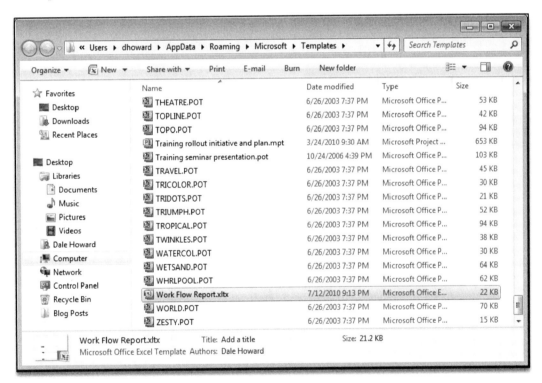

Figure 11 - 58: Templates folder

Module 12

Project Closure

Learning Objectives

After completing this module, you will be able to:

- Understand and use project closure methodologies
- Close a completed project in Microsoft Project 2010
- Save a completed project as a project template
- Compare a completed project with the original project using the Compare Projects tool

Inside Module 12

Using Project Closure Methodologies

The final stage of every project is the closure stage, regardless of whether you complete or cancel the project. Project closure should include the following aspects:

- Update and complete all documents associated with the project, including the Microsoft Project 2010 project file.

- Analyze the project management process using a Lessons Learned (aka "Post Mortem") meeting. You should primarily focus on project successes and effectiveness, but remember to look at project issues and failures, unforeseen risks, project variance and change requests as well as communication problems.

Do not play the "blame game" at your Lessons Learned meeting. Instead, MSProjectExperts recommends that you use this meeting to improve your project management skills so that your next project receives the benefits gained at the meeting. Stress to your project team members that the Lessons Learned meeting helps them to function better as project team members.

- Distribute a Lessons Learned report to all parties interested in your project, including project team members.

- Save all project documents in an archived project repository for future reference.

- Release project team members to work on other projects.

- If your organization maintains a resource skills database, update the database to reflect new skills and increased proficiency gains your resources realized while working on your project.

The Project Management Institute (PMI) recommends that you run a closure process at the end of every phase in addition to the closure process you use at the end of the project.

Closing a Project

To close the Microsoft Project 2010 project file, you should complete the following steps:

1. Cancel unnecessary tasks.

2. Enter actual progress for tasks completed during the final reporting period.

3. Set to 100% complete all remaining milestone tasks.

4. If necessary or desired, save the completed project as a project template.

5. Compare the original project with the completed project using the *Compare Projects* tool.

With the exception of #2, I discuss each step separately.

Cancelling Unnecessary Tasks

During the task planning process you undoubtedly included tasks in the project that you did not need to complete the project. MSProjectExperts recommends that you **do not delete** an unnecessary task, since deleting the task generates negative variance that you cannot possibly track or analyze in your project in the absence of the deleted task. Your project might show under budget on both work and cost, but you have no way of knowing WHY it is under budget! Instead, **cancel** the unnecessary task so that you can maintain the historical record of baselined tasks in the project and analyze the negative variance caused by cancelling the task.

For example, consider the task shown in Figure 12 - 1. The project sponsor elected to cancel the Phase I Review task after learning that the task was not necessary to complete the project work. Therefore, you need to cancel this task in the project.

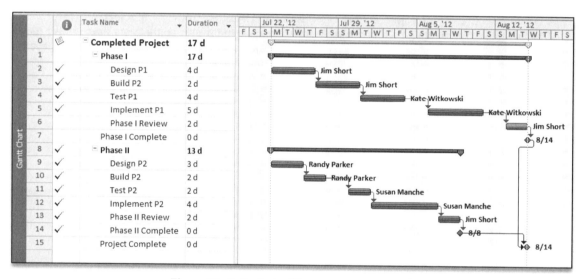

Figure 12 - 1: Project with an unnecessary task

Microsoft Project 2010 offers two different ways to cancel unnecessary tasks. If you use the **Standard** version of the software, you should use the custom process I recommend in this book. If you use the **Professional** version of the software, you can cancel a task using the *Inactivate Task* feature that is not available in the Standard version of the software.

Cancelling a Task Using Microsoft Project Standard 2010

To cancel an unnecessary task using the **Standard** version of Microsoft Project 2010, I recommend you use the following process:

1. Click the *View* tab to display the *View* ribbon.

2. Click the *Gantt Chart* button in the *Task Views* section of the *View* ribbon to display the *Gantt Chart* view.

3. In the *Data* section of the *View* ribbon, click the *Tables* pick list and select the *Work* table.

4. Drag the split bar to the right to expose the *Remaining Work* column.

5. Set the *Remaining Work* value to *0 hours* for the cancelled task.

6. In the *Data* section of the *View* ribbon, click the *Tables* pick list and select the *Entry* table.

When you set the *Remaining Work* value to *0 hours*, Microsoft Project 2010 recalculates the *Duration* to *0 days*, and displays the task using the milestone symbol as shown in Figure 12 - 2.

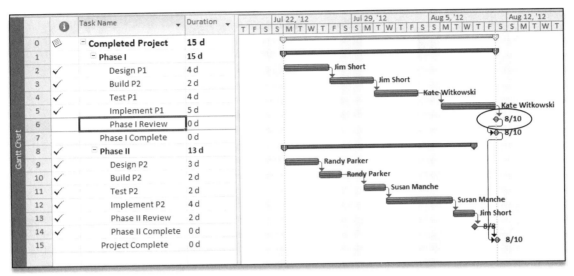

Figure 12 - 2: Cancelled task displayed as a milestone

7. Click the *Task* tab to display the *Task* ribbon.

8. Click the *100%* button in the *Schedule* section of the *Task* ribbon.

> Although it may seem illogical, you must mark the cancelled task as *100% complete*. Before Microsoft Project 2010 can mark the project as completed, you must mark every task as *100% complete*, including cancelled tasks.

9. Click the *Task Notes* button in the *Properties* section of the *Task* ribbon.

10. On the *Notes* page of the *Task Information* dialog, click the *Bulleted List* button and then enter a note documenting the reason for cancelling the task.

11. Click the *OK* button when finished.

12. In the Gantt chart, double-click the milestone symbol for the cancelled task (the black diamond). Microsoft Project 2010 displays the *Format Bar* dialog shown in Figure 12 - 3.

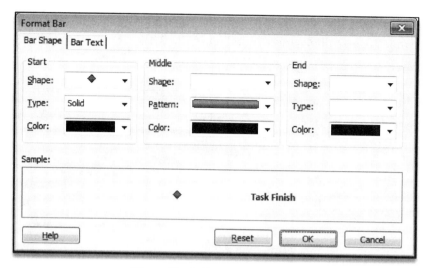

Figure 12 - 3: Format Bar dialog

13. In the *Start* section of the *Format Bar* dialog, click the *Shape* pick list and select a symbol to use in the Gantt chart for the cancelled task. For example, you might pick the solid circle near the bottom of the list.

14. In the *Start* section of the *Format Bar* dialog, click the *Color* pick list and select a color for the cancelled task symbol. For example, you might pick the *Green* color in the *Standard Colors* section of the list.

15. Click the *OK* button. The system displays a unique symbol for the cancelled task, as shown in Figure 12 - 4.

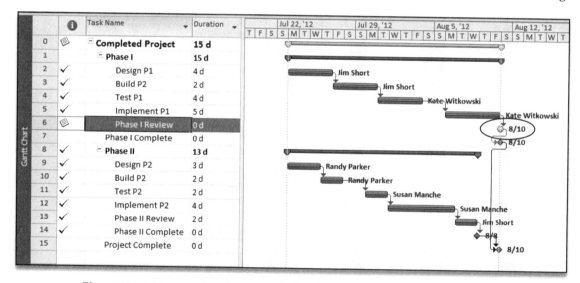

Figure 12 - 4: New symbol for a cancelled task with cell background formatting

In addition to completing the previous steps, you may also want to apply cell background formatting to the cancelled task, as shown in Figure 12 - 4. Using a unique cell background color for all cancelled tasks makes them stand out in the completed project.

Cancelling a Task Using Microsoft Project Professional 2010

To cancel an unnecessary task using the **Professional** version of Microsoft Project 2010, complete the following steps:

1. Click the *Task* tab to display the *Task* ribbon.

2. Select the task and then click the *Inactivate* button in the *Schedule* section of the *Task* ribbon. Figure 12 - 5 shows the *Inactivate* button on the *Task* ribbon, along with its floating tooltip.

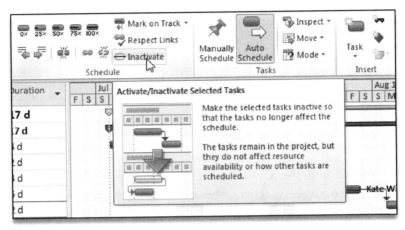

Figure 12 - 5: Inactivate button and tooltip

3. Click the *Task Notes* button in the *Properties* section of the *Task* ribbon.

4. On the *Notes* page of the *Task Information* dialog, click the *Bulleted List* button and then enter a note documenting the reason for cancelling the task.

5. Click the *OK* button when finished.

Figure 12 - 6 shows the original project shown previously in Figure 12 - 1, but after setting the Phase I Review task to *Inactive* status using the *Inactivate* button. When you cancel a task using the *Inactivate* button, Microsoft Project 2010 does the following:

- The system formats the text of the *Inactive* task using the strikethrough font effect and the gray font color.

- The system formats the Gantt bar of the *Inactive* task using a hollow (unfilled) pattern.

- The system treats the *Inactive* task as if it has 0h of remaining work. This means the *Inactive* task no longer affects resource availability for resources assigned to the task, as indicated in the tooltip shown previously in Figure 12 - 5.

- Although the system continues to show link lines for the *Inactive* task, the system schedules successor tasks as if they are **not linked** to the *Inactive* task. This means that the duration of the *Inactive* task no longer affects the schedule of successor tasks, also indicated in the tooltip shown previously in Figure 12 - 5.

591

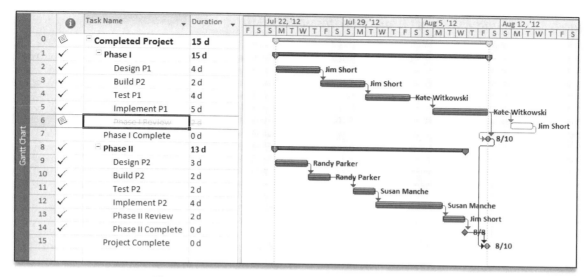

Figure 12 - 6: Phase I Review task set to Inactive status

Figure 12 - 7 shows the *Inactive* task with the *Work* table applied in the *Gantt Chart* view. Notice that the system **did not** set the *Remaining Work* to *0h*. Notice also that the system shows **-16h** of work variance in the *Variance* column for the Phase I summary task and for the *Project Summary Task*, caused by inactivating a task with 16h of work on it.

	Task Name	Work	Baseline	Variance	Actual	Remaining	% W. Comp.
0	**Completed Project**	**224 h**	**240 h**	**-16 h**	**224 h**	**0 h**	**100%**
1	**Phase I**	**120 h**	**136 h**	**-16 h**	**120 h**	**0 h**	**100%**
2	Design P1	32 h	32 h	0 h	32 h	0 h	100%
3	Build P2	16 h	16 h	0 h	16 h	0 h	100%
4	Test P1	32 h	32 h	0 h	32 h	0 h	100%
5	Implement P1	40 h	40 h	0 h	40 h	0 h	100%
6	Phase I Review	16 h	16 h	0 h	0 h	16 h	0%
7	Phase I Complete	0 h	0 h	0 h	0 h	0 h	0%
8	**Phase II**	**104 h**	**104 h**	**0 h**	**104 h**	**0 h**	**100%**
9	Design P2	24 h	24 h	0 h	24 h	0 h	100%
10	Build P2	16 h	16 h	0 h	16 h	0 h	100%
11	Test P2	16 h	16 h	0 h	16 h	0 h	100%
12	Implement P2	32 h	32 h	0 h	32 h	0 h	100%
13	Phase II Review	16 h	16 h	0 h	16 h	0 h	100%
14	Phase II Complete	0 h	0 h	0 h	0 h	0 h	100%
15	Project Complete	0 h	0 h	0 h	0 h	0 h	0%

Figure 12 - 7: Work table shows cancelled tasks

Remember that when you set a task to *Inactive* status, Microsoft Project 2010 schedules successor tasks as if they are **not linked** to the *Inactive* task. Because of this, you should link successor tasks for the *Inactive* task to the nearest *Active* predecessor task to reset the project schedule from that point forward. Figure 12 - 8 shows the project after linking the Implement P1 task to the Phase I Complete milestone task.

You do not need to mark the *Inactive* task to 100% complete, since Microsoft Project 2010 treats the *Inactive* task as if it does not exist. If fact, if you try to mark the *Inactive* task as 100% complete, the system will not let you do it.

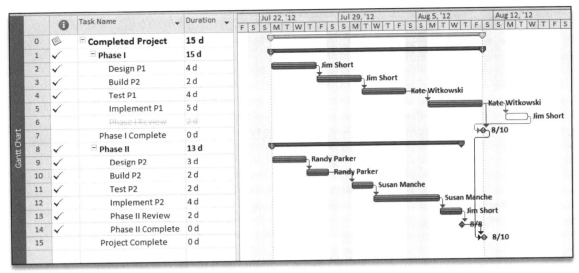

Figure 12 - 8: Link the Implement P1 task to the Phase I Complete milestone task

Warning: Microsoft Project 2010 does not allow you to cancel a completed task or an in-progress task by setting it to *Inactive* status. To cancel the uncompleted work in an in-progress task, apply the task *Work* table and then set the *Remaining Work* value to *0h* for the task.

Marking Milestones as Complete

To mark a milestone as complete, use the following process:

1. Click the *Task* tab to display the *Task* ribbon.

2. Select the milestone task and then click the *100%* button in the *Schedule* section of the *Task* ribbon.

Microsoft Project 2010 marks the milestone task as 100% complete by entering a date in the *Actual Start* and *Actual Finish* fields and by displaying a completed task indicator (blue check mark) in the *Indicators* column for the task. When you set every task to 100% complete in the project plan, Microsoft Project 2010 automatically marks the Project Summary Task (Row 0) 100% complete as shown in Figure 12 - 9.

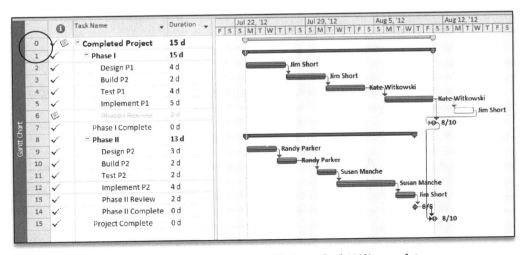

Figure 12 - 9: Project Summary Task marked 100% complete

Hands On Exercise

Exercise 12-1 for Microsoft Project STANDARD 2010 Users

The current date is Monday, April 21, 2014. Project team members completed work on the Training Advisor Deployment project during the previous week. The Provide Training Advisor Classes task finished one day earlier than expected. The project sponsor decided to cancel the Provide Post Training Support task due to a budget cutback for the project.

1. Open the **Training Advisor 12.mpp** sample file.

2. Click the *Task* tab to display the *Task* ribbon.

3. Right-click on the *Select All* button and select the *Work* table in the shortcut menu.

4. Scroll down so that you can see task ID #40, the *Provide Training Advisor Classes* task, and then drag the split bar to the right side so that you can see the *Remaining Work* column.

5. In the *Work* table, enter *0h* in the *Remaining Work* column for the *Provide Training Advisor Classes* task.

Notice that when you set the *Remaining Work* value to *0h* for this in-progress task, Microsoft Project 2010 marked the task as 100% complete automatically.

6. For task ID #41, the *Provide Post Training Support* task, set the *Remaining Work* value to *0h* to cancel this unneeded task.

7. If you see a *Planning Wizard* dialog about a scheduling conflict, select the *Continue* option and click the *OK* button.

8. Right-click on the *Select All* button and select the *Entry* table in the shortcut menu.

9. Dock the split bar on the right edge of the *Duration* column.

Notice in the Gantt chart that Microsoft Project 2010 shows the cancelled task using a milestone symbol (a black diamond).

10. Select task ID #41, the *Provide Post Training Support* task, and then click the *Task Notes* button in the *Properties* section of the *Task* ribbon.

11. On the *Notes* page of the *Task Information* dialog, add a task note to document the reason for cancelling the task (budget cutback).

12. Click the *OK* button to close the *Task Information* dialog.

13. In the Gantt chart, double-click the milestone symbol for the *Provide Post Training Support* task.

14. In the *Start* section of the *Format Bar* dialog, click the *Shape* pick list and select a symbol other than the diamond to use in the Gantt chart for the cancelled task..

15. In the *Start* section of the *Format Bar* dialog, click the *Color* pick list and select a color for the cancelled task symbol.

16. Click the *OK* button to close the *Format Bar* dialog.

Notice that the system displays a unique symbol for the cancelled task.

17. Save but **do not** close the **Training Advisor 12.mpp** sample file.

Exercise 12-1 for Microsoft Project PROFESSIONAL 2010 Users

The current date is Monday, April 21, 2014. Project team members completed work on the Training Advisor Deployment project during the previous week. The Provide Training Advisor Classes task finished one day earlier than expected. The project sponsor decided to cancel the Provide Post Training Support task due to a budget cutback for the project.

1. Open the **Training Advisor 12.mpp** sample file.

2. Click the *Task* tab to display the *Task* ribbon.

3. Right-click on the *Select All* button and select the *Work* table on the shortcut menu.

4. Scroll down so that you can see task ID #40, the *Provide Training Advisor Classes* task, and then drag the split bar to the right side so that you can see the *Remaining Work* column.

5. In the *Work* table, enter *0h* in the *Remaining Work* column for the *Provide Training Advisor Classes* task.

Notice that when you set the *Remaining Work* value to *0h* for this in-progress task, Microsoft Project 2010 marked the task as 100% complete automatically.

6. Right-click on the *Select All* button and select the *Entry* table on the shortcut menu.

7. Dock the split bar on the right edge of the *Duration* column.

8. Select task ID #41, the *Provide Post Training Support* task, and then click the *Inactivate* button in the *Schedule* section of the *Task* ribbon.

9. If you see a *Planning Wizard* dialog about a scheduling conflict, select the *Continue* option and click the *OK* button.

10. Select task ID #40, the *Provide Training Advisor Classes* task, then press and hold the **Control** key on your computer keyboard and select task ID# 42, the *Training Complete* milestone task.

11. Click the *Link Tasks* button in the *Schedule* section of the *Task* ribbon.

12. Save but **do not** close the **Training Advisor 12.mpp** sample file.

Exercise 12-2

Mark all milestone tasks as 100% complete to complete the Training Advisor Deployment project.

1. Return to the **Training Advisor 12.mpp** sample file.

2. Select task IDs #42 and #43, the *Training Complete* and *Project Complete* milestone tasks, and then click the *100%* button in the *Schedule* section of the *Task* ribbon.

3. Examine the *Indicators* column for the Project Summary Task (Row 0) and notice the blue check-mark in this column, indicating the project is totally complete.

4. Save but **do not** close the **Training Advisor 12.mpp** sample file.

Saving a Completed Project as a Template

If you believe you may base one or more future projects on the completed project, then you should save the completed project as a project template. Before saving the project as a template, you need to "clean up" the project to prepare it for use as a template. To "clean up" a complete project for use as a template, complete the following steps:

1. Open the project and save it using a **new name**, such as by appending the words *Saved for Template* to the end of the file name. This prevents you from accidentally saving the "cleaned up" project over your final, completed project.

2. Click the *Task* tab to display the *Task* ribbon.

3. Click the *Select All* button to select all tasks in the project.

4. Click the *Information* button in the *Properties* section of the *Task* ribbon.

5. In the *Multiple Task Information* dialog, select the *General* tab and enter 0% in the *Percent complete* field.

6. In the *Multiple Task Information* dialog, select the *Advanced* tab.

7. On the *Advanced* tab of the dialog, click the *Constraint type* pick list and select the *As Soon As Possible* item on the list.

8. On the *Advanced* tab of the dialog, click the *Calendar* pick list and select the *None* option.

9. Click the *OK* button to close the *Multiple Task Information* dialog.

10. For each task with a deadline date, double-click each task individually, click the *Advanced* tab in the *Task Information* dialog, delete the value in the *Deadline* field, and then click the *OK* button.

11. Using the **Control** key on your computer keyboard, select any tasks containing notes that you wish to remove.

12. In the *Editing* section of the *Task* ribbon, click the *Clear* pick list button and select the *Notes* item on the list.

 Project templates should not contain *constraints* or *deadline dates*. Users of the project template should set *constraints* and *deadline dates* on an "as needed" basis for each new project created from the project template. Furthermore, project templates should not contain notes that document the history of completing the project. Instead, use notes in the project template to guide the project manager on how to plan the project properly.

13. Click the *Select All* button to select all tasks in the project again.

14. In the *Editing* section of the *Task* ribbon, click the *Clear* pick list button and select the *Clear Formatting* item on the list.

15. Set the *Task Mode* value to either *Manually Schedule* or *Autoschedule* for selected tasks, as needed.

16. Set all *Inactive* tasks to *Active* status by selecting the tasks and unclicking the *Inactivate* button in the *Schedule* section of the *Task* ribbon (Microsoft Project **Professional** 2010 users only).

> In a large project, the fastest way to identify all *Inactive* tasks is to apply the default group named *Active v. Inactive*. To apply this group, click the *View* tab to display the *View* ribbon, click the *Group By* pick list, and then select the *Active v. Inactive* group. The group containing *Inactive* tasks appears at the top of the project. You can select all of the *Inactive* tasks as a block and then unclick the *Inactivate* button on the *Task* ribbon to reset all of them to *Active* status. When finished, return to the *View* ribbon and click the *Group By* pick list again, and then select the *[No Group]* group.

17. Select all tasks except for the Project Summary Task (Row 0) and then click the *Resource* tab to display the *Resource* ribbon.

18. Click the *Assign Resources* button in the *Assignments* section of the *Resource* ribbon, select all resources in the *Assign Resources* dialog, click the *Remove* button, and then click the *Close* button.

> If you use *generic* resources in your organization, you may want to go one step further and replace your named resources with their corresponding *generic* resources. For example, replace a *human* resource named Mickey Cobb with a *generic* resource named SQL DBA.

19. In the *View* section of the *Resource* ribbon, click the *Team Planner* pick list button and select the *Resource Sheet* view.

20. Click the *Select All* button and then press the **Delete** key on your computer keyboard to delete all of the resources on the project team.

> The preceding step is an optional step if you build a completely new project team each time you create a new project. If you use a dedicated project team, skip the preceding step. If you want to create a template that includes *generic* resources, use a more selective approach to avoid deleting the *generic* resources from your plan.

21. Click the *Task* tab to display the *Task* ribbon.

22. Click the *Gantt Chart* button in the *View* section of the *Task* ribbon to reapply the *Gantt Chart* view.

23. Reset the *Gantt Chart* view to its default settings by clicking the *Gantt Chart* pick list button in the *View* section of the *Task* ribbon and then clicking the *Reset to Default* item on the list.

In addition to the preceding steps, you may also need to remove task splits caused by entering actual work hours on a daily basis in the timephased grid of the *Resource Usage* view. Whenever you enter *0h* on the *Actual Work* line of the timephased grid for any time period during the life of a task, Microsoft Project 2010 automatically creates a task split to show no work performed during that time period. For example, notice that there is a task split resulting from the entry of daily progress in the project shown in Figure 12 - 10.

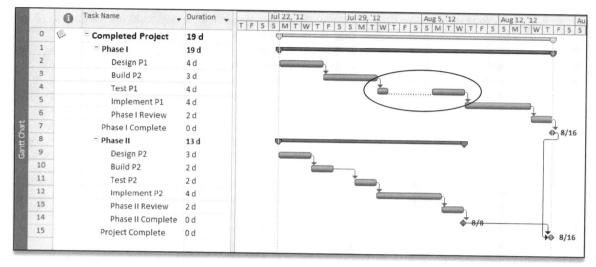

Figure 12 - 10: Task splits resulting from daily Actual Work entries

To remove a task split, position your mouse pointer over the right-most portion of the split task, click and hold, and then drag the split portion to the left until it rejoins the left-most split portion. When you release the mouse button, Microsoft Project 2010 rejoins the split portions of the task's Gantt bar. If a task contains multiple splits, repeat this process for every split section until you reassemble a complete, unbroken Gantt bar for the task.

Since the completed project contains the final *Duration* value of every task, which might include a fraction such as *6.5 days*, you may want to set the fractions to whole numbers. For example, you might want to change a *Duration* value of *6.5 days* to either *6 days* or *7 days*.

To save your "cleaned up" project as a project template, complete the following steps:

1. Click the *File* tab and then click the *Save As* item in the *Backstage* menu.

2. In the *Save As* dialog, enter a name for the template in the *File name* field.

3. Click the *Save as type* pick list and select the *Project Template (*.mpt)* item as shown in Figure 12 - 11.

After you select the *Project Template (*.mpt)* item on the *Save as type* pick list, Microsoft Project 2010 navigates to the default templates folder on your hard drive automatically.

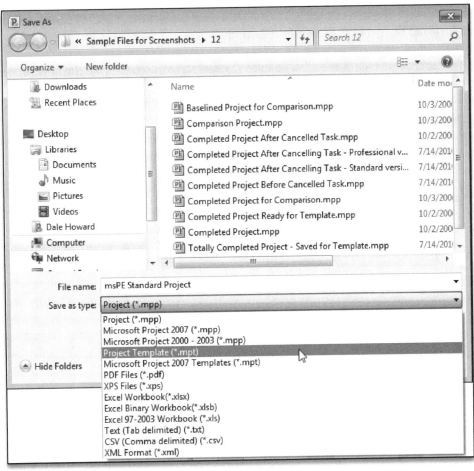

Figure 12 - 11: Save As dialog when saving a project template

4. Click the *Save* button. Microsoft Project 2010 displays the *Save As Template* dialog shown in Figure 12 - 12.

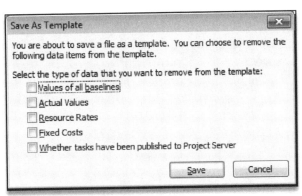

Figure 12 - 12: Save As Template dialog

5. In the *Save As Template* dialog, select **at least** the first two checkboxes, and then click the *OK* button.

You do not need to select the *Resource Rates* option if you already deleted all resources from the project team, or if you opt not to clear actual resources from your project, as might be the case with a dedicated project team using consistent resource rates. You should select the *Fixed Costs* option if you added extra task costs in the *Fixed Cost* column as part of entering actual progress on tasks. Do not select the *Fixed Costs* option if your fixed cost amounts represent planned task costs in the project. Select the final option, *Whether tasks have been published to Project Server*, only if you use Microsoft Project Server 2010 and the project is an enterprise project.

6.   Click the *File* tab and then click the *Close* item in the *Backstage* menu to close the new project template.

7.   If prompted to save the changes in a confirmation dialog, click the *Yes* button to save the latest changes to the project template file.

Creating a New Project from a Template

To create a new project from the project template, complete the following steps:

1.   Click the *File* tab and then click the *New* item in the *Backstage* menu. Microsoft Project 2010 displays the *New* page in the *Backstage* as shown in Figure 12 - 13.

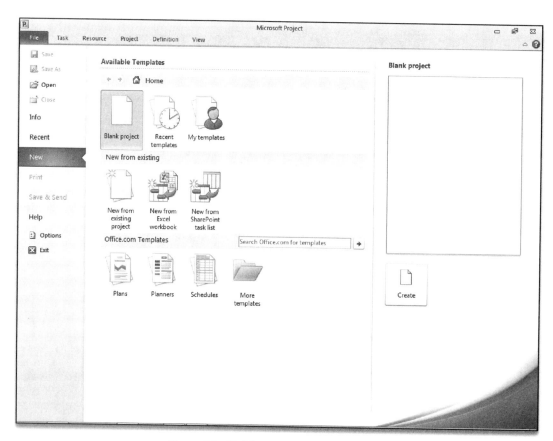

Figure 12 - 13: New page in the Backstage

2.   In the *Available Templates* section of the *New* page, click the *My templates* icon. The system displays the *New* dialog shown in Figure 12 - 14.

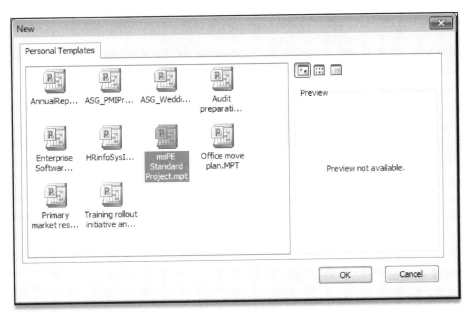

Figure 12 - 14: New dialog

3. On the *Personal Templates* tab in the dialog, select the template you want to use and click the *OK* button to create a new project from the template.

Hands On Exercise

Exercise 12-3

Clean up the tasks in the Training Advisor Deployment project to prepare to save it as a project template.

1. Return to the **Training Advisor 12.mpp** sample file.

2. Click the *File* tab and then click the *Save As* item in the *Backstage* menu.

3. In the *Save As* dialog, save your file using the new name **Training Advisor Project – Saved for Template.mpp**.

Warning: Do not skip the preceding step in this exercise. You **must** save the Training Advisor 12.mpp project file using a new name to protect the original sample file for use later in this module.

4. Click the *Task* tab to display the *Task* ribbon.

5. Click the *Select All* button to select all tasks in the project.

6. Click the *Information* button in the *Properties* section of the *Task* ribbon.

7. In the *Multiple Task Information* dialog, select the *General* tab and enter 0% in the *Percent complete* field.

8. In the *Multiple Task Information* dialog, select the *Advanced* tab.

9. On the *Advanced* tab of the dialog, click the *Constraint type* pick list and select the *As Soon As Possible* item on the list.

10. On the *Advanced* tab of the dialog, click the *Calendar* pick list and select the *None* option.

11. Click the *OK* button to close the *Multiple Task Information* dialog.

12. Double-click task ID #43, the *Project Complete* milestone task.

13. On the *Advanced* tab of the *Task Information* dialog, **delete** the date in the *Deadline* field, and then click the *OK* button.

14. Click the *Select All* button to select all tasks in the project again.

15. In the *Editing* section of the *Task* ribbon, click the *Clear* pick list button and select the *Notes* item on the list.

16. In the *Editing* section of the *Task* ribbon, click the *Clear* pick list button again and select the *Clear Formatting* item on the list.

17. Select task ID #40, the *Provide Training Advisor Classes* task, and then click the *Manually Schedule* button in the *Tasks* section of the *Task* ribbon.

18. Select task ID #41, the *Provide Post Training Support* task, and then unclick the *Inactivate* button in the *Schedule* section of the *Task* ribbon to set this task back to *Active* status.

19. Click the *View* tab to display the *View* ribbon.

20. In the *Zoom* section of the *View* ribbon, click the *Timescale* pick list and select the *Days* item on the list.

21. Click the *Task* tab to display the *Task* ribbon.

22. Select task ID #20, the *Load and Configure Software* task, and then click the *Scroll to Task* button in the *Editing* section of the *Task* ribbon.

23. Position your mouse pointer over the right-most portion of the split task part of this task's Gantt bar, click and hold, and then drag the split portion to the left until it rejoins the left-most split portion of the Gantt bar.

24. Select task ID #32, the *Create Training Module 01* task, and then click the *Scroll to Task* button again.

25. Remove the task split in the Gantt bar for this task as well.

26. Click the *Gantt Chart* pick list button in the *View* section of the *Task* ribbon and select the *Reset to Default* item on the list.

27. When prompted in a confirmation dialog, click the *Yes* button.

28. Widen the *Task Name* column as needed and then dock the split bar on the right edge of the *Duration* column.

29. Scroll to the top of the project and select task ID #0, the Project Summary Task, and then click the *Scroll to Task* button one final time.

30. Save but **do not** close the **Training Advisor Project – Saved for Template.mpp** sample file.

Exercise 12-4

Clean up the resources in the Training Advisor Deployment project to prepare to save it as a project template.

1. Return to the **Training Advisor Project – Saved for Template.mpp** sample file.

2. Select all tasks in the project **except for** the Project Summary Task (Row 0) and then click the *Resource* tab to display the *Resource* ribbon.

3. Click the *Assign Resources* button in the *Assignments* section of the *Resource* ribbon, select all resources in the *Assign Resources* dialog, and click the *Remove* button.

4. When prompted in a warning dialog about removing actual values, click the *Yes* button.

5. Click the *Close* button to close the *Assign Resources* dialog.

6. In the *View* section of the *Resource* ribbon, click the *Team Planner* pick list button and select the *Resource Sheet* view.

7. Click the *Select All* button to select all resources on the project team, and then press the **Delete** key on your computer keyboard to delete them.

8. Click the *Task* tab to display the *Task* ribbon.

9. Click the *Gantt* Chart button in the *View* section of the *Task* ribbon to reapply the view.

10. Save but **do not** close the **Training Advisor Project – Saved for Template.mpp** sample file.

Exercise 12-5

Save the "cleaned up" Training Advisor Deployment project file as a project template.

1. Return to the Training **Advisor Project – Saved for Template.mpp** sample file.

2. Click the *File* tab and then click the *Save As* item in the *Backstage* menu.

3. In the *Save As* dialog, enter the name *Software Rollout* in the *File name* field.

4. Click the *Save as* type pick list and select the *Project Template (*.mpt)* item in the list.

5. Click the Save button.

6. In the *Save As Template* dialog, select all of the options and then click the *Save* button.

7. Close the Software **Rollout.mpt** project template file.

8. When prompted to save changes in a confirmation dialog, click the *Yes* button.

Exercise 12-6

Create a new project from the Software Rollout project template.

1. Click the *File* tab and then click the *New* tab in the *Backstage* menu.

2. In the *Available Templates* section of the *New* page, click the *My templates* icon.

3. In the *New* dialog, select the *Software Rollout* project template and then click the *OK* button.

4. Close but **do not** save your new project.

Using the Compare Project Versions Tool

Microsoft Project 2010 includes a *Compare Project Versions* tool that you can use to study the differences between two projects. It is particularly useful for studying the changes between the original project and its completed counterpart or with other versions you save along the way. To use the *Compare Project Versions* tool for this purpose you **must** save a copy of your original baselined project before you begin entering progress in your production project. To use the *Compare Project Versions* tool, complete the following steps:

1. Open the earlier version of your project, such as the copy of the project you saved after baselining the project.

2. Open the later version of your project, such as the final completed version of the project.

3. Click the *Project* tab to display the *Project* ribbon.

4. Click the *Compare Projects* button in the *Reports* section of the *Project* ribbon. Microsoft Project 2010 displays the *Compare Project Versions* dialog shown in Figure 12 - 15.

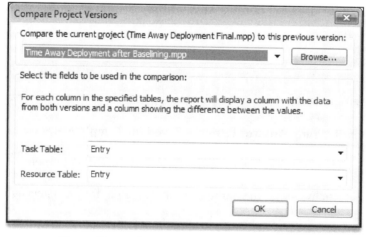

Figure 12 - 15: Compare Project Versions dialog

5. Click the pick list at the top of the dialog and select the earlier version, if necessary.

6. Click the *Task Table* pick list and select the table containing the task data you want to compare.

7. Click the *Resource Table* pick list and select the table containing the resource data you want to compare.

8. Click the *OK* button.

The system finds the differences between the two selected projects, and then displays the *Comparison Report* view shown in Figure 12 - 16. Notice that the *Comparison Report* view consists of a combination of three project windows, a *Legend* window, and the *Compare Projects* ribbon.

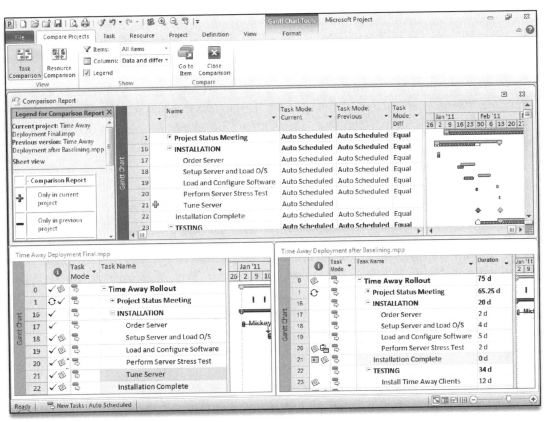

Figure 12 - 16: Comparison Report for two projects

By default, the *Comparison Report* view shows the results of task comparisons first. The bottom two panes show you the two projects compared using the *Compare Project Versions* tool. In the *Comparison Report* pane at the top, you see a special comparison project that contains the task comparison results between these two projects. Because I selected the task *Entry* table for comparison, notice that the first three columns in this comparison project include the *Task Mode: Current*, *Task Mode: Previous*, and *Task Mode: Diff* columns. To see the comparison between other columns of data in your selected task table, scroll to the right in the table shown in the comparison project. If you selected the task *Entry* table for comparison, then the comparison project includes additional columns that compare the *Duration, Start, Finish, Predecessors*, and *Resource Names* columns.

To understand all of the symbols shown in the comparison project, refer to the *Legend for Comparison Report* pane in the upper left corner of the *Comparison Report* view. The *Legend for Comparison Report* pane contains two sections. Refer to the information in the *Sheet View* section to understand the indicators shown in the *Indicators* column of the comparison project. Refer to the *Gantt Chart* section to understand the Gantt bars shown in the *Gantt Chart* portion of the comparison project.

To compare the resource information between the two projects, click the *Resource Comparison* button in the *View* section of the *Compare Projects* ribbon. The system displays a similar *Comparison Report* view, except with the *Resource Sheet* view in all three project windows. Again, the *Legend for Comparison Report* pane helps you to understand the indicators shown in the *Indicators* column in the comparison project. Click the *Task Comparison* button to return to the *Comparison Report* view for tasks.

Click the *Items* pick list in the *Show* section of the *Compare Projects* ribbon to choose the exact type of comparison data you want to see in the *Comparison Report* view. For example, to see only the tasks with differences between the two projects, select the *All Differences* item on the *Items* pick list. Click the *Columns* pick list in the *Show* section of the *Compare Projects* ribbon to choose the sets of columns you want to see in the *Comparison Report* view. By default, the system selects the *Dates and Differences* item on the *Columns* pick list. This means that you see a set of three columns for every column in the selected task table, such as the *Task Mode: Current*, *Task Mode: Previous*, and *Task Mode: Diff* columns shown previously in Figure 12 - 16.

If you understand the indicators shown in the comparison project, deselect the *Legend* checkbox in the *Show* section of the *Compare Projects* ribbon. Microsoft Project 2010 closes the *Legend for Comparison Report* pane and expands the comparison project in the top pane.

To focus your analysis on an individual task in the *Comparison Report* view, select the task in any of the three project panes and then click the *Go to Item* button in the *Compare* section of the *Compare Projects* ribbon. The system selects the task in all three project panes and scrolls to the Gantt bars for the selected tasks as shown in Figure 12 - 17. Notice that I selected the Verify Server Connectivity task in the comparison project pane and clicked the *Go to Item* button to view this task in all three project panes. Notice the "question mark" indicator for this task in the *Indicators* column of the comparison project, which means that I renamed the task, by the way. Finally, in the *Legend for Comparison Report* pane notice that the question mark indicator means that I changed the name of this task in the later version of the project.

To close the bottom two project panes, click the *Close Comparison* button. The system leaves open the comparison project pane and the *Legend for Comparison Report* pane for further analysis. If you want to save the comparison project for additional analysis, you may do so as well.

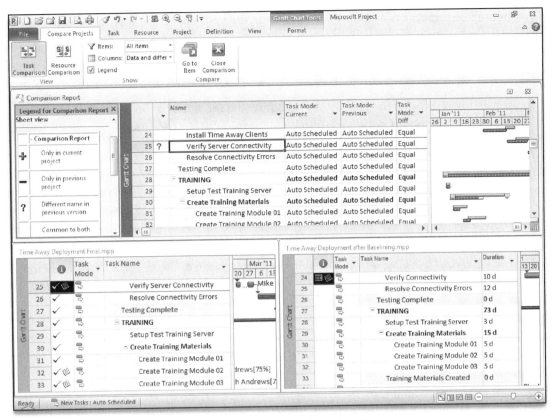

Figure 12 - 17: Go to Item for selected task

Hands On Exercise

Exercise 12-7

Use the *Compare Project Versions* tool to compare the baselined and completed versions of the Training Advisor Deployment project.

1. Open the **Training Advisor Original.mpp** sample file.

2. Open the **Training Advisor 12.mpp** sample file as well.

3. Click the *Project* tab to display the *Project* ribbon.

4. Click the *Compare Projects* button in the *Reports* section of the *Project* ribbon.

5. In the *Compare Project Versions* dialog, make sure the pick list at the top displays the *Training Advisor Original.mpp* sample file.

6. In the *Compare Project versions* dialog, leave all other default settings in place and then click the *OK* button.

7. In the *Comparison Report* pane at the top, drag the split bar all the way to the right side to view more columns in the table. You may need to scroll to the right to see all of the columns.

8. Examine each set of columns in the *Comparison Report* pane and look for differences for the tasks in each project. Widen columns, if necessary, to examine the information in each column.

9. Scroll down through the task list and examine the indicators shown in the *Indicators* column in the *Comparison Report* pane. Determine the meaning of the indicators using the *Legend for Comparison Report* pane.

Notice the new tasks added to the project during the execution stage, and notice the renamed task as well.

10. In the *Comparison Report* pane, select task ID #40, the *Provide Training Advisor Classes* task, and then click the *Go to Item* button in the *Compare* section of the *Compare Projects* ribbon.

11. In the bottom two project panes, determine the original name of the task and its new name.

12. Click the *Resource Comparison* button in the *View* section of the *Compare Projects* ribbon.

13. Examine the indicators shown in the *Indicators* column for every resource.

Notice the new resource, Sarah Baker, added to the project during the execution stage.

14. Click the *Task Comparison* button in the *View* section of the *Compare Projects* ribbon.

15. Close the *Legend for Comparison Report* sidepane.

16. In the *Show* section of the *Compare Projects* ribbon, click the *Items* pick list and select the *All Differences* item on the list.

17. In the *Show* section of the *Compare Projects* ribbon, click the *Columns* pick list and select the *Differences columns only* item on the list.

18. In the *Comparison Report* pane, examine each of the columns that show differences.

19. Click the *Close Comparison* button in the *Compare* section of the *Compare Projects* ribbon.

20. Close the **Comparison Report** project file without saving it.

21. Save and close the **Training Advisor Original.mpp** sample file.

22. Save and close the **Training Advisor 12.mpp** sample file as well.

Index

D

E

F

G

H

I

K

O

P

You may also need these books!

Buy direct from our website or your favorite bookseller

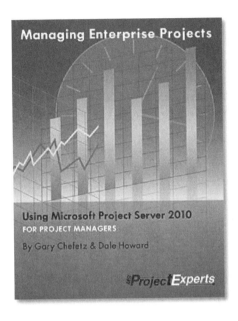

Managing Enterprise Projects Using Microsoft Project Server 2010

ISBN 978-1-934240-11-3

This is an unprecedented learning guide and reference for project managers who use the Microsoft EPM platform. Our goal in writing this training/reference manual is to help you build on your knowledge of the stand-alone tool by mastering the enterprise project management environment. Follow our best practices to success and heed our warnings to avoid the pitfalls.

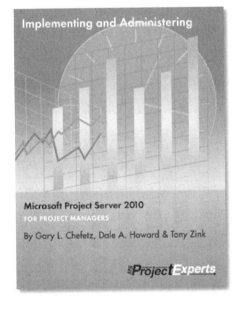

Implementing and Administering Microsoft Project Server 2010

ISBN 978-1-934240-09-0

Implementing and Administering Microsoft Project Sever 2010 is your essential reference guide for installing, configuring and deploying Project Server to your enterprise. This book begins with the organizational strategies you need to succeed with an EPM deployment and follows through with an implementation plan and step-by-step instructions for installing, configuring and deploying the Project Server 2010 platform to your organization. Loaded with best practices, warnings and tips from Project Sever gurus Gary Chefetz and Dale Howard, Implementing and Administering Microsoft Project Server sets the gold standard for Project Server implementation.

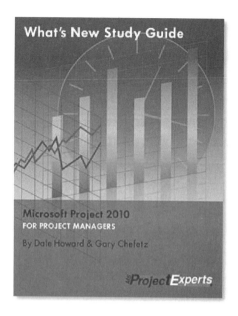

What's New Study Guide Microsoft Project 2010

ISBN 978-1-934240-16-8

A learning guide to get you up to speed with the revolutionary new features in Microsoft Office Project 2010. Learn how to use manually scheduled tasks, the team planner, and the new user interface. The content of this book derives from the Ultimate Study Guide: Foundations, Microsoft Project 2010.

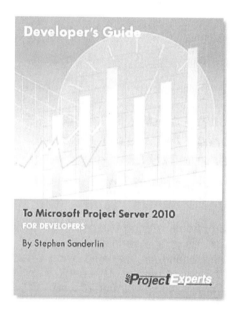

Developer's Guide To Microsoft Project Server 2010

ISBN 978-1-934240-08-3

The first book covering development for Project Server. A complete guide to the PSI, including sample code that you can use to build your own solutions.

CONSULTING

TRAINING

BOOKS AND COURSEWARE

SUPPORT

You deserve the best, do not settle for less! MSProjectExperts is a Microsoft Gold Certified Partner specializing in Microsoft Office Project Server since its first release. This is not something we "also do," it's all we do. Microsoft recognizes our consultants as being among the world's top experts with three Microsoft Project MVPs on staff.

MSProjectExperts

90 John Street, Suite 404

New York, NY 10038

(646) 736-1688

To learn more about MSProjectExperts:

http://www.msprojectexperts.com

For the best Project and Project Server training available:

http://www.projectservertraining.com

To learn more about our books:

http://www.projectserverbooks.com

For FAQs and other free support:

http://www.projectserverexperts.com